THE SONG OF SONGS

THE SONG OF SONGS

A mystical exposition
by
Father Juan González Arintero, O.P.

Translated by

James Valender, M.A.
and
Jose' L. Morales, Ph.D.

Published by: The Dominican Nuns
Monastery of the Holy Name
Cincinnati, Ohio U.S.A.   1974

Dedicated

with love and gratitude

to

REVEREND MOTHER MARY IMELDA, O. P.

and to the

DOMINICAN MONASTERY
OF THE
HOLY NAME

Cincinnati, Ohio

in remembrance of
the 50th anniversary
of her Religious Profession

1925 — 1975

JOSÉ L. MORALES

TRANSLATOR'S NOTE:

For the quotations from St. John of the Cross we have used *The Collected Works of St. John of the Cross,* translated by Kieran Kavanaugh, O.C.D. and Otilio Rodriguez, O.C.D. (New York: Doubleday and Co., 1964). For the quotations from St. Teresa we have used *The Complete Works of St. Teresa,* 3 vols. translated and edited by E. Allison Peers (London and New York: Sheed and Ward, 1963). All other translations are our own.

The Song of Songs *is a unique book, and of all the books of the Old Testament the one preferred by mystics and poets. It is, therefore, not suprising that is has been the subject of many commentaries. In recent times attempts have been made to interpret it as a dramatic work, but mistakenly. For, on the contrary, we believe that the allegorical interpretation — which, in substance, is the traditional interpretation of Jews and Christians — must be upheld.*

Whoever has read the Bible, whether the Old or the New Testament, will have noticed the extensive use made of the symbolic element. Jehovah, having selected Israel as His chosen nation through which He would bring about Messianic salvation, began by establishing a bilateral pact with it. Here we have the first image. Jehovah and Israel are two allies. The nations that surrounded Israel were constituted as kingdoms, and Israel looked upon Jehovah as their King, and His domain as their Kingdom. Here we have the origin of another image, the Kingdom of God, the Kingdom of Heaven. The Israelites possessed a vast number of sheep; the patriarchs of Israel were above all shepherds. Hence another image, that of Jehovah as the Shepherd of Israel, and Israel as God's flock, which He pastures through the intermediaries of kings, prophets and priests. But the favorite image used for portraying the relationship between Jehovah and His chosen people is that of marriage. Jehovah is the Spouse, Israel the Bride, and the Temple is the house where the conjugal relations, always spiritual in character, take place. This image is fully developed by Hosea and Ezekiel; but as early as Exodus, Jehovah appears to Israel as a jealous God, and in the books of the prophets the commission of sin, especially the sin of idolatry, is called infidelity or adultery. In the Gospel the Kingdom of Heaven is on several occasions compared to a wedding feast. St. Paul says he betrothed the Corinthians to the Spouse, Christ, and St. John in the Apocalypse gives us the image of the Lamb with Jerusalem His Bride.

Now, in the post-exilic era, a sage, who was also an eminent poet, took this image and developed it, including in it a series of scenes and songs, and using his native marriage customs and perhaps also those of neighboring countries, which differed very little, as a basis for his work; for material, he had a great abundance afforded him by the prophets with all their Messianic predictions. However, the Song, being so optimistic, cannot correspond to the historic time of Israel which the historians and prophets show us to have been so bleak, but to the Messianic age, in which the Messianic predictions are depicted with such rosy-colored hues. Such a beautiful, pure and youthful Bride could not be the Israel or the Jerusalem that the prophets describe as being completely given over to idolatry, her hands stained with the blood of the oppressed poor or of the innocent sacrificed to pagan gods. Therefore, when we speak of allegory we do not mean an unbroken continuous metaphor in which all the elements, verbs, nouns, adjectives, have their special transcribed meaning. Only a few examples of this kind of allegory are offered us by St. John in his Gospel. We speak of the allegories given us by the prophets, fully developed but displaying an abundance of purely ornamental elements. If we read through the long chapters 16 and 23 of Ezekiel in which the prophet describes the history of Israel's relations with Jehovah we shall see this outstanding element of amplification in which it would be pointless to seek any meaning apart from that of underlining the essential elements of the allegory. It is true that the ancient fathers and commentators made no distinction between these two kinds of elements; but we believe that the present exegesis, which seeks above all the literal sense of the Bible, achieves more when these two kinds of elements are distinguished and when each one is given what is appropriate to it.

In the Song of Songs *the mystical commentators also tend to discard the interpretation of minimal details so as to see more quickly the great mysteries it contains. In themselves,*

such expositions are often to be admired for the doctrine they
contain, but not as an exposition of the sacred text. The
authors of these interpretations, men filled with mystical
knowledge and the Spirit of God, offer us wonderful pages of
spiritual doctrine, but doctrine which we cannot consider to be
contained in the biblical text, unless we argue as St. Augustine
does in his Confessions, that the Holy Spirit was the source of
these expositions, that He inspired their authors, and that since
they were good and holy, He approved them and made them
His own. But this exegetic method, in which the authors seek to
harmonize their interpretations with those of Scripture, was not
adopted by the Church or by modern scientists.

   In the Song of Songs, however, we have the complete
meaning of the doctrine as expressed in Sacred Scripture, which
is today gaining ground among commentators. Let us look at it.
This book celebrates Jehovah's marriage to Israel in Messianic
times just as the Prophets, enlightened by the Holy Spirit,
envisioned it to be. What is the fulfillment of these predictions
made known to us in the Gospels? For no one will doubt that
there is a substantial similarity between the predictions of the
prophets and the experiences of the apostles, even though there
may be accidental differences due to the manner in which they
were conceived and expressed. However, there is no doubt that
Jehovah of the Song is Jesus Christ, God and Man, and that
Israel is "the Israel of God" of St. Paul, the Israel formed by the
children of God, in faith.

   We can go still further. In the Old Testament Jehovah's
relations with Israel began by His relations with the nation, but
gradually these became more individual; His dealings are with
souls, who alone have an eternal existence and destiny. All the
elements that constitute His formal relations with the people of
God as a whole, that is, of the Church, are directed toward the
life of souls. These are then the true brides of Christ, and this is
what the Apostle truly meant when he wrote. "I have betrothed
you to one husband that I may present you as a chaste virgin to

*Christ (II Cor. 11, 2). This is precisely St. John's meaning when
he speaks to us of the eternal wedding of the Lamb in the
Apocalypse.*

*We can go yet one step further, reflecting that if in
marriage the legal bond which unites the two spouses is a
relationship which, as the logically-minded would say, allows
for nothing more and nothing less; nonetheless to this union of
nature and grace, love has been added, which unites hearts; and
this is what is essential in the spiritual marriage of Jesus Christ
with souls, which is the subject of the* Song of Songs. *Now, this
love, which is charity, poured into hearts by the Holy Spirit is
present in varying degrees in each soul; hence the special
application of its meaning in the Canticle to those most highly
favored ones, to those of whom St. John says that they have
been permitted to follow the Lamb wherever He goes and to
sing a song that they only are permitted to sing. For this reason
it is particularly applicable to mystical souls, and more
especially to the Most Blessed Virgin. All this is merely the
development of different applications of the same literal
meaning, the theological meaning which is mystical union of
souls with God through charity "which never passes away" (I
Cor. 13, 8).*

*The commentary of Father Arintero is based on this
principle, which, as our readers will see, is no fantasy but
something that stems from the very nature of Sacred Scripture
and from divine revelation and which the Holy Spirit has sought
gradually to communicate to mankind, according to the state of
the soul and its capacity to understand and assimilate it.*

*Added to this is another principle which has not the firm
basis of the first, that of coverting the Song into a perfect
allegory, in which all its elements would have a special meaning,
always related to the one previously mentioned, of the love
between Jesus Christ and mystical souls. No, the Song is not an
allegory like the one the Lord uses in St. John when He says: "I
am the true vine, and My Father is the keeper of the vineyard.*

*Every branch in me that bears no fruit He cuts away, and every
branch that does bear fruit He prunes to make it bear even
more"* (John 15, 1-2,s.). *In this Gospel allegory, each noun and
verb has a special meaning within the overall meaning of the
soul's relations with Christ. All this belongs to the literal
meaning of the Gospel, and is therefore clear and beyond
reasonable doubt.*

The same is not true of the Song of Songs. *It is composed
of songs in which poetic images and expressions abound, by
means of which the Spouse and Bride woo one another and
declare their mutual love. This is the general sense, and here,
too, there seems no room for any reasonable doubt. But any
attempt to be more precise and to study the details of the
manifestations of mystical life, the stages of its development,
the trials undergone, etc., all this is subject to considerable
doubt. For this reason it is not surprising that mystical
interpreters, unless they copy one another, differ very greatly
one from another, and no scientific exegetic value can be
conceded to them. Normally the souls of these expounders are
full of God; some, like Father Arintero, have their minds
enriched with mystical doctrine or with doctrine restricted to a
more or less scientific trend and take the* Song of Songs *as a
canvas on which they sometimes strive to portray works of
marvelous beauty. That is, they expound spiritual experiences
that are of lofty, edifying and of theological worth their pens
being guided by the Holy Spirit to enrich the mystical doctrine
in the Church. Pious souls who read these pages without undue
concern for scientific exegesis will there find abundant food for
their sustenance.*

*Such is Fr. Arintero's commentary, enriched by his
prodigious erudition, a work which offers us countless passages
from the Holy Fathers and learned expounders, rich in doctrine
and suffused with holiness. In this commentary Fr. Arintero,
the author of* The Mystical Evolution *and many other spiritual
works, offers us that same doctrine, expressed in a form*

suggested by the inspired Book while at the same time giving its words marvelous meanings which cannot easily be found in the text itself, but which agree with those revealed by the Holy Spirit through other books of Scripture and through works compiled by inspired authors by whom the Holy Spirit speaks to His Church. What more could be desired by those who seek, not knowledge which sometimes puffs up, but charity which always edifies? For this reason we do not hesitate to recommend to souls a work whose worth is guaranteed first by the name of its author, and then by the repeated editions it has undergone.

FATHER ALBERTO COLUNGA, O.P.

CONTENTS

CONTENTS

The Song of Songs of Solomon, *the Song* par excellence, *is a divine* epithalamium *inspired by the Holy Spirit and included in the books of the Old Testament. With great vividness it represents or symbolizes, in the form of a human betrothal between Solomon and the Shulamite, or between a shepherd and a young shepherdess, and through the tender love that exists between them, the ineffable loves of Christ His Mystical Bride, the Holy Catholic Church and for the Most Blessed Virgin, the very model and epitome of all the Church stands for and the example for all holy souls, revealing to us the ineffable mysteries of the spiritual betrothal that the Divine Word wishes to celebrate with all such souls.*

The characters *who take part in this song are many. The principle ones are the Spouse and the Bride, who usually are represented as shepherds, and sometimes as farm laborers or gardeners, although they often appear as kings; the* young maids and the daughters of Zion, *the Bride's friends, who aspire to this divine betrothal; and the daughters of Jerusalem, vulgar and completely profane souls encountered along the paths of this mystical love. The* friends of the Spouse *also appear, representing sometimes His ministers on earth, sometimes His angels and saints in Heaven.*

The human author *of this book, as its own title indicates and as nearly the entire Judaical and Christian tradition supposes, appears to be King Solomon himself. Nevertheless, certain modern critics, basing their argument upon the way in which this character is presented, a way that Solomon would not have chosen, and upon the Aramaean and the Chaldean expressions that are to be found there, attempt to make it date from a much later period, according to many, from the time of Nehemiah and Esdras; this opinion continues to gain ground. Even if this were so, and even if this king were considered only as a model or figure for the true Spouse, Jesus Christ, who is celebrated there, just as they attribute the book of* Wisdom *to him, although it is not his, this would be of little importance to the matter at hand. For as St. Gregory the Great would express it, what we find truly edifying is to know that it was the Holy Spirit Himself Who dictated the Sacred Scriptures, and not the human instrument used by Him for the purpose of writing them.*

The whole Judaic and Christian tradition is in perfect accord in recognizing the spiritual and mystical sense *of this wonderful* Song, *always seeing in it the most eloquent testimony of the tender love and infinite bond linking God with His chosen people, and especially with those happy and privileged souls who receive the grace to respond to Him. Thus Rabbi Eleazar, President of the Sanhedrin, near the year 90 (Anno Domini), had condemned the opinion of the School of Schammai that interpreted the Song quite literally, believing that all that was being celebrated was a human betrothal.[1] In the same way, the second General Council of Constantinople (553) condemned the opinion of Theodore of Mopsuestia (360 — 429) who was the first Christian to view this book as a simple nuptial song written to celebrate Solomon's marriage to the Egyptian princess. Therefore this opinion is quite unacceptable whatever rationalist critics may say.*

Admitting the mystical or spiritual sense principally intended by the Holy Spirit, it might be well to state here, as elsewhere in the Old Testament, a literal historical *event served as a basis for it; and this is what Bossuet, Calmet and other*

---

1.   "Never did anyone in Israel," retorted the distinguished Akiba energetically, "ever dare to doubt that this Canticle was a sacred book ... All the hagiographers are saints but the *Song* is sacrosanct."

Catholic commentators claimed, arguing that this book literally refers to Solomon's nuptials and that this even takes on a spiritual significance, representing the nuptials of Christ with the Church and with every soul in a state of grace.

Although this opinion has not been rejected and could very easily be maintained since it offers a priori *a certain semblance of truth, it in fact raises many very serious problems that make it unacceptable and therefore has very few reputable supporters. Therefore the majority of Catholics, and even the Jews themselves, take the whole of this Song, not as it reads* literally, *but metaphorically or allegorically, considering it to be a true rhetorical allegory, that is to say, an extended metaphor, like the parable of the* Prodigal Son, *or the* Vineyard *(Luke 15, 11; 20, 9-16) of the Sower, or the wedding-feast for the King's son (Matt. 13,3; 22,2), in which the meaning that Bossuet holds to be secondary or figurative is seen to be the true, primary, and literal sense. This mystical or spiritual sense, then, is the only true literal sense, the only one intended by the Holy Spirit, and even by the human author himself, who simply used those images and natural comparisons to symbolize the purest supernatural love.* "Itaque tota hujus libri oratio," *writes Fr. Luis de León (in Ch. 1, Prol.),* "figurata est, et allegorica."[2]

To convince ourselves that the text cannot refer to any human betrothal we have only to study the apparently quite arbitrary way in which the character and condition of these incomparable spouses change at every step. They manifest themselves at times as kings, or gardeners, but more often appear as simple shepherds, using comparisons very common to shepherds but which would sound utterly improper on the lips of kings. It is impossible to imagine how the daughter of

---

2. This does not mean that we deny that there could be an *initial figurative sense* that is not *mystical* but strictly speaking *'historically literal'* — such as Jehovah's love for His chosen people — and which serves as a base for a fuller, *more figurative* and properly *mystical* sense, such as the love of Jesus for each of His holy souls; and it is this meaning that is the principal concern of our humble *exposition;* for all these expressions of divine love can easily fit into a single and very broad *figurative sense.*

Pharaoh, or any other of the wives of the pompous kings of Israel is going to wander by night in search of him, through the streets or through the "huts of the shepherds, her companions," like a humble shepherd-girl; or that she will become brown in the sun, being made "to look after the vines."

In other words, if they really were shepherds or farm workers they could hardly appear as kings, in all their splendor and possessed of great riches.

On the other hand, there are very many lines that taken in their strictly literal sense *belong neither to kings, nor to shepherds, nor to any specific person; if these were not taken metaphorically they would sound far too vulgar or ridiculous to be found on the lips of an inspired writer, whose words, being truly divine, always serve to instruct us* (II Tim. 3,16). *In this way the detailed description, for example, of the whole of the body or of its various members, with the attributes given to each of them or the objects with which they are compared, would seem almost scandalous, did they not distinctly represent the good qualities of the soul, just as the great diversity of plants and flowers there mentioned must, and does, represent the beautiful variety and sweet scent of virtues.*

Interpreting it in this way, there is no reason to search in the written word for more than is strictly necessary to establish the metaphor and its meaning; no need to tarry over details that the simile or analogy rarely goes into, but always directing one's heart and thought to the sublime heights that are there indicated. Otherwise our attention would be drawn to that material form which is in itself totally incapable of giving edification or of uplifting the heart. Here perhaps better than anywhere else, we see the truth of the apostle's saying (II Cor. 3,6): the written letters bring death, but the spirit gives life.

Moreover, Bossuet's division of the Song into seven parts that correspond to the seven day celebration of the Hebrew wedding-feast, is too arbitrary and has scarcely any foundation in the sequence of the narrative or in the narrative itself, in which these consecutive days of celebration are often interrupted at a time when one would least expect it. Because of this, this division has now come to be rejected by everyone.

Almost the same could be said of the division made by others who consider it to be a kind of drama in five acts: Act One, I, 1 — II, 7; Act Two, II, 8 — III, 5: Act Three, III, 6 — V, 1; Act Four, V, 2 — VIII, 4; Act Five, VIII, 5-16. The end of Acts One, Two and Four are indicated by the king's command, not to awaken the bride, *and in Act Three by a similar charge (V, 1), but mysterious sleeps have no special value in a human drama, although they do have, as we shall see, very great value in indicating the great stages of mystical life.*

If it is seen in a literary sense as a pastoral drama, *we will search in vain for a unity of plan, or of place, or for any definite purpose, nor will we find any surprising denouement or any lively dialogue, etc. Rather than a single poem, it would perhaps seem to be made up of scattered parts of various poems, without any further inference than that which the identity of the characters might be able to give them, although these latter* change their condition at every step.

On the other hand, if we see it as a mystical idyll, *that is to say, if we take it in that lofty spiritual, metaphorical sense, that unique sense recognized by tradition, we will discover within it a grandiose plan that corresponds to the soul's progress in the life of the spirit; and what at first appear to be disconnected passages become very beautiful descriptions of the principal successive stages of the spiritual life, stages which are presented as though they follow instantaneously one upon another, or after a short space of time, while in fact they involve long periods lasting months and even years... Its various parts, then, cannot be called* acts *or* scenes, *but* cantos *that form, as Meighan says, "an* idyll *involving two (principal) characters, a canticle in dialogue form."*

The principal phases or sections are separated or indicated, as we said, by the Bride's mystical sleeps that the Spouse orders

not to be disturbed (II, 7; III, 5; VIII, 4), sleeps from which she
therefore emerges greatly enriched. They extend, to be precise,
from what precedes the first sleep, the beginner's *state, to what*
succeeds the final one, the stage of the perfect, all the rest
belonging to the successive stages of those more or less
advanced, *who eventually, from the second sleep onward, and*
especially after the second calling of the Beloved (V, 2), could
well be considered almost perfect, *if not indeed fully perfect,*
for this is how Fr. Luis de León[3] *sees them. With even better*
reason they could, and even should be taken for such after the
third and final surrender of the soul to the Lord, as though
confirming forever all her promises to be faithful to Him with
the words: I am His . . .

*St. Ambrose has, in fact, noted (*De Isaac et anima, *Ch. 8),*
that these three surrenders of the mystical Bride (II, 16; VI, 2;
VII, 10), "must correspond to three successive stages: the first
indicating her initiation and formation in virtue, the second, her
progress in virtue, and the third, her complete perfection. In the
first, the stage of spiritual infancy, she perceives supernatural
things as though in darkness . . . ; in the second, she inhales the
fragrance of her Beloved, Who appears to her among lilies . . . ;
in the third, she is confirmed in grace, thereby giving the Divine
Word a resting place in her own heart, so that He might always
be turned *toward her, gazing at her with utmost satisfaction;*
and thus, with great confidence she can invite Him to go out
into the fields in her company."

This is how it develops into a most beautiful idyll formed
by a series of cantos that correspond to the different parts or
phases of the mystical life.

We can agree, therefore, with St. John of the Cross when
he writes in his Spiritual Canticle *that: "these stanzas begin*

---

3.   He maintains, in fact, in his latin Exposition (ch I), that in this book there is a
      description of the stage of love that every pious soul can, if she wishes, pass
      through systematically, from the first to the last; and that the three great
      divisions of spiritual life are separated by the words *Vox Dilecti* of chapters 2
      and 5.

*with a soul's initial steps in the service of God and continue
until she reaches spiritual marriage, the ultimate state of
perfection. They refer consequently, to the three states or, ways
of spiritual perfection . . . through which a soul passes . . . The
initial stanzas treat of the state of beginners, that of the
purgative way. The subsequent ones deal with the state of
proficients in which the spiritual espousal is effected, that is, of
the* illuminative way. *The stanzas following these refer to the*
unitive way, *that of the perfect, where the* spiritual marriage
takes place.

*But bearing in mind the three divisions mentioned and
how this advanced stage is excessively prolonged, we think it
preferable to divide the divine* Song *into* four parts: *1st, that of*
beginners, *of souls who are beginning to* follow the Lord; *2nd,
that of the proficient or* advanced, *that is to say, of those who
follow Him truly and who already live in a certain familarity or*
union with Him; *3rd, that of the* well advanced *and* almost
perfect, *in whom He* lives *and reigns through the intimate union
of* Betrothal; *and the 4th, that of the perfect who are*
transformed and made one with Him (Spiritual Marriage). *Even
here one could add a further state of* consummate perfection —
*in so far as such perfection is possible in this life — which would
begin in the third sleep (VIII, 3-4).*

*Others, — and not without reason — feel authorized to
admit as many as six different cantos that correspond to as
many sections or progressive stages.* [4]

*In this way we discover a wonderful order which, from a
purely human point of view, could not be discerned or even
suspected.*

---

4.   According to Fillion (Introd. to *Song*), "the song can be divided into six
     different parts, which seem fairly complete in form and content: 1st canto I, 1
     — 11, 7; 2nd, II, 8 — III, 5; 3rd, III, 6 — V, 1; 4th, V, 2 — VI, 8; 5th, VI, 9 —
     VIII, 4; 6th, VIII, 5 — 14. In the events described in the different cantos there
     is a very marked ascending gradation; Christ and His Church (or the pious
     soul) loving each other more and more, giving each other greater and greater
     proof of their celestial and reciprocal love, their union becoming more and
     more intimate in each canto."

The similarity between this poem and Greek drama is to be found in the introduction of the chorus, which interrupts the dialogue, making it much more amenable, and invests it with a certain elevated tone of religious lyricism that transcends all the base and abject thoughts that might come to mind. This choir is at times composed of the friends, companions or emulators of the Bride, then again of the friends of the Spouse.

This admirable Spouse, *Who is none other than the Word incarnate, Who became man for no other purpose than to* deify us, *celebrating with our poor souls the eternal Betrothal — having gained, attracted, purified, beautified, adorned, enriched and . . . deified our souls through His divine Action — can easily be recognized in all the successive stages described there: now as the* Good Shepherd *Who knows His sheep, calls them by name, induces them to follow Him into the richest pastures and giving them nothing less than* eternal life *(John 10,11,14,27,28); then again as a powerful* King *Who invites us to reign with Him, to share His throne, provided we accompany Him in His labors and sufferings* (Luke 22,29; Rev. 3,21); *or as a vine-dresser who keeps a large vineyard and hires laborers to tend it, or who leases it* (Matt. 9.38; 20 and 21); *and even as the true Vine . . .* (John 15,1) *that yields the most precious wine that makes maidens* flourish (Zech. 9,17).

Thus, the souls that He deigns to take for His brides are of every different kind, and all of them together will be His only bride, the Holy Church, the chaste virgin, worthy of being presented to Christ (II Cor. 11,2).

The Church, then is normally the Bride *par excellence, although at times, and in a very special way, the Bride is the Blessed Virgin who appeared before Him, always "encountering peace", always pure and "beautiful like an army in battle array"; and thus she serves as a prototype of the Church and as its epitome. This title of* Bride *is also to be applied to all just souls who, according to their fidelity to grace, are being purified and sanctified so as to become worthy of being presented before Him, like small churches "stainless and spotless", and like "closed gardens" where He can take His delight, for He has His delight in dwelling with the children of men (Prov. 8.31).*

Because He desires to take His delight in every soul, no one is excluded from His invitations of love: the doors to these intimate communications are not intentionally closed to anyone. Therefore, those who sincerely desire it "are given the power to become the children of God," and therefore His brothers are intimate friends whose souls He can finally take to Himself as faithful Brides. [5]

The familiar contact and mystical betrothal of God with His souls. — *The immense love that the Divine Word has for us induced Him to use all manner of loving intercourse with us — the most intimate and affectionate relations that could ever be imagined. For, not satisfied with being Redeemer, Shepherd, Physician, Lord, Father, Brother, Friend, etc., He desires to become nothing less than the true Spouse of souls; and this is the title that He treasures most, since it indicates the deepest and tenderest of loves. No other name could be found that expresses so vividly the intimacy that He wished to establish with us, says St. Bernard (Serm. 7 in Cant. n.2), than those of Spouse and Bride who share everything: riches, the table, the home, the bed. He even wanted to be of the same flesh and blood as we, assuming our own nature so that we might participate in His, giving us His Own Body to eat and His most Precious Blood to drink so that we might have eternal life, thereby participating ever more abundantly, in His Own life-giving Spirit, Whose fullness dwells in Him, to be unreservedly communicated to others according to His grace*

5.   "Every soul, however laden with sins and shrouded by vice it may be," writes St. Bernard (*Serm.* 83 *in Cant.*) in agreement with St. Augustine (*Manual,* ch. 18), "cannot only breathe with the hope of forgiveness, but confidently aspire to contract the most intimate union with the King of Angels and celebrate the mystical betrothal with the divine Word."

"Then let those who still do not experience such singular favors believe in this Love," he adds (*Serm.* 84), "so as to be able one day, through faith, to reap the fruit of the experience of this wonderful and divine betrothal."

(John *1,16; 3,34; 6,55; 10,10; Eph. 4,7), since all those who adhere to Him become one Spirit with Him (I Cor. 6,17).*

Thus the Psalmist presents Him to us (Ps. 19,6), as a giant descending from Heaven, to ascend later to its highest region, but rising as Spouse, *and endeavoring to enkindle in all souls, without exception, the fire of His divine love (ibid; 7;* Luke *12,49). In* Hosea *(2,19,20) He promises to betroth us to Him in righteousness and in judgement, in loving kindness and in mercy . . . : something which is brought about in baptism, then ratified in the course of a holy life . . . and finally consummated in glory, and to some extent here on earth in souls who have gained the heights of mystical life where the now indissoluble* Spiritual Marriage *is celebrated. In* Jeremiah *(2,2) and in* Ezekiel *(16, ff.), Jerusalem appears as the Bride chosen by God Himself; and it is for this reason that its infidelities are painted in the blackest colors of adultery. The Baptist declares himself to be a friend of the Divine Spouse Who comes to win and enamor souls (John 3,29); and He Himself compares the Kingdom of Heaven to a king celebrating his son's wedding (Matt. 22,2). St. Paul pictures the Church, the true Kingdom of God on earth as Christ's bride (Eph. 5,29); and finally the* Apocalypse *(19, 7) celebrates the eternal nuptials of the Lamb of God.*

Thus, this Canticle *is the divine* epithalamium *par excellence in which the Eternal Father, through all ages seeks to celebrate the mystical wedding of His Only-Begotten with the Bride that He had destined for Him; and in it, in a marvelous way, we are told of the wonders of the love that this Divine Spouse holds for us (John 3,16), and of His prodigious condescension in stooping down to our insignificance so as to raise us up to His infinite greatness.*

"Here," says Fr. Luis de León (Prologue to Trans.), "we see vividly portrayed the amorous fires of true lovers, the kindled desires, the constant anxiety, the grievous anguish that absence and fear produce within them . . . ; in short, all those feelings that impassioned lovers usually feel are seen here, but

so acute and delicate because divine love is so much more intense and pure, than human love. Divine love is expressed in the most exquisite words, the gentlest endearments, the most unusual and most beautiful comparisons ever written or heard; and because of this, the book is difficult for anyone to read, and dangerous for the young and for those not yet advanced or steadfast in virtue; for in no other written work is the passion of love explained with greater force and significance . . . It is quite clear and generally agreed upon that in these Songs *the character of King Solomon and his bride . . . who use these endearing expressions, the Incarnation of Christ is explained and His eternal love for His Church together with other mysterious secrets of considerable consequence;"* — as are all the secrets communicated by Him to the happy souls who truly love Him.

We must, then, says Tirino, consider this sublime Canticle as a kind of spiritual colloquy between Jesus Christ and His Church, and every soul that is solidly Christian, and thus a member of that Church and His Bride. Christ here fulfills two functions or roles: the first as that of the wisest Master, teaching the highest truths and unfolding the most ineffable mysteries involved in our sanctification. In the second He appears as the most loving and tender Spouse, extolling in an unbelievable way the prerogatives of His sweet Bride, and at the same time adorning her, enriching her and heaping graces and ineffable gifts upon her. In the same way as the Church every just soul plays two, or rather three roles, namely: that of disciple, that of bride, and finally that of mother of many other souls; usually these souls are accorded the name of maidens, or daughters of Zion, or daughters of Jerusalem. *The latter names are usually given to those who are still very worldly, and so scarcely understand the ways of the spirit; the former being given to the purer and more advanced who are already inhaling the divine fragrance of virtue.*

The content of this divine colloquy and holy conversation

is, as befits the persons involved, most useful and pleasing and sublimely uplifting, so that the whole of the Canticle becomes one of the sweetest, most delightful

The excellent features of this Canticle. *There is no poem comparable to this one, which is quite rightly referred to simply as* The Song. *What reading, we join St. Bernard in asking (*Serm. 1, in Cant.*), could be more agreeable, or could do more to instruct, edify and delight than the perusal of these ineffable mysteries hidden beneath the surface of this divine Epithalamium, which begins with the sign of peace, the holy kiss of the true Solomon to this Bride, the Church, and to all just souls, and ends with the most marvelous display of an infinite love . . . ? We have no doubt whatsoever, he goes on, that this wonderful poem, with its exalted purpose, its singular unction and delicacy, excels not only all profane peoms but also all the other Canticles found in Sacred Scripture whose truths it contains. Let those who know this through experience thus speak of it, so that those who have not savored its ineffable delights, may thus become desirous not only of knowing them in theory, but also of experiencing them for themselves:* Sui singulari dignitate, et suavitate cunctis merito antecellit; quia caeterorum omnium est fructus. Experti recognoscant, inexperti inardescant desiderio non tam congnoscendi, quam experiendi.

*For this reason it is to be hoped that, as Fr. Juan de los Angeles says (*Considerations on the Song, *Prael VI), "the fruits of this reading will be most gratifying . . . It is a spiritual garden for the regalement of souls, where they can make sweet-smelling bouquets of different flowers for their own pleasure and enjoyment. Here they begin to estimate the value of God's love, its accomplishments, demands, achievements and the obstacles that separate them from it. Here they will come to know its many sudden appearances and its performances, so different from those that we see today in people who call themselves spiritual; in this way many will be undeceived and return to the truth." For here, indeed, they will find "wonderful*

instruction for their guidance, if they have such a desire, to make
progress in mystical theology and communication with God
through the outpourings of His gratuitous, delectable and
seraphic love that forms the basis of these Songs.

In this way, when readily the description given in Holy
Scripture of this spiritual wedding and the mutual feeling of the
Spouse, we can readily remove from our minds any base or
worldly idea that a human betrothal might suggest to us, so as
to fix our attention solely on the most exalted truths that these
comparisons communicate to pure minds that thirst after God.
As a result, the mind is free to understand and attain that
ineffable union that this same Spirit of love seeks to establish
between Jesus and His souls . . .

"You must bear in mind," remarked St. Bernard once
again (Serm. 45, n. 7-8), *"that it is the Spirit Who speaks here,*
and therefore you have to understand the things He tells you in
a spiritual way. Therefore, when you hear or read that the Word
and the soul speak to one another and gaze at one another, do
not think or imagine that human words are spoken by either, or
that corporal images are used in this mutual gaze . . . Since the
spoken word of God is spiritual, and the response of the soul to
that word is also spiritual, they each have their own way of
speaking to one another. The language of the Word is certainly
the evidence *of His condescension; and that of the soul the*
fervor *of her devotion. The soul that does not possess this*
spiritual tongue is dumb and lowly, and can in no way converse
with the Word. Therefore, when the Word says to the soul: How
beautiful you are, *and calls her* His love, *He infuses in her what*
is needed to spiritualize her love for Him, and at the same time,
He gives her the sure knowledge *that she is loved. Thus when*
she calls the Word her Beloved . . . she attributes to Him,
without fraud or invention, this fact that she loves Him and is
loved by Him, while admiring His condescension and wondering
at such a profound favor."

All these things are like red-hot coals which inflame pure

*and generous hearts with divine love and inspire them to
respond eagerly to the One Who loves them so profoundly.*

*Nevertheless, there will always be those whose hearts are
too gross to behold in these material images taken from sensory
love, the ineffable wonders of that* beautiful love, *that higher
love which is completely celestial, spiritual and divine, and
about which they scarcely know anything. Such holy
occurrences, we would add, are not for such people. These
precious pearls must not be cast before swine* (Matt. 7,6).[6]

*For this reason the Hebrews were careful not to let anyone
read this book until they had reached a mature age in which
there was at least the good sense needed to view it with the
proper reverence. But we Christians have no such prohibition,
for we have already received the first-fruits of the Spirit with
which to free ourselves, if we so will, from the bondage of the
written word that kills, and to establish ourselves in this divine
love that shines through it, understanding it to be the fruit of
the Spirit Who brings life (II Cor. 3,6). Furthermore, we must
all have some knowledge of this most exalted doctrine if we are
to attain the desired perfection.*

*Mystical doctrine, Clement of Alexandria has remarked
(Stromat., 1, V, Ch. 10), ought to be known by all who are
perfect. Thus, it should be placed within the reach of all, so that
everyone can become and show themselves truly "perfect in
Christ":* Quem nos annuntiamus, *said the apostle (*Col, *1,
28)*... docentes omnem hominem in omni sapientia, ut
exhibeamus omnem hominem perfectum in Christo Jesu. *For
this reason he earnestly prayed for all the faithful, that they
might be filled with all wisdom and spiritual knowledge so as to
know the will of God fully and know how to* please Him in all
things: Non cessamus pro vobis orantes, et postulantes ut
impleamini agnitione voluntatis ejus *in omni sapientia et
intellectu spiritali,* ut ambuletis digne Deo per omnia

---

6.   "Whoever sets out to read this book with profane eyes and a heart full of
     carnal love," writes Petit (Introd. *in Cant.*), "will encounter the written word
     that kills instead of the spirit that gives life."

placentes, in omni opere bone fructificantes, et crescentes in scienta Dei *(Ibid. 9-10).*

Without this divine science the soul cannot be considered a perfect Christian although, on the other hand, unless she is already to some extent perfect, she will have difficulty in understanding the mysterious language of Wisdom (I Cor. 2,6).

The mystical Bride, says Origen (Prologue to Song), *is called perfect. "Being the bride of the* perfect *Man she must be perfect for her to receive the words of His perfect doctrine."*

However, in order to reach such lofty perfection she must prepare herself gradually and at every stage.

Therefore, it is wrong to refuse to use this sacred work as a help to our spiritual progress because we fear to encounter words or expressions that could be taken in a wrong sense. This attitude was energetically condemned by St. Teresa when she wrote (Conceptions of the Love of God, Ch. 1). *"You may think that in these* Canticles *there are some things which might have been said in a different way . . . I have heard some people say that they actually tried not to listen to them. O God, what miserable creatures we are! . . . The Lord grants us great favors by showing us the good things which come to the soul that loves Him and by encouraging it till it can hold converse with His Majesty and delight in Him; yet from these favors we derive only fears and we attribute meanings to them that well display the little love we feel for God . . . We think it impossible for a soul to hold such converse with God as this . . . (But there are certain people) to whom it has brought such abundant blessing, such joy and such complete security from fear that they have often felt bound to give special praises to Our Lord for having provided such a salutary help for souls who love Him with a fervent love. This unfathomable love on God's part has led them to see and understand that God can really so humble Himself; their experience alone would not have sufficed to remove their fears when the Lord granted them such favors, but in this they see the anchorhold of their security.*

"I know someone who for many years had misgivings about this and nothing could reassure her until it pleased the Lord that she should hear some texts from the Canticles *which assured her that her soul was being well guided. For, as I have said, she then realized that it is possible for a soul enamored by her Spouse to experience all these joys and raptures human agonies and afflictions and delights and happiness in Him, when she has left all worldly joys for love of Him and has given up self and placed herself wholly in His hands . . .*

"(I conclude by advising you . . .) not to be surprised at the tender words in Scripture that pass between God and the soul. What amazes and bewilders me more, considering what we are, is the love which He had for us, and still has. Nevertheless, He has such love and there are certainly no words by which He could make it known more clearly than He has already manifested by His actions."

Thus, it does not matter that the unrefined realism of our age is unable, through its own fault, to reach the sublime heights of this beautiful love; because fortunately, there will always be those, and they are more numerous today than is generally thought, who are sufficiently pure in heart to perceive in these similes and figures, to a greater or lesser extent, the sublime realities that they represent; and imbibing the things of the Spirit (Rom. 8, 5), and beholding these supernatural splendors, they are able to climb the heights to attain them until they finally behold God in Zion and there delight eternally in Him.

Shocking expressions and difficulties that arise. *It is true that in this Canticle there are many things that are very difficult to understand, and not a few expressions that are apt to disconcert or shock at first sight, being apparently very daring and, of course, very different from the kind generally used today; and certain descriptions which, to human eyes, might well seem too realistic. Simple spiritual souls, however, who utterly refuse to read profane and unacceptable books, far from finding any base or coarse idea in this poem, encounter the purest*

*delights in it, being much more uplifted and enchanted by it
than by any other book. They know very well, as St. Teresa
says, that although material things are mentioned, it is as
though they signified nothing corporal, but were purely of the
spirit; for this love is completely spiritual and divine, and
whoever sees anything else is not yet ready to read or
understand this work; and so these favored souls never even
dream of taking it literally, but rather, fully realizing that it is
through the different parts of the body that the hidden
conditions of the soul and the singular qualities of the mystical
spouses are portrayed, they understand better than anyone the
appropriateness of using certain terms and expressions that
could well seem shocking to others.*

*With respect to this, however, it must be pointed out that
many of the things which surprise or shock us today, and, as a
result, are very difficult to understand, for example, the
comparison that is made between teeth and hair, flocks of sheep
and goats, would heardly surprise us if we lived among
shepherds, even less so in those times and circumstances, when
the meaning of these expressions that seem so obscure today
was perfectly clear.*

*In general, the obscurity of this book derives above all
from the loftiness of ideas and the sublimity of feelings, with
which someone who is not to some extent initiated in the
ineffable mysteries of divine love can scarcely be acquainted. As
Fr. Luis de León remarks (loc. cit.) this obscure or difficult
language is to be found "in all works where any great passions
or feelings, especially of love, are roused, for the intellect then
becomes incoherent and confused. However, once the thread of
these vehement passions has been understood, these reasonings
correspond marvelously to the affections they display,
affections which are born one from the other in natural
harmony. The reason of this seeming incoherence is found in
the fact that when a strong passion predominates, the tongue
does not follow the heart and all it desires to say and so it*

expresses these lofty sentiments haltingly and without
connection. Sometimes reason begins to function at the
beginning of the experience, at other times not until the end,
disregarding the beginning; for, just as he who loves feels deeply
what he says, so it seems to him that whatever he writes will be
understood by others, for passion, with its strength and
incredible haste, rushes his tongue and his heart from one
affection to another, and in this way his words are disconnected
for they correspond to the vehement movement of the passions
and the impressions they make on the mind of the one who
utters them; all this is misunderstood and misjudged by anyone
who does not experience it."

For this reason, "in this sacred epithalamium," as St.
Bernard observes (Serm. 79), the affections should be given
more consideration than the words. Holy love — the only
purpose and content of this book — does not display itself in
words, but in what it effects. Love is what says everything here;
so that whoever seeks to understand what is written in this
work, let him first learn how to love. Whoever does not love will
exhaust himself pointlessly in listening to or reading the canticle
of love; for it is absolutely impossible that its expressions of fire
be understood by a heart that is frigid. Just as a person who
does not know Greek cannot understand this language when it
is spoken . . . so the same is true of the language of divine love
which seems foreign and strange to one who does not love."

Not just any love is sufficient: in order to attain it, the
soul who aspires to the mystical betrothal must full understand
the requirements demanded by this love. It is through
communication with the Divine Word, as St. Lawrence Justinian
remarks, that we learn the art of loving Him and the language of
His love.

"The second cause of obscurity," continues Fr. Luis, "is
the fact that it has been written in Hebrew, by construction
and nature a language of few words and disconnected phrases,
and words that have a diversity of meanings; and also the fact

that the style and opinions of the people of those days were so different from what is generally held today; hence we find the comparisons that this book uses, when the spouse or bride seeks to praise more highly the beauty of the other, both new and strange and quite lacking in the niceties of expression."

Opportuneness. *Hence the* advantage *and even the* necessity *of explaining it clearly and of bringing it within the compass of all pious souls who ardently desire to be inspired and edified by such lofty reading. This opportuneness is indisputable, in spite of all the arguments that might be used against it. For Holy Church places the* Breviary *in everyone's hands, hoping that all will take part, just as they always have done, in the liturgical office. And we see included in the* Breviary *nearly the whole of this Canticle, its precious lessons embalming with divine perfumes, the festivities of the Blessed Virgin and of the saints most enkindled by the love of God, and thus becoming the delight of every pure soul. There all that understand Latin can see or hear it, whether they are men or women, adults or children. A simple and brief explanation is given so that what cannot be comprehended may be correctly understood and the fruit that the Church desires may be gathered from it.*[7]

This, no doubt, was what moved St. Francis de Sales to try to put it, as much as possible, within the reach of all the readers of his Devout Life; *and this, too, because of our own insufficiency inspired us to explain it in detail, in class, to our pupils who were studying Holy Scripture (1915-1916), so that they might understand it properly in the choir, and in turn preach it in a sacred manner from the pulpit, without running the risk of quoting it with disastrous results, as often happens to*

---

7.   Although it is clear that it cannot be placed indiscriminately in everyone's hands, it is nonetheless true, as Fillion observes, that "it breathes forth — in its smallest details as in its entirety — an immaculate purity, a sacred holiness, and (that) there is nothing in it that is unworthy of the Spirit of God.

In every age the most chaste and exalted of souls have found their delights there and have wondrously availed themselves of it in becoming enkindled by the love of God."

those who do not study it. We, therefore, think we are wise to accede to the pious requests of several very devoted religious (the Reparadoras of Madrid) who, for their greater good, asked us to explain to them, in a brief series of talks the great mysteries of spiritual life so concisely and marvelously expounded there. And since one of them (Mother Mary of the G. P.) noted down these explanations and summarized them with all the precision one could possible desire, it seems to us only right, in view of the interest many have shown in taking advantage of these notes, that we now accede to a double request that we publish them immediately as they stood, in a simple and concise form that will help many good souls who will be content with them; and that later, we amplify them for their greater usefulness, giving a more complete and detailed exposition that would satisfy the desires of those who would not be content with so little.

Having already published the first version, entitled A very Brief Exposition of the Song of Songs according to the Version of Father Scio, *for the use of spiritual persons,* [8] *we believe the moment has now come to publish the second or more extensive version as well, with the new title of* A Mystical Exposition of the Song of Songs. *In editing it we have tried to join together the previous notes with others taken in class by our students, and to complete them by studying the matter in greater details and at greater length. At the same time we have kept much closer to the Hebrew text, the sense of which we have always kept very much in mind,* [9] *although not abandoning thereby the general tenor of the Vulgate, in which version expressions are found, consecrated by the continual use of the Church, and to which nearly all our readers have grown accustomed. We have taken care to corroborate our poor doctrine by the knowledge and testimonies of the Holy Fathers, the great mystics and the masters of the spiritual life, so that it might thus achieve a*

8.   Vergara, typography of the Holy Rosary, 1918, 48 pages in 4°. (out of print).
9.   For greater clarity we have preserved the parallelism of the phrases (that is to say, the form of the Hebrew verse) in our version.

twofold end: namely, to awaken desire for that special unction to which this poem holds the secret, and the solidity and security needed to infuse into souls tranquillity and confidence. We also endeavored, as far as possible, to make certain that this Exposition *should be of use not only to many souls eager to become advanced in the spiritual life and to grow in intimate union with God, but also to all those who want to know the ways of the spirit, the wonders of mystical life and the mysteries of this beautiful love in greater depth.*

However, that we may not write at too great a length, we restricted ourselves principally to the mystical betrothal of the Divine Word with all faithful souls, and merely indicated at times what relates to the Church, or to the Synagogue and to the Blessed Virgin; for that exposition actually belongs to a different kind of work, dogmatic, exegetic or apologetic in nature.

Because of our own meager understanding and lack of experience, this task may appear too bold; however, we do not on that account wish to abandon it as we believe it to be very necessary. We trust, then, in the goodness of the Lord to help us carry it out in the right way, seeking inspiration from those meaningful words with which the Mystical Doctor, St. Teresa used to encourage herself (loc. cit.): *"I still think that the time I have spent in writing this will have been well employed, since I have been pondering over matters so divine that I have not deserved even to hear them spoken of."*

If we study it with love, perhaps we shall manage to grow more and more in our appreciation of it, and to take greater care in our preparation so as to be able to experience it; meanwhile we shall be glad to help others grow in appreciation and to reap from the fruit that we ourselves were unable to reap until now. May we be able to instruct others in this doctrine, at least as far as is possible, even if we are unable to do so through our example; hoping that our discreet readers will not be too demanding, but will accept this humble service, and with their fervent prayers will endeavor to assist our weakness and lukewarmness, bearing in mind what St. John Climacus has to say about this subject (Spiritual Ladder, Ch. 26): *"Do not be a hard and severe judge, when you meet persons who teach sublime things and yet live heedlessly; for often the defect in works is compensated by a usefulness of doctrine. No two people are the same. some are distinguished more by their words than by their works, and others more by their works than by their words. Those are few who have everything."*

Therefore, as the Prince of the Apostles charges us (I Peter, 4, 10), *we must all try to administer the grace received in the best way possible, to the benefit of others, so that we become "good stewards responsible for all these different graces of God."*

May He deign to bless this humble work and make it serve His greater glory, and to advance the good of so many souls thirsting for this doctrine, who are eager and who need to know the sublime mysteries of divine love, but who have no one to teach them how they might drink of the mystical waters of divine wisdom . . . ! May He bless it, for such works are so urgently needed, works that He Himself is calling us, in so many ways, to undertake . . . !

"Certainly," remarked the mellifluous Doctor, St. Bernard (Serm. 39, n. 5), *"when I recall this verse* (Ps. 119, 130): O God, the unfolding of your word inspires and enlightens the very young, *I think I must pause to explain these mysteries.* For the Spirit of Wisdom is merciful (Wisdom 16), *and delights in finding a kind and diligent teacher who willingly endeavors to satisfy students and uninformed persons, although he himself possesses very modest talents. Divine Wisdom assures us* (Ecclesiasticus 24, 31), *that* those who are engaged in clarifying His celestial doctrine will have eternal life as their reward; *a prize that they would certainly want to win . . . Since there are also great mysteries hidden here in this work, even in words that seem very simple and clear, my speaking of them will be of*

some profit even to the highly informed and intelligent."

There can be no doubt that a true exposition of these divine words, apart from "enlightening the very young", can enlighten and inspire many who are already "adults in Christ", or who consider themselves to be such, revealing quite clearly to them many of the truths of the mystical life which greatly interest them and which have become disfigured or obscured through the centuries. Thus we trust in divine mercy that these expositions will serve to confirm and complement all we have said in The Mystical Evolution *and, above all, in the* Mystical Questions, *and that they may help to encourage many souls to enter into intimate communication with God, to search for the hidden treasure of His Kingdom which is in our own hearts, to possess the precious pearl of His inestimable love, and achieve that exalted wisdom that is offered to all and that invites us all with its ineffable communications.*[10]

May every devout soul thirsting for God, then, read or listen attentively to this wonderful Song *and try to understand and repeat what the Bride says, so as to be worthy one day of themselves hearing what is said to her, and meanwhile at least have the good fortune of the young maidens that accompany her or of the friends and companions of the Spouse.*

There are many, in fact, who are not concerned about obtaining these divine favors for themselves, for they do not know how to appreciate them and cannot find anyone who will give them an explanation of them, or encourage them to enter resolutely upon the beautiful paths of justice, and the delightful ways of wisdom and holy love. However when they behold the ardent desires of the mystical Bride so vividly expressed in this sublime Canticle *how can they fail to be enkindled with similar desires, and join her in calling out for Him who with His divine fragrance draws all simple and pure souls to Himself and captivates* all the upright in heart? *If the just were able to love and desire Him in this way so many centuries before the*

10.   *Prov.* 8 − 9; *Is.* 55, 1; *Matt.* 11, 28 − 29; *John* 7, 37; *Rev.* 21, 6; 22, 17.

Incarnation of the Word, how much more ought we to respond to Him, having seen Him converse with men on earth and shower them with graces?

What, then, should every sincere Christian soul do now, who beholds these wonderful mysteries accomplished, and experiences the miracles of love that God offers her in His desire to raise her to these sublime heights, considering that He made her from the time of her baptism nothing less than His daughter, sister and bride . . . ? What can she do to respond to such generosity and with what desires should she try to prepare herself to become the worthy bride of the Word? What less could she do than fear, reverence, satisfy and love Him with all her heart, and try to please Him in all things, following faithfully in His ways and serving Him with all her strength and might? And what less could He demand of her? This is, indeed, what is demanded in the ancient law where it says (Deut. 10, 12): Et nunc Israel, quid Dominus petit a te, nisi ut timeas Deum tuum, et ambules in viis ejus, et diligas eum, ac servias Deo tuo in toto corde tuo et in tota anima tua . . . ?

But now, in this new law of love, after He has shown Himself to us so "full of grace and truth . . ." so that we all might receive of His fullness, and having deigned to reveal Himself in the glory proper to the Only Begotten of the Father, so as to win hearts and enkindle the whole world with His divine fire, how can we but love and desire Him with our whole soul, continually crying out and sighing for Him, unable to live but in and by Him? If, in short, He was already so urgently desired in the Old Testament when He could be seen only in darkness and at a great distance, how shall we desire Him, seeing Him so near and in all His enchanting reality . . . ?

Let all faithful souls, then, enthusiastically intone this sublime and ever-new canticle of love, and with their fervor compensate to some extent for the coldness, indifference and disdain with which so many others respond to the infinite goodness of the divine Lover . . . !

Salamanca. The Feast of the Holy
Name of Jesus, January 1918

CHAPTER I

Synopsis

The soul thirsty for God begins in a kind of swoon, crying out and sighing for intimate union with Him in Whom she already knows all her good and true help are to be found. (v. 2). She shows how lovable and desirable the divine Spouse is, and how He steals hearts that are pure (v. 3). She turns to Him, as to her Savior, begging Him for His grace and fortitude; and at once declares that she has already achieved more than she could possibly desire, and explains the joy she feels (v. 4). Back again with the daughters of Jerusalem she answers the vain accusations they direct at her for having begun this new life of love and fervor, making known the hidden beauty of this life, while at the same time recognizing her own exterior ugliness, brought about for her own humiliation by the will or permission of God, an ugliness which she regrets not having been able to avoid since she has been overladen with work (v. 5-6). Tired of being with creatures she asks the Love of her heart to tell her where she can find Him, rest near Him and be nourished by Him (v. 7). He teaches her the ordinary path followed by His faithful sheep, of obedience to the shepherds, of abnegation, mortification and surveillance of the senses, and of directing the appetites and the disordered inclinations (v. 8). Pleased to see that she is so determined and brave and that she is now beginning to triumph over herself through the *active purgation*, He rejoices greatly (v. 9-10), promising her, for further encouragement, to enrich her with His precious gifts, truly beautifying her with all manner of virtues and graces (v. 11). She now manages to regale Him with the sweet perfume of her prayers and sacrifices, gazing at Him in the principal mysteries of His most holy life (v. 12). And with the continual memory of the sorrows and joys of Christ and with the virtue of His Blood, she now begins to become truly purified, beautified and consoled (v. 13-14). Greatly pleased, He celebrates the singular beauty of this soul who has now become His true love, and the new light and purity of intention that He sees shining in her eyes (v. 15). She then returns this praise to Him and, venturing to look upon Him as her sweet Spouse, offers Him the bed of her own heart which, thanks to Him, is now entirely beautiful, sweet-smelling and incorruptible (v. 16-17).

1.   The Song of Songs by Solomon.

THE BRIDE
2.   *Let Him kiss me*[a] *with the kisses of His mouth;*
     for Your love is better than wine
3.   *more fragrant than the best ointments.*
     Your name is as oil poured forth:
     that is why the maidens love You.
4.   *Draw me: we shall run after You*
     following the scent of Your ointments[b].
     The King brought me into His mansions[c].
     We shall be glad and rejoice in You.
     praising Your love above wine.
     The upright love you![d]

a.   This sudden change of persons: *Let Him kiss me... Your love...* is characteristic of Biblical language. Origen believes that line one is addressed to God the Father and line two to the Son Who, being so much desired, reveals Himself to her.
b.   This line: *following the scent of Your ointments* is not to be found in the Hebrew.
c.   Hebrew: Will bring me into His intimate rooms. Septuagint: into His bedroom.
d.   Hebrew: We shall praise Your love above wine: You are rightly (recte) loved; or the righteous love You. The Septuagint: Let us rejoice in You; and we shall love Your breasts that are more pleasing than wine. Righteousness loves You.

5. *I am black but lovely, daughters of Jerusalem*
   like the tents of Kedar[e]
   like the pavilions of Salmah.
6. *Take no notice of my swarthiness,*
   it is the sun that has burned me.
   My mother's sons turned against me[f],
   they made me look after the vineyards,
   and I have not looked after my own.
7. *Tell me, then, you whom my heart loves:*
   where will you lead your flock to gaze,
   where will you rest it at noon?
   That I may no more wander like a vagabond
   beside the flocks of your companions.

THE SPOUSE

8. *If you do not know this, O loveliest of women,*
   follow the tracks of the flocks,
   and take your kids to graze
   close by the shepherds' tents.
9. *To my mare harnessed to Pharaoh's chariot*
   I compare you, my love.
10. *Your cheeks show fair between their pendants of pearls*
    and your neck within its necklaces.
11. *We shall make you golden earrings*
    and beads of silver[g].

THE BRIDE

12. *While the King rested on His couch,*
    my nard yielded its perfume[h].

---

e.   The Kedar Arabs were nomads who lived between Arabia and Babylonia; their tents were made of goats' skin that were nearly always black.

f.   Hebrew: grew angry.

g.   This verse and verse nine refer to the head-dress worn in those days from which little chains, or threads of pearls or jewels would hang, carrying some small figure which could well be like that of a turtle-dove. These same or very similar adornments are still worn by orientals.

h.   It was customary to pour censers of sweet-smelling scents over the more important guests at a banquet. (Cf. *Luke* 7:37; *Matt.* 26:7; *John* 12:3).

13. *My Beloved is a sachet of myrrh*
     lying between my breasts[i].
14. *My Beloved is a cluster of henna flowers*[j].
     among the vineyards of Engedi.

THE SPOUSE

15. *How beautiful you are, my love,*
     how beautiful you are!
     Your eyes are dove's eyes[k].

THE BRIDE

16. *How beautiful you are, my Beloved, and how gracious!*[l]
     Our bed is of flowers.
17. *The beams of our rooms are of cedar*
     the paneling of cypress.

Exposition

FIRST SECTION
The soul in pursuit of the Lord: the way of purgation, proper to beginners.

Verse two.   Let him kiss me with the kisses of his mouth. . .

This ineffable *kiss of God* which is the intimate and most
perfect union with Him through the full communication of His
Spirit, although the last to be achieved is the first that is and
should be desired by every soul that truly aspires to enjoy Him
eternally in glory and, insofar as it is possible, in this life here,

---

i.   The young girls in the East used to carry on their breast little bundles or
       packets of myrrh, a bitter and very aromatic resinous substance produced by
       the *Balsamodendron myrrha.*
j.   The henna *(Lawsonia .inernis)* is "a bush whose leaves were used by the
       Egyptians in their toilette, a custom which was adopted by the Jews and
       which spread throughout the East. It becomes laden with clusters of golden
       flowers, hanging from flesh-colored boughs which provide a pleasing contrast
       to the refreshing green of the leaves. Because of their sweet scent these flowers
       were highly valued by Israel women, who made small bouquets and crowns
       from them to wear on their breasts and heads." E. Rimmel.
k.   Hebrew and the Septuagint: Your eyes (are) doves, or like doves.
l.   Hebrew: delightful, sweet.

for only in this way will she be able to find her well-being, her happiness and rest, and completely fulfill the purpose for which she was created.

This Divine Spirit, observes St. Bernard (*In Cant. Serm.* 8, no. 2), "was communicated by the Savior to His disciples in the form of breath (*John* 20:22), which was like a kiss from Him, so that we might understand that it proceeds from the Father and the Son, as a true shared kiss."

Such is the ineffable kiss of God! "The Holy Spirit," exclaims Sauve (*Jesus Intimo,* Pref.), "the happiness, the immense joy that the first Two Persons receive from each Other; the Holy Spirit, Their bond, Their infinitely intimate unity, and also Their link with our soul; the Holy Spirit, the consummation of divine life. . .the peace and rest of the soul."

This Divine Spirit, agrees Ruysbroeck, is "an embrace that intimately penetrates the Father, the Son, and all the Saints in delightful union."

"*Spiritus Sanctus spiritus amoris est, spiritus oris Dei osculum oris Dei,*" in his turn exclaims the servant of God Fr. José de San Benito.

Such, then, is "the sweet kiss of his mouth for which the enamored soul so ardently beseeches the Divine Spouse; for she becomes united in love with Him through this ineffable communication of His Spirit, a communication which contains all the marvels of God's charity."

It can also be said that in these words the soul prays for divine Love, seeing that she cannot achieve it on her own. In this way, "the mouth", notes Fr. Gracian, "is the desire; and God's Love is nothing but the joining of our desire with the desire of Christ, to want what Christ wants, to desire what He desires, to surrender our own will to the divine, and to be in peace with Him; for when it is pleasurable, sweet and gentle and a gift, love is very properly signified by the mouth. And since the soul does not have it from her own resources. . . , she asks for it from God. . ."

"When the soul is enlightened with the light of grace," wrote a most devout Dominican Tertiary from Naples, María de los Dolores, "she knows how worthy of being loved the Lord alone is, and so the whole of creation becomes worthless in her eyes. But knowing her own weakness she asks the divine Spouse to imprint His mystical kiss the seal of His love, upon her, to draw her to Him with His breath and make her live by His Spirit. . .In this way the soul will no longer live in herself, but in Jesus Christ by Whom she was attracted. Oh Kiss! more desirable than any other gift! Only You can lead us to the end of our desires; only You can bring the consummation of that celestial betrothal contracted in the holy baptism."

The kiss of His mouth, says St. Gregory, is the same love that He reveals to us in His holy inspirations and with which He changes us so that we are made to fall deeply in love and finally are left transformed in Him.

The mystical Bride discovers her happiness and the fullness of all that is good, for she encounters the Supreme Good and manages to possess Him in such a way that she comes to be one with Him. . . "The soul is certainly happy," writes Fr. Juan de los Angeles "and a thousand times happy, in that *kiss of God,* when without any intermediary He joins her to Him, when she becomes transformed and deified and, dying to herself and to all that is not God, she lives only that which is God. . .Many were carried away by the sweetness of the *kiss of God* and *deified* during the rapture."

"What a divine kiss!", he exclaims again (*Considerac.* Ch. I), "and how worthy of every admiration, for it is not the joining of mouth with mouth but where God is joined and united with man."

". . .*Osculetur me.* . .: means: 'May I be permitted to take from your sweet mouth that most holy Spirit of which I have already received a part, from whose communication I possess life and spirit, and whose first taste I found so sweet that in comparison even wine, which usually cheers men's hearts, is insipid and unsatisfying.' "

"In that divine contact," he adds, "in that mystical kissing of the holy soul by the celestial Spouse — she dies in herself and He alone remains living within her, their lives now exchanged, each given to the other. Oh, supreme transformation! Oh, most just desire of the soul! Repeat again and again, Oh blessed Bride: *Let Him kiss me with the kisses of His mouth*. . .for there is nothing you could pray to the Spouse for that is more to His liking than this sacred kiss, for which you leave yourself and become transformed in Him, and He in you. In this transformation He takes upon Himself your weaknesses and communicates to you the strength of His Spirit."

". . .I say that the Spouse's kiss that the Bride here asks for is a most worthy effect of a certain tenderness and intimate consolation communicated to the soul by means of a very secret delight: a kiss that she asks for confidently, since love gives her the confidence to do so."

For this reason, "when you hear or read these things", remarked Philon, Bishop of Carpacia (in *Cant.*), "you must understand that everything here is entirely pure, chaste, and sacred; they are the most divine communications of His celestial gifts, where there is nothing carnal or corruptible, base or gross, but rather everything is entirely virtuous. In this way you will prevent your soul from becoming stained or from receiving a mortal wound, where it could well find spiritual refection and a salutary medicine. For the spiritual kiss of God excels and surpasses physical pleasures as much as the light does the dark, as much as life does death, and the eternal the fleeting. For,. . .just as there are physical kisses, so there are spiritual ones; the former carnal and corruptible, the latter celestial and totally divine."

But so as to be able to reach the sublime heights of the divine mouth, the soul must first remain as long as she can in the kiss of the feet of the Crucified Christ, doing penance for her sins with tears of compunction. Resting at these most sacred feet she will soon reach the open wound in His Side, in whose kiss she now begins to take on the image of Christ, through the fire of divine Love that she feels there, and through the faithful imitation of His virtues of which she will become enamored. Resting in that sweet wound, she will then reach the mouth of the Word and receive from Him the ineffable and mystical kiss of peace which completely transforms her in Him; thus achieving the complete perfection that is possible in this life, as the Eternal Father declared to St. Catherine of Siena (Dialogue, Ch. 26).

Osculetur me. . . "Oh, dear God," exclaims the Ven. Mariana de San José, foundress of the Augustinian 'Recoletas', " and what great things this holy soul here asked for, and how she abbreviated all the most substantial requests!". . . "It would seem impudent for her to venture to ask such a great favor, such an extraordinary demonstration of love, so bluntly and without a word of courtesy. But those who understand and know what real distrust of self is, what the profound annihilation, contempt and hatred of self are, will have already experienced the great graces that then follow this divine favor, and will have learned how the Lord gives to them all the help and encouragement they need that they may find the true life. . .

"*There is no other road,* Lord, nor could there be, for me to love and serve You, but that You touch me and give me Your divine peace. Let this touch come, then, for if the Lord gives it to us it will surely reveal all that is caused to be felt and enjoyed when the favor that the Bride is requesting is conceded to her; for being well advanced in the school of God, she is able to ask exceedingly great mercies, and they will be granted to her. . .

"There is no day of rest as long as this Holy Spirit that vivifies souls fails to be communicated to her; and although now touched with this fire, she is not content but asks and wishes that they become one; that, leaving her spirit in the keeping of her Spouse, He will give her His Own, so that she can then say

(*Gal.* 2,20): *Vivo autem jam non ego: vivit vero in me Christus*. . .For she fully realizes that when this Lord opens His mouth, it is to teach the highest knowledge, just as He did in the case of the eight Beatitudes, where the Evangelist writes that He opened His mouth and said (*Matt.* 5) *Beati pauperes spiritu*. . .Since the Bride knows what is done and the marvels achieved by this divine Breath, she asks Christ, our Good, that He make her one with Him. . . She no longer wants to be taught by intermediaries, but wishes that the Holy Spirit be her Master."

This, then, is the aspiration of the mystical Bride, who as St. Bernard remarks, is *any soul in love with God and full of longing to possess and enjoy Him*. For this Bride will not be content to receive the wage paid to a *servant*, nor with the doctrine accorded to the *disciple*, nor even with the very inheritance that is due to *children*; she will not be content with simple gifts, however great and wonderful they may be, but above all and before all else she seeks the Sovereign Giver Himself; she wants to be filled with His Divine Spirit so as thereby to become one spirit with Him. This is the aspiration of every soul who is truly pious and full of fervor, every soul worthy to be called *Christian.*

This soul, knowing very well that her ultimate end and true happiness are to be found in the full possession of God through the Beatific Vision, and never being able to remain satisfied as long as He in some way or other fails to reveal to her His glory (*Ps.* 17:15), she feels as though impelled to show, at times with sighs and cries that break out from the depths of her heart, how anxious she is to enjoy Him now, praying to the Father of mercies and to the God of all consolation, that He deign to give her His peace and the joy of His well-being, by kissing her with His sweet kiss.

"Could I desire and ask for a more precious and sublime favor," writes the Blessed Suso (*Letter* V) "Than that Jesus should show me His loving face and give me His kiss of infinite love? Who could doubt that that is the whole of Paradise?"

"The more the soul knows God," writes St. John of the Cross (*Spiritual Canticle*, Stanza 6), "the greater becomes her desire and anguish to see Him, for. . .there is nothing that can cure her pain save the presence and sight of her Beloved. . .Any soul with authentic love cannot be satified until she really possesses God."

And she will truly love Him if she loves Him for Himself, because, *He is Who He* is, seeking His greater honor and glory in all things, living only in Him and through Him.

"The soul can know clearly whether or not she loves God purely. If she loves Him, her heart or love will not be set on herself or her own satisfaction and profit, but upon pleasing God and giving Him honor and glory. . .Whether the heart has been truly stolen by God will be evident. . .if it has longings for God; or if it finds no satisfaction in anything but Him" (*ibid*, Stanza 9).

It is then that she will truly come to possess Him and begin to receive *the kiss of His mouth.*

This *mouth* of God the Father is His very Son, the eternal splendor of His glory and the Word of His virtue through Whom in the fullness of time He saw fit to reveal Himself to us and speak to us words of eternal life (*Hebr.* 1:2; I *John* 1:1-2); and the *kiss* of this Divine Mouth is the very sovereign Spirit of Love which proceeds at one and the same time from the Father and the Son and is their eternal bond of union in which is contained all the virtue and stability of the heavens, founded upon the Word of the Father. The Christian soul seeks an ineffable communication from the Divine Spirit that allows her to participate in the Father and the Son and causes her to know them both: *"Petit ergo audenter dari sibi osculum, hoc est Spiritum illum in quo sibi et Filius reveletur et Peter. Trinae ergo hujus agnitionis infundi sibi gratiam quantum quidem capi in carne mortali potest, sponsa petit, cum osculum petit."* (St. Bernard, *In Cant., Serm.* 8).

In this way pious souls pray for the most intimate union possible with their God, their all, in Whom, as they know, is to be found their inheritance and all their good and happiness, forever repeating to themselves the words of the Psalmist (*Ps.* 73:28): *My joy lies in being close to God and in placing all my hope in Him.* (For) *anyone who is joined to the Lord is one spirit with Him* (I *Cor.* 6:17). In short, they pray for "a most wonderful knowledge of the Three Divine Persons which would be like a foretaste of eternal life making them thenceforth burn forever in living flames of inextinguishable love." (*Mystical Questions* la. ed. p. 119).

"Once," recounts the Blessed Suso (*Treatise of the Union of the Soul with God, III*), "I saw spiritually that the heart of my heavenly Father was applying itself to mine in an ineffable way. Indeed, I heard the divine Heart, the divine Wisdom, without form or image, speaking to me in the depth of my heart, and in rapture of joy I cried out: 'Oh my dearly Beloved, my only Love, here I am embracing Your very Divinity, heart to heart! Oh God, more lovable than all things lovable! He who loves continues to be different from the object of his love, but You, the infinite Sweetness of true love, You pour Yourself forth like a perfume into the hearts of those that love You. You penetrate with Your whole being into the very essence of their souls, You embrace them divinely and remain united to them through the bonds of an infinite love. . .' "

"The perfections of love that this most loving Lord gives to souls," wrote in his turn the blessed Father Hoyos (*Life* by Vriante, 1884 p. 44), "are such that they are credible only to those who have had experience of them. It is a flash of glory. . ., a heavenly madness. . .: it is when the soul is enjoying that divine breast, rejoicing in the arms of her Beloved. . .it is a sweet destruction, a melting away, an enkindling, an endless burning in flames of love."

Whoever has experienced this in some way cannot help but pray over and over again, stopping at nothing, asking for that mercy sought by the Bride: *Kiss me. . .*

"O my Lord and my God," exclaims St. Teresa (*Conceptions,* Ch. I), "what words are these for a worm to use to its Creator! Blessed be Thou, Lord, Who hast taught us in so many different ways! Who would dare to use these words, my King, save by Thy permission? It is an astonishing thing, and it may well be thought astounding for me to say that they may be used by anyone whatsoever. . . I confess that the words may be taken in many senses, but the soul that is afire with love so that she hardly knows what she is saying is interested in none of them, but wishes only to repeat the words themselves. . . Why should we be astounded at this?. . . Do we not approach the Most Holy Sacrament? I have even wondered if the Bride was asking here for this favor which Christ afterwards gave us. . . These words, if taken literally would strike fear into anyone who was in a normal state of mind when he uttered them. But in anyone, Lord, whom love for Thee has drawn right out of himself Thou wilt pardon the use of them, and even of more words of the kind, notwithstanding their presumption. And if a kiss denotes peace and friendship, my Lord, why will not souls beg of Thee to give it to them? What better thing could we ask, O Lord, than that which I ask of Thee — that Thou wilt give me this peace, *with a kissof Thy mouth?*"

"For this reason, daughters, I advise you always to pray with the Bride for this sweet peace, for in this way all the little fears of the world are kept in control. . . Is it not clear that whomsoever God is so merciful as to join with Him in such friendship, must be left enriched in His goodness. . .?"

"So my Lord, I ask Thee for nothing else in this life but that Thou shouldst *kiss me with a kiss of Thy mouth;* and let this be in such a way, Lord of my life, that, even if I should desire to withdraw from this friendship and union, my will may ever be so subject to Thine that I shall be unable to leave Thee " (*Ibid.,* Ch. 3).

"Oh, how great is the strength of love!", exclaimed the

mellifluous St. Bernard (*In Cant., Serm.,* 7, n.3).

"Oh, what trust and freedom it gives to the soul possessed by it! What clearer proof *that perfect love banishes every fear?* (I *John* 4:18)." In this state the soul's only concern is to become more and more united with the Divine Spouse, seeking, through the mystical kiss that she asks of Him, to be filled with the Holy Spirit, so that the breath of this loving Paraclete might illumine her with His lights and kindle in her the flames of His love, giving her a taste of the wonders of celestial wisdom and of the sweet seasoning of divine grace; for both gifts contain within them the favor of the holy kiss, the light of knowledge and a most substantial solid devotion: *Petit osculum, id est, Spiritum Sanctum, per quem accipiat simul et scientiae gustum, et gratiae condimentum...Utrumque enim munus simul fert osculi gratia, et cognitionis lumen, et devotionis pinguedinem"* (Ibid., *Serm.* 8, n.6.).

Blessed Grignon de Montfort writes (*Orat.* in *Vraie dévot. à la V.*), "since the Holy Spirit is the only Divine Person Who does not produce another within the Divinity, it is this Spirit Who forms and produces all these Divine Persons outside the Divinity; for, all the saints that have been and that will be are the work of His love."

For this reason He cherishes them and, as it were, suckles them at His breast (*Is.* 66, 11-13). And these sweet *breasts,* His sweet *loves* (that of God and of one's neighbor), that He pours into our hearts (*Rom.* 5:5), fragrant with the most precious ointments of His gifts and favors, will "surpass the wine" of worldly pleasures and that of spiritual consolation. That is how the mystical *Bride,* the soul enamored of God dares to ask for the divine kiss refusing to be content with anything less; for as St. Francis de Sales remarks (*Love of God,* I, Ch. 9), "in expressing her first desire, she pretends nothing save a chaste union with her Spouse, protesting that it is the only end to which she aspires and for which she longs."

The Hebrew text puts *kisses* in the plural, undoubtedly

(writes St. Ambrose)" so as to indicate the extent and ardor of the soul's desires; for the soul that loves greatly. . .wants the Word to bestow on her many kisses so that, being full of the lights of His knowledge and receiving from Him the pledge and gifts of His Love she might join the Prophet in saying, overcome with joy (*Ps.* 119:131) *'I opened my mouth and drew toward me His Divine Spirit.'*

"It is this completely spiritual kiss by which the soul is united with the Word and through which a transfusion of the Divine Spirit is brought about within her. . .just as those who give one another the kiss of peace not only join lips but pour forth (so to speak) their hearts and souls into those of the other."

It was for this kiss that the patriarchs and prophets and all the ancient saints clamored and sighed with longing; and it is for this kiss that all we Christians ought to sigh with greater ardor still, following the example of the Holy Virgin, so as not to be unworthy of the name. But, alas!" exclaimed St. Bernard (*Serm.* 2 in *Cant.*), "I can scarcely hold back tears for the suffering and shame that the insensibility of the men of today awakens within me. For who today is as delighted by the fulfillment of His grace as the ancient Fathers were by the mere promise of it. . .? In those days every perfect man would exclaim: 'How much longer will the mouths of the prophets have to continue announcing it to us'. Let Him kiss me now with the kisses of His mouth, He Who is more beautiful than all the children of men! I am not content with listening to Moses, for he seems to me to be stammering. . .Jeremiah does not know how to speak for he is still just a child, and to me the other prophets are as though dumb when compared to Him Whom the Father annointed with the oil of His Divine Spirit above all mortals. Do not speak to me, then, in them or through them; for His words, the efficacious and living words of God, to me are so many kisses of peace, not precisely through the joining of lips, this tending to bring a false peace of heart; but rather because with these words He communicates to the soul an infusion of sovereign joys, a revelation and knowledge of the most divine secrets, and an admirable blend of supernatural lights and internal illustrations."

"What, oh Divine Word," asks St. Mary Magdalene of Pazzi, "are the *kisses* that you give to the soul your bride? A kiss of peace, a kiss of union, a kiss of wisdom, a kiss of order, a kiss of love, a kiss of well-being, a kiss of knowledge: *kisses that are incomprehensible to all flesh.* With these sweet divine kisses the Word consoles all those who suffer and are distressed to see the offences committed against Him... All ye who have intelligence come to the Word and embrace Him and sate yourselves with His kisses!"

"Love," said St. Thomas of Villanueva (*In Cant.* I), is the most absolute Lord that recognizes neither majesty nor reverence, it holds everything against a single measure, it dares all and considers all things licit and for this reason we have to be· indulgent with love."

"The soul is fully aware," adds the saintly abbot already cited (*Serm.* 9), "that she does not even deserve the kiss of the Lord's feet, but love and need force her to desire even the kiss of His mouth, unable to content herself with less: "Non quiesco, ait, nisi *osculetur me osculo oris sui:* Gratias de osculo pedum gratias et de manus; sed si cura est illi ulla de me *osculetur me osculo oris sui... Accepi, fateor, meritis potiora,* sed prorsus inferiora votis... Ne quaeso causemini praesumptionem, ubi affectio urget. Pudor sane reclamat, sed superat amor."

"With such longings the soul seeks the Divine Word," he repeats, (*Serm.* 85), "because she needs it for her perfect correction and enlightenment, for her to become well founded in virtue, for her to be reformed in wisdom, to conform herself to Him in all things and join herself to Him and so be able to produce the fruits of life: *Quaerit anima Verbum, cui consentiat ad correptionem, quo illuminetur ad cognitionem, cui innitatur ad virtutem, quo reformetur ad sapientiam, cui conformetur ad decorem, cui maritetur ad foecundatem, quo fruatur ad jucunditatem. Propter has omnes causes quaerit anima Verbum.*"

We can all, then, join this pious writer in exclaiming "Oh Spouse of my soul, my Jesus! Deign to give me those kisses of Your mouth, filling me with the gifts of Your Spirit, so that there might be within me nothing but words of wisdom, nor any love but that of justice nor any other taste but that for chastity and purity!"

But in spite of all these ardent desires no one ought to presume, or attempt to climb at a stroke to the most sublime heights, omitting to pass through the intermediary stages; no one ought to try to receive the kiss of the divine lips without first of all having well purified his own with the kiss of His Sacred Feet, Hands and Side, transfixed by our love. "The soul laden with sins and still subject to the passions of the flesh," observes the same mellifluous Doctor (*Serm.* 3 In *Cant.*) "should not rashly rise up to the mouth of the pure Spouse; but, on the contrary, she ought to throw herself at His divine feet, and dismayed, like the publican fix her eyes on the ground, not even daring to look up. . . Do not disdain to remain in a place in which the repentant sinner rids herself of the weight of her sins and dresses herself again in sanctity and purity. . . Like this happy penitent prostrate before the feet of the Savior, she must concern herself only with embracing them, kissing them and sprinkling them with her tears, not so as to wash them, but so as to be worthy of being washed herself; and. . .finally to hear from His mouth words of such consolation as these (*Luke* 7:47): 'Your sins are forgiven you'; or again these other words: 'Rise up, rise up, captive daughter of Zion' " (*Is.* 52:2).

"And this is not sufficient", he continues, "for the distance from the Spouse's feet to His mouth is still very great for one to pass suddenly from one extreme to the other: *Longus saltus, et arduus, est de pede ad os*. . . Having emerged yesterday from the mud, do you now dare today to present yourself before the Spouse and touch the face of the very King of Glory with your own? No, no: first pass by the kiss of His hand. . .with candor and purity and fruits worthy of penitence, which are the works of piety. . .giving Him all the glory and attributing nothing to yourself. . .; and this is how you can promise to yourself to escape from the mud in which you were, and aspire to higher and more sublime things."

Then having arrived at the kiss of the side, and perceiving there the beating of the loving heart and, caressed by the breast of divine consolation, she cannot help but feel fully confident to approach Him and receive the peace of His mouth and pray to Him adding:

For your breasts (loves) are more delightful than wine.

Here the soul, ceasing to talk to herself and to creatures, and addressing herself directly to Him for Whom she so longs, tells Him the cause of her longings and ardent desires, praising the sweetness of His sacred breasts, of His loving heart, that is, of His affectionate *love,* and of His ineffable communications and consolations, comparing them to wine which similarly gives comfort and regales, and which is usually understood to be worldly comfort and consolation. Allusion seems to be made here to what would happen in those days, and what happens even today sometimes when someone faints or passes out, when they try to revive or comfort him with wine, giving him sweet scents to breathe in. She, seeing herself faint with love, and presuming that her companions were trying to comfort her in this way, for it is very frequent to see how everyone tries to distract the souls who sigh for God, in vain offering them false or miserly pleasures and worldly gifts, fleeing from this disturbing and harmful conversation, she addresses herself to her Beloved to tell Him that in Him alone can she find her consolation and help, and thus to all gifts and comforts she resolutely prefers the ineffable sweetness of His sweet breasts, to which He Himself promised to bring us and with which He promised to caress us with a more than maternal affection (*Is.* 66, 11-13), until we become enraptured in His divine delights. It is from these sacred breasts from which tender virtuous souls "like new-born babes, receive the milk of justice, of consolation, affection and gifts, that they need to grow in virtue, and because they ought to long and in fact will long ardently if they have already begun to taste how sweet and gentle is the Lord" (I *Peter* 2:2-3). It is there that the adults now drink a love that is not only sweeter and more intoxicating than wine, more capable of attracting, winning, captivating, embalming with their fragrance than all other scents however rich and precious they may be, a love stronger than death, triumphing over all.

We can say that these breasts are the very Divinity and Sacred Humanity of our sweetest Savior, full as they are of an affection that is such that, with ineffable sweetness, it nourishes, comforts and strengthens the soul and makes it grow in all kinds of virtues and breathe an atmosphere of such purity and sanctity that it penetrates and wins hearts for God; and finally will leave the soul so enraptured and ecstatic and so full of strength that she will be able to do wonders of love and suffer all kinds of martyrdoms, if necessary, for the glory of the Beloved.

"The love which proceeds from the two natures, human and divine, united in the person of Jesus Christ," says Maria de los Dolores, "is more intoxicating than wine. And just as wine warms the heart and, intoxicating, causes the man as it were to leave himself, to be unafraid of dangers, so divine love warms souls and causes them to fear nothing, not even death itself."

For this reason they will exclaim in exhilaration:

Your loves are more delightful than wine.

"What tremendous secrets", writes St. Teresa (*Conceptions*, Ch. 4) "there are in these words! May our Lord grant us to experience them. When in His mercy His Majesty is pleased to fulfill this petition of the Bride, the friendship which He begins

to establish with the soul is one which only those of you who
may experience it will understand. . . The soul feels within itself
such great sweetness that it is well aware of our Lord's nearness
to it. . . When it is not so much absorbed in this sweetness, the
experience comes in another way. Both the inward and outward
man seem to receive comfort, just as if into the marrow of the
bones had been poured the sweetest of ointments, resembling a
fragrant perfume . . . that pervades our whole being. Just so does
it seem to be with this sweet love of our God. It enters the soul
with great sweetness, and berings it such joy and satisfaction that
it cannot understand how or in what way this blessing is
entering it. . . In the friendship which the Lord now reveals to
the soul, He desires to have such intimacy with it that nothing
can separate them. Great truths are communicated to it; for this
light which dazzles it because it cannot understand what it is,
shows it the vanity of the world. It does not see the Good
Master teaching it, although it knows *He is at its side.* But it
receives such good instruction and is so much strengthened in
the virtues that it does not know itself nor can it do anything or
say anything but give praises to the Lord. When experiencing
this joy, it is so deeply inebriated and absorbed that it seems to
be beside itself and in a kind of divine intoxication, knowing
not what it is desiring or saying or asking for. . . Awakening
from that sleep and heavenly inebriation, she is like one dazed
and stupefied; well, I think, may her sacred folly wring these
words from her: *"Thy breasts are better than wine".* . . . Oh,
my daughters, may our Lord grant you to understand, or,
rather, to taste, for in no other way can it be understood, how
the soul rejoices when this happens to it. Let worldlings come
with all their possessions, their riches, their delights. . .even if all
these could be enjoyed without the trials that they bring in
their train, which is impossible, they could not in a thousand
years cause the happiness enjoyed in a single moment by a soul
brought hither by the Lord."
    But what will happen when these ineffable communica-

tions go even further. . .?

"When this most wealthy Spouse," adds the same saint (*ibid.*) "desires to enrich and comfort the Bride still more, He draws her so closely to Him that she is like one who swoons from excess of pleasure and joy and seems to be suspended in those divine arms and drawn near to that sacred side and to those divine breasts. Sustained by that divine milk with which her Spouse continually nourishes her and growing in grace so that she may be enabled to receive His comforts, she can do nothing but rejoice. . ."

"*Your breasts are more delightful than wine.* . . Much would have to be said here," observes Fr. Gracian in turn, "about these breasts and all that God gives there to enamored souls and in comparison to which the *wine* of worldly wisdom and human prudence is of little worth. For from the love of Christ's wound arise the sweet-smelling heroic virtues, thanks to which the soul becomes exemplary; these virtues being indicated by the sweet-smelling ointments mentioned by the bride."

These breasts, according to Fr. Juan de los Angeles, are meant to signify spiritual nourishment, that is to say, the doctrine of the gospel and the gifts and fruits of the Holy Spirit, with which the Holy Spouse sustains His Church.

"I like to think," he adds a little later, "that by breasts what is principally meant here are the secret words and intimate feelings of Christ, and also the wonderful caresses and consolations with which on occasions and at intervals He visits and regales the soul. His are these words spoken by Isaiah (66: 10-11): *Rejoice with Jerusalem and be glad with her all you that love her. . .so that you may suck and be satisfied with the breasts of her consolations. . .*" Great is the satisfaction that a soul derives from the doctrine of the gospel, so that the Spouse's heart or mouth was like breasts that continually gave forth the milk of doctrine and grace. . .

"The gift of the breasts of God is such that no one can

know it unless he experiences it; there are no words which suffice to say what it is in itself. Because of this whenever the Holy Scripture seeks to give us an idea of these gifts and delights, there being nothing which completely explains it, it sets forth many ideas so that each will say its part, which in truth is very little. Sometimes it calls them *manna,* which was very sweet-tasting. . .; here they are *better than wine,* indicating a greater tenderness; *breasts,* the breasts of the mother are not as sweet and delicious to the child as the delights of God are delightful to him who tastes them. . . But because those of us who live in the flesh are unable to come to the knowledge of virtue and the pleasures of the spirit save through the taste and savor of that which the flesh savors and takes pleasure in, the Holy Spirit often makes these comparisons. . .so that, having seen how much better and more advantageous are the riches of the soul than those of the body, we might renounce the latter and take up the former."

Here, then, is "the treasure hidden in the ground of the soul for which a man digs and finds; having found it he craves it so vehemently that he sells all he has, denies himself all things that have to do with pleasure, so as to possess this ground — that is to say, these gifts. The Holy Spirit is the treasure of God and of the soul, for He is the nexus of love, the embrace and penetration that pierces and enfolds all interior spirits in fruitive unity; and the Spirit Himself is the Love which causes lovers to faint and be consumed in the furnance of love." Ruysbroeck, *The Kingdom of Those Who Love God,* Ch. 35.

These divine breasts, as we said, represent the love for God and for one's neighbor together with all the favors and graces that nourish and promote it within the soul, and together with all the ineffable delights that our Lord reserves for those that love and revere Him. At the same time, in the opinion of many learned people, they can represent the Old and New Testaments infused with the love of the Celestial Spouse. According to St. Ambrose they represent moreover the Sacraments with which the Divine Savior comforts, restores and regales us, and especially the Holy Eucharist, which is the Sacrament of His Love, where He so intimately binds Himself to our hearts so as to kindle them in celestial fire. For this reason the saintly Doctor (*De Sacram.*, 1, 5, Ch. V) exhorts souls that are pure to approach this adorable sacrament where the Good Lord so affectionately waits to join them and incorporate them into Himself and at the same time be kissed and embraced by them.

Thus they will come to know the incomparable fragrance exhaled by those divine breasts and will excitedly exclaim:

Your loves are more delightful than wine!
(v. 3)   *More fragrant than the best ointments.*
Your name is an oil poured out,
and that is why the maidens love you.

These maidens or *young girls "adolescentulae"* are those souls that are pure, or fairly well purified of worldly pleasures, who are feeling or capable of feeling the divine fragrance of piety and inner life and are becoming strongly desirous of serving God sincerely. They are the true *beginners* in *spiritual life,* who, even if they appear serious-mined and grey-haired or are sixty or seventy years old, are still *children in virtue* and as such need to be attracted and won with gifts. Even when they love tenderly, they still love in too imperfect a way, are still far from *burning* and *fainting* in pure *love.*

For these *"little maidens"* the sweet name of Jesus, or His Sacred Humanity, is their entire delight and the object of their affections, represented by the ointments or perfumes to which girls used to be, and still are, so attached. Thus the sweet fragrance of the name of the Savior, a balsam poured into as many devotions and pious institutions as are generated within the Holy Church, causes those souls that are pure, and those that through purification have become like children, to come to Him, and, entering into His mystical kingdom, to succeed in loving Him truly, and even with ardor and *to an extreme degree,* and so deserve to enjoy one day His intimate union and communication. They will then not be looked upon as *children* but as *ones perfect in Christ.*

The *young girls,* remarks St. Bernard (*Serm.* 19), here represent souls who have made little advance in virtue, who, being still children in Him, need to be sustained with milk and oil, that is to say, with the tender memory of the life, passion and death of the Savior which, in their state, is what most moves them to love Him.

"Thus the love of these friends of the Bride," he continues (*Serm.* 20), "being that of those who are still beginners, is in some way carnal, insofar as its principal concern is for the very flesh of Jesus Christ and all that this Lord did for us. Filled with this tender love, it is with very great ease that they are moved to compunction when they hear this matter spoken about. There is nothing that they listen to with greater pleasure or read with greater affection, or meditate over with greater or sweeter feeling. . . When they pray before a sacred image of the Man-God, whether newly born, or at the breast, or preaching, or dying on the Cross, or ascending up to the heavens or at some other stage in His life, they feel their hearts full of love for virtue and full of hatred for vice. . . In this way the Invisible One makes Himself visible so as to attract the hearts of carnal men to the spiritual love of His Sacred Humanity, men who could only love Him in a carnal (or human) way. Thereby, gradually, and through progressive stages, He elevates them to a more spiritual and purer love. . . Let those souls, then, that are novices in virtue rest here in the shade of this good God, souls that do not feel strong enough to bear the sun's rays. Let them be sustained by the sweetness of the flesh of Jesus Christ as long as they are still unable to acquire the knowledge and taste of things that belong properly to the Spirit of God. Let them be consoled with this material consolation until the Vivifying Spirit visits them, possesses them and lifts them to the exalted degree of love of those who can join the apostle in saying (II *Cor.* 5:16) *Et si cognovimus Christum secundum carnem, sed nunc jam non novimus: although we once knew Christ in the flesh, that is not how we know Him now."*

But the celestial fragrance of the mysteries of the Humanity of Christ will always be attracting pure and sincere souls to this, the only way which can lead to the delightful and spacious regions of light and life that are the mysteries of the Divinity, wherein it is not possible to enter save through Him Who is also the only gate that leads to salvation and true repose; although both the gate and the way, as St. Augustine observes, are for us to pass by and not to stop. But only the young maidens, humble and pure souls, are able to feel and savor the gentleness and sweetness of the mysteries of Jesus.

"Only the humble", writes Fray Juan de Los Angeles in support of Enrique Harpio (*In Cant.,* I), "are allowed to experience the sweet smell and fragrance of this name. The proud also possess this balsam, but it is closed; they have it in books but not in their hearts; they have it externally in the written word, but not within themselves, in their siprit; their hands touch the vase that is full and sealed, but they do not open it to anoint themselves. . . What is the good of reading and re-reading His Holy Name in books if you do not imprint the efficacy of its virtues in your way of life. . .?"

Thus, observes Calmet, the souls that are pure, the maidens (or, as the Hebrew text has it, the *virgins*), renouncing the corruption of worldly intercourse and the concupiscence of the flesh, are drawn towards loving the Divine Spouse, first with tenderness and then with ardor, through the sweet smell of the gifts of grace and of the Holy Spirit with which the Father anointed Him, a smell which He is forever emitting so as to win them. Indeed, the name of *Christ,* which means *Anointed* spreads throughout the world through evangelical preaching and holy *Christian* conversation; and is poured like a divine balsam over sincere hearts, curing and comforting and renewing them and keeping them from corruption. In this way thousands and thousands of souls attracted by the softness of this sweet name, not only renounce the corruption and deceptions of the world, but soon they themselves become the *sweet smell of Christ*, working for the salvation of many.

Speaking of those divine perfumes the V. M. Mariana de San José does well in saying: "It is not only the Lord Who exhales them but also the souls that He touches and anoints with them, and from a very great distance it can be seen that these are souls are nourished by the divine breasts, for the flowers of their virtues are very beautiful. . . It is recognized that they are souls who follow the Lamb. I would even venture to say that they are not the only ones who take in the sweetness of these most precious scents, but that all who try these breasts will enjoy their benefit and reward."

Such, oh sweet Master, is the nature of Your blessed name, and such is the name by which everyone, even Your enemies, knows You: "Oil or balsam, poured forth" — Christ, Anointed with all the graces and gifts for our comfort and well-being. You are truly what they call You: Christ-Jesus, that is to say, the Anointed Savior Who brings us every wealth and remedy, and possesses all the delights with which He steals the pure in heart and Who is deserving of infinite praise.

For this reason, writes Maria Dolorosa, the enamored soul tells Him "that simply to name Him brings the scent of grace, just as the *balsam that is poured out* gaves *off* fragrance. And just as oil keeps lamps alight, so the name of Jesus, imprinted in souls, keeps the lamp of love aflame within them and enlightens them, showing them the way of the divine law." Moreover, she adds, the effusion of this grace, together with the wine of supernatural love, cures the wounds of sins; and because of this mercy Jesus comes to be loved by these *young girls,* that is to say, by recently cured souls, still tender in virtue.

Once well founded in virtue these mystical maidens will succeed in loving Him in such a way that, attracted by His divine fragrance they will run after Him in incalculable numbers and with giant strides. For His fragrance is such as is proper to

Him Who is the depository of all the graces, beauties, sweetnesses, scents, and gifts of the Holy Spirit.

Thus, although to pursue Him requires so many self-denials and crucifixions and seems to offer only sacrifices, deprivation, suffering and abuse, we nonetheless see how in every century and in every kind of person, place and condition, thousands and thousands of virgins throng around Him, dedicating themselves to His service and to His love; and countless are the happy souls who have been, and continue to be, so captivated by Him, so enraptured and drawn by His ineffable sweetness that they think only of pleasing Him, praising Him and exalting Him and in seeing how they can sacrifice themselves more and more for His honor and glory. . .

Because of this, since the day of Circumcision when He first began to shed His most precious redeeming and life-giving Blood, when He was given the glorious name of Jesus that so warms, captivates and stirs hearts as though by its light everything had changed in appearance; since that day a whole new era has begun for all that are His, and indeed for the entire universe, an era which is the *era of grace*. . ., since He has truly shown Himself to be the Only-Begotten Son of the Eternal Father, *full of grace and truth, so that we might all receive of His fulness* (*John* I:14-16).

Since then, mysteriously attracted by this *Spouse of blood,* so many, indeed "countless" (*Song* 6:8) souls, have like the Wise Men gone in pursuit of Him, and so many of them with such courage and generosity that the whole of mankind stands in admiration and amazement.

Thus, it was clearly seen how our sweet Jesus was the true Desire of all people (*Agg.* 2:8); and we see how He is and deserves to be called the *Beloved par excellence.* For, indeed, not only is He the Beloved of men but even of the angels (I *Peter* 1:12); and He is not only the happy *Beloved* of the Eternal Father Whose love is worth infinitely more than that of all men and angels put together and Who loves only those whom

He sees adorned with the image and splendor in which His own Wisdom is decked (*Wis.* 7:28; I *Cor.* 1:24), and of *His Beloved Son in Whom He is well pleased* (*Matt.* 3:17); (II *Peter* 1:17; *Eph.* 1:6); but as a certain pious author writes, "it is wonderful to see the throng of those who throughout history have loved this true Lover, and the unprecedented fervor and perfection with which He is loved. . . Life itself would not be long enough to recount all that the lovers of Jesus tell Him so as to show Him how much they love Him. For the love of this Beloved and for His pleasure what has not been done by an infinite number of people? They have left their country, they have rid themselves of their possessions, they have renounced the love of flesh and blood and, greater still, have renounced their love of themselves. Because of the Beloved, poverty has been their riches, the desert their paradise, torments their pleasures and persecutions their rest. So that Jesus might dwell within them they chose to die to all things and even to strip themselves of everything and disfigure themselves so that the love of Jesus might be the form, the life, the being, the doing and even the suffering within them. Oh, what great love! Oh, sweet fire for whom souls are burning! For You, Lord, tender maidens embraced death; for You feminine weakness withstood fire, wild beasts and the severest of torments. Your purest love peopled the deserts; by loving You, oh Sweetest Good! a soul is purified, inflamed, enlightened, uplifted, enraptured and completely transported."

Therefore, "you children, praise the Lord, praise the holy name of the Lord. Blessed be the name of the Lord henceforth and forever. From the rising of the sun to the going down of the same, the Lord's name is to be praised." (*Ps.* 113; 1-3)

"Then praise, oh christian soul," exhorts the V. Granada (*Vita Christi, in Circumc.*), "praise, embrace and kiss this holy name that is sweeter than honey, richer than oil, more soothing than balsam, and more powerful than all the powers of the world. This is the name desired by the patriarchs, longed for by the prophets, and repeated and hymned by every generation. This is the name that angels adore, that devils fear, from which opposing forces flee, and at whose invocation sinners are saved. This is the name that bears the life, health and happiness of the whole of mankind and upon which all these depend."

"Blessed be this name," exclaims once more the same Venerable Father (*Serm. in Circumc.*, Ch. 1,ii), "blessed be this health, and blessed the day when such news was heard in the world. Oh, glorious name! Oh, sweet name of priceless virtue and reverence, invented by God in His eternity and brought down from heaven by angels. . . Oh name of all delight and consolation! Oh glorious name, worthy of being written and engraved in our hearts!"

"Your name, oh Divine Word," exclaims in her turn St. Mary Magdalen of Pazzi (5th P., excl. 3rd), "calms the wrath of the Father, delights the angels and the blessed and instills fear in the devils. In this name it is that the Eternal Father gives us His graces: may You vouchsafe, then, to write it with Your Blood in the hearts of Your brides. . . It is a name of goodness and if they keep it in their hearts, what else but words of goodness can spring from their lips. . .? Oh, how sweet are the words of those who keep it in their hearts!. . . What wonderful music to hear them pronounce this sacred name, by which we attract to ourselves the gaze of the Eternal Father, cause angels to want to see us in their company and become frightening to devils."

"Oh Jesus, our sweet Lord! How wonderful in Your name in all the earth! Above the heavens is your majesty chanted by the mouths of children, babes in arms. You set Your stronghold firm against Your foes to subdue enemies and rebels." (*Ps.* 8, 2-3)

"The excellence of this holy Name," writes Fr. Juan de Los Angeles "refers to its sovereignty, sweetness and utility. . . Its sovereignty showed itself when our Lord invoked it to bring about the curing of the sick, the resurrection of the dead, the casting out of devils. . .the protection from every kind of

danger. . . *In nomine meo demonia ejicient.* . .(*Mark* 16,27). . .
St. Paul describes this Majesty of the Divine Name very well
when he wrote that: *In nomine Jesu omne genu flectatur.* . ."
(*Phil.* 2,10).

As far as its sweetness and utility are concerned one has
only to observe how it attracts and captivates hearts, winning,
healing and renewing them. . . "The name of Jesus," continues
the same writer, "is a balsam poured out for mankind, the
antidote and panacea that the Lord gave to the Church and that
He wanted to be carried everywhere for the good and remedy of
all." This was the purpose for which Saul was chosen: "to carry
it as proven medicine with which to heal souls and bodies." *In
nomine Jesu,* said St. Peter to the lame man (*Acts* 3,6), *surge et
ambula* he then stood up and, jumping with joy, gave thanks to
the Lord. In the same way this name was a collyrium to the
blind and a most efficient cure to the melancholy and sick in
heart. In short, it is medicine that came down from heaven, for
there is no medicine so effective and universal on earth. An
angel received this name from the mouth of God and with great
reverence brought in into the world and placed it in the ear and
heart of the Virgin, whence it spread into the Church. . . (*Luke*
2,21).

"*Oleum effusum nomen tuum.* Jesus is balsam extracted
from the very heart of God, a name in which God sacrificed
Himself, and with which He showed His love for the world, and
in which He gave all that He possessed. . . What more could He
have given us, in giving us His Son? Or, what did He *not* give us
when He gave Him to us? *Quomodo cum illo non omnia nobis
donavit?* (*Rom.* 8,32).

"For this reason St. Bernard said that although the Spouse
has many names, Jesus is His proper name. It is the name He
was born with and which is, as it were, embedded in His being;
for, as I said just now, all that is in Christ is goodness and this is
proclaiming and activating His name. The Lord wanted His
name to demonstrate the great love that He has for us. . ."

"Isaiah," observes in his turn the Venerable Tome de Jesus (*Trabajos de J.*, 7.), "prophesied that our Lord would have many other names, which were: Swift Thief, Emmanuel, which means *God with us;* Wonderful, Counsellor, Prince of Peace, God, Father of the world to come, and others. All these are declarations of the Holy Name of Jesus, for to be truly Jesus, which means Savior, like a swift and vigorous thief, He would have to rescue souls from the power of the devil and from the blindness and ills which were causing their perdition; He would have to be God, yet walk among men; the Teacher and Counsellor of the wonderful doctrine with which He would save us from our faults, reconciling us with God and establishing a peace between heaven and earth. He would have to be the Father and Author of eternal life, open the gates of heaven and give it to those who deserved it. His kingdom would have to be without end, as indeed it is. All this is what is meant by perfect Savior and all this is contained in the Holy Name of Jesus. . ., Who is our Savior in heaven and on earth. And since Christ is our Savior, He wanted His Holy Name of Jesus to be dreaded in hell, extolled on earth, and adored in heaven, that all just souls should find their pleasure and delight in it; the sinning, their remedy for all their ills, the endangered, safety; the reposing, contentment; the needy, succour; the wayfarers, hope; the cold, warmth; the devout, love; the fearful, strength; the sad, joy; riches, their source; and evils, their redemption."

"The principal thing which I wish to communicate," said the sweet Jesus to His confidante Sr. Benigna Consolata, a Visitandine who died in Como in 1916 in the odor of sanctity, "is that I am all love; and the greatest pain that can be caused Me is for people to doubt My goodness. My heart is not only compassionate but is glad when it finds much to restore, provided that there is no wickedness. If you only knew how much I would work within a soul, even if it were full of shortcomings, if only it would let Me. Love does not need anything, but should not encounter any resistance. Frequently

what I require from a soul in order to make it holy, is that it
should let Me act... Imperfections, provided they are not
loved, cannot displease Me. The soul ought to use them as so
many steps with which to climb up to Me, through humility,
trust, and love. I descend to the soul that humiliates itself and I
go out to look for it in its nothingness so as to unite Myself to
it."

"The Son of God came into the world," adds Fray
Angeles, "for the joy of the world; He came anointed as to a
wedding feast; He came to dispel melancholy and sorrow from
the hearts of men, who knew only how to weep and grieve. St.
Paul said (*Rom.* 14,12) that the *kingdom of God means
righteousness and peace and joy brought by the Holy Spirit.*"
And indeed these three things are inseparable: for where there is
righteousness there is peace, and where there is peace and
righteousness there is contentment and perpetual joy which no
event can prevent or disturb, as the sage testifies (*Prov.* 12,21).

...*And that is why the maidens love you.* The name of
Jesus is a name that spreads and becomes absorbed in the soul
like oil (*Ps.* 109,18), entering into its most secret and intimate
regions, leaving no corner unvisited and uncomforted. It is not a
highsounding name that frightens and awakens fear, but soft
and loving, inviting and provoking the maidens to love, a name
which, heard in the ear or spoken with the mouth, enters into
the sphere of the soul, wins over the heart and, inspiring it with
love, draws it behind it, a name which, once known, encourages
us and gives trust to await the Lord without fear, a name which
teaches the how and when of the divine praise: *Secundum
nomen tuum, ita et laus tua in fines terrae* (*Ps.* 48,11), a name
which sums up all that God has done for men and about which
Isaiah says (*Is.* 26,8) *Domine...nomen tuum, et memoriale
tuum in desiderio animae meae...*

...This is the fruit of the name of Jesus Christ: the love
left toward Him by the maidens, those souls that are pure and
innocent. First of all this oil, divine love, is poured forth; and

then the maiden's love is pursued... Sometimes this love and
desire grow so great that certain souls are carried away and
transported into a kind of exalted contemplation when, going
out of themselves, their understanding, enlightened by divine
light, reaches such a sovereign height that it exceeds all human
power and possibility and achieves such a wonderful union with
God that it seems more divine than human. Then love and
desire know a much greater satisfaction than that which they
previously enjoyed."

But as Ricardo says, "divine love is insatiable; it is all
consuming and the greater it becomes, the greater the need and
hunger that it causes to be felt, for, by letting its delights be
enjoyed, it awakens insatiable desires for delights greater still.
Oh good God, whose love is the soul's nourishment! How is it
that You sustain Your lovers in such a way that they become
more and more hungry if not because You are at one and the
same time nourishemnt and appetite, satiety and renewed
hunger? This wonderful hunger for You cannot be possessed by
anyone who has not savored You; and for this reason You
nourish the soul so as to make it desire more and more, so as to
teach it to have this divine, insatiable hunger."

The mystical Bride praises and celebrates this blessed
name, viewing it as *oil or balsam poured forth* whose sweet
smell comforts, regales and transports her, always awakening
within her renewed and greater desires, while attracting and
captivating the hearts of countless maidens that are sighing for
such a good. For, by these precious words: *Your name is an oil
poured forth*...says Petit, are meant the urgent desires felt by
pure souls to become brides of Jesus and, thereby, to be worthy
as such to bear this same name; *oil* whose principle properties
are those of curing, soothing, nourishing and enlightening; and
poured forth so as better to communicate to all its ineffable
virtues and thus excite even more the love of these mystical
maidens.

"With a single inner communication from the Lord,"

observes the Ven. M. Mariana de San Jose *"this soul suddenly*
feels a profound sweetness in such a way that she can say for
her the time has now come when not only grace is apportioned
to her, but this loving Spouse of hers pours Himself forth to her
in great abundance; and it happens that simply upon hearing His
name, she enjoys an abundant peace. . . The marks of her old
wounds are healed and are completely removed with this divine
oil. . . *Adolescentulae* are pure souls devoid of all things,those
that are already free from the worldly stench and from things of
the world. They are the ones that will take and enjoy this divine
oil; and considering it to be precious above all things, they let
themselves be swept away by divine love, which is the fruit of
the appreciation that must accompany the search and pursuit of
the Lord. . .

If we give ourselves to it with steadfast resolution we shall
understand and enjoy the sweet mercies that are to be enjoyed
in this divine oil poured forth. Thus we shall truly abandon all
things and do what that wise merchant in the gospel did (Matt.
13,46), who sold all his jewels and riches so as to be able to buy
that precious pearl."

"Oh blessed name!" exclaims St. Bernard (*Serm.* 15 *in
Cant.*), "Oh name poured forth in every corner. . .! Fullness was
poured forth so that we all might receive life from it. This is the
glorious name that enlightens souls when it is preached, that
instructs hearts when it is thought of, and cures them when it
is invoked. Does not your heart stir, perchance, when you recall
this name? What is there that does more to restore the senses, to
encourage virtues, to confirm good habits, to sustain holy
desires and to promote chaste affections and thoughts than this
sweet name? My soul finds unsavory all food that is not
seasoned with this oil. . . If you write, I do not enjoy reading it
unless I find Jesus within it; if you discuss or converse, I do not
enjoy such conversation unless it includes mention of His Holy
Name. Jesus is honey in one's mouth, melody in one's ear and
joy in one's heart. This wonderful name is also medicine for our

souls. If anyone is sad, let Jesus enter his heart and then come
to his lips, and as this light issues forth, the dark clouds will be
dispelled and serenity will return. . . There is nothing which
curbs the path of anger, which deflates the haughtiness of pride,
heals the wound of envy, extinguishes the flame of lust and
moderates the thirst of avarice as the devout invocation and
memory of this sweet name. . . For, my soul, you have this
precious remedy enclosed within the vase of the name of Jesus,
which is the common medicine for all infirmities. Therefore,
bear it always in your heart and in your hands, so that your
thoughts and deeds might be guided by it."

Thus, we shall indeed follow Him, even if only as the
tender maidens who were the Bride's companions, so that later,
through her example and His grace, we may succeed in loving
and following Him as adults in Christ, as perfect men who no
longer weep, but remain forever steadfast and, alone, bear His
cross, serve God and adore and love Him *in spirit and in truth*.

"For although this devotion to the flesh or Humanity of
Christ," adds St. Bernard (*Serm.* 20), "is a gift and a very great
grace of the Holy Spirit, nonetheless I believe I am right in
maintaining that this love is still carnal in comparison with that
in which the pious soul delights not so much in the Word
Incarnate, as in this same Word as Wisdom, as Truth and as the
very Justice and Sanctity of God, together with the other
properties of His Divinity, for all this is Jesus Christ for us, God
the Father having given Him to us, as St. Paul says (I *Cor.* 1,30),
to be *our wisdom, and our virtue, and our holiness and our
freedom*. Who would say that the love of a soul who is inspired
to tender compassion by the Crucified Christ and who, easily
moved by the sweet memory of His Passion, remains virtuous,
pious and pure, is the same as that of the soul who is always
enkindled by zeal for justice, who is always most anxious to
defend the truth and who places all its effort in the knowledge
and preservation of wisdom. . .? Comparing, then, the effects of
one love with another, surely everyone will recognize that this

spiritual love is more sublime and perfect than this other love
that we have called rigorous. . .? But, although it is not as
perfect, this other love is nonetheless very good and sufficiently
effective to triumph over the world and concupiscence. . .; and
through a living faith it will go on growing and become more
spiritual reaching its plenitude when with the help of the Holy
Spirit, souls feel such strength that not even the worst trials and
torments nor death itself could turn them away from the paths
of justice."

"The soul that belongs to this group of maidens," writes
St. Lawrence Justinian (*De casto Connubio Verbi et animae* c.
18), "can enter the courtyard of the King, but not into His
rooms; receives gifts but not kisses and full of confusion sees
how the Bride goes on in while she herself is left outside.
Nevertheless she takes courage hoping eventually to be admitted
after her, and achieve with supplications what she cannot obtain
through her own merits: "Nam etsi transactarum confidit se
indulgentiam recipisse culparum, non tamen laetari audet
tamquam sponsa singulari privilegio charitatis. In commune
ingressa est atrium Regis, sed non in arcanum Sponsi cubiculum:
Recipit munera, nequaquam autem oscula, vidit introeuntem
Sponsam, et pudore perfusam se foris derelictam. . . Consolatur
tamen se prophetico sermone, qui ait (*Ps.* 45): *Adducentur Regi
virgines post eam.* . . Nam et plerumque quod non praevaluit
amor, potuit humilis longanimitas, et quod nen impetravit
meritum, obtinuit importuna petitio."

Thus, he adds, no one has any reason to be discouraged,
and all ought to trust in the goodness of the Word. Delay in
receiving does not prevent one from receiving, in one's proper
time, a good one hundred times as great: "Nemo de Verbi
bonitate diffidat nemo de se desperet. Plerumque quod dari
differtur ad tempus, suo deinde tempore traditur centuplicatum;
similiter et qui postremus ad nuptias accessit; primus recubuit."

We all ought, then to join the same saint in repeating (Ch.
19): Since my soul is unworthy to be looked upon as Bride,

would that it were worthy to be considered least among the maidens! *Non enim sponsae me vindico dignitatem. Utinam vel adolescentularum inveniar minimus!*

Let us, therefore, imitate these mystical maidens and join the great St. Augustine who, when his soul had become one of them, exclaimed (*Medit.*, Ch. 36 — 37): "O most sweet, kind, loving, beloved, precious, desired, lovely and beautiful Lord! I beg You to fill my heart with the abundance of your sweetness and love, so that I might never desire or think anything worldly, but only love You and have You on my lips and in my heart. With Your own hand, write in my soul the wonderful memory of Your sweet name in such a way that no forgetfulness could ever efface it. . . Also give me that clear sign of Your love — that perennial source of tears. . . Let them reveal all the love that my soul feels for You, for it cannot hold them back because of the tremendous sweetness of Your love. . . Make me run after You, following the fragrance of Your precious ointments; support me and guide me so that I may not fall away. . ."

v. 4)   *Draw me: we will run after you*
                 pursuing the scent of your ointments.

Such is the language of souls desiring perfection but who are still dismayed by the roughness of the road that leads to Calvary; nevertheless they truly wish to travel along it. These souls desire to seek Him Whom they begin to recognize as the Source of all good. Feeling themselves not strong enough to follow Him, or to follow Him as closely as they would like, they pray to Him to attract them to Himself, and with His most efficacious grace to move and support them in such a way that, with great strides, they might not only go after, but *run after Him, pursuing the scent of His ointments.*

"This soul is taking the right attitude," says M. Mariana de San José, "for the Lord to be merciful to her. Not forgetting her lowliness, but being always aware of how little she can do without the help of the Spouse, she likes this abject condition and humility. Thus we see that she does not speak a word that is not enveloped in this holy, charming virtue, whose beauty wins the eyes of her King and Lord. In this way she will obtain not only that for which she asks, but other very great mercies besides."

Full of confidence, she hopes that, like herself many other souls will be moved, inspired no doubt by her words or by the sweet fragrance of her own example and virtue. This is what we often see happen; for, as St. Teresa pointed out, when a soul gives herself completely to our Lord, she always manages to take many other souls with her or to draw them after her. That is why the Bride says: *Draw me. . .and we will run,* that is to say, all those of us who are inspired by the same desires.

"Oh Jesus!" exclaims St. Teresita (Sa Vie, Ch. 11), "there is thus no need to say that when You attract me, You attract the souls I love. This simple word is enough: *Attract me!* Yes, when a soul lets herself be captivated by the sweet scent of Your perfumes, she will not run alone, but all those she loves will be drawn after her, as a natural consequence of her attraction to You!"

It is when they are burning with love that they will really begin to feel the need to empty themselves and strip themselves of everything that prevents them from running after Him, or stands in the way of the intimate union and communication that they so long for. It is then that they learn to love the cross, the self-denial, humiliation, self-annihilation necessary to be able to follow Christ faithfully and to participate in His light and love, for Him to become everything within them, for in Him they find everything united in one. For this reason, now knowing very well their own weakness, they cannot fail to sigh and cry out, ceaselessly praying to be *carried along* by the virtue of His favor, that is, by the gifts of His Divine Spirit, thereby to be able to follow with complete faithfulness, hurriedly *running* after Him, captivated by His love.

Oh, the priceless efficacy of the virtue of the Word! Oh, what wonderful wisdom, which in this way knows how, and is able to, inspire, heal, win, attract, strengthen, console, enlighten, captivate, wound and change hearts to possess them fully, impressing its very feelings upon them and filling them with delights!

"Draw me, and we will run. . . which is as good as to say," writes Fr. La Puente (*La Perfec. en gener.,* tr. 2, c. 11), "I shall not run alone, but with many others whom I shall inspire to run with me by my example. But in this pursuit they will not go after me but after You, for their goal will be to imitate not me but You. If they were to imitate me it would only be in the way in which I imitate You, following my example since it conforms to Yours. Nor will they run solely because of the scent of my ointments but because they will smell the sweet perfume of Yours, savoring within them the sweetness of Your gifts."

O powerful love of God," exclaims St. Teresa (*Exclamations,* 2), how different are Your fruits from those produced by love of this world! For love of this world desires no companions, fearing lest they may take from it what it possesses. But love for my God increases more and more as it learns that more and more souls love Him. . . Thus the soul seeks ways of finding companionship and is glad to abandon its own possessions thinking that this may help others in some degree to strive to attain it."

"These two utterances," observes Fr. Juan de los Angeles, "are punctuated differently by different interpreters. Some prefer: *Trahe me: post te curremus;* Others: *Trahe me post te: curremus,* etc. Both interpretations maintain a single sense and indicate that the Bride is eager to follow the Spouse, to tread in His footsteps, since to keep up with Him is impossible. . .

"*Curremus.* The Bride speaks of herself and of her maidens. We shall run together. For it is not in the nature of love to pursue its goal with slow and deliberate step, but rather to cease walking and to run (*Ps.* 51), and occasionally to fly along its hurried and impetuous course."

But "the only one to run," remarks St. Gregory M. "is she

who is drawn, for she who is not assisted by divine grace, must
necessarily be held back by the hindrance of her own
corruption... She who is drawn, then, is she who runs, for
willingly following the bonds of love and strengthened with the
love of grace, she is able to break away from all obstacles
without difficulty. There is no reason for us to marvel at this,
for she is following the scent of the ointments; when she
experiences and savors the sweetness of the spiritual gifts, what
is there in this world that can stop Christ's bride from running
after Him? There the soul is regaled and refreshed with the
softness of the ointments, and, smelling with the sense of
discretion, receives the sweet odor of charity. After having first
spoken in the singular, the soul passes to the plural, adding: 'We
will run after You.' for in the love of God it has found the
second precept of loving one's neighbor. Thus instructed, the
Bride tries to see that we, too, participate in the sweetness that
she enjoys within herself."

In much the same way, St. Bernard and other authors
point out that the love of the Bride shines forth in these words
in a very special way, of this Bride who wants to have many
companions in her consolations although finding herself alone
in her trials; for to be drawn or borne along implies a certain
violence while to run in the pursuit of such fragrance indicates
joy...

These sweet-smelling ointments that attract them are,
according to St. Bernard (*Serm.* 22), the most precious gifts of
the Holy Spirit, or also the Divine mercies, the wonderful
miracles worked in the world, or the fame of the Spouse's
name, or finally the evangelical doctrine, whose sweet fragrance
certainly exceeds that of all other aromas, and which refreshes
and comforts the interior senses of the soul and sometimes the
exterior ones as well.

For, as St. Augustine remarks (*De Spiritu et animo*):
"There are two kinds of senses in man: one interior and the
other exterior, and both have their good in which they find

recreation. The interior sense, in the contemplation of the
Divinity; the exterior, in the contemplation of His Humanity.
One of the reasons why God became man was to beatify the
whole of man in Him; so that man's whole turning should be to
God and his entire love should be in Him; and so that with the
senses of the flesh His own most holy flesh might be seen and,
with the sense of the soul in contemplation, His Divinity. This is
man's entire good; that interiorly and exteriorly he would find
nourishment in his Maker: nourishment for his body in the
humanity of his Savior, and nourishment for his soul in the
Divinity of the Creator."

That mysterious *sense of smell* with which pious souls
perceive and follow the divine fragrance, is one of the five
spiritual senses that are so sublimely described to us by Origen,
St. Albert the Great and St. Bonaventure, and with which the
beauty of God is to some extent glimpsed here below, in this
experimental science that is proper to mystical life. "With these
senses," writes the Seraphic Doctor (*Breviloquii,* p. 3, Ch. 6),
"man is made ready for contemplation... With them the
sublime beauty of Christ the Divine Spouse is seen in the form
of splendor, His sublime harmony is heard as Word: His sublime
sweetness is tasted in the form of wisdom, which comprises
both things, words and splendor; His sublime fragrance is sensed
as the Word inspired in the heart; and finally with the sense of
touch His sublime delicateness is perceived as the Word
Incarnate Which dwells corporally among men and offers
Himself to us to be felt, embraced and kissed with ardent
love... These interior senses...give mental perceptions of the
truth contemplated in the Divine Spouse... Thus we stand
before the throne of Solomon, where the most wise and truly
gentle and loving King is seated and for Whom holy souls long;
with this fervent longing our spirit is enraptured and we join the
Bride in saying: *"Let us run in the pursuit of the scent of your
ointments..."*

With these brief words: *"Trahe me:* attract me or draw me

after You. . ." the Bride indicates very clearly how ardent her desires, how sincere the love she feels for her Divine Spouse, and how sharp at the same time the feeling of her own weakness. Finding herself ready to break with everything in order to following Him, she does not see how she can do so unless He Himself carry her. These words, as Cardinal Hugo observes, mean: "Come to my help, comfort me and give me strength so that, in spite of the resistance and weakness of my flesh, I might follow You as I wish."

"This," writes Enrique Harpio (*Theol. Mysticae*, 1.1 Ch. 36), "is a clamoring of the soul that detests human consolations and delights and fervently desires divine ones. But it notes the violence it must do to itself if it is accustomed to the joys of the senses in order to renounce them and prepare itself to search for those of Heaven. It asks then, to be drawn or carried along; for this indicates the violence that must be done to its natural inclinations, and therefore beseeches it the help of God."

For this reason, the Lord told us (*Matt.* 11, 12), that the kingdom of Heaven suffers violence. . .because, in trying to acquire it, we find opposition within ourselves. In this way, observes Fr. Juan de los Angeles (*in Cant.* 1, 3), "the violence or coercion is not done to the Kingdom, but to ourselves and to our evil inclinations. This is what the Bride means when she says: *Draw me,* which is to say, move me to follow You with promises or threats if need be, test me with trials, attract me with rewards, use with me whatever means You like, whether it be to comfort, punish or enlighten me. For she knows very well that she cannot attain these supernatural communications unless she is sustained by grace. . .

"The Bride wishes to be united to the Divine Word, her Spouse, with a bond that can never be undone. With this anxious and just desire is the knowledge of her own weakness and insignificance. She prays for union and for the grace needed to attain it. There are many things in the present life which prevent the fulfilling of the Bride's desire. There are domestic

worries, public and private business. There are the delightful
and flattering attractions of the flesh; there are all kinds of
pleasures that distract, divert, moderate, stifle, arrest and
oppress the soul, preventing it from going straight to God, and
often from even raising its thoughts to Him. . . What she is
asking for her is something very great indeed. She asks that,
despising and renouncing all things of worldly worth, she might
think only of Him, and love only Him, as though removed and
freed from the troubles and ties of the flesh. This is the meaning
of the phrase *Draw me. . .*: my will is to follow You, my desire
is to be united with You, my longing to be lifted far above the
earth; But I am not sufficient in myself to bring about what I so
much want. . . If you do not draw me and snatch me from the
claws of the cares and desires of the world, how shall I be able
to follow You, how shall I abide with You?"

These two phrases, he adds, are very important: *Draw me*
and *let us run;* the first since "it is a kind of violence
and. . .announces the efficacy of divine grace;" the second
because "it points to the ease with which our free will is carried
along, without prejudice to its freedom. . . In saying *Draw me,*
the soul admits that it has to be carried along (as it were) in this
movement; and in adding *curremus, let us run,* it shows how
"God offers His grace and the maidens their hands. The
ordinary way to God is *by the scent of His ointments. . .*

"Some walk, others run, others fly, others are carried,
others transported, and I stand still for I have no love! For as St.
Augustine said, love is the power in the soul that makes it run
and fly, that raises it from the things of earth to those of
Heaven, that transports it to the Beloved and gains it access into
the inner wine-cellar and chambers of the eternal King. But, it is
a terrible thing, my Lord, that a great force should be needed
for gravity to carry a stone to its center. . .that I should remain
attached to the motionless earth when You are my center and
my sphere, and my soul made to rest in You. . .! If no
creature can be still when away from its center, how am I going

to be, when I am away from You, Who are my center? O
infinite Center, infinitely good, and infinitely attractive! Why
do You not transport me and carry me to You?. . ."

"Draw me!" exclaims St. Augustine (*Medit.* 4), "so that I
might delight in running after You, following Your divine
scent. . ."

Draw me!, then, will be the fervent exclamation of the
anxious soul, recalling the words used by the Savior Himself
(*John* 6, 44; 12, 32): *"No one can come to Me unless he is
drawn by the Father who sent Me"*, and *"without Me you can
do nothing. . ."* But it will cry out full of confidence, knowing
how well-disposed the Lord is to grant this blessing to those
who ask Him for it from their hearts, as He assured us through
His prophets saying (*Hosea* 11. 4; cf. *Jer.* 2,2): *I (shall lead)
them with reins of kindness.*

Thus, just as the Caananite woman cried out, so the soul
thirsting for justice cries out after Him, aspiring to be worthy of
His graces; and if it continues to cry out, says St. Lawrence
Justinian, it will not be long before it will be comforted,
consoled and encouraged not to give up.

This is indeed so, for once Jesus has seen this humble and
generous disposition in a soul, imploring His help, determined
to follow Him in all things, whatever the cost, renouncing all
claims to itself and its own ways in perfect surrender, then it
seems He cannot bear any further delay, and pushing everything
aside, hurries to bring it inside, if not yet into the mystical
wine-cellar of His infinite love, at least into one of the many
secret chambers that He holds in readiness for it, *to make it
joyful in His house of prayer* (*Isaiah* 56, 7). In this house, which
is the pure heart, He causes it to taste something of the
mysterious hidden manna that He offers to the victorious (*Rev.*
2, 17), something of the ineffable sweetness that He has hidden
for those that fear Him (*Ps.* 31, 20).

With just this *something* the soul will emerge so changed,
so strengthened and decided, that, full of fervor, admiration

enthusiasm, she will exclaim:

The King has brought me into his rooms!. . .

"This soul must have had a wonderful and efficacious way
of prayer," writes the V. Mariana, "for the Lord attends to her
so well that not only does He fill her with abundant hope of
receiving what she asks for. . .but He even turns to her, brings
her into His private chamber and shows her His secrets and
treasures. There He treats her such that He causes her to leave
herself, and after this kind of rapture, when she returns to
creatures, she asks them to help her give thanks to her Spouse
for such an extraordinary grace, saying: *Exultabimus et
laetabimur in te.* . . O Lord, if only I were able to understand
the language of this Bride, and could walk behind the Master
that guides her, so that I might enter in and become the
companion of such lovers. . .! How easy it would be for You to
enable us all to enter in!"

"Here we are taught," she adds, "not to seek entrance on
our own, or by our own labour and effort, until our Divine King
brings us in Himself; let us remain at the entrance hall of His
Palace, recognizing that whatever place His Majesty allocates
to us is more than we deserve; that even if we were to spend
thirty thousand years in patience and humility, it would be
little in view of the riches that await us. . . But perhaps we are
too negligent, for if we were to take more care in keeping the
precepts and counsels of the Lord, we would find ourselves
within His celestial chamber. . .and there He would let us to
taste His gifts so that we might delight in Him. . .

"What this chamber is and what it is like the soul does not
tell us nor does the Spouse want her to do so, thus revealing His
wish that we all search for it. . . and in this way He will come
out to meet us and turn our poverty into riches. . . Wishing to
find an occasion to communicate Himself to us, it seems that
the Holy Spirit prefers here to keep secret the chamber into
which He introduces His beloved Brides, so that the desire to
find this treasure hidden in the Divine land of perfection, where

the worldly see only misery, thorns and trials, might bring us to
discover that sweet powerful voice that calls us, saying (*Is.* 55):
Oh, come to the waters all you who are thirsty. . . These riches
will be given us quite freely if we leave our lukewarm life and
things of this world. He will give us waters that will satisfy us. . .
For all that the Lord desires is our good, and for Him to give us
these mercies He wants us to go out in search of Him. He has no
need of us whatsoever, but moved by the deep and tender love
that He has for us, He would like to draw us and communicate
Himself to us. Since He is preparing us and yearns to bestow on
us His mercies, to which He continually invites us in the words
cited above, He will not delay long in introducing us into the
chamber of which the soul here speaks. Although the way
seems rough and the virtues difficult to attain. . .it is later
realized how securely the suffering soul has been conducted to
the freedom of this heavenly mansion."

The Kingly chambers the Bride speaks of, then, are the
mystical *mansions* into which the Lord begins to introduce the
souls that are truly in search of Him and that give themselves to
Him generously, to reward them with the sweetnesses and gifts
of the infused prayer of *recollection* or *quiet,* for the great
efforts and sacrifices made for His love. He gives them the light,
health and strength, which they would never have obtained
through their own endeavors alone.

After this they can speak, through their own experience,
of the sweetness and gentleness of God, and unable to contain
themselves, being so full of holy joy, they want to proclaim this
out loud so that all might be encouraged to search for this
hidden treasure.

Introduxit me. . . Which means, said Theodoret:
"recondita mihi sua consilia patefecit, Mysterium a saeculis et
generationibus absconditum, mihi indicavit. Thesauros
absconditos atque invisibiles operuit mihi."

While the young maidens are running, says St. Gregory of
Nyssa (*Orat.* 1, *in Cant.*), she has already gained entrance: "Enim

vero animae quae ad virtutis perfectionem necdum pervenerunt
...cursuras se ad metam quam unguentorum odor ostendit,
pollicetur. At perfectior anima versus anteriora majori cum
impetu contendens metam ipsam jam assecuta est, qua cursus
absolvitur, ac digna thesaurorum in penetralibus abditorum
fruitione ducitur."

Indeed, apart from the enlightenment and consolation
normally received through the faithful practice of virtue "there
is," writes St. John Climacus (*Spiritual Ladder* Ch. 26),
"another singular enlightenment and joy which lifts the soul out
of itself and unites it with Christ...in a secret and ineffable
way. This occurs when the soul is touched by the hand of God
with a most fervent love, and enlightened, or rather abundantly
filled with intellectual light, by which she becomes so united,
absorbed and transformed in God Himself, that she begins to
faint and become caught up and enveloped in the spring of that
most clear splendor and transported to the riches of His glory.
Thus...she comes to deny herself and to repose, sleep and
delight in her own Creator. This is what *Mystical Theology*
consists in: the affective and loving knowledge of God through
that sublime gift of the Holy Spirit and the end of all gifts:
Wisdom. When thus enkindled, the soul knows through
experience the savor of God and through this wisest love
becomes one with Him."

Introduxit me rex in cellaria sua. "Cellaria vero Sponsi,"
writes Juan de J. M., "sunt duo, divina videlicet contemplatio,
et ex ea orta dilectio. Quae sane cellaria, et vini et unguentorum
quaedam quasi promptuaria nuncupari possunt, vini quidem,
propter charitatis ardorem, et sobriam amoris ibi excitati
ebrietatem; unguentorum vero, propter delicias, quas ibi anima
percipit, internis voluptatibus a Sponso delinita, specialique
Spiritus Sancti unctione delibuta... Hic autem sponsa tot bonis
aucta...quasi mentis excessum patitur... Alterum cellarium,
contemplatio divina est, valde quidem recondita, et hujus
saeculi sapientibus clausa, in qua viget ea Sponsi notitia, quae

affectuosa, seu affectuum excitatrix nuncupari solet, quam qui experiri cupit, a tumultibus externis longe avocandus, et in cordis intima introducendus est. Alterum autem cellarium, amor intimus est, in cordis centro defixus, in quem mundus neutiquam penetrare valet; neque enim in externorum se amorem effundens, in amorem illum medullus permeantem, Deoque interne fruentem, caelique gaudia praelibantem, qui justorum proprius est, se valet insinuare."

"Whoever enters this hidden and most secret Sanctuary of God," says St. Bernard (*Serm.* 25), "for however short a span of time, in such wise that nothing and no one can distract or trouble him through the scattering of the senses, or the burden of cares, or the remorse for sins, or the harassment of a wandering imagination, this soul can then say in all truth: *The King has brought me into His rooms.* Oh, what a truly tranquil place, which fully deserves to be called a place of rest, there where God is neither angry nor busy, but brings us to know what is His good, acceptable and perfect will! (*Rom.* 12, 2). This divine vision does not inspire terror, but rather encouragement and hope; it does not provoke a restless curiosity but rather quiets it; nor does it tire the senses, but rather calms them and gives them rest. It is here in this happy quiet where God rests, showing Himself to be the peaceful King that brings calm to all things, so that to look at Him in quiet is the best rest."

But, "how is it," asks Fr. Juan de los Angeles (*in Cant.*, I,3), "that, God's sweetness and gifts being of such virtue and efficacy. . .we rarely or never come to experience them?" St. Augustine replies in one word: *Christus,* inquit, *est sapientia animae purificatae,* which means that the wisdom of the Father is sweet and pleasant only to those who have their soul's palate free from the vices, cares and pleasures of the world. . .

"He took His own up the mountain so as to show them His glory, but those who did not ascend neither saw nor knew it. He who is to enjoy the delights and gifts of the Spirit and His divine consolations must climb up and abandon worldly cares, must forsake the delights and gifts of the flesh. . ."

This is the difference between the delights communicated to souls by God and those offered them by Satan; Satan of course, pretends they are otherwise, but this is mere appearance, for they are in fact deadly poison. . . What God shows and offers His own is, on the surface, in outward appearance, both unattractive and of little worth; but once tasted, sweeter than honey. . . In order to enjoy the riches that are to be found in the chambers of the Spouse, the heart's palate must be purified and unsullied. . . St. Bonaventure (*Solliloquy,* Ch. II), writes that if the soul is to enjoy the divine sweetness it must be purified, exercised and uplifted. When purified the soul has the fragrance of the Bride and her maidens; when exercised, like the prophet it tastes the sweetness of God; when uplifted, it sometimes attains to intoxication. I repeat that the soul must be purified and free from sins and disorderly affections; free and disengaged from passing consolations and from the inordinate love of all creatures. For according to St. Bernard, whoever thinks or persuades himself that Heavenly sweetness can be mixed with ashes, divine balsam with poisonous pleasure, and the gifts and anointing of the Holy Spirit with the attractions and enticements of the present century, is very much mistaken indeed."

Enrique Harpio (*Theo. Myst.* 1.1. Ch. 39) believes that in some way or other these *Kingly chambers* include the *wine Chamber;* and therefore "they really contain all the treasures of the inner sweetness of divine contemplation; for, this very contemplation which, according to St. Basil, is the light of the heart, the mansion of the Holy Spirit, the joy of the mind, the garden of delights, the paradise of the soul, the recreation and peace of the spirit, can quite rightly be considered, according to Origen, the true center from which the fullness of all gifts is dispensed. For the contemplation of the mysteries within is a resplendent light for the whole soul: it is the room wherein the scents of all the virtues are inhaled, where the unction of all the divine gifts is felt, and where the ineffable treasures of Heavenly delights are enjoyed, the waters of salutary wisdom are imbibed, the divine sweetness most deliciously savored, and the soul intoxicated with divine love that makes it go out of itself and enjoy a foretaste of the joys of glory."

But between these chambers and the mystical wine-cellar that will be mentioned later, and between the gifts that are given to the soul in the one place and the other, "there is, I think," quite rightly observes Fr. Juan de los Angeles, "considerable difference. . . For in the first place the Spouse reveals to the soul His secrets, and in the second gives it to drink of His wine; in the one, the soul is enlightened, in the other, enraptured. . ."

Nevertheless with this superior light comes peace, health, rest, and with such ineffable sweetness and delight that it seems to the soul that it could never forget them, and so bring it to despise and forget all worldly pleasures; so that the soul says

> *The King has brought me into his rooms!*
> *You will be our joy and our gladness.*
> *We shall praise your love above wine;*
> *How right it is to love you.*

It has been translated: *That we might rejoice in You. . .* "Such, indeed," writes Petit, "is the supplication of the faithful souls aspiring to perfection. They beg God to fill them more and more with His favors and blessings, and when they see someone more advanced in virtue, they take courage from his example and strive to imitate him."

What perhaps previously seemed to them boldness, singularity or madness, they now begin to defend as the only sanity and wisdom acceptable to the laws of love, wondering how it is that the others do not understand this. This is way the Bride finishes here with an exclamation condemning the ungodly, saying: truly the *right of heart* or as the Hebrew puts it, *the rightnesses love you;* or alternatively, *it is rightly or with*

good reason that You are loved. Which is to say: those who
have any sense or rightness cannot help but love You madly;
whoever does not love You in this way is not sensible, is very
stupid. This is what St. John of the Cross says the worldly wise
are to the *divinely wise,* just as the divinely wise are to the
worldly. Thus there will always be those who consider rectitude
little less than foolishness; and they will be those very servants
who, presuming to be pious and friendly, have strong ties with
the worldly; so that, despite all that they say, they clearly show
themselves to be lacking this uprightness of heart. Whoever
possessed it would show it in really loving Jesus Christ and in
loving His servants as members of His Mystical Body, without
ever judging ill of them (II *Cor.* 13, 5), and thus would go on
loving them more and more as they themselves become more
upright of heart. Only those who love Jesus in this way are
living rightly, as the upright in heart. "True wisdom, which is
true love," writes P. Avrillon *(Ano afectivo),* does not know
what detours are. It goes straight to God by a single path which
is always the shortest and straightest. It possesses no other
artifice but innocence, and no other finesse but Christian
simplicity. The upright heart searches for and loves God, and
God alone, says St. Augustine (in *Ps.* 77). Since the light of
divine love always illuminates its steps, it never makes a false
one; since the fire of this love burns it without reserve, it never
admits any other flames... And since it is the love of God that
causes it to love and that it is the Spirit of love Who is loving
within it, it is impossible for it not to love wisely."

Although the rest in these intimate chambers where such
lessons are learned, is usually of a short duration, normally only
about half an hour (the half-hour of that mysterious silence that
was made in Heaven, *Rev.* 8, 1), "the memory of these divine
experiences," observes Fr. Juan de los Angeles, "lasts for a very
long time, as do the happiness and joy, for the soul has only to
recall those moments for it to leap with joy and boundless
delight and even to cry out and do the most unusual things...

All of which means quite simply that with these memories come happiness, joy or jubilation and a kind of re-tasting which, as the Prophet says (*Ps.* 145, 17) announces the magnitude of the sweetness of God, with which the soul was replenished: *Memoriam abundantiae suavitatis tuae eructabunt.* "

Thus the soul will exclaim that, without knowing how, she was brought into those portentous mansions, unknown to mortals, and that she will never forget all that she experienced there; but she does not tell us anything about what was revealed to her, still less what she felt, for this is nearly always so ineffable that it defies description of any kind. We must be content with the Bride's exclamation, or by this other one from St. John of the Cross: "I entered in where I knew not, and remained not knowing transcending all knowledge. . ."

She alone is introduced, for her companions are not yet worthy of such a favor, but they rejoice with her nonetheless and she with them.

But there is something wrong if they always remain this tender in virtue and never become worthy enough to be brought in to hear the divine secrets.

Although it is not always possible to give an account of, or explain what happens to the soul during these intimate and divine communications, the soul will always carry with her certain very clear signs that will witness to the fact that she really has been in the region of light. These signs, says Hugo, will come from the same light that we turn to in order to dispel our own darkness: the light of holy fear, the light of truth, the light of charity. . . How could we know that we had been there if we did not come out illuminated?

According to Fray Luis de León, when the Bride says: *The King has brought me into his rooms* "she forgets that she is speaking as a shepherdess and thus calls Him by His name, for love always brings such familiarity with it; or perhaps it is a part of that language, as it is of ours, for anyone that is loved very greatly to be addressed as *My King.*"

Moreover, "He lives in our souls," remarks St. Mary Magdalen of Pazzi (2aP., Ch. 13), "as Spouse, King, Father or Brother, according to the purity and love and particular disposition that He encounters in each one of us."

He brought me in, although spoken in the past tense, could well be understood in the future, as something that will certainly happen very shortly, and that is how the commentator understands it. But the joy with which the Bride concludes is clear proof that she is speaking from experience, and although it perhaps seems to us too soon, she reveals quite definitely that she has received this grace. By having recounted it in this way, following directly after her request, we realize how ready Our Lord is to grant this grace to all who truly ask Him for it, although at times, in order to test and purify souls further He will make them wait days and even years... We have already said that these vivid expressions are disconnected images which describe many things very quickly, as though they followed one immediately upon the other, whereas actually in themselves they demand quite some considerable time for them to be achieved.

As a result souls are made more confident of finding God quickly, provided they are truly looking for Him, for we can see from this how close He always is to those that invoke Him and do so in all truth (*Ps.* 145, 18). Pious and sincere souls are greatly encouraged to seek Him more eagerly, sure of finding Him, as it has been promised to them.

Far from being discouraged by their own weakness, this same weakness serves as a stimulus to invoke Him even more, for it makes them see how much they need Him. The more that the Bride who is ardently longing to be united with her Spouse loves Him, says St. Ambrose (*De Isaac,* Ch. 3), the more earnestly she will beg Him to deign to draw her after Him, so that she might follow Him along His swift path and not remain exposed to great dangers: *Festinat ad Verbum, et rogat ut attrahatur, ne forte derelinquatur... Et quia videt se imparem tantae velocitati, dicit: Attrahe nos."*

Running after Him in this way she will soon find Him and eventually all her desires will be satisfied to the full. "If a person is seeking God," observes St. John of the Cross (*Living Flame of Love,* 3), "His beloved is seeking him much more. If a soul directs to God its loving desires, which are as fragrant to Him as the pillar of smoke rising from the aromatic spices of myrrh and incense (*Sg.* 3:6), God sends it the fragrance of His ointments by which He draws it and makes it run after Him (*Sg.* 1:3), and these are His divine inspirations and touches. Since these are His, they are always bound and regulated by the perfection of His law and of faith... Thus it should be understood that the desire for Himself which God grants in all His favors of unguents and fragrant anointings is a preparation for other more precious and delicate ointments, made more according to the quality of God, until the soul is so delicately and purely prepared that it merits union with Him and substantial transformation in all its faculties."

"Then," advises St. Bernard (*Serm.* 21), "let the Bride say and with sighing: Carry me, my Spouse, behind You, for corruptible flesh weighs my soul down... Indeed, she needs to be carried and not by anyone except by Him Who said: *Without Me you can do nothing.* She is absolutely dependent upon help from the Spouse in being able to run after Him, imitating His virtues and in taking Him as a model and example for her life. Above all she needs all His protection if she is to deny herself, embrace His cross and follow Him...

"But, oh sweet Jesus! How few there are who want to set out and follow You and yet there is no one who would not want to come to the place of Your dwelling! Knowing that in Your right hand endless joys are to be found (*Ps.* 16, 10), they long to enjoy You, but not to imitate You; everyone wants to reign with You, but not to suffer with You: *Omnes volunt te frui, et non ita imitari; coregnare cupiunt, sed non compati...,* *consequi, sed non sequi...,* wanting to find You without looking for You, wanting to die like saints but not to live like them... But this is not the language of Your beloved Bride. Having abandoned everything for love of You, she wants only to follow after You, never leaving Your footprints, walking with You wherever You go. She knows very well how attractive and beautiful are Your ways and how peaceful and sure Your paths, and that *whoever follows You does not walk in darkness (John 6, 44)*. She asks You, and earnestly begs You to take her with You, knowing very well that *Your justice is as exalted as the highest mountains* and it is impossible for her to reach such heights by her own strength alone... She asks to be carried by the Son, given her by the Father to be her guide and example, and to instruct and teach her the paths of prudence, giving her the law of life and of discipline."

With this help that the Lord is quick to grant to all who truly ask Him, we could all without exception run after Him following the scented trail of His perfumes.

"What excuses could anyone put forward," he goes on to ask (*Serm.* 22), "for not running after the aroma of these ointments unless it be someone whom this scent of life has unfortunately not yet reached? Anyone who does not smell this vital fragrance poured forth everywhere, and not smelling it does not run after it, is undoubtedly dead or full of corruption... As far as we are concerned, sweet Jesus, we cannot help but run after You, seeing Your wonderful sweetness and gentleness and recognizing that You would certainly never abandon the poor nor reject the sinner... Thus, we shall all run after the sweet scent of Your wonderful mercies, although we might not all pursue them with the same ardor, some being more impressed by the scent of Your wisdom, and others by the hope of forgiveness through penitence; the former are more moved to the practice of virtue by Your powerful example, while the latter are more inspired with holy desires by the memory of Your Passion."

But just as the Sacred Spouse has different kinds of scents

with which to win and attract souls, and hence the different gifts they receive enabling them to pursue Him along the paths of virtue and the practice of piety, so, writes the same Saint (*Serm.* 23), "the rooms of the Spouse are numerous and diverse, and not everyone who enters enjoys His wonderful presence in the same way, but each one according to the will of the Eternal Father. For it is not we who chose Him, but He who chose us and assigned us the place as was pleasing to Him, so that we might be where He Himself saw fit to place us. . . In these different mansions which the Heavenly Spouse has for receiving souls who follow Him, all these, whether queens or maidens, receive the fortune that corresponds to their merit, until such a time when through the gift of contemplation they are able to go further and enter into the joys of their Lord and examine the sweet and hidden secrets of the Spouse."

Because of the way that He treats them there and the impressions they receive, they will often forget about things here below, and will be scorned and laughed at by those who do not understand the delightful mysteries of this *interior life,* which is the most beautiful and worthy part of Christian life: *Decor enim vitae est in illa* (*Eccles.* 6, 31). Thus the desire to justify themselves will sometimes move them to make excuses and defend themselves.

v. 5)   *I am black but lovely, daughters of Jerusalem,*
            like the tents of Kedar,
            like the pavilions of Salmah.

Here begins another scene in which the Bride appears as a mere humble working-girl. This suggests that some time must have elapsed since she was allowed to enter the King's chambers and that since then she has been criticised because of her new way of life. She now replies to the tacit censure or rebuke made by the *daughters of Jerusalem,* recognizing that she is, indeed, black or *swarthy,* but not for the reasons they suggest in their efforts to draw her away from the course she has undertaken, but on the contrary, that she is so because she is still unable to pursue it with the perfection she would like. She says that she really is black because of her own human weaknesses of which she has been unable to strip herself, and above all because of what she acquires through her inevitable contacts with creatures. But in spite of all this she is beautiful because of what she has of God, that is because of His divine grace which continues to increase through this intimate communication. She is black in the eyes of the profane, but deep within, thanks to the presence of her Divine Lord pouring forth His love in torrents, she is more beautiful than ever.

"May God free us from outward appearances that invite praise from those who see them, whenever they are occasioned by vanity," writes Fr. Gracian. "A soul is much more sure when it wears all its glory *on the inside*. This is why, when speaking with those that despise her for not having an outward appearance worthy of praise, the Bride replies: *I am black, but beautiful. . .*"

"The soul says: *Sed formosa. . .*", observes the V. Mariana, "because once it has become truly humble it is able to list its own virtues without lapsing into vanity, for it views them from its lowly state, as the holy Bride did here. The first thing that she says is: *Nigra sum. . .* Although she sees that she is rich, she recognizes that all her riches come from her Spouse, it was He who generously gave them to her and that she was less deserving than all other creatures. In this way, because of her low estate, her virtues seem to her all the more beautiful. Just as rich embroidery stands out much better against a dark background, so it is with her, she says, and she will never forget this, for the favors would not be such as they are and so pure were she to be forgetful of her own nothingness. . . This is what the Bride is doing, as though instructed by the Holy Spirit, never leaving her post which is the nothingness of her own harvest, keeping her gaze always fixed upon it, even though her Sacred Spouse grant her further favors."

But the soul cannot fail to acknowledge these favors

gratefully: "for we can scarcely love," she adds, "unless we recognize our obligation to love. Thus what will best stir us to love is to recall the love that Our Lord has for us and all that He does for us is done with infinite love, and that with this same love He forgives us, suffers and waits."

Because of the goodness of this sweet Love that is so pleased to favor the soul and laden it with graces, she comes to look not only like the tents of Kedar which had a very abject appearance outwardly, being made of black goat-skins, but were rich and luxurious within, and like the pavilions of Solomon which were made of skins on the outside but were nevertheless worthy royal mansions. Truly, *the beauty of this King's daughter is hidden there within (Ps.* 45,13).

I am black, says the Church," writes Maria de la Dolorosa, "because I walk in the darkness of faith, but *beautiful as the pavilions of Solomon* because I am enriched with every grace and because I have Jesus, both as God and as man, hidden within the Blessed Sacrament."

"Black, because of what I possess on my own part," writes Fr. La puente (*Guia* espirit., 2,9) "and because of what I outwardly appear to be in the estimation of the world, but beautiful because of the grace I possess in the most secret and hidden regions of my soul and because of the esteem of God Who gave it to me. He in His infinite wisdom, a wisdom more wonderful than that of Solomon, was able to unite such blackness with such beauty within His Church and within each holy soul, that in the one it should recognize itself and found itself upon humility, and that in the other it should know its Benefactor and become rooted in charity, loving Him Who loved it so much that He became man and gave Himself in death for it. . ."

"The reason," writes Fr. Luis de León, "why the Church, that is, the company of the just and any one of them has a dark and ugly outward appearance is quite clear because of the little attention and importance or rather, because of the very bad treatment the world gives them, for it would seem that there are none poorer, more beaten down and forsaken than those who have to do with goodness and virtue, when in fact they are loved and favored by God and their souls are filled with incomparable beauty."

"*Nigra sum. . .*" writes St. Thomas, "id est, deformis persecutionibus, et aerumnis quas sustineo; *sed formosa,* decore virtutum."

"The Church's persecutions, heresies and scandals," observes Scio, "give it a very gloomy outward appearance; but inside it is seen to be full of wealth, magnificence and beauty, for it is adorned with the most sublime virtues and contains within it a large army of just men and saints."

"If we consider," writes St. Bernard (*in Cant. Serm.* 25), "how humble, beaten-down and worthless in our eyes saints often outwardly appear to be, while inwardly, at the same time, they are contemplating with unveiled faces the glory of God, *growing brighter and brighter as they are turned into the Image they reflect* (II *Cor.* 3, 18), if we were to censure them for their blackness, each one of them would undoubtedly reply: *I am black, yes, but beautiful.* We have excellent proof of this in the Apostle St. Paul (II *Cor.* 10), who, because of his humble outward appearance and because of the many trials he had undergone, seemed despicable and, indeed, was despised, and yet could truly boast of having been taken up into the third Heaven. . . Would you still call this soul black, O daughters of Jerusalem? *Hanc vos dicitis nigram?* It might be black in your eyes, but in the eyes of the angels and even of God Himself it is beautiful. What wonderful blackness this is that causes the soul to be inspired with candor of spirit, the light of wisdom and the purity of conscience: '*Felix nigredo, quae mentis candorem parit, lumen scientiae, conscientiae puritatem.*'"

But those who do not see these precious things, or who do not want to see or recognize them, however often they shine forth, these people, and they tend to be numerous and those that stand nearest, will never cease ridiculing such a soul, always ready to persecute, insult or throw scorn on it in a thousand different ways. Thus we see that *anyone who tries to live devoted to Christ is certain to be attacked* (II *Tim.* 3, 12), and especially by those who formerly praised them the most, and by their own friends who now show themselves to be their greatest enemies because of their continual concern to please their interior Guest and to attend to His slightest suggestions, with which He instructs them and wins their souls. As St. John of the Cross and St. Teresa observe, being still unable, until they reach the highest stage of union in which they are greatly comforted, to be both Mary and Martha at the same time, they tend, much against their own will, to be forgetful or absent-minded in their affairs, something which God allows in order that their purification might be all the greater, but which causes them to be called lazy, stupid and useless. They encounter opposition in everything, and even their greatest works will be interpreted in the worst way. Their silence, modesty, discipline, observance and composure will be considered strange and extravagant, melancholic, neurasthenic or haughty and scornful of others; their fasting and austerity a farce, or an abuse of health; or on the other hand, their most basic requirements will be called a luxury and their ardent desire to devote themselves to prayer is censured as laziness of sloth, and a wish to waste time. . .

At every step they are quick to point out all their past and present faults, exaggerating and disfiguring them dreadfully, when in the past they would perhaps applaud them or at least forgive them.

Whoever really wishes to give himself to God will not be forgiven or pardoned anything by the worldly, still less by those who are lax or lukewarm in their faith; for these, seeing their own weakness, slovenliness and disorderly life condemned by the fervor, fidelity and exemplary behavior of these others, will never cease reproaching and ridiculing them all they can, telling them, among other things, that "since they began to become saints or to try to pass as *mystics*. . .or as more spiritual than others," they have become much worse, setting a bad example and giving everyone much to talk about, and that if they glory in their piety and fervor, boasting of having received special graces from Heaven, it is in vain, for God could scarcely give such favors to those who commit so many imperfections and manifest faults. They say there would be nothing surprising about these faults in other people, such as themselves, who do not make such boasts (as though they were not also obliged to sanctify themselves or even to keep the commandments) but are intolerable in those who exult so much in themselves and scorn the rest.

"It is an outcry," says St. Teresa (*Sixth Mansions,* Ch. 1), "made by people with whom such a person is acquainted, and even by those with whom she is not acquainted, and who she never in her life supposed would think about her at all. 'How holy she's getting!' they exclaim, or 'she's only going to extremes to deceive the world and make other people appear in a bad light, when really they are better Christians than she is without any of these extravagences!' (Notice, by the way, that she is not really indulging in any 'extravagances' at all; she is only trying to live up to her Profession.) Then persons whom she had thought her friends abandon her and it is they who say the worst things of all."

Perhaps they think they are doing her a great favor and under the pretext that with all her "strange and idle ways" she might become useless, disturbed or, as they say, "lose her mind". They try to impose occupations and work on her, when she so sorely needs rest, like Mary, at the feet of the Lord, to receive light and strength with which to come to know herself, to correct herself properly and fulfill and that she is required to do.

Seeing that this poor soul is overwhelmed by so many concerns, when she is so weak in virtue, it is hardly surprising, indeed it is only to be expected, that at times she will fail to keep watch over herself, while having to attend to others. Being the object of so much derision when she feels most oppressed within and most in need of some kind of comfort or alleviation, would it be at all strange if she acted a little harshly or if, like a beginner, she allowed herself to become a little impatient? This *blacknes of the face* is noticed and censured by everyone, and principally by the *daughters of Jerusalem,* those of the same religion, or by those who desire to appear good and devout, but who content themselves with a mediocre and negligent life, which they call the *ordinary way* or the *smooth and well-trodden path.* . . Thus they never tire of branding the fervent as "strange, peculiar, odd," if not deluded, demented, bigoted, hypocritical, fanatical and other such "compliments" of the same order, so frequent in this kind of "devout" people who are capable of detecting a speck in the eye of their neighbor, but who cannot even see the beam from a wine-press in their own. They do not want to look at themselves, but rather to criticize their brothers, just as the old Accuser did (*Rev.* 12, 10). They do not see that they are completely without charity and justice and yet exaggerate a very slight outward imperfection in others without wishing to observe the beauty that shines within. . .

Those who are thus surprised or shocked to detect some inevitable little defect in pious souls as though it were possible from the outset to reach immediately the heights of sanctity and at once live on earth like true angels rather than as travellers along the way, and who therefore mock them and despise their enlightenment and fervor as mere illusion and fraud, could very well be countered with this reply from St. John of the Cross (*Spirit. Cant.,* stanza 33): "Souls, you who do not know of, nor recognize these favors, do not marvel that the Heavenly King has granted such admirable ones, as even to bring me to His secret love. For though of myself I am dark, He so frequently fixed His eyes on me, after having looked at me the first time, that He was not satisfied until He had espoused me to Himself and brought me to the inner chamber of His love." "The soul, then," he adds, "is absorbed in a divine life, withdrawn from its natural appetites and from all that is secular and temporal; it is brought into the King's cellars, where it rejoices in its Beloved, remembering His breasts more than wine, saying: *Although I am black, I am beautiful, daughters of Jerusalem,* for my natural black color was changed into the beauty of the Heavenly King." (*Living Flame of Love,* II)

"But," observes St. Bernard, "saints ought to glory not only in their inner beauty, but also in their outer blackness itself, since they have nothing which does not work toward their greater good. . . Thus spoke the Apostle (II *Cor.* 13 9-10): *I shall be very happy to make my weaknesses my special boast so that the power of Christ may be the more manifest in me. . . For it is when I am weak that I am strong.* The Bride quite rightly glories in the very thing that her rivals would use to insult her, boasting not only of being beautiful, but also of being dark. She is not ashamed of a darkness which she knows very well that her Spouse had Himself chosen for her sake, greatly desiring as she does to be like Him; so that for her there can be nothing as honorable as to share the ignominy suffered by her Savior. Hence that cry of joy and happiness (*Gal.* 3, 24): *May God free me from boasting of anything save of the cross of my Lord Jesus Christ.* For whoever really loves and really wants to be grateful to the Crucified Lord, cannot fail to rejoice in the ignominy of the cross: *Grata ignominia Crucis ei qui Crucifixo ingratus non est.* This is, indeed, a kind of darkness, but one which makes me like my sweet Master."

"O what humility and excellence the Bride possesses!" exclaims the saintly Abbot on another occasion (*Serm.* 27) "being at one and the same time a tent of Kedar and sanctuary of the Most High; an earthly dwelling and a Heavenly palace; a mud house and a Kingly chamber; a body of death and a temple of light; in short, despicable to the eyes of the proud, while a lovable Bride to the eyes of Christ. *She is dark but beautiful, O daughters of Jerusalem;* for although the afflictions and troubles of this exile disfigure her and take away her color, she is adorned by a celestial beauty which shines throughout her."

She can well join St. John of the Cross in declaring (*Spir. Cant.* v. 29): "I lost myself and was found." By which, he adds, "the soul answers the tacit reproof of those in the world who usually criticize persons who are entirely given to God and think these persons excessive in their conduct, estrangement and withdrawal, asserting that they are useless in important matters and lost to what the world esteems. The soul skilfully answers this reprimand, boldly facing it and all the other possible reproofs of the world; for having reached the intimate love of God, she considers everything else of little consequence. But this is not all. She even proclaims how she has acted and rejoices and glories in having lost the world and herself for her Beloved... That they might see the gain of her loss and not think it an absurdity or a delusion, she declares that her loss was her gain... He who loves is not abashed before the world because of the works he performs for God, nor even if everybody condemns them does he hide them in shame. Whoever is ashamed to confess the Son of God before men, by failing to perform His works, will discover that the Son of God, as is recorded in Luke, will be ashamed to confess him before the Father. (*Lk.* 9, 26). The soul possessing the spirit of love glories rather in beholding that she has achieved this work in praise of her Beloved and lost all the things of this world."

These are not the only things that are lost, but also the soul's pious practices, its ordinary ways of seeking and serving God. This often causes great astonishment and is rigorously censored by all those who like to adhere to their own methods and endeavors. But, as the mystical Doctor goes on to add, "a soul treading the spiritual road has reached such a point that she has lost all roads and natural methods in her communion with God, and no longer seeks Him by reflections, or forms, or sentiments, nor by any other way of creatures and the senses, but has advanced beyond them all and beyond all modes and manners, and enjoys communion with God in faith and love. Then it is said that God is her gain, because she has certainly lost all that is not God and all that she is in herself."

These words of the Bride, as St. Bernard remarks (*Serm.* 29), can also be applied to the *daughters of this century* who like to criticise devout souls, calling them indiscreet in their penance, austerity and lengthy praying, maintaining that is how they have grown so weak so to become pale and discolored. To such worldly wise people who are so abundant, even in the holiest places, the fervent soul can well reply: this weakness and paleness in my body gives vigor and strength to my spirit; the very rays of my divine Sun, Jesus, caused it for my good. In this way the Church and every loving soul rejoices and glories in seeing itself black and discolored through love of its Spouse, attributing this not to this own endeavors, but to the grace and mercy of God.

"The daughters of Jerusalem are amazed to see the Bride like that," says the Blessed Suso (*3rd letter*), "But the Holy Spirit means that all faithful souls who are afflicted, discouraged, darkened and continually tried by God with the heaviest crosses, if they persist with patience and supernatural submission, become the most intimate and highly favored in the Heavenly court."

"The Hebrew word," writes Fr. Juan de los Angeles, "means not only beautiful, but graceful, lovable and desirable. . . In truth there is nothing as lovable. . .as a soul who is worthy of being Christ's Bride. Nor can anything be found without, which will deprive her of the beauty within: neither the baseness of her country, nor her lowly origins, nor the poverty of her family nor her past life . . . once her soul is purified through faith and adorned and embellished with charity and the other virtues. Who can call me a fool or an ignoramus if I have within me the Spirit of God in Whom are all the treasures of wisdom and knowledge . . . ? The Bride quite rightly considers herself loved by her Spouse and worthy of His bed-chamber and embraces, although outwardly appearing dark, ignoble and dull like the tents of Kedar. She holds within herself the Holy Spirit and is His temple, a daughter of promise . . . and a citizen of Heaven. What does she care if the daughters of Jerusalem call her black? For she takes pride in the fact that a dark, tanned appearance is not acquired by idling at home, nor by reclining on padded pillows, but by undergoing trials and suffering the heat of the sun and the inclemencies of the weather. In truth, the less bright the outer clarity and the more reviled the body, the nearer the soul will be to the Crucified Christ. This is *not* a cause of sadness, but it fills the soul with a very great joy, as St. Paul says of himself (II *Cor.* 7,4): *I am filled with consolation and my joy is overflowing.*"

But since the *daughters of this world* and the very *daughters of Jerusalem,* that is, persons who are devout only to a degree, do not understand this language of the spirit and cannot be governed by supernatural principles, the interior soul time and time again finds, or believes itself to be obliged to justify itself, very much against its own will. It gives new explanations, so as to avoid these puerile and pharasaical "scandals", and above all to prevent insult and abuse that it may be able to follow quietly the path along which God leads it, although at times the more advanced will prefer to keep silent.

v. 6   *Take no notice of my swarthiness,*
          it is the sun that has burned me.
          My mother's sons turned their anger on me,
          they made me look after the vineyards.
          Had I only looked after my own!

That is, they foolishly placed in her care more vineyards than her very limited strength could look after properly, with the result that she did not keep the vineyard of her own soul free from every imperfection. She begins by openly confessing that her dealings with the world or the excess of duties

darkened her face; but she thinks she ought to avow that this
will not prevent her from being more beautiful than she was
before entering the chambers of the King. She recognizes her
imperfection, her *blackness,* but shows how this blackness was
inevitable, given her incapacity to manage all the work and
duties entrusted to her. The blame lies principally with those
who abuse her in this way, heedless of her weakness. Her
mother's sons have turned their anger on her. Between children
of the same father and different mothers this would not be so
surprising; in such situations there is often rivalry and
antipathy, while true and intimate brotherhood would be
expected between those who are children of the same mother.
In this case, however, it is precisely these latter, the most
intimate and best loved, those who manifested the greatest
confidence in her and who she hoped would support and
encourage her; it is these, who are the first to turn against her,
thus fulfilling Our Lord's saying (*Matt.* 10, 36) that a spiritual
man's worst enemies shall be of his own household.

"It is true to say," observes Fr. Luis de León, "that her
brothers did this violence to her, for there is no other person
more opposed to true virtue and more keen in persecuting it
than those who profess it in title and outward appearances only;
those who are most indebted and obliged to us, more often than
not we find to be our very worst enemies."

"Among the persecutions and insults that do most to
darken honor in this world," adds Fr. Gracian, "there are none
to match those caused by one's own brothers and sisters
(especially if they are held to be holy. . .), for, since everyone
believes them, the persecuted person cannot raise his head. . .
And so he resolves to accept the insults, to live the whole of life
without men's esteem, withdrawing into the inner life of his
heart so as to love, fear and hope only in God."

"The war waged against the Bride by her brothers,"
declared Fr. Juan de los Angeles, "was designed to prevent her
from having what she so much desired: union with the heavenly

Spouse. . . Ridiculing her dark and discolored appearance they maintained she was not fit for so sovereign a betrothal. Justifying herself she says: Take no notice of my swarthiness, for I have already told you that I am nonetheless very beautiful. . . , and the dark color is accidental. She could well add: It was long toil that made me black, for I was white. . . *Decolaravit me sol.* The work that my brothers had me do made me dark like this. *Pugnaverunt.* . . In order to do away with my love for my Spouse, they first of all put me to tending the vineyards, together with other duties and tasks I was obliged to perform. They then cut me off from the company of the shepherds, two things which do much to weaken one's will, and drain away one's love, however great it may be; that is the absence of the good that is sought after, and too much involvement in other things. . . It is quite clear that a person involved in many things cannot be fulfilling his duties to himself."

They made me look after the vineyards. . .

As Scio remarks, these words are often repeated by holy prelates and by all those whom charity and obedience "oblige to watch over others who do not feel capable of looking after themselves. Through this dealing and conversation with men, even the most holy fall into some kind of error; they are thus to be heard continually sighing for solitude and retreat."

"Taking vineyards to mean souls," writes the holy Abbot of Clairvaux (*Serm.* 30), "I often reproach myself for having taken on the care of other souls without being even capable of caring for my own. . . Certainly those who put me to looking after vineyards must have fully realized how badly I kept my own. But, alas! How long did I keep it uncultivated and deserted. . .? When I became converted to the Lord I confess that I began to care for it a little better, but not as much as I ought. . . How much harm was done to you, my vineyard, even then when I was beginning to show you a little more care? How many and how wonderful were the clusters of good works contaminated by my anger, stolen from me by pride, or spoiled and ruined by conceit? How much has my vineyard suffered from the beguilements of gluttony, from the vice of idleness or from the pusillanimity and storminess of the spirit? This was the condition it was in and yet *they made me look after the vineyards* without considering what needed to be done to mine or what had been done, heedless of the Apostle's words (I *Tim.* 3, 5): *How can any man who does not understand how to manage his own family have responsibility for the Church of God?*"

He adds: "I am amazed by the boldness and temerity of many who, while doing no more than gathering thistles and thorns from their own vineyards, are not ashamed to want to meddle in caring for those of the Lord. Such people deserve to be called usurpers and thieves rather than custodians and cultivators. But, alas! How many risks to which I see my own vineyard still exposed and myself unable to tend to them because of having to tend to so many others. . . ! With its fences broken down, *all who pass by the way can steal its fruit.* (Ps. 80, 13). It is exposed to the onslaughts of sadness and anger, and defenseless against the motions of impatience. . . There is no way of seeing myself free of these evils, nor of escaping from these troubles, nor do I have time even to pray. What floods of tears could I shed sufficiently to water the sterile land of my neglected soul. . . ?

"O, how many there are," exclaims Fr. Juan de los Angeles, "who could say of themselves: They made me look after other vineyards and I failed to look after my own! 'Other' is everything that has to do with the flesh and with the senses of the body, and 'one's own' is all that has to do with the soul. The world cares only for the former; no one remembers the latter."

Here then are the many ways in which a soul can say that she is dark, for she has been tanned by the sun and has not cared for her vineyard because she has been busy caring for those of others. By this care (in so far as it is prejudicial) are meant the excessive 'outside' activities and dealings with people; and by this sun that discolors is meant, as Scio explains, "the flame of the trials and tribulations that afflict the Church and every soul. . . That color is not natural but acquired from having been out in the sun, and then not by her own wishes but through compulsion."

The Church, says St. Thomas, can well tell its faithful: "Take no notice of my dismal and despicable outward appearance but be attentive to my inner beauty: *Nolite me considerare quod fusca sim;* id est, quod tribulationibus afficiar, quod persecutionibus opprimar; *quia decoloravit me sol,* id est fervor persecutionis splendorem in me quodammodo offuscavit; et illam attendite, non illa quae foris pati videor: Tale est quod Apostolus dicit: *Nolite deficere in tribulationibus meis pro vobis, quae est gloria vestra."*

In every fervent person, says Fr. Avrillon, "the laborious exercise of penitence has darkened their flesh and withered their complexion; but the practice of love has embellished their soul."

According to Cardinal Hugo, "these are words with which the Bride encourages the young maidens, souls just beginning, to have patience and to persevere through trials, and with which she reprimands the petulance of murmurers, as though to say: 'My friends, do you want to enter into intimate communications with Our Lord . . . ? Be steadfast then, and do not cower before the troubles and afflictions that you see me suffer at the hands of my enemies. Yes, I am blackened by the trials that surround me; but I am beautiful nonetheless, for inwardly I glory in my suffering and weakness so that the virtue of Christ might shine forth in me.' These words can also be applied to the Church which, because of its penitent souls and still more because of its sinners has become blackened and yet which, thanks to the just, is so very beautiful; black in its very active members, and beautiful in its contemplatives . . . ; in short, black in the eyes of the godless but extremely beautiful in the eyes of the angels. . ."

Filon, Bishop of Carpacia, gives a favorable interpretation to this scorching or *burning of the sun,* understanding the Bride to mean: "Do not despise me for the blackness of my offences, for Christ the Sun of Justice has now enlightened me and removed such ugliness." Agreeing with this interpretation is the explanation given by the Ven. Mariana: 'Through my own doings and birth and through the other offences I have committed, I am dark; for I abandoned myself to the harmful winds and suns of my appetites, mistaking darkness for light. . . , but do not despise me, for the night has now fled from me and the day of my redemption and salvation has dawned; I have had such purifications that although the outside is ugly and coarse, the inside is as beautiful as the tents of Kedar."

Thus, she goes on to add, "the more gifts she receives from the King, the more she is grieved and the more deeply she knows the nothingness from which He saved her. So it seems to me that, giving herself completely to an ardent feeling of gratitude and appreciating with the full force of her heart the fact that the Lord should have turned His gaze to so lowly a creature and given her such great mercies, she says: 'I am black, I admit, and you have good reason to be surprised. . . But when He gazed upon me, His look was so beneficial that my wounds were healed and I became as beautiful as the tents of Kedar which looked so ugly on the outside, but which were so rich and beautiful on the inside — rooms where princes would take up lodgings.'. . . That, it seems to us, is how the Spouse works; finding no one in the world who will receive Him and give Him lodging, He enters these tents that He has made and enriched with His most generous hand; and here He takes His recreation and delight with the children of men, that is, with the heroic works of souls full of strong desires — souls who are unknown to the world, for they try to hide themselves and to see that their works are not seen by anyone except their own Spouse. Since men do not see the beauty hidden within the despised outward appearances, they move away from such people and dismiss them as sad and dejected. This is the blackness of which the Bride speaks here."

If carnal men were once to know this hidden treasure that so enriches and embellishes holy souls inwardly, how much they would desire and seek after it, imitating these souls instead of scorning and mocking them!

If they could only see how poor, base and abominable they really are, however much they might be esteemed and honored by the world, how eagerly they would try to acquire this heavenly treasure, being completely without it. How much they would then prefer to be taken for madmen, as the saints were, rather than to be as they are in the eyes of God . . . !

"O, if men only knew," exclaimed St. Rose of Lima, "how wonderful grace is, how beautiful, how noble, how precious, what riches it carries hidden within it, what treasures, what joys and delights; they would undoubtedly employ all their intelligence and care in seeking out afflictions and troubles, they would scour the world in search of pains, illnesses and torments solely in order to acquire the wonderful gift of grace. This is the merchandise and the interest won by patience. No one would complain of the cross nor of the trials that fall to their lot if they but knew the scales on which they are weighed for distribution among men."

They would consider and focus their attention upon this, if they were wise, rather than upon simple appearances; and they would live in truth, and not under illusions and mistakenly as they unfortunately do now.

"In the Hebrew," says Fr. Juan de los Angeles, "instead of *considerare* is written *despicere*. 'Do not scorn me for my swarthiness, for this is not natural in me, but rather accidental. . . It was not of my own free-will that I went out in the sun, but rather was forced to do so by my brothers: they beat me to such an extent that they forced me to leave my

corner, my own convenience, the couch and pillow and go out
into the fields. *Posuerunt me custodem...* I had my own
vineyard and I failed to look after it so as not to go out into the
sun; and they made me look after the vineyards of others ... !

"St. Paul gives permission for souls to see to the needs of
the saints. (*Rom.* 12, 13), but in such a way that it will not
interfere with prayer and communication with God. Moreover,
Christ our Savior, when talking to Martha who is busily engaged
in seeing to many things He needs, says to her: *'Unum est
necessarium.'* What is this one thing, so famous in the lives of
saints, so necessary and so preferable to all Martha's cares and
attentions? I would say that it is the condition that is absolutely
essential to devoting oneself entirely to God, and which requires
the heart to be undivided and not distracted by many different
things... In order to communicate with Him alone you have to
be alone; in order to reach God, who is one, you have to be one;
do not let your heart become divided, nor apportioned among
the world's delights, but rather, despising them all in the name
of the one of which all things partake and with infinite
advantage, remain one... This *one* was what the saints sought
after in the deserts and retreats of Thebes and Egypt. This was
the goal of that wise merchant who sold all that he had in order
to buy the one fine pearl (*Matt.* 13, 45) It is this that we must
all long for in all our actions, intentions and contemplations,
and when we achieve it, we are sure to become like Mary. Our
contemplation of things divine may now be as lofty as we
would like, but there are times when we are kept from it,
sometimes through our own fault, other times not. This, it
seems, the Bride seeks to excuse when she says: *Posuerunt me
custodem vineis...*"

Unless this responsibility is made obligatory, quite clearly,
as the same author goes on to point out, "to argue that she did
not look after her own vineyard because she was looking after
her brothers seems a very poor excuse. It is an evil that has
severed many from a loving and familiar communication with

God and the cause of many a downfall. Many say: Neighbors! Neighbors! They would do better to remain in a corner, forgetful of them and all things, remembering only their Creator. The harm incurred by a soul who is absent from God, failing to communicate with Him in prayer, is very great. But no less great is the harm incurred by voluntary activities, undertaken with greater or lesser fervor, and even by those who are obliged to accept offices, from which God in His mercy preserve us.

When these activities, however, are not voluntary but imposed through obedience, or through the very love of Christ which *moves* one (II *Cor.* 5, 14), and one really longs to live free from such duties so as to leave the heart free to devote itself entirely to *unum necessarium,* Our Lord is able to make up for one's involuntary deficiencies in such an excellent way that everything being done in His love, redounds to the good of one's own soul, and at the same time to His greater glory, to the benefit of one's fellow-men and to the general good of the Church.

This, according to St. Bernard (*Serm.* 30), is what happens to those who are able to sacrifice themselves and make themselves all things for all people, forgetting themselves and their own convenience, for the glory of God and the good of their brothers. "The perfect man," he states, "can also say that he did not look after his vineyard, in the sense in which the Savior tells us in the Gospel: *He who would lose his soul for Me, shall save it.* The only person who ought to be considered worthy and capable of being put in charge of vineyards is he whom the care of his own vineyard does not prevent from diligently watching over those others placed in his care, not seeking his own ends but those of many. In this way St. Peter was charged to look after the vineyard of the Church: unworried by being imprisoned and put to death for Christ, his love for his own vineyard did not prevent him from tending to others entrusted to him. In the same way St. Paul was charged

with the vast uncultivated vineyard of the gentiles, being
constantly ready to sacrifice himself for it... You too, if you
deny your own will, if you completely renounce the pleasures
of the flesh, if you crucify you body with its vices and desires,
and mortify your members, mental powers and senses, you will
become an imitator of St. Paul... and a disciple of Jesus Christ,
so happily losing your soul for His love — a soul that you would
do wisely to lose so as to save, rather than save and so lose. For
anyone who wants to save his life shall lose it." (*Matt.* 16, 25).

Very tired of giving explanations in vain to those *who do
not want to know how to do good* (*Ps.* 36, 4), the mystical
Bride suddenly turns to the only one who can always
understand her, comfort her and help her in all things, to Him
Who stole her heart and from Whom she cannot live separated
even for a moment.

Therefore, she begins to look upon Him as Shepherd, and
wants to become like one of His many faithful sheep, as well as a
humble shepherd-girl.

v. 7)   *Tell me then, you whom my heart loves:*
          Where will you lead Your flock to graze
          where will you rest it at noon?
          That I may no more wander like a vagabond
          beside the flocks of your companions.

Having justified her color," writes Fr. Luis de León, she
turns to speak with her Spouse and, unable to bear the delay
any longer, asks to know where He is with His flock, resolving
to go out in search of Him. True love does not set store by
trivial matters of good-upbringing and points of honor, nor does
it wait until it has first been invited, but rather is the first to
offer itself and give of itself; and although the Bride has called
to her Spouse for His assistance and He has not replied, she does
not become any less anxious, or any more careful of her honor,
but rather her desire grows stronger. Since He does not come, she
decides to go out in search of Him... It does not matter in fact
that, since the Spouse is, as we suppose Him to be, absent, He

can neither hear the Bride's requests nor satisfy them; for in the case of true and intense love a thousand like impossibilities occur. Absorbed in such an ardent love, the senses are blinded, and, deceiving themselves, they believe all their thoughts to be possible and feasible. On the one hand the Bride speaks to the Spouse as though He were present before her and she could see and hear Him, and on the other hand she does not know where He is, but is determined to find Him wherever He might be; and since this might be the cause of her losing herself, she adds: 'That I may not wander like a vagabond beside the flock of Your companions."

Here the Bride is asking what, in his turn, Thomas à Kempis will also ask (*Bk.* 3, Ch. 2): "That *You* speak to me Lord, not Moses or any of the prophets, but You Who are the light and inspiration of all the prophets; for You alone, without them, can teach me with perfection; but they, without You, can achieve nothing. They can speak words, but cannot communicate spirit. They speak very well, but if You are silent, they do not kindle the heart. . ." The soul, indeed, asks to be tended and guided not according to the ways and reasons of men, whose judgements she so often finds to be mistaken or whose words leave her barren and cold if not disconcerted, but rather by Him Who is never mistaken and Whose words are all life. Since He has hidden Himself from her, she asks Him to show her where and how she can find Him; for she sighs only for Him, and her dealings with those that do not understand these secrets of divine love become even more painful and unbearable to her.

Thus, she asks *Him Whom her soul loves,*Who is now not to be confused with anyone, to reveal Himself to her, to quell her loving desires, not to hide Himself from her so much, to be a good Shepherd and kindly tell her where He is grazing His beloved sheep, which is the watering-place where He takes them during the heat of the midday; for now she wants to be tended only by Him. . .

Once a soul has come into contact with God, even if it be only on one of the lowest levels of mystical contemplation, she will now long only to be in continual communication with that divine Lover that completely won her over and Who is now the only one that her soul loves, being unable to love anything else save through Him and in Him.

This is what she asks Him, and she asks Him for it as earnestly as she knows how, calling Him by the sweet name of her *Beloved*.

She calls Him this, says Niseno, since there is no other name she could give Him which could better show to Him her love, nor which could more ardently declare it, for this love with which she loves Him is the effect of the love which He first showed to her when, seeing her black, He shed His Blood that she might become beautiful. . . And thus, full of trust, she turns to Him to explain the imminent danger she otherwise runs of losing her way or of wandering off, by following incorrect advice or examples, or by letting herself be led by imprudent guides or by shepherds *who have led their sheep astray, who have left them wandering in the mountains, who have gone from mountain to hill, forgetting to lead them to their resting-place (Jerem. 50, 6).*

"I say that the Bride is very discreet," remarks Fr. Juan de los Angeles, "for, having to ask for something so great, as we shall see, in order to win her Spouse, she pledges nothing but the deep and heart-felt love she has for Him. This is the only thing that God values and that man can say is his. . . This is the treasure that we possess, if we possess any treasure at all, and even then if it is of any value it is only because of the grace of God; for since the will is to a certain extent all things, and love leads it where it will . . ., he who loves gives everything to his beloved. For this reason, so often in the Holy Bible God asks us for this love, for when we give it to Him, we give Him all the wealth we possess and all that we have of any worth. Whoever denies Him this love, even if he were to give Him the whole world, can give Him nothing, for nothing is his that lies outside the realm of the will and of love things which are free and which suffer violence in man. Love is truly precious and in itself without any other gift lovable, acceptable, sweet and gentle; and without it, everything else is neither lovable, acceptable nor desirable. As St. Bernard put it: 'Love is enough in itself, in itself it is pleasing; it is its own merit and reward. . .' Therefore the Bride, wanting to win her Spouse and find fulfillment for her desire, pledges nothing else nor justifies her asking Him to tell her where He rests at midday, with anything save her love for Him, and then not half-heartedly and in the company of another, but alone and with all her heart.

"The 'midday' that the Bride here wants to enjoy is, in the opinion of most commentators, that place where the uncontaminated light reaches its zenith and where, in utter silence, far from the madding world, Christ's voice alone is heard, a voice which sounds in her ears noiselessly and with incomparable delight, transfixing the holy souls of the glorious flock that surrounds Him, moving them to an ecstasy in which they live only in their Shepherd."

Although she asks to rest with Him in the bosom of the Father and at the same time to be instructed in the mysteries of the Divinity, she is not thereby asking to enjoy these things as the blessed do in the perpetual midday of eternal glory but only as befits travellers along the way. "It seems to me," adds the same Fr. Juan, "that the Bride is here not asking for the spiritual food and quiet of glory, but for those of the doctrine and sacraments with which the Holy Shepherd feeds and tends His perfect souls, in both active and contemplative life. Speaking with all due propriety, at midday the Shepherd rests, the flock drinks, ruminates and is refreshed, and in the afternoon returns to its pastures; this is different from what happens in glory, for there will be no night nor any temporal succession.

Origen understands midday to be the splendor of the divine Majesty; St. Jerome, those secrets of the heart by which

the soul receives from the Divine Word the clearest communication and the loftiest knowledge; St. Gregory, the ardor of
vices and hence our need for the shade and refreshment of the
Holy Spirit to prevent us from being enkindled; Cardinal Hugo,
the Church of the perfect where the Spouse rests and quietly
enjoys the noon-day... Whatever it may be, the request is lofty
and full of love: it asks for quiet, instruction and knowledge
that is both clear and free from error: it asks for light
untroubled by darkness, it asks for the company of the Spouse
with Whom the soul wants to be completely alone, for love does
not consent to the dividing or sharing of the heart."

She turns to Him, then, Whom she loves with all her soul.
Indeed, it is to Him alone that we must direct ourselves, and
from Him that we must learn to find the recollection and *rest
for our souls* that we so much long for (*Matt.* 11, 28-29). It is
He that we must always follow if we are to be sure of the path
and not expose ourselves to deviations and deceptions (*Jn.* 8,
12, 31-32). He alone can guide us with complete security and
lead us to the abundant pastures where His flock lacks nothing
(*Ps.* 23, 1). It is through Him that these pastures must be
entered, for He is the true *Gate* as well as the true *Shepherd*
Who knows His sheep and is known by them, and "all those who
enter through Him *will be safe, and will go in (into the
mysteries of His Divinity) and go out (into the mysteries of His
Humanity), and will be sure of finding pasture.*

This is how souls can be treated as God's favorite flock,
being saved, instructed, recreated the refreshed with the
precious corn of the chosen and the wine that produces virgins
(*Zechar.* 9, 16-17). For the very "Lamb Who is at the throne of
God will be their Shepherd and will lead them to the springs of
living water" (*Rev.* 7, 17), and to the living spring of sanctity
and grace which is His most Sacred Heart, wherein are
contained all the treasures of wisdom and divine knowledge
(*Col.* 2,3).

The spiritual food that this sweet Savior gives to His sheep is sometimes His sacred mysteries, His wonderful examples and words of eternal life, spoken by His divine mouth or through those of His ministers, with which He delights, comforts and inspires souls, urging them on to all kinds of virtues. Sometimes it is His very flesh and blood which He continually offers in the Sacrament of the Altar to all those who approach Him with a true hunger and thirst for justice, satisfying and strengthening them, filling them full of life and every grace in accordance with their own readiness, bringing them to breathe His heavenly fragrance and participate in His very purity and sanctity and in all His graces, by which they grow spiritually and become lovable and precious in the eyes of God, useful to their neighbors and capable of all kinds of good works.

Whoever has tasted this divine food and enjoyed the loving relationship with the sweet Spouse will be able to think of nothing else and will be wearied by the things of the world.

Once the soul has contemplated Him, remarks St. Lawrence Justinian, she cries out anxiously for Him to reveal Himself to her again, absolutely sure that if she persists in her diligence she will obtain what she asks for and will find the Person she is looking for; and by purifying her heart she will succeed in seeing Him that she loves and in being nourished by Him.

The place where they *rest at midday* and where His faithful sheep seek to lie next to Him, is now the Tabor where He sometimes appears to them transfigured, raising them up in loftly contemplation; now the Sacred Tabernacle, where at every hour devout souls can visit Him, find Him, and receive from Him, although hidden with the veil of faith, very great consolation and inspiration; now Calvary itself, on the holy cross where He slept that divine sleep of Love that triumphed over death, and where He would like His brides to be sleeping on the day of tribulation, resting in His shade so as to be able to savor His sweet fruits (*Song* 2, 3); now the bosom or right hand of the Father, where He is awaiting them amidst the splendors of His glory, and where they long to see Him and delight in Him in eternal rest, free from all danger; now the breast of His most Blessed Mother, where He found the greatest delights that He could have had in dwelling with the sons of men, and where everyone can find Him so easily; and now the pure in heart and loves like Mary where He also comes to graze, as though to take rest from the evil treatment given Him by the worldly and the ungrateful.

"*At midday*," writes St. Thomas, "that is to say in the heat of persecutions, temptations and trials," when in a special way the faithful soul, just like Holy Church, tries to find where her Good Shepherd Jesus is resting, so as to attend always to Him, to rest trustingly on His breast or beneath His loving gaze, and so as not to expose herself to the errors, seductions and deceptions of the false shepherds bad companions and advisors.

She very diligently tries to find out which are the hearts where He enjoys His greatest delights, so that she can go there as though to a place of fine pasture, of refuge and repose, following examples of singular virtue, or searching for support and imploring prayers, and learning in this way to prepare her own heart and to offer it to the Lord so that she also might be instructed and find rest, since He has promised to accompany His own in times of trouble, to encourage them, to protect them from every danger and to bring them to glory (*Ps.* 91, 15).

Ubi pascas; "that is," writes Enrique Harpio (*Theol. Myst.,* 1, 1, Ch. 47), "in whomsoever you find spiritual food, in the doers of good works, in other words, in those who dedicate themselves fervently and faithfully to the active life; and *ubi cubes,* wherever you rest, wherever you find inner repose, which is to be found in true contemplatives. For the active are His Cenacle, and the contemplatives His chamber or place of rest; and at midday, or in other words, in the fervor of contemplation, or else of tribulation."

With respect to the Church, many holy Fathers this "heat

of midday" means the persecutions suffered by it (Casiodoro, Bede, Filon Carp.). "Never were the faithful more closely attached to their Shepherd Jesus Christ than during those dangerous times. Never was their fervor greater nor their virtue more pure. Those who lost sight of the Shepherd went astray and fell into heresy or idolatry" *(Petit).*

The name of shepherd is so fitting a name for Jesus, writes Fr. Juan de los Angeles, "that although in the Scriptures He is given many different names, none was more highly valued by Him and so openly as this one. *Ego Sum* He says *(Jn.* 11, 14), *Pastor bonus.* . . Before He was born in the flesh He tended the angels and all the creatures; for all without exception have their eyes fixed on Him, depending on Him for their sustenance *(Ps.* 104, 27; 145, 15). Then when He is born, He fed men with His Spirit and then with His flesh and blood. . . When men are carried up to Heaven, He will also be their Shepherd there; and as long as His sheep live, which will be for all eternity, He will live with them, communicating to them His very life, as their Shepherd and as their Food. St. Peter calls Him the *Prince of shepherds* (I *Peter,* 5,4). . .

Of even greater wonder, and underlining even more clearly how well suited to Christ this role of shepherd is, is the fact that this tending of His flock is not a single act of tending but adopts as many forms as the needs and conditions of His sheep demand. The pasture is measured according to the hunger that each possesses, and this means knowing the names of His sheep and calling each one by his own name. The weak are fed in one way, the strong in another; the perfect this way, the imperfect that way. It was for this reason that St. Peter called Christ's grace manifold (I, 4, 10); for it takes a different form in each soul. . .

"The perfect government is that of Christ, for it governs with a living law, always understanding what is best, and always wanting that good that it understands. This way of governing was maintained by the Apostle who, as he says (I *Cor.* 9,22), made himself all things to all men in order to save them all. From which it is clear that the office of the shepherd, if he is worthy of this name, embraces many offices, all of which he himself must administer. So that it is Christ Who calls us, sets us right, heals,purifies and sanctifies us, delights us, sustains us and dresses us in His glory; as can be seen in Ezekiel (Ch. 34) who dwells at length upon what Christ was to do for His sheep."

"The Word," confirms St. Mary Magdalen of Pazzi (*Works* Part 3, Ch. 9), "leads His sheep to the pleasant meadows of His Humanity, where the freshest pastures of the gifts and fruits of the Holy Spirit are to be found. What is more, He feeds them with His own substance, giving them His Body and His Blood; and those to whom it is given to know a higher state of grace savor the most precious food of the interior communications that God pours into the soul. . . There others find an even more sublime nourishment, a foretaste, in this life, of the joys of heaven. But which is the watering-place, O Word! You Yourself, You are, *Fons Sapientiae.* You call out loud to everyone: *If anyone thirsts, come to Me and drink.* To the Samaritan woman You said that the soul who drinks of the water that You give, will see living water springing to eternal life.

After watering His sheep, the Good Shepherd washes them. How? With His Own blood: *Lavit nos in Sanguine Suo.* Then when He has washed them He takes up His shears to shear them; which is what happens to the soul when she is in fear or pain, or amidst temptations and humiliations. God rids her of her appetites and desires, her passions and self-love, in accordance with His divine will. Before shearing them He ties their feet and throws them to the ground. God also enchains all our feelings and affections so that the soul is left quite desolate and without any kind of comfort . . . thrown to the ground by the knowledge of her own wretchedness and desolation. . . No one, however strong he is, can reach perfection without first having been sheared by the Lord, either through inner affliction or outer suffering."

"Jesus also feeds His sheep," observes Maria Dolorosa, "that is, simple and obedient souls, through the mouths of His ministers; and He rests on the Altar in the Sacrament of the Eucharist, where He shows us the strength of His love just as He did on Calvary, like the sun that shines with greatest force at midday."

Ne vagari incipiam. "She does not say: that I might go wandering," remarks Fr. Juan de los Angeles, "but: that I might not begin to go wandering. I feel sure that our total perdition is incurred in beginning to go astray and to follow different studies and cares. Whoever begins to go astray can be sure that he is going to have to sweat and suffer many trials rather than be safe and at rest and in unity, a unity which cannot be found but in God; and it is in God and nowhere else that the Bride reaches for this.

"Gerson (Tr. 84 *super Mag.*) says that her desire here is to feed with the One Who gives nourishment, and to rest with Him Who gives rest, thus fleeing from all wandering and from the divisions among the shepherds who fail to follow the single, eternal Shepherd Who, in His Gospel, promises rest and refreshment to the tired and weary. . .

"May God free us from vague, wandering thoughts in prayer, for, apart from wasting time, the soul runs the risk of falling into many kinds of temptations born of idleness and distraction."

"What are you looking for, little man?" asks St. Augustine. "What are you looking for, wandering after many different things? Search for Him Who, being One, embraces all things, and your disquiet and your wandering will cease."

So the mystical Bride joins Job in saying (17, 3-4): *Free me, Lord, and place me beside You, and then let anyone raise his hand against me. For his heart knows no discipline and he shall prevail. . .*

"The faithful soul," says Scio, "who is searching for the true and good Shepherd Who is Jesus Christ, hears no other voice. She asks Him to show her the place where He rests; for otherwise she will become lost. This is expressed even more vividly in the Hebrew, where it says: *Why shall I be like the one who goes away to join the flocks of her companions?"*

To express it more clearly, as Maria Dolorosa explains, "it is as though she were to say: I want to be led by You, O Divine Shepherd, like so many of Your sheep that rest in Your safety at midday. . . For I am determined to follow You in the same way that sheep follow the voice of their shepherd, and I do not want to try any other food but that which comes from You. Here the soul shows herself ready to deny herself every kind of satisfaction, however proper or necessary it might be, so as to feed only from the food which her Spouse offers her, resting in the fulfillment of His will."

Thus, "that this thirsting soul might speak with her Bridegroom and be united with Him in this life through union of love," observes St. John of the Cross (*Spirit. Cant.* stanza I), "it would be well for us to answer for her Spouse, since she asks Him, and point out the place where He is most surely hidden. She may then surely find Him there with the perfection and delight possible in this life, and thus not wander in vain after the footprints of her companions. It should be known that the Word, the Son of God, together with the Father and the Holy Spirit, is hidden by His essence and His presence in the innermost being of the soul. A person who wants to find Him should leave all things through affection and will, enter within himself in deepest recollection, and regard things as though they were nonexistent. St. Augustine, addressing God in the *Soliloquies* (30) said: *I did not find You without Lord, because I wrongly sought You without, Who were within. . .*

"Oh, then, soul, most beautiful among all the creatures, so anxious to know the dwelling place of your Beloved that you may go in quest of Him and be united with Him. . . This is something of immense gladness for you, to see that all your good and hope is so close to you. . . What more do you want, O

soul! And what else do you search for outside when within
yourself you possess your riches, delights, satisfactions, fullness
and kingdom, your Beloved Whom you desire and seek?. . .
Desire Him there, adore Him there. Do not go in pursuit of Him
outside yourself. You will only become distracted and wearied
thereby. . .

"Yet you inquire: Since He Whom my soul loves is within
me, why do I not find Him or experience Him? The reason is
that He remains concealed and you do not also conceal yourself
in order to encounter and *experience* Him. . . Remaining hidden
with Him, you will *experience Him in hiding,* and love and
enjoy Him in hiding, and you will delight with Him in hiding,
that is, in a way transcending all language and feeling. . . If like
Moses (*Ex.* 33, 22) she hides herself in the cleft of the rock, in
the real imitation of the perfect life of the Son of God, her
Bridegroom, she will merit that, while God protects her with
His right hand, *He will show her His shoulders,* which means He
will bring her to the high perfection of union with the Son of
God, her Spouse, and transformation in Him through love. In
this union she experiences such closeness to Him and is so
instructed and wise in His mysteries that, as for knowing Him in
this life, she has no need to say, *"Where have You hidden?"*

She calls Him 'Beloved' to move Him more to answer her
prayer. When God is loved He very readily answers the request
of His lover. . . A person can truthfully call God Beloved when
he is wholly with Him, does not allow his heart attachment to
anything outside of Him, and thereby ordinarily centers his
mind on Him. . . Some call the Bridegroom Beloved, whereas He
is not really their Beloved because their heart is not wholly set
on Him. As a result their petition is not of much value in His
sight. They do not obtain their request until through perseverance in prayer they keep their spirit more continually with
God and their heart with its affectionate love more entirely set
on Him. Nothing is obtained from God except by love."

For this reason faithful souls cannot help but cry out,

saying: *Show me, my Beloved, where You lead Your flock to graze.* . . "With these words," writes F. La Puente (*Guia* Tr. 3, c. 6), "the Holy Spirit briefly depicts for us the principal things we can desire and aspire to in contemplative life, and in the most exalted stage of that life, together with the two most effective motivating forces for attaining such things. First of all, fear: not servile but filial, for this aspiration is not that of slaves or of day-labourers, but of children and true friends, who fear blame and punishment if they were to leave the presence of thier heavenly Father and begin to wander after the flocks of false shepherds . . . Fearing this, then, . . . with generous magnanimity, trusting in the goodness of God, and with the holy boldness that this gives her, the soul says to Him; Oh, my Beloved, Whom my soul wishes to love as its only Spouse, show me the pastures where You lead Your sheep to graze, that I might go and collect myself there with You and with them, so that I might not wander astray and be misled by different thoughts and affections. . . , with the danger of falling into many errors, deceived by those who consider themselves to be Your companions, when they are in fact Your enemies. But I am not content with this but also ask You to show me the place where they rest in quiet. . .

"Oh, how great is Christian magnanimity! How high it flies with its desire and prayer! Do not be daunted by the meagreness of your worth, nor by the greatness of God's gifts; for from a God as great as ours we should not ask for small things, in keeping with our own smallness, but very great things, in keeping with His greatness. And if we ask Him for them with great faith there is no doubt, says St. Bernard (*Serm. 26 in Cant.*) that they will not be denied us. Pray, then, to God for so perfect a recollection of your heart in all its thoughts and affections that it will exclude the disorderly wandering after creatures, fearing not only lest you go astray, which is worthy of blame, but what is more, as the Bride says *Ne vagari incipiam:* fearing lest you even begin to go astray. Oh, how worthy is the generosity of such a bride! Who is there who does not begin to wander off in prayer, suffering distractions or the beginning of some deception or other. . .? But the perfect, when confronted by distraction or deceit, recognize it as such, resist it and suppress it. . . They fervently desire to be so far removed from distraction that they might not even detect a suspicion of it. . . O Beloved of my soul, come to my heart and remain there permanently so that I may not wander after creatures, for if You are not with me, I shall then begin to pursue them. In truth, says St. Gregory, in quo Christus not cubat vagatur: 'he who does not rest in Christ, wanders like a vagabond. For if the quiet, gentle spirit of Christ does not fill him, he will lapse into all kinds of imaginings and worldly affections. . .' But if he receives the Spirit of Christ, this will bring him to collect himself. . .in such a way that he will be untroubled by the things of the world.

"The other principle thing motivating us to ask God for the sublimity of contemplation is love, whose nature it is to inspire us to want to see the person that we love; and it is very effective in urging this Lord to show us His serene countenance. . . You, Lord, said (*Jn.* 14, 21): If anyone loves Me, I shall love him and show Myself to him; fulfill, then, what You promised and show Yourself to my soul that loves You."

In this way, as this holy writer goes on to add (tr. 4, c. 15, SV), we can see how the perfect keeper of the five senses, "which gently but efficiently restrains them, is the fruit of prayer and contemplation. For, since the soul sees, hears, tastes and feels so much of God within herself, she has no wish to see, hear or taste anything that is outside of her. And since the inner delights are greater by far than the outer ones, once the first are known, the second become quite tiresome. . . St. John Climacus (*Escala* c. 14) says that gluttony cannot be completely overcome until there has been a taste of the inner sweetness of the soul. Generally speaking no one will completely reject sensual pleasures until they begin to know the spiritual delights of the inner communication with God."

"Well, then, my Lord God," exclaims St. Augustine
(*Manual,* c. 30-31), "teach my soul the way and the place in
which I am to find You. . . If you are everywhere how is it that
I do not see You before me? In truth, You dwell in a light
which is inaccessible. How am I going to attain a light which is
unattainable. . .? O mighty Lord, what will this banished servant
of Yours do, that is so far away from You . . .? He longs to see
You and is very, very far from Your presence. He wants to
reach You and yet the light in which You dwell is inaccessible.
He wants to find You and yet is unable. . .

"How long, Lord, are You going to forget us? How long
are You going to keep You face hidden from us. . .? When will
You enlighten our eyes and shows us Your countenance . . . ?
Look at us, Lord, and hear us. Enlighten us and show Yourself
to us . . . for without You we are in a sorry state. Since You
encourage and invite us, now favor and help us. . . Hungry, I
began to look for You, do not leave me forsaken and without
support. . . Teach me to look for You; for neither can I look for
You if You do not teach me, nor can I find You if You
Yourself do not reveal and show Yourself. So that: make me
look for You desiring You, making me desire You looking for
You, make me find You loving You, and having found You,
make me love You."

That is how all the saints long for God and that is how all
the great spiritual masters teach us to long for Him: fervently,
trustingly and lovingly, because without Him we can do nothing
and because He Himself wants us to search for Him anxiously so
as to make us feel all the more the strength of His love.

Marceline Pauper, when meditating one day on those
words spoken by St. Andrew to Our Lord (*John* 1, 38-39):
Master, where do You live? and on the reply he received: *Come
and see,* ventured to ask the same question when she went to
receive Holy Communion, to which she had the consolation of
receiving the same reply. "Then," she adds, (*Letter* of 8 Dec.

1701), "He brought me to see His eternal mansion in the breast of the Father... He repeated to me once more: *Come and see,* and then brought me to see His second mansion in the breast of the Holy Virgin, where He was pleased to remain because of the purity and humility of Our Blessed Mother. Then again I was told: *Come and see,* and my sweet Savior showed me His Cross and told me: *I take delight in purity; the breast of My Father is the very essence of purity; that of My Mother is by virtue pure; and here is the purity of suffering and love. And then He said to me: I dwell in purity."*

"My daughter," said the Divine Master on another occasion to the Blessed Crescencia Hoess, "I dwell readily in a pure heart and there have My delights. Happy they who are pure of heart, for they shall see God."

Not only those who are fortunate to be pure, having lost none of their baptismal innocence, but all those who purify themselves sufficiently, washing themselves in the blood of the Lamb and purging themselves with the fire of the Holy Spirit which kindles within them fervent desires for God. All who do this will surely, as is promised them (*Matt.* 5.8), attain the joy of seeing Him, although it may be in a different way.

As St. Bernard remarks (Sermon 31, *in Cant.*), "to souls who burn with holy desires the Divine Word, their Spouse, reveals Himself frequently and under different forms: *Studiosis mentibus Verbum Sponsus frequenter apparet, et non sub una specie...* We already know how often He used to treat the ancient patriarchs with that familiarity with which He communicated Himself to them by means of certain external signs or voices, although not in the same way to all, but as the Apostle says (*Hebr.* 1, 1): at various times and in various different ways... There is another kind of divine vision which is as different from these as it is more interior, when God condescends to visit the soul who seeks Him and who, with ardent desire and burning love, is dedicated to this search. The sure sign of His coming to these souls, as we are told by one who knew from experience, is that a *fire will precede Him and will burn up His enemies around Him* (*Ps.* 97, 3). The ardor of holy desires must precede His presence in every soul in which He is to take lodging, destroying the stain of vice and preparing an abode for the Lord. The soul will know that this sweet Lord is now near when she feels herself to be enkindled by this heavenly fire. . .

"Souls who frequently sigh in this way, who ceaselessly pray and suffer from the intensity of their yearnings, when they see the One they desire taking pity on them and coming out to meet them, can then, I believe, say in the words of the prophet Jeremiah (*Lam.* 3, 25): *You are good, Lord, to those that place their hope in You, to the soul who truly looks for You.* . . His very angel who accompanies her everywhere will ceaselessly admonish her by frequent inspirations telling her (*Ps.* 37, 4): *Delight in the Lord and He will give you what your heart desires. . . Put your hope in the Lord and follow His ways. . . Even though He delay in coming, wait for Him, for He will surely come, He will not tarry* (*Habak.* 2, 3).

"The soul who loves in this way will not remain satisfied with that simple revelation that the Spouse made to many people in ancient time through creatures, by means of visions and dreams, but with that special prerogative of receiving Him, of having Him descend from Heaven into the most intimate and secret recesses of her heart, and thus possessing Him Whom she desires, not figuratively but by means of a real communication, not through signs but through the affections: *Non figuratum sed infusum; non apparentem, sed afficientem.* There is no doubt that the more interior the visit is, the more delightful it is. The Word does not shout aloud, but penetrates; does not speak, but is efficacious; does not deafen the ears by His thunder but caresses with holy affection. . .

"Yet I would still not venture to say that He reveals Himself *as He is,* for in this way He reveals nothing except *what He is.* Nor would I say that this manifestation is continual and familiar, even in very devout souls, nor that it is the same or uniform in all of them. The enjoyment of the divine presence varies and differs according to the desires with which these souls are inspired. The infused taste of supernatural sweetness delights the soul's palate in various ways, according to her various appetites."

"Thus," he adds, "to some He reveals Himself as the most loving Spouse, to others as the Physician Who comes equipped with oil and various ointments with which to cure and comfort souls that are weak, sickly or delicate, and for this reason called *maidens;* to others He reveals Himself as the Traveler or Pilgrim Who accompanies them on their pilgrimage and Who, with His loving conversation makes them forget their troubles and sets their hearts on fire (*Luke* 24, 32). Finally, He goes out to meet others as a very rich Father of families. . .or like a magnificent and powerful King Who desires to overcome the pusillanimity of His poor little Bride and to arouse her desires, showing her all the priceless treasures of His glory, all the abundance of His wine-presses and store-houses, all the harvest of His gardens and fields, and finally bringing her into His most intimate and secret chambers. The heart of the Spouse now trusts in her and conceals nothing from her whom He has redeemed as one in need, has tested as a faithful soul, and embraces as a loving Bride. He never ceases to reveal Himself, in one way or another, to those who faithfully seek Him, so as thereby to fulfill the promise He made to us when He said (*Matt.* 23, 10): *I shall be with you until the end of time.* . . In all these ways He shows Himself to be sweet, gentle and full of mercy. . . Perhaps He appears here as a Shepherd Whom the Bride asks: *Where are you pasturing. . .?* in order to show that the Good Shepherd is He *Who gives His life for His sheep.* Together with His life, He gives His very flesh, the former as the price, the latter as the sustenance. O what an extraordinary wonder, that He Himself is our Shepherd, our food and our redemption."

"But who is capable," adds the same saint (*Serm.* 32), "of

searching and penetrating the ineffable affections and merit that the Divine Spouse brings to the soul with His multiform graces...? If any of us can join the prophet in saying (*Ps.* 73, 28): *My joy lies in being close to God,* if there is anyone who is so full of desires that he longs to see himself free from the bonds of the body so as to be with Christ, provided that he earnestly desires it with a burning thirst and is continually conscious of it, he will certainly receive the Word as Spouse when He condescends to visit him, at the happy hour when he feels himself interiorly embraced as though by the secure arms of Divine Wisdom, and feels his soul being infused in this way with the sweetness of holy love. While still living in this mortal body, his heart's desires are granted (*Ps.* 21, 4), although only in part and for a very short time. Even when sought after with great vigilance and prayer, and with much affliction and sorrow, He, revealing Himself, again slips out of the soul's grasp just when he thinks he has Him most firmly in his embrace... And even though He return and again yield to his requests, He allows Himself only to be held, not retained... If the devout soul were to persist in his requests and cries, He would again return to him so as to assure him that his prayers were not in vain (*Ps.* 21), but would soon leave him once more and not allow Himself to be seen by him until he had again sought Him with his whole heart. This is how it is possible, even in this mortal life, to enjoy frequently the presence of the Spouse, although his happiness is not permanent or complete, for while the visits give joy, the vicissitudes cause distress... But all souls do not enjoy even these transitory visits, only those whose great devotion, ardent desire and sweet affection bear witness that they are brides and worthy, when visited by the Word, to have Him reveal Himself to them as Spouse.

"Whoever still lacks these exalted affections, but instead feels a great contrition at the thought of all his sins ... does not seek the Spouse but the Physician, and therefore will not receive caresses, but cures for his ills... Do we not often feel and experience this in prayer when we see ourselves still tempted by present trials and tormented by those of the past? How often, by Your visits, sweet Jesus, You have freed me from very great sorrows! How often, after my great cries and inexpressible moans and sobs, You have anointed my wounded conscience with the unction of Your mercy and poured the oil of Your holy joy over it? How often have I not begun my prayer almost in a state of despair and then finished it feeling joyful and confident of forgiveness? Those who have felt these affections know very well that Our Lord Jesus Christ is truly the Physician *who heals the contrite in heart and binds up their wounds (Ps. 147, 3)."*

There are other souls, finally, who anxiously search for Him, but who are also fearful, seeing how liable they are to make mistakes or be deceived through lack of competent guides. To these, in this instance, He reveals Himself as both the Shepherd and the Master Who will teach them the paths of life, in order to be able to fill them with joy by the revelation of His heavenly countenance (*Ps.* 16, 11).

v. 8)   *If you do not know this, O loveliest of women,*
         follow the tracks of the flock,
         and take your kids to graze
         close by the shepherds' tents.

"A generous heart," says Fr. Luis de León, "cannot allow one who loves Him to suffer for Him very long, and therefore, tells His Bride to follow the tracks of the flock, for by these she will find Him... This is an indication to the souls of the just that the path to finding God and virtue is not the one that each soul would like to imagine, but the well-trodden path of a vast number of saintly and learned persons who have gone before us and led holy lives.

This is the first lesson that the Divine Master gives us in His sacred Gospel (*Matt.* 16, 24): *"If anyone wants to be a follower of Mine, let him renounce himself and take up his cross and follow Me..."* That, in substance, is what He wishes to convey

now, as He appears for the first time in this sublime *Canticle* of
His love.

While presenting Himself to us as Shepherd and Master, He
does not wish us to forget the fact that He is also our Spouse, *et
Ipse tamquam Sponsus*...that He has come from the heights of
Heaven to win souls on earth and to kindle the divine fire
within them (*Luke* 12, 49; *Ps.* 19, 6). With supreme tenderness
He calls the soul *the loveliest of women* for that is what His
grace has made her and will go on making her, ever increasingly;
for *whoever follows Him will not walk in darkness, but will
have the light of life* (*John* 8, 12).

If you do not know this... If you do not know where I
am grazing My sheep and where I take them to rest, if you are
not able to feel Me within you as you would wish, search for Me
along the ordinary paths of meditation by considering My
works and mysteries. Follow the tracks of the flock, not of the
lost, not travelling along the well-trodden paths of the worldly,
slothful, and comfort-loving, the broad way which so many
follow blindly to their perdition, but along the holy, pure and
narrow way of abnegation and justice (*Is.* 35, 8-9), which is the
only way that leads to life and true rest (*Matt.* 7, 13-14).
Follow the footsteps of the saints and all My faithful servants,
those happy sheep who *hear My voice and follow Me, and to
whom I give eternal life, and whom no one will ever steal from
Me.* (*John* 10, 27-28). If you are unable to find Me in the
sweetness and tenderness that you so desire and that brings you
such benefit and consolation, or if you cannot hear the
whistling with which I, as *Good Shepherd,* direct My sheep to
the best pastures, or to the watering-place and rest of *infused
recollection* and *quiet,* leave yourself, all your pleasures and
comforts, and set out very early before dawn breaks, when
everything is still, where nothing and no one can impede you or
stand in your way; for those who seek Me early shall find Me
(*Prov.* 8, 17). Even if it is completely dark, by following the
sweet scent of the examples and virtues of the saints, you will

discover the secure path that they pursued, the path of abnegation and sacrifice, where you will not lose yourself. Meanwhile, *take your kids* (undisciplined affections) *to graze* on holy things, so that they might grow very fond of them and indifferent to things that are worldly; employ your words, initiatives and deeds to this end, and work as best you are able with My ordinary grace; take great care to keep your senses, mental powers, passions and inclination subdued and well-ordered; and try to live in obedience to the direction of the prelates and priests I have given you, that in My name they might carefully watch over you and diligently instruct you until the time comes for Me to instruct you Myself. . . Then you can join with My servant St. John of the Cross in singing:

> One dark night,
> Fired with Love's urgent longings —
> Ah, the sheer grace!
> I went out unseen
> My house being now all stilled;
>   In darkness and secure,
> By the secret ladder, disguised,
>   Ah, the sheer grace!
> In darkness and concealment,
> My house being now all stilled;
>   On that glad night,
> In secret, for no one saw me,
> Nor did I look at anything,
> With no other light or guide
> Than the one that burned in my heart;
>   This guided me
> More surely that the light of noon
> To where He waited for me
>   — Him I knew so well —
> In a place where no one else appeared.

"Whenever He comes," writes Ruysbroeck (*Adorn. of the Wedding* 2, 8), "Christ asks of us a special going out of ourselves

so as to lead a life that corresponds to His coming. For in the
same way in which Christ moves, presses, urges, draws, touches
and influences us, we must go out and engage ourselves in
interior exercises, if we really want to be perfect. But if we
resist the Holy Spirit with a different kind of life, we shall
clearly be deprived of his inner impulse and stimulus, and shall
likewise remain completely without virtue. On the other hand,
if we try to be faithful and obedient in all things, and if we
continually long for Him Whom we ought so much to love,
there will be no delay in receiving His consoling visit."

"Well then, little man," exclaims Enrique Harpio (*Theol.
Myst.*, 1,1, Ch. 49), "abandon your pursuits, quiet these
tumultuous thoughts, devote yourself completely to God and
rest in Him. Enter into yourself and cast out of your soul
anything which is not God, or which does not help you to
search for Him and delight in Him in wonderful contemplation."

"Flee then, faithful soul, searching for your Beloved in
solitude and silence," adds Fr. Juan de los Angeles, "so as to
taste and drink His ineffable sweetness; there, cast yourself
down and drink your fill, for this fountain will never dry up
unless you begin to tire of it. . . This is the place where the
Bride can rest with the Spouse at midday in the fervor of
contemplation. Oh, truly a place of rest and one that can well
be called the King's chamber, where He reveals Himself gentle
and sweet, and eager to communicate His *good and acceptable
and perfect will* (Rom. 12, 2). . . ! Oh, soul! Why do you not
aspire to this place where the Divine Spouse sleeps and rests and
where your rest is to be found? Join the Bride in repeating over
and over again and with great affection: *Indica mihi. . .ubi
pascas. . .*"

If you do this it will not be long before you are heard and
cared for, as she was.

"It seems," says the V. Mariana de San José, "that His
delay in speaking to her was in accordance with the great love
that He has for her. . . For although He has given her favors and

graces, He has told her nothing; she is the one who until now has spoken and revealed her suffering and longing, for ardent feelings are mixed with extreme suffering. . . This soul was so enkindled in love that her longings drew Him to look upon her and give to her with infinite power what she asked. And He, would seem no longer able to refrain from responding to His beloved Bride who so anxiously begged Him to show her the place where He rested at midday. . .

"God bless me! How startled this soul must have been in this state, and how fearful that her beloved Lord was about to leave her, for she believes she is with Him in the most secret place. Since the communication which He gives her there causes the consoling feelings that overwhelm her to increase, she urges the Lord to tell her where He rests at midday, to reassure herself and enable her to enjoy that goodness without fear of being confused, or worrying whether it is a whim, or another of her enemies' deceptions, for anxiety about this is not the least of the crosses that her Lord asks of her. Perhaps, moved by her tribulation, He now wants to unburden her of her suffering and lets her know the mercies He has shown her are truly from Him, for in her humility she doubted if they were.

Thus He says to her: . . . If you think that the mercies I show you are so great that you cannot believe they are Mine in view of your own unworthiness . . . , go out and see how much you have gained since I have given you such favors, and keeping these, the flock, always in sight, graze and give rest to your desires, giving an account of them to those whom I have placed in My Church as the soul's guides and teachers. In other words, they will tell you the value of the precious stones I have given you and show you how to exercise these desires, which are the little kids that must be led to graze through the exercise of the virtues and through mortification.

"It seems to me that this is one of the places where the Lord most shows to us the great love He has for us, and something of this can be gathered from the way in which He called her the loveliest of women. We can also see the reverence and respect with which the soul always spoke to the Lord and which made her worthy of her Spouse's showing her this path that is so true and certain which, if followed under the direction of those He placed in His Church as teachers and guides for souls, offers a very restful short-cut to the attainment of perfection. . .

"I have heard from many people that they begin on this way but then abandon it, saying that their Father Confessor does not understand them and therefore they decide to look for another one. I fear that this is because they do not want to go where they are led, nor do they want to abandon their own way which is full of their own petty ideas conceived by their vanity and self-esteem. O what falsehood I have seen, and what riches these souls lose by refusing to overcome the difficulties they encounter . . . ! Just as soon as the Lord wants to enrich them they turn their backs on Him simply because they do not want to suffer a little. . . On the other hand the favors that He bestows when this self-negation is embraced in His name can hardly be imagined. . .

"From this obedience to directors the Lord also draws forth very great riches so that these shepherds, His creatures and the sheep of His flock, might know and praise Him, seeing His works and mercies, when He bestows so many on His Bride through His power alone. By this manifestation they might know that the progress of souls should be attributed not to the direction of others or to their explanation of doctrine, but to the grace of the Lord. Although at times He seems to halt His divine work until the soul reaches the feet of the confessor, whatever happens, the Divine Spouse is the direct Master, Sometimes He acts on His own, sometimes in the way we have described. . . Happiness consists in being among the chosen. Let Him select the path that leads us to Him. Undoubtedly, when a soul reaches such a lofty state of communication with the Lord He gives her access and in some way makes her a companion of that holy assembly of the blessed in Heaven where He normally dwells. It is perhaps there that He gives her this grace, where she lives with those heavenly shepherds who knew so well how to tend their flocks, their senses and mental powers. The Spouse gives them to her as good teachers, as models by which to learn how to govern her own life. By living in their company she can say that her life and conversation are in Heaven, where her desires (the kids) take their recreation; there she lives sustained by the spiritual food of Heaven. At least the Lord permits her to set up her dwelling place there, and to enjoy Him, if not always, certainly at times during that perfect midday rest. ...

"But although this Lord is the Master it is not good for any soul who faithfully wants to make progress to be satisfied with this experience; for without a guide she will often be deceived, but with one never, for the Master will never instruct contrary to the law of God. This will be seen later, and will be shown by His Majesty, for He has written His law in the hearts of those who search for Him, and should the written law be lacking, in these souls the living law will be found; the Legislator Himself dwells within them. If they do not let themselves be deceived He will enlighten them so that they can read this divine writing that the holy King David (*Ps.* 119) so often asked the Lord to show him in His commandments and justifications."

In these words spoken by the Spouse there is, then, nothing resembling censure for a lack of self-knowledge or for a certain concealed presumption, as many have imagined, following too closely to the literal wording of the verse as it appears in the Vulgate: *Si ignoras te.* From the context and above all, from the Hebrew text it is quite clear that this *te* is redundant, a redundancy which is faithfully transmitted in the Spanish translation of the original: *Si no te lo sabes.** This

---

* Translator's note: It is impossible to translate this redundancy into English.

means, then: If you do not know what you ask Me, if you do not know where I am; cannot possibly mean: If you do not know yourself well or presume of yourself.

He is far from reprimanding her here, for He begins calling her *loveliest of women* and then goes on to praise her as He does in the following verses (8 — 10). Nor was there anything worthy of reproof in the ardent desire of the soul to learn about Him so as to search for Him and succeed in pleasing Him in everything, just as there was nothing reprehensible in the still bolder act of asking for His mystical *kiss.* For there is no competent director who would not praise, recommend and try to arouse such desires for God as being very necessary and beneficial.

Hence the error of all those who, basing their opinion on a false understanding of this passage, dissuade faithful souls from trying to attain, in as far as they are able, to the intimate and divine communications to which the Lord Himself has invited them in a thousand ways and at every hour (*Rev.* 3, 20; 22, 17; *Matt.* 11, 28; *John* 7, 37), so as to prevent them from *wandering off* after creatures.

"He is so pleased by the Bride's desire," says Maria de los Dolores, "that He calls her *most beautiful.* If you want to please Me, He tells her, go out. . . and follow in the tracks of the saints who already form My flock in Heaven; do what they did, and with your prayers and good example, lead to the priests seated in the tribunal of penitence those lost souls who, like kids, are unaccustomed to following the shepherds' voices."

In short, what the Spouse wishes to tell her now is that if she is still not able to find Him through infused contemplation, she should look for Him through ordinary, or discursive, prayer and through the practice of good works, certain of sooner or later finding Him in this mystical way that she so much desires, fulfilling His divine promise (*Matt.* 7, 7): *Search and you will find,* or as the *Ladder of Paradise* interprets it: "Search *meditating,* and you will find *contemplating.*" If you cannot find Me within your own heart, go out and travel along the ordinary path of meditation and imitation of My works, after the example of My faithful sheep. In this way your desires will finally be fully realized.

Meditation upon and imitation of Our Lord's virtues, says the V. Mariana de San José (in *Cant.* 1), "is the straight path to the holy mountain where Christ Our Lord has His home and tabernacle which is true contemplation. Following this path the soul will succeed in passing through this glorious gate. . . , which is the entrance way to those celestial experiences the Lord allows His chosen ones to enjoy here in this life. However, it will cost them the same suffering as that endured by this Bride."

To the very brave and enterprising who are not content with what is commonly called "the ordinary way", to those who aspire to what is greatest and most pleasing to God, always attempting the greatest possible perfection of virtue, "there is no doubt," says St. Bernard (*Sermon. 32*), "that since by the greatness of their faith, they deserve to attain the fullness of sanctity . . . the Spouse will reveal Himself to them, delighting in exalting them and pouring His light and truth over them so as to lead them to His Holy Mountain and bring them into His wonderful Tabernacle, enabling them to exclaim (*Luke* 1, 49): 'The Almighty has done great things for me.' Indeed, their eyes will see the King in His beauty (*Is.* 33, 17). They will see Him go before them to the greenest part of the desert, to the beds of roses, to the lilies of the valleys, to the most pleasant parts of the gardens, to the parts watered by fountains, to the delights of the store-houses, to the fragrance of spices, and finally to the most concealed and secret recess of His Own mansion. These are the treasures of wisdom and knowledge hidden in the Spouse, — the food of life prepared by Him in order to sustain holy souls. Happy the man who satisfies all his desires here! (*Ps.* 127, 5). . . Happy the soul who has the Divine Word as an inseparable companion, being always kind and affectionate to her; for, always enjoying His sweet company .she will find herself free from the attacks of the passions and will redeem the time lost! She will no longer experience tiredness or fatigue ... The more we trust in the Lord the greater will be the gifts that we receive from His hands ... For this reason the Bride asks Him to tell her where He pastures ... ready to be fed by Him and to always feed with Him under His direction."

How far she is, then, from being censured for what made her so worthy of praise!

If we stop to consider it we will perhaps come to see that the very redundancy in the expression *Si ignoras te* is not without its own mystery ... It is as much as to say: If you do not know it for yourself, for your own direction, even though you know it for the enlightenment, consolation and direction of others ..., go out of yourself, abandon your own opinions and knowledge, and follow the footsteps of the saints, trying to place yourself under the direction of a wise and discreet spiritual guide who will lead you where you would lose your way on your own, and will teach you what very often you cannot know 'for yourself', however much you may know it for the good of others. Now, at least as a general rule, no one is a good judge of, or guide for himself, and therefore if the Lord does not supply any special light or grace, or the fruits of long experience, even the wisest and most famous directors and spiritual teachers need someone else to enlighten and direct them if they are not to expose themselves to error.

This, has a special application in the beginnings of spiritual life which is the state the soul now finds herself and it ought therefore to be kept very much in mind by those who are still novices in religious life and who need to know whom they are to follow and imitate and how and by whom they are to be governed and instructed.

By these flocks and shepherds, says Fr. Juan de los Angeles, are meant not just any, but very "special flocks and special shepherds; as though He were to say ...: Follow the flocks and the tracks of the sheep of God and take your kids to graze next to the tents of those great and outstanding shepherds . . . Imitate the examples of My chosen ones for, from the beginning of the world there has always been and there will continue to be in My Church, not a few but many who have follow and will always follow My true shepherds."

The Lord wishes, he adds, that those who embrace religious life, "first of all watch the tracks of His flock and go to His shepherds' tents, which are the spiritual fathers, the prelates, and founders of the Orders who, although dead, left their doctrine imprinted there; that they may lead a monastic life in the place where they will find someone to instruct them, to awaken and encourage them in the service of God, someone to spur them on if they are weak in virtue, someone to halt them if they go ahead, someone to put them right again if they go astray; so that these others will be their eyes, will govern and direct them until carnal desires have been tamed, until worldly covetousness has been overcome and the soul has gained its strength; then they will be able to manage for themselves and govern others, then solitudes and deserts can follow. . . But when they are novices, He orders them to follow the tracks of the chosen flocks and to graze next to the shepherds' tents, so as to obey them and never stray from their direction."

In this way, little kids can be taken to mean all *beginners,* of whom the mystical Bride must take a special care. "The grown flock," observes the same writer, "can freely graze in the sweet pastures of Sacred Scripture and the sacraments; for as the Apostle said, they have their senses disciplined; but the little kids, common people, those new in virtue, *juxta tabernacula pastorum,* must not move away from the shepherds' tents. Taking the words literally, the kids are never allowed to graze far from the shepherds' fold, because of the danger of wolves and other harmful animals . . . I repeat, those who are perfect and confirmed in grace can, without danger, go and graze further away, can converse with sinners, argue with heretics, retire into the secrecy of the desert, live in solitude; but those who are still children in virtue, in need of the milk, government and direction of their spiritual fathers run considerable risk if they try to graze freely."

Thus, he adds, the Lord here seems to say to whoever is looking for Him, "If you follow the tracks of My flock you cannot fail to find Me, for I am a Shepherd Who never fails in His duty; I always tend My flock."

This is how the soul is commanded to go out and set off for the place where the Lord is awaiting her . . . On two other occasions (III, 2; V, 5-11) she will go out completely in the dark and each time in a much more sublime way, as Ruysbroeck points out, until she loses herself completely in Him Who so mysteriously calls and draws her. Then it will be to continue singing with our great mystical poet:

O guiding night!
O night more lovely than the dawn!
O night that has united
The Lover with His beloved,
Transforming the beloved in her Lover . . . !

Here the Divine Spouse is content to call her "loveliest among women," charging her to follow faithfully the tracks of His flock.

"This calling her the most beautiful," observes the Venerable Mariana, "could well cause us concern if we did not know from long experience that the Lord treats many souls as though each were the only one, the beloved Benjamin. Just as each soul's merits must be different, for there are different degrees of glory in Heaven for those who enter, so here in this life this singular beauty must come from that in which they excel. For each soul is the most beautiful in that particular virtue in which she excels, whatever her fortune and opportunities. She is very beautiful, for she attained grace in the loving eyes of her Spouse Who speakers of all praises her as the most beautiful of all . . . He did not want to leave these words in any doubt, so as to show His Bride the love He has for her and the mercies He has done her. Although He has sent her to His ministers that they might tell her about them, He Himself cannot desist from disclosing to her the value of the jewels He has given her."

v. 9)   *To my mare harnessed to Pharaoh's chariot*
              I compare you, my love.

This is another scene in which the soul is supposedly following faithfully the footprints of her Divine Spouse. Seeing her so brave and determined to follow Him whatever the cost, disciplining herself, denying herself in everything so as to give pleasure to Him, setting her appetites in order and subjecting them to the yoke of obedience so as faithfully to follow in the footsteps of the saints, He is now apparently unable to restrain Himself any longer. Immediately He begins to show her the special care He has for her, caressing and cherishing her like a child, praising her beauty and valor and with very tender words commending her for these initial triumphs, so as to encourage her to follow ever more resolutely the paths of virtue.

For this reason, having already called her *most beautiful,* undoubtedly because of the holiness of the desires He saw in her, now seeing her truly executing these by her ardent pursuit of Him, He compares her (according to the Vulgate) to His *cavalry,* (according to the Hebrew) to His loveliest mare which, with elegant strength and rich adornments, pulls a beautiful chariot resembling those that Pharaoh used to drive. Other similes can be applied even more appropriately to the Church and the Blessed Virgin.

v. 10)   *Your cheeks show fair between their pendants*
              and your neck within its necklaces.

The Spouse continues praising the soul's beauty, graciously comparing her cheeks with those of the turtle-dove, according to the Vulgate, or with the turtle-dove itself, or with certain little figures of this bird which apparently they wore at that time as adornments for their faces, or thinking how well it would look between pendants of pearls or jewels which would adorn it like a head-dress. In the same way He compares her neck with those most richly adorned with pearls and jewels. This, in substance, is what the text says, however much the wording may lend itself to different interpratations.

The soul resembles this beautiful, chaste and solitary little bird, for indeed she has become a mystical turtle dove ever since the King saw fit to bring her into His chambers. It annoys her to go out into the bustle of people, for she loves solitude and her cooing is like the sighing of purity, fidelity and innocence. The turtle-dove, says St. Gregory the Great, is an image of the holy soul, faithful to her Divine Spouse and who, in His absence, never ceases to moan and sigh because of the ardent desires she has of possessing Him.

"You who hear this, if you do not want to hear in vain what is written for your good, and who seriously wish that your soul might become the bride of God Himself," says St. Bernard (*Serm.* 40), "try to see to it that both cheeks of your endeavor possess the same purity and beauty as this chaste bird, searching for God alone and living in solitude with Him, and thus raised up above yourself . . . Sit alone, like the turtle-dove. Have nothing to do with the world, let communication with people be unimportant to you: *Forget your nation and your ancestral home, and then the King will fall in love with your beauty (Ps. 45, 11).* O soul, perservere in solitude, so as to belong only to Him Whom you have chosen to be your only heritage; flee from the public and even from your own servants . . . Perhaps you do not know that you have such a chaste Spouse that He will be unwilling to honor you with His presence unless He finds you alone. Flee away, then, as much as you can, at least mentally, in your intentions, in your devotion and spirit. For your King and Lord . . . seeks the solitude of the spirit and not that of the body, although the latter will also be useful to you, if you have the opportunity, to withdraw the body to a retreat, above all for the purpose of prayer . . . The solitude that we are all told to keep, unreservedly, is that of the spirit and of the soul; for you will be really alone if your thoughts are not distracted like those of the majority of people, if you do not become attached to passing things, if you despise what the multitudes love, and abstain from what others desire, in this way avoiding quarrels and forgetting wrongs that you have received. Unless you do this you will never be truly alone, however much you may be so physically. Do you now understand how you can be alone in the midst of a crowd, and how, even in solitude, you can still find yourself in very bad company?"

When the soul thus begins to live alone like the turtle-dove so as to please only her Divine Spouse, He lavishes a thousand caresses and consolations upon her, saying: *Your neck (is) like pearls, or as though between necklaces of pearls.*

Later He will compare it to the tower of David, which is a fortress, or tower of strength; now He speaks of ornaments, praising her as one would a child, telling her how very beautiful she is and how very beautiful He Himself will make her with precious gifts, leaving her laden with graces and riches. To express it more clearly, it is as if He were to say: Your chaste cheeks are already beautiful, and your neck is elegant: but how much more beautiful you will appear when your neck is adorned with necklaces of virtues and your cheeks with the rich pendants of gifts and fruits . . . ! For I am going to adorn and enrich you with all these so that you may thus become truly beautiful. And these divine words effect what they say, producing in the soul a beauty that is entirely celestial and in which God Himself takes His delight and can say to her: *Pulchrae sunt genae tuae* . . . "It seems," says the Ven. Mariana de San José (*in Cant.* 1), "that the Spouse is gazing at Himself . . . in this soul, as though in a mirror in which He can see Himself, and in this soul He sees those divine splendors of His divine being with which she is enlightened. Accomplishing such wonderful and exquisite things in her, like a painter who is perfecting a finished picture, at every touch of high-light he murmurs words of satisfaction to himself . . . If seems that this is the way in which the Lord is producing divine touches of beauty in the soul, bringing them to light as He pronounces them with His lips. It happens just this way, that often His gifts are not recognized until what His secret, sweet voice has uttered is brought about in the soul. For His words are works, in short, words of life. Those who experience it know this very well. This soul now passively hears and receives mercies, allowing the Lord to work within her, doing almost as little as the wax which receives the imprint of a seal when it is soft, as I believe the Bride now to be. If we go on, we will discover she not only confesses that she is pliable but that she is melting with love . . . As I say, beholding Himself in the soul, it seems this sovereign King never tires of praising her and telling her, quite openly now, how beautiful she is, looking for new ways and words with which to show her the great love which He has for her and the joy He has in gazing at her."

"Do not think," she adds, "that this very holy Spouse is percipitate, nor that He says sweet things to the soul before time; for. . . His works are heavy with the infallible weight of His secret knowledge. He knows very well that He can now praise this soul without her becoming proud; on the contrary, each favor makes her more aware of her misery and nothingness, and seems to put on her a burden heavier than an entire world, of infinite weight, causing her to follow profound paths of humility which bring her more and more self-knowledge and, at the same time, knowledge of the goodness and richness of her Spouse and Lord, to Whom she offers herself again and again that she might be more completely possessed by this Prince Who, with such care and solicitude, loves and seeks her. Because of these effects and many loftier still, the Lord speaks these words to His sweet Bride, words with which He discloses and brings to light the work that He is doing within her . . .

"We can also understand this as praise of a penitent and mortified soul. Perhaps He was gazing at her cheeks streaming with tears of grief because of her sins which had caused the absence of her Lord. I believe that for His Majesty no angels' water is as sweet as the tears of a soul who, loving Him, is grieved at having offended Him . . . He praises her penitence and mortification . . . for an unmortified soul will not be praised by the Spouse, since mortification is the seasoning which must accompany every spiritual exercise and without which perfection cannot be attained . . . It is the continual discipline of all that gives pleasure or satisfaction, and when the soul disregards this solicitude, the blemishes will come to the surface. Mortification is a beauty that cannot be feigned, just as the lack of it cannot be concealed or, at least, will quickly be discovered . . . This mortification deciphers very great mysteries, is the treasure-house of every virtue, the mother of humility, custodian of virginity, the most certain gateway to prayer, and the path along which we shall soon find the Spouse . . . seeming narrow at first, but soon broadening out as the way becomes clear to us."

v. 11)   *We shall make you golden earrings*
                 and beads of silver.

These mysterious earrings, or murenulas, with which she is to be exquisitely adorned are undoubtedly the gifts, graces and lights of the Holy Spirit which, firmly linked with the most precious virtues, will at one and the same time truly beautify, enrich and fortify her, making her obedient to divine movement and inspirations until through them she will eventually become great and rich, enjoying these treasures as her own possession which are at present borrowed, being lent to her by the Spouse Himself that He might delight in her. These little *turtle-dove* figures into which the earrings are shaped, symbolize the Holy Spirit, just as gold, according to interpreters, symbolizes charity and the most precious gifts, the beads humility*, and silver the

---

* Translator's note: The Spanish word used here is *gusanillo,* which is not strictly speaking a bead but rather the gold or silver twist or design a bead may well possess. *Gusanillo* literally means 'small warm' or 'grub', and hence it lends itself to symbolize humility.

innocence of life and the purity of habits with which she will surely fill the Spouse with delight. Being adornments for the ears they indicate the special graces heard, as it were, in the form of words of life, which He wishes to communicate to her through them.

In order to encourage the Bride, then, who is confused and frightened at seeing herself praised, the Lord, writes the V. Mariana, goes on to say to her, *"We shall make you golden earrings and beads of silver."* As if to say, "I will reveal in My words the flaming love I have for you and also your own nothingness, so that these two truths being heard by you may become embedded in the most intimate part of your spirit, leaving you so steadfast that it would be impossible for you to grow vain or attribute to yourself any of the considerable good that I have placed within you. Gracious me! If the Lord were to give us these precious earrings, how much more would be their worth than all the riches of Potosi! What wonderfully precious mercy! . . . There is nothing that strengthens a soul more than the knowledge of the goodness and love of this Lord for us. When this knowledge is true and profound, it causes the soul to sink into the very depth of its nothingness. When these two truths enter and take root in her, it is a sign that she already possesses these earrings which the Lord places on her when her understanding becomes filled with His truths. Hence . . . the esteem and reverence with which she approaches the Lord and the contentment when she realizes that by His hand alone she is to be and can be enriched. For this reason she takes joy in her poverty, discovering traces of God in past failures; for she sees that they are mended in such lofty ways. In this way she becomes better prepared to receive more of the light that shines forth from the gold of the earrings we are discussing. Thus instead of weeping over her weaknesses, she converts them into beads of silver, no longer horrible worms* that cause pain and

*See previous Translator's Note.

affliction, but wrought in silver, which are pleasing in the sight of the Spouse, and in the sight of the soul herself, thus lifting her from the abyss of her lowly estate into the love and goodness of the Lord.

"It seems to me that the ears where these earrings are placed are very secret channels possessed by the understanding through which the soul receives the communications and truths already mentioned. These truths and communications beautify her and fill her with splendors of love, making her appear to be of a different race and of a higher lineage than before; at the same time, so delicate that they can well be illusory, for they are such as to be much desired and sought after; but, if they are genuine, neither our enemies nor our imagination will be able to feign them ... It is the language used for those chosen and loved by this richest Spouse, Who speaks so secretly and privately that He does not even instruct with words, but with a secret communication ... He will fill His beloved with unnumbered truths by merely placing these earrings upon her ... Happy is the soul who merits to receive this mercy; for the Spouse is thus bringing her closer to Him and preparing her for that secret communication of love, the path along which He gives her the earrings that He has promised. With these she so charms the Spouse that she will no longer need any contrivance to attract Him to her; all discourse and consideration will be left aside; ... for the Lord has so transformed this soul according to His own wishes that, as King David would say (*Ps.* 123, 2): *Sicut oculi ancillae in manibus dominae suae* ... This Bride is now so dependent upon His divine gaze that for her there is no other rest than this dependence. ..

I have said that here there are no words for this language is very secret: simply the vision of the sovereign Lord and the soul's own nothingness together with His desire to adorn her with these golden earrings and beads of silver. This alone suffices to ennoble and enlighten her to such a degree that it leaves her more beautiful than visible creatures ever could. She sees that this is so, for the improvement in this state is such that it cannot be concealed. She does not become proud because of this, but rather loves the Lord all the more seeing how His love for her is gratuitous and how only through His goodness does she receive these mercies."

v. 12)   *While the King rested on his couch*
                    my nard yielded its perfume.

Adorned with such precious graces, far from attributing them to herself or flattering herself on account of them, the soul tries to use them according to the divine wishes, recognizing that they are borrowed and that they must not be left idle, but must be used to the greater glory of Him Who thus favored her; for it is very characteristic of divine favors to cause humility and astonishment in the soul, and the greater they are the more they humiliate; even though, in spite of this it is possible to later abuse them all and try to attribute them to herself. But here, forgetting herself, she thinks only of how she can honor and treat her Beloved in a way that is worthy, gazing at Him reclining on His *couch* or special bed from which people used to eat in those times. These *bed-tables* or *reclinatorios*** on which the Beloved rests and celebrates His banquets with His friends are numerous and of various kinds. According to interpreters, the principal one is eternal, in the bosom of the Father; the second, temporal, in the bosom of the Blessed Virgin; the third the manger; the fourth the one He really used on many occasions when eating with His disciples, as on the occasion when Mary Magdalen anointed it with sweet perfumes; the fifth the cross; the sixth the tomb; the seventh that which He occupies reigning at the right hand of the Father. To these, of course, must be added the tabernacle where every day He truly celebrates the costly banquet of His mystical marriage with faithful souls; and also these very souls in whose hearts He loves to rest and takes His delights, feeding on the precious

*Translator's note: *Reclinatorio* can be translated as 'couch' but here means quite simply 'an object to lean upon'.

fruits of every virtue. In all of them (although each in its own way) He invites and regales His friends and is at the same time the One Who is regaled and delighted by His true Brides with sweet conversation, tender affection and the loving occupation of adoration and blessing, of reparation and expiation, of prayer and praise, whose fragrances, symbolized by those of the nard, are exceedingly pleasing to Him.

This sweet-smelling nard was first composed of the desires and prayers of the holy patriarchs and prophets sighing for His birth while they saw Him resting in the bosom of His Eternal Father until they prevailed upon Him to descend into His Mother's breast. The *reclinatorio* of the cross is formed by the cries of compassion, the tears and great afflictions with which His faithful followers (that is to say, those who really love Him) accompany Him. In the *reclinatorio* of their own hearts all fervent souls will be offering these, continually trying to praise and accompany this Divine Guest with the most tender affection Who thus deigns to dwell within us, glorifying and worthily carrying God within our own body (*I Cor.* 6, 20), exalting and sanctifying Christ in our hearts (*I Peter* 3, 15), and offering Him there continual sacrifices of love and self-denial, of humility and adoration. Then, as St. Bernard says (*Serm.* 42), "your fragrance will be devotion, your scent the good name gained by your conduct, diffusing itself to others for whom everywhere you will be *the sweet fragrance of Jesus Christ.*"

With respect to this, Origen observed and Fr. Juan de los Angeles recalls, "that although the nard has its own scent, it is not hers that the Bride is said to give, but that of the Spouse . . . The nard yields *His* perfume; as if to say: the nard is mine, but the scent comes from the King. The sanctity and virtue of the saints, through the contact in living faith that they have with Christ, have the same fragrance as Christ Himself. So that St. Paul can say: *Christi bonus odor sumus Deo.* We are the good odor of God because we have the fragrance of Christ deep within us. In short, what the Bride says is that her nard never communicated or spread its scent until she sat at table with her Spouse: no virtue can be pleasing to God, nor can it have any supernatural value, unless it bears the fragrance of Christ. As the Apostle says (*Eph.* 1, 6), in Him we are acceptable to the Heavenly Father . . . Hence all works of piety that are to imitate the nature of the nard and spread their sweet scent must possess this 'reclining' toward the Spouse. It is the source of the genuine tears shed in hatred and abhorrence of sin . . . ; from here stems profitable fasting, efficacious and sure penitence; in short, all the services of the the Christian, which like the nard, are usually sweet-smelling to God.

Thus *my nard;* my own understanding, united with that of My Savior gives forth a celestial and divine scent.

When the King was in his bed . . . "In these beds," observes Fr. Gracian, "Jesus Christ finds delight and takes His rest, and the soul, embraced by Him and lovingly united to Him in each one of them, exercises exemplary and heroic virtue that is compared to the nard . . . Contemplating Christ in the heart of the Heavenly Father and loving Him as the infinite God, causes love to shine in her soul accompanied by the heroic virtue of magnanimity or greatness of heart with which she despises and scorns all created things when compared to God. When through contemplation she joins Christ in Mary's virginal womb, or adores Him resting in her pure arms and there loves Him, she obtains through her chaste love purity of conscience. Taking up Christ's cross she receives patience in her trials and cannot but die to herself for His love. By contemplating Him in the Holy Sacrament of the Altar she acquires love of her neighbor and is able to join with all other creatures of Heaven and on earth in order to love Him more. The soul loves Christ in Heaven with celestial joy and happiness, with herself with recollection, and in her neighbor's soul with mercy and humility . . . May God give her to understand this through experience.

"What are the seats and where the places in which the King of Heaven gives a banquet to His chosen ones, but the

celebrations of the mysteries of His life? And what is the nard
that yields its scent in the presence of the King but the most
precious virtues that He delights in? The nard is a very small
herb . . . whose fragrance is stronger the smaller the nard itself is;.
thus it represents humility — which denotes littleness, charity
and devotion and causes the soul to yield sweet-smelling
affections and exemplary works. All these virtues are in action
when the King is before them reclining in His seat; for if you
gaze at Him in any of His mysteries you will be urged to humble
yourself to the very abyss of your nothingness, partly through
the humiliation that your sins deserve, partly because of the
incomparable humility of the King shining in the examples of
His life . . . O sovereign King, seeing You so humbled, my nard
will bring forth its scent. It will not be my scent but Yours,
produced by Your virtue and by Your example and akin to the
scent of humility which your nard diffuses which is so much
more excellent than mine, because it is a far greater comparison
for the Creator to humble Himself than for the creature to do
so. But I join my nard with Yours, my humility and humiliation
with Yours, so that both together might bring forth a fragrance
so pleasing to You, and pleasing to Your Father, that they
become worthy of finding grace in His presence.

"In the presence of this sovereign King the nard of charity
also yields its own fragrance of loving affection, like that of the
King Himself, and according to the necessity and disposition of
the soul who gazes at Him. For if you are sorry for your sins,
you will bring forth sentiments of loving contrition, seeing how
the Lord looks upon them and what He does and has suffered in
order to redeem you and forgive them. Like another Mary
Magdalen you must kneel at His feet with this sweet-smelling
nard ointment with which to anoint them, uniting your
anguished soul with His, and asking forgiveness and reparation
for your sins. If you breathe its fragrance with the hope that He
has forgiven you, the nard will yield affections of gratitude and
praise. Like Mary Magdalen herself you will gain courage to

anoint His head, uniting your fervent desires for great perfection with the wonderful works that He performed, seeking to be as a mystical member with your Head, so that you might receive from Him an emanation of eternal life. How is it possible for the nard of charity to fail to yield its enkindled love when placed next to the infinite fire of love?" (La Puente, *Guia espiritual,* tr. 2, Ch. 12, para. 3)

Like the little herb which "gives forth more scent the more trodden down it is," says the V. Mariana de San José, "the soul here says that her nard now yields its scent: she suffers scorn and delights in persecution; the voices and cries of her enemies are now like sweet music to her, and her heart finds rest in no other exercise: this is the one that gladdens and consoles her. She does not attribute the fragrance and virtue of the nard to herself, but to the Spouse Who is the One Who gives her life. Thus every syllable of the line speaks of humility. She does not call the Lord Spouse or Friend, but King. Judging herself to be so lowly and unworthy she does not dare to say: when the King is in my bed, etc., although she very well could do so. Rather she says: in *His bed,* her heart and soul, made and adorned by Him with His own hand and with His divine wisdom, so transforming her that He can quite openly call her the King's bed. O my Lord! How precious must be the soul who is Your bed . . . , Your rest . . . , rest for her God . . . ! For this soft and restful bed is the heart of the humble and meek; this is the bed wherein the Lord takes His rest, in Whose presence her nard will give forth much fragrance in suffering abuse, mortification and temptation, being strong even though all the inmates of hell were lined up against her. There is nothing stronger than a humble soul, nothing will disturb her . . . O gracious God, how wonderful it is to be with such souls! How manifest it is that they are living temples of the Lord and that His majesty is dwelling within their mansion . . . !"

When this begins to occur with more stability, he adds, "there are no longer any desires to die, to suffer and so on, which usually exist in souls who truly serve and seek the Spouse. Here there is quite simply a continuous act of resigned surrender, of being silent and reverencing the goodness of this tranquil King, a sinking and hiding of oneself in Him, a feeling of having too much of everything and realizing that every suffering or labor is a pleasure and great good in comparison with what one deserves . . . Hers is now the true life and so this Bride is always making sacrifices acceptable to her King, living in spirit and in truth. One of the virtues humble souls possess is that of being sustained and upheld by truth. When praised they do not become boastful, or when reproached, do not grow dejected; neither can they be taken by surprise for they have anchored their hearts in truth and so are full of the spirit of consummate Truth. From these souls the light will never be hidden; they will always find it, or rather, they have it, for the King has already chosen them for His bed of rest."

The soul thus becomes more and more pure, fragrant and beautiful with the same virtue and fragrance as the Spouse, on Whom she wishes to model herself in all things, embracing Him intimately and drawing Him close to her heart. *Her nard* is now the continual remembrance of the mysteries of the Savior, Who will thus cause her always to exhale the sweet fragrance of His life. The vision of Him 'reclined' on the cross becomes a very bitter but extremely precious myrrh whose fragrance emblams her and preserves her from all corruption, leading her to help preserve all those close to her.

"The Bride goes on to count," adds Fr. Gracian, "the good things that are bestowed upon her by the love of Christ when, brought before Him, He actually loves and contemplates her. One of the principal things is a loving compunction; a sweet and pleasing reproof that God gives the soul, informing her of the defects for which she is normally responsible . . . The myrrh represents this revelation . . . Thus when Jesus Christ dwells in the soul's breasts (which are understanding and will through contemplation and love), He sweetly reproves His Bride, telling her of her faults." The Bride, tasting this sweet bitterness and being thankful for it, says:

v. 13)   *A bundle of myrrh is my Beloved unto me,*
         he will lie between my breasts.

With the loving and bitter memory of the crucified Christ which the soul wishes to impress deep in her heart, she will be continually encouraged to suffer for Him and with Him, and thus become modeled on the *Lord of suffering,* no longer wishing to glory in anything save the cross of Christ, participating fully in the suffering, ignominy and bitterness of His passion and death, so as to become completely purified and renewed in the virtue of His Resurrection, continually diffusing His sweet fragrance before God and before men. Thus she carries Him in her breast like *"a little bundle"* of myrrh.

"She wants all in heaven and on earth to know," says the V. Mariana de San José, "that she no longer belongs to herself, to the world, to honor or to any other but this powerful King Who is so full of love for her, and with Whom she is so much in love that her only request is for eyes that will gaze at Him as her sole treasure. Therefore she keeps Him where women usually keep their richest and brightest jewels and things which they desire to keep safely guarded . . .

"However, in spite of this she does not say she has placed Him there but rather that she will do so. She is waiting for the Spouse to agree, for although she loves Him as we have seen, she respects Him as Father and Master, and so awaits His request to place Him in her heart. This is the manner in which Our Lord often works, showing and teaching His secrets and then not allowing them to be experienced."

He will not delay long in giving us His sweetness and gentleness if we truly try to imitate Him and accompany Him as we ought in His suffering. It is very just that we should share in them, being so culpable and needing so much to purify ourselves and expiate our sins; hence the greatness of His sufferings for us, He Who is all holiness, purity and innocence.

Be they great or small, He wants us to accept joyfully the sufferings He sends for our own good; receiving them as health-giving medicines placing them on our hearts as tokens of His love and profound friendship.

Although all have to suffer, whether they wish to or not, there are few who are able to make this necessity a virtue, bearing their trials with patience and resignation as the Lord commands us all to do. And still fewer are they who suffer with complete peace, conformity and even with joy, trying to bear their sorrows lovingly in their hearts. Because of this the majority never come to experience the sweetness of the cross, for this is born of the unction of divine love. If one truly loves God everything becomes very easy, and most sorrows become ineffably sweet, in so far as the soul sees how they help her toward union with her sweet Lord.

"What is this, holy Bride!" exclaims the V. Maria de San José, D.C. "You call the Beloved a little bundle of bitter myrrh? See how those of us who also bear the name 'Bride of the Beloved' are scandalized. For to us He seems sweet and gentle and more so the nearer one draws to His heart. He is delight, sweetness, pleasure, consolation: He is all love. For this reason we follow after Him, abandoning parents, relations, friends and all that the world esteems. We deny ourselves and He draws us after Him with the fragrance of His name. Has He then been placed between your breasts as a bundle of myrrh? Well then, how dare you maintain that He is bitter, in front of so many witnesses who have not known what you have experienced of His infinite sweetness? Take care that those who do not understand your language will not suspect you are jealously trying to keep Him to yourself . . .

"O daughters of Eve! You are deceived as she was! Adam is not your spouse with whom you are to share the sweet apple, but Jesus Christ Who pays for this sweetness by suffering the bitterness and torment of the cross. If you are to give Him your hand as Bride, the nail must join your hand to His. He is a

Spouse of blood, and you must cloth yourself in this mantle and livery if you desire the King to love your beauty and if you are to be like Him . . . If the thorns have not wounded you, it is a clear sign that the Spouse has not embraced you and given you the kiss of peace, for if you had received His kiss, you would certainly have tasted of the bitterness of the gall that fills His mouth. O my good Lord! It is little that You should be myrrh to us for we were gall to You; and in tasting it You should be myrrh to us for we were gall to You; and in tasting it You sought to remove from the daughters of Eve the bitterness of the apple that our mother ate. O, happy and blessed is the Bride to whom You are as myrrh between her breasts! Who could describe all the happiness and sweetness in this so-called bitterness! Is there any joy on earth equal to that of suffering for You? Where else is true wisdom to be found but in suffering and the cross? To whom do You reveal Your loving Heart but to the afflicted heart that comes to You . . . ? Unhappy, gross and ignorant are those who do not know what it is to suffer for Christ . . . Who taught me to wait for You; who urges me to search for You; who has brought me to experience what faith tells me, so that what before I only *believed,* I now *touch* and *know by sight* — who but You. You Who strengthen the weak, raise up the fallen, instruct the ignorant, make Yourself known to children, accompany the sorrowful, hear the requests of those who call upon You, free those that serve You, reward those who suffer and are silent, and above all, make the trials suffered for Your sake more desirable than the riches and pleasures of our times (however incredible this may seem to the worldly) . . . The gall and bitterness of tribulations were the salutary collyrium which opened my eyes . . . O sweet Spouse . . . , may I have You like a bundle of myrrh between my breasts as the holy Bride has You, who, being well instructed by You, prays that she might embrace and possess You without affliction . . . for it is not a burden which weighs down but a bouquet which delights and refreshes."

"This *bouquet* or *little bundle of myrrh*," adds Fr. Gracian, "also represents the passion of Jesus Christ that must remain fixed in the memory, understanding and will."

St. Bernard, expressing what he felt about this, wrote (*Serm.* 43): "Since the time of my conversion instead of reflecting upon the merits that I knew I lacked I tried to make a little bundle of myrrh composed of all my Lord's trials and sufferings. I tried always to bring Him into my heart, dwelling there with Him, contemplating first of all the want and poverty in His actions and mysteries as a Child, then pondering His trials as a Preacher, the exhaustion of His journeys, His vigils while praying, His fasts, His tears and compassion for sinners, the deceits of His enemies, and finally the accusations, insults, jeers, beatings, thorns, nails and other infamous sufferings that are described in the Holy Gospels. From all this myrrh I did not omit that which they made Him drink when nailed to the cross, where He took upon Himself the bitterness of my sins, nor that ointment of myrrh with which they finally anointed Him in the tomb, thus consecrating the future incorruptibility of my body. As long as I live, therefore, I shall awaken within myself and spread abroad the remembrance of the redundant abundance of the sweetness of these scents, recalling always the mercies of the Lord that restored life to me. . . This *little bundle of myrrh* was certainly reserved for me; no one, then, will deprive me of it; I shall place it and keep it always in my heart. My wisdom is in pondering it; here I find all I need for my justification, the plenitude of knowledge, the riches of health and the abundant treasure of merit. Here I am given a precious drink that is sometimes salubriously bitter, sometimes a sweet unction causing ineffable consolation. It encourages me in adversity and humiliates me in success; and amidst the joys and sorrows of this present life leads me along the sure path, avoiding the dangers that are to be found on both sides. Thus, to know Jesus, to know the crucified Christ will always be the sublime philosophy of my life."

Inter ubera mea commorabitur. "Id est," says St. Thomas, "in cordis mei memoria aeternaliter habebitur, et numquam tantorum beneficiorum obliviscar; sed sive in prosperis sive in adversis sim recordabor ejus qui me dilexit, et mortuus est pro me."

"Imagine, then," says Fr. La Puente (*Guia* tr. 2. ch.13 para.2), that your Beloved is like a tree of myrrh that distills myrrh through its pores; if the bark is punctured and split it distills a greater abundance. The entire life of Jesus was a continual cross of poverty, scorn, suffering and trials, sometimes of His Own choice, at other times through the acceptance of those willed by His persecutors who maltreated Him; these He constantly distilled with His love... You must arrive at this blessed tree; on your way, meditate on His appalling sufferings, retaining some in your memory so as to contemplate them slowly, placing them, as St. Bernard says, not on your shoulders but in your heart, that your contemplation might be uninterrupted and full of love with the tender affections of compassion for all that He suffered for your salvation, and of gratitude for having suffered them. But be not content with this. Take for yourself (as St. Gregory says, *in Cant.,* 1), another little bundle of mortifications and virtues similar to Him, and truly desire to imitate His nakedness and humiliation, His suffering and trials, so as to have occasion to practice His poverty and humility, His patience and fervent zeal, tying this bouquet with the affection, of love and charity which is the bond of perfection (*Col.* 3,14). However much myrrh you take it will not be a heavy weight for you but a very light little bundle; for love lightens it and converts the bitterness of the flesh into the sweetness of the spirit. How could anything that God as a Child suffered for you through His great love be but a little bundle? How could you fail to enshrine in your heart what He cherished in His? How could you carry hidden on your shoulder what He kept always before His eyes? Do not take just one virtue but make a bouquet of them all, for one alone will be a weight, but all together they provide alleviation. When united with the Beloved Who adorned Himself with all the virtues, you will discover that humility makes poverty sweet, patience is sweetened by charity, and charity softens humility; a difficulty encountered in one virtue is overcome through the possession of another. O my Beloved, from now on You will be a bouquet of strong-scented myrrh, for it I love You whatever I see in You will be delightful to me. The scent, because it is Yours, will comfort and inspire me . . . : I love You as You love me and it will be sweet for me to suffer what You suffered."

It is important to note that in the Hebrew the Bride here does not say "my Beloved" but my *Love;* she speaks in an abstract term," writes Fr. Juan de los Angeles, "signifying her love is well placed, being in Him alone. *My love* is an expression of great assurance, being exclusive, and says more than my *Beloved* or my *Loved One,* for . . . whoever says *my love* leaves no room in her heart for anything but that which deserves such a name. . . It is as much as to say: He Who draws all my love after Himself, not leaving any love for anyone but Himself, is for me a bundle of myrrh. . . For just as other women often use various perfumes, she prefers to robe and delight herself in the fragrance of her Beloved . . . as though saying: my perfumed bouquet is my Beloved; He is my finery and He alone occupies my heart; He is my Love — — no more can be said."

This will incite her to model herself completely on Him, even at the cost of sacrifice. Because of this, as the writer goes on to add: "There always have been, there always are and always will be souls who are in love with Christ. There will always be living examples of this blessed desire; there will always be a thirst for Him; there will always be sweet longings and faithful witnesses of this kindling of the heart. Light would fail to radiate from the sun before the world would be devoid of souls who love and adore Christ. This love supports the world which is held in His hand to prevent it from falling. The world is nothing without those in it who are burning with love for

Christ. . .

"Therefore, what degrees of perfection will love lack, of what qualities will it stand in need, seeing that it is from the Holy Spirit? Could it be anything less than love born of God and therefore worthy of Him, and is the very same love as that which enkindles the angels in Heaven. All the loves with which men love one another here on earth are but shadows and very imperfect reflections of this love produced within those who love Christ. That is why He is the Beloved *par excellence*: because God enables us to love Him with a love that is unique and far surpassing other loves. The Holy Scriptures quite fittingly call this love hunger and thirst, in as much as the more one loves Christ, the more one desires to love Him. It can grow so strong and powerful that persecutors can take out a martyr's heart but cannot take away his love."

Here then begins the most helpful part of the *passive purifications* which the soul generously accepts to complement and conclude the the *active* ones which she has been cultivating; although with all her endeavors she has been unable to achieve the graces which she seeks and which she needs if she is to enter into intimate communication with God; for these active purifications are practiced until He Himself intervenes to heal her with this very precious, mystical myrrh. We know that myrrh is medicinal and very aromatic, but extremely bitter, and is used to embalm or preserve from corruption. This means that to free ourselves from the contagion of the world and to overcome the evil in creatures, Divine Wisdom, although always attracting and captivating with His sweet scent, before allowing His faithful one to experience the ineffable sweetness reserved for her, begins by embittering the soul's palate so as to truly purify her. Thus, when the soul, attracted by the sweet fragrance of Christ, has entered the way of voluntary mortification, God then sends *passive* purifications, which are much more painful than those which the soul can inflict upon herself; but at the same time are far more efficacious and beneficial. She overflows with joy in the midst of them, seeing how they restore her "health", so that by dying she returns to life.

v. 14)   *My Beloved for me is a cluster of camphire*
              in the vineyards of Engedi.

The enamored soul being purified now forgets the bitterness of the myrrh so as to think only of the beauty of the Spouse Who she now can see, or in some way or other feel, and contemplate with ineffable pleasure; thus she exclaims: *My Beloved for me is a cluster of camphire* . . . a flower extremely beautiful, sweet-smelling and valuable. It is as though she were to say: if in the mysteries of Your passion and death You were for me a bundle of very bitter myrrh, this bitterness has been changed into ineffable sweetness as You bring me to participate in the mysteries of Your Resurrection, as You reveal Yourself to me in Your joys and triumphs, in Your glorious Ascension, in the communication of Your Holy Spirit with His inestimable graces and sweet scents of life, and in the daily partaking of Your Chalice full of the mystical wine of Engedi with which You delight our hearts, and cleanse and beautify us with Your very blood.

"If you have already lamented your sins," says St. Bernard, "then taste the bitterness of myrrh; but if you now feel within you the effects of a new life it is a sign that bitterness has changed into sweetness for you . . ."

Thus the soul will deserve these words from the Spouse:

v. 15)   *How beautiful you are, my love,*
              how beautiful you are!
              Your eyes are doves.

It is as if He were to say to her: I see that you act as a true friend, filling Me with satisfaction and contentment; in you I have My delights, your dove-like eyes steal My heart; your simplicity, your purity of intention and trusting surrender delight Me. . . Indeed, He praises her eyes comparing them to those of a dove, because of the grace and simplicity with which

He sees them shine; for this soul now has great infused light. Therefore, in deep self-knowledge and knowledge of God's goodness, she neither relies on herself nor attributes anything of this to herself. He is no longer content to tell her she *looks* beautiful, but repeatedly and full of admiration tells her that indeed she *is* beautiful, in so far as her eyes are her singleness of purpose.

"How great and how tender is the heart of the Divine Spouse." exclaims Maria de los Dolorosa. "He seems to forget His greatness and speaks to His beloved Bride as though enraptured, twice calling her beautiful; indeed she has been made beautiful with His grace; she is also beautiful because of her own cooperation with the working of grace. Your eyes, He says, are those of a dove, for you please Me with the purity of intention that you show in your actions. O my sweet Jesus! Who was it that formed these eyes in Your Bride but You and Your grace? Why then do You declare Yourself so captivated by them? Yet love of its very nature makes what belongs to each the possession of both.

She is thus truly beautiful, because of the dove-like simplicity with which she gazes at and contemplates Him. Fr. Juan de los Angeles explains, "what beautifies the soul most is what the Bride has declared of her Spouse: namely, that He was for her *a little bundle of myrrh placed firmly between her breasts,* and *a cluster of camphire in the vineyards of Engedi;* by which, as we saw, she meant that Christ was her one and only pleasure, and that to Him was directed all her love and affection, whether He showed Himself to be bitter, like myrrh, or sweet and delightful like a cluster of camphire. The greatest beauty one can have and that which makes it most pleasing in His divine eyes is this conformity of the soul with God."

It must also be pointed out, however, that "although the Spouse here calls His Bride *beautiful* He does not do so as in Chapter IV, where He says she is *entirely* so; here He says that only her eyes are beautiful. You are beautiful; this beauty is in your eyes which are like those of a simple dove. . . From the clear and simple eye come works that are pure and pleasing to God, but from the evil eye. . .works of darkness. . . The devil is especially vigilant to vitiate and corrupt the purity of intention in the acts of those who are endeavoring to practice virtue. *Hostes ejus in capite (Lam.* 1,5) . . . The evil eye. . .belongs to her who, ceasing to look at God, turns her gaze upon the things of the world. On the other hand, she is very virtuous who, ceasing to look upon the world, having found nothing there that can satisfy her, directs her gaze always to God; in this way everything she does beautifies her and makes her precious in the eyes of God, attracting to herself God's gaze and blessings until the Eternal Lord finds His delight and satisfaction in her."

Once when St. Gertrude (*Revel.* 1, 1, Ch. XI) said to the Lord, "I find no pleasure on earth but in You alone," He deigned to reply, "and without you I find no delight in Heaven or on earth; for through love, I associate you with all My joys, and with you I enjoy all My comforts, and the greater they are for Me, the more fruitful they are for you." Not content with this, He added further (1. 3, Ch. V): "My love is so linked with yours that I cannot live happily without you." "The eye of My Divinity is ineffably pleased to gaze upon you whom I made so beautiful and so pleasing to Me in all things, through all the graces and favors with which I have enriched you. My divine ear receives like the sound of the sweetest harmony the words of love you address to Me, praying to Me for sinners or for souls in purgatory or when you reprimand or instruct, or in any other way utter a word for My greater glory. Even when this proves to be of no use to anyone, simply because of your *good will and purity of intention that has Me as its sole object,* your voice sounds sweetly in My ears, and moves Me to the very depth of my heart. At the same time the hope that makes you constantly long for Me, yields a fragrance very pleasing to Me. Your sighs and desires are more gratifying to My taste than the most delicious dishes. In short, in your love I find the delights of the sweetest embraces" (*ib.* 1, 3, Ch. L). "No spouse has ever been able to enjoy the caresses of his bride as much as I have even in the brief moments when My chosen ones give Me their hearts that I might delight in them" (1, 4 Ch. 38).

"O, a thousand times happy," exclaims the Ven. Mariana de San José," is the soul who is beautiful in the eyes of the Lord; indeed, far happier is she for He Himself declares her beauty, repeating *How beautiful you are, my love, how beautiful you are.* If she is Your love, my Lord, how could anyone ever doubt she is beautiful? Your words suffice to tell us that she is more beautiful than could ever be described. This is the beauty one should seek and desire and of which it is right to be jealous; for what the world calls beauty is but vanity and ugliness.

. . .*Oculi tui columbarum.* It is impossible to describe the depths of mercy that the Lord communicates to the soul with these words as He begins to reveal to her how much and how tenderly He loves her. Such a flood of goodness can be known only by her who receives it, and even she only rarely experiences it after much progress has been made in humility. . . For now that the soul is well instructed in this divine science, the beloved Spouse cannot resist manifesting His love and affection for her; therefore He says to her: *Ecce tu pulchra.* . . Mention has been made elsewhere of how the Lord's words are effective; they give life to the soul who hears them, and so it is. One moment dryness and oblivion fill the soul and in the next, by a word from the Lord, she is transformed in such a way that she no longer seems herself. . .

"Although there are various expressions by which the Lord instructs souls and gives them His mercies, none annihilate and overwhelm them as these words of tenderness. They require a careful examination, for the effects produced are considerable. And if the latter are lacking, then they cannot be words spoken by the Lord, even in the case of very advanced souls; rather they are forged by the imagination of a devout soul who is guilty of nothing but ignorance. I believe there are many such souls, even among people of considerable virtue. . . But the soul to whom the Lord truly speaks is like a shaft or dart of fire shot by Him, so active that at the moment when she understands that little word spoken to her, she becomes so united with the Word Who uttered it as to become, so to speak, annihilated. In this state she fixes her gaze on Him Who wounded her, and at the sight of the fact that she cannot be saved or wounded by any other hand, her eyes become like those of a dove, and, searching for the source of the fire that passed through her, she finds it in the depth of her own nothingness."

These effusions of God's love in His faithful servants and intimate friends can undoubtedly only be understood by souls that are so humble and pure that they there find recreation and inspiration.

If everyone endeavors to read these things with spiritual perception, purifying and simplifying their lives more and more and asking God to give them a pure and simple heart with an innocent dove-like gaze, they will one day surely be restored to spiritual health and will receive His divine revelations as He speaks to them with tenderness.

Then the faithful Bride hastens to return this praise to the Lord, giving Him the glory that belongs to Him, declaring that it was from Him that she received this beauty, that to Him she owes and for Him alone wants all that she possesses.

v. 16)   *How beautiful you are, my Beloved,*
            and how delightful!
            Our bed is of flowers:
v. 17)   *The beams of our houses are of cedar*
            the paneling of cypress.

You are indeed truly beautiful and are so in Yourself. In You are all graces and delights, and to Your goodness alone is due whatever beauty my soul may have and the ability to now contemplate our bed that is so full of flowers and so adorned with virtues, and our mansion that is so rich and precious. If, then, the poor little house of my soul is now a bed of flowers for You, a delightful mansion and like a pleasant garden, it is because You Yourself diffused all Your graces there, and taught me to remove from there everything that was displeasing to Your divine eyes.

He is indeed exceedingly beautiful in as far as He is God, like the eternal splendor of the glory of the Father and delightful in as far as He is man, being "full of grace and truth" that we all might receive of His fullness (*John I,* 14-16; *Hebr.* 1, 3; *Ps.* 44, 3).

However, this resplendent beauty that so stirs the Bride's heart, could never have been seen by her, says St. Bernard (*in Cant.* Serm. 45) had she not already had dove-like eyes. These reveal divine wonders to her and force her to join the saint himself in exclaiming: My Jesus, how beautiful You are as God to Your angels who see You in the sacred splendors of Your eternity...! And how delightful to me in the very despoilment of such beauty! For where You utterly despoiled Yourself for my love, where You, divine Light, completely stripped Yourself of Your natural splendor there Your mercy radiated more and Your divinity shone forth with the refulgence of Your graces ... What light You shed for me, O Star of Jacob! (*Num.* 24, 17). What a delightful Flower springing from the stem of Jesse! (*Is.* 11, 1) What a welcome Light in the midst of the darkness, coming from on high to visit me! Everywhere my Lord Jesus, You show Yourself to be beautiful to the eyes of the loving souls: beautiful in Heaven and beautiful on Calvary, beautiful reigning among the angels and beautiful hanging between thieves; beautiful sitting at the right hand of God the Father and beautiful dying on the cross for us."

"When the Bride hears Christ's expressions of love, she is almost beside herself, finding no other terms with which to show her affection than those which she heard from her Beloved. She tells Him that He is full of grace — 'delightful' — that she does not tire of hearing His words, wishing Him to be continually speaking in her heart. Since she longs to rest in the love of her sweet Lord, she adds: *Our bed is of flowers.* She speaks thus of her heart, which is now her Spouse's, because He with His grace has formed it in such a way that a God is able to rest in it as though in a flower-strewn bridal chamber; that is to say, adorned with all kinds of virtues that have sprung from His blood." (Maria Dolorosa)

Ecce tu pulcher... "What a wonderful thing it is to see a soul in this happy state," exclaims the Ven. Mariana de San José, "being now able to have loving discourse with her God. These conversations are not composed by the mind nor are they the soul's own speech, but rather they are produced by the presence and operation of divine wisdom which is enlightening the soul, working through the wonderful gift of Our Lord's Spirit and the Gift of Himself Whom, as the object of her contemplation, she has discovered within her very heart. When the soul thus finds this little grain of fire that the Lord has sown in her heart, gazing at Him she says: *How beautiful You are my Beloved,* etc. Your beauty gladdens the very depths of my heart where, as the flower-strewn Spouse and resplendent Sun You work new wonders and unseen mercies. Here is where the soul longs to be consumed in praising her Lord and speaking many tender words because of those things which He tells her; ineffable truths which are incredible to anyone who does not know the infinite love He has for those with whom He communicates... O what pleasures are enjoyed by those who hear this sweetest Nightingale sing! How short the hours and days become!... The soul emerges from these communications not wishing to hear the praise of human or worldly things: she is far from the things of this earth. . ." (*Phil.* 3, 20).

This is how He so truly beautifies her, and wishes to beautify all of us until we become, if we wish, nothing but flower-strewn beds in which He can take recreation and rest as He delights in doing.

The soul is, indeed, a flower-strewn bed when in a state of

contemplation, continually exhaling the sweetest affections, which to the eyes of the Lord are the most sweetly-scented flowers. It is there that she, at the same time, rests in the divine approbation, later to leave in order to collect new flowers of virtue and good works with which to regale and delight the Spouse and deserve other new and more wonderful favors from Him.

"Since the virtues of the Bride," writes St. John of the Cross, "are perfect and she enjoys habitual peace in the visits of her Beloved, she sometimes has a sublime enjoyment of their sweetness and fragrance when her Beloved touches these virtues, just as man enjoys the sweetness and beauty of flowers and lilies when having blossomed, he picks them. In many of these visits the soul sees within herself all her virtues by means of the light caused by the Bridegroom. And then in a wonderful ecstasy of love she gathers them together and offers them to Him. . . This all occurs interiorly. The soul feels that the Beloved is within her as in His own bed. She offers herself together with her virtues, which is the greatest service she can render Him. Thus one of the most outstanding delights she receives in her interior communion with God comes from this gift of herself to her Beloved." (*Spirit. Cant.*, Introd. to Stanza 16)

Having God within her, resting as though in a flowery bed in her own heart beautified by Him and adorned with virtues, she will gradually become conscious of the fact that she herself is entirely within Him until she eventually comes to rest, not in a bed of flowers but in the very Flower of all beauty, the Sacred Heart. . .

When the soul reaches such a high degree of perfection and union, her sweet bed, says the great mystical Doctor, "is none other than her very Bridegroom, the Word, the Son of God, as will soon be seen upon Whom she reclines through the union of love. She calls her bed a flourishing one because her Bridegroom is not only flourishing, but the very Flower of the fields and the Lily of the valleys. . . Thus the soul reclines not merely upon the bed of flowers but upon the Flower Itself, the Son of God, Who bears within Himself divine fragrance, grace and beauty, as He likewise declares through David: The beauty of the field is with me (*Ps.* 50, 11). The soul thus relates in song the properties and graces of her bed." (*Spirit. Cant.*, Introd. to Stanza 24)

The Saint continues his commentary on the same stanza: "This bed of the soul is the Bridegroom, the Son of God, Who is in flower for the soul. Now that she is united with and reclines upon Him and has become His bride, her Beloved's breast and love is communicated to her. This means that He communicates to her His wisdom, secrets, graces, virtues and gifts, and that through them He makes her so beautiful and rich and so imbues her with delights that it seems to her she rests upon a bed, made of a variety of fragrant divine flowers that delight with their touch and refresh with their scent. Very appropriately does she call this union with God through love a 'bed in flower'. . . She calls it 'our' because both have the same virtues and the same love (which are the Beloved's) and both have the same delight. . . She also says that it is in flower because the virtues of the soul in this state are now perfect and heroic. This, though, could not have come about until the bed had flowered through the soul's perfect union with God."

In order to attain such a happy state, "what is important here and now to gather or learn from this holy Bride," says the Ven. Mariana de San José, "is that we should not recline or rest in any other bed but in Christ Our Lord. He must be our resting place as we repose sometimes in the example of His life, other times reclining on His merits, still other times hiding ourselves in the sanctuary of His sweet heart, a refuge and rest during all our sufferings and misery, where all is secure. . . O what a soft, safe bed is Christ's heart! How secure are the bonds of the precious cypress of His Divinity! The construction of this bed is such that only the Designer Who built it knows its quality and excellence. . . This indicates just how priceless it is; so we need

speak no more about it, but would do well, instead, to adore it
and make ourselves worthy of its enjoyment, for the Lord
Himself built it that we might truly call it *ours.*"

As far as the soul is concerned, in order that the flowers
with which she is adorned always be sweet-smelling and fresh,
says Fr. Juan de los Angeles, "they must be constantly renewed.
The flower of a good work quickly withers, dries and loses its
pleasing scent if it is not replaced by another. We are not to be
content with doing good today or tomorrow, but throughout
the whole of life; for in this way one's interior is strewn with
flowers and the Spouse approaches with pleasure, sleeps and
rests as though in His own soft, comfortable bed.

"And . . . she does not say 'our bed' but our 'little bed' is
strewn with flowers . . . ; either because in this life the bed in
which God sleeps with the soul is narrow and there is only room
for the two of them in it . . . or because it is merely a couch in
which to spend the siesta, to rest a little, avoiding the extreme
heat of the sun."

St. Thomas of Villanova observed that the Bride does not
say "the beams of our house" but "of our houses"; for, as with
the soul, the body itself must also be the house or mansion of
God, as the Apostle says (I *Cor.* 6, 19-20): *An nescitis quoniam
membra vestra templum sunt Spiritus Sancti, qui habitat in
vobis. . .? Glorificate. . .Deum in corpore vestro.*

"The beams of these houses," says Fr. Juan de los Angeles,
"are the virtues. Part of them belong to reason, part of them to
the appetite of the senses. . . And included here are the infused
and acquired virtues . . . which, interlinked and connected, make
the building firm and stable. They are made of cedar, which
allow neither wood-worm nor moth to enter, and therefore are
solid and eternal."

"The house and room where the Spouse dwells," remarks
Fr. Gracian, "is founded upon solid virtues, which are the
beams of cedar, and adorned with the gifts of the Holy Spirit,
which are the *paneling of cypress.* Within this house is the

flowery bed, which is the true replica of the crucified Christ."

Thus, although every soul in a state of grace is Christ's mansion, only the very contemplative souls, being already full of the beauty and fragrance of all the virtues, are His *flowery bed* where He is so pleased to recline; and in this bed He grows more and more pleased and delighted as He sees them become beautified in love, adorned with the most fragrant flowers of virtues, and made incorruptible through continual mortification and the spirit of sacrifice. However, His favorite bed and mansion is the Holy Virgin, the mystical mansion of peace and house of gold that divine Wisdom made for Himself, placing seven wonderful pillars within her; and there He will again seek to introduce every holy soul (Ch. III, 4; VIII, 2).

In her own way, the Church is also this bed, as is *every house of God* and every community that is truly *religious.*

Indeed, "the Spouse's bed," says St. Bernard (*Serm.* 46), "is every monastery where the peace of God reigns due to its separation from the world; for these holy places are truly full of beautiful and sweet-smelling flowers because of the example of so many fervent souls that live there, because of the teaching of their zealous prelates, and because of the sweet scent that is yielded by the blossoming observance of the holy rule. . .

"When the Bride says *'our bed'* and *'our houses'* or *'rooms',* these expressions do not indicate a usurpation but rather a profound love, as a result of the confidence with which the excesses of His love make her speak to Him, causing her to consider as her own those things which are His Whom she so much loves. She neither can nor ought to believe that she is separated from His house and company while, forgetful of self, she carefully works for His greater glory. . . Then she glories in the common possession of wealth shared with Him with Whom she knows herself to be intimately united in the bonds of love. This is not the language of the soul who has not yet denied her own will; such a soul lies alone in her own bed, or rather, does not live alone, but accompanied by her passions to which she is but a worthless slave."

On the other hand, she who loves God with all her heart, having already renounced herself, does not dwell in herself but in Him and with Him and so is free of all enslavement, enjoying holy liberty of spirit. She will not hesitate to call the Lord and Creator of all, her *Beloved*. It is also to be noted, observes the same Saint (Serm. 45), "that she does not call Him simply *Beloved*, but *my Beloved*, indicating something personally hers. What a wonderful vision or communication this is that so ennobles and increases her confidence, that she dares to call the Lord of all, not *Lord* but *Beloved*. . .! She speaks familiarly to the Spouse and sees Him face to face, just as Moses had done, and not through signs and figures (*Exod.* 33, 11). Thus she calls Him beautiful and delightful, for this is how He deigned to reveal Himself to her spirit in this sublime vision or communication. Her eyes, then, saw the King in His splendor and majesty but they did not see Him as King. One prophet sees Him seated on a high throne (*Is.* 6, 1); another sees Him face to face, as he himself tells (*Gen.* 32, 30); but my opinion is that this vision that the Bride has just been favored with is better than all these other visions — or at least, is preferable. If to the others He appeared as Lord filling them with the fear that is inseparable from the majesty of such a holy and awesome name, if I were given the choice I would far more happily choose the Bride's vision, being to my mind so much more loving and noble, having been born of love which is the very height of perfection. There is undoubtedly a great difference between appearing awesome in His counsel to the children of men, and showing Himself to the Bride to be more beautiful and delightful than any mortal (*Ps.* 66, 5; 45, 3).

With these expressions of pure love, the Bride invites Him to come to her again to rest and delight in her heart, it being filled with an ineffable joy by the very act of His deigning to make it a pleasant dwelling-place for Himself. As though she were to say: Come then, my Beloved, You Who are beauty itself and all my delight, come to the bed which with Your power and help I have prepared for You in the little house of my soul. See how, thanks to You, it is all covered with sweet-scented flowers, although before it was covered with sharp and fetid thorns. . . The beams of Your house are of cedar, that it to say, incorruptible and aromatic, my body being now enclosed in Your dying "so that Your life also might be made manifest in my mortal flesh" (II *Cor.* 4, 10); so that when all passing desires are dead there might only dwell within me those holy affections that are to perfume You forever. The roof or paneling is of funeral cypress, the symbol of the mystical death for which I long, no longer desiring to live but in You and for You and finding all my joy in this world in being crucified with you (*Gal.* 2, 19; 6, 14). Your very cross, placed in the middle of my heart is our flowery bed where all Your virtues shine and where Your very fragrance can be perceived and Your purity and incorruptibility (symbolized by those precious and sweet-smelling beams) can be shared. And she says that it is 'flowery', *Floridus* "as though saying," writes the V. Mariana, "let no one think that our bed is hard and rough, for my Spouse built nothing but a bed of flowers. . . And then He made our cross easier, when He let Himself fear His own (which His love made ours), taking for Himself the bitterness of the cup."

With respect to the Church, according to M. Maria de los Dolores, these *houses* or *rooms* represent its members, its faithful whose souls are in their bodies as though in houses which they must eventually leave at the moment of death. But these houses have beams of cedar which are the crosses that Jesus sends them to make them incorruptible through patience. . . She then says that the *paneling is of cypress,* indicating that, with the thought of death that awaits them and that will put an end to all their labors, faithful souls rejoice in the cross that brings them into the heavenly Kingdom" . . . O my sweet Good! With a single loving gaze You can also form Your room in me, making my thoughts incorruptible and my will unswerving in virtue: thus You will rest in me and I in You."

In this way the crucified Christ — considered scandalous by the Jews and stupid by the Gentiles — for the Church and for each soul that is enamored by the fragrance of His life, He becomes the true *Anointed,* full of grace, Who draws all pure hearts after Him and Whom the upright in heart cannot help but love; the *Desired One* of the nations, in Whom all peoples hope to find salvation. In short, *Christ is* the power and wisdom of God (I *Cor.* I, 23-24).

How rightly, then, must He be ardently desired by all sincere souls, by all hearts thirsting for truth and justice . . . !

Although all can and should desire this intimate communication with the Divine Wisdom Who has thus sought to have His delights with us, it would nonetheless be very presumptuous and forward to want to receive this at once and to address Him familiarly without beforehand preparing a worthy mansion and purifying the lips that aspire to His kiss of peace. It is madness to try to reach the exalted heights of the unitive way in a single leap without passing through the stages of the purgative and illuminative ways; and it is madness to try to approach God so as to communicate intimately with Him while remaining unwilling to strip oneself of worldly affections to cloth oneself in the wedding garment of perfect charity, or to prepare a bed for the divine Spouse that is to His satisfaction.

"If then, you desire to reach the quiet of contemplation," observes St. Bernard (*Serm.* 46), "you do very well; but take care not to forget the flowers that you saw adorning the Bride's bed. Try to adorn your own with good works . . . preparing yourself through the faithful exercise of every virtue for the holy leisure and rest of contemplation. For to do otherwise. . . is to invert the order of things: to wish to rest without having worked, to receive the prize without having deserved it, and to eat without chewing your food. This is contrary to what the Apostle stipulates (*I Thes.,* 3, 10). . . The delights of contemplation are due entirely to obedience to the divine commands. Rid yourself of all though of your own will or convenience . . . , for the Spouse will not want to come and rest with you in a bed of thistles in place of flowers. . . And if yours is still dirty and foul-smelling, how can you dare to invite the very King of glory. . .? Endeavor first of all, then, to wash it well with tears of penitence . . . and when you have it well adorned with the flowers of virtues, then with these you can invite the Spouse to come, just as the Bride did."

"As far as the spiritual house of God is concerned," he adds (*ib.*), "you must bear in mind that this can be achieved only by those who are led and guided by the Spirit of God, not by those who live according to the flesh. *The temple of God is sacred,* says the Apostle (I *Cor.* 3, 17), *and you are that temple.* Take care, then, to preserve this spiritual building; to s : that, as it is being erected, it does not sway and fall because it has been well cemented and supported by strong beams of virtues. Take care, I repeat, to secure it with firm and indestructible beams; that is to say, with the holy fear of the Lord which lasts through all eternity; with that *patience of the poor which,* it is said, *shall not perish forever* (*Ps.* 9, 19); with a long-suffering and forbearance capable of keeping this holy building steady and unyielding beneath even the greatest weight until the coming of eternal happiness; for as the Savior says (*Matt.* 10, 22), only *the man who stands firm to the end will be saved.* Try above all to maintain it through charity which never dies. . .

"Also try as much as you are able to reinforce these beams with others of equal worth and beauty for the adornment and stability of the paneling: with the gifts of knowledge and wisdom, of prophesy and healing, the interpretation of Holy Scripture and with the other supernatural graces which are all *useful* in beautifying the building, although not *necessary* for salvation. Concerning the acquisition of such precious gifts, I have no precept, but it is most laudable to try to achieve them, although with discretion."

With these gifts the soul will undoubtedly be able to serve

the Spouse more perfectly and delight Him with new pleasures. For this reason the Apostle desires us to know of all these spiritual graces that give greater glory to God and edification to the Church, and even to yearn for the greatest of them (*I Cor.* 12, 1, 31; 14, 1-12, 20, 39).

Synopsis

The colloquy between the Spouse and the Bride continues,
He attracting her and inspiring her to love Him while telling
her how she must behave to please Him (v. 1-2); and she
celebrating the glory of her Beloved, and proclaiming how
much she owes Him, having found her happiness and rest
in Him and having grown intoxicated by the wine of His love (v.
3-4). Swooning from the excess of this love she asks to be
comforted with sweet-smelling flowers and receives the
tenderest caresses from Him Whom she so much desires (v. 5-6);
and He commands that she be not roused from her first
mystical sleep (v. 7). Now dreaming always of Him, she hears
Him speak and sees Him come to invite her to a new and much
more perfect life where she would flourish with all kinds of
virtues and good works, although having to suffer the pruning
of new purifications; and where much beautified and coming to
dwell continually in His very wounds, she would please and
regale Him with her graceful presence and with her sweet
dove-like cooing, with which she will begin to be helpful to
other souls (v. 8-14). Prior to this, however, she must destroy
even the slightest disorderly affection, or allow it to be
destroyed within her, so as to be completely His and to enjoy
Him while it is *day*. Then the frightening shades of the awesome
night will fall and, losing sight of Him she will never cease to
call out to Him in great anguish (v. 15-17).

THE SPOUSE

1. *I am the flower of the field*[a]
   and the lily of the valleys.[b]

2. *As a lily among the thistles*
   so is my love among the maidens.

THE BRIDE

3. *As an apple tree among the wild trees*
   so is my Beloved among the young men.
   In his longed-for shade I am seated
   and his fruit is sweet to my taste.

4. *He has brought me into his wine-cellar*
   and set love within me.[c]

5. *Sustain me with flowers,*[d] *comfort me with apples;*
   for I am sick with love.

6. *His left arm is under my head*
   his right embraces me.

THE SPOUSE

7. *I charge you, daughters of Jerusalem*
   by the gazelles, by the hinds of the fields
   not to stir my love, nor rouse her
   until she please.

THE BRIDE

8. *The voice of my Beloved! See how he comes*
   leaping on the mountains, bounding over the hills!

a. In Hebrew: *a narcissus of Sharon.*

b. The Hebrew word means: a flower with six leaves, and it is not easy to establish which flower this is. In the Septuagint and the Vulgate it is translated as lily or lily of the field, and could well be another liliaceous like the hyacinth or the tulip.

c. Literally: "and his banner over me (is) love;" that is to say, he has imposed his law of laws within me.

d. Septuagint: *Make me a bed of apples for I am stricken with love.* Simmacus: *Make me a bed of flowers.* — Fr. Luis de León: "Inspire me, surround me with cups of wine, encompass me with apples . . ."

9. *My Beloved is like a gazelle, like a young stag.*
    See where he stands behind our wall
    looking in through the windows [e]
    peering through the lattice.
10. *My Beloved lifts up his voice and says to me*

THE SPOUSE
Rise up, hurry, my love,
my dove, my beauty and come. [f]
11. *For see, winter is past*
    the rains are over and gone.
12. *The flowers appear on our earth.*
    Pruning time has come.
    The season of glad songs has come,
    the cooing of the turtle-dove is heard in our fields.
13. *The fig tree is forming its first figs* [g]
    and the blossoming vines give out their fragrance.
    Arise then, my love, my beauty, and come.
14. *My dove, hiding in the clefts of the rock*
    in the opening in the wall [h]
    show me your face
    let me hear your voice;
    for your voice is sweet and your face is beautiful.
15. *Catch the little foxes for us*
    that destroy the vineyards,
    for our vineyard is in flower.

THE BRIDE
16. *My Beloved is mine and I am his.*
    He pastures among the lilies;

e.   In Hebrew: "window", in the singular
f.   In Hebrew: "My Beloved speaks and tells me: arise, my love, my lovely one,
     and come!" — The Septuagint added: "my dove" and the Vulgate did the
     same. The "hurry" is not to be found in either the Hebrew or the Septuagint.
g.   In Palestine the fig tree sometime produces three crops: in June, August and
     at the beginning of winter. When winter is over the first figs begin to appear.
h.   In Hebrew: "in the coverts of the cliffs".

17.   *until the day blows and the shadows flee;*[i]
      Turn, my Beloved, and be like a gazelle
      a young stag on the mountains of Bether.[j]

Exposition

v. 1)   *I am the flower of the field*
                         and the lily of the valleys.

Since the Bride had just considered the beauty and
fragrance of her flower-strewn bed the Spouse tells her and
everyone that He Himself is the Flower *par excellence* in which
all delights are to be found, and that where He graciously
manifests Himself, all becomes a flowery meadow. The flower
of the field grows spontaneously without need of cultivation,
and tends to be more beautiful and often more fragrant: thus
this incomparable Flower of the root of Jesse that sprang forth
in the field of Mary's virginal heart through the overshadowing
of the Holy Spirit, untouched by any human instrument,
embalmed with Its divine fragrance not one particular garden
but the whole world, captivating, enrapturing and attracting it
with Its beauty. The Hebrew reads: The narcissus of Sharon,
which is a white and very fragrant flower and thus symbolizes
very well the Savior's sanctity and purity together with His
aroma of life. He is also the iris, or rather the lily (as He used
often to be called) or lily of the fields, which has the same
characteristics and best represents Him Whom St. Bernard calls
"the crown of the humble" (*Serm.* 47).

"We are told," adds the holy Abbot, "that the just shall
grow like the lily (*Hosea* 14, 6). Who is the just man but he who
is humble...? The true just man is he who keeps himself as

i.   In the Hebrew this phrase is connected with the one that follows and not to
      the one that precedes. (v. 16)
j.   In the Hebrew: "on the steep mountains, or mountains that separate us"
      (according to those that consider *bether* a crude appellative "division" and not
      a proper noun). According to Eusebio, the Mountains of Bether were two
      miles from Jerusalem.

humble as the valleys. If, then, we have the good fortune to be recognized by the Lord as truly humble souls, our works will be precious like this flower, and our blossoms will exhale an eternal fragrance before the Divine Majesty."

"He is called *the lily of the valleys,*" writes Maria de la Dolorosa, "because He takes pleasure in humble souls and infuses within them the beautiful purity that He finds so pleasing; for being a lily, He pastures among the lilies. But since He is in the valleys, they prefer to walk in the humility of a hidden and silent life and find Him more easily among these humble souls."

Fr. Juan de los Angeles observes that it is precisely from the Hebrew *susanim* that the Castilian *azucena* (lily) is derived, therefore *azucena* is the proper translation of *lilium* in the Vulgate, and not *lirio,* more properly, 'iris', as it is normally rendered by most translators because of the apparent similarity of the words. The lily, as Titelman remarked, has two colors: on the outside its leaves are very white, and on the inside, as though drawn from the very center of the flower are three yellow streaks of gold, symbolizing the Humanity and Divinity of Our Lord. That outer whiteness represents the very pure human nature that He took upon Himself through His love for us; and the inner golden color represents the divine nature hidden beneath the human. The Savior Himself celebrates the beauty of that flower of the field (*Matt.* 6,28), and like that flower, He here reveals Himself to be at the disposition of all, so that all who wish may enjoy Him: *et eo fruantur quicumque velit,* but always provided they are humble.

This must not be just any kind of humility. One must be humble in heart, says the Ven. Mariana de San José, "for this Divine Lily to be born within and become one with the soul. If humility is not in one's heart, it will not be humility, nor will the Lord be one's lily. . . Whose excellence is such that not even Solomon in all his regalia was robed in such colors (*Matt.* 6, 29). This lily, whose color he could not extract, is the flower of the

humble, and the humble are so much more advanced than
Solomon that they not only are able to copy its color in adorning
themselves, but actually put on the lily itself, making such a
beautiful and wonderful garment that each one looks like a
Solomon, though far more resplendent and wise. Through
lowliness and scorn they clothed themselves in Jesus Christ and
so became kings; eventually they will arrive at beatitude, since
here they were kingly over their passions, imitating this Divine
Lily. . .

   "This good is enjoyed by those souls who are humble, who
strip themselves of self in such a way that there is room in their
hearts for this precious flower whose roots yield a wonderful
scent, and with which they achieve that cleanliness of which
Our Lord says (*Matt. 5, 8*): *Happy are the pure in heart for they
shall see God;* as though to say, the humble in heart. Through
faith they see Him even in this life, representing Him as the
flower of the valleys, which yields such pleasures and comforts
in souls where it dwells. . . that one can only beg the Lord to
show souls and bring them to taste this ineffable good which
His love alone can and will bestow, if we are ready to imitate
Him . . . This knowledge of God . . . is communicated to the
humble . . . in whom, this lily and its precious fragrant roots are
to be found growing. . . The scent of this lily is preserved in
such pure hearts as these, emptied of themselves and of the
things of this world, and with this they will see God not only in
the next life, but *before leaving this mortality,* through a
communication of the wisdom of the Father that is so clear that
the soul cannot fail to delight and love much more than can be
expressed."

   "The knowledge of Christ," writes Fr. Gracian, "is what
most moves one to love Him. God is not loved only when He is
not known. When the Spouse, therefore, wants to draw the
Bride to Himself He identifies Himself with the flower and the
lily . . . as though to say . . . no one will prevent you from
obtaining this Flower if you desire it; for I am not enclosed or

locked in, but am the Flower of the field, accessible to all who want Me. . ."

As the Flower of the field, He is within the reach of all who desire Him. It cannot be said that He is reserved for privileged souls only, as flowers in an enclosed garden are. He is also the Gate of the enclosed garden wherein are kept the hidden mysteries of the Divinity. All can and should arrive at the Gate and knock so that it will be opened to them (Matt. 7, 7). All can find Him and follow Him Who is the true *Way*, so as to become enlightened by Him, the *Truth*, and be worthy of having Him as *eternal Life* (*John* 8, 12). . . The man who finds Him finds life (*Prov.* 8, 35). In short, all can approach and reach Him Who deigned to tell us: *Come to Me all of you.* . .(*Matt.* 11, 28).

As the Flower of the field and true Blossom of the root of Jesse, full of all the fragrances emanating from the Holy Spirit, the more lovingly one encounters Him, the more one is permeated with His divine fragrance. "If you wish to breathe in My fragrance," wrote the Blessed Francis Possadas, speaking in His Name (*Carta del Esposo*, para. XII), "come into contact with Me, do not let go of My hand and you will see how you will walk in the perfume of these scents, as the brides do."

But in order to treat Him as one ought one must turn to the sweet "Mother of fair love" in whom "the grace of every way and every truth" is to be found, and together with it "all hope of life and virtue" (*Ecclus.* 24, 24-25), and behind whom the mystical maidens are led to the King (*Ps.* 45, 15).

She is, in fact, the gracious rod born of the root of Jesse: in her grows the Flower of all beauty in Whom all graces are to be found (*Is.* 11, 1-5).

"The root of the Patriarch Jesse," says St. Ambrose (*De Spiritu* S. 1. 2c. V.), "is the Jewish race; the stem, Mary; and the Flower of Mary, Jesus Christ, . . . springing from her virginal womb, as He Himself says: *I am the flower of the field.*"

"This Flower," adds St. Jerome (*in Is.* 1. 4, Ch. 11), "has as many leaves as there are ministries and examples of virtue in the Church. If you wish to possess such a precious Flower, try to move with your prayers the beautiful stem in which it was born; for if by the very loftiness of its Divinity, the Flower is so exalted that it seems inaccessible, through the piety of the stem that so easily inclines to our requests, the Flower comes within our reach. While the Flower is very rare, being the only one in Heaven and on earth, It is nevertheless very common, unenclosed by any walled garden, in the fields, at the disposal of all who pass by.

"It should be noted," says Fr. Juan de los Angeles (*in Cant.* 2, 1), "that the Spouse does not say: I am the Flower of the gardens, but rather: I am the Flower of the field; so that it might be understood that He is available to everyone especially to those who wish to pick Him. The flowers of enclosed gardens belong exclusively to their owners who alone can enjoy them; but the flowers of the field are denied to no one, being the common property of all and for all to pick and enjoy. Thus Christ is the Flower of all, and for all: *Clara est, et quae nunquam marcescit sapientia, et jacile videtur ab his qui diligunt eam, et invenitur ab iis qui quaerunt illam* (*Ws.* 6, 13). . . As St. Matthew said, this treasure is not hidden in a fortress or inaccessible place, nor enclosed behind a strong wall, but in the fields. . . It is easily found by whoever searches for it diligently. This Treasure and Flower is in the fields for everyone, easily found by the poor and rich alike, by the wise man and the unlearned, by the Gentile and the Jew. . . It will be the Fountain, revealed and manifested to all (*Zech.* 13, 1); all will be able to be washed in It, even though their sins be extremely black. . . The truth is that if Christ, as a Flower, belongs to all. . . He belongs more particularly and efficaciously to the humble (represented by the valleys)."

That we might all see and appreciate this Flower better, it is shown to us on the heights of Calvary. On this holy mountain, writes Blosius, summarizing Tauler (*Explic. de la Pas.*

Ch. 16), "is to be found the Flower of the field and the *Lily* of the valleys the sovereign Fruit of the earth... Here is without doubt the beautiful Lily of our valley, Its brilliant whiteness suffusing the whole world with Its beauty and filling it with the perfume of Its virtue. From this Flower come streaks of gold, the very Divinity that is hidden beneath the white leaves of the purest Humanity. Rejoice then for our earth is now adorned with such precious Fruit; let the laments cease in our valley of tears ... for the flower that was formerly tainted ... has now produced countless lilies among whom, says the enamored soul, her Beloved walks and takes recreation. Our valley has produced as many lilies as there are men on earth who are pure in heart and love God; and in such men the Spouse takes much delight. He undoubtedly is that excellent Lily from Whose seed the others were born and took their form, their beauty and their scent. This Lily's fragrance puts serpents to flight and does away with all corruption."

In order to humble this soul, to strengthen the week and encourage the downhearted, "writes the Ven. Mariana de San José," He says that He Who is the joy of the blessed, is the *Flower of* the field ... , as if to say: I do not love and favor you alone, I am not for you alone, but for everyone, searching and calling to everyone, giving Myself so freely to them that I place Myself in the field, that whoever wishes may not only see Me and enjoy My fragrance, but also ... may pick and take Me in their hands and lift Me to their nose and eyes where they can see at close range the goodness and love with which I wish them to come to Me...

"O Divine Flower! If only I could manage to say something of all that You represent, of all that those who look for You find in You and of the great comfort that we miserable sinners can receive from You... What would have become of me if You had not become the *flower of the field and lily of the valleys,* appearing in the middle of my twisted paths that I might find You there and love You more than these abhorrent things that we children of Adam pursue?. . .

Although all those who follow Him are very beautiful flowers, their charms are not to be compared with those of the Flower of flowers, Whose virtue is the source for all souls. He, therefore, says to the soul: *I am the flower of the field,* etc., for although He considers her to be flowery. . . He wants her to realize that all these infinite gifts come from her association with this Flower Which is He Himself. He is in the field, accessible to all souls who desire Him; He has gifts to give to all and will be a Flower for all Whose fragrance rich and poor can enjoy. He has such a strong desire to give Himself to them that He will do all this to help them seek and follow Him. . . O, how Our Lord here shows how graciously He gives Himself; for in order to possess Him one has only to desire it. Thus when He says: *I am the flower of the field,* He gives us to understand: Do not think that because I am infinite in power, wealth, beauty and mercy that I am difficult to find; for I am the Flower of the field and if you want Me you can pick Me. . . O what happy hands are they that reach out to the Lord and in which He is held, for it is impossible for them not to be left extremely enriched. . . I repeat that because the Lord is a Flower, He delights to be held in the hands of men. As one soul expressed it, He never seemed more beautiful than when the priest held Him in His hands; for in no way do we see His goodness and His love for us better than in this Holy Sacrament. . .

This Flower was not content to give Himself at low cost but wanted this giving of Himself to cost Him dear; and it seems to us in giving ourselves to Him we only return what He has dearly paid for and we consider ourselves, and really are, His dearly bought possession and in so many ways. . . For just as flowers serve to delight and comfort men, and their juices to restore their health, so, after the Lord became the Flower, He alone is our comfort and the true salvation of the soul. I think He also said this to His Bride in order to win her confidence; for since she has Him, He will not let her fall, nor become ill."

Some suppose that these words are spoken by the Bride herself that she in order to win her Spouse's heart even more, praises the flower-strewn bed indicating which flowers they are, saying: I am the little flower of the field; and when she adds "the lily of the valleys" they believe that this is attributed to Him, as though she were to say: "I am the rose of the field, and You the Lily of the valley, showing how well the beauty of the one announces the beauty of the Other" (Fr. Luis de León).

The introduction of this "you", that is not contained nor indicated in any way in the text, is altogether too arbitrary; and as a result, if the words are really spoken by the Bride, the whole passage must be attributed to her, without there being any sign of self-praise, since she is not rebuked for this, but simply advised as how to preserve all her freshness. Therefore she would only mean to say: I, a wild, abandoned little flower, growing without any cultivation, took life as though by chance among the thickets and lived in decay and uselessness, destined soon to die and be burned... The Bride does not display her *graces*, as some would suppose, in order to please the Spouse, but rather her own *lack of grace* so as to give Him the glory for everything... Applying this to the spiritual soul living in the world, it means: I was not raised in the cloister among examples of holiness, nor have I been guided by a good spiritual director, as many other privileged souls are. I have lived in the world surrounded by dangers, in a valley glutted with miasmas, where, unable to develop fully, I would have died of suffocation... And in spite of everything You have chosen me and taken me as Yours. How can I ever thank you sufficiently...'

If this is applied to the Church, then, says Calmet, the Bride can well take pride in being the flower of the field and lily of the valley, for the purity and sweet fragrance which distinguish it from all sects and heresies, and for the heroic virtues of so many holy martyrs, confessors and virgins who by their purity, innocence and holy lives were the sweet fragrance of Christ and His faithful imitators.

v. 2)   *As a lily among the thistles*
              so is my love among the maidens.

The difference in beauty and fragrance between the
thistles and the lily is the same difference as that which exists,
or should exist, between My love and the other maidens. A
flower which lives vigorously among thistles is all the more
appreciated the more repulsive are the thistles that surround it;
their ugliness brings out its beauty. He does not say she now *is* a
lily, but rather that she should try to become one, and to
become as one surrounded by thistles. Thus in these words the
Divine Spouse declares which His true Brides are, and how those
souls that aspire to be His Brides and to live in intimate
friendship with Him should proceed. My Brides, He says, should
be like Me — the Flower of the fields — living like lilies among
the thistles; for the soul in whom I take pleasure and make the
chosen object of My favors must so excel in the fragrance and
splendor of her virtues that other maidens in comparison look
like thistles, thorns and brambles. Lilies among thistles also
because it is only through the thorns of mortification that the
freshness of chastity is kept pure. I surround the faithful and
mortified soul with many thorns of tribulations so as to keep
her more secure and always fragrant and beautiful. I surround
her in this way so that she cannot escape from My hands, nor
become contaminated through contact with creatures (Blessed
Suso, *Eternal Wisdom* Ch. 19). To the mortifications which I
impose on her she, of her own accord, adds many more, that
My beauty, fragrance and very life may shine forth in her all the
more clearly (II *Cor.* 4, 10).

"Just as the lily among the thistles keeps itself safe,
without the danger of any strange hand coming to touch it, so,"
says Maria Dolorosa, "the Bride keeps herself pure among the
thorns of mortifications."

These thistles are, more often than not, the very daughters
of Jerusalem who would and hurt her in a thousand ways,
although at the same time they form a wall which keeps the

worldly away and preserves this precious flower from coming into contact with them. But in as much as they prick, says St. Bernard (*Serm.* 48), they are not good: *Non bonae filiae quae pungunt.*

Nevertheless, they always serve to bring out the goodness and beauty of the holy soul, so that her Beloved might look upon her with greater pleasure and render her greater praise. For just as human lovers usually shower praises on the object of their love, so the Divine Spouse, says St. Bonaventure (*Serm. de Sancta Agnete V. et M.*), celebrates His beloved Bride, comparing her to a lily among the thistles. In the whiteness of the sweet-smelling lily He praises her spotless beauty; in the surrounding thorns, her suffering and shedding of blood; in the word 'love' He declares His consuming desire; in comparing her with the other maidens, taken to be in general just souls, He proclaims her excellence, for she stands out above all, like a rose amid its thorns. This is that we might learn, first of all, to love the flower of incorruption; secondly, to suffer the thorns of tribulations that keep and preserve it; thirdly, to maintain the fervor of charity that makes us His love; fourthly, to desire the companionship of the blessed, who are roses and lilies without thorns to give offence or provide defence.

All those who thus try to imitate the mystical Bride will eventually receive the same affection from the Lord.

"We must not believe," writes the Ven. Mariana de San José (*in Cant.* 2,) "that it is just one soul that is favored by the Spouse; for even were the number of perfect and just souls in the Church militant not a matter of faith we know that His infinite love would not allow Him ever to crease searching for souls to whom He can communicate Himself; and for this reason we must believe that He has many and they are such as deserve all the favors He grants them, for He *makes them worthy to receive them*. But the wisdom and wealth that He has to give are so great that each soul with good reason might think she is the beloved Benjamin, for each soul must excel in some

particular virtue; and since there are so many mines on the way
to Heaven and perfection is so high, there are different seats for
everyone and different exercises . . .

"For of this Bride it is now said that as a lily is among
thistles, so is she among the maidens. She exceeds them as much
as the lily exceeds the thistles. This should not surprise us, for
any growth in grace is of much greater worth than could ever be
imagined. What should be appreciated here is the manifestation
of love that the Spouse shows the soul, comparing her to a lily,
having previously given Himself the name of Lily, establishing
this analogy so that we might understand something of His
quality and now it seems He wants to do the same that we may
understand the Bride's quality as though they were equal.
Although they are not and cannot be equal, the nature of love is
to adapt one to the object of one's love. Since He sees
that . . . we cannot be true gods, He wants to give Himself so
entirely that we might appear like Him; at every step calling
Himself the Son of man. His ardent desire to be like us, and we
like Him urges Him to use the same analogy He used for Himself
for His Bride, calling her a lily, and so excellent a one that all
the other maidens are like thistles in comparison. Happy is the
soul whom the Lord so favors and enriches that if He is a lily
she is also, and so fair and beautiful in His eyes that all other
maidens are thistles in comparison. If He were to say this solely
of the Blessed Virgin, I would say the Lord was right; but that
He should say this of other souls is something astonishing. If we
consider the infinite desire the Lord has to communicate
Himself to souls, we will cease to be surprised that those whom
He chooses for His lofty communication are such as they are; for
with every deeper understanding of Himself that He gives, He
transforms, making them so beautiful, rich and excellent that in
comparison, other souls, even daughters of Jerusalem, are but
thistles."

"The advantage," says Fr. Juan de los Angeles, "of one
soul, who merited being called the Spouse's love, over others

who are not so called, is the same advantage that the rose has over the thorns that surround it. But who would pay close attention to the tenderness and delicacy of the rose, the soul, and the danger it faces from the base company of thorns, but one who fears such company, however favored that soul is by the Divine Spouse? You are a tender flower, my soul, and live perpetually among the thorns of sins and sinners, of devils and wretchedness; you must watch, fear and be careful. You live among scorpions, said God to *Ez.* 2, 2-6, watch where you place your foot. . . Just at one who walks barefoot over ground that is thorny and full of thistles must take care where he treads so as not to hurt himself at every step, so the soul in love with God must always be careful to avoid dangers and occasions of sin, so as not to hurt herself with any sinful thorn. The rose among thorns was the symbol of a good surrounded by things evil."

St. Ambrose (in *Ps.* 99) points out that the Spouse does not say "As a lily among the thistles so is My love among the *strangers,*" but *"among the daughters".* Therefore we can see better that these very people who live closely with us, or who at least make pretence of a certain piety, are those who most prick us like sharp thorns. "Thorns," says Fr. Juan, "because of their evil habits; daughters because of the communion of the sacraments. This is the greatest suffering and grief that my own brother should be a thorn to me, hurting and afflicting me. Among such thorns we must of necessity grieve. Finally the apostle's words are quite clear and firm (II *Tim.* 3, 12): *Anyone who tries to live in devotion to Christ is certain to suffer persecution."*

"Let no one deceive himself," continues St. Ambrose, "saying that tribulations were for our fathers, and that we are now free of them . . . If you do not suffer any tribulation for Christ, see whether it is not because you still have not begun to live piously according to Him."

As long as the soul lives in mortal flesh, she must live among thorns, suffering disquiet, temptation and tribulation. If,

as the Spouse proclaims, she is a true lily, then, says St. Bernard
(*Serm.* 48) "consider how careful and vigilant she must be to
preserve a beauty surrounded on all sides by thorns that hurt and
prick all that they touch; and all the more so when this delicate
flower is scarcely able to resist the slightest prick without being
pierced and ruined. Do you now understand how right and
necessary are the prophet's words (*Ps.* 2, 11) exhorting us to
serve the Lord with fear. . .? Confirming that this is how the
soul should be, as a lily among thorns, he added (*Ps.* 31, 4):
Change me into You, my God, seeing that I am surrounded by
wretchedness and that thorns pierce me on every side. A happy
piercing indeed, whose pain worked towards his conversion.
You too will be happily pierced if you truly feel contrition.
Bene pungeris, si compungeris. . . This torn is certainly sin;
thorns are afflictions, false brethren and all the evils that
surround us. . . O white lily! O tender, delicate flower! See how
cautiously and carefully you must walk among so many
unbelievers and profaners and see how you can walk safely
among so many thorns! The whole world is full of them; they
are in the earth, in the air, and even in your own flesh. . .

"But *be of good cheer,* the Lord tells us (*John* 16, 33), *for
I have conquered the world.* Even if you are pricked and pierced
on all sides by all manner of thistles and ills do not let this
dismay or discourage you. Remember that 'sufferings bring
patience, and patience brings perseverance, and perseverance
brings hope. This hope is not deceptive, because the love of God
has been poured into our hearts by the Holy Spirit Who has
been given us' (*Rom.* 5, 3-5). Also bear in mind how the lilies lie
among thorns and how the Lord takes such care to preserve a
flower that so quickly disappears, for, how much greater care
will He not surely show His beloved Bride?. . .

"*Like the lily among the thistles.* . . A certain sign of
singular virtue is to remain virtuous even in the midst of sinners,
and to preserve the purity of innocence, Christian sweetness and
gentleness among those who only try to do us harm. . . Let us

be like that and our souls will be loved by the Lord and they will hear from His divine voice the same praise that He attributes to the Bride."

The lily among thistles is the holy soul; it is the Blessed Virgin among all other women, conceived without the stain of sin and full of every kind of grace; it is also Holy Mother Chruch, surrounded as She is by a whole crowd of sects, heresies and superstitions that continually try in vain to drown or taint her. But the Church stands firm, trusting in the Savior's promise; and the more impugned, persecuted and troubled She is, the more brilliantly she shines with the splendor of divine truth and purity of life. Both the Virgin and the Church are truly flowers of the field that "grow maintained only by Heaven and by His mercy." (Fr. Luis de León).

When the wind blows the thistles, says Fr. Avrillón, its thorns pierce the lily on all sides. But how does this beautiful flower avenge herself of such abuse? Simply by using her wounds as mouths through which to exhale the precious scent with which she embalms these same cruel thorns . . . , and with them all that surrounds her.

This is what the soul in the love of Jesus must do: in the midst of suffering, breathe out the divine fragrance of that precious Lily of the valleys, and be like Him, always flourishing (*Ecclesiasticus* 39, 19), so as to contribute with her self-denial, spirit of sacrifice and silent suffering, to the salvation of all. The more afflicted the mystical Bride is, the greater the divine fragrance she will exhale, and the more gracious and beautiful she will appear, thereby deserving to be compared to a *lily among thistles*.

v. 3)   *As an apple tree among the wild trees*
             so is my Beloved among the young men.

Being very grateful for, but confused by this wonderful comparison, far from appropriating all the praise to herself, the soul seeks to return it with interest to the Spouse, with this new comparison. The difference between a lily, which has only a

pleasing smell and appearance, and an apple tree, which apart
from being beautiful and sweet smelling, yields wonderful fruit
and gives welcome shade, is very obvious. Clearly the apple tree
far exceeds those rough, unproductive wild trees that represent
the other sons of Adam. From the latter nothing can be hoped
for, since in themselves they can produce nothing that is good.
He alone gives sweet and delightful fruits with which to redeem
all the ills of the world, being the true Tree of Life, symbolized
by the apple tree, which here means every kind of fruit-bearing
tree.

   Sicut malus. . . "In these words," writes the Ven. Mariana
de San José "we see how enlightened this happy soul is and how
full of love. She replied with such excellent praise and so easily
and quickly, a swift response being a sign of burning love and a
desire to do nothing but replay and correspond with her
Beloved, as she calls Him; for she no longer looks to see if they
will notice her or not; she wants everyone to know that she has
a Master, that she belongs to this Lord and wants to proclaim
His graces. . . She announces the wonderful greatness of her
Spouse, comparing Him to the apple tree among the wild trees.
The beauty does not come from being large, for the wild trees
are bigger and taller than the apple tree. This could be seen in
the Lord . . . : *Parvulus Filius* . . . The apple tree is a small tree
but is so fertile that in its very first year it blossoms and gives
fruit. This is what the Spouse did: when He was born He was a
flower that gave forth fruit. Eight days later He shed His blood
for the first time, guaranteeing the abundance of His mercies.
When the Bride considers these truths. . .she says to Him: My
Spouse, if I am as beautiful as a lily among thistles, You are as
beautiful as an apple tree among wild trees, being so fertile and
abundant. To You I am simply a lily without fruit, no more
than a pleasant and beautiful appearance, so weak that anyone
who touches it will stain it. For me You are an apple tree in
Whose shade I rest, and Whose sweet fruit is pleasing to my
taste. The apple tree's excellent qualities and characteristics are

many. . . It does not wait for the leaves to appear before blossoming as other trees do. For the first thing which it yields is its blossom, and then its fruit. As the fruit grows the tree fills out with leaves which is what Christ did, for when the leaf of human nature sprouted, the most perfect Flower emerged already fully formed and complete. Then He gave us the very early fruit of His tears, and eight days later His blood, thus beginning the work of our Redemption, softening the hard earth of our hearts with the tears from His eyes."

In his longed-for shade I am seated
and his fruit is sweet to my taste.

Thinking of Christ as the precious Apple Tree or as the Tree of Life, as opposed to the other apple tree in which she found death, the soul sees Him hanging from the holy Tree of the Cross and there she sits to slowly contemplate the ineffable mysteries of a love stronger than death itself that moved Him in this way to sacrifice Himself for us so as to give us life. Meditating very seriously every day upon the mysteries of the Passion and the Redemption, of the expiation and the sacrifice, she comes to know the delicate taste of the fruits of the cross. The cross will no longer be solely a flowery bed in which to rest, but a beautiful apple tree that protects with its shade and that gives fruit that is very sweet once it is ripe, although beforehand very bitter as its skin would indicate. Once this skin is removed and the fruit is chewed with affectionate meditation, having allowed it to ripen with proper perseverence, the soul will begin to taste the ineffable sweetness of this hidden manna that God keeps for those who overcome themselves in this way (*Rev.* 2, 17). "Oh, if only people knew the value of the cross," exclaims St. Margaret M. (*Works* v. 2, p. 49), "it would not be rejected in the way that it is, but rather it would be so loved and cherished that it would become the only source of pleasure." Through love of the cross, therefore, one can be sure to receive God's favors.

Indeed "No one enjoys greater consolation," the Blessed

Suso was told by *Eternal Wisdom,* "than those who are touched
by My cross. For the soul who is glad to drink the chalice of My
sufferings will receive My sweetnesses in abundance. If the skin
is bitter, the fruit is delicious." "Affliction," he adds (Ch. 19),
"separates man from the world and brings him nearer to
Heaven. . . From the cross springs humility, purity of
conscience, fervor of spirit, peace and tranquillity of soul,
discretion, recollection, charity and all the good things that
come with it. . ."

   In order to be able to experience this taste of Heaven, says
St. Bonaventure (*Serm. I in Dom. Sexages.*), the soul must be
seated, her gaze resting lovingly on the Beloved, and not tiring
herself with rambling discourse: *"Sedi*: Non discurri per mentis
distractionem, quia *qui minoratur actu, percipiet sapientiam*
(*Ecclesiasticus* 38, 25). *Et tunc fructus ejus dulcis gutturi meo,*
propter sapientialem oblectationem."

   When your soul is thus seated in His shade, He will let you
feel ineffably His adorable presence and will finally bring you to
taste the divine sweetness of His loving communication, and it
will seem to you that He has been formed and born (*Gal.* 4, 19)
in your very heart.

   "From this sweetness," writes Ruysbroeck (*The Wedding
Adornment* 1, 3. Ch. 19), "comes a chaste pleasure in the heart
and in all the sensitive forces; for whoever experiences it feels as
though surrounded and embraced within by the divine bond of
love. And this pleasure and inner consolation fill the body and
soul more copiously than any earthly pleasure, even if it were
all concentrated in one man, presuming that such a thing were
possible. In this delight or chaste pleasure, through His gifts
God communicates and pours Himself into men's hearts with
such perceptible joy and consolation that they overflow in
abundance. Thus whoever receives these consolations knows
how truly miserable the people are who live without this divine
charity. This delight melts the heart and makes it overflow with
such abundance of inner joy that it cannot be contained."

Sub umbra illius. . . "Before telling us of the sweetness of the fruit," remarks the Ven. Mariana, "she says that she sat down beneath the shade of the Apple Tree, without which she could not enjoy its sweetness, for only the Lord's shade gives men wisdom. . . It is as though she were to say: I no longer enjoy the contemplation of the mysteries of Christ in a fleeting or hurried way, but rather it is with immutability and quiet that I enjoy the sweetness of His fruits. For this is a grace that the Spouse communicates to the soul, a grace of great consolation that prepares her even more than the previous communications. This grace robes her in her wedding garment, and thus is more deeply settled within her and she sat down. . . The soul's sitting in the shade of the Apple Tree is a great mercy and favor given to one who is already rich in the exercise of virtues and has already undergone the trials and complete mortification of the senses and mental powers. Although we are often given to experience something of what is communicated by the Holy Spirit we do not do so as profoundly as the Bride does here; for when she comes to sit in the shade of this divine Apple Tree she does so only after her love for her Spouse has been stripped of all its wishes, so that she stands divested with this Tree as her only protection. She is completely alone and, because she is, she does well to sit in this divine shade which will prevent any serpent from reaching her."

There she receives the blessing of the Lord and the mercy of her Savior (*Ps.* 24, 5), being much improved and advanced in all things.

"The changes are so great," she adds, "that the soul does not seem the same as she was; for she is now the mistress and has gained strength from the fruits that she tasted, which are in a manner of speaking the same obscure mysteries of faith as before, but now so limitless and unveiled through the purity of her understanding that the entire soul comes to know their sweetness. The shade of this Tree . . . is such a sovereign good that it is no less than God Himself . . .

"In the shade of the One she desires, her understanding falls quiet and the bustle of her mental powers is stilled, allowing her to enjoy the rest and refreshment of His shade, and not merely fleetingly as before... These graces are now deeply seated... *I sat down,* by which she would seem to mean: It is no longer through my own effort... or through discourse or personal communications that I enjoy Him, but through a quiet and peaceful possession. Formerly she desired Him, now she enjoys Him, and is so fearless of His leaving her that she seems to be telling us that she has Him entirely as she wishes,... She is unrestrained so as to benefit from all that she consumes of the divine fruit of this Tree, a Tree that is not wild and sterile but productive, bearing such incomparable fruit so sweet to the Bride's taste and so substantial that with this fruit she can travel the long journey that will lead her to God on Zion."

The fruit of this Tree of Life which is so delicious to the palate, says St. Ambrose (*in Exod.* Ch. 16), "is spiritual manna, or the dew of divine wisdom which the Son of God bestows on those who ardently search for Him; a dew which fertilizes the sterility of souls flooding them with an ineffable sweetness. Whoever knows through experience the delight and worth of this mystical wisdom, will never yearn for any other food..."

Indeed, everything else causes revulsion as long as one is unable to taste this divine sweetness again. "The Bride quite rightly, then," says St. Bernard (*Serm.* 48), "longed for the shade of the One from Whom she hoped to receive both the refreshment and sustenance that she needed. For although wild trees protect with their shade they do not serve to support life, and still less do they provide perpetual fruit for the preservation of health. There is only one Author of life, just as there is only one Mediator between God and men: Jesus Christ, Who says to His Bride: *I am your salvation.* Because of this, she constantly sought Christ's shade in a very special way since, in addition to the cool refreshment He gives her against the heat of vice, He fills her with the sweet delight of virtues. 'I sat in the shade of

Him that I had desired.' The shade is His flesh, the shade is faith. . . Can I not glory in the fact that His Own flesh serves as shade for me every time that I eat of It in the Eucharist?"

This indeed is the sweet fruit of the cross: *Sacramentum Passionis Christi* as St. Thomas calls it, that is so good and pleasing to the palate of the fervent soul so that through this fruit the soul becomes transformed into Christ. . .

As far as the Church is concerned, writes Maria Dolorosa, "she is seated next to the Tree of the Cross and tastes the fruit of this Tree, which is the transubstantiated Christ, Who sustains her members and infuses whoever receives this fruit with the sweetness of His grace."

"The prophet Jeremiah," continues the holy Abbot of Clairvaux, "says that Christ is our strength. . .: *beneath His shadow we shall live among the nations* (*Lamentations* 4, 20). Take care, then, to live like the prophet beneath the shadow of Christ, so that one day you might reign with Him in His light. . . In His flesh He is the shadow of faith; in His spirit He is the light of the soul."

"The shadow of Jesus Christ," adds St. Gregory the Great "is the protection of the Holy Spirit who shelters with His grace all the souls that He visits, cooling the heat of temptations from within with His sweet breath, at the same time giving them the means to recover their strength and to run more swiftly up into the heavens. To sit in His shade is also to rest in contemplating Him, which not only protects us but gives us renewed strength with which to help our neighbors."

It should be noted that the Bride does not say she desired the shade, but her Beloved Himself; for the desire of the holy soul always goes straight to God, however difficult it is for her to see Him in this life and however impossible to enjoy Him except in darkness and then usually only for a very brief space of time.

"She sat down," writes Fr. Juan de los Angeles, "and not for ever; she enjoyed the shade, but not for long; she ate of the fruit so as to pursue her journey. . ."

"Here," says St. Teresa (*Conceptions*, Ch. 5), "she likens Him to nothing less than an apple-tree and says that His fruit is sweet to her palate. O souls that practice prayer, savor all these words! In how many ways can we think of our God! To how many different kinds of food can we compare Him! For He is manna, the taste of which is to each of us as we wish it to be . . Oh, that one could express all that the Lord signifies by it! . . . How well protected is the soul when the Lord sets it in so wondrous a place! Well indeed may it sit down and feel secure! . . . God gives these sublime consolations, and grants these great favors to persons who have labored greatly in His service and desired His love and tried to live so that all their actions may be pleasing to His Majesty. . . Putting themselves beneath the protection of the Lord, they desire none other. And how well they do to trust His Majesty, for thus they obtain the fulfillment of all they have desired! And how fortunate is the soul that has merited to dwell under this shadow . . . ! The soul seems to be wholly engulfed and protected by a shadow, and, as it were, a cloud of the Godhead, whence come to it certain influences and a dew so delectable as to free it immediately, and with good reason, from the weariness caused it by the things of the world. The kind of rest which comes to the soul here is such that it is fatigued even by having to breathe. . . A person in this state has no need, for any purpose, to move her hand, or to rise (I mean by this to practice meditation), for the Lord is giving her the fruit from the apple-tree with which she compares her Beloved: He picks it and cooks it and almost eats it for her. And so she says: 'His fruit is sweet to my palate.' For here all is enjoyment, without any labor of the faculties. . . Already the soul has said that she is enjoying the sustenance of His divine breasts. . . Now that she is more mature, He gradually prepares her to receive more. He stays her up with apples, for He desires her to understand more and more how bound she is to serve and to suffer. . ."

"When she says that she sat in the shade of the One she desired," writes the Ven. Mariana, "she means stripping herself of all her own wishes and surrendering herself into the hands or providence of God. . . which is as much as to say: I now quietly and steadily enjoy and sustain myself with the mysteries of Christ, although not with the clarity with which they will be seen in Heaven, but here in shadow. For all the light that is enjoyed here is like a shadow in comparison with that which is to be seen in Heaven. Since she tells us that she sat in the shade of her Beloved, she has Him near her. How close will He be to whichever soul is able to make the same renunciation as this Bride when she came to sit so near her Spouse, that He might cover her with His shade. . .? It seems to me that this shade is a complete giving of ourselves to whatever Our Lord would do with us: so devoted a *Fiat voluntas tua*. . . that the soul strips herself completely of her own will, that He might order and govern her in all things, leading her with His hand so that she might steadily enjoy the shade of this tree of love, where the soul is seated in wise simplicity and rich poverty, removed from all discursive communication, abandoned and stripped possessing nothing save her own nudity. It is in this state that the soul is able to enjoy the shade of the Spouse, abandoning herself completely into His hands; and here we behold the *Fiat* of which we spoke. . .

"This is the state in which the support and shadow of God are enjoyed. What this good is can be neither described nor merited; for this shadow is an illustrious cloud, heavily laden with the goods of grace, which the soul enjoys through a communication in which the Beloved makes her His Own. She calls these goods sweetest fruits, 'fruits', not only to fit in with the metaphor of the tree, but also because they actually are His fruits for without the Beloved the soul would not taste them. They are sweet to her taste for they were produced with infinite love for her good, a love which makes her capable of receiving these fruits, and supporting her so that she may be able to enjoy them . . . She now not only benefits from the Spouse's goods, but consumes them, and seem to become transformed into them: *Et fructus ejus dulcis*. . . The soul is now sustained by the fruits of Christ, and not just any fruits but those which have an essential sweetness and good taste, for previously many favors were bestowed by the Beloved's servants, but now it is the Lord Himself Who gives HImself and Who becomes so intimate with her that she enjoys His shadow and His fruit. . . "Which is what she said, that she sat down and lived without any deliberate sins, and with very few semi-deliberate ones, ate and tasted the sweetness of the fruit of this divine Tree. For to eat the fruits is one thing, and to taste their sweetness is quite another; not everyone knows their taste, only those who live depending upon the will of the Lord . . . Now that the soul has been made capable of tasting divine things, in this shadow she is shown the divinity of the fruit of this tree that she tastes not only through faith but with such clear certainty that she seems to be very close to beatitude; at least, she sees that she is with Him Who is the beatitude of those in Heaven. In order to receive all these mercies the Lord Himself must grant His favor and cast His shadow."

"Moreover", she adds, "we are such that with His sweetnesses the Lord prepares us to follow Him happily wherever He leads us. If the taste and fruit of the tree of Paradise killed us, at its foot He wants His souls to receive new life . . ., elevating the gifts that He first gave us through His passion and death, with other favors and testimonies of His love."

But although these favors are so divine, they are offered to all of us and all of us could enjoy them if we truly prepared ourselves to receive them instead of being deaf to His loving invitations. For as the same servant of God goes on to say: "our appetite and desire come to wish not so much the things that we long for but rather only that which the Lord wishes to communicate to us. He hastens, therefore, to give

Himself to such souls, and waits only for them to allow themselves to be enriched by Him. This is all that the Bride does: sit in the shade and eat the fruits of the Tree of Life. Enjoying them steadily (or sitting down) in quiet and rest, *she will taste the seven fruits* of this Tree, which are gifts of the Holy Spirit, with which the soul is so enriched and adorned that it is very fitting that she should be the Bride of the Most High."

Sub umbra illius... "The shadow of Christ the Lord," says Sr. Teresa of J.M. (*Coment.* XXV), "refers to the sacramental graces, for His Majesty is in the Holy Sacrament like a tree full of fruit. This fruit is the grace that He won for us through His works and merits, and this grace is the fruit of the sacraments but especially of the sacrament of the Holy Eucharist, because it contains the Divine Tree, Jesus Christ Himself, Who is producing this fruit in great abundance, and communicating and distributing it with great generosity... The Bride sits and dwells not only in the shadow... but with eyes of faith penetrates this Divine Tree and takes Its fruit which is so very pleasing to her palate, for as we have said, it gives grace which is so mild and gentle."

The faithful soul becomes so fixed in the contemplation of the crucified Christ, or the transubstantiated Christ, and becomes so full of the graces of His Spirit that perhaps she cannot help but join the Bride in suddenly exlaiming:

v. 4)   *He has brought me into his wine cellar*
              and ordered love within me.

"Then when the Bride had eaten," continues Sr. Teresa, "she says that He brought her into the cellar of His sweet, divine wines and ordered charity within her... Having now eaten, the Bride would quite obviously have to drink..., having received and tasted the grace given by this Blessed Sacrament it was only to be expected that through this grace she would also receive and taste an increase in charity, for this food and drink are inseparable... to be found in the same measure and to the same degree. For this reason she says: *Ordinavit in me*

charitatem; which is as much as to say: in the measure and to
the degree in which He gave me the food of grace He ordered
charity to be given to me to drink, seeing to it that grace and
charity were so ordered in me that the one should not exceed
the other even to a slight degree. The Spouse had brought His
Bride into His wine-cellar before, but that was at the very
beginning and they had been together so little that she called
Him King, not daring to call Him her Spouse; and then she does
not say that He gave her drink, only that they were happy to
see the immensity and strength of those divine wines of love"
(Sr. Teresa, *Coment* XXV).

After savoring the mysteries of the passion by suffering
with the suffering Christ, the soul comes to drink the new wine
of His Precious Blood pressed on Calvary; and this wine that
engenders virgins fills her with ineffable delights, causes her to
faint, leaving her as though drunk and sick with love, while at
the same time becoming the object of God's wonderful love and
of His divine pleasure.

First, however, she must rest in the shadow of the cross
and savor the fruits of this mystical Tree of Life; she must be
led into the storeroom or cellar where the precious wine is kept
in preparation for the Lamb's wedding. This wine-cellar is the
fifth of St. Teresa's interior mansions of the soul, and the
precious wine that is kept there is a sublime communication of
the Spirit of Wisdom that produces inebriation in the soul
during lofty contemplation. From this she emerges changed,
unrecognizable, and so strong and inspired that it seems as
though she has enlisted for a war of divine love.

Here, indeed, the soul is intoxicated by the abundance of
the house of God, drinking unchecked from the torrent of His
delights. Here the soul tastes His ineffable sweetness and
receives His secret communications so that she now knows
through experience that He is the source of life and that only
with His infused light can she see the light well (*Ps* 36, 9-10).

The Hebrew text reads: *He brought me into the guest*

chamber, that is, into the cenacle. Now, when the soul visits this mystical cenacle where the great feast of love is celebrated, she truly begins to be intimate with the heavenly Lover, and eventually manages to be led where she so much desires to be led, to the place where the precious, intoxicating wines are kept together with all the great divine treasures and where she can drink until satiated and transported, and then emerge inebriated with love and enriched with all kinds of celestial goods.

"This cenacle," writes María de la Dolorosa, "is the Church, the feast — Holy Communion, the wine-cellar — contemplation. The Bride says that she was led in there because, just as the Lord has called us to His Church and invited us to His Eucharistic Table, so He brings the soul to contemplation when and how He likes; she would strive in vain to enter on her own, for she would never succeed in doing so unless she was brought in there by her Divine Spouse. In contemplation, just as in Holy Communion, He marks the soul with the seal of His love, giving her those loving raptures that manifest themselves even externally. She is left as though wounded, all athirst with love for her loving Lord, but a thirst that is sweet, not raging; resigned, not violent."

"This, as I understand it," writes St. Teresa, speaking of the prayer of union (*Interior Castle* V, 1), "is the cellar where the Lord is pleased to put us, when He wills and as He wills. But we cannot enter by any efforts of our own; His Majesty must put us right into the center of our soul and must enter there Himself; and, in order that He may the better show us His wonders it is His pleasure that our will, which has entirely surrendered itself to Him, should have no part in this. Nor does He desire the door of the faculties and senses, which are all asleep, to be opened to Him; He will come into the center of the soul without using a door, as He did when He came into His disciples' presence and said *Pax vobis.* "

Introduxit me. . . "From the seat and shade," writes the Ven. Mariana de San José "she is taken to a more secret and interior place but it is not she that advances because she cannot make these ascents on her own nor by any other favor save by the hand of the Lord Himself Who was casting His shade over her, making her a shelter so that she could remain in silence, removed from everything in order to be captured without any impediment to this wonderful wine. I would say that this Room is Christ Our Lord. . . wherein are stored all the treasures of the Father and of the Holy Spirit, and of the infinite wisdom of this very Word Incarnate, outside of Whom there is nothing that is truly good. For, since the Bride was so well prepared and supported by the shade and proximity of the Lord, as though leading her by the hand, He brought her into this wine-cellar, which is an escape from the imaginary into the essential."

Although, as she adds, the soul must not try to enter on her own, but wait for the Lord to bring her in; "if she perseveres and keeps in step with the Spouse, following Him through humility, when she least expects it He will take her by the hand and lead her to a place which she will never want to leave. There the Holy Spirit wants to show His beloved sweet Bride His fortune and divine treasure and bring her into the store-room. He shows her its mysteries and promises and gives her them to taste to prove to her that she is not being deceived . . . manifesting the spirit of His holy law and the truths of faith. This is not all; He even instructs her in letters without her ever having studied them. He brings her to a fine appreciation of the Holy Scriptures, not to mention Theology, which the saints learned in this wine-cellar. And thus it happens that an unlearned woman can become so enlightened that what the Lord teaches in one hour could not be learned in many years at school. . .

"But, leaving aside this meaning or way of tasting the wines in this cellar, let us return to what I began to say, that to enter into these sweet joys and delights was above all to know that they are communicated to the soul when the soul is united with God. This, then, seems to be the wine-cellar in which

charity arranges within the soul all that was disorderly. O what
gifts! What delights! What riches! What glories! What divine
communications these are! O Lord, who but You could be so
merciful? Who else would be so generous as to give himself?
Who is there so wise that all infinity is contained within such a
small vessel, and then not contained within but freely poured
out . . . ?

"Well, into this wine-cellar the King brought her . . . not
only so as to show her their pricelessness but that by
discovering how lovable His attributes are . . . she might
recognize the good reasons she has for loving her sovereign
Spouse . . . each communication affecting her like a red-hot
coal . . . Or let us say that each is like a drink she takes from the
wine and is such that she is so enraptured that her understanding does not comprehend as it usually does, nor can she
remember anything save her present good, nor does she love
anything save this Lord Who is communicating Himself to her in
love . . . If she loves, she loves with His love, as one who no
longer belongs to herself but to Him Who orders love within
her. Thus He, by His hand, placed a mayor, as it were, within
this fortress that it might be ruled and governed by the Three
Persons rather than by the faculties; here it is the Third Person
Who shines forth and directs the Bride in a most marvelous
way . . .

"By His hand, then, she was brought into the wine-cellar
where she constantly enjoyed the King's treasures . . . The
movement of entering is the first step in enjoying them; and the
goods are such that one only has to look at them to be
delighted beyond words . . . Here she only says that the King
brought her into the wine-cellar but because of the con-
sequences of this we have to believe that she was given these
wines to taste and that she drank from them in great
abundance . . . for she came to enjoy the order of charity . . .
They say of wine that it comforts . . . that it cheers and warms
the heart . . . Well, all this the Lord does to the soul here . . .

returning to her what she lost through sin . . . , He strengthens her, which is necessary if she is to be able to receive so many gifts, . . . He warms her heart and cauterizes her will, that her lukewarmness might disappear and the divine fire give such communications of itself that she may become full of joy and consolation. Receiving these goods she, through the Holy Trinity, becomes a store-house and treasury of sanctification. All three Divine Persons speak to her here and communicate themselves to her with admirable distinction. Here she works with divine strength, for the order that charity establishes places each thing in its rightful place; in other words, the Bride's faculties are filled with these three wines: the memory with the Being of the Father, the understanding with Infinite Wisdom, and the will with the Holy Spirit. Not only does this order effect happiness in the soul, but God's goodness and love are such that He takes this happy soul as His own interior resting-place. He fulfills this desire when the soul has reached this degree of fulfillment. The soul, with this profound good, the presence and possession of her God and Spouse . . . loves Him with divine love; for her will is placed in God and so she loves with the Love of God; at the same time she understands with the Wisdom of God, and rejoices in the eternal Being of her Lord."

This, then, is where *charity is truly ordered,* for this charity does not manifest the wonderful order that it possesses until the soul is brought into the mystical wine-cellar where, intoxicated like the disciples in the Cenacle, she comes to love God because of Who He is and without the incentive of self-love; for truly experiencing God with the mystical gift of wisdom, the soul esteems Him as the highest Good and despises all that is not Him or that does not pertain to Him. That is why mystical life, that is, contemplation which is infused in the soul when led into this mansion, is so desirable, for it is through this that one learns to fulfill the first commandment perfectly: *You must love your God with all your heart, with all your soul, with*

all your mind and with all your strength (Mark 30, 13). This
cannot be achieved by our own efforts alone, nor in our own
human way, but rather by letting ourselves be completely
possessed by the Divine Spirit so as to proceed in the *divine way*
as true and faithful children of God (*Rom.* 8, 14) with He
Himself ordering the charity within us (Cf. *Mystical Questions*
1, p. 87; 4, p. 398).

Origin (in *Hom.* II) supposes that these words are spoken
by the Spouse Who wants to enter our souls as the King of love,
and says to all those that believe in Him: *Introducite me in
domum vini;* and adds: "Cur tam dui foris maneo?*Ecce sto ad
hostium et pulso...(Apoc.* 3, 20) ...Et nunc eadem dicit
Sermo Divinus... Vobis quoque catechumenis loquitur:
Introducite me. Introducite, non simpliciter in domum, sed in
domum vini, impleatur vino laetitiae, vino Spiritus Sancti anima
vestra, et sic introducite in domum vestram Sponsum, Verbum,
Sapientiam, Veritatem." That is how holy love will be ordered,
and is later wonderfully explained when he says: "When man
loves what he should not love, or loves with greater love than
the thing deserves or with less than it merits, then love is not
ordered within him. Very few have this order, which consists in
loving God without measure, with all one's heart, with all one's
soul, with all one's mind, giving to God the Creator and our
Father all that we are and possess. If we do not love Him as
much as our strength allows it is clear that we do not have our
love ordered. With respect to one's neighbor, love him as
yourself, as you are required as a member of the same body and
being united to the same Head, always remembering that one
owes more love to the worthier or more important members."

Those who have perfect charity, therefore, says the Ven.
Granada (*Memorial,* tr. 7: *Concerning the Love of God* Ch. 1, i)
"live an angelic and supernatural life, and so can be called angels
on earth; for they converse on earth only with the body while
the rest is in Heaven. This is what the spirit, life and
conversation of *all the saints* were like; and it is by imitating

them that *the faithful* must direct their intentions and desires."
In this way they will soon find the peace and fulfillment they
desire.

He goes on to add, "not just any degree of charity is
sufficient to give man this peace and inner fulfillment of which
we speak, but only *perfect charity.* To achieve this it should be
noted that as this virtue grows, so it works greater and more
excellent affections within the soul. First of all, charity — *when
ordered by God* — brings with it a *knowledge* and *experience* of
the goodness, sweetness and nobility of God; from this
enlightment comes an intense ardor of the will; from this ardor
a wonderful delight; from this delight an impassioned desire for
God; from desire a new fulfillment; from this fulfillment an
intoxication; from this intoxication flows a security and
complete trust in God, where our soul rests and has its *spiritual
sabbath with Him.* It seems that these eight steps are linked
together in such a way that one leads into another. . . For this
knowledge is followed by a great fire and burning. . . And this
by a very sweet delight which is that hidden manna that no one
knows save those who have tasted it (*Rev.* 2, 17); and it is a
natural consequence of walking in the company of love and
proceeding from it. . . And since spiritual things are so excellent
and so divine that the more they are tasted the more they are
desired, from this tasting proceeds an enkindled desire to enjoy
and possess this treasure. . . This desire gives way to satisfaction
— in as far as this is possible in this life — because God does not
fill His souls with desires simply in order to torment them but
rather into order to fulfill them and prepare them for still
greater things to come. Thus. . . it is He Who gives His souls
desire and satisfaction, and with satisfaction such an intense
dislike for things of the world that the soul considers them as
though they were beneath her feet, and thus is at rest, happy
and content with His sweetness alone, finding in Him the
composite of all possible pleasures and joys: she knows through
experience that *in nothing else can the rational creature find*

complete rest but in Him alone. . .

"And the happiness of these last two stages (security and rest) the Lord promised, through Isaiah, to His chosen ones when He said (*Is.* 32, 18): *And my people shall dwell in the beauty of peace, and in the tabernacles of trust, and in complete rest and furnished with every good.* This, my brother, is the Kingdom of Heaven on earth and the paradise of delights that we can enjoy in this exile; and this is the treasure hidden from the eyes of the world in the country, as described in the Gospel, and for which the wise merchant sells all that he has in order to obtain it."

"Who is he, then," he continues, "who having heard this news and knowing that divine grace is as available for him as it is for all the saints, does not go in through this door to enjoy such great goodness, here in this life?" "The perfection of Christian life," he adds, "consists in the perfection of charity. . .; so this life will be more or less perfect to the same extent in which one is more or less perfectly charitable. . . Perfect charity in this life is that which powerfully resists and rejects all that weakens and keeps the soul from this *actual love of God.* . . The more inflamed the feeling of charity and the more united to God *through actual love.* . . the more perfect it will be, being morelike that of those who dwell in Heaven who with all their strength are always and actually enkindled with the love of God. This love is what mystical theologians call *unitive* love. . . The prime concern of the servant of God is to do all that is possible to keep the soul always united with God *through prayer, contemplation and actual love. . .*"

"Whoever desires to possess perfect charity," says St. Gregory the Great (*Moral. in Job,* 1, VI, Ch. V), "must not only try to expand his activity, but also the heights of his contemplation."

"This," says St. Thomas, "is what true perfection in this life consists in: getting as near as possible, through a most perfect actual love, to the perfection of the blessed."

Ordered charity within me. "O words," exclaims St. Teresa (*Conceptions,* Ch. 6), "never to be forgotten by the soul to which Our Lord gives such favors!. . . Blessed is the sleep, and happy inebriation, wherein the Spouse supplies what the soul cannot attain and bestows on it so marvelous an 'order' that, though all the faculties are dead or asleep, love remains alive. The Lord ordains that it shall work, without knowing how, and that so marvelously that, in complete purity, the soul becomes one with the very Lord of love, Who is God. . . He sees that the Bride is lost to herself and enraptured for love of Him, and that the very strength of love has taken from her the power of understanding, so that she may love him the more. . . Meanwhile God sets love in order in the soul so that it may well know how to please Him, both then and also later, the intellect being unaware of it. But it becomes well aware of it later on, when it sees the soul so wonderfully enamored and decorated with precious stones and pearls, which are the virtues, that it is amazed and can only say: 'Who is she that has been like the sun?' O true King, how rightly did the Bride give Thee this name! For in a moment Thou canst bestow riches, and so endow a soul with them that it will enjoy them forever. How well is love set in order in such a soul! . . .

"*The King set in order charity in me,* and He sets it in order in such a way that the soul loses the love which it had for the world, and that which it had for itself turns into indifference. The soul's love for its neighbors and for its enemies would be thought incredible if it were not proved by experience. It has grown greatly; while its love for God so far exceeds all limits that weak nature is oppressed beyond endurance and, seeing that it is fainting and at the point of death cries: *Stay me up with flowers. . .*"

The Hebrew text, instead of *ordered charity within me,* reads: *The banner He raises over me is His love;* or *His banner over me is His love* which means His love serves as an unfurled banner so that we can follow Him everywhere as though in a battle of love... For this reason the soul was led into the wine-cellar of divine contemplation, whose sign or banner is burning love.

His pure love now reigns in me, banishing all servile fear; and indeed He so ordered it that the soul loves no one now but Him and what He Himself wants her to love and in the way that He wishes; or, as St. Thomas says, He has placed a well ordered love in me such that, denying myself and renouncing self-love, I love myself and my neighbor only through Him and love Him for Himself and above all things.

This is the best possible way in which we will fulfill His holy will in all things. For, as St. Margaret Mary remarks (*Oeuvres* t. 2, p. 229): "Only the pure love of God is capable of moving us to do all to please Him; and only this perfect love will enable us to do it in the way that pleases Him, and it is not possible for there to be any other way of knowing how to do all that is pleasing to Him."

"It should be known," says St. John of the Cross (*Spirit. Cant.* stanza 26), "that however spiritual a soul may be there always remains, until she reaches this state of perfection, some little cluster of appetites, satisfactions, and other imperfections, natural or spiritual, after which she follows, in an effort to pasture and satisfy it... Some have more and others less of this flock, and they follow until, having entered the interior wine-cellar to drink, all transformed in love, they lose it entirely. In this wine-cellar these swarms of imperfections are more easily consumed than the rust and tarnish of metal is consumed by fire. Thus the soul now feels free of all the childish likes and trifles which she pursued." Thus, should we not urgently seek and try to win at whatever cost such a great good that frees us from all our miseries?

"Would that the King would bring us into His wine-cellar," exclaims Fr. Juan de los Angeles, "and let us even just taste that miraculous wine, even were it to bring us the trouble it brought the apostles when they drank it and were taken for drunkards;

as though wine could teach strange languages and not confuse its own . . . ! It is a wine which, then taken by youths and maidens, gives them a thirst for virginity."

We could all receive this favor in accordance with our needs were we to really try to achieve it by preparing ourselves in the proper way. According to St. Jerome (*Epist. ad Damasum*), "the coming of the Son of God into the world gave pure souls access to the room where this wine is kept. God always had a wine-cellar; but He spoke with His loved ones in the doorway, and would bring wine for them to drink there in a limited amount. After He became man, He removed the high lintel that prevented souls from entering the divine wine-cellar (*Is.* 6, 4), and made the entrance open and free, not to all, but to those whom the King wants to enter. This is why it says: *Introduxit me Rex. . .* One does not enter according to one's own free will but in accordance with the wishes of the Eternal King. It is a gift for friends and very close friends: the friend drinks and the very close friend becomes intoxicated. Some are told (*Ps. 34, 9*): "O taste and see how sweet the Lord is;" others are told to open their mouths. . . (*Ps. 81, 11*). *Richard writes* that: "only those whom the Lord led out of Egypt and brought into His wine-cellar are told: *Open your mouth wide and I will fill it.* The promise is a very great one, as is its secret. What do the Egyptians hunger and thirst after? Temporal and carnal things. And those that left Egypt? Spiritual and celestial things. The latter are told to open wide their mouths for they will be given what they desire without measure. What is the mouth of inner hunger but the heart's desire. . . ? Open your mouth, then, and increase your desires as much as you are able; for the greater you make them (with respect to spiritual goods) the more capacity you will have to contain them, the happier you will be . . . So not be shy in desiring nor cowardly in asking, but open your heart and soul as much as you can, for however much you manage to do so, it will never be too much. Whoever merited entry into the wine-cellar of the Eternal King can well increase their desire sure that they will have more than enough wine to become intoxicated."

On the other hand, he continues, "until the soul enters this wine-cellar, everything is thirst, entreaty and poverty and there is nothing to satisfy or fill the breasts and empty spaces of the heart. The wine-cellar means satisfaction, the fulfillment of desire, joy, abundance and rapture. If it were not so, neither would the Bride boast of having gone into the wine-cellar, nor would she speak to her maidens about it as though it were something wonderful."

"The soul," he adds summarizing Tauler (*Serm. 1 Dom. p. Epiph.*), "is left so strengthened and renewed that to her death seems very little for her to suffer for her Beloved. Like another St. Paul, she defies all ills, judging herself to be superior to them all, and very powerful in everything through Him Who strengthens her. This is part of the intoxication, because those who have drunk from the wine are very daring and fear nothing. . .

"When God sees the soul surrender herself completely and unreservedly to the taste and consolation of this very sweet and strong wine that He gave her to drink freely, He takes it away and hides it, filling the soul with such bitterness and pain that it seems as though she had never tasted God nor ever known what joy is. Why all this? So as to draw her to Him, by bringing her first to forget creatures through the gift of His celestial wine, and then to leave her to herself so that she can realize in this way what she is capable of doing through God and what she is able to do when left to her own devices. In the state of inebriation her desire went far beyond what was required of her, it sometimes being controlled, sometimes not; but in this state of poverty and misery she can hardly utter a single word. . .

"The Bride drinks and drinks without restraint; for she enters the wine-cellar and leaves it with charity well-ordered. When God's friends first drink from the delicious wine of His sweetness, they cannot retain it: it stirs about within them, it intoxicates them and they become disordered in some way. But by transporting them in this way beyond themselves and their own strength, and by drawing them into Him, God communicates Himself to them in such a different and far more excellent way that from now on everything is ordered within them; it is thus that we must consider the Bride. . . 'Here God ordered the Bride marvelously,' says Tauler, 'and brought her along wonderful deserted paths into the depths of His divinity, into Himself, and there He gave her what is impossible to achieve or describe through the outer senses because it is beyond them and beyond all human understanding. And, indeed, He saved her and gave her the taste of eternal life: *Re ipsa namque vitae aeternae vera quaedam praelibatio fuit.*' "

"The *Introduxit me*," writes the Ven. Mariana, "in my opinion, is the act of letting oneself be instructed by this Lord, of paying such close attention to what He teaches that the soul thereby comes to be enlightened and wise, that no other affection dwells within her but charity, that the Holy Spirit becomes the true Master of her house. . . By obeying Him and following His voice she reached this room, and merited . . . that love should be her master and love should be her direction and life. For love is the order of life, and life itself for this soul, as she says here: *and He ordered charity within me.* Thus this soul's life is now the Holy Spirit, Who is Love. If the soul's life and occupation is the Holy Spirit . . . and if she has no other life but this love she can quite rightly call Him my Life; for He truly is her Life, and is the One Who gives her life and orders it, showing her how the immortal Lord gave His own life that she too might have life."

The fruits are such that the soul seems to begin to live among the angels and saints in Heaven; and the same servant of God describes them very well from her own experience, on another occasion, when she writes: "It seemed to me that the faculties were full of riches and that they worked marvelously without hindering one another, for the Holy Spirit was guiding them. It is not like other kinds of prayer in which only the will seems to work: for the soul has now reached such a state that all her faculties seem to have the powers of those in the Kingdom of Heaven . . . for her kingdom is in God and she cannot love anyone but Him, nor understand anything except His wishes . . . ; and so it seems to me that it was said of these people that *Justo non est imposita lex,* because those who reach this point keep all laws in just keeping one and this one law is the law of love. . . This is the sign that they follow, and this voice is always heard there, there is no other, and this same voice guides and gives light. O what virtues are taught here! How perfect are those who dwell here, accomplishing by their example *more in a single day than could be achieved any other way in a thousand years.*"

This demands a complete and trusting surrender into God's hands, from which come sanction and recompense.

"When through love we deny our own will and give ourselves to that of God in such a way that we no longer wish for anything except what God wishes, then," writes Ruysbroeck (*The Seven Guardians of Love,* Ch. 13), "we make a profession of true sanctity to God, whatever our condition, whatever our state in life. However, when we seek to be certain and sure, instead of trusting in God, when our will wants and does not want, it is still not yet united with the divine will . . . and we cannot profess love but must remain novices. . . When love recovers and burns within us to such an exalted degree that it completely destroys within us all such imperfect love, all pain and fear of losing and hope of gaining . . . and all that by which we seek our own ends, then there will be a pure, clean and perfect charity. In this *cella vinaria* not only is love set in order but all the other virtues as well, for here is to be found their source, their life, their growth, their sustenance and their conservation, in their proper order and variety of expression according to the action performed and the habits acquired. Charity, however, rests with the Beloved in the inner chamber, beyond reason and beyond the exercise of virtue as such; there . . . the soul has all that she can desire and long for, never having to look outside herself for anything, for she has God within her and is enraptured in her ascent to God, being stripped of everything. She is made to transcend reason when ordinary means fail and in happy ignorance without hesitation, she is captivated by love."

St. John of the Cross, in his turn, explains (Stanza 26): "He put me in the secret wine-cellar . . . means that when I was put in His love, He gave me love to drink; or, more clearly and properly speaking: He put His charity in order in me, accommodating and appropriating His Own charity to me. Hence the soul drinks of the Beloved's very Own love, which He infuses in her." This is how she will come to be possessed by divine love and united and transformed in the One she loves. For, "As the drink is diffused through all the members and veins of the body, so this communication is diffused substantially in the whole soul, or better, the soul is transformed into God. In this transformation she drinks of God in her substance and in her spiritual faculties. With the intellect she drinks wisdom and knowledge; with the will, sweetest love; and with the memory she drinks refreshment and delight in the remembrance and feeling of glory."

"Although these wines," writes Fr. la Puente (*Guia*, tr. 2, Ch. 1), "are sometimes given to a soul to taste outside this wine-cellar, when Our Lord communicates them to her without any previous cause, more normally they are given in abundance only to those who have entered in through prayer, meditation and contemplation, they follow the inspiration of the King of Heaven Who guides them and leads them with His hand moving their wills to open wide their mouths so that they may be filled with heavenly affection. This is comparable to wine for it gladdens the heart and dispels all sadness; it strengthens the soul for the service of God removing all human fear; it excites the spirit stirring about like new wine surging with desires for magnificent things, sloughing off all idleness in undertaking them; and sometimes with a holy intoxication it makes man forget himself and all things on earth and undertake things that far exceed his strength. Although his principal strength is in the spirit, often in its overflow, the spirit communicates some to the flesh, bringing the flesh with it into the wine-cellar and giving it to drink the wines it has drunk from, so that both the heart and the flesh delight together in God (*Ps.* 84, 3). . .

"But in this entry the King of Heaven Himself must order charity, putting order in the affections." "He establishes this order," he adds, "by raising over our hearts the banner of the pure love of God, which is the heart's new law, coming from the New Man Jesus Christ. . . And because this Sovereign Captain and Eternal King raised His banner of love when He was on the cross, through meditation you are to enter the wine-cellar, which is His Sacred Heart, through the doors of His wounds so that you might there be enraptured by the flaming affection that is enkindled from meditating on His loving works. O King of Heaven Who brought Your beloved Bride into the wine-cellar of heavenly wines, for were You not to bring her in she would be unable to enter on her own, bring me also into its innermost part so that I might leave with such a desire to attain virtue, that I may achieve perfection for Your sake. Amen."

"He brought me into the wine-cellar and I followed Him, offering no resistance to being led into this mystical darkness and to being cut off from discourse and the human mode of meditation through the repose of contemplation; for the banner which draws me after it and which I follow, just as soldiers, follow their banner, is the banner of His love. It follows that whoever is not mad loves whoever he knows loves him; and loving him, he trusts in him; and trusting in him he lets himself be led unquestioningly wherever the other wishes; for he will lead him only to a place where he will profit. In the Scriptures wine signifies all that is joy and delight; so that to enter into the wine-cellar is to inhabit and enjoy, and not partially but entirely, all the greatest joy." (M. León)

We could all enjoy this great happiness if we were to try to be docile to the invitations of God and to follow the banner of pure love, renouncing human ways and intentions. Therefore "whoever you are," writes St. Bernard (*Serm.* 49), "you too will be able to say that the Spouse brought you into the mystical wine-cellar provided that you recollect your spirit with the proper care, strip yourself of importunate cares and enter alone into the house of prayer; and placing yourself there in His divine presence, with the hand of your desire you touch the gates of glory, presenting yourself before the heavenly choirs with fervent devotion, for the prayer of the just man penetrates the heavens, weeping in their sight because of the miseries and troubles that afflict you, and at the same time, showing them your needs through continual weeping and inexpressible moaning so as to move them to compassion. If you do this, I again assure you that you also will enter the wine-cellar of divine love, for I cannot do less than believe Him Who said (*Matt.* 7, 7) *Ask and you shall receive.* For if you continue to call out you will never leave His presence unfulfilled. Rather, when you have prayed in this way you will return to the company of your brethren full of grace and charity, you will be unable to contain the fervor of your burning heart and, however hard you try, you will not succeed in concealing the gifts you have received. Generously communicating these graces to them, you will not only make yourself lovable to them, but will also become worthy of the admiration of the rest, and will also have the right to glory in having indeed been brought into the wine-cellar like the Bride. I advise you just one thing and that is to take great care not to attribute it to yourself, but to the Lord."

In the Church, according to some fathers, this *wine-cellar* is meant to be the Holy Scriptures in which holy souls find their hearts' delights; according to others it is the gifts and graces of the Holy Spirit with which the Savior promised to enrich souls;

it is in this wine-cellar or store-room that the mystical wine and holy oil — fortitude, wisdom, devotion and love — are kept... (Petit).

v. 5)   *Sustain me with flowers, comfort me with apples,*
         for I am sick with love.

When the soul drinks this spiritual wine she becomes so enraptured that she faints, unable to bear the natural weakness resulting from such an abundance and excess of favors and gifts. Asking for some alleviation, she explains the cause of her sickness, saying she is as though pierced by shafts of divine love, as we read in the Septuagint: *because I am stricken with love.* As a remedy she asks for objects whose fragrance will sustain, strengthen and restore her to herself again. It should be noted that the Hebrew word *aschischoth,* translated as *flowers,* is more commonly interpreted as perfume boxes or flasks of wine, which would undoubtedly produce even greater rapture in the soul. To be sustained and revived from her faint, therefore, she asks to be given the very same thing that caused this sickness, for the love-stricken soul can be cured only by being stricken further; and she will not be completely cured until she is wholly dissolved in a wound of love (cf. *The Mystical Evolution,* p. 501). For this reason, being now so enraptured, she desires even greater rapture.

"The flowers and apples the Bride asks for in order to be revived from her faint," writes Scio, "are the flowers and fruits of that same tree in whose shade she had been sitting. In the suffering and bitterness of this state souls find consolation in the words, virtues and example of the Crucified Christ." Her cure then, is to be found in the fragrance of virtues. She strives to sustain herself with the flowers of virtue and fruits of good works to please the Bridegroom and to find rest in His loving arms. In practicing these through love of her Spouse, she begins to spend herself with ardor and zeal to the great benefit of her neighbors, thus producing precious fruits of good works that will comfort, strengthen and sustain her, and she will gain more and even greater gifts and consolations. With these she will recover her true health as she experiences the pain of this blessed wound more and more intensely, impelling her to cry out:

I am stricken with charity. . . "Whoever does not know the pain of this wound," says St. Gregory (*Homil. XV in Ezech.* 40, 7), "is ill in his very health. But when the soul begins to cry out with heavenly desire and to experience love's wound, then although previously ill with 'good health', she now becomes healthier by being stricken. . . One thing normally consoles the soul who is sick with the desire to gaze upon her Spouse: the fact of seeing that others are cured by and benefit from His doctrine. . . For this reason she says: *Sustain me with flowers, comfort me with apples, for I am sick with love.* What are these flowers but souls who are beginning to do good and to exhale the fragrance of holy desires? And what are these apples but perfect souls who transform holy desires into fruits of good works? Thus, sick with love, she asks to be sustained with flowers and comforted with apples because during the time she is not given to see the One she desires, she finds great consolation and joy in the progress made by others. Therefore the holy soul sick with love must be sustained with flowers and apples, so that, unable to contemplate the face of God, she might find rest in the good works of her neighbor."

Fr. Juan de los Angeles writes, "St. Gregory understands these flowers to refer to those souls who are beginners, weak in virtue, or newly converted to the faith; and the apples to refer to the last thing to appear on the tree, that is, to souls who are perfect. The former the Bride wants near her so as to help them; the latter so as to imitate them; for the love-sick soul, tried by the absence of her Beloved, has only this consolation and relief: the conversion and progress made by other souls. . . In *Ecclesiasticus* (39, 17-19) the just are called flowers and fruits: *Obaudite me divini fructus.* . . 'Listen to me, divine fruits, and blossom like the rose that grows on the bank of a watercourse.

Give off a sweet smell like incense, flower like the lily, spread
your fragrance abroad, sing a song of praise blessing the Lord
for all His works.' There could be no clearer confirmation of
this than what St. Gregory says, that the just are divine flowers
and fruits with which the Bride wants to see herself surrounded
and adorned... Gilberto Genebrardo adds... that this is a very
famous passage for the invocation of saints, to whom the
Church here calls in great anguish: "ut ipsorum precibus eam in
hoc mundo fulcire velint, et constipare, quia Sponso suo
abeunte in coelum, vel ab ea discente in animi diliquium rapitur,
ejusque amicos sanctos invocare cogitur, ut ipsorum orationum,
instar incensi, aut florum odore confirmata, immensi amoris
impetum, quo jam languet, et frangat, et moderetur...

"I am sure that by flowers and apples the Bride here means
particular favors and spiritual gifts, which will either comfort
love's sickness or moderate its forcefulness.

"The love-sick soul is one who is completely merged into
the love of her heavenly Spouse, so that forgetful of herself and
all around her, she is as though oblivious and without feeling,
satisfied by nothing save the sight of her Beloved... How
happy, how very, very happy is the soul who is sick with divine
love! And how unhappy is she who suffers the sickness, or more
precisely, the madness of death of worldly love...! Those who
share the Bride's sickness are they, and they alone, who gain
entrance into the wine-cellar of the Eternal King and drink the
wine that enraptures all who partake of it, bearing them up to
God, transforming the human into the divine."

Thus these souls continually cry out from the depths of
their hearts, ardently longing for the One Who so wounded
them; and they faint dying because they cannot die, longing to
leave this mortal body at once so as to fly to Him, no longer
able to bear earthly conversation and the abject company of
creatures feeling strange and out of place in their midst...

Fulcite me floribus... "I am not content," writes Sr.
Teresa of J.M. (Coment. XV), "Merely to be sick, rather my

Spouse Who is the very Flower of the field must come to me
and sustain me... And feed me with the divine apples of the
heavenly Paradise, the three Divine Persons. He must feed me in
such a way that I am filled and wholly satisfied. Until this
happens I shall always be sick and my spirit will always be
fainting."

In these souls the words of the Lord Himself are fulfilled:
Ego occidam, et ego vivere faciam, which Sr. Teresa of J.M., in
her *Commentaries on Several Passages in the Holy Scriptures*
(XII), interprets in this way: "I have slain you with respect to
all things of the world and the senses to give you life with
respect to things spiritual and divine. I wound you with the fire
of My love and with this I will cure you of any earthly or
sensual affection. There is no one that can or could ever take
you from My hand, for I shall keep you and protect you in a
most wonderful way."

Thus, says St. Teresa (*Inter. Castle*, V, ii), it is wonderful
to see "the restlessness of this little butterfly, though it has
never been quieter or more at rest in its life! ... It knows not
where to settle and make its abode. By comparison with the
abode it has had, everything it sees on earth leaves it
dissatisfied, especially when God has again and again given it
this wine which almost every time has brought it some new
blessing. It sets no store by the things it did when it was a
worm... It has wings now; how can it be content to crawl along
slowly when it is able to fly? All that it can do for God seems to
it slight by comparison with its desires. It even attaches little
importance to what the saints endured, knowing by experience
how the Lord helps and transforms a soul, so that it seems no
longer to be itself or even its own likeness. For the weakness
which it used to think it had when it came to doing penance is
now turned into strength... Everything wearies it, because it
has proved that it can find no true rest in creatures... But
where will the poor little creature go?... What trials begin
afresh for this soul! Who would think such a thing possible after

it has received so signal a favor?. . . Oh, the greatness of God!
Only a few years since, perhaps only a few days, this soul was
thinking of nothing but itself. Who has plunged it into such
grievous anxieties?. . . The grief I am referring to is not like that
caused by these kinds of meditation. . . That grief does not like
that caused by these kinds of meditation. . . That giref does not
reach to the depths of our being, as does this grief, which,
without any effort on the soul's part, and sometimes against its
will, seems to tear it to pieces and grind it to powder. What
then, is this grief? Whence does it come . . . ? Have you not heard
concerning the Bride. . .that *God put her in the cellar of wine
and ordained charity in her?* Well, that is the position here. The
soul has now delivered itself into His hands and His great love
has so completely subdued it that it neither knows nor desires
anything save that God shall do with it what He wills. . . His will
is that, without understanding how, the soul shall go thence
sealed with His seal."

"But . . . , how is this? asks the V. Mariana de St. José
"We have just said that He ordered charity within her . . . and
now the Bride tells us that she is sick and needs flowers and
apples to strengthen her . . . How are we to explain these
riches in the light of such poverty and need? The truth is that
this is very great wealth, for whoever loves God possesses
every good . . . This sickness with which the soul emerges is
true health . . . If we understand this to be the loathing and
disgust the soul feels for worldly things after she has tasted
the divine . . . it is an effect produced in the Bride by having
entered the wine-cellar . . . Another effect is the anguish and
very sweet pain at being unable to give anything to the
Lord, for everything has been given to her in love. She loves
greatly but without giving anything to the Beloved. The soul is
troubled and filled with anguish with the realization that she
has nothing to give, nor anything with which to repay a part of
what she owes; and says: *Fulcite me.* . . 'Sustain me with apples
and flowers' which are intense desires and ardent affections, for

she finds herself without them, with only a flame burning within her. She desires to throw more fuel on the fire to be secure for she knows its worth and does not wish to be deprived of it. Therefore she asks for flowers, which when enkindled are fragrant, and for apples or works beautiful and pleasing to the Spouse, not finding these within herself to give Him.

Oh, in what a state the soul must have been when she left that room of union where she received so much from the Spouse! For although His gifts are eternal our capability is so limited that it cannot always enjoy them in this... the experience as described here cannot be enjoyed for more than a very brief space of time... Although the soul remains the same, she will normally take a long time to completely regain the use of her senses... Eventually she emerges completely enkindled in love, not a passionate love, nor anything which will disturb the serenity of natural judgement, but rather a wisdom that dispels all ignorance, a light that enlightens the understanding, for everything that is not wisdom flees. For there is no true wisdom save in the love of this Spouse, He Who is infinite Wisdom giving Himself completely to the miserable creature. When He enlightens her that she might know His goodness, He also enkindles her with this light so that she becomes lost... leaving herself she enters into Him saying 'I am sick, sustain me with flowers...'

"O Lord, would there were many sick with this sickness, and ordered in charity which would be their queen and mistress within them rather than rejected in lukewarm souls such and I am! But the enkindled soul is a sea of love... she is a sea of love... she utters words of love revealing her longings and desires, desires to do the works of one who now has life; for contrary to bodily sickness which drains away life, her sickness bestows it, and not to be ill with this love-sickness is death. Truly this is a good of inestimable worth, but since the body is imperfect, it cannot bear it, so it groans... while esteeming it above all else. Sometimes it happens that the body fears its own death while the soul loves the good it possesses. . .The whole cure resides in being disencumbered of mortality . . . giving rise to torment and to a secret and very painful martyrdom. . . This yearning is so strong that it would soon destroy her were she not to find her cure; and even were she to give her life to find it, she would regard it as bought cheaply . . . as the soul in this state considers herself fortunate to give her life for her Lord. This is also her grief that later she will find no way of losing her life for His love, and to live without dying for Him is more difficult than life itself. How little the worldly believe this, living only to indulge in their pleasures! How little they know of the sweetness of leaving everything for the Spouse . . .! Nothing but these flowers and fruits can satisfy the Bride who has experienced His presence, therefore asking for them is her continual occupation. But one thing ought to be carefully noted here: what is passing through her soul, for before entering the wine-cellar, she was full of longing to enter, her every care being directed towards speeding her progress along the path to the tasting of these wines. . . After entering, she seems to leave it thirstier still, with greater longings, and with a more ardent efficacy in searching for ways to give and surrender herself more to love. She came with yearnings and burning desires which made life insupportable, for she was, as it were, dying of love; and emerges with a love yet more inflamed. . .

"Perhaps she is lamenting that she is not dying from this sickness, but only sick or weak and needs to be given flowers of the lives of the saints to be strengthened by imitating them and by learning from the fruits of their sufferings and severe mortification. She anxiously begs for opportunities to exercise herself; for as we have already said, she will die if she cannot have them. No one sick with this wound would want to be without it, and quite rightly so. Some souls, however, suffer it with a very sweet, continual lament. The pains of this sickness are so delectable and precious that only those who suffer them can comprehend them and, I believe, only He Who wounded the soul knows this."

"To fall into this kind of fainting," says St. Ambrose in (*Ps.* 118, 81), "is to dwell only upon that which is desired, to be intimately united with it, to be dissolved and, as it were, transformed into the loved object. The more the soul is weakened with the vehemence and ardor of such desires, the more she feels the increase of charity within her; just as the more ardently she desires to be united with Him Who is her true salvation, so the more strongly and intensely she feels these faintings within her; but through them she overcomes her human weaknesses and robes herself in divine virtue and strength."

Let us all, then be like the Ven. Grananda (*Comp. de Doct. espir.*, Ch. 26), crying out day and night: "Give me grace, Lord to love You with all my heart, with all my soul and with all my being, as You command us to do. . .O precious, fragrant, delectable Spouse! O my heart's sweetness! O my soul's life and my spirit's happy rest! O Lord, wound the deepest part of my soul with the shafts of your love and enrapture it with the wine of Your perfect charity. . . When will You carry me off, submerge, transport and hide me within You, where I might never perish?"

Charity will be perfect, he adds (*Memorial*, tr. 7, Ch. 2), "when man despises all ephemeral things and takes no pleasure or disorderly satisfaction in any of them, but rather, all his pleasure, love, cares, desires and thoughts are in God with such continuity that his heart is always, or nearly always placed in God, finding no rest apart from Him and finding it only in Him. When he lives in this way only for God, dying to everything else, and when with the greatness of His love he triumphs over all other loves, then he will have entered the cellar of precious wines of the true Solomon where, inebriated with this wine of love he will forget all things, even himself for God."

No one has any reason to become fainthearted, for if he perservere in asking and in trying to be completely faithful, maintaining himself continually in the presence of God, sooner or later "the Lord will see fit," says the Ven. Tome de Jesus (*Trabajos de Jesus;* aviso 12), "to open the door, to dispel the mist and bring him into the house of the sweet-smelling wines of His love, and order charity in his soul. Then, when He speaks all human tongues will cease and he will rest and sleep in peace and in God Himself."

"It is understood," writes the Ven. Mariana finally, "that the tasting of these wines is gained through prayer and enjoyed through the union of the soul with God. If the wine-cellar is Christ Our Lord, all wines are in Him . . . and the straight road to reach this room is the imitation of His life. He is the Gate through which we pass into the joys and treasures of the Father."

Souls who have begun to enjoy these intimate communications of the Divine Spouse also experience many other sufferings when they see themselves deprived of His sweet presence and placed in darkness and barrenness. Then they ask to be comforted with the precious fragrance which comes from the remembrance of the Savior's words, works, and sufferings.

It is not surprising, observes St. Bernard (*Serm.* 51), "that when the Bride has been favored not only with the presence but also with the companionship and familiar conversation of the Spouse, and brought into His very chamber, which is the innermost recess of His heart, it is not surprising, that she should fall into a kind of faint wondering at such excesses and carried away by vehement desires to see herself in the quiet possession of the One she loves. For the more painful His absence is, the more welcome His presence has to be. And certainly, after having sat in the shade of her Beloved, having eaten at His table, and having drunk from His very chalice, it is only natural that, seeing herself without Him now, she should return to her companions to tell them that her suffering is the effect of the love with which she burns, asking them to help her by comforting her with flowers until she can again return to her

Beloved, for His delay fills her with an intolerable torment: *Refrigerata umbra, cibata fructu potata calice... molestissime sustinet demorantem....*" So we see that holy souls, unable on many occasions to bear the heat of the fire of divine love, faint and so are deprived, either wholly or in part, of the use of their external senses. In such a situation they sometimes really need to be comforted with flowers and apples, that is, with the words and examples of their sweet Spouse in Whose life, passion and death they always find the most opportune remedy for all their ills, and courage to exercise themselves in things that are pleasing to God, and with which they will merit new visits and favors. "Ergo ex bonis operibus," adds the mellifluous Doctor, "recipit consolationem mens assueta quieti, quoties sibi (ut assolet) lux contemplationis subtrahitur."

"She asks to be renewed with flowers that please her tender Lover...; she asks for the fruits of His blood to make her beautiful in His eyes, for her only care is to please the Spouse, and all her efforts are to this end." (Maria de la Dolorosa, *Illustr. sul Cantico,* 2,5)

Stay me up with flowers. These flowers have a different perfume from any that we know on earth. I understand the Bride to mean that she is asking to be enabled to accomplish great things in the service of Our Lord and her neighbor, and for the sake of this she rejoices to lose her delight and pleasure; for, although it belongs rather to the active life than to the contemplative, and she will apparently be the loser if this petition is granted, yet, when the soul is in this state, Martha and Mary never fail, as it were, to work together. The interior part of the soul is spent in the active life, and in things which seem to be exterior; but, when active works proceed from this source, they are like wondrous and sweetly scented flowers. The tree from which they come is love of God for His own sake alone, without self-interest; and the perfume of these flowers is wafted abroad, to the profit of many; it is a perfume which does not vanish quickly, but endures, and works great blessings... This, I think,

must be one of the greatest comforts on earth, to see good
coming to souls through one's own agency. It is then, that one
enjoys the most delicious fruit of these flowers. Happy are they
to whom the Lord grants these favors and strictly are they
bound to serve Him. . . One of these souls does more good by
her words and deeds than many whose intentions are soiled
with the dust of our sensuality and with some measure of self-
interest.

So it is not long before she is rewarded with new and
ineffable consolations.
v. 6)   *His left hand is under my head,*
               and his right embraces me.
The first phrase could very well be interpreted to indicate
a strong desire that will not take long in being satisfied. It is as
though she were to say, writes Maria Dolorosa: "There is no
creature in Heaven or on earth that can support my head by
influencing my spirit. You alone, Divine Spouse, Who have
wounded me and left Your seal upon me, You alone can
support me in my fainting, by embracing me and placing me
next to Your heart. . ."
When the soul faints, through the force of divine love, the
One Who really supports her is Jesus Christ with the
remembrance, the power and efficacy of His sufferings and the
grace with which He makes her faithful in following His
example and imitating His virtues. Supporting her very well
with His *left hand,* that is with the adversities, trials and
humiliations which He sends her for some time so as to prevent
her from fainting. . . He will then comfort and console her with
the ineffable caresses of His *right hand,* in which, says the
Psalmist *there are everlasting pleasures (Ps.* 16, 11), and with
His strength will defend, protect and prevent her from receiving
any serious or lasting injury from all her adversaries. For the
soul who imitates and loves Jesus will always have enemies; if
no others she will have those of her immediate surroundings
who are always ready to trouble her under every kind of

pretext: these are the *daughters of Jerusalem.*

According to Fr. Gracian, the Divine Spouse's left arm can also be taken to mean His Providence in temporal things, for when the soul, in raptures of love, casts these things into oblivion, placing them as it were beneath her head, she succeeds in being embraced by the right arm which provides her with an abundance of eternal things bringing her to enjoy now the delights of glory.

In the Church, the Spouse's left and right, says Petit, are persecutions and peace; His left afflicts and humiliates, His right uplifts and supports. In her persecutions and afflictions the Church needs the assistance of this right hand to prevent her from succumbing; and when prospering, afflictions and adversities prevent her from lessening in fervor. And so, just like souls, the Church is sustained by these vicissitudes.

But the Lord sends adversity to His Own Spouses only in order to purify and uplift them, making them worthy and capable of receiving greater consolations and favors. For this reason when the devout soul sees herself supported by the Lord's *left hand,* that is, the passing adversities and humiliations, then she can hope for God's consolation with greatest confidence, saying that since *His left hand is under my head* at the moment, later *with His right He will embrace me.*

Thus she will be completely comforted and restored and will consider all her efforts, however great and extraordinary, as well spent.

"How much strength and courage will the soul recover from her Beloved's presence," says St. Bernard (*Serm.* 51), "having become faint and ill simply through His being absent! He does not allow His beloved Bride, then, to be troubled for long, but without delay presents Himself to her for it is impossible for Him not to fly, to the one He had called with such ardent longing and desire. Finding, moreover, during His absence a great faithfulness in good works and a great application in the practice of virtues as revealed by the flowers

and fruits with which she asks her companions to strengthen
her, the Spouse now wants to bring her to enjoy new favors and
to bestow new graces upon her, embracing her tenderly. . .
Happy the soul that rests on the Heart of Jesus Christ and
reclines in the arms of the Divine Word!"

"Happy is the soul," exclaims St. Ambrose (in *Ps.* 118),
"who has the good fortune to be so embraced by Divine
Wisdom! And what great hands these are that thus caress and
cherish her! They are, indeed, hands that embrace the whole
soul and that encompass and fortify her on every side when she
has reached the spiritual marriage with the Word of God. This is
certainly the soul under whose head the Eternal Wisdom places
His left hand, stretching forth His right hand so as to embrace
her and support her in her entire body of works and acts of
virtue."

"O good God!" exclaims Fr. Juan de los Angeles, "How
well You fulfill the function of Lover caressing souls who seek
their consolation and peace of heart in You alone! . . . But what
will a soul feel when God embraces her and brings her so closely
to Him?. . . I believe this is something that cannot be described
with any words or reasoning; and I also believe that whoever
experiences it most is most reserved in speaking about it; his
experience deprives him of speech and imposes silence upon
him. For there is so much for the soul to experience that she is
completely occupied, being free for nothing else."

Thus, in extreme peace and tranquillity she sleeps and rests
in God and God watches over her.

v. 7)   *I charge you, daughters of Jerusalem,*
            by the gazelles, by the hinds of the fields
            not to stir my love nor rouse her
            until she please.

This is how the first section or Song ends, with this
mystical dream in which the holy Bride begins to possess the
Good she so longed for: "Tenet eum quem quaesivit, et
abundantia caritatis fruitur." (Gietmann, *h.* 1)

Do not stir my Beloved... "The word 'Beloved', 'Dilectam'," says the Ven. Mariana, "although very brief is one of the words most filled with love and affection in these songs."

In the Hebrew, instead of 'Beloved', we read 'Love'. "This Spouse's endearment is very great," writes Fr. Juan de los Angeles, "for He so loves His Bride that He does not call her, concretely as it were, His Beloved, but rather love itself, in the abstract. He is so in love with her that He considers her a unique and singular pleasure and the delight of His heart. How she pleases Him for, seeing her asleep, He guards her sleep and charges all the daughters of Jerusalem...not to stir or rouse her until she please.... This shows that this sleep is of such a kind that the one who is asleep has freedom of will, and that there is something here that sleeps and something most important that keeps watch."

"How lovable the heavenly Spouse is!" exclaims Maria de la Dolorosa. "Scarcely has He heard the Bride ask Him to support her, than straightway He attends to her, pressing her closely to His Heart. When she sees herself embraced in this way, the soul rests in her Beloved and sleeps keeping watch, only her hearing remaining free..."

It is to be imagined, then, that the soul is here deeply asleep with a redundant abundance of consolations. Her companions, tired of waiting for her and displeased at seeing her so quiet, try to rouse her and urge her to join them in the usual exercises or to instruct them, to encourage and edify them with her company. But the Spouse rigorously hinders and withholds them from rousing her for their purposes of good works that they value so highly and in which they want to see her now occupied.

So we see how the Lord not only comes quickly to console souls who suffer for His love, and embraces and caresses them so that they might rest on His Own Heart; but He also keeps watch to see that no one disturbs them. There, indeed, the soul sleeps the sweet sleep of mystical contemplation, still enraptured by the new wine from the Divine Spouse's wine-cellar. He esteems this sleep so highly, considers it to be so necessary and beneficial that at whatever cost He wants it to last as long as is necessary, without anyone daring to interrupt it. For this reason He charges the 'daughters of Jerusalem', those devout souls who still do not understand these mysteries, not to waken her until she please; and charges them by all that interests their zeal, by *the gazelles and hinds of the field,* that is, the sinners and misguided to whose pursuit they want the Bride to dedicate herself, believing that she is wasting her time sleeping in holy contemplation, this divine sleep of love, as if external works are all that matters. In order to correct this lamentable mistake, He earnestly charges them not to waken her until it is time, for she accomplishes more by being *asleep* like this, more even for the good of her neighbors, than all she could possibly achieve through great work and labor in active life. For it is here that she gains strength and receives knowledge and skill; it is here that she pleads with God for the conversion and advancement of souls, and acquires the ability to attract, win, soften and change hearts; and finally, it is here that she enters into the Spirit of Divine Love so as later to exhale everywhere the sweet fragrance of Jesus Christ with which to win countless hearts for Him.

"What a sweet sleep is had, "exclaims Fr. La Puente (*Guía* tr. 3, Ch. 1), "resting in the arms of God and on Christ's breast. It is He Who occasions this sleep and protects it! O what sovereign goods He communicates to the soul that sleeps in this way, for He watches over the sleep in which these are received! O how awake the soul is to interior things, for she is given the free-will to awake whenever she pleases! This sleep does not interrupt understanding but rather intensifies it; it is not an image of death, but rather the sign of a very worthy life!"

Those who do not live this new life, still do not have their spiritual senses sufficiently awake to know fully the mysteries of the Kingdom of God; thus they are often lamentably mistaken, believing that everything is to be achieved through effort and industry alone, scarcely leaving any place for divine grace.

How much more good active souls would do, says St. John of the Cross (*Spirit. Cant.* Stanza 29), "if at least half of the time they spend in activity were spent with God in prayer!" When souls have reached perfection they are no longer harmed by contact with creatures for even when in their midst they are in continual prayer. But before reaching this state, they cannot accomplish all this and need to be comforted in this mystical wine-cellar where charity is ordered. This well-ordered charity begins by attending to its own progress, without, however, neglecting that of one's neighbors.

No less than three times in this Canticle the Spouse orders that His beloved's sleep be not disturbed or interrupted, and He does so in three different tones that change as the soul enters more deeply into the intimacy of His divine love. From this it can be seen how extremely necessary is the Eternal Wisdom's charge, made with such insistence and earnestness, and how lamentable it is to go against it, under vain pretexts.

But this hindrance on the part of the *daughters of Jerusalem* is helped rather than opposed, as should be the case, by many bad directors who, St. John of the Cross remarks (*Living Flame of Love,* Stanza 3), "not understanding souls that tread the path of quiet and solitary contemplation think these souls idle since they themselves have not reached it and do not know what it is to part with discursive meditation. They impede them and hamper the peace of restful and quiet contemplation, which God of His Own was according them, by making them walk along the path of meditation and imaginative reflection and perform interior acts. In doing this, they cause these souls to experience great repugnance, dryness, and distraction when they want to remain in their holy idleness and quiet and peaceful recollection . . . ; they cause them aridity of spirit, and deprive them of the precious anointings God was bestowing on them in solitude and tranquillity... These directors do not know the ways of the Spirit. They do a great injury to God and show disrespect toward Him by intruding with a rough hand where He is working. It cost God a great deal to bring these souls to this stage, and He highly values His work of having introduced them into this solitude and emptiness regarding their faculties and activity so that He might speak to their hearts, which is what He always desires... The extent to which He values this tranquility and sleep or annihilation of sense, is clear in the entreaty, so notable and efficacious, which He made in the Canticle: I adjure you daughters of Jerusalem etc., by which He indicates how much He loves solitary sleep and forgetfulness... Yet these directors do not want the soul to rest and remain quiet, but want it always to labor and work, so that consequently it does not allow room for God's work and ruins and effaces through its own activity what He is doing."

That is why He is so pleased to see her rest like this, and with such tender care watches to see that no one disturbs such a necessary, holy and salutary sleep.

"What wonderful condescension and favor the Spouse shows," says St. Bernard (*Serm.* 51), "in bringing the contemplative soul to rest in His own most loving breast, seeing that no one disturb or bother her, whatever the serious matters or concerns that may arise, and not allowing her to be roused in any way until she herself should please."

"O man, what could you ever have experienced like that which has just been communicated to you from the heart of the Most High? What idea will you form for yourself of what awaits the soul in Heaven who, on earth, has already known the intimacy of being embraced by God Himself, of being sheltered in His breast and protected and guarded with the greatest care to see that nothing trouble or rouse her until she so please?" (Ibid. *Serm.* 52).

There is certainly great relevance in what is symbolized by this wonderful and repeated episode of the mystical Bride. The majority of so called Christians, imprudently eager to increase the Kingdom of God by anxiously pursuing little wild animals or lost sheep so as to bring them straightway to Christ's fold, despise what they wrongly call the 'passive virtues' but which are precisely the most characteristic virtues of the true *Christian* life; and thus they are displeased with cloistered religious and other persons of contemplative life, or look upon them with scorn, imagining that in the twentieth century everything is done and ought to be done by that feverish exterior activity called *Americanism*. Like so many over diligent Marthas they want to take Mary away from Jesus' side by keeping her busy in external ministry and work. But today as on that occasion Jesus comes out in the defense of contemplative souls, censuring *Americanism* through the mouths of His friends and vicars, earnestly entreating the over-active, by the very love of these unbelievers or the misdirected whom they would *pursue* for His sake, not to disturb or rouse these happy souls from their mystical sleep; that is, according to how much you love these unbelievers for My sake, do I command you not to awaken her because her sleep of contemplation procures more good for them than if she were awake, doing active works for their salvation; but rather try to imitate these happy souls for they are the *lightning conductors* of His anger, the *perpetual sacrifices* with which He is appeased, and the expiatory *victims* whose sweet scent gives Him pleasure. With the graces they obtain they soften the hard-hearted to listen to the voice of truth, and with the sweet scent of Christ that they exhale, they attract and win them. Thus, with the blessing of the Most High, they manage to achieve in one day, or in a few hours, what others (who do not have this scent) fail to achieve in many months and years of ardent zeal which is not *secundum scientiam*.

There is some reason for God preserving the world in spite of all men's sins. What would become of the world, St. Teresa was asked, were it not for the religious? For this very reason the great reformer tried to found so many refuges for contemplative souls where, as though in true enclosed gardens, the Lord might come and find pleasure, their love and faithfulness winning from Him pardon for the world corrupted and defiled by Luther. In view of the fact that sins are increasing and that at the same time efforts are being made to suppress and banish these mystical lightning conductors, there can be no doubt that today more than ever God is venting His fury upon the ungodly nations. . .

"The contemplative orders," M. Maria Dominica Clara of the Cross, O.P. was told by an angel, "are necessary now more than ever to the Church, being called as they are, through their life of penitence and expiation and through their prayers day and night, to appease the diving justice, to halt the punishment and cause the grace of God's mercy to descend upon the guilty world."

The apostolic orders ought always to depend upon prayer and sacrifice.

"I have called you to an apostolic order, that of my servant Dominic, "Our Lord told Sr. Maria Josefa Kumi (*Life,* Ch. IX), "for I have chosen you to fish for souls. You will win a great many of them with this love that crucifies you." Again, in 1814, He deigned to tell her (*Ibid.,* Ch. XIX): "For every drop of blood that is wrung so violently from your heart, I promise you I will bring a soul from out of the darkness of sin and love of worldly things. You will feel within you the reconciliation of justice and mercy."

We shall soon see how the apparent *idleness* and the mystical sleep of contemplative souls are a wonderful preparation for an apostolic activity more intense and fruitful than that of any active soul.

From now on, a new life begins for the soul, a life in which she lives only in God, thinks only of God, dreams only of God and works only for God, Whose glory she anxiously desires and with Whose zeal she is enkindled, all her communication being now with Heaven. From now on new and vast horizons are opened up to her and as it were a new world is revealed to her through which her Divine Spouse will lead her, arousing her from her sweet sleep, so that through her awakened mystical senses she may perceive the wonders of God.

SECOND SECTION
The soul in God: The illuminative way

v. 8) *The voice of my beloved! See how he comes leaping on the mountains, bounding over the hills!*

The Bride is still asleep, but her heart . . . dreams, and dreams of what she loves. . . She thinks she can clearly hear the voice of her Beloved, she makes sure that it is He, and sees Him coming toward her in great haste leaping over the mountains and hills, which are the *sacred mountains* and *eternal hills;* the mountains where He pours forth His blessings, namely, the great saints that follow in His footsteps. . . And she is not deceived. . .

"In that rest she hears her Beloved's voice reassuring her of His love. She sees Him now on Calvary, now on the Mount of Olives . . . now on the slopes of the Church." Maria Dolorosa.

Just like the enamored soul, but to a much greater degree, the holy Catholic Church, accustomed as she is to hearing her Spouse's voice and the voice of all those who come in His name, is able to distinguish it very well from the voice of impostors, and does not let herself be taken unawares by them as other churches do. By their voice and words she has recognized all those wolves who have come to her dressed in sheep's clothing: "In this way she unmasked the heretics, the hypocrites, the false reformers, the corruptors of her doctrine and morality, the enemies of her practices and traditions; and with her vigilance and fortitude she managed to thwart all their designs" (Petit.)

This Bride's very delicate sensibility will seem incredible to hearts who do not love; but those who love God understand it perfectly well.

"Love's concern is so great and is so anxiously searching for whom it desires," writes Fr. Luis de León, "that it recognizes his among a thousand footsteps, hears him among dreams and sees him behind walls; finally, love of its very nature compels souls in whom it reigns to act very differently from the ordinary experience of men, so that those who do not feel this affection cannot believe it. They consider it a miracle or rather, madness, to see and hear such things."

Fr. Juan de los Angeles says, "it is well that she is asleep. She hears Him, recognizes His voice and awakens saying: It is the voice of my Beloved calling me, and inviting me to go and work for His love. For it is God's way to often withdraw the special delight of contemplation that we may turn to the exercises of the active life, as He taught us through the words of Ezekiel (1, 8). Et manus hominis sub pennis eorum. Human hands were seen under the wings so that, once the flight of contemplation was over, the contemplative soul might be exercised in some work of virtue."

In this mystical sleep of contemplation the soul not only rests and gains spiritual strength, but is more alert and more attentive to listen for the voice of the Beloved and to carry out immediately whatever He should see fit to command her. Here she is enlightened with divine lights and revelations, as the apostle desires and prays for all (Ephes. 1, 18). With these lights, the eternal origin of the Word, His coming into the world and the treasures of the spiritual heritage that He came to entrust to pure hearts, are all revealed to her. Here she sees how the prayer that she made before (1, 6) has now been heard, and thus Christ Himself, her Beloved, the One desired by the people, the Eternal Hills, comes to be her Master and lets her hear His voice: Vox Dilecti! . . . Oh sweet and powerful voice . . . ! And what a sweet, wonderful and exalted science He teachers her. . . ! It is the voice of Truth speaking in silence, showing the soul the paths of life in just one word, and by its very presence ravishing the heart and liberating it from all bondage (John 8, 31-32).

It is the voice of my Beloved: "In this kind of spiritual quiet," remarks Fr. Gracian, "God enlightens the loving soul with the highest and most divine mysteries of the faith: the mystery of the Holy Trinity, of the Incarnation, of the Transfiguration, of the fruits of the cross, of the Resurrection and Ascension... And when this light enters prayer it does so instantly, in the blinking of an eye; for there is no goat or hart that runs more swiftly. . ."

Let us now consider, says St. Ambrose (in *Ps.* 118, Oct. v.1), the leaping the Divine Spouse does to reach souls: He leaps from the height of Heaven into the breast of the Virgin, from here into the crib, into the Temple, from the Temple to Jordan, from Jordan . . . to Calvary and the cross, and from the cross to the grave and from the grave He ascends to Heaven again. It is He the prophet speaks of when he says: *He went out with ardor to travel along His way like a giant; he went out from the highest part of Heaven and returned to this height.* He leapt over the mountains so as to reach His Bride; and even now He descends every day upon His saints from the bosom of the Father. Would that I too, tough a miserable sinner, could experience His coming within me! Would that my soul could truly say: *See how He comes!* For He certainly does not come to the soul whose affection is tied to the earth, but to those who are on the mountains, that is to say, to those whose hearts are liberated from the world and lifted up to Heaven. Since the soul of the just is the Bride of the Divine Word, when this soul feels herself filled with holy desires, when she prays without ceasing, when with all her strength she longs and sighs for the Spouse, she thinks she can in some way hear His voice although she sitll cannot see Him, but has within her an intimate awareness of the presence of God.

The *Ordinary Gloss* understands these mountains and hills to be those generous souls who, through their great virtue and purity of life, rise above the level of the ordinary and everyday, and ascend to the great heights of contemplation. It is there that the Divine Spouse leaps, for He visits these lofty hearts with frequent illuminations, although not halting His course for long, but leaping as it were. And according to St. Thomas He leaps over the highest mountains because He surpasses them all in everything and does not stop on them for very long.

"Finally," says Fr. Juan de los Angeles, "there is no reason to despair of being saved, having such a wonderful and merciful Lord Who comes leaping and bounding across mountains and hills to do us good."

If we understand these latter to be the proud and powerful of this century, "it is nice to think," he says, "that God always leaps His way through them like a hart or mountain-goat that never stays, for He never finds a seat among them. He dashes rapidly through them until He reaches His beloved Bride who is waiting and longing for Him."

Our Lord said to St. Mechtilde (*Revelations,* Introd., V): "I have always sought out the littlest and most humble so as to heap My spiritual gifts upon them. The high mountains cannot receive the revelation of My graces, for My Holy Spirit makes these graces run down-into the humble valleys." It is towards these valleys that the Lord comes leaping and bounding, as He told the same saint, saying to her (Part 2, Ch. 3): "The eagerness of the bee in heading for the green fields in search of flowers is no greater than Mine in coming to a soul when she calls Me." He would undoubtedly come with even greater eagerness if she were no longer content with just calling to Him but prepared to receive Him with the greatest fervor possible.

To this end He sends His Spirit to prepare all hearts, and to renew them (*Ps.* 104, 30) making a dwelling place within them that is pleasing to Him. But the majority are always resisting His divine inspirations and grieving the sweet Host and Consoler of souls; as a result when the Savior comes to visit them He usually finds many doors closed and many ears deaf.

"The Holy Spirit," says St. Mary Magdalen de Pazzi (*Part 1,* Ch. 27), "with the weight and lightness of His goodness and love halts with us and swiftly inclines toward all souls ready to receive Him. Who could ever describe the wonderful effects that He produces wherever He is received. He speaks without saying anything, and His sublime silence is understood by all . . . He gives Himself only in so far as He wishes, although He is ready to communicate Himself fully to souls that He finds well-disposed."

"My Divine Spirit," said our Lord to Sr. Catherine of Jesus Mary (*Autob.*, Part 2, Ch. 65), "always descends to pour forth His gifts into hearts, although with greater abundance on this day (Pentecost). And if He were capable of disconsolateness being Consolor and All-consolation He would return to Heaven disconsolate at not having found every heart disposed to receive Him. *He refuses no one: He seeks all;* but you see how few receive Him being so ungrateful, turning Him away discourteously by not being prepared to receive Him." Hence the coldness that Jesus usually finds nearly everywhere, thus obliging Him to leap about in search of hearts that will admit Him and receive His graces.

"O with what pity and tenderness this Lord fills me," exclaims the V. Mariana de S. José (*Life* 1, 1, Ch. 15), "when I see Him so rich with gifts and so poor in hearts! For this has forced Him to place so many in mine that has always been so worthless. O what desire this gives me to cry out to all creatures to turn to the Lord so as to be filled with endless riches surpassing all understanding! Let Him tell them and call them with that great voice with which He revives the dead, for the dead are those who do not actively and truly search for Him. . . They do not know what they are losing."

Thus we see how "He has never ceased leaping for," according to Fr. La Puente (*Perf. Gen.*, tr. 4, 6.5), "every day He also comes leaping from Heaven into the Sacrament, in churches everywhere, and from the Sacrament He leaps into the breasts of many men, visiting them all so as to delight and enrich them. Although it says that He comes leaping to indicate

His speed and joy in coming, He also comes with seriousness and rest, halting as long as is necessary for our good, fulfilling the promise He made on the night of the Supper (*John* 14, 28): *I am going away and shall return to you.* He comes during the consecration of the Sacrament; He goes when the sacramental graces come to an end. He goes away in so far as He is man; He remains in so far as He is God. He sometimes goes away with respect to the perceptible favors that He bestows; He remains with respect to the graces and gifts of virtues that He concedes; and although He comes as a traveler and wayfarer He brings with Him all His treasures which He generously distributes to the people He visits."

If, then, we never experience His coming to visit us, we do well to lament this and to say, with even better reason than St. Bernard (*Serm.* 45): "Alas! My Lord visits the mountains around me but never comes to me! Am I perhaps one of the hills over which the Spouse leaps without touching it? I can see one soul with wonderful abstinence and another with singular patience; the one surpasses himself in contemplation, the other enters the heavens through the insistence of his prayer; and others have various outstanding virtues, like mountains that are visited by the Lord, where the Spouse of holy souls leaps and rejoices. But I, the wretch that I am, feeling none of this, what am I but one of the mountains of Gelboe that, because of my sins, the Lord fails to visit while graciously visiting all the other mountains?"

Never to receive these divine visits in any way is, as the great masters of the spirit tell us, a very clear sign of how little advanced we are; it shows how little we love God, undeserving of this proof of His love for us; for, if we truly loved Him and tried to please Him in everything, He would not fail to come to us and manifest Himself in some way, as He has expressly promised us (*John* 14, 21-23). If we had a clean heart and simple, pure and loving eyes like those of the Bride we would soon manage not only to *experience* Him and *hear* His words of life, but would also in some way *see Him.*

v. 9)   *My beloved is like a gazelle, like a young stag.*
            See where he stands behind our wall
            looking in through the windows
            peering through the lattice.

Here it is clearly shown how quickly God comes to console His own souls, to cheer them with His visit, especially in times of affliction and tribulation. If He ever flees or turns away from the soul, His love, He does so imitating the way of these gracious little animals, the gazelle and the stag, which from time to time turn their heads around.

He is also like them, says St. John of the Cross (*Spiritual Canticle,* Stanza 1), "not only because He is withdrawn and solitary and flees from companions like the stag, but also because of the swiftness with which He shows and then hides Himself. He usually visits devout souls in order to gladden and liven them, and then leaves in order to try, humble, and teach them."

Thus Christ never leaves the soul so abandoned and alone in the midst of all the rigors with which He tries her that some time or other He does not reveal a little of Himself to her or does not let her hear His sweet voice so as to wound, captivate and inspire her all the more with love.

"What most moves the soul to love God is when the Spouse pierces her heart with His divine eyes, enrapturing, subduing, slaying and over coming her. This gaze . . . is normally a kind of inner vision that is strong, effective and full of love. . . For although she cannot see who is gazing at her, knowing that it is He and she is in His presence, she loves Him, readies herself within and works with carefulness, diligence and pleasure" (Gracián).

With these words, remarks the Ven. Mariana, the soul describes "the speed with which the Holy Spirit comes to her aid and to the aid of the just who place all their trust in Him. The same is meant by the words that follow: *He stands behind our wall,* meaning that she will not be dismayed because He will not abandon her completely, that His absences will not be longer than her own weakness is able to bear. He will always be there close-by to assist her, gazing through the windows, that are the soul's sighs and cries, and through the lattice, whose opening is very narrow because of her fear of falling, the result of her weakness or of her lack of trust in His mercy and goodness. Learning all these paths her confidence grows stronger so as to advance further. . ."

"The Spouse," says Maria Dolorosa, "gazes as it were through the lattice and the windows, and with this gaze gives fortitude to souls suffering together and shows the persecutors the limits beyond which they cannot lift a finger against the Bride."

She compares Him, therefore, to the gazelle and young stag not only for the grace and speed with which they move and run and with which she hopes to see Him come but also because of the characteristic they have of turning their heads; for if He flees from her she at least wants Him to turn His head around to look at her. But He also resembles them in another respect, in returning often by circling around and stopping rather than fleeing by a straight path. She goes on to add: *See where he stands behind our wall, looking in at the window and peering through the lattice.*

The Bride can now feel Him almost beside her for only a wall of earth, a thin mud wall according to the Hebrew text, separates them.

Behind the wall of the Sacred Humanity the soul discovers or in some way is aware of the presence of the Divinity of Christ, and behind the lattice of the tabernacle and the veil of the sacramental graces and the outline of the mystical darkness, with the eyes of living faith she sees Him hidden in the Sacrament of the altar and in her own heart. She sees clearly how He lies in wait for us there, hiding Himself more or less, playing hide-and-seek as it were, concealing the fire of His love

so as to enkindle and win hers all the more, But however much
He hides in the heart in which He is pleased to dwell, says St.
John of the Cross (*Living Flame,* Stanza 4, v. 3), He always
gives signs of His presence by which the soul sometimes feels
and enjoys Him, tasting His sweetness. This she tastes with the
gift of wisdom which was communicated to us that we might
know by experience the gifts that are received (I *Cor.* 2, 12-16;
I *John* 5, 20); and she feels and perceives and hears Him
through the spiritual senses through which she comes to acquire
such certainty and sureness that at times, with a special light,
she can clearly perceive whether a soul is or is not in grace and
therefore whether or not she is a living temple of Christ; and on
entering the Church she does not need to look to find out
where the ciborium is but goes straight to it as though her heart
were drawn there by instinct. Feeling and hearing Him, she tries
to be very attentive to His suggestions and instructions.

En Ipse stat post parietem! . . . That is to say: It is He and
no one else that I now feel very close beside me. . . It is He
Who, beneath the veil of faith, as though through a lattice, lets
me see Him a little and deigns to look at me. . . So that the soul
can no longer be content with any other, longing only for Him;
and so she can say with St. John of the Cross (*Spiritual
Canticle,* Stanza 6):

> Do not send me
> Any more messengers,
> They cannot tell me what I must hear. . .

For this reason St. Bernard (*Serm.* 21) tells us that there is a
truly divine gaze when God of His own accord sees fit to visit
the soul that searches for Him: *Est divina inspectio. . .cum per
seipsum dignatur invisere Deus animam quaerentem se.* The
Bride, he adds, cannot be content with anything less than this
visitation and communication by the Word, carried out in
reality and not merely in figures and representations.

The servant of God, Sr. Catherine of J. M. and J., a
Dominican nun from Quito (1717 — 1795), being very troubled

at having heard a certain theologian say that it was not the Lord Himself but an angel who spoke and comforted souls in His name, fell to lamenting, saying (*Autobiography,* Part 2, Ch. 41): "But Lord, what does the soul feel during these apparitions, for apart from the joy of that presence there is nothing more to enjoy? And the Lord replied: "Leave that to the theologians and the books that they are laboring with in vain, for they do not understand; the truth is that I am the One Who comes to delight souls and nothing is impossible for Me. And as proof of this see how when I appear, the soul does not and cannot see any other end but Me, Myself, in person. And if during the apparition the soul receives light to see some greater end, then it would be an angel." (Cf. St. Teresa, *Interior Castle,* 5, Ch. 9).

Hortulanus understands this *looking through the windows* to be the visits the Lord makes to souls enlightening and consoling them in a very clear and manifest way; and since He does this so inconspicuously that they hardly see Him, He looks at them as it were *through a lattice.*

"As though trying to search out His Bride's most hidden feelings," writes St. Ambrose (*Serm.* 6, *in Ps.* 118), "sometimes He remains away from her so that she might look for Him anxiously; and sometimes He presents Himself before her, delighting her and heaping her with favors; hence the fact that He looks at her through a lattice, partly showing Himself and partly hiding Himself so as to provoke her to greater love."

He stands behind our wall. . ., observes Fr. La Puente (*Guia* tr. 3, Ch. 6): "the wall of our body and the coarseness of our understanding prevents us from seeing Him, although He stands behind the lattice of creatures, seeing us without being seen. Yet. . . *En Ipse stat.* Look, for He is undoubtedly there, and I feel His presence. . . This kind of presence is communicated by the Lord in contemplation, with a celestial light that reveals Him in a way which is better felt than described for we are given to feel that He is truly with us, and without seeing anything we feel that we are in the company of a

Majesty of immense grandeur that moves us to extreme reverence and admiration, and our whole spirit is recollected so as to gaze upon Him attentively. . . O eternal God, send Your sovereign light from Heaven that I might see You even if only behind this lattice, for by feeling Your presence I will enjoy the rich gifts that You bring with it."

"Behind the wall of this body," says Sr. Teresa of J.M. (*Comment.* II), "He is looking with my eyes and speaking with my tongue and so on. I also feel beside me, outside, the company of Christ the Man in an intellectual way, not by picturing Him in any way in the imagination but by attending to the fact that He is always gazing at me and accompanying me wherever I go, ordering me to do all that I have to do, even eating, sleeping and the rest; and my wish is to do everything solely to please and obey Him, without my ever looking up when He does not wish or without His will or permission."

Those who never feel Him or never long to see Him or to receive His sweet loving gaze, nor ever listen or attend to Him as their lovable Spouse or as their tender Father, nor even as the faithful Master of all truth Who comes to correct and undeceive us, will have to suffer His other gaze as the *awesome Judge of the children of men.* Upon these too, who are not His sons or friends, upon these "the Lord looked down from Heaven to see if there were any that understood and sought God; but they had all turned aside and became tainted, and there was not one that did good, no, not one (*Ps.* 14, 2-3). And against those who have turned aside and do not wish to be converted He will cast the terrible burden of His just wrath when, as He promised. . . He will come to judge Jerusalem, and the daughters of Jerusalem, with a light that reveals all.

"O what a penetrating eye this is!" exclaims St. Bernard (*Serm.* 55). "Nothing will be left hidden, nothing will escape His rigorous inspection, for He will examine even the most concealed parts of the heart (*Ps.* 7, 10). What assurance, then, can Babylon have if Jerusalem is to be subjected to such a rigorous examination!"

But those who love Him and attend to Him as the Bride does, He loves and appears to them all full of love (*Prov.* 8, 17), He calls to them with the greatest sweetness, speaking to them in many ways.

v. 10)   *My Beloved lifts up his voice*
              and says to me
              Rise up, hurry, my love
              my dove, my beautiful one and come.

"The soul in a sublime experience of glory," writes St. John of the Cross (*Living Flame of Love,* Stanza 1), "feels and understands most distinctly all these things which the Holy Spirit shows it. . ."

But the Lord has many ways of calling to souls according to the state and disposition they are in.

"O God, the strength of my salvation!" exclaimed St. Augustine (*Medit.,* Ch. 2)". . . I go astray and You call to me over and over again, I resist You and You invite me, I am idle and You rouse me, I am converted and You embrace me, I am ignorant and You instruct me, I am sad and You cheer me, I fall and You lift me up, You restore me after the fall, You give me all I ask You for, You let me find You when I look for You and You open the door when I call. So that, Lord God of my life, I do not know what excuse I could have. Now, Father of mercies and God of all consolation . . . grant me the joy of Your countenance that by loving You I might receive all that You promised me . . . inspire me as to what I must think of You, teach me what words I must use to invoke You and give me works with which to please You."

With this wonderful call, writes Maria de la Dolorosa, He seems to be telling her: "Do not waste your time in recalling your sins; you should now think only of loving Me. I have made you My love, I have given you the wings of a dove with which your heart can fly to Me . . . ; and My love has made you beautiful in My eyes; rise up, then, from these memories and come to Me with love.

"The winter of the past life has now ended with that flood
of defects; the spring has now arrived, prepare your soul to
produce fruits of virtue together with the flowers of holy
desires."

Surge... "Neque enim satis habuit," writes Soto Mayor,
"paulo ante semel dixisse: *Surge, propera...nisi* rursus per
repetitionem adderet: *Surge...veni.* Quadoquidem etiam atque
etiam jure suo petere non dedignatur a sponsa, cui tam multa et
magna beneficia praestiterat et eum sequatur, atque delitiis
verni temporis cum liberate fruatur, quasi vero ipse beneficium
acciperet et non potius daret."

No one, then, has any right to excuse himself from hearing
this loving call that is like a request from the Divine Lover...
This would be a terrible negligence.

"Indignum est enim prorsus, atque praeposterum,"
continues Soto Mayor, "ut anima hominis, quantum vis alias
peccatrix, obtemperare nolit, et obsequi recuset, vel repugnare
audeat Deo, id est, Sponso caelesti tam blande et amantur eam
vocanti, seu provocanti atque excitanti, imo vero etiam atque
etiam obnixe roganti et deprecanti, ut se ducem ad salutem et
libertatem et beatam vitam..., sequi velit... Surge... Veni...
Nempe, ut eum ad salutem et perfectam libertatem id est ad
praestaniora at diviniora sequatur libens, et cito, id est, magna
cum celeritate et alacritate. Quemadmodum par est probam et
charissimam sponsam talem ac tantum Sponsum vocantem
atque manuducentem sequi."

Every time that He calls us in this way He offers us the
graces necessary to follow Him progressively to the peaks of
sanctity.

"Hic," says St. Gregory of Nyssa (*In Cant.* Orat. 5), "video
sponsam a Sermone divino velut in itinere, quo per gradus
sursum tenditur, per virtutis ascensum, quasi manu duci...
Semper nimirum excitari nos oportet nec unquam est
quiescendum, etiamsi cursu proprius ad scopum perveniamus.

Quoties ergo tum verbum hoc, *surge,* tum alterum illud, *veni, Sermo* Dei proferit, *toties facultatem ascendendi ad potiora largitur.*"

The words *Rise up,* according to the Ven. Mariana, signify "a rising up of the spirit above our wretchedness and a readiness to give oneself as the Spouse gives Himself. They express also the revelation of His love, and this is shown in the words that He says: *Hurry my love, my dove, my beautiful one.* These are like exalted splendors manifesting how this love gives itself to the Bride, and with each radiance He more and more inspires her love, enriching her and bringing her closer to Him; thus she becomes more and more like Him as He gives her this beauty that He speaks of here. The phrase *and come* is that which completely prepares her so that she can become one with Him, just as fire converts wood into flame.

In this way the Spouse calls to her to rise up not only from her imperfections, but also sometimes from the flowery bed of contemplation, for the day is now dawning for her spiritually and it is time for her to go out and work for the good of souls. Having entered the wine-cellar and rested and regained strength from the mystical sleep, she does not rise up 'before light' nor 'before having rested' (*Ps.* 127, 2), and she is therefore prepared to carry out the work of God effectively, She goes now full of assurance since she goes with Him and at His invitation.

These words *Surge. . .et veni* are, says St. Thomas, a loving invitation that the Divine Spouse makes the soul to practice works that are full of devotion and for the good of all. It is as though He were to say to her: "Rise up from this sweet room; from the quiet and repose in which your only care is to please Me, to praise Me and to converse lovingly with Me; and hurry off and exercise yourself for the good of your neighbors, so that by your preaching and good example you might move them to practice virtue and obtain salvation for their souls."

It should also be noted, writes Fr. Juan de los Angeles, "that the same Person Who charged the daughters of Jerusalem

not to awaken His beloved from the sweet sleep of contemplation now awakens her so that she can go and help her neighbors
ex charitate. Prayer must be put aside when one's brothers'
needs require it. *Orationi instantes, necessitatibus sanctorum
communicantes (Rom.* 12-3).

My love, my dove, my beautiful one. . . "O devout soul,"
exclaims Origen (*in Cant.*), "how wonderfully you are praised
here; but the praise is not for what comes from you but for
what comes from Him Who loves you. For by faith in Him you
are powerful, through hope you shine, through love you radiate,
through justice you are resplendent. . . Come, then along the
path of perfect charity, loving God with your whole heart, with
your whole being; with all your understanding, without any
opposition or resistance from your will; with all your mind,
without your memory forgetting or neglecting anything; for if
you are lacking in any of these you are not progressing in a full
and perfect way."

"*My love,*" explains Fr. Juan de los Angeles, agreeing with
St. Gregory, "because you love Me and I love you; *dove* because
of the simplicity that the Holy Spirit has communicated to you;
beautiful, because you are made in My likeness. *Surge.* Rise up
from temporal things to things spiritual and hurry. . ."

In this way, with sweet words such as these, the Divine
Spouse inspires her to hasten to follow Him undismayed
wherever He might go. And indeed, as Vercelense says (*in
Cant.*), "there is nothing that contributes more effectively to
the soul's continual progress than these loving invitations which
she makes to God and God to her. . . The whole course of love
consists in insistently repeating them. That is why the Divine
Spouse tells her: *Rise up. . .*"

"The three commands: *Rise up, hurry, come,*" according
to Scio, "correspond to three kinds of persons that God calls to
Himself through the efficacy of His grace. The first, *rise up,* is
directed to those who are *beginning* to follow the Spouse; the
second, *hurry,* to those who are *making progress* in His service;

and the third, *come,* to the *perfect* who merit entry into the wine-cellar. In the same way to each of these three classes of souls there is a corresponding name of endearment that the Spouse uses to call His Bride: *my love, my dove* (this does not appear here in the Hebrew text but in verse 14), *my beautiful one.* The first applies to those who have left the miserable state of sin; the second to those who serve Him faithfully; and the third to those who already have all the adornment of the virtues within them."

It seemed to St. Mecthtilde (*Revel.,* Part 2, Ch. 1) that the heart of Jesus was calling her saying: "Come and repent and confess your sins, come and find comfort, come and be blessed. Come, My love, and receive all that a friend can give his friend. Come, My sister, and possess the eternal heritage which I have acquired for you with My Precious Blood. Come, My Bride, and enjoy My Divinity."

Rise up and hurry... "O, if only the Divine Spirit would reveal to you what is meant by these comparisons," exclaims Fr. La Puente (*Perf. Gen.,* tr. 3 Ch. 13), "you would undoubtedly be moved to attempt the exalted conversion and perfection that He urges you to seek with these words. What He tells you is to rise up from your sad and tearful state... so as to begin a new and totally converted life and to exercise yourself fervently in the works of sanctity with which this is achieved."

v. 11)   *For winter is past,*
                    the rains are over and gone.

Winter is past, although it will return. It is now time to go out into the fields to work. "The winter," says Scio, "represents the temptations, aridities and miseries of human life; and the rains, the exterior persecutions and other trials."

"Just as spring succeeds winter," says Maria Dolorosa, "so, after a time of persecution and grief God gives His Church a time of prosperity and joy. While she is grieving, tribulations rain down upon the bodies and souls of all kinds of persons, the ungodly being exalted and His children being ground into the

dust. . . But He, far from allowing His children to yield and be
defeated, reminds them that He has the time of peace and
consolation prepared for them. . ."

"When the winter's water goes away and the salutary
summer water of wisdom arrives," says Fray Juan de los
Angeles, "it not only does not prevent those walking along the
paths of eternity, but encourages, instructs and directs them so
that they will not go astray. It lifts up our spirit, it makes it leap
and brings it into the secret of eternity. It is the water that,
through St. John (4, 14), Christ promises to those that are His:
*Aqua quam Ego dabo ei, fiet in eo fons squae salientis in vitam
aeternam.* It is water that springs from the fountain of life,
which is God Himself, lifting up our thought and meditation
through the desire for eternal things. . . It extinguishes our
thirst for temporal and transitory things; for this water is
springing from within us and we cannot thirst but for God, for
as He says (*Ecclesiasticus* 24, 29): *They who drink Me will
thirst for more.* O how wonderful it is to drink from this water!
A single drop would make us nimble and swift for these
journeys to Heaven and would give us the strength to combat
every obstacle that might stand in our way and would make us
leap; not leaps towards temporal things but towards the eternal,
until we enter the secret chamber of the Divinity of the Lord."

"This," adds the author of the treatise *De 7 Itiner., (Itin.*
3), "is the sweet, flowery path along which the soul progresses,
once the storms are over, in search of the Divine Spouse's secret
retreat."

v. 12)   *The flowers appeared on our earth.*

That is to say, the frosts, the gloom and trials of the
purgative way are now over, although not completely and
forever; and the joyful spring of the *illuminative way* appears,
smiling and blossoming. . . "giving to understand," says the
Ven. Mariana, "that she, who was so subject to the misery and
weakness of sin, is now earth giving forth flowers; for she was
the inheritance and property of both; and since she is now the

possession of the Spouse Who is her Lord and Master, He has tended her with His water which is His presence and assistance; and in this way she gives forth flowers. . ."

On our earth. . . How full of love these words are and how appropriate for setting our hearts aflame. . .

"Nusquam, ut opinor," says St. Bernard (*Serm.* 59, in Cant), "de caelo sic locutum reperies, nusquam alibi de terra. Adverte igitur quantae sit suavitatis Deum caeli dicere: *In terra nostra.* Quique terrigenae et filii hominum audite: *Magnificavit Dominus facere nobiscum.* Multum illi cum terra, multum cum sponsa, quam de terra sibi asciscere placuit. *In terra,* inquit, *nostra.* Non plane principatum sonat vox ista, sed consortium, sed familiaritatem. Tanquam Sponsus hoc dicit, non tanquam Dominus. Amor loquitur, qui dominium nescit."

It is as though He were to say to her, remarks Maria Dolorosa: "In the earth of your heart, which is now Mine through the bond of love which unites us, flowers of the virtue of fortitude now appear which were not there before; it is important, then, to prune away everything superfluous so that these flowers can produce good fruit. I was not able to do so before because you were still young in virtue. Now that you are grown these useless branches must be pruned with the cutting-irons of tribulations; your will is resolved to embrace all that pleases me; and in the solitude of your spirit you are like the turtle-dove that moans with longing to please its companion."

Pruning time has come

In natural terms, spring does not seem the most appropriate time for pruning. But in the soul it is always pruning time; and now that it seems she has stripped and rid herself of the main obstacles to growing in virtue, when she has done all that she, for her part, can do to purify herself, she must submit to another and much deeper purification, which she must undergo passively. She must abandon herself into the hands of the Divine Gardener so that He can prune her according to His wishes. For it is no longer a matter of pruning certain inordinate affections which spring up and drain away the sap of the solid virtues; but rather of pruning the very discourse that tires the understanding, and certain affections of the will that are too sensitive, together with the hidden fondness for spiritual consolations, in so far as they prevent the soul from going straight to the God of all consolation.

The task of pruning is partly entrusted to superiors and directors, but it is God Himself Who is to complete it and bring it to its perfection, with the touch of the Finger of His right hand, that is, with His Holy Spirit, Whose mysterious action takes place during the *dark nights* of the *passive purgations* of the soul. And we must not only abandon ourselves to this passive pruning, suffering the divine action, allowing God to do and undo within us whatever He pleases, knowing that everything is for our own good, but must prepare ourselves and cooperate whenever necessary with our own action. "For who among us is there," asked St. Bernard (*Serm.* 58), "who has trimmed the superfluous shoots of his vine so perfectly that he is not in need of new trimming? Believe me, my brothers, that even what was once pruned begins to shoot again. . . One pruning is not enough but many prunings are required, or rather, we should always be pruning as long as we are able; for if we do not want to deceive ourselves we shall always find something to prune within us. . . Let us prune away concupiscence so as to strengthen ourselves in piety."

Pruning time has come. . . "On vines they prune those shoots," says the Vercelence "that, if left, produce fruit in great quantity but of inferior quality. A similar thing happens in the soul where there are inclinations and dispositions which could be very fruitful in active life but would harm the contemplative life which produces more precious fruits, since this life possesses the better part. . . We must rid ourselves, then, of the images of creatures and of the discourses of the understanding so that through contemplation we might be able to perceive in a super-intellectual way the rays of divine light: *Quoties ergo superintellectualiter exercemur ad divinum radium, toties opus est ut resecemus intellectuales operationes et creaturarum similitudines.*"

"See how I act, My daughter," the Eternal Father said to St. Catherine of Siena (*Dialogues*, Ch. 24), "toward My servants who are united to My much beloved Son. . . I prune them so that they will bear much fruit, and fruit that is not coarse but excellent in quality. The shoots on the vine are cut off so that the wine will be better and more abundant. . . And I Who am the true Vinedresser do the same with My servants, pruning them with tribulation, so that their virtue is tested and gives more abundant and more perfect fruits."

"The flowery vineyards," says Hugo, "are the fertile faculties and talents of the contemplative soul where, as the true tree of life in paradise, divine Wisdom is planted and bears fruit; of this happy soul inhabited by the Divine Gardener Who cultivates them in the way He knows and thus fills them with flowers and sweet scents: flowers because of the Word of truth; and sweet-smelling and fragrant because of the spirit of charity."

With respect to the holy Church, "after the winter of persecutions that she had to suffer at the hands of the Jews and gentiles, *flowers appeared* in the earth of her children, cultivated by Jesus Christ and His Apostles; and what before seemed a sterile, thorny desert is now a beautiful garden adorned and perfumed with great examples of heroic virtue. But since there were not a few imperfect, cowardly or unworthy Christians among so many saints, it was then most necessary to *prune the vine,* using the harsh rule of suffering and rebuke to subdue the passions and correct the disorders." (Petit-Calmet)

> *The voice of the turtledove was heard*
> *in our land.*

v. 13) *The fig began to form its first figs,*
   and the blossoming vines gave out their fragrance.

All these things are clear signs of spring and therefore of the *illuminative way* in which the soul now not only blossoms with beautiful virtues, but moaning like the turtle-dove, truly begins to be, like the fig tree, full of sweetness for others, keeping all the bitterness for herself. That is how she begins to give sweet fruits of life and to exhale the sweet fragrance of Christ, Who is the *true Vine* with Whom she is now very closely joined, as the shoots are to the vine.

"The soul cannot be united and communicate intimately with God," wrote Origen (*in Cant.* 1, 4, Hom. 4), "unless she is first rid of the entire winter of troubles and coldness and every storm of vice and sin, so that she can be strengthened in truth and not blown along by any wind. When this happens and she no longer feels moved by any vain desires, then virtues will begin to flower vigorously within her. Pruning time for her mind will also come when it will be necessary to cut away everything that is superfluous or useless in her thoughts and feelings so that a pure spiritual science can grow with vigor. Then she will also hear the voice of the turtle-dove, that is to say, of that mystical wisdom the good preacher communicates to those who are perfect, the lofty divine wisdom that is hidden in the mystery (I *Cor.* 2, 6-7). This is what is indicated by the voice of the turtle-dove, a bird which dwells in solitary places.

. . .By the first figs that the fig tree produces we are given to understand the fruits of the Holy Spirit. . . There is in the soul, then, as it were, a fig tree which gives forth fruit; a vine in blossom that gives of sweet scent, a vine whose shoots the heavenly Father Himself, as Divine Gardener, undertakes to prune so that they can give abundant fruit. . . The soul has reached, then, the happy spring of peace and tranquillity when the divine Word appears, gladly banishing the clouds of sin and bringing virtues to flower within her, to yield precious fruits of good works: *Fit ergo tranquilitas animae apparente ei Verbo Dei, et cessante peccato, et ita demum, florente vinea, incipient virtutes atque arbusta bonorum operum fructum germinare.*"

"The first fruits," explains Maria Dolorosa, "have now appeared on the tree of love which, like a fig tree, protects you with the shade of its branches, and comforts you with the sweetness of its fruits: the vines of My virtues have blossomed causing you to perceive the scent of good example; rise up, My love, for I have brought you into My friendship and since you have not resisted this grace, you have become beautiful; rise up then from the rest of your solitude, and come and carry the cross that you might be worthy of the crown."

Surge. . . Thus the invitation to go out into the fields is repeated after this long description which is so beautiful that it has rightly been said there is none to equal it among the Latin and Greek classics. The spiritual spring of the flowering of all the Christian virtues, together with the song of the mystical turtle-dove inviting the soul to go out and do great works of devotion in a fruitful apostolate, fully deserves to be celebrated in this way.

Rise up, my love, my beautiful one, and come.

This is what matters most: that she should go on truly progressing and getting as close as she can to the divine Model, that she rise up from her miseries and imperfections and hasten quickly to Him, being beautified and illumined more and more with the splendor of His virtues as she graudally draws closer (*Ps.* 33, 6), and boldly advances along the paths of holiness and justice so as to follow Him faithfully, for *all those who follow Him do not walk in darkness but have the light of life (John 8, 12)*; in this way she will become intimately united with Him and yield abundant fruit (*John* 15, 5).

v. 14)   *My dove hiding in the clefts of the rock,*
          in the opening in the wall:
          show me your face,
          let me hear your voice;
          for your voice is sweet
          and your face is beautiful.

This *rock* and *wall* — or defensive wall — where the

mystical dove has her dwelling is Christ Himself; the *clefts*, the wounds in His hands and feet; the *opening in the wall*, the opening in His loving side. When the soul has made her dwelling here and has cleansed and beautified herself in His Blood and become enkindled in the ardor of that divine fire . . . ; and when she has then entered the secret wine-cellar where charity is ordered; it is then that she has become beautiful and graceful in the eyes of her Spouse and that He tells her to show Him her face and let Him hear her voice which cannot fail to be sweet, as St. Bernard says, now that her entire presence is so pleasing and gracious. She will lift up her voice, then, a voice of joy and salvation (*Ps.* 117, 15), and with it will delight and please her Spouse, for this voice is sweet not only in its continual songs of praise but also in the words of life and encouragement that it utters, beginning to be, through her divine attraction and delight, a powerful enticement to souls.

It is from these *mysterious clefts in the rock* that pure souls can raise their inner eyes to contemplate the divine mysteries, and it is there that they are made capable of communicating to others what they have contemplated. It is there that they are able in some way to see the glory of the Word, as of the Only-Begotten of the Father full of grace and truth and receive from His fullness (*John* 1) whatever they may need for themselves or to communicate to others. . .

Let me hear your voice. . . "What love God shows for a pure soul!" exclaims Fr. Juan de los Angeles. "It seems that He has no other occupation than that of gazing upon her face and listening to her voice. . . *Show me your face and let me hear your voice. . .* What wonderful words! *For your voice is sweet and your face is beautiful.* Blessed be such a lover! But what is this face so beautiful that it draws God after it? And what is the voice that He finds so pleasing? I believe that it is the inner disposition and harmony of the spiritual faculties by which man represents the image of God. . . To show Him this face is to direct all our mind and affection to Him . . ."

Sonet vox tua. . . These words, says Soto Mayor, could refer to a canticle, or rather to a sweet conversation: "ad colloquia seu potius soliloquia illa amatoria, arcana secreta, quibus animae sanctae atque perfectae, divino amore flagrantes, ex abundantia quadam et fiducia amoris, et quasi extasim patientes interdum privatim et familiariter utuntur, et alloquuntur Sponsum ipsum divinum; quibusque vicissim ipse Sponsus divinus animas sanctas atque perfectas, divino ejus amore flagrantes, similiter . . . , quasi amicam et sponsam alloquitur."

"The Bride's voice that the Spouse longs to hear," says Fr. Juan de los Angeles (*Lucha espir.*, Part 2, Ch. XI), "is interpreted by the Hebrews to refer to the prayer of the saints which is sweeter to the Spouse than all the music and harmony in the world. And the Chaladic expounder says: "Let me hear your voice beause your sweet voice is in prayer and in the house of the sanctuary, and your beautiful face is in the virtuous works."

"There is nothing more delightful to the Divine Spouse," adds Fr. Juan de los Angeles, "than to see us in His Church coverting all the soul's powers to Him, from the highest to the lowest, and approaching Him with all our affection. It is then that our voice is especially pleasing to Him, as when we lament past sins, or confess our own nothingness, our sickness and misery, or ask for what He wants us to ask, or when we thank Him for all the good we have received from His generous and bountiful hand."

He is also extremely pleased by the voice that brings words of salvation to its neighbors while winning them and attracting them with the beauty of good example and the delight of good works.

Show me your face and let me hear your voice. . .

The same author, in agreeing with St. Thomas adds: "You, My beloved, who have withdrawn and hidden yourself in the quiet of your contemplation and do not let yourself be seen by anyone, come out into the public and show your neighbors the beauty of your works, that by your example they might be encouraged to do good works. Then the soul shows her face to God, and, for the profit and edification of her neighbors, tells them how great is the inner beauty of virtue" (*Matt.* 5, 16).

"My God, You want those to whom You communicate these lights to bring others to share in them," says St. Mary Magdalen de Pazzi (*Part* 2, Ch. 4), "for a virtue which is not communicated is only half a virtue."

Your voice, your whole voice, not only the voice joyfully praising Me, but the voice of salvation for its neighbors, with its pious exhortations and preaching of My holy doctrine.

"The celestial Spouse is extremely pleased when His Gospel is preached with purity and sincerity and with no other aim than that of pleasing Him and edifying souls. . . *Let your voice sound in my ears,* not in those of men, indicating the motive ministers of God must have in the preaching of the Gospel" Fr. Angeles.

Show me your face. . . "It is as though saying," writes the Ven. Mariana, "that He now has her in a state to declare herself as His and to reveal the paths of the Lord, which are her voice which He here orders to sound forth. And it seems that it has already done so. . . *For your voice is sweet. . .* As if to say: your words and good works already move and inspire souls to follow Me. If Our Lord wants a soul to do this. . . and she does not, she has much to account for; and if she does do this what riches will be hers and what glory this exercise will bring to the Lord. But this must be after the will of the Spouse has been fully proven and ascertained, revealing itself in many ways to those who truly wish to know it."

"The Spouse wants his beloved," agrees Maria Dolorosa, "to come out from the clefts in the rock and from the opening in the wall; that is, He wants her not to be concerned with human appraisal nor to be fearful of any dangers but to practice devotion for the salvation of souls. In this way He will see the

Bride's beautiful face, He will hear that voice that He finds so pleasing because He hears it teaching the ignorant the path to salvation. A soul who in this way attempts to bring about the salvation of her neighbor without being concerned with human respect, defending the rights of the Lord, becomes beautiful in the eyes of God. But she should not get involved in this unless she is called by God; for otherwise, instead of winning other souls she will lose her own."

As can be seen quite clearly, in these last verses (10-14) the Divine Master, Who is the very *Truth,* teaches the soul the true *way* of *life,* concentrating the whole of mystical science into a very few words. In just these three progressive words *Surge, propera, veni,* spiritual teachers, as has been shown, usually see the outlining of the three principal stages in Christian life, or, what are called the three *ways*: the *purgative, illuminative* and *unitive* ways, to each of which there is a corresponding state in which the soul is still *beginning,* is *progressing,* or is *perfect,* and is addressed as *amica mea, columba mea, formosa mea* respectively. *Rise up* from the grave of sin, *hurry* along the paths of justice, and *come* and hide yourself in My wounds and *be united with Me.* Rise up, My *love,* for I gave you My grace with which you recovered My love and could then stand and walk in My presence; hurry, My *dove,* for I have given you the gifts of My Spirit the mystical *wings* with which you can not only run with the gift of fortitude, but fly with the gifts of understanding and wisdom until you find your rest (*Ps.* 55, 7); and I have saved you and made your eyes beautiful with the precious ointment of charity (*Rev.* 3, 18), and with perfect simplicity and purity of intention; come and be united with Me, My *beautiful one,* for you are indeed beautiful, with all the graces with which I have enriched you, after washing away the stains of your sins and imperfections.

This mystical little shepherd-girl is now becoming truly beautiful and perfect, an example of those souls worthy of soon being admitted into intimate union with God. It is for this

reason that the Divine Spouse addresses her in this way, telling
her that the winter of the purgation of the *senses* is now over,
and that the spring of flowers of infused virtues and of the
purgation of the *spirit* has now come, the time for the pruning
of the most hidden of the disorderly affections and of certain
exuberant off-shoots that stifle the soul's vigor; and it is also the
time for moaning like the turtle-dove, feeling compassion for
Christ and living with Him at the foot of the cross. The fig tree
that produces spiritual sweetness in the doing of good works
begins to yield fruit; the vine of the sweet fruits of the Holy
Spirit now gives off its precious scent promising an abundance
in the autumn. But for this to be so, He tells her, you must
come to Me and be completely united with Me, for its only in
Me that you are able to yield fruit in abundance, and without
Me you can do nothing. Hide yourself, then, like an innocent
dove in My wounds, especially in the wound in My side so close
to My Heart that it reaches it; and there you will have impressed
upon you the living sentiments with which it is beating:
sweetness, true humility and the spirit of sacrifice, until you
become moulded in My form and can act with My Own virtues
and carry out My Own works.

There the mystical dove will not only learn to moan and
coo in a way that pleases her Beloved, raising her head now and
again so as to give Him greater joy, but will regain strength and
spirit with which to leave the ark and to fly without risk over a
world buried in mud, carrying the olive branch in her mouth,
and will begin to be useful to many souls; for, when her work is
directed purely to the greater glory of God and to the good of
others, she will not alight upon soiled ground. Her voice and her
presence and her very feet will be precious and pleasing to the
eyes of God.

The soul learns this sciences and gains this virtue and
strength in her mystical sleep. . .!

It is very interesting to read what St. Bernard has to say
about this and his comments deserve being quoted at length:

"Look at the Bride's devotion," he says (*Serm.* 57), "see how carefully she watches the Spouse coming and how she afterwards records all His movements with the greatest diligence. The Spouse comes, runs etc. and nothing escapes the Bride's watchfulness. . . He comes to her with the love and desires of His mercy. . . , presenting Himself to those that come out to meet Him. . . , speaking to souls, teaching and persuading them about the Kingdom of God. This is the way in which the Spouse comes: the blessings and riches of salvation always accompany Him and all His doings give rise to delight and cause an abundant fullness of ineffably pleasing affects. And since the soul loves Him, she watches and observes all this. Happy is the soul whom the Lord finds watchful! He will not pass without stopping but will visit her and tell her sweet things, speaking to her as His Beloved. And listen to what she says: *See how my beloved speaks* to me. . .

"Her Beloved comes to her, then, with words of love, and not of reproach. She is not among those whom the Lord rebukes because they were absorbed in vain speculation and failed to observe the time of His coming; but rather, as careful and watchful as ever, from afar off she noticed Him and saw Him coming, leaping because of the speed with which He was approaching, passing over the proud, and through humility drawing near to His humble Bride. . . Listen finally to what He tells her: *Rise up, hurry, my beloved, my dove, my beautiful one.* O how happy is the soul who merits this praise! Who is there among us so watchful and careful in observing the time of His visitation. . . that at the moment when He comes and knocks at the door of his heart, he opens it to Him? All this is also applicable to the Church and to each one of us as members of it, so that we all ought to participate in these blessings. What, then, of St. Paul's affirmation (*Rom.* 8, 16) that *the Divine Spirit Himself bears witness to our spirit that we are children of God?* And how are we to be children if we do not share in His inheritance? Our own spiritual poverty is clear proof of the carelessness and negligence in which we live. Whoever among us that, in the words of the sage (*Ecclesiasticus* 39, 6), dedicates his whole heart, from dawn, to the Lord Who made him, praying in the presence of the Most High and longing with all his heart to prepare, as Isaiah says, the ways of the Lord, and to make the paths of God straight (*Is.* 40, 3) in such a way that he can join the prophet king in saying (*Ps.* 25, 15): *My eyes are always on God*... surely *he will receive the blessing from the Lord, and righteousness from the God of his salvation* (*Ps.* 24, 5); whoever does this will undoubtedly be *visited by the Lord, and very often.* He will always know the time of His coming, however secretly this modest Lover visits him in spirit. The chaste and watchful soul will see Him coming, then, even if He is very far from her... for He Himself tells us (*Prov.* 8, 17) that *those who seek Me early shall find Me.* That is how the Bride, who is truly looking for Him, comes to know even the desires of the One Who comes running towards her. She will see when He approaches and when she has Him before her and, moreover, with blessed eyes will see her Beloved's eyes gazing at her, and finally from His mouth will hear the words of joy and love when He calls her *His love*... You, too, can be sure that it is He Who is present before you if you see that you are burning in His love or are enkindled in the grief of your sins... It is written (*Ps.* 97, 3) that *a fire precedes Him as He goes* and that *He Himself is a consuming fire* (*Deut.* 4, 24). The first fire is sent to move and prepare you and at the same time to advise and warn you... The second consumes by turns and purifies, burning with sweetness... It is certainly consuming, but acts in such a way against vice that at the same time it communicates to the soul a kind of ineffable unction. By the virtues, then, with which you see yourself improved, and by the love in which you feel yourself to be enkindled, you will recognize the presence of the Lord within you...

"Certainly, once every stain of sin has been consumed in this fire, this pure and serene conscience is followed by a sudden and extraordinary expanding of the soul and by a certain infusion of celestial light which illumines the understanding so that it can possess knowledge of the Scriptures or enter into the divine mysteries. Then the eye that gazes at you is undoubtedly the eye of Him Who. . . makes your light shine like the dawn amid darkness (*Is.* 58, 8). These gazes of mercy are succeeded by a voice that softly and sweetly touches upon and explains the divine will, a voice that is none other than love itself which, unable to lie idle, never ceases to urge and compel the soul towards all that leads to the greater honor and glory of God. Finally, the Bride hears Him tell her to rise up and run, and undoubtedly to run nowhere but to the gaining of souls. Indeed it is very characteristic of true and chaste contemplation that the soul should feel so enkindled in divine fire and at times possess such extraordinary devotion and such an intense desire to search out and find, for God, souls who will love Him in the same way, that she very willingly leaves the holy inactivity of contemplation to dedicate herself to the work of preaching. Once her desires are satisfied, she returns to do the work of Mary, and the more she is mindful of the precious fruits that she has received from this holy inactivity, the more ardently she returns. When she again enjoys the taste of contemplation, she again, with greater courage and her usual joy, renews her efforts to win more souls. . .

"You have, it seems to me, in the Bride these three things: *preaching, prayer* and *contemplation* — recommended and indicated in the three words *love* (or *beloved*) *dove* and *beautiful.* For the soul that earnestly and faithfully works for her Spouse, preaching, advising, and serving Him, is rightly called His *love,* just as the soul who, beseeching Him in prayer and lamenting her own sins, never ceasing to reconcile divine mercies, is rightly called His *dove.* And the soul burning with celestial desires, and clothed in the splendor and beauty of divine contemplation is rightly called *beautiful.*"

"The face and voice of any soul who proceeds in this

way," he adds (*Serm.* 62), "are always pleasing to the Lord; the face for its purity, the voice for its confession, since *confession* and *purity* and *holiness* are things that are always *present before Him* (*Ps.* 96, 6). Thus those that have these graces will come to hear the Spouse say to them: *Show me your face, let me hear your voice.* In every contemplative soul the voice is admiration and thanksgiving so also is preaching. The Lord is especially pleased and delighted in these clefts and this cavern from which He hears the sound of voice of gratitude, admiration and praise."

"It is," says St. Lawrence Justinian, "a safe and impregnable refuge that all should know and where all can go for shelter; a refuge that the enemies do not venture to approach, terrified by the presence of the Spouse and even by that of the Bride herself, souls are welcome where they will very soon begin to taste ineffable delights. It is offered to all: it is open to all."

"When you begin to pray," said our Lord to St. Veronica Juliani (*Diary,* 1 May 1697), "you must place yourself in My wounds, for these are My brides' chambers and the chambers of all the souls that are dear to Me."

"And there is no reason to fear," continues St. Bernard, "that any one who wishes to enter here will be refused, on the contrary he is invited in. *Go into the hollows of the rocks, into the caverns of the earth for fear of the Lord and for the glory of His Majesty* (*Is.* 2, 20). The soul that is still weak . . . is shown this hollow where she can find shelter and take comfort and gain strength so that she can be given access to the inner secrets of the Word which only the strong in virtue and pure in heart reach. . . But the soul who makes her dwelling in those divine pierced hands and feet will undoubtedly regain complete health very quickly. What is there that is as efficient in healing the wounds in our conscience and purifying the inner vision of the soul, as the continual meditation on the wounds of Jesus Christ? But as long as the soul is not completely pure and well, I do not understand how the Spouse's words *Show me your face...* can be applied to her. How could the soul who is told to hide in the hollow dare to show it and to raise her voice? And why is she told this if not because she is neither beautiful nor fit to be seen? A soul will not be worthy of being seen as long as she is not ready and prepared for seeing.

When, through her stay in the hollow (the kiss of the divine feet), she has progressed so far in healing her inner vision that she can now *directly contemplate the glory of God,* then she will speak confidently of what she sees there, meriting the attention of her Spouse, and pleasing Him through the beauty of her face and the sweetness of her voice. The face of that soul who can now look upon the clarity of God must be pleasing to Him: *Placeat necesse est facies, quae in Dei claritatem intendere potest.* But she could do none of this were she not herself already clean, pure and lucid, *transformed into the very same image of clarity* that her inner eye is seeing... Once she is able, through her purity, to look upon the pure Truth, the Spouse will want to see her face and hear her voice.

"Just how pleased the Spouse is by the preaching of truth with purity of conscience, is shown in what immediately follows: *For her voice is sweet.* This does not mean that He finds her face displeasing, for He explains adding: *And your face is beautiful.* Inner beauty is nothing else put purity. Many pleased God with this alone without preaching; but He was never pleased by preaching not accompanied with this purity. Truth is not revealed to the impure, nor is wisdom communicated to the unclean... Would you like to know who it is that I call impure? Those who long for human applause, who fail to preach the Gospel in a disinterested way... It is not to the proud but to the sincere that truth is revealed."

v. 15)   *Catch the little foxes for us*
                that destroy the vineyards,
                for our vineyard is in flower.

Here the Divine Spouse ceases speaking to the Bride's heart

and addresses His faithful friends and ministers, charging them to take very special care of this privileged soul, now considered a true vine; and speaking in her name also, since she is now very closely identified with Him, He charges them to catch the little foxes of certain disordered attachments or affections, or other little defects that pass unnoticed, but which, unless they are quickly eradicated, will gradually and secretly ruin her, changing her from His chosen vine and the garden of His delights into a true desert (*Is.* 5, 6; *Jerem.* 12, 10-11). The little foxes, according to Maria Dolorosa, are also the various thoughts which have the appearance of God but which are really prompted by the devil in his efforts to trouble the soul and ruin the vine of God's purposes.

According to many Fathers (Origen, Augustine, Gregory, Cassiodorus, Bede etc.), in the Church these little foxes, or jackals. (very common in Palestine where they do great damage in the vineyards), represent the heresies that destroy the Savior's vine; therefore He charges His apostles, prelates, preachers and doctors to catch these little foxes: *Cum proditur dolus, cum fraus aperitur, cum convincitur falsitas, rectissime tunc dicitur capta vulpes.* St. Bernard (*in Cant. Serm.* 64).

"The Spouse had said," remarks Fr. Juan de los angeles, "that the vines in flower yielded their scent, and He now charges those entrusted with looking after the churches (represented by the vineyards) to defend them against the attacks of heretics and perverse men. The heretics are called little foxes because by feigning humility they deceive and ruin the Church. . . And they are to be feared chiefly because of the flowers; that is to say, because of the damage that can be done to those who have not yet produced fruits of perfection, for, as St. Gregory says, the less mature a soul is in virtue the more quickly it can be led astray."

"These false doctors who destroy the Lord's vine in this way," writes St. Augustine (in *Ps.* 80), are "as clever as foxes and equally skilled in hiding and in deceiving, but at the same

time easy to recognize because of the foul odor they leave
behind them."

As far as the vine of the soul is concerned: "What are the
little foxes," asks Fr. La Puente (*Guía espiritual,* tr. 4, Ch. 14),
"if not the disordered imaginings and affections which with art
and cunning enter the heart and gnaw away at the shoots of the
virtues planted there? These are difficult to catch for they use
their cunning and smallness to hide themselves, entering under
the disguise of virtue, gradually, with great cleverness."

But, as St. Teresa would say, in a room where plenty of
light enters no cobweb remains hidden. The light here
communicated to the soul in this close intimacy with her
Spouse reveals within her not only these little affections but
numerous other faults or imperfections as well that begin to
germ and sprout again and would very gradually grow stronger
doing damage if not now nipped in the bud. She herself wants
to be free not only of the conspicuous and noticeable faults
which she had already been rooting out, but also of her slightest
and most hidden faults and of all that might prevent her from
advancing in virtue and from pleasing her Spouse. For this
reason, both in His name and in hers, He Himself charges His
friends who are entrusted with the care of this vine to *catch
these little foxes* for them before they can do any considerable
damage. Here, then, according to spiritual teachers, we are
taught one of the most important rules of Christian life, which
is the extreme care that must be taken to avoid and get rid of
even the slightest defects, however harmless they might appear
to be, and to try to destroy them as soon as they begin. Do not
let them grow to become the cause of our ruin or to prevent us
from harvesting the fruits which God wishes to gather within
us: *Principii obsta. . .*

In the vine of the just, too, there is another kind of little
foxes similar to those which attack the Church, the most
damaging of which, according to Fr. Juan de los Angeles, are
the hidden detractors and those who blandly flatter one. Both

can be caught with favors and gifts, with admonition and fervent prayer and so will not do harm to the flowering vine. The flower is a new life; for modesty in clothing, moderation in speaking, serenity, gravity and composure are signs of the fruits that are to come.

"These spiritual vines," writes St. Bernard (*Serm.* 63), "should be seen only as referring to those pious people whose souls, being well cultivated, yield the fruits of salvation. And what is said of the Kingdom of God (*Luke* 17, 21) that it is within us can also be said of these vines of the God of armies. The Gospel assures us (*Matt.* 21, 43) that the Kingdom of God will be given to those who will produce its fruits which are those St. Paul enumerates saying (*Gal.* 5, 22): *The fruit of the Spirit is love, joy, peace, longsuffering, gentleness, goodness, faith, meekness, temperance.* Advancement in these constitutes our progress. *Fructus isti, profectus nostri.* This growth is very acceptable to the Spouse, Who is entrusted with the care of our salvation . . . , He considers them to be His Own fruits. He carefully watches them develop, is pleased to see how they begin to sprout and then looks after them with the greatest solicitude for our good and for His, for, since we are His, He is interested in our progress. He therefore orders the cunning little foxes to be caught in time to prevent them from later robbing the new fruits."

There words *Catch the foxes,* etc. could just as well, or perhaps even better, be spoken by the Bride, who, now delighting in her Beloved and considering her possessions as belonging to both Him and her, speaks in the name of both, and so lets Him hear her voice with this kind of canticle: *Catch the little foxes for us. . .*

"Desirous that neither the envious and malicious devils," writes St. John of the Cross (*Spirit. Cant.,* Stanza 16)," nor the wild, sensory appetites, nor the various wanderings of the imagination, nor any other knowledge or awareness hamper the continuance of this interior delight of love, which is the flower

of her vineyard, the bride invokes the angels, telling them to
catch all these disturbances and keep them from interfering
with the interior exercise of love, in the delight of which the
virtues and graces are communicated and enjoyed by the soul
and by the Son of God. . . The vineyard spoken of is the
nursery of all the virtues in this holy soul; these virtues supply
her with a sweet-tasting wine. The vineyard is in flower when
the soul is united with her Bridegroom according to the will and
gladdened in Him according to all these virtues together. . . The
soul calls all this harmonious composite of appetites and
sensory movements 'foxes' because. . . as foxes pretend to be
asleep when they are out to catch their prey, so all these
appetites and sensory powers are tranquil and asleep until these
flowers of virtues rise and blossom in the soul in an exercise of
love. At that moment, then, it seems that the sensual flowers of
the appetites and sense powers awaken and arise in the sensory
part of the soul in an effort to contradict the spirit and reign in
their place. . . He does not say 'catch me' but 'catch us' because
she is speaking of both herself and the Beloved. They are united
and enjoying the flowers of the vine . . . At this stage . . . it will
happen that all her virtues are suddenly and clearly revealed in
their perfection and that they give her immense sweetness and
pleasure. The soul feels that these virtues are both in her and in
God so that they seem to form a very flowering and pleasant
vineyard belonging to the Bridegroom as well as to herself and
in which they both feed and delight. She then gathers all these
virtues and makes very joyous acts of love in each of them and
in all together. She offers this bouquet to the Beloved with
remarkable tenderness and sweetness of love."

But she is afraid nevertheless, lacking confidence in herself,
and the more enriched she is the more she is afraid. For, as Fr.
Juan de los Angeles observes, "this is what the gifts of God
effect in the humble soul: the greater the gifts are the more
abject she feels herself to be, and she does not use these gifts for
her own pride and vanity but so as to become even

more submissive and modest in her work. She therefore not only flees away from great dangers but also from every risk. . . This soul is extremely well favored and has seen the gifts of the Beloved, and yet, in spite of this, does not feel secure. She is afraid and asks Him to remove the difficulties . . . , she is afraid of the little foxes . . . as though saying: I am not afraid of the enemy who attacks me openly and with the full force of his ferocity, for I can recognize him from afar off . . . ; I fear him when he tries to harm me with astuteness and cunning, secretly and with craft. . ."

All this occurs in the flowering *spiritual spring* that commences when the soul begins to enter fully into the illuminative way, proper to advanced souls. For, as St. Bonaventure and St. John of the Cross (*Dark Night* 1, Ch. 1-7) quite clearly teach, as long as souls have not been lifted up more or less to contemplation, they are still *beginners,* they are still completely immersed in the *winter* of the *purgative way.* And, as St. Alfonsus Rodriguez said, they receive the light through cracks and crevices. It is only when God *illumines* them, darkening them with His *dim rays* in the first steps of contemplation, that they truly begin to *progress,* showing that they now have the light of life with which to take their works out of darkness and continue advancing along the illuminative way in the continual presence of God, following paths of sanctity and justice. After they have succeeded in entering the *royal chambers,* where through experience they now see how the upright in heart love God, their own hearts dilate and they begin to run in His divine service and in the faithful fulfillment of His holy Will. And when they leave these mystical *wine-cellars* where charity is ordered and perfected, they hurry along the paths of God without tiring, as though aided by supernatural wings with which they can, as it were, fly and quickly climb up to great heights (*Is.* 40, 31). It is then that they not only flower, but also begin to produce mature fruits of life. Thus the state of those whose habitual way of praying is discursive or meditative is represented by this mystical winter; the first stages of infused prayer are represented by the happy spring; and the great heights of contemplation in which souls lose themselves so as to live in God are the summertime and autumn, when they bear not only pleasing flowers but mature fruit of virtues and good works. *"Animae non sublevatae,"* says the Seraphic Doctor (in *Hexamer.,* Serm. XX), *sunt quasi in hieme; sed quae sunt sublevatae ad mediocrem contemplationem sunt quasi in vere; sed quae elevatae sunt ad excessus extaticos sunt quasi in aestate, et percipiunt fructus autumnales."*

v. 16)   *My beloved is mine and I am his.*
            He pastures his flock among the lilies.

The Bride can say this in all truth and sureness, and celebrate it with her song, for through experience she sees that He is everything for her since she was captivated by His divine fragrance and by the pasture that He gives His faithful sheep. She resolves to follow Him truly in everything without refusing Him anything, surrendering to Him her whole heart and all that she has.

"What wonderful kindness," exclaims P. Massoulie (*Tr. de l'Amour de Dieu,* Part 1, Ch. 7), "that a God should thus allow Himself be possessed by this soul, as though there were no other soul in the entire universe! How happy must the soul be who, possessing God, is united with Him, and loses herself living only in Him! Are these laws not the laws of the truest, purest and most perfect friendship, loving one another by giving oneself one to the other?"

As we shall see, the soul will repeat this beautiful phrase, or this happy triumphant song, as many as three times, and each time in a more exalted tone, and in a more intimate and truer sense, as the strength of love continues to grow uninterruptedly.

Now, very grateful because she begins to see better what He is for her, she sincerely and truly wants to respond saying *And I am his. . .* She will then feel herself to be more and more

intimately possessed by Him, and, knowing through experience that she is completely His, she rejoices at this exclaiming with admiration, gratitude and satisfaction *I am my beloved's*...
Marveling to see how divinely He responds to this complete giving of herself, being completely hers and turning always towards her as though He had nothing else to think about, she adds: *And he is turned towards me.*

Moved by love and by a strong desire to please her Beloved in everything and never to deny Him anything, she now begins to be anxious, in order to please Him more, to destroy all those hidden little attachments and defects which it cost her so much trouble to discover and which, without her noticing it, could do her great harm and prevent her from attaining the union that she so much desires. As soon as she surrenders herself completely into the hands of the Lord that He might work in her whatever He wishes, she resolves to sacrifice for love of Him the things that cause imperfection in her or prevent her from being united with Him. She then begins to experience Him as her sweet Lord and most loving Spouse, Who is so pleased to take recreation in souls that are pure. He takes His delights in her as long as the mystical *day* of illumination lasts, with its happy clear light, and until the terrible *night* comes with its sad shadows and darkness when the Spouse flees away and hides...

The compact words spoken here by the Bride: *My beloved is mine,* are full of meaning beyond anything we could ever imagine, and only those who experience these mysteries of love can understand them. "We do not know," observes St. Bernard (*Serm.* 67-68), "what it is she says because we do not know what she feels. Tell us, then, O blessed soul, what is your Beloved for you, and what are you for Him...? But such feelings cannot be described or understood, only experienced. If she speaks in this way, it is because feeling herself to be full of ineffable delights in the presence of Him Who is now the sole object of all her desires, unable to remain completely silent or, on the other hand, to express the abundance of wonderful things she feels within herself, she breaks out into these expressions, not in order to explain herself but rather to relieve her feelings. The mouth speaks from the abundance of the heart, but does not speak in accordance with the fullness that is to be found there. . . What she utters here is a kind of transport of love, loving sighs rather than words. . . *He is mine,* that is, because of the goodness and mercy with which He has deigned to provide me with His love and grace; and *I am His* because I do not want to be ungrateful and want to respond with all my affection. . . *He is for me* because of the care that He takes for my sanctification, and *I am for Him* because of my desire to work for His greater glory and to fulfill His Holy Will in everything.

"The knowledge of what her Beloved is for her is so exalted," says the V. Palafox (*Varon de deseos,* Part 3, 3), "that she cannot find words with which to explain it. For if she were to say: *My beloved is* my Spouse, she could say that 'Spouse' is very little for He is also her Father. If she were to say: *My beloved is* my Father, she could say that 'Father' is not enough for He is also her Friend. If she were to say: *My beloved is* my true Friend, she could say that this is not enough for He is also her Lord. And if she were to call Him Lord she could then add that Lord is not enough for He is also God. And for me He is something else apart from God, for He is God and Redeemer. . . Recognizing that she could not sufficiently explain what she felt except with the affection of her inner heart, she explains by silence what the tongue is unable to express. In the same way, after having said *My beloved for me,* without being able to explain what her Beloved is for her, she says: *and I for my beloved,* also without being able to say what she is for her Beloved. For if she were to say: I am my Beloved's lover, she would then think: I am not worthy of being a lover being so full of self-love. . . In this way, by breaking off in her explanation she achieves more; the less she says the more she communicates."

The very learned Fr. Paz, O.P. (*Conm.*) offers no less than four interpretations of this passage. 1st, *My beloved is for me,* that is to say, is befitting to me, *and I for him.* It is as though saying: Each for each, 'He for me and I for Him.' He is white and red and I shall try to be so by imitating His virtues; He is white because of the incomparable purity of His life, and red because of the outpouring of His Precious Blood in death. And I want to be this for Him, keeping my heart pure and stainless in His presence and bringing myself to be torn in grief and to pour forth blood in remembrance of my past sins.

2nd, 'He is for me,' communicating His grace to me enabling me to accomplish good works; and 'I for Him, faithfully cooperating and making sure that His grace is not received in vain within me. And both things, divine grace and our own cooperation, are absolutely necessary for producing the fruits of life.

3rd, He is everything and in everything for my good and advantage; and I wish to be wholly for His honor and glory. For me He was born and lived, and for my love He gave Himself up and suffered; for my good He died, destroying my death with His Own, that I should live no longer for myself but for Him Who died and was raised to life for me. (II *Cor.* 5, 15; cf. *Rom.* 14, 7-9). For whom should I live, asks St. Bernard, but for Him without Whom I would have no life? He Who offered His life for me quite rightly claims my own.

4th, 'My Beloved for me' is all that I can desire; for He is my entire Good, the complete and absolute Good that embraces every good and that can satisfy all my desires. For this reason she did not state in concrete terms what her Beloved was for her, but limited herself to saying *My beloved for me . . .* since He is incomparably more than all that could be said or even thought. *And I for him,* all that I am and am capable of. She refrains from saying what she is, so as to avoid boasting and because it is but slight in comparison with what she would like to be for Him.

She finds it is not enough to say she is His servant, sister, daughter, friend, bride . . . for all that she is or may be she wants to recast in love of her Spouse.

"What are you to Him?" also asks Fr. Juan de Los Angeles. "What He is to you, we have already seen; what you are for Him we are told, is *Ego illi.* And she goes no further; she makes no mention of the holy thoughts she offers Him, nor of the frequent prayers, nor of the long vigils, nor of the works of piety in which she is occupied, nor of the souls in whom she serves Him, for this is but little with which to return His love. What she says is: *Ego illi.* I am wholly His, all that I am. It is a reply which, while not equalling her Spouse's generosity, at least imitates it in her careful attentiveness, disposition and service. What God is for the soul is out of all proportion in comparison with what the soul is for God, but there is a similarity. . . There is all the difference between finiteness and infinity in their favors, but they are very similar. He loves me as Creator; I love Him as a creature, but I do nonetheless love Him. And since all that God wants of us it that we love Him, He is content simply with our love. All the other affections of the soul, together with the exercises and arts, have some goal beyond themselves, but the affection of love asks only for love. Love is the favor and the reward, the demand and the payment, for nothing is deserving of love but love. . . He is all mine and I am all His and there is nothing to be more said. . . He is cut according to the measure of my will, and I according to His."

But . . . how can she show that she is now her Beloved's, completely His, and in accordance with His desire . . . ?

"Now I see, my Spouse," exclaims St. Teresa (*Conceptions,* Ch. 4), "that Thou art mine, I cannot deny it. For my sake didst Thou suffer these great trials, for my sake didst Thou endure these scourgings, for my sake hast Thou remained with us in the Most Holy Sacrament, and now that Thou dost bestow on me these exceeding great marks of Thy love. Then . . . what can I do for my Spouse? . . . How can I be

Thine, my God?. . . He allows us to think that He needs us —
He, this true Lover, my Spouse and my Good. Then, daughters,
since He allows us to think this, let us exclaim once more: 'My
beloved to me and I to my beloved!' Thou to me, Lord! If Thou
comest to me, how can I doubt that I can render Thee great
services? Henceforth, then, Lord, I would forget myself and
look solely at the ways in which I can serve Thee and have no
will save Thine own."

"O how great is Your generosity!" exclaims St. Mary
Magdalen de Pazzi (*Part* 2, Ch. 6). "You are our Father, our
Spouse, our Lord, our Brother. . . For my part, I do not want to
halt at this word 'Pater'; I want to reach the contemplation of
Your divine attributes. . . But seeing at the same time that You
are so beautiful, so lovable, so good, so sweet and gracious,
neither shall I be content with the simple contemplation of
Your greatness and divinity, but will take the liberty of calling
You my Spouse, of considering You as such, of embracing You,
and loving You as my chaste and tender Spouse, for without
You, My beloved Spouse, I would never enjoy any peace!
Without You I cannot live, without You I am nothing, without
You I can do nothing, nor do I want to do anything or want
anything. . . If You were to give me every happiness, every
pleasure that can be enjoyed on earth, all the strength of the
strong, all the wisdom of the wise, the graces and virtues of all
creatures, all this without You would be a hell to me. And if
You were to give me hell with all its horrid torments, provided
that I had You I would consider it a paradise."

"This expression *Dilectus meus,*" says the V. Mariana de
San José, "is so mysterious and sweet that it seems to me
impossible to give it a true explanation; and I have not seen any
commentary which would seem to explain it completely. For it
is a cipher of all the delights and excellences of love, a blend of
expressions of love so sweet and beautiful that it is not
surprising that it cannot be explained. Thus, so as not to take a
long time in describing the state in which love held her, she

explains it in these very few words: *My beloved for me and I for him.* It is as though to say: He and I understand one another . . . like one who has encountered his own likeness. But who made her like the Spouse? It was He Himself Who made her like Him, with His grace, with His gifts, with His favors and expressions of love. In short, like One Who was espoused to her in faith is the impression He made on her; both of them should live keeping themselves the one for the other with all faithfulness and care. Here she sees Him, recognizes Him and thanks Him, The Bride here calls these thanksgivings and responses 'lilies', among which the Spouse pastures, that is to say, as long as the souls's responses to Him continue, He will remain present with her, provided that the Bride does not become neglectful, for in neglecting her duty the day passes away and the shadows of night begin to fall. . ."

If this intimacy comes to reign between Jesus and a soul conceived in sin, what will not happen between Him and His Holy Church? Above all, what will not happen between Him and His Immaculate Mother. . .?

"O who could ever understand," asks M. Olier (*Pensées choisies,* 1916, p. 94), "what Mary is to Jesus, and what Jesus is to Mary. If the terms bride, sister, beloved and all-beautiful are inadequate for the Son of God to express His sentiments for His Church, what words are there which could show us His feelings of love and tenderness for the Holy Virgin? This most lovable Jesus fills her so completely that He does not leave her room to love anything except her Beloved. When she wishes to work, it is always in Him and through Him . . . ; and she can have nothing which is not for Him."

For he pastures among the lilies, that is to say, He exhales a fragrance so sweet that it is as if He fed Himself upon them, or as if He had spent the whole day among the sweetest-smelling flowers. The Septuagint translates it as *He pastures (his flock) among the lilies,* picturing Him as a Shepherd who leads His sheep to a field full of these flowers, with whose scent He becomes perfumed and also perfumes His sheep.

Then, as St. Lawrence Justinian observes, the soul can be very sure of being entirely His, and He hers, because the fragrance of life that embalms gives witness to this fact. Her integrity and pure love inspire this firm trust within her.

O, to be fed by so sweet and loving a Shepherd . . . !

Who pastures among the lilies. . . "He is a wonderful shepherd," writes St. Gregory of Nyssa (*Orat. 5 in Cant.*); for He does not pasture His sheep with hay but with pure lilies. He does not want His own flock to feed from the coarse pastures of the world which will make them bestial and earthly. For it is written that all flesh is hay (*Is.* 9, 6), that is to say, as long as one is living in the flesh. But whoever lives by the Spirit of God is not only freed from corruption, but also becomes one spirit with Him, and thus he himself becomes a most fragrant lily of purity, converted into the very nature of this divine food."

A truly *divine* food . . . ! For the "Lily of the valleys and Flower of the field" feeds us with His Own flesh and blood which is full of every fragrance and beauty and which He communicates to His faithful sheep so as to make them the gardens of His delights. "What a Shepherd!" exclaims St. John Chrysostom, "He feeds His flock with His Own blood!"

And who but He could also give *eternal life*?

"Happy the soul'" exclaims Fr. Juan de los Angeles, "who has been made God's garden, adorned and beautified with a variety of virtues! There He finds entertainment and recreation . . . *Qui pascitur inter lilia,* because of their purity, as though she were to say: I have a most pure Spouse Who has the color and fragrance of Heaven, and Who pastures both His flock and Himself among souls whose minds are pure and who are endowed with most beautiful and resplendent virtues. . . This Divine Shepherd's flock will not die of hunger, nor will it feed on rough pastures. The pastures are such that the Shepherd also feeds on them. Thus there is no mystery in the ambiguity of the word that means both to give food and to be fed. He gives food and is fed in graceful pastures and in sweet, flowering places."

Here the words of St. John in the Apocalypse are in some way fulfilled: *non esurient amplius. . . , quia Agnus qui in medio throni est reget eos. . .*

"Only of Christ can it be said," continues Fr. Juan de los Angeles, "that He is not only our Lamb, that is, Host and Sacrifice, but also our King and Shepherd and such a loving Shepherd that when He feeds His sheep He too is fed.

By pasturing, or pasturing His sheep among the lilies, we are quite clearly given to understand the fragrance and purity that He breathes and brings souls to breathe. "His pasturing among the lilies," according to St. Bernard, (*Serm.* 71), "is His delighting in the beauty and fragrance of virtues. . . When He feeds, He feeds us, and feeding us He Himself is fed and regaled, for our profit is the tastiest morsel to Him. . . Heaping spiritual joy upon us, He is glad to see our gain. My penitence is food to Him, my salvation is food to Him and I myself am food to Him. . . I am eaten by Him when He reprimands me, chewed and swallowed when He instructs me, digested when He renews and transforms me, assimilated when my life becomes like His: *Mandor cum arguor, glutior cum instituor, decoquor cum immutor, digeror cum transformor, unior cum conformor.* Do not be surprised at this, for in fact He eats us and is eaten by us so as to unite us more intimately with Him . . . May He eat me, then, that He might have me within Him, and may He be eaten by me that I might also have Him within me. In this way our unity and conformity will be complete, I living in Him and He in me."

"It should be noted," says St. John of the Cross (*Spirit. Cant.,* Stanza 17), "that the soul does not say the Beloved will feed on the flowers, but *amid the flowers.* He feeds on the soul, transforming her into Himself, now that she is prepared and seasoned with the flowers of virtues, gifts and perfections, the seasonings with which, and among which, He feeds on her. By means of the Holy Spirit, Who prepares the dwelling, these virtues delight the Son of God so that through them He may feed more on the love of the soul. This is characteristic of the Bridegroom, to unite Himself with the soul amid the fragrance of these flowers."

v. 17)   . . .*until the day blows and the shadows sink.*
          Return, my beloved, and be like a gazelle,
          a young stag on the mountains of Bether.

This blowing of the day is the fresh evening breeze which is very much looked forward to in Palestine when the days are hot. Then, when evening falls, *the shadows flee,* (as in the Hebrew text), their darkness lengthening and disappearing to give way to the night. This intimate communication with the Divine Spouse, this most enjoyable giving of one another lasts only until the evening breeze begins to blow, the shadows lengthen and the dark, dreadful night of the soul arrives, a time when in order to further purify, assay and refine her love and faithfulness, the Sun of Justice seems to abandon her completely, leaving her sadly forlorn and forsaken as though in complete solitude, encircled in thick darkness and surrounded by foes. For as "night falls, all the forest animals come out. . . (until) the Sun rises and they retire (before It) (*Ps.* 104, 20-23)."

This dreadful *night* will be repeated over and over again until the soul is purified of all from which our sinful nature needs purification so that it can come to the intimate and stable union with the God of all purity and holiness. Only while the evening breeze is still blowing and the night is still drawing nigh, only as long as the light of day still shines can she feel her Beloved grazing among the lilies, can she enjoy Him and speak to Him those words that give her such consolation and delight. For when the shadows sink and the mystical night begins, when she is lost in her darkness, she scarcely knows whose she is, nor can she find Him Whom she loves with all her heart, nor is she able at times even to call to Him, however near He is to her, or rather however hidden He is in the depth of her heart, secretly protecting her and taking pleasure in seeing how she sighs for

Him. But she, although more safe than ever, seeing only wild beasts surrounding and menacing her, believes that she is lost. . .

For this reason, scarcely has she mentioned the night than she trembles and prays immediately for the return of day, for her Sun to appear again for she can no longer live a single moment without seeing her sweet Lord. Thus she cries out to Him loudly, saying *Return*. . .! Return with the speed of the gazelle . . . , since You are fleeing and leaving me, be as this little animal or the stag. Look back occasionally and let me see Your Face even at the top of Bether, the mountain of *Separation* which prevents me from seeing You, or on the true *Bether,* the mountain of prayer, that separated me from the world, a mountain full of fragrance that You find so pleasing and delightful.

"Because she places her love in Him," writes the V. Mariana, "she lets Him do in her whatever is His Will. She beseeches Him only that this withdrawal be like that of the stag, never letting her out of His sight, so that in this way she may not fall or forget Him, and asks that He return soon so that the time of His absence might pass quickly. She asks that like the young stag watching from the top of the mountain, He never cease looking at her, thus preventing her enemies from offending her, for they would not dare to do so in His sight."

Your visit, she will tell the Lord, borrowing the words of Job (10, 11), *kept and preserved my spirit.* Fr. La Puente (*Guia,* tr. 1, Ch. 20) writes, "without Your visitation neither the life of grace which You gave me, nor the gifts which through Your mercy You communicated to me, nor the Spirit of Heaven which You infused into me, none of these can last, and without them I would fall from the mountain of mortification, which would become a sad death for me, and I would climb down from the hill of prayer converting it into a painful distraction."

Thus she will be, as it were, forced to say over and over again, *Return! Return!*

"My Lord," exclaimed the Blessed Suso (*Eternal Wisdom,*

Ch. 13), "You are such a sweet, beautiful, divine, incomprehensible Friend that even if all the angels were to speak to me of You they would not satisfy my heart nor would they prevent it from longing for Your presence. Do I not love You more than the whole of Heaven? Where then is the faithfulness of Your love? The Bride whose heart You have captivated awaits You, desires You, sighs, groans and dies for Your presence, from the depths of her heart she is crying out: *Return, return. . . Lord!* You hear the cries and groans of the soul who loves You and yet You remain silent! . . ."

Very often, writes Fr. Juan de los Angeles (*h.* 1), not only is Christ very present in a soul but "He directs and governs her and is, as it were, her soul and spirit, and yet He is not felt or known by the soul herself. Hence her longing and anguish, and the frequent repetition of the word *Revertere. . .* He is present and pretends to be absent though hearing the *Revertere. . .*

But when the Beloved is absent, he continues, "there is nothing that can give the soul consolation. Having learned to love nothing but God, she can be consoled only by Him. . . Only He Who dwells in the soul can comfort her. He although often absent from the joy and delight of the just by not entering the faculties, is never absent from their merit, being present, though hidden in the depth and essence of their souls. The former is more delightful but the latter more profitable. . .

"O the ways of God! You love a soul with great tenderness and yet sometimes You put her in such great difficulties and to such an extent that it seems that You have forgotten her and changed from being her friend into being her enemy! And why, Holy Spouse? So as to test her faith, so that it can be seen that she loves You, so as increase her desires, so that she might anxiously look for You and once she has found You not let You go. Thus You increase the care, the vigilance and the merit."

Revertere. . . "What is this, O ardent soul," asks St. Bernard (*Serm.* 73), "the Beloved of your heart has just

departed and already you are telling Him to return?. . . Have
you forgotten anything important? Forgetting, in fact,
everything which is not her Beloved she even forgot herself. And
although she does not lack the light of reason she now does not
seem to be completely sane. . . The excessive violence of love
leaves her distressed. . . *Return my beloved,* she tells Him when
He has scarcely begun to leave her. Nor is she content with this
but begs Him to come running, and running no less than with
the speed of the gazelle. . .

"But such an inopportune call," he continues (*Serm.* 74),
"is a clear sign of the excessive love of the one, and of the
ineffable kindliness of the Other. . . *Return,* she tells Him. . .
Who could give me a worthy explanation of this coming and
going of the Word?. . . Whence can He come and whither can He
go, seeing that He fills everything and is everywhere present. . .?
Using the figurative language with which God Himself
sometimes chooses to speak to us. . .we would say that the
soul s Divine Spouse comes to her as He pleases and leaves her
when and how He likes; and we understand these comings and
absences to refer not to movements of the Word but to the
sensibility of the soul. When the soul feels grace within her, she
knows He is present; when she does not feel it she complains
that He has left her and once again begs for His presence, saying
(*Ps.* 27, 8): My Lord, my eyes do seek You, and I am always
longing to see You. But is it strange that she should seek for
Him so anxiously when, being deprived of His sweet company,
she finds everything loathsome and tedious and nothing can
console her? For her only remedy is to search for Him with
greater care and to call to Him in the greatest truth. This is the
way to oblige Him to return: by calling to Him with strong and
urgent desires. . . Is not desire itself a true voice? A voice it is,
indeed, and a very powerful one. *Lord, You have heard the
voice of the humble,* said the prophet (*Ps.* 9, 17). When the
Word is absent, then, a continual desire always remains in the
loving soul like a ceaseless clamoring for His return: Verbo

igitur abeunte, una interim et continua animae vox continuum
desiderium ejus, tamquam unum continuumque revertere,
donec veniat.

"Give me, then, a soul that is visited frequently by the
Word, that is inspired by His closeness, that is made hungry by
His absence, and strengthened again by the joy of His presence,
that is brought to true disdain of all things through the holy
inactivity of contemplation. To such a soul as this I would not
hesitate to give the name of Bride, all that the Holy Spirit says
about her. For every soul that longs for the return of her
Beloved in this way, thus shows that *she has already merited His
presence,* although not as much as she would like. Otherwise she
would not say *return,* but *come.* And perhaps He has left
precisely in order to be urged more ardently to return, and
thereafter to be possessed more firmly. *Forte ideo subtraxit se
quo avidius revocaretur, teneretur fortius,* just as on another
occasion He pretended to go further away, not because this was
His purpose but because He wanted to hear them say (*Luke* 22,
27): *Stay with us, Lord...* The same words the soul now
repeats over and over again with devout yearning Passing on, He
wants to be halted; and leaving He wants someone to call Him
back... He goes away and returns as He pleases, visiting His
chosen ones very early so as later to test them with His
absence... These comings and goings of the Word take place in
the soul for her good, as it is written (*John* 14, 28): *I am going
away and shall return to you,* and shortly afterwards (16, 16):
*In a short time you will no longer see Me, and then a short time
later you will see Me again.* O, 'a very short time' indeed! How
very, very long it is! O holy Lord, You call the time that we
spend without seeing You *very short!...* Well, this very short
time is for me a very long time, indeed an excessively long time.
This absence is very short for what I deserve, yes, but very long
for what I desire... And the loving soul, moved by her urgent
desires, forgets her nothingness and, closing her eyes to the
majesty of the Beloved, opens them to the joy of possessing

Him, placing her hope of salvation in Him and working without fear. Bold and daring, she calls out to the Word again, confidently beseeching Him to renew His delights, treating her with His accustomed freedom, not as Lord but as her Beloved, saying to Him: *Revertere. . .dilecte mi. . .*"

These visits, he adds, can be recognized very clearly by the salutary effects they produce. Thus, although we cannot fathom His ways, since this "Word of God is living and efficacious, "as soon as He entered my sleeping soul, He awoke it, moved it, softened it, melted it, wounding my heart which was sick and as hard as stone. He also began to tear out, destroy, building and plant, to water the barrenness of my heart, to light up its darkness, to discover its secret breasts, to inflame what was cold, and to straighten the crooked, and convert the rough ground into smooth paths, so that my soul blessed the Lord. . . Sometimes entering my soul as Spouse, the Word gave no perceptible sign of His entry. . . Only through the movement of my heart did I notice His presence; just as through my abandoning of vice and the mortification of my carnal affections I came to know the power of His arm; just as through the secret repression of my hidden faults I came to admire the depth of His wisdom; just as through a certain improvement in my habits I experienced the goodness of His sweetness; and just as through my inner renewal and reform I came in some way to perceive the image of His beauty, remaining stunned, as it were, wondering at the abundance of His greatness.

As soon as the Word leaves, everything begins to languish, to become numb and cold. . .and here for me is the clear sign of His absence, my soul remains sad until He returns again and until it recognizes Him by the new ardor in my heart.

"Having these experiences of the Word, is it strange, then, that I should take the liberty and use the Bride's words to oblige Him to return when He leaves me?. . . As long as I live I shall have the habit of crying out for the return of the Word with the cry *Return!* And I shall repeat this as often as He is absent from me, ceaselessly crying out, like someone running after a person who is escaping, with an ardent desire in my heart that He return and restore to me the joy of His salvation, giving Himself to me."

"It comes to pass," writes Fr. Gracian, "that the soul is disconsolate, dry, lukewarm and alone, for it seems to her that her Spouse has left her, since she does not enjoy His sweet and gentle presence as she is accustomed to do. She calls to Him to return to her presence saying *Revertere*. . . As though to say: Return, my Lord, and comfort my soul with all the swiftness and lightness that You usually show in coming to console me, and may I feel mercies and gifts like those You gave the world on Mount Sinai. . . and that You gave on Mount Calvary. . . that is to say, a strong desire to keep the law of God and to imitate His passion. This desire usually comes after the abandonment; for these *two mountains* are called the *mountains of Bether, beter* in Hebrew meaning house of separation; and when it seems that God abandons the soul, leaving her to suffer barrenness, He will usually return with greater delights and fruits to those souls that persevere in love and prayer."

Since it is the Holy Spirit Who moves the faithful Bride in this way to cry out with all her heart *Return! Come back!*. . . let him who hears her continuous cry and does not want to remain deaf to the voice of the Holy Spirit, say and repeat *Come!*. . .

In this way he will freely receive the water of life. Come, then, Jesus, come! . . .

Et Spiritus et Sponsa dicunt: Veni. Et qui audit dicat: Veni. . . Et qui vult, accipiat aquam vitae, gratis. Veni Domine Jesu! (Rev. 22, 17, 20).

Synopsis

The soul has entered fully into the *mystical night*, which is repeated and prolonged for her purification, and in which she believes herself to be plunged into the greatest abandonment being unable to find her Beloved in the bed of prayer (v. 1); the courage and resolution with which she goes out to search and ask for Him (v. 2-3); how through faithfulness, meekness and generosity she finds Him and ardently embraces Him, unwilling now to let Him go until He has taken full possession of her as her true Spouse and absolute Master (v. 4). Another mystical dream and another command not to disturb it (v. 5)... The way in which the soul leaves completely renewed, breathing out the fragrance of prayer, mortification and every virtue (v. 6). The guard for the bed of the true Solomon, His wonderful litter, and the mysteries of His coronation celebrated by the Bride herself (v. 7-11).

THE BRIDE

1. *In my bed, in the nights, I sought him*
   whom my soul loves:
   I sought but did not find him.
2. *I will rise and go through the city:*
   through the streets and the squares
   I will seek him whom my soul loves.
   I sought but did not find him.
3. *The watchmen who guard the city found me:* [a]
   Have you seen him whom my soul loves?

a.   In the Hebrew: *The guards who go about the city...*

4. *Scarcely had I passed them*
   than I found him whom my soul loves.
   I held him fast and would not let him go
   till I had brought him into my mother's house,
   into the room of her who conceived me.

THE SPOUSE

5. *I charge you daughters of Jerusalem,*
   by the gazelles, by the hinds of the field,
   not to stir my love or rouse her,
   until she please to wake.

CHORUS (*friends of the Spouse or Bride*)

6. *Who is this coming up from the desert*
   like a column of smoke,
   perfumed with myrrh and frankincense
   and every kind of scented powders?[b]

THE BRIDE

7. *See, it is Solomon's bed.*
   Around it are sixty champions,
   of the most valiant of Israel;

8. *they are all armed with swords*
   being expert in war.
   Each man has his sword at his side
   because of fear in the night.[c]

9. *King Solomon has made himself a litter*
   of wood from Lebanon.

10. *The pillars he has made of silver*
    the couch of gold,
    the ascent of purple;
    its interior is adorned with precious things

b.   In the Hebrew: *What is this (or who is this)... like columns of smoke,*
     breathing of myrrh and frankincense, and every perfume of the merchants.

c.   So as to avoid any surprises that might occur. According to Dionysios of
     Helicarnaso, it was also a custom among the Romans to guard the royal bed
     during the night.

for the daughters of Jerusalem. [d]

11.   *Daughters of Zion, come out and see King Solomon,*
      wearing the diadem with which his mother crowned him
      on his wedding day,
      on the day of his heart's joy.

Exposition

v. 1)   *In my bed in the nights I sought Him*
          whom my soul loves:
          I sought but did not find him.

The *nights* came, and long *nights*, one after another; and
their darkness is such that the more the soul seeks God in
prayer the less she seems to find Him. What was formerly a bed
of rest and happiness no longer seems to be so, but is rather a
bed of torment and pain, of bitterness, anguish and mortal
afflictions. It is in this desolation and forlornness, in this
terrible abandonment and solitude, enveloped in the frightening
darkness of the mystical *night* that the soul will become
completely purified and shine like a diamond of inestimable
worth. She calls out to Him, and searches for Him more
diligently than ever, seeking ways to discover Him again. What is
the favorite place for this search if not the mystical bed of
prayer where so often by merely calling to Him or, when least
expected He would show Himself to her, heaping ineffable gifts
upon her?

Here she finds only a depressing void and desolation that
fill her with such loathing and repugnance that she would prefer
to do any other work than to remain in such barrenness and
violence. Yet she perseveres, hour after hour, night after night,

d.   The *media* of the Vulgate is neuter plural, signifying *those things in the
     middle,* hence *its interior. Charitate* is a Hebrewism, the noun substituting for
     the adjective *valuable* or *precious; propter* here is *for,* or *to please.* The
     Hebrew reads: "Within, an embroidery (or work) of love for the daughters
     of Jerusalem."

knowing that perseverance is always rewarded and that Jesus prayed at greater length when He was in agony.

Experiencing such delay and not knowing what to do nor how to find Him whom she so much desired, she is compelled to go out, however inopportune this may be, riding roughshod over everything, to ask for Him of those who might know, and to search for Him where she knows He is usually to be found: occupied in winning souls or working for the greater honor and glory of His Eternal Father. It is her duty to go in search of Him wherever her own obligations call her, for this is the clear expression of the will of God, urging or moving her in the exercise of many works of piety and mercy. We must search for Him in the *city* of God: in the service of Holy Church, in the *streets* and *squares* of our duties where we can in some way discover His tracks or those of His faithful followers that might give us some news of Him, or wherever the interests of God or the needs of our neighbor call us. At times, then, as St. Teresa advises, we ought to exercise ourselves in exterior works of piety or devotion by which our souls are prepared to surrender themselves again more fruitfully to contemplation, thereby winning the heart of God and deserving to be heard and consoled more quickly, as Isaiah says (58, 7-11): *Share your bread with the hungry... Then will your light shine like the dawn and your wound be quickly healed... Cry and the Lord will answer; call and He will say: I am here... When you give relief to the oppressed your light will rise in the darkness, and your shadows become like noon. And the Lord will always guide you to true rest and will fill your soul with splendor... and you will be like a watered garden, like a spring whose waters never run dry...* (Cf. *The Mystical Evolution*, pp358-70)

"If you only knew," said Our Lord to Sr. Benigna Consolata, "how willingly I rest in a charitable heart! There I find my delights and bring the soul to enjoy them, flooding her with peace, joy and celestial consolation."

The mystical brides must not, because of this, abandon

their retreat or become distracted or dissipated, or wander away from the paths of Jesus, for if they were to do so, in vain would they imagine that they were out in search of Him. . .

"These squares where they fail to find the Spouse (and where it is impossible to find Him)," says the Ven. Mariana de San José, "are a remedy I have often seen Him use. . . when in difficult times souls are distracted by some occupation or other that is not so much illicit as indifferent, and which is such as to keep them from prayer. . . As a result of this, souls usually suffer and are plunged into very dangerous torments and calamities, even falling to such an extent that only with very great difficulty can they be saved. The truth is that, in order to look for the Spouse, the soul must not flee from Him but, on the contrary, must cry out perseveringly at the threshold of His house, for if she remains there, He will come out in search of her and when found, she will receive new favors and mercies. He does not abandon the Bride, although He does hide so as to see if she is able to suffer for His sake, and also if she will profitably use her talents to search for Him, even at the cost of abuse and her very blood, for a love untested is worth very little."

She looks for the Beloved of her soul in all this darkness, in the bed of her heart, and does not find Him. "O how great the pain is that she suffers while she is in this state!" exclaims María Dolorosa. "On the one hand, she is resigned to accept God's will; on the other hand, she cannot be at peace fearing that it was through her own fault that her Lord left her. She continually asks herself the cause of this very painful absence and although she cannot find it she cannot rid herself of this fear. Whoever is greatly in love is very fearful of displeasing the object of this love. In this way she searches for Him and does not find Him. It is only in order to bring her to experience her own insufficiency and weakness that from time to time He permits this darkness to fall, refusing to attend to the Bride's calls until He is pleased to show Himself to her again."

"The Spouse did not return at the Bride's cries," writes St.

Bernard (*Serm.* 75) "undoubtedly so as to quicken her desires, to try her affection and to enkindle her more and more in divine love. These trials are more the product of pretence than of indignation. They are stratagems to make the soul continue seeking Him for although He was called He did not come. Perhaps if He is sought after He will allow Himself to be found as it is promised in the Gospel (*Matt.* 7, 8): *Search and you will find*. . . Enkindled in greater desires to find her Beloved, the loving Bride goes out in search of Him with all the ardor of her soul. She searches for Him first of all in the bed and in no way can find Him. . . And it should be noted that she has not gone out vainly searching for Him on just one occasion, on just one night; for she tells us that many were the sleepless nights she spent looking for Him."

Quaesivi. . . quaesivi. "A repetition that indicates the care with which she searches and the anguish that she suffers. Quem diligit. . . These words also, expressing a very strong affection, are often repeated in this passage. *Et non inveni.* What a penetrating sadness is conveyed by this simple little phrase!" (Fillion)

Thus the poor little Bride cannot fail to join the Ven. Palafox in exclaiming (*Varón de deseos,* Part 2 *Sent.* X): "Come lament with me the sadness of my soul. I sought my Beloved there and did not find Him. . . When I thought I had Him in my heart I found my heart empty of God and full of myself. I thought I had You, Jesus, and that it was You that I felt and loved, but it was I who was living there. . . I looked for You in my heart: *In lectulo meo,* and not in a heart that is Yours but in a heart that is mine. Instead of looking for You as I ought, in the desire to serve You, I looked for You in the pleasure of enjoying You. Instead of looking for You as I ought, in the love of praising You, I looked for You in the security of feeling You near. I looked for You for myself when I ought to have looked for myself for You; to have adored You for You and to have come to live in myself without myself, so that You alone could

dwell within me. When shall I stop living in myself? When shall I
stop losing myself deep within myself. . . ? O Lord, strip my
heart that I might leave it and join You, and You, my God,
enter into it! Just as the soul animates the body so You
animate my soul. May Your will govern it, may Your love
govern it, may Your inspirations guide it and may Your charity
inflame it."

What will this poor soul do, then, in such sad solitude?
v. 2)   *I will rise and go through the city:*
               through the streets and the squares
               I will seek him whom my soul loves.
               I sought but did not find him.

"Here," says the Ven. Mariana de San José, "the soul
usually suffers the very painful anguish of absence. It is suffered
quite justifiably, for what could a soul miss if she has her Lord.
And if she does not have Him, who is there that can give her
companionship, and what life can she have now that she is
without life. . . ? That is how it appears to souls who know love,
when it seems to them that He has gone and left them. When
the Lord causes this pain to be felt there is nothing that can be
compared to it; and when they meet souls who are distressed by
the loss of worldly goods, whatever they might be, it seems to
them a very vile thing that they harbor any grief at all for such
things. Apart from being so afflicted, the soul ardently desires
to suffer even more, and to end her life in the grip of this
anguish which keeps her so exhausted, even wishing to have the
combined strength of all creatures with which to surrender
herself to it the more. Even still her heart is not satisfied for,
since her loss is infinite, she will not rest until her suffering is
infinite. Besides this, there is all the anguish that stems from her
willingness to have died a thousand times rather than to have
given Him cause to leave her; and the anxiety of wondering
whether she, in fact, gave Him this cause, and how she can
repair this with physical torments if need be. Since the suffering
increases as she sees that after her first efforts she still has not

found Him, she says: If what I have done already has not been sufficient, *I will rise and go through the city,* etc. It is as though she says: I shall thoroughly search out the corners of my soul and will see whether there is any obstacle preventing the Spouse from entering it. I shall pass through the narrow streets which are the paths and ways which He walked leaving the traces of His footsteps. If I did not watch carefully enough or did not walk as He wished, I shall correct myself and perhaps in this way I shall find Him."

She rises in the state of dryness and desolation in which she finds herself, and in spite of the fear that such darkness could cause in her, she resolves to pass along the most trodden paths of the mystical *city of God,* the methods, devotions and pious practices by which she used to find Him, remembering that, as St. Teresa points out (*Life,* Ch. 13 and 18), no state of prayer is so lofty that occasionally one does not have to return to the beginning stages again. She sets out along these sacred streets where the way of searching for the Kingdom of God and His justice is preached, and passes through these squares where mystical talents are negotiated in the service of the heavenly King and where, with all that one possesses, one can buy the 'hidden treasure' and the 'precious pearl', and where with supplications and tears, with fasting and penitence and alms and other works of piety and mercy one obtains from Him the grace and virtue with which to please and serve Him as He likes, and to be deserving of His favors. But not even in this way does she find Him, for as she adds: *I sought but did not find him. . .*

How could she say this since she does indeed find Him in the faithful fulfillment of her duty? She says this because she is not aware of this finding, because she has not found the Lord in the perceptible or joyful way that she desires. The truth is that He is very close to her and very much within her when she searches for Him in this way.

"You should know, my daughter," our Lord told Gemma Galgani (*Biography,* Ch. 21), "that while you were suffering I was always near you. . . After the darkness will come the light, and then you will abound in clarity. . . If you truly love Me, you must love Me even in darkness. With souls that are dear to Me I like to entertain Myself in games of love. Do not be afflicted if I pretend to abandon you and do not believe that this is a punishment; it is only something My love has invented to take you completely away from creatures and to unite you to Me. When it seems to you that I am leaving you, you should know that quite the contrary is true, that I am embracing you all the more closely. . . Be of good cheer for after the struggle will come the peace. What you need is faithfulness and love."

"My Jesus," exclaimed Sr. Benigna Consolata, "how have You been able to allow this state to last so long? 'It was for your good; I want to prepare you to receive new graces; I have deprived you of consolation to give you the opportunity of practising perfect charity. An *Ave Maria* said not during fervor but as a pure act of the will in times of aridity is of much greater worth in My sight than a whole rosary recited in the midst of consolations. Write this to comfort souls."

"You are tiring yourself out calling to Me," He once told St. Veronica Juliani (*Diary*, Sept. 8, 1696), "and here I am with you." Although it seems to the soul that she is without God, for she is searching for Him she can be consoled to know that this searching for Him comes from God and this aspiring to attain Him is to possess Him. Even though there be no feelings of it, she who has love already has Him Who is contained in love" (*Palafox*, 1. cit.).

"Whoever looks for God," said St. Augustine (De vita beata), "is not without God even if he has not yet found Him."

He alone can console the soul and comfort her in this apparent abandonment.

"Even if the whole world were to join together in consoling her," says the Ven. Mariana de San José, "it would not be enough, and all creatures put together could not fill the void in the soul . . . ; the more she remembers what she has lost, the greater the pain, the higher her esteem for the Spouse, and the emptier everything becomes without Him. . . But the Spouse did not leave the Bride like this, nor in fact was He absent except with regard to the senses, suspending those lights and touches that He gave her by which she might feel and know Him perceptibly. It is clear that it was no more than this, for she had these desires which are extremely precious. . ., this is an excellent disposition for; making more rapid progress and extending the soul's capacity to receive greater mercies from the Spouse."

This is no small mercy that He gives her in encouraging her to perservere.

"The Bride's constancy," adds St. Bernard (*loc. cit*), "is truly astounding and her courage prodigious! To get up by night, to go about the streets unassisted, to pass through the city asking all she meets for her soul's Beloved, undeterred even by a thousand obstacles and difficulties, and refusing to let either the hour of her rest, or the modesty becoming her quality and sex, or the fear instilled by the darkness and shadows of the night to dampen the vehemence of her desires. These desires are still frustrated and in spite of all her diligence she has achieved nothing. What purpose could the Spouse have in hiding Himself so tenaciously that He gives rise to displeasure . . . and could well lead to despair. . .? I understand that such pretense (if it can be called this) would be pious and useful to the Bride as long as she was content with calling out to Him. . . But now that she is looking for Him and looking for Him again so diligently, how is it that she does not find Him? How is it that the Spouse is sought after so carefully and with so much zeal and yet does not let Himself be found either in the bed, or in the city, or anywhere, when He Himself promised us (*Matt. 7, 7*): *Seek and you shall find?* Jeremiah, speaking with God, says: Lord, You are good to the soul that seeks You. . . Nevertheless there are three reasons why many of those who go out in search of the Lord do not find Him; namely, by searching for Him at the wrong time, or in a way or place that is not befitting. For if any time were right for looking for Him, in vain would the Prophet tell us: *Seek the Lord while He may be found. . .* (*Is.* 55, 6); from which it can be inferred that the time will come when it will not be possible to find Him. That is why he adds that we should call upon Him while He is near us. . . We are now at the right time and in the days of salvation; undoubtedly at the right time to search for and call upon Him; at the time when He usually makes His presence known even before He has been invoked. For listen to His solemn promise (*Is.* 65, 24): *Before you call me I will tell you: here I am. . .* Since God must be sought through good works let us try to practice them and do good to all while we have time. . . The most opportune time for finding Him is the present, when whoever looks for Him will surely find Him providing that he looks for Him where He is to be found and in the way which is befitting."

The true reason for the Bride not finding Him despite the fervor and diligence with which she looks for Him is that she searches for Him in a way that is not altogether befitting, going out in this way at such an improper hour without anyone to guide or direct her to where He is to be found; without a light and a guide she is searching for Him by night, running the risk of losing her way. Although it may be a time to look for Him, it is still not the time when He can be found, at least not by searching for Him in this way. In fact, adds St. Bernard, "we must consider all the time that we spend in searching for the Spouse as true night; for, were it to be daytime for those searching for Him, He would at once make Himself present to them and they would no longer need to look for Him."

"If the Sun of Justice," observes St. John Climacus (*Spiritual Ladder*, Ch. 26), "after having dawned in our soul, ever set within us, hiding from us His gracious presence and the light of His consolation, there would then be darkness in the soul and *night* would fall; for during this absence man finds everything dark and concealed and it seems that the light is not to be found anywhere and the sky becomes like metal and the earth like iron. There he is enveloped in such darkness of passions and confusion of thoughts that at times he suspects he has completely lost divine grace. For on this *night,* which is when this darkness occurs in the soul, every wild beast of the forest passes through us. . . that is, the fierce and bestial passions of anger and impatience. . . beasts which walk about during this time, roaring to take from us the hope of persevering in the good that we have begun. . . When the Sun appears again however all these wild beasts of passions and temptations withdraw and disappear and retire to their dwellings, that is to say, to hearts that are carnal and sensual."

The night arrives again and the soul returns to her sad solitude and to her search for the One she loves . . .

In my bed, she says, in a state of unspeakable suffering; *in the night,* in a state of darkness, of inability to pray, to feel, to reason, *I sought Him Whom my soul loves.* How can she look for Him if she lies quiet in her bed of suffering, experiencing her nothingness? Precisely by being resigned to her own incapability, her nothingness and the impossibility of her looking for Him: this is the best and surest sign that she is truly looking for Him; for in this way she trusts in Him alone.

It seems to her that this is mere idleness, that she is not doing what she could and ought to be doing; she tends to watch what the others do to follow them, and she goes out into the streets: the spiritual exercises, readings and conversations whereby perfection and the way of finding Him are taught, to see if through the ordinary paths, practices, methods and procedures she can find what she is seeking so earnestly. But in vain: *the entire city,* that is to say the entire sphere of the Church, of sermons, feast days, pilgrimages, devotions and readings which move others — all this she passes through, trying to imitate whatever good example she observes in whatever kind of person, but without discovering the secret that she is seeking.

I sought but did not find him.

"When she finds herself separated from Him," writes Fr. Gracian (*h.* 1), "the loving soul goes in search of her Christ in every place she can. She searches for Him within herself, trying to achieve spiritual quiet and suspension of the senses but often these efforts are to no avail. . . and so she says: In lectulo meo. . . On other occasions she rises to meditate. . . And thus says *I will rise and through. . . the streets and the squares I will seek my Beloved*. . . I shall lift my thoughts to Heaven; I shall meditate on the lives of the saints, both of those who followed the narrow active life, and of those who pursued the contemplative life and walked through the broad squares of divine love. . .; but even with all this I do not find Him."

Nothing that she can see and hear without, can fill her within; neither the works of charity and devotion, nor the care of the sick, nor the splendor of fellowship can produce a lasting impression upon her. She always feel herself to be *alone* and devoid of the good for which she longs.

What must she do? It seems impossible for her to turn to her spiritual *directors,* for now she finds in them only greater emptiness and confusion. Where can she find the kind that she desires? But God provides for her need: without her having to look for them they come out to meet her; she finds them in her darkness and nothingness and, forgetful of herself and of everything, she addresses them asking for her Beloved. These are the true watchmen: attentive, zealous, vigilant and providential. What do they tell her? The text does not say, but it is clear: they surely tell her that they understand her and advise her to rest quietly; not to leave her path without a light or guide and to continue sighing and hoping in this way. . . They tell her to be brave and to persevere in looking for Him, for this absence is not an abandonment, but something devised by love itself. "Do not think yourself abandoned," said our Father St. Dominic's favorite disciple and first successor, the Blessed Jordan to the Blessed Dian (*Letter* 28); "do not think yourself abandoned because you feel great aridity and desolation. . . The Lord does this for some time so that you will search for Him with greater ardor, and looking for Him will find Him with greater consolation, and finding Him will be united more intimately with Him, and possessing Him will never lose Him again. . . With the two arms of prayer and contrition you will have Him close to you and you will never let Him go."

"She did not find God, her soul's Beloved," says M. Sorazu (*Spiritual Life*, Ch. 19), "while she looked for Him in her own bed, in herself, nor did she find Him in the streets and squares of creation until, separated from creatures and from herself, she followed the advice of the men of God and established herself in God Himself, in Whom she must now see all of creation, including herself. For although it is true that God can be found in creatures, this is not the way for souls who are now called to dwell in God's bosom, withdrawn from everything and transported beyond themselves, just as the Word dwells in the Father. . ."

"When the soul is in aridity like this," remarks Fr. Gracian, "it is good advice to take a devout book, to listen to a sermon, a talk or a discourse given by a learned and spiritual servant of God. The spirit is normally uplifted through good doctrine; and thus she says: *The watchmen found me. . .*"

Indeed, when she follows the advice of these watchmen and advances a little, Jesus makes His presence felt with all the swiftness of a beam of light, and forgetting her past worries she rushes forth to embrace Him.

v. 3)   *The watchmen who guard the city found me:*
          Have you seen him whom my soul loves?

While she was doing all she could on her part to find Him Who had so stolen her heart, she is surprised by the watchmen and guards of the holy city, that is, by the prelates, confessors or directors responsible for watching over souls, and who, at the Spouse's wishes, now go out to meet her to enlighten her with His lights. When she sees them, though, without waiting for

them to ask her what she is doing there at such a time and
without giving them any further explanation, she addresses
them as true representatives of God and anxiously asks after the
sole object of her love, which supposes that they must know
who this is. Then we see how she tries to follow their directions
and advice most scrupulously, and even to exceed it. This is
how she eventually finds Him.

v. 4)   *Scarcely had I passed them*
                 than I found him whom my soul loves.

"Love does not give up hope even if it fails to find news of
what it seeks and desires; it becomes more enkindled and thus
the Bride went out and found for herself what they could not
show her. It is a cause for much wonder and admiration that,
previously she looked at length for Him and did not find Him,
but when she left the city-guards she then found Him. It can be
understood from this that in the most hopeless things, when all
human wisdom and endeavor are exhausted, then is God most
ready to come to our aid. Together with this, it can be seen that
the reason why many search for Christ for a long time and
through numerous trials without finding Him, while others find
Him more quickly, is because these search for Him where He is;
and the others do not find Him because they search for Him,
not where He is, but where they would like to find Him; serving
Him in those things that they like most and that are most
pleasing to them, reflecting their own particular inclinations and
opinions" (Fr. Luis de Leon).

"Whoever sets out to search for Christ," says St. Ambrose
(*De Isaac,* Ch. 5), "avoids looking for Him in idleness and
pleasure. He is neither in the bed, nor in the rich and wonderful
halls of justice, but on the cross, in humiliations, in poverty
and in trials; He is always among those who join together in His
name and who fear Him. . . Let those who want to find Jesus
Christ and taste how sweet the Lord is, go out of themselves. . .
deny their own passions and appetites as the Gospel prescribes
and the Spouse will then surely show Himself to them and will

be theirs. Let them imitate Mary Magdalen who rushed to the
tomb of her Beloved before dawn and did not halt nor rest until
she found the sole Master of her heart."

"The soul," says St. John of the Cross, (*Spiritual Canticle,*
Stanza 3), "is aware that her sighs and prayers, . . . are not
sufficient for her to find her Beloved. Since the desire in which
she seeks Him is authentic and her love intense she does not
want to leave any possible means untried. . . Even after she has
done everything, she is dissatisfied and thinks she has done
nothing. And accordingly . . . she desires to look for Him herself
through works . . . practicing the virtues and engaging in the
spiritual exercises of both the active and the contemplative
life. . . And mindful of the words of the Beloved, *Seek and you
shall find* (*Lk.* 11, 9), the soul decides to go out . . . to seek Him
through works that she may not be left without finding Him.
Many desire that God cost them no more than words, and even
these they say badly. They scarcely desire to do anything
for Him that might cost them something . . . if they were not to
receive thereby some delight from God in their mouth and
heart. They will not even take one step to mortify themselves
and sacrifice some of their satisfactions, comforts, and useless
desires. Yet unless they go in search for God they will not find
Him, no matter how much they cry for Him. The Bride of the
Canticle cried after Him but did not find Him until she went
out looking for Him. . . She says that she found Him after
undergoing some trials. He who seeks God and yet desires his
own satisfaction and rest, seeks Him at night and thus will not
find Him. He who looks for Him through the practice and
works of the virtues and rises from the bed of his own
satisfaction and delight, seeks Him by day and thus *will find
Him.* . . The Bridegroom Himself points this out in the Book of
Wisdom (*Wis.* 6, 13-15). . . . This passage indicates that when the
soul has departed from the house of her own free will and the
bed of her own satisfaction, *she will find outside divine
Wisdom. . .*"

"The loving Bridegroom of souls cannot long watch them suffering alone. . . because as He says through Zacharias, their afflictions touch Him in the apple of His eye (*Za.* 2, 8); especially when these afflictions are the outcome of love for Him. . ." (*ibid.*, Introd. Stanza II).

"Who," asks St. Bernard (*Serm.* 76), "are these watchmen guarding the city, but those whom the Savior declares as blessed (*Luke* 12, 37), provided that He finds them keeping watch at the hour of His coming? O what fine sentries are they who, passing whole nights in prayer, are very careful to be on their guard against the deceits of the enemy, ready to thwart their schemes, to break their snares and to frustrate all their machinations! These are they who truly love their brothers and the entire Christian nation, who never cease to pray for them and for the holy city of the Church. These, who are very careful to look after the sheep that the Lord entrusted to them, devote their hearts to keeping watch from very early dawn, and to praying in the presence of the Most High. They keep watch and pray knowing their own inadequacy,, and aware that were the Lord not to guard the city, in vain would they keep watch to guard it (*Ps.* 127, 1). Since the Lord tells us (*Mark* 14, 38): Keep watch and pray, lest you fall into temptation, it is clear that without this double exercise of the faithful and the care of the guards neither the city, nor the Bride, nor the sheep can enjoy any safety. . .

"Be on your guard, then, priests and others of you charged with this ministry of looking after souls! Keep watch over yourselves and over the precious trust that has been given to you! It is a *city;* guard it and see there is concord. It is a *Bride;* take care of her adornment. They are *sheep;* feed them."

"But let us now see," adds the holy Abbot (*Serm.* 77), "how it is that the Bride while not finding Him for Whom she was looking, yet was found by those for whom she was not looking. Let this be carefully heeded by those of you who do not hesitate or fear to enter the paths of life without a guide or director; who want to be masters in the spiritual art at the same time as disciples, and not content with this, search for proselytes, thus becoming 'the blind leading the blind'. How many of these we have seen stray from the straight road at such peril. . . ! Let those who work in this way bear in mind then, that they must proceed with much caution in the future, learning from the Bride, who could in no way find the One she desired until she had first been met by those whose direction and teaching she had to make use of in discerning and knowing her Beloved. . . Whoever fails to turn to his director places himself in the hands of the seducer. Whoever abandons his sheep and leaves them unguarded is more a keeper of wolves than of sheep."

It should be noted, as St. Bernard observes (*Serm.* 78), "that before the sentries speak one word to her, the Bride asks after her Beloved, and as though inspired by God, is the first to speak to her guides asking them: *Have you seen him whom my soul loves?*. . . Had she herself not been prepared by the grace of the Holy Spirit she would never have dared to address those she meets with such familiarity, and to ask for Him from whom this Divine Spirit proceeds. Thus she did not wait for them to ask why she had come but she herself spoke to them, and undoubtedly from the abundance of her heart."

"O violent Love!" continues the holy Doctor (*Serm.* 79). "O vehement, enkindled, impetuous Love Who allow one to think only of You, causing all else to provoke loathing. . . ! You upset the order of things, You do not observe their use, nor do You show concern for means and circumstances, triumphing over everything and captivating for Your sake whatever seems convenient and reasonable. Whatever this soul thinks and says refers solely to You and nothing exists for her apart from You — so great is the power with which You made Yourself Master of her heart and tongue! *Have you seen him,* she says, *whom my soul loves,* as though the sentries already knew of Whom she was thinking. O Bride, you ask for Him Whom your soul loves?

Has He no name perchance? And who are you and Who is
He...? The language of divine love seems strange to one who
does not love. But since these sentries had also received the gift
of love from the same Spirit, they know what this Divine Spirit
says, and understanding the language of love, immediately reply
in the same language, that is, with loving desires and pious
affections. In a short time she is so well informed about what
she asked that she can straightway say: *Scarcely had I passed
them than I found him whom my soul loves...* It was right, in
fact, that the Bride should meet those who must bring her to
know the truth, but not that she should stay there, for had she
not gone on ahead she would not have found Him for Whom
she was looking, We must suppose that this was what they
advised her for they did not preach themselves but their Lord
Jesus Christ Who is undoubtedly far above them and Who said
(Ecclesiasticus 24, 26) Approach me you who desire me."

According to the Angelic Master these guards are the holy
doctors who, as St. Gregory says, cheer and inspire us with their
words and writings. We must however study their doctrine very
carefully, going beyond the pure materiality of their phrases
and truly penetrate into the Divine Word.

"The watchmen who guard the city of the Church,"
repeats Fr. Gracian, "are the doctors and teachers who write
good spiritual and devout books or who preach piously and for
the good of consciences; and it happens that once a soul reads a
devout book or hears Christ spoken of, she recollects herself
and gladly returns to the devotion she had lost. When she finds
Him in this way, she embraces Him and strives never to let Him
go until she reaches the beatitude of glory which is her Mother,
the beloved Jerusalem. With this strength she is transported
again and rests in inner silence and in prayer of union..."

She did not find Him when she looked for Him in her own
bed, that is to say, in her own way or where she would find
herself; nor did she find Him in the streets and squares of
conversation and communication with creatures, nor in their

ways of behaving and thinking. It was only when she left them
and herself and, faithfully following the advice of her directors,
ascended above all creation so as to lose herself in God, that she
was able to find Him.

"*Scarcely had I passed them* — in my search for God where
they themselves had told me He would be, beyond creation, in
the bed of the Divinity — *than I found him whom my soul
loves; I held him fast,* with my understanding and will, *and will
not let him go till I have brought him into my mother's
house.* . . until I have brought Him into my own heart through
the mystical and divine contemplation that I long for and until
He has sanctified me as He sanctifies the angels and saints who
possess Him through perfect assimilation in glory. *I shall not let
him go*. . . . this is what the soul does at this time, retaining her
God and not letting Him go for a minute, tirelessly endeavoring
to bring Him into her heart, now under the aspect of one divine
perfection, now another, conceiving an understanding of these
perfections and allowing them to fructify in her to the degree
that God has predestined. It is impossible to describe the
wonderful activity carried on by the soul in her daring, and at
the same time, resigned and holy efforts to become Godlike (M.
Sorazu, loc. cit.).

> *I found him whom my soul loves*
> *I held him fast and would not let him go*
> *till I had brought him into my mother's house,*
> *into the room of her who conceived me.*

"After the soul has searched for her Beloved throughout
the night," observes St. Ambrose (*De Isaac,* Ch. 5), ". . . He
finally takes pity on her and goes out to meet her; and she says:
I have him and will not let him go. It is then that she imbibes the
divine mysteries in torrents and, intoxicated with the wine of
charity, falls into unspeakable ecstasy."

The most holy Lover of souls could not allow the soul who
loved Him so much and who so resolutely and generously
searched for Him, to wait any longer. Seeing her do even more

than was required by her guides, He straightway goes out to meet her and presents Himself to her. Thus, as the Sun of Justice rises for her, the shadows disappear, the wild beasts flee with all their fears and anguish, and all is peace and joy. Therefore she cries out in gladness: *I found him. . . I embraced him, I will not let him go now. . .* until I have made Him the absolute Master of this house that I inherited from my mother, my fallen nature, and which, when purified by Him and adorned with His graces, can offer Him a sweet flowery bed wherein to rest. . . Thus she brings Him into the place where she felt His absence so keenly and where she sought Him so painfully.

Her mother's house is also her family, her religion, her community. . . ; she wants to bring Him in there with renewed fervor and with new graces and blessings. . . She does not want to let Him go, says St. Augustine (*Meditations,* Ch. 25, no. 2) until she has come to reign with Him in the house of that other great Mother of ours, the heavenly Jerusalem.

Because she did what she was ordered, and her generosity even extended beyond this, and because she was faithful and fervent, she can now exclaim in transports of joy that she has found Him with her understanding, held Him with her will, and will not let Him go, but rather will try to bring Him into her own heart through mystical contemplation, assimilating one after another all His ineffable perfections.

He allows Himself to be captured and this soul's grasp is so strong that she thinks it is impossible for anyone to snatch from her, only Beloved in Whom all her good is to be found; and that she will manage to bring Him into the place where she knows He is delighted to dwell and reign, which is her own heart, and also 'the room of her who conceived me'; that is the celestial room of *life in Mary,* the Mother who brought her into the inner Life of the Spirit and who at the same time, as St. Grignon observes, has the key to the mystical wine-cellar with which she can bring in whoever she pleases.

St. Gregory of Nyssa and St. Ambrose understand house
and room to be the Bride's own heart and the upper part of the
soul where the Holy Spirit dwells adorning and enriching her
with His precious gifts and with all His supernatural virtues. It is
here that the Bride herself seeks to enthrone her sweet Beloved
and enter into the most intimate relationship and familiarity
with Him, and where she hopes perpetually to enjoy His
presence and company, to feed from His words of eternal life,
to learn His impenetrable secrets, and in all security and
confidence benefit from His ineffable consolations and most
loving communications.

Nec dimittam. . . "Negat sponsa," says Soto Mayor, "non
se libere dimissuram esse Sponsum, quem jam comprehensum
tenebat, donec. . , ipsa a Sponso suo plene ac penitus omnia
arcana et sublimia mysteria, quae scire cupiebat, edoceretur."

She wants, said Ricardo, to bring Him into the innermost
part of the house where she can converse with Him alone and
hear most intimate secrets from His mouth.

I have him and will not let him go. . . "It is true,"
according to Fr. Gracian, "that when the soul is in the prayer of
quiet she will never want to leave it, nor concern herself with
any other exercise." She sees that nothing can be as beneficial
to her as this intimate relationship with the Savior.

With respect to the Church, this mother into whose house
she must bring Him, is the Synagogue, which she will come to
know at the end of the world, and in such a way, says St.
Gregory, that she will come to have the most intimate
communications with Him.

Tenui eum, nec dimittam. "A saintly patriarch," adds St.
Bernard (*Serm.* 79), "said: *I will not let you go until you bless
me (Gen.* 32, 26). This soul does the same and much more, for
even though He blesses her she will not let Him go. What I want,
she says, is not just Your blessing, but You Yourself. For, apart
from You, whom have I in heaven and who is there upon the
earth that I desire? (*Ps.* 73, 25). I shall not let You go then, not

even if You give me Your blessing. . . But perhaps He Himself is no less eager to be held, for He said (*Prov.* 8, 3): *My delights are to be with the children of men.* . . What stronger union could there be than this, sustained by the firm and vehement will of both? If she holds firmly to Him, He also has her firmly grasped as she herself declares when she says (*Ps.* 73, 23): *You held my right hand.* Holding on to Him and being held by Him, how is it possible for her to fall? She is clasped to Him through the firmness of her faith and the fervor of her devotion; but she could not hold Him in this way for very long unless she was also supported by Him. It is the Lord Who, with His power and mercy, supports her."

O the wonders of divine love! . . . O how incomparable is the joy of the soul united with God, made one with the Word and Seat of Divine Wisdom . . . !

"Every soul enamored of God," says St. Liguori, "is always certain to find and embrace Him with faith and charity in the Holy Eucharist. . . In it, how frequently this strong faith is transformed into a kind of vision or locution in which the voice of the Beloved is heard, speaking words of eternal life and of ineffable mysteries. . . !"

These expressions of the Bride can more properly still be applied to the Church herself, whose union with Christ is indissoluble; however much trouble it costs to hold Him, the Church will never let Him go, until the end of the world when she will have the satisfaction of bringing Him into the house of her mother the Synagogue, in whose bosom she was formed. Nor will He let the Church go, or allow the Church to let Him go, for we have His unbreakable promise to remain with her forever (*Matt.* 28, 20). "So from then on," adds St. Bernard (ib.), "neither Christianity, nor. faith, nor the Church's charity have ever been lacking on this earth. The fierce floods came and the strong winds blew and violently beat against her; but they could not demolish her because she is founded upon the Rock Who is Christ Himself. For this reason, neither the vain argumentation or the word-spinning of philosophers, nor the subtleties of heretics, nor the swords of tyrants have been able, or even will be able, to detach the Church from the love of God which is in Jesus Christ (*Rom.* 8, 39), so tightly is she clasped to the One Whom her soul loves and so happy is her union with Him!"

With good reason the holy Bride can joyfully exclaim: *I have him and will not let him go. . .* Her ardent desires were not in vain for, transported at once in lofty contemplation and enraptured with the delights of divine love, she remained submerged in a profound sleep; one so sweet and fruitful for her and of such satisfaction to her Beloved that He Himself once again undertakes to see to it that she is not awakened, repeating His order that her emulators dare not to disturb her.

v. 5)   *I charge you daughters of Jerusalem*
              by the gazelles, by the hinds of the field
              not to stir my love, nor rouse her
              until she please to wake.

Jealous of the good enjoyed by these happy souls who, like Mary, chose the better part, Jesus again charges the over-solicitious and disorderly Marthas, by the same objects of their solicitude and love, not to awaken His Beloved until she, whose will is identified with the divine will, considers it time to awaken. From this it can be seen how good, beneficial and pleasing to God is this mystical sleep, as He again sternly orders that she be not disturbed; for there, in such intimate union with God, the soul undoubtedly gives greater glory to God and benefits to the Church and herself in a very short time, then she would through much action and less union.

"The Spouse is greatly pleased," writes Maria de la Dolorosa, "to see His Beloved resting on His breast; and so He charges souls still young in prayer not to awake her until she pleases. They do not understand this sleep of ecstasy in which they see the mystical Bride enrapt. Perhaps thinking that it is one of the numerous faints that women often suffer, they try to help her, shaking her or giving her scents. Meanwhile the soul in such a state of adoration will usually be aware of everything, have a keen ear, however much she might be unable to move or speak or open her eyes. She is disturbed to see others looking at her but is unable to do anything to prevent it. For this reason the Spouse does not want her to be troubled, and so that she might know how concerned He is, He charges the daughters of Jerusalem . . . by the things that they most love."

Fr. Luis de León supposes that this second command is made by the Bride herself who, in reply to the first, now wants her sweet Love to rest peacefully in the bed that she has prepared for Him. Since this bed is her own heart, when He rests there it is she herself who rests and sleeps the mystical sleep, while her heart keeps watch, sweet perfumes that are so rare on earth.

THIRD SECTION
God in the soul: Betrothal

The union contracted in this second sleep is the intimate and uninterrupted sleep of the soul transported into the mystical *betrothal* of the soul who is now in the first stages of the ineffable *transforming union* where God *lives and reigns within her and works through her.* She is so *advanced* now that she is the cause for much admiration and could well be considered relatively *perfect* although strictly speaking she is still not perfect.

v. 6)   *Who is this coming up from the desert*
          like a column of smoke
          perfumed with myrrh and frankincense
          and every kind of scented powders?

It is not known whether it is the daughters of Jerusalem who say this, or the Bride's maiden friends, or, as seems most probable, the Spouse's friends or the angels in Heaven who are astonished to see this precious column of incense coming up from the desert and barren land of the world, fragrant with the perfumes of all the virtues, and which, to the great joy of those dwelling in Heaven, is gradually rising up from this loving bosom.

"When she reaches this stage of prayer," says María de la Dolorosa, "she rises up to God like a column of incense through her desire to sacrifice herself for His glory... It is for this reason that the Spouse, rewarding these desires as though they were already realized, presents His Beloved to the angels who say: Who is this coming up from the desert... ?"

While the holy soul rests beneath the guard and protection of her Divine Lover, choirs of His friends sing at His gates, wondering to see her so rich in gifts and merits, so beautiful and perfumed with graces and virtues, and so exalted and transformed with the strength of love that enkindles her. How beautiful she is as she ascends and how imposing, a living supplication represented by this column of smoke! (Cf. *Ps.* 141, 2). This mystical smoke is formed from the myrrh of mortification, from the incense of devotion and from all the other aromatic spices which the Divine Gardener planted in His own heart and cultivated. All noble hearts must yield before these souls who are espoused to Christ and who endeavor to be worthy of His most notable favors, as they see how highly they have been exalted and the inconceivable good that they do in the world, keeping numerous other souls from corruption with the fragrance of their virtues, winning them for God. Thus God wants the virtue which, until now had remained hidden, to radiate and manifest itself for the good of many and to be, at times, the object of great praise (M. Leon) even though this might then provoke new controversy.

This has a very special application to the Church and to the Blessed Virgin; to the Church, as it rises fragrant and beautiful above all the sects that are born and remain in this sad desert while she mounts up to God; and to the Virgin, especially in her Immaculate Conception, in her happy birth and in her glorious Assumption, when she appears embalmed with the singular fragrance of her gifts and virtues, glorifying God with ineffable delight, and exalted above every human and angelic creature.

Furthermore, it is applicable not only to the very advanced but also, in a certain sense, to every devout soul. All must ever bear in mind that the incense of prayers that they must offer to God are to be joined to the fragrance of every virtue, accompanied especially by that of myrrh, which symbolizes mortification of the flesh and is a memorial of the burial of Jesus Christ, and of our mystical death and burial with Him through baptism. "When the devout soul," writes St. Gregory the Great, "mortifies her flesh to keep it safe from the gangrene of vice, it is as though she were applying myrrh to a dead body to free it from eternal corruption. When, through the vehemence and ardor of her holy desires she rises up into the heavens, diligently banishing from her heart every sinful or useless thought, she then makes of her own heart a censer from which, enkindled in the fire of charity, rises a column of the most fragrant and exquisite smoke into the presence of God." "It is in this fire," he adds, "that the just exhale the fragrance of their prayers and virtues which have a scent whose delicacy is measured by the extent to which it has been purified of every worldly composition to be able to please God as the Bride does."

Like a rod of smoke. . . "When the incense burns," says Fr. Gracian, "the smoke at first appears very slender like a small rod, but then it extends and spreads throughout the room filling it with a fragrant and delectable scent. In the same way the loving soul attains to an exemplary life, for she takes the incense of prayer and the myrrh of mortification with the interior acts of other virtues and casts them upon the hot coals of the love of God.

Although, at the beginning, whoever proceeds in this way is not known or esteemed in the world, he will later give off the sweet odor of sanctity, and at the end of his life his name and reputation will be known throughout the Church and will serve as a model and example for many others."

Thus the holy soul will oblige many to exclaim in wonder: *Who is this . . . ?*

"As though to say," writes Fr. La Puenta (*Guia,* tr. 4, Ch. 12), "Who is this soul who, living in the desert of the world and in the exercises of penitence, climbs and grows in them like incense or a little rod of smoke? A little rod, because she climbs with humility and is young in heart; of scented smoke, because she does not climb with the splendor of joy but with weeping and tearful eyes, full of fragrance and great sweetness. From where does this smoke proceed? From the myrrh of the mortification of her flesh and from the incense of prayer that accompany her, and from all kinds of scented powders, which are the acts of other moral virtues, milled through mortification and prudence so that they can be bound and joined to one another helping each other in a kind of brotherhood. But it is not enough for the smoke to appear: they must all cast themselves on the hot-coals of charity that are in the censer of the contrite heart, and with the force of this fire they advance and grow in every perfection. O happy is the soul who rises up before the Divine Majesty with such a precious scent! O what a blessed ascent is this that edifies men, fills angels with wonder and gives God Himself such great delight!"

"By making mention of every kind of scented powder," writes the V. Granada (*Memorial,* tr. 7: Love of God, Ch. 5), "the whole spectrum of virtues needed for this ascent is indicated. However, the special mention of myrrh and incense — which are mortification and prayer — indicates that these two virtues are especially helpful in this transformation; for the one mortifies whatever in the soul is contrary to God; and the other unites her to Him, making her one spirit with Him."

v. 7)   *See, it is Solomon's bed.*
               Around it are sixty champions,
               of the most valiant of Israel;

v. 8)   *they are all armed with swords*
                being expert in war.
                Each man has his sword at his side
                because of fears in the night.

These words seem to be spoken by the Bride herself who, as though blushing to hear such praise, seeks to direct it to the glory of her Spouse to Whom she owes everything in her that is worthy of praise and admiration. It is as though to say: do not praise me but Him to Whom everything that you revere in me belongs. Behold His bed, what riches it exhibits and how well defended it is; and do not wonder at the graces and strength that are communicated to me there.

We have already seen that the bed of the true Solomon can be the bosom of the Eternal Father, the bosom of the Blessed Virgin, the crib, the cross, the ciborium. . . and also, in a special way, the heart of every soul where He has His delight and where He comes to rest, to celebrate the mystical betrothal with her. All these various beds are not only sustained, adorned and enriched with great virtues and inestimable treasures of graces, but also protected or guarded by legions of angles (cf. *Matt.* 25, 53), symbolized by these sixty valiant guards.

"In these loving dispositions," says Maria de la Dolorosa, "she comes to be the bed for her Beloved, the true Solomon, Who knows how to lead souls, giving them true wisdom. In order to show His Bride how carefully He guards her, He points out all the angels defending her. O, the loving heart of God! Not content with loving souls to the extent of shedding Your Own blood for them, You entrust them to the protection of Your angels who will constantly watch over them. In this way You make them so much Yours that You have all your delight resting in them, and they have all their love placed in You."

According to St. Gregory, the bed of the Bride's heart is, in some way, guarded by all the saints and great servants of God who protect her with their words, examples and spirit of prayer.

Thus, although the soul appears to be alone and

surrounded by danger, she nonetheless feels by the prayers of the just and comforted by the continual presence, not only of her holy guardian angel, but also of innumerable angels that God sends to protect and defend her (*Ps.* 91, 11; cf. St. Teresa *Life* Ch. 21); and in this way she can join Elisha in confidently proclaiming (*Kings* II, 6, 16): *Have no fear, there are more on our side than on theirs.* We could all witness this reality if our eyes, like those of the prophet's fearful servant, were opened by faith (*ibid.* 17).

Because of this, the princes of darkness who, with their infernal cunning, make secret attacks which cause these nightly fears, never manage to take her by surprise, nor succeed in harming or disturbing her however much they encourage the world and the flesh to assault her. Who but these angels carry her as though in the palms of their hands so that she will not stumble against anything, and teach her to flee even the slightest occasion of sinning and to avoid dangers of which she, in her innocence is unaware?

These faithful friends of ours and valiant defenders always have their swords at hand that we can see how quick they are to fight for souls who implore their help and protection, how ready to free them from every attack, however sudden it may be, and to resist all their enemies and put them to flight. This is carried out in a special way in the many attacks which God allows the soul to suffer in the two dark nights, *of the sense* and *of the spirit,* where she experiences such fear. These are the *nocturnal fears* against which He deigns to protect her. Trust fully, then, in Him Who is your strength and refuge, but fear yourself, and you will see how you are never better defended or nearer to triumphing over everything or more carefree. Never more laden with precious trophies or overflowing with merits, never richer in virtue and grace than when you think you are alone like this, in the dark, surrounded by enemies, and abandoned in a terrible desert, with no other recourse but to hope against all hope in the mercy of Him Who never abandons those who cry out to Him from their hearts. *He helps them in times of trouble (Ps. 9, 10) bringing all things to work together for the greater good of those who love Him (Rom. 8, 28).*

"See how carefully," adds Maria de la Dolorosa, "the Lord guards the soul who loves Him, ordering His angels to defend her always, with the sword of His power ever ready. He wants them to be continually giving her firm inspiration to prevent temptations from prevailing over her during the night of her present life."

Solomon's bed is also guarded by zealous priests and directors who, with discretion and sacred wisdom, watch over the good of those souls entrusted to them, always ready to defend them with the sharp spiritual sword of the true word of God, elucidated in their own example.

"O divine Solomon!" exclaims Fr. Puente (*Guía,* tr. 4, Ch. 14), "O true King of peace! How truly you desire rest as though in your own bed! You are not content with the care that You Yourself take to defend her but in addition, You want armies of guardian angels to surround and defend her, angels chosen from among the strongest in Heaven that see Your Holy Face. They are always on guard and ready to defend her with the sharp swords of their strong inspirations, warning her against dangers and adversities. You want her to be surrounded by the strong men of Your Church, by the Holy Fathers who went before us and by those who now govern in Your name, and who, by word and example, guard and encourage her, preserving her peace and integrity without any disturbance or violation. Furthermore she is surrounded and defended, Lord, by sixty valiant men of Your house, which are the heroic virtues and gifts that you have communicated to her for her defence and safety, each one carrying a sword with which to destroy and vanquish the enemy should he dare to trouble her. What is perfect chastity but one of these strong men who guards the heart . . . ? What are humility and spiritual poverty but strong men of Your house who guard Your bed against the vain desires for honors and riches, annihilating them before they can disturb the soul? What are the seven Gifts but seven strong guards, direct and immediate instruments of the Holy Spirit, which by their divine actuation fortify the heart against the onslaughts of her enemies? O Supreme Guard of men, how grateful I am for the guards that You place around my heart that is so sorely in need of them! O Prince of Peace, may the heavenly ranks bless You for the guards You chose to preserve the peace of the heart in which You dwell!"

v. 9)   *King Solomon has made himself a litter*
             of wood from Lebanon.
v. 10)   *The pillars he has made of silver,*
             the couch of gold,
             the ascent of purple;
             its interior is adorned with precious things
             for the daughters of Jerusalem.

To praise even more all the greatness and magnificence of her Spouse, the Bride, after considering His bed, then begins to describe and reveal the riches of His portable throne or chair, litter or chariot (for all these can be used to translate the word *ferculum*), as though adding in joy and admiration: "Well, what can one say of the throne that He has built for Himself, a throne whose beauty is only matched by its richness, a throne made completely of silver, gold and purple worked in an extraordinary and wonderful way? Where it says: *its interior adorned with love* (or *precious things*) the Hebrew word also means enkindled, which is to say that with its beauty and richness it enkindled the daughters of Jerusalem in love and stirred their affection" (M. Leon).

The true Solomon's portable throne, royal seat, chariot and litter symbolize every soul in the state of grace. The more replete they are with spiritual riches and charity, the more attraction they have with which to win other souls, represented by these *daughters of Jerusalem,* who thus come to be enkindled in divine love. Every good Christian is, in fact, the *bearer of Christ,* or the *bearer of God* (*Cristoforo* or *Teoforo*), as St. Ignatius the Martyr called himself, and as we ought to consider ourselves to proceed with proper sanctity and reverence: *"Do you not know,"* writes the Apostle (I *Cor.* 3, 16; 6, 19-20), *"that your bodies are the temple of the Spirit Who dwells within you. . .? You are not your own. . . Therefore glorify and bear God in your body."*

This throne must be built by the heavenly Solomon Himself and is constructed from the incorruptible, beautiful and sweet-smelling wood from Lebanon, which is the fragrant and solid infused virtues that have been planted in the heart by the divine Husbandman; virtues which are immaculately pure, secure and firm, always exhaling the sweet scent of Christ and never that of self-love, as happens with those who are motivated by human esteem.

"The divine Solomon," writes Maria Dolorosa, "molds the soul into a magnificent chariot in which He reclines while embalming her with His grace in such a way that He makes her as incorruptible as the timbers of Lebanon. . . We are told that the King Himself builds it, for only Jesus Christ can make us the object of His gratification."

She is supported, moreover, by *pillars of silver,* which are the seven gifts of the Holy Spirit, given to us as a support and supplement to the virtues, enabling these to work with fullest perfection and heroism.

The *couch of gold* is the charity that is now well ordered in her through holy contemplation; it is there that the King of kings rests and has His delight. *The ascent is of purple,* dyed and beautified with the most Precious Blood of the Divine Lamb, which gives us the means, the virtue and strength to ascend to God. By simply imitating Christ and sharing in His sufferings we can come to be His thrones. With each sacrifice for love of Him we are preparing for His entry, offering, as it were, a step for Him to climb in order to rest in our hearts.

The *interior* of this beautiful litter is *replete* with unheard of *riches and precious things,* or covered with emblems of love and fruits of that same divine love, which are the twelve fruits of the Holy Spirit, the most outstanding being charity and peace in which the loving *King of Peace* delights so much.

Peace is the atmosphere in which He dwells. That is why St. Margaret Mary said: "Always keep your soul in peace; and thus you will come to be the *throne of God.*"

Made beautiful in this way, the heart of the fervent soul becomes worthy to be borne to the heavenly Solomon, as a living throne or litter, and thus fills the daughters of Jerusalem, or ordinary souls, with holy envy and draws them after it, enkindling them in the love of the sovereign Author of as many wonderful things as are discovered in the interior life.

All this can be applied in a special way to the Blessed Virgin who "so worthily bore the Son of the Eternal Father" and whose precious Heart is the true *Seat of Divine Wisdom,* as well as the *Ciborium of the Holy Spirit.*

In the mystical body of Holy Church, according to St. Thomas, these pillars of silver are formed by the apostles and apostolic men, the couch of gold, the doctors in whose celestial doctrine others rest, the ascent of purple, the martyrs. . . What shall we do, he then asks, together with St. Gregory, those of us who do not serve in any of these capacities. . . ? Let us have charity for it is this that covers the interior of this Litter, and with it we shall have all we need.

With this, indeed, as St. Thérèse of the Child said, we shall have everything. We shall be at the same time apostles, doctors and martyrs and shall undoubtedly win many souls for God.

This throne is represented in the Church, moreover, by the interior ciborium of devout hearts and by the magnificently adorned monstrances which even more inspire reverence, adoration and fervor. It is especially in these that the Lord desires to rest and to be carried with a burning love.

Thus, when the Ven. Mariana of Jesus, called the Lily of Madrid, was one day about to receive the Sacrament and did not have courage to do so in view of her own unworthiness, she said to Him most lovingly, "My Lord, this ciborium in which you now rest is much clearer and more beautiful." But He replied, "It does not love Me . . . !" "From which," she adds, "I understood how much He prefers to dwell in our souls, rather than in gold, silver or precious stones . . . that are incapable of loving Him."

Living in holiness, to be able to dwell with the Lord and bear Him in our hearts, and endeavoring to adorn them with the finest and most precious charity, we shall not only come to be worthy thrones for Him where He can rest contentedly and take His delight, but eventually, even without realizing it, we shall succeed in communicating Him to many souls, carrying Him like living litters or monstrances wherever He pleases, that all might honor, love and respect Him, and thereby also share in His abundant grace.

The Ven. Ana María of St. Joseph, who lived in the odor of sanctity in the Convent of the Discalced Franciscans of Salamanca, recalls that often after receiving communion she felt herself mysteriously being borne away as the Lord's throne from which He would delight to pour forth His blessings, even to the furthest "cities and kingdoms". When she was transported like this she would hear Jesus say: Come, let them all ask for Me, for I am in Ana's heart. . . Here I will let Myself be taken." "Sometimes," she continues, "He says to me: Let us go to Japan for I have many friends there who are working for the conversion of souls, and we must visit and strengthen them. . . At other times, after communion, I seem to be carried along bearing the Blessed Sacrament in my heart and I see that many souls are adoring Him while He distributes many graces."

The Holy Eucharist Itself is also a kind of litter hiding the Divine Solomon so as better to win souls and enkindle in them the fire that He brought into the world.

"Who will fail to be inflamed and enkindled in the love of this heavenly King," asks Fr. Luis de la Puente (*Perf. Gener.,* tr.

4, Ch. 5), "when they see Him so afire with His own love and with it, inflaming us? What heart could be so cold that, if it looks at this litter in the right light, could resist the darts of fire that the Savior, from within this litter, is scattering? O daughters of Jerusalem, come and see King Solomon in the litter that He built to come and visit you, to walk with you and honor you with His presence, enriching you with His grace and enkindling you with His love! This litter is also the throne from which He governs you as King, the *cathedra* from which He teaches you as Master, the bridal-chamber where He delights you as Spouse, and the table where He sustains you as Father. From these He cures you as Physician, defends you as Captain, governs you as Priest, and gives you milk as your Mother.

"But if you want me to tell you outright why He is in this litter, so that you can come to love Him Who has so much love for you, you must understand that He comes with the purpose of *setting Himself as a seal upon your hearts and upon your arms* (8, 6), impressing in your souls the likeness of His glorious virtues, enabling you also to become His litters within which He can traverse the world. O soul, communicating so worthily, behold your dignity! You are the litter of the true King Solomon, where He is present in the flesh while the sacramental species remain, and afterwards, united to your spirit through His grace. The presence of the Lord makes you like a cedar from Mount Lebanon, white because of your innocence, large because of your magnanimity and incorruptible because of your fortitude. He works the pillars of silver within you, adorning you and strengthening you with His gifts and virtues. He makes you His couch of gold, resting in you, and you in Him, through intimate familiarity and loving contemplation. So as to be able to ascend and rest in you, He makes His steps and stairs, covering them in purple, moving you and helping you to practice various acts of mortification by which your patience and obedience are perfected; with the purple of ridicule so that you can wear the purple of glory and humble yourself outwardly so as to rise interiorly to Him. Above all, He Himself is within you *accensus et combustus,* inflamed and enkindled in the love that He has for you, so that you can become inflamed and enkindled in His own love." "The Eucharist," says St. John Damascene (*Lib. 4 Fidei,* Ch. 14)," is a flaming red-hot coal of fire, because the flesh of Christ is united with the fire of the divinity; and we receive it *ut participatione divine ignis igniamur, et deificemur,* so that by participating in this divine fire we also become inflamed and are deified or exalted through our great similarity to God. . . The Septuagint interpreters translate it as: the interior of this litter was adorned with precious stones, meaning here, stones shining like hot-coals. . ."

"O what a divine chariot the soul rests in!" exclaims Fr. Gracian. "What a state of security! O how free from danger her spirit is, when the Spouse builds these things within her spirit: first of all, purity in all her faculties, this is what is meant by *wood from Mount Lebanon,* because Lebanon, in Hebrew, means whiteness; secondly, hearing the word of God . . . , and receiving His divine inspirations, which are the *columns of silver;* for silver, because of its sound, represents the divine word . . . and finally adorned throughout in the charity and love of God."

"Happy is the soul," exclaims St. Bernard (*in Cant. Serm.* 27), "who is told: *Come, my chosen one, in you I shall place my throne.* And you, my soul, why are you sad and why do you disturb me? Do you think that perhaps you too could find room within yourself for the Lord? What place is there within us able to accommodate so much glory and capable of containing such greatness? Would that we were worthy to adore Him in the place where His feet trod! Who will at least allow me to follow in the footsteps of any holy soul that He has chosen for His dwelling-place? But were He to see fit to anoint my soul as well with the unction of mercy, thereby expanding it, I too would perhaps manage to find within me, if not a 'large and well prepared cenacle where He can rest with His disciples', at least a place where He can rest His head. Far away from me I can see those happy souls of whom it is said, (II *Cor.* 6): *I will dwell in them and walk in them.* O how wonderful will be the soul's greatness and how excellent her merits when she is thus worthy to receive the Divine Majesty and capable of lodging Him within her... The soul must certainly be very free of all worldly cares and stripped of all human desires, concupiscence and curiosity before she can be converted into a heaven and dwelling-place for the Most High. Otherwise, *how can she be still and know that He is God?* (*Ps.* 47, 9)... Then she needs to grow and expand in order to be capable of receiving Him, and this capacity is given to her by love, as the apostle says (II *Cor.*, 6): *Extend yourselves in love...* In this way the soul grows and expands spiritually. She grows not in substance but in virtue; she grows in glory, she *grows into a holy temple in the Lord;* she grows and progresses until she becomes a *perfect man, fully mature with the fullness of Christ Himself* (*Ephes.* 2, 21; 4, 13)... Here, then, are the heavens that the Church has within her, being herself in her universality a great heaven that stretches from one sea to the other..."

"When we live in this union with our Lord," wrote M. Margarita Maria Doëns (1842-1884; cf. *Life,* Ch. IX), "we are called to do good as though we were another sacrament... We filter and spread this good around us almost without realizing it. Just as the Holy Eucharist gradually works within us, so we in our turn work for Jesus... Just as He, during His mortal life, communicated Himself to all who approached Him, He wants to continue communicating Himself through us to all who surround us. At times I seem to hear Him saying in the depth of my soul: 'Take Me, My daughter, and give the whole of Me to these souls for I am completely at your disposal for this purpose. Give Me to them in a smile, in a kind word, in an act of charity.' "

"Then," said Sr. Elizabeth of the Trinity (*Memoirs,* p. 138), "we shall console the Heart of Jesus... and presenting us

to the Father, He will be able to say: I am glorified in them. . .
Since Our Lord dwells within our souls, His prayer is ours, and I
would like continually to take part in it, being like a small vase
in the fountain, so that I can then communicate life,
overflowing with these torrents of infinite love."

Enthroning Jesus in this way, we could all join this fervent
Carmelite in joyfully proclaiming (*ib.*, p. 331): "I have found
Heaven on earth, since God is Heaven and God is in my soul.
The day that I understood this, everything became clear to me,"

If the Lord is to enlighten us also and bring us to know
everything through experience, we must join St. Augustine in
repeating (*Manual,* Ch. 5): *O God, the light of hearts that see
You, the life of souls that love You, and the strength of the
thoughts that seek You!... Come, I beseech You, into my
heart, and enrapture it with the abundance of Your delights so
that I forget all temporal things... and am always united to
You with a holy love... !"* Amen.

v. 11)   *Daughters of Zion, come out and see
              King Solomon wearing the diadem with
              which his mother crowned him
              on his wedding day,
              on the day of his heart's joy.*

The Bride who now knows through experience that she
herself, her own heart, is her Spouse's mystical litter, cannot
help but invite the daughters of Zion, that is to say, pious souls
who now have their dwelling-place near the Sacred Tabernacle
or who are among the *maidens* who desire to follow the Divine
Lamb (*Song* 6, 7-8) to come out and see Him in her, with the
crown with which His Mother crowned Him. The Holy Virgin
did, indeed, crown Him in her own way, giving Him the
precious, passible flesh of the Sacred Humanity in which the
Word is wed for ever to human nature. Through His love for us,
He who is infinite, immense and unsuffering becomes small and
passible so as to redeem and win us with His excessive kindness.
His step-mother the Synagogue then also crowned Him but with

a crown of thorns, when on the Cross He betrothed Himself to the Church and to faithful souls. Both are days of joy to His most loving Heart.

However, the true "day of His Heart's joy" is not so much that of His Betrothal with the soul, as that day when the soul, as His worthy Bride, succeeds, through the Holy Virgin, in offering Him a most precious crown of virtues, merits and sufferings.

According to Maria de la Dolorosa these *daughters of Zion* are souls weak in virtue who, even when resigning themselves to their trials, still want to see themselves free of them. Such a soul "is called a young girl because she still does not know the value of suffering; but a young girl of Zion, not of Jerusalem, since she has already made some progress in perfection. In order to encourage her, the angels tell her to leave the thought of her anguish and to look at the divine Solomon full of wisdom and majesty, who, in order to satisfy the love He has for her, offers to wear a crown, not of precious stones, as befits His glory, but of piercing thorns, and precisely on the day when He was wed to souls on the wood of the Cross... Let it be added that He received that diadem on the day of His heart's joy so that it can be seen with what transports of love Christ endured such cruel torments. In view of the Redeemer's suffering, the soul resigns herself and suffers in peace."

"Come!" exclaims Fr. Gracian. "Leave behind your sins, temptations, imperfections, your self-love and desires. If you want to walk with safety in the chariot of love, if you want to rest and defend yourself against your enemies in King Solomon's bed, if you want to lead an exemplary life, like a small rod of smoke exhaling incense and myrrh, search for Christ as He walks with the cross on His shoulders crowned with the crown of thorns... walking happily with it, as though on the way to betrothal and to marriage; for His heart's joy is to die for you so as to save you."

The daughters of Zion here could also refer to contemplative souls when God calls them to engage in works in His holy service.

Egredimini filiae Sion... "As though to say," writes Sr. Teresa of Jesus Mary, "Come out, you daughters of Zion, you contemplative souls, and see King Solomon, wearing a crown of thorns with which His mother crowned Him... *Ecce Rex vester,* said Pilate. It seems that the Eternal Father addresses these same words to contemplative souls, as though saying: Look at your King, this divine Man Who is so tormented and humiliated, follow Him along the path of Trials, do not always be resting in the bed and leisure of contemplation. *Egredimini.* Come out and exercise the other works to which I call you, accompany your Spouse, for it is He Himself Who is knocking at the door, wanting to accompany you and to join you in doing these works of active life; you cannot excuse yourself, for He will go away and you will lose everything."

So, fervent Christians, look and wonder! See Christ wedding Himself to a soul! And then see Him triumphing within her...! See Him wearing His crown of ignominy with which He triumphs over our pride, and, afflicted and oppressed beneath the weight of our sins, consoles the daughters of Jerusalem who weep to see Him so demeaned (*Luke* 23, 28)! And see Him adorning His Bride with another similar crown, bringing her to share in His sufferings that she might also share in His glory. Contemplate this mutual surrender, this exchange of interests and even of hearts, and see how the holy Bride abounds with joy and overflows with delights in the midst of all her afflictions, giving such satisfaction to her Beloved and winning souls for Him. Thus, she herself is "His *joy* and His *crown*" (*Phil.* 4, 1).

"Like the good shepherd rejoicing and holding on his shoulders the lost sheep..." writes St. John of the Cross (*Introd.* to Stanza 22), "This loving Shepherd and Bridegroom rejoices. And it is wonderful to see His pleasure in carrying the rescued, perfected soul on His shoulders held there by His hands in this desired union. Not only does He Himself rejoice, but He also makes the angels and holy souls share in His gladness, saying in the words of the Canticle: *Go forth daughters of Sion and behold King Solomon in the crown with which his mother crowned him...* By these words He called the soul His crown, His bride, and the joy of His heart, and He takes her now in His arms and goes forth with her as the bridegroom."

As such, He brings her to share in all that is His, in His sufferings and in His consolations.

"Our Lord," St. Margaret Mary wrote in regard to this (*Oeuvres Compl.*, 1867, II, 32), "has seen fit to give me a small share in His crown of thorns that is all the more precious to me for being a continuous suffering, often preventing me from sleeping and even from resting my head. This makes me pass some *most delightful* nights in the company of my Jesus suffering through love."

"The more deeply these thorns pierced the sacred head of the Spouse," writes St. Mary Magdalen of Pazzi (*Part* 1, Ch. 17), "the more consolations they bring to the Bride. Not all the thorns of His crown wounded Him, for some faced outwards; and these, O Beloved Spouse, You have reserved for Your chosen ones, so that they can share in Your sufferings... If You had kept them all for Yourself, they would not have been able to share in Your afflictions, and would have been deprived of the immense treasures contained within Your divine head. Those that entered therein, made openings through which souls could see the secrets of Your wisdom... This crown is the glory, consolation and delight of Your Bride."

Go forth, then, O daughters of Zion, and see your King, exclaims St. Bernard (*Serm.* 50), "go forth from servitude of the flesh into freedom of the spirit. For although His kingdom is not of this world, He is nonetheless King of this world. In this exile He governs and motivates our good works, in judgment it is He Who discerns merits, and in His kingdom it is He Who distributes and apportions crowns and rewards... Wearing the crown with which His mother crowned Him, He appears full of mercy and as a model for us. He also wears on His forehead a crown of misery and opprobrium with which His step-mother crowned Him, and with which He looks extremely despicable. Likewise He carries on His head a crown of justice with which the imitators of His virtues have crowned Him, and with this He appears awesome. Finally, He wears the crown of glory with which His Father crowned Him, appearing most wonderful to us. Let sinners look, then, and contemplate their King crowned in misery so as to become converted; let the daughters of Zion gaze upon His crown of justice and will perish, but the saints will adore Him with the crown of glory so as to rejoice with Him eternally."

Even in this life they abound with joy in the midst of all their tribulations, receiving as a reward for their trials ineffable consolations and singular graces, as happens to the mystical Bride.

"It seemed to me," says Sr. Teresa of Jesus Mary (*Com.* XIII), "that the day when the Divine Lord made such a special betrothal and union with my soul was the day that He called the day of His betrothal. Since His Majesty is so pleased and delighted that a soul should reach this state and that she should become one with Him, through the infinite love that He has for her, He also calls His betrothal day, the day of His Heart's joy."

"At the beginning of this espousal," says St. John of the Cross (*Spirit. Cant.*, Stanzas 14-15), "God communicates to the soul great things about Himself, beautifies her with grandeur and majesty, adorns her with gifts and virtues, and clothes her with the knowledge and honor of God, as the betrothed is clothed on the day of her betrothal. Not only do her vehement yearnings and complaints of love cease, but, in being graced with the blessings mentioned, a state of peace and delight and gentleness of love begins in her. This state is indicated in these stanzas, in which she does no more than tell in song her Beloved's grandeurs, which she knows and enjoys in Him through this union of espousal. Thus. . . she no longer speaks of sufferings and longings as she did before, but of the communion and exchange of sweet and peaceful love with her Beloved, because now in this state all those sufferings have ceased. . . The soul sees and tastes abundance and inestimable riches in this divine union. She finds all the rest and recreation she desires, and understands secrets and strange knowledge of God, which is another one of the foods that taste best to her. . . She has the feeling of being filled with blessings and of being empty of evils and far removed from them. And above all she understands and enjoys inestimable refreshment of love which confirms her in love.

But this confirmation in love is not yet complete, for the soul still has not reached full perfection and achieved all the peace and rest that she desires."

"Although the Bride," he adds (stanza 15), "enjoys so much good in these visits of the state of espousal, still she suffers from her Beloved's withdrawals and from disturbances and afflictions in her sensory part and from the devil; all of these cease in the state of marriage."

Synopsis

After the mystical Bride has so delicately returned to her Spouse the praises which she received from the chorus of friends, and after she has encouraged the daughters of Zion to contemplate Him, full of gratitude He now begins to extol her in a wonderful way, celebrating her singular beauty in pastoral language, using words of praise in exalting her principal parts, beginning with her eyes (v. 1-5), and then going on to consider the gentleness and perfection of her entire being (v. 7). At the same time He invites her to search for Him in the rough and lofty place of mortification and prayer (v. 6), and then (v. 8) to imitate and follow Him in the apostolate, whereby she will be enriched and crowned with the trophies of great victories. He then shows how much the soul loves and is enamored of this most perfect active life, which is now the mature fruit of contemplation, pointing out her purity of intention, ardent zeal, sweetness and gentleness in everything, the exquisite fragrance of her fervor and of all her excellent virtues (v. 9-14), with which she wins and attracts her neighbors, for whom she herself now becomes a fountain of graces watering beautiful gardens (v. 15). But her own garden, with the sweet breath of the Holy Spirit that He Himself sends her, will yield, for the glory of God and the good of souls, a fragrance that is completely heavenly (v. 16).

THE SPOUSE

1. *How beautiful you are, my love, how beautiful you are!*
   You have doves' eyes
   without what is hidden within. [a]
   Your hair is like flocks of goats
   that came up from Mount Gilead. [b]

2. *Your teeth are like a flock of shorn sheep*
   that came out from washing.
   Each one has its twin
   and not one among them is barren.

3. *Your lips are a scarlet thread*
   and your speech is sweet.
   Your cheeks are like a piece of pomegranate [c]
   without what your veil covers. [d]

4. *Your neck is like the tower of David*
   built with bastions, [e]
   hung around with a thousand shields
   each the armor of mighty men.

5. *Your two breasts are like two young roes that are twins*
   that feed among the lilies.

6. *Before the day blows and the shadows flee*
   I will go to the mountain of myrrh.
   to the hill of frankincense.

7. *You are wholly beautiful, my love,*
   and without a blemish.

8. *Come from Lebanon, my Bride,*
   come from Lebanon, come.
   You will be crowned [f] *from the top of Amana,*
   from the top of Shenir and Hermon,

a.   Hebrew: *Behind your veil.* Fr. Luis de León: "Your dove-like eyes within your locks."
b.   Since Jerusalem was high up they used the expression come up as synonymous with come, even when the other places were higher.
c.   Hebrew: *Like half a pomegranate.*
d.   Hebrew: *Behind your veil.*
e.   Hebrew: *Built to be an armory . . .*
f.   Hebrew: *Look from the top . . .*

> *from the dens of lions,*
> *from the mountains of leopards.*

9. *You have wounded my heart, my sister, my Bride,*
   you have wounded my heart with one of your eyes[g]
   with one lock[h] from your neck.

10. *How beautiful are your loves, my sister, my Bride![i]*
    Your loves are more delicious than wine!
    And your perfumes more fragrant than all other scents.

11. *Your lips, my Bride, are like the filtering of the honeycomb.*
    Honey and milk are under your tongue,
    and the scent of your garments
    is like the scent of incense.

12. *You are an enclosed garden, my sister, my Bride,*
    an enclosed garden, a sealed fountain.

13. *Your shoots are a paradise of pomegranate trees*
    with all kinds of fruits, camphire and spikenard,

14. *Spikenard and saffron, calamus and cinnamon,*
    with all the trees of Lebanon,[j]
    myrrh and aloes, with all the most precious perfumes.

15. *(You are) a fountain for gardens, a well of living waters*
    that flow down impulsively from Lebanon.

16. *Rise up, north wind, and come south wind,*
    and blow upon my garden
    to spread its sweet smell around.

Exposition

v. 1)   *How beautiful you are, my love,*
        how beautiful you are!
        You have doves' eyes
        without what is hidden within.

g. Or else: "with just one of your glances" (one was enough).
h. Hebrew: *a pearl*
i. Hebrew: "What spells lie in your love . . . !"
j. Hebrew: "with all the trees *that produce incense*..." or "with all the most precious balsams."

Now that the Bride has been raised to the mystical betrothal in which there takes place an exhcange of desires and even of hearts (cf. *Myst. Evolut.* pp. 420-429), and now that she has begun to watch ardently for the glory of her Spouse, as He Himself charged St. Teresa saying: *From now on, you will be a true Bride and will watch for My honor;* He in His turn begins to respond with divine generosity, fulfilling what He had earlier promised to St. Catherine of Siena: *Think of Me and I shall think of you.* Greatly pleased in this way by the Bride's love and faithfulness and happy to see her so closely modeled upon Him, He breaks into these expressions of praise whose meaning is symbolic and completely spiritual, and thus full of ineffable mysteries, all the more wonderful because of the infinite goodness of God that they manifest and because of the marvelous familiarity with which He deigns to communicate with men.

"The union and intimacy of human betrothal," says Fr. Luis de León, "is nothing in comparison with this. No spouse ever used such tender and ardent expressions as those which God addresses to the happy soul who has been raised to the mystical betrothal.

Not long ago a soul who knew the Lord through experience said (cf. *Myst. Evolut.* p. 231): "To those who are enriched by the action of His Holy Spirit, Jesus is a passionate Lover and the sweetest and gentlest Spouse... Through the gifts of the Holy Spirit, the soul is to Jesus Christ a beloved and gentle bride, because of the sweet and delightful fruits that these gifts produce within her."

"The gifts of friendship the Bridegroom bestows on the soul in this state are inestimable," writes St. John of the Cross (Introd. to Stanza 34), "and the praises and endearing expressions of love which frequently pass between the two are indescribable. She praises and thanks Him and He extols, praises and thanks her."

He begins marveling at her beauty and, captivated by it,

twice repeats *How beautiful you are!* . . . For without any doubt such she truly is now to a very exalted degree, not only because of the many graces that she has received up to now and to which she faithfully corresponded, but also because of the great tests and purifications that she suffered for His love and in which she so generously let herself be cleansed; and lastly, because of the works of devotion exercised by her. It is because of this that her eyes are like doves' eyes, for the charity, simplicity and purity of intention with which she proceeds in all things, some of which can be observed in her innocent and loving gaze, although most of it remains within hidden behind the veil of modesty and discretion. This is precisely what pleased the Divine Spouse most, and He seems to be telling her: You are now truly beautiful for I can see you full of My sentiments, My zeal, My pure love; what you are now seeking in everything is truly My honor and glory; and the many souls that you attract to Me and that come to adorn you like a beautiful head of hair, look like flocks of goats coming from Gilead, where the sons of Ruben dwelt, up toward the true land of promise.

Quam pulchra es! "She seems so beautiful to Him," writes Sr. Teresa of Jesus Mary (XIV), "that He is not content to say it just once, but delights in repeating it when looking at her again. Then He says: *oculi tui columbarum:* your eyes, that is, your understanding, are like two divine doves: one, the Holy Spirit, Who is usually represented by the figure of a dove because when He gazes upon and knows the Divine Essence that He receives from the Father and the Son, He does so with a most pure, simple and loving look. Secondly, He wants to compare this look with yours because it does not try to know or attain with discourse or reasoning what is beyond the soul's capacity, but rather submits itself with holy simplicity and obedience to what God knows and to what faith tells it. Thirdly, the other dove is the holy soul of Christ . . . Although His understanding clearly sees God as He is, He nonetheless fails to comprehend Him.

Thus He too, in His own way, submits and surrenders Himself to what God knows, and looks at Him with a straight and simple gaze which is how your eyes are like this dove. And all three ways of looking become one through the union of your soul to Him, revealing to you more secrets than you could attain through the ordinary light of faith."

"Your eyes," says Fr. Gracian, "are your intentions, and when your intention is sincere and without the gall of malice, like that of a dove . . . *the whole body* of your conscience will be filled with light (*Luke* 11, 36). Consequently, external works performed with purity of intention will bear much fruit in addition to the merit one receives from exercising the love of God by a correct intention."

When we look at our neighbors without judging ill of them, but rather, consider them as images of God, members of Jesus Christ and living temples in whom the Holy Trinity dwells, we shall then become accustomed to treat them with the proper love and respect; in this way we will always see them with doves' eyes, and this habit will lift us into very lofty regions of thought.

With respect to the Church, these eyes are the prelates, priests, doctors, apostles and prophets, and all those truly enlightened by God for the good of others. The words *without what is hidden within*, "allude," says María Dolorosa, "to the sacrament of the Eucharist in which He Himself, the God-Man, is hidden beneath the veil of the sacred accidents.

Your hair is like flocks of goats
that came up from Mount Gilead.

Goats jump and leap about the steep rocks; this is what the Bride's hair is like. As if to say: your hair, that is, your thoughts, which before were vain and disorderly like goats scattered over the mountains of Gilead, is now in order, and has a heavenly sheen like goats on their way to the Holy City. It can also be interpreted as: your hair is black and resplendent like that of a flock of goats on Gilead. For the numerous goats with silky hair clinging to the slopes of the hills, gave a very good picture of the Bride's fine, abundant hair (Fillion).

Your hair is like flocks of goats . . . "With these words," writes Fr. Gracian, "the Spouse means that He wants His Bride to have lofty and continual thoughts of God and of His service, born of the desire to suffer martyrdom for Christ. He says like flocks of goats because these like to wander off along steep rocks and climb the highest cliffs . . . ; and Gilead, in Hebrew, means mountain of witness, which is the same as desire for martyrdom, for 'martyr' in Greek means witness. So when the soul fills her heart with the thought of doing whatever she can, even of dying for God, all other desires seem to her unworthy. Thus she always employs herslef in lofty aspirations and exalted yearnings."

Just as hair grows naturally from the head, so in the spiritual world, holy thoughts and plans for good works spring from the soul without effort or attention. These are spread abroad very quickly, crossing crags and jumping mountains until a group of brave and agile souls are formed, like flocks of goats, but leading always toward the Sanctuary. "The hair," says María Dolorosa, "represents the thoughts of the loving soul, which are always intent on the supreme end."

"Your thoughts," comments Sr. Teresa of J.M. (*Coment.* XIV), "are like flocks of goats that came up from Gilead, which represent humility and self contempt. Because of these you do not consider yourself worthy of being compared to sheep or lambs, which is customary, but to young goats, to which sinners are generally compared. You hold and consider yourself to be one of them, and even worse than they, in so far as you are responsible. In this way you are able to climb so high, for the beginning of the ascent is on this mountain: *quae ascenderunt de monte Galaad.*"

"These thoughts," explains St. Luis Beltran (*Works*, vol. 1), "are like goats passing through the mountains of contemplation, the heavenly heights: they are not earthly and low because you live as though you were not on earth.. . ."

"Capilli tui. . . ," explains John of J. M., "cogitationes tuae, persimiles capillis a capite ortis, imitantur capras e montis Galaad declivio ad verticem propter pabula salutarium herbarum conscendentes. Cogitas enim frequentur, quomodo . . . per me ceu montem excelsum, cordis ascensionibus et meritis possis ascendere, et salutaria sacramentorum medicamina ex me orta velut salutares e monte plantas carpere valeas."

"In so far as it applies to the Blessed Virgin, her hair," says Sorazu, "is her divine thoughts, fertile like the flocks of goats grazing on Mount Gilead, and perfumed like their fleece or wool, for they are impregnated with charity, humility . . . and all the virtues. These thoughts rise up to God, to the Divinity and sacred Humanity of Christ (represented by Mount Gilead), with order and harmony like a flock, all directed to the same end of divine glory and God's eternal blessing.

"What a rich mountain Christ's Sacred Humanity is, fertile in all kinds of fruit and aromatic plants! Is it strange that the virgin, whose thoughts pasture on this holy Gilead, should be so beautiful, so rich in ideas and conceptions, so wholly divine in the eyes of God and men, and that she should perfume the atmosphere of the world and Heaven itself with the fragrance of her virtues and her divine thoughts . . . ? No, it is not strange, because she must, of necessity, be divinely fertile and marvelously divine in thoughts, words, works and desires, pasturing as she does on the mystical Gilead of the Sacred Humanity of Christ, infinite Wisdom, and feeding from His virtues and divine perfections. She must also necessarily be raised to the Divinity because she is deified as she reproduces within her soul Christ, true God and true Man, with all His virtues and perfections.

"O my God, may all souls who are joined together in a single flock through the bonds of faith and charity be brought by You to the mountain of Your Humanity, and may they, feed upon Your virtues and perfections until they achieve perfect development in the supernatural order and enjoy Your clear vision in Heaven. Amen."

With respect to the Church, this hair, adds María Dolorosa, "represents the faithful, who have still not reached the perfection of following blindly, like lambs, the voice of their divine Shepherd; but who generally leap about the precipices like goats taking evil for good."

It should be noted that there is considerable difficulty in understanding these comparisons, for as Fr. Luis de León says, "the majority are foreign or unknown to common usage and style, and some of them seem to go contrary to what they would describe." Nevertheless, he adds, "since the whole Song is to be understood in a spiritual sense, the parts of the Bride which are praised are the various virtues that are to be found in just men explained by means of the parts of the body. The comparison, apparently contradictory on the surface, expresses very well the beauty of the soul, and this is the proper interpretation of the words." "If it is carefully considered," he goes on, "this comparison is not lacking in grace and propriety bearing in mind who it is who speaks and what it is that is especially being praised in this Bride's hair. The one who speaks is a shepherd, and since he will speak as a shepherd, nothing could be more appropriate than for him to compare his beloved's hair to a large flock of goats at the top of a high mountain, thereby showing its great abundance and color, since it is black and shining like goats feeding on that mountain. He especially said black, because hair that color was highly valued by the people of those lands ... Similar to this is the comparison which follows:

v. 2)   *Your teeth are like a flock of shorn sheep*
               that came out from washing, etc.

which, apart from being pastoral, bears great significance, and is apropriate for conveying the intended thought. The good quality of teeth depends on their being small, white, equal and close together, all of which is clearly indicated in this

comparison; they are small and close together because they are
like a flock of sheep, who always go about in a close group;
they are white, because they are coming from washing; they are
equal, because *there is not a sick or barren one among them.*"

Your teeth are like flocks of sheep... Her reading,
meditations, and the affections with which she pastures on holy
doctrine so as to assimilate it fully ... the sentiments and ideas
with which she ruminates ... are gentle and peaceful like sheep,
and form flocks because of the many souls that are attracted by
her virtue. Without realizing it, a soul who is fully in love with
the Lord finds herself surrounded by other pure souls (being
washed and shorn); and these are not inactive but rather are
tireless apostles and propagandists, who in turn conquer others
(their twins). An interior soul who is always *ruminating* in this
way soon forms a flock of spiritual daughters. She never lives
alone.

"By teeth," writes Fr. Gracian, "the Spouse refers to the
soul's reasoning and meditation. For just as the teeth munch,
shred and grind what is to be eaten, so meditation works upon
what is to be contemplated. He says they are flocks of sheep
because sheep are docile; and they come up from the washing
with two lambs each, meaning that our meditation must always
be quiet, pure, docile and peaceful, and must end in the love of
God and love of our neighbor, for these are the two lambs of
good meditation."

"*Dentes tui*, that is," says John of J.M.: "Meditatio tua,
qua velut dentibus quibusdam mea dogmata frustillatim
concerpis ... similis est gregibus ovium, quae tonsae, quae
ablutae, quae agminatim gradientes sunt. Est tonsa, resectis
affectibus terrenis; est abluta lacrimis, mentisque puritate, ex
ablutione hac nitens et candida. Est concinna et more gregum
agminatim gradiens, cum rationum serie et quodam velut
agmine in voluntatem impetum facit. Haec meditatio de
lacrimarum lavacro, amoris motu ascendit tot gradibus quot
motus efficit in voluntate."

These beautiful teeth represent the diligence with which
the soul, hungry for justice, uses her faculties in masticating and
ruminating the word of God. They are flawless as is the Bride's
inner application, one which is productive, yielding abundant
fruits of eternal life. He thus means to say: the teeth with which
you feed and ruminate My teachings are white and identical,
just as My doctrine is so refined, pure and ground for you to
digest and assimilate without any foreign substances; and when
you expound it, you become a faithful echo of My words,
feeding and nourishing many souls for Me as fruits of true love
which is never barren nor idle.

The soul happily betrothed to Jesus, hungers for divine
pastures: for celestial doctrine, for prayer, for love, for works of
piety and zeal . . . She wants to nourish herself with everything
good that she encounters, and it seems that nothing is sufficient
to satisfy her. The image of her as a *rearing* sheep is thus very
appropriate, for such sheep develop a greedy hunger well known
to shepherds. But she will be even more hungry if they *shear* her,
and more still if they *wash* her, and the most if she *nurturing
twin lambs* . . . The Bride finds herself in these conditions: they
have shorn her of the burden of wordly and earthly cares; she
comes out of the *bath* of Christ's own blood and out of the
waters of many tribulations in which she is washed and purified;
and she *rears two lambs,* namely, the love of God and of her
neighbor, who take from her all her strength, even the beating
of her heart . . .

"The Bride's mouth," says Sr. Teresa (XIV), "undoubtedly
represents the will. For as God said through David: Dilata os
tuum et implebo illud; that is, open your will and your desire
and I will fill it . . . The teeth in this mouth are the affections,
the instruments with which the soul assimilates its spiritual
nourishment, just as the teeth are the instruments with which
the body takes its corporal nourishment. The Spouse says that
His Bride's affections and desires are as strong as teeth, and they
are like flocks that have been shorn of their wool; that is,

everything that is soft, luxurious and pliable like wool. The Bride's affections are now stripped of everything that is of flesh and blood, self-love and all that is worldly; but in addition, in divine love the Bride is deprived even of all that is merely sensible and sweet. These affections that are as strong as teeth are employed not only in easy things . . . which cause little trouble, but also in difficult matters which the soul desires and longs for. They seek to be employed in a love that is strong, solid, purely spiritual and divine, united to the same love with which God loves Himself and that with which the will of Christ's soul embraces the Godhead. These three loves and wills become so unified as to be one most ardent affection. The Bride must be very pure, unsullied and without blemish if her will is to be so joined and take part in such a union. That is why He not only says the sheep were shorn, but that they were coming up from washing . . . And this is not all: He goes on to add that they each bore fruit, double fruit, and none was barren. Affections and desires must bear fruit and produce good works, and double works, both interior and exterior, loving God and one's neighbor."

"As applied to the Church," says St. Gregory the Great," by these *teeth* are meant the priests and preachers who, when they expound the Holy Scriptures, shred the doctrine so that it can be fully understood and digested by the faithful, just as mothers cut up the food that they are going to give their children."

"The quality of good teeth," observes Maria Dolorosa, "represents the principal virtues of priests. They must above all be fully united in love to Jesus Christ and to His religion, just as teeth are joined to the gums . . . They must be free from everything so that they can assimilate the divine word . . . They must be pure in heart and body so that they do not stain it . . . They must take care to guard themselves in His holy ministry, like teeth enclosed in the mouth, without ever mixing in temporal affairs . . . The image comparing them to sheep coming out from washing shows that they must be as gentle as lambs with sinners . . ."

"They are like *washed* sheep," writes Scio, "because of the whiteness and purity of their holiness and life; *shorn,* because turning away from the cares of the world, they tend only to the ministry of the word, striping themselves of all earthly goods as religious do through their vow of poverty. They are *with twins,* because they engender in the hearts of their spiritual children the love of God and the love of their neighbor; *not one among them is barren,* because they produce within themselves and in others a wonderful harvest of good works."

v. 3)   *Your lips are a scarlet thread,*
                         and your speech is sweet.

These scarlet lips represent charity flowing from within and breaking forth in words that are sweet both to the ears of God and one's neighbor, and so impassioned as to win hearts. In other words, it seems as though the Spouse is telling her: these lips that admirably preach My doctrine are red and inflamed like scarlet because of the ardor of your love. Your speech is always kindled and inspired by this divine love that can accomplish all things, can suffer all things, that is always kind (I *Cor.* 13, 4), attracts, moves, captivates and ravishes . . . To this is added the enchantment of your cheeks that are ruddy and fair because of your ardent zeal, your spirit of sacrifice, and the whiteness of your soul, with which you win for Me all who observe you well. *Your cheeks are,* in fact, *like a piece of pomegranate:* they are inflamed and beautified through your desire to do and to suffer so much for My love, and all this, *without what is hidden within,* or *without what your locks hide.* For the greatest glory and beauty of this happy 'daughter of the King' is within (Ps. 45, 14); her ardent desires go far beyond what is outwardly visible in what she does and suffers, the best part remaining concealed behind the locks of her humility or the veil of her modesty.

Sicut vitta coccinea . . . "That is to say," writes Sr. Teresa of J.M. (*Comment.* XIV),"the part of this will and love outwardly apparent, represented by the lips, seems to me to be like a crimson or scarlet thread. These clearly show that what is within is healthy and without the obstruction of sin, for this is the metaphor David used when he said *Omnis inquitas oppilavit os suum.* For, just as poor bodily function due to some inner obstruction can be detected in the appearance of discolored and pale lips; so too, the inner channels of the spirit's blockage by sin (channels through which God communicates Himself to the soul) can be detected in a kind of colorless behavior that has neither warmth nor love but rather is cold and lukewarm, like the lips of a person who is ill. To show how far removed the Bride is from any such obstruction caused by sin, and how open her spiritual channels are to receive the movements from God, the Spouse extols the color of her lips for they are so inflamed and her conduct is so fervent and inspired that it seems she is catching fire. This color and these lips are said to be a single thread, indicating the few words spoken by the Bride, which thus emerge like drops distilled from honey-combs. And so He says: *eloquium tuum dulce;* and a little further on He adds: *Favus distillans labia tua,* because beneath her tongue she has honey and milk ... which ... represent the Holy Spirit communicated to her by the Spouse in the form of a tongue ... Since the Holy Spirit is the Bride's tongue, it is clear that her words must be sweet. He says that this honey and milk, representing the Holy Spirit, are under the Bride's tongue, hidden within her, as it were, so as to move her and use her as an instrument.

"... The Bride's cheeks, which form the principal and most prominent part of her face, can be interpreted as her conscience. He compares this to pieces of pomegranate, because this fruit is supreme among all other fruits, and because of the peace the soul has when, having defeated all her enemies, she is crowned queen and victoriously enjoys her kingdom in peace. He says pieces of pomegranate which means an open pomegranate divided up, indicating . . . that she can reveal herself to the whole world because she employs no duplicity or deceit, but is rather all sincerity and truth . . ."

"He tells her that her cheeks are like pomegranate," writes María de la Dolorosa, "so as to show that she has become a living image of His passion, not only because of what she suffers outwardly with happiness and joy, but much more because of her hidden desires for suffering."

So Augustine (In *Ps.* 44) did well to recommend this mystical Bride's inner beauty to every faithful soul: "You too," he said, "are betrothed to the same God . . . It is He Who has given you the pledge and the dowry for this wedding. Through Him you possess the beauty with which you are adorned . . . Take care, then, not to seek in your good works your own glory, but only that of God. Be content with the testimony of the One Who searches the secret recesses of your heart for it is He Who will reward the good He finds in you. He Who sees what is hidden undoubtedly loves hidden virtue; and the Author of the Bride's beauty loves this inner beauty with the purpose of Himself being loved there. Do not take satisfaction, then, from the honors and praises bestowed by those who see you only outwardly."

In the Church these scarlet lips are the evangelical preachers, whose sermons must offer the beauty and splendor of scarlet, stemming from their ardent love and from their zeal for the glory of God and the good of souls. The good preacher should always have his lips as though dyed with the blood of Christ and purified with the sacred fire of the altar, so as to be able to speak with such a spirit and exemplary life that, as St. Gregory says, he makes his teaching pleasing and assimilable. Thus this scarlet color refers to the flames of love with which they enkindle the faithful, to whom they worthily announce the word of God.

Your cheeks are like pieces of pomegranate
without what is hidden within (without what your veil covers)

When the soul is enkindled in the love of God and her neighbor, however well she keeps it hidden within her where it is known only to the Divine Spouse, it cannot fail to manifest itself to some extent outwardly, as a burning fire, lighting up her face; although this, like the pomegranate, remains a very pale red, because of the modesty and purity with which she does everything.

Without what is hidden within. "What the pomegranate has hidden is the inside of the seeds, white though covered with a brightly colored juice. In the same way the most intimate and hidden part of the conscience is pure and white, for it is always washed in the blood of the Lamb. Enveloping this purity and whiteness is the flaming fluid of love. The pomegranate also has many seeds, all identical and close together, with small golden skins that bind and preserve them; and in the same way, the Bride has all her neighbors united with her, loving them all equally and embracing them with the thin golden fabric of charity," Sr. Teresa (*Comment.* XIV).

The pale-red color of the pomegranate also represents the modesty and purity of Holy Church together with the ardor of her divine charity. These *cheeks,* the vehicle of her modesty and the mirror in which her inner beauty is reflected, are the Christian virgins, who, as St. Cyprian says (*De habitu virgin.*) are the most illustrious part of the Lord's flock and the glory and honor of the Church: *Flos ecclesiastici germinis, decus atque ornamentum gratiae spiritualis . . . Illustrior portio gregis Christi.*

Having described the beauty of her head, the divine Lover now goes on to describe the beauty of her body, beginning with her neck.

v. 4)   *Your neck is like the tower of David*
              built with bastions,
              hung around with a thousand shields,
              each the armor of mighty men.

Here we see the Spouse praising the soul's true and solid fortitude, comparing it to the tower of David with its bastions.

The shields that are hanging there are the trophies of the soul's victories over the world, the devil and the flesh. And the various arms with which she overcame them are all kinds of heroic virtues, with which, like the great saints, she did battle, carried along with zeal for the glory of God.

Sicut turris David . . . "She is compared to the tower of David," says Sr. Teresa of J.M. (*Comment.* XIV), "because in this soul My chosen ones defend themselves against their enemies, as though in a very strong tower; and I built bastions within her where all can take refuge, and these bastions are My virtues; and she is hung with shields and arms so as to fight those who are not strong members of My militia." "As though He were to say," she adds (*ibid.*), "your fortitude, constancy and perseverance, represented by your neck, are like a tower, and not just any tower, but like that of David, where there are shields and arms for the strong."

"In comparing her *neck* to the *tower of David*," says María Dolorosa, "her faith is being praised, for, in souls in a state of grace, faith is strong and operative. It resists all the attacks of temptations through the grace that fortifies it within, and shows this fortitude outwardly in working freely, without fearing danger when it is a question of the glory of God, just like martyrs."

This steadfastness comes to the soul through continual prayer which, like the neck, joins and unites us with Christ, our Head, so that we can receive from Him virtues and strength we need. Taking refuge there, we defend ourselves and triumph over all the attacks of our enemies.

"We have no better defense in our battles," says Fr. Gracian, "than prayer; for it is the neck through which the nourishment of grace comes to us from our Head, Jesus Christ . . . It is like the tower of David . . . We must turn to prayer in order to fend off all evil thoughts, asking God for His favor and defence, which are the shields and strong arms with which we resist the blows of our enemies."

All this amounts to His saying to her: the neck of this noble boldness given to you by My intimacy with you and by the ardor of My holy zeal, is solid and impregnable; for, placing your trust in the power of My Name which is a most solid tower, like David you resist every kind of attack and even come out of this fortress so as to attack those besieging you and put them to flight, enriching yourself with the spoils.

This fits the Church wonderfully as it triumphs over all heresies. The doctrine, examples and portents of its most holy doctors form the defences of this impregnable tower; it is these, together with all the zealous preachers of truth, who make up this solid neck of the Church. This is especially true of the Blessed Virgin who, through her incomparable excellence, unites the whole Mystical Body with the divine Head.

Your two breasts are like two young roes that are twins that feed among the lilies.

The Bride's mystical breasts are her love of God and neighbor: with these she feeds and rears Jesus in souls that are very small and young. These souls should not be fed with any other milk but that of purity, truth, sound doctrine and holy conversation, breathing always an atmosphere embalmed with the fragrance of great examples of virtue. This is why these breasts are compared to two beautiful young roes or musk-deer feeding among the lilies. They are twins because of the supreme harmony with which these two loves are combined in souls who have reached the lofty state of union in the betrothal, where they can now feed all their spiritual children with holy examples and words of life.

"With these two affections that must always be derived from prayer, namely, love of God and of one's neighbor," writes Fr. Gracian, "the soul nourishes all her works, words and thoughts, and gives them the milk of merit. This is why the Spouse calls them two breasts. He says that they are like twin kids born from the same womb; for a soul will love God in as much as she loves her neighbor, and will love her neighbor in as much as she loves God. As St. John says: *Anyone who says 'I love God,' and hates his brother, is a liar, since a man who does not love the brother that he can see cannot love God, whom he has never seen.* (I *John* 4, 20). These two desires must be pure and free from sin . . . that is why He says they feed among lilies. They must last the whole of life, the soul perservering in them until the night of death."

"Here, then," as María Dolorosa says, "in praising her two breasts, Jesus is praising the two loves that exist in the Bride's heart . . . ; both are young, being *twin roes,* but they *feed among lilies,* because the soul does not love out of self-interest, but is concerned only for the glory of the Spouse and for the good of souls, *until . . . the shadows flee* from this miserable life."

This is applicable in a special way to Holy Mother Church, and even more so to the Blessed Virgin, suckling her divine Child, and nourishing us with Him.

"These two breasts," says Sr. Teresa (loc. cit.), "can also be interpreted as love and fear, which are like two kids (or young roes) sprung from the same womb; because love and fear must be very loving and friendly brothers, never leaving each other's side. He points out that they are small, for in this life they can always, and must always be growing. He compares them to young goats because they are inclined to walk across rough and craggy ground and to climb up swiftly over difficult things. Love and filial fear have the same inclination, tending always towards trials and difficulties, and running swiftly through them. He says that these two kids are from the same womb, because love and filial fear are both born together from the knowledge the Bride has of her Beloved; for she loves Him in the measure that she knows Him, and this in turn determines the extent of reverence and fear with which she stands before Him. The Spouse says that these young goats feed among lilies, for they share the same food; namely, the Spouse Himself, Who said He was the Lily of the valleys . . . These two beautiful little kids feed on His divine words as upon leaves, and not only on

His leaves, but on the Lily Itself. When love boldly enters the inside of this Lily in order to feed on those gold threads, that is on the divine Essence, it does not dare to enter in without its brother and companion, fear, who accompanies it in trembling as they stand before that infinite Majesty, more frightened of displeasing Him than of a thousand deaths; for, if love enjoys the infinite riches of the Lord, fear is sad to see Him offended. If love seeks to feed on the immense greatness of Christ's love, delighting in such possession; fear feels the pains and afflictions suffered by that sacred Soul in redeeming our sins, and is afraid of not sufficiently benefiting from them. If love wants to feed and delight in the glory enjoyed by the sacred body of this Lord, fear trembles at the infinite price He paid to buy us and the account that is going to be asked of us. Therefore, love does not take a single step unaccompanied by his friend and brother. This fear is not that described by St. John which does away with perfect love, for since they are twins and born of the same knowledge, the one does not impede the other, but rather they help one another and grow in step . . ,"

"The breasts of the Church," says Soto Mayor, "are the two Testaments on which we feed so as to grow in grace and virtue until we become conformed to the divine Model. The breasts are also, according to St. Gregory (*Moral.* 1, 31, Ch. 22), the holy preachers who, drawing from the Sacred Heart, abound in divine love and beneficial knowledge gained in supernatural contemplation, and thus are able to nourish souls with their sweet and sound doctrine.

And since this is the milk that nourishes them the faculties that produce it, that is to say, the mind and the will, could also be called the mystical Bride's breasts.

"What are these breasts," asks Fr. La Puente (*Guia,* tr. 3, Ch. X), "but the understanding and the will that God placed together in the soul? These, united with God in knowledge and love, are filled with the milk of divine consolation, and are happy and full of rejoicing; diligent and fervent like young

goats, they accompany one another, and feed among the lilies
of the divine mysteries for as long as the day of this mortal life
lasts . . . They are not like goats wrinkled with old age, but kids
growing every day in fervor, preserving their youthful vigor and
renewing their youth like the eagle . . .

"The sweet Spouse later says to them: Come, My friends,
and see Me climbing the mountain of myrrh and the hill of
incense; climb up with Me, both of you, so as to preserve your
union. Then the understanding climbs to the very peak of the
myrrh by attaining perfect denial of itself, of its own judgment,
of all its reasonings and thoughts; so as to submit them to God
and to join them to Him, in order to have the same sentiments
as His own; and the will accompanies it mortifying all its wishes
so as to unite them with the divine will, forcing its appetites,
the flesh and everything it possesses to climb the same
mountain with it. From there, both friends pass to the hill of
incense, helping one another in prayer and in communication
with God in such fervor that their garments, which are all the
other works, smell of incense because they flow from prayer.
v. 6)   *Before the day blows and the shadows flee*
             I will go to the mountain of myrrh,
             to the hill of frankincense.
We already know that the myrrh here represents mortification, and the incense prayer. It is wherever these scents are
breathed in all their purity; that is, on the mountains and hills
where they are produced that the Divine Spouse promises to
take recreation and where He is sure to be found until night
draws nigh. Both prayer and mortification must go together if
Jesus is to be found among them; and then, *only for as long as
the day lasts and until the shadows begin to fall.* This phrase
could well be added to the previous one, indicating that the
praising of the Bride's breasts and the feeding among the lilies
lasts only as long as the day; for at night these little animals
retire since they graze only during the day. But the meaning is
the same. It is as though the Lord were to say to the soul: as

long as the day of My lights and consolations lasts, when a man can walk without stumbling and do what must be done (*John* 9, 4; 11 9-10; 12, 35), or until the dark *night* comes when you think yourself forsaken, follow Me to the places where I take solace and recreation; to this mystical mountain of myrrh and hill of incense. There you will easily find Me until night falls and I retire hiding Myself from your view so as to further enkindle your desires and purify your love, purging and beautifying you so that you can enjoy all the more My lights and consolations, and win more souls for Me.

The Lord gives us to understand, as María de la Dolorosa says, that "the soul must go with Him to the hill of incense, that represents prayer in general, and to the mountain of myrrh, which is the contemplation of His bitter sufferings; so as to drink a part of the chalice which, through love for her, He drank to the dregs.

Calvary and the Garden of Olives were really *the mountain of myrrh and the hill of incense for Jesus*, for it was there that He prayed at such length and suffered such bitterness. This mountain and hill also represent in a mystical sense souls who are outstanding for their spirit of sacrifice and prayer.

"The Spouse goes to *the mountain of myrrh and to the hill of incense*," says St. Gregory the Great, "for *He frequently* and *very easily visits* all who ceaselessly strive to climb up to these heights and to reach the summit through mortification of all their passions, and whose pure, humble prayers ascend to Heaven like a sweet, immensely pleasing incense. These are really the exercises of virtue with which the Church in general and each faithful soul in particular become pure and holy, fighting against vice through mortification of the flesh and senses, and daily washing themselves of their sins with tears so as to please their Divine Spouse, in Whose sole presence they wish to appear beautiful and lovable. Promoting such pious endeavors with His grace, He eventually leads them to the fulfillment of their desires, and therefore praises them: *Cujus*

*conatum ad effectum Sponsus per gratiam suam ducit, opusque
suum in sponsa benigne laudat . . ."*

"The Spouse," says Fr. Gracian, "calls the height of
mortification the mountain of myrrh, and lofty prayer the hill
of incense . . . From this prayer and mortification . . . is born,
together with the love of God and one's neighbor, . . . true
purity whereby the soul lives without the stain of sins and
faults. Thus the Spouse says: *You are wholly beautiful. . . "*

No one has the right to complain that she cannot find the
Lord for He promises that He will let Himself be found by those
who search for Him in this way. St. Thomas observes that they
themselves become changed into the mountains that the Lord
visits: *Mons ergo myrrhae et collis thuris, sunt excelsae animae
sanctorum per contemplationem. Promittit ergo Sponsus se ad
montem myrrhae venturum, et ad collem thuris, quia illas
mentes sua visitatione dignatur inhabitare, quae membra cum
vitiis et concupiscentiis mortificant, quae etiam seipsas per
sancta orationum studia Deo gratum sacrificium faciunt.*

Prayer without moritifcation is very often subject to
illusions, and cannot be trusted. Mortification without the spirit
of prayer is, as in the case of flagellants, both presumptuous and
vain. That is why to Tobias St. Raphael said: *Prayer is good
with fasting,* by which we can understand any kind of
mortification.

I will go to the mountain of myrrh . . . "That is to say,"
writes Fr. La Puente (*Guia* tr. 1, Ch. 20), "I will go and visit and
inspire those climbing the mountain of mortification and the
hill of prayer, and I will happily console those who have
reached the summit . . . The purpose of God's visits is to help
and inspire us in these exercises, and reward the care that we
put into them . . . For this reason Our Lord visits His friends
chiefly on two occasions: when they are undergoing mortification and penance or are in some trouble or affliction; and when
they are preparing for prayer or are engaged in it, especially if it
is lengthy and toilsome because subject to distractions and

aridities."

"What else," says St. Gregory, "is the mountain of myrrh but strong and lofty mortification in work? What is the hill of incense but great humility in prayer?"

When you are full of bitterness and very troubled, "you must understand," adds Fr. La Puente (*Perf. en gener.* tr. 5, Ch. 5), "that you are a tree planted on the mountain of myrrh, near Jesus Christ your Savior, Who always lived on this mountain. Just as when these trees, distilling little myrrh through the pores, are pierced and barked in several places so that they can distill myrrh in great abundance; so when the Lord sees you yielding very little myrrh through voluntary mortifications, He seeks to pierce you with illness and pain to give you an opportunity of mortifying yourself. Thus you must try to be a fertile tree of myrrh through patience, and not a thorn through impatience."

In this way you will purify yourself of all your stains, and your soul will seem gracious in the eyes of God.

v. 7)   *You are wholly beautiful, my love*
                 and without a blemish.

With frequent changes between light and darkness, between the happy and consoling visits in which the soul is encouraged and comforted with virtue from Heaven, and the sad absences and desolations that force her to be well grounded in humility, she sees through experience that nothing she possesses is hers. She gives continual proof of fortitude and perseverance, of pure faith and disinterested love. By these frequent alterations she gradually restrains and purifies herself in everything, becoming strengthened in the inner life through the virtue of the Holy Spirit until she reaches the full perfection and expansion of the theological virtues by which she is intimately united with God. Thus, pleased with her, "having praised her, and having studied and named each part individually, not content with this, He adds: tota pulchra es, amica mea . . . you are wholly beautiful My love and without a blemish. Not because you are free from any stains of imperfections through the frailty of human nature, but because of the great care and diligence with which we both proceed to have them washed away at once with My blood. You are thus left so white, pure and beautiful, so unmarred, that it seems I can say you are without blemish, because these imperfections are neither habitual nor voluntary" (Sr. Teresa, XIV).

He wants to dedicate her fully to His divine work; and so as to recommend her to the faithful and to induce her to total commitment, He Himself undertakes to praise and celebrate the virtues He now sees in her and the store of graces with which she is adorned, calling out to her: *You are wholly beautiful and without blemish...!* Such the soul must be if, like Moses, she is to penetrate the mystical darkness and communicate intimately and familiarly with the God of all holiness. No one can see His eternal splendors if he has not first died to all that is transitory and been born again in a new and glorious life.

This wonderful praise is now real, and not merely a kind of flattery. For the Spouse does not address these words to the soul as He formerly did, in order to encourage her; now she really is adorned in graces, gifts and virtues and without the blemish of attachments, faults and voluntary or conscious imperfections. For He now has her closely modeled on Himself, sharing to a high degree in His own lights, beauties and perfections. Before breaking forth into a new song in praise of His Beloved because of the triumphs that He will achieve through her, He prepared her, with this general praise, for the difficult and glorious mission that He is going to entrust to her. He states that she is fit for it, celebrating this immaculate purity in which she is now clothed, the ardent zeal that enkindles her within and consumes the remains of faults and imperfections and which, shining forth, makes her so beautiful; and the rich mantle of virtues and gifts with which she is enriched and adorned, and at the same time protected so as to go and win souls for Him without offering any resistance, since it is now He who lives and works within her . . .

"In this new intimate union with Him that the Lord gave this soul," writes the Ven. Mariana de San José of herself in July, 1615 (*Life*, 1, 3, Ch. 28), "it seemed in that silence that He was filling her with a most secret wisdom, not by pouring Himself into her soul as He is wont, but by making her the mistress of His very love and of His infinite wisdom; with this love she loved Him, and with this understanding she understood Him . . . The Lord showed that the working of the soul is not her own, but is the work of His powerful hand. All her movements and actions are now those of her divine Master, although He makes her the mistress of these works as much as if she were to do them alone. Thus He considers Himself well paid, pleased and served, for everything that He sees in her seems beautiful to Him. I understood the truth of the words He speaks to the Bride: *Tota pulchra es amica mea* . . . And when the Lord speaks these words to the soul there is a flood of ineffable riches . . . "He has left me not wanting to love or enjoy anything else . . . nor can my soul be inclined to any virtue or gift but that of silencing all my desires and appetites; aspiring to no other good, however spiritual it might be . . . It knows only that it has abandoned itself, that He has taken it as His Own, so as to work new mercies through and with it . . . Thus the soul is wholly employed in self surrender, desiring no other employment, because this divine Master has shown it that all its yearnings and affections are . . . an obstacle to the perfect work that He is doing."

v. 8)   *Come from Lebanon, my Bride,*
         come from Lebanon, come.
         You will be crowned from the top of Amana
         from the top of Shenir and Hermon,
         from the dens of lions,
         from the mountains of leopards.

This is one of the passages in which the mystical sense of the divine Song, the sense truly intended by the Holy Spirit, most visibly transcends the matter of the symbol; that is the King's betrothal represented by it, which could be attributed to a human agency. For it is inconceivable that Solomon could invite his queen to win such a crown as this.

The Lebanon spoken of here is not the famous mountain in Phoenicia but what is called in the books of Kings *Saltus Libani* or 'wood of Lebanon': one of the royal sites near Jerusalem where it is known that this monarch built a country house for his bride, the daughter of the King of Egypt. It is from this mystical place of recreation and spiritual retreat that the divine Solomon calls her who, having been fully purified and beautified through a submergence in the Spirit, has now become His Bride. He calls her so as to crown her, not with flowers, but with piercing thorns, glorious trophies which, like Him, she herself must collect on the rough and dangerous heights of Amana, of Shenir and Hermon where many terrible wild animals have their lairs. How clearly does this daring image, which could never have occured to a worldly lover, convey the extremity of love the Son of God has for souls, and likewise the degree of love He demands of His Brides in contributing to His work of salvation . . . !

Similarly, as the Lord's disciples, after being filled with the virtue of the Holy Spirit, were called away from the Cenacle and the Mount of Olives to proclaim the Good News through all Judea and Samaria and then to all the corners of the world, in spite of the dangers they would encounter; in the same way, Christ calls His perfect Brides to leave the place of their delights and bitter purifications and go out to win souls for Him; exercising the visible and invisible apostolate that He sees fit to entrust to them; accomplishing very difficult and dangerous undertakings that demand supernatural courage. In this way they will eventually deserve to be crowned with trophies won from these mountains, and from these caves of lions and leopards.

This is where the truly faithful soul will one day be called

when, full of the strength of the Holy Spirit, she can, in her
efforts to communicate this virtue to others, expose herself
with impunity to the dangerous commerce of the world; passing
like a sheep among wolves in order to convert the wolves into
sheep . . . It is now that she is called to true Christian action,
and not merely once; she is called three times and most
insistently. For after the mystical betrothal has been reached by
the soul the Beloved wants her to leave her retreat, the repose
of prayer and delight in His intimacy; and go to fight for His
glory and for the salvation of souls, even if to do this she has to
enter lions' caves and go up into mountains infested with
leopards. She is offered a crown of wild animals' teeth; that is,
of great opposition, trials and tribulations. This is the crown of
the apostolic soul. This was St. Paul's crown and it was the
crown of our Father St. Dominic, and of all those who have
inherited his evangelical and intrepid spirit.

"O my God!" exclaimed a pious commentator, "What
reasons have You for so earnestly inviting Your Bride to follow
You? Why, in order to oblige her to do this, do You call her as
many as three times and offer to make her share in Your
crowns . . . ? *Veni, veni veni coronaberis.* Do you not know that
all her dreams and ardent desires are to be united with You and
to possess You? All this You know very well. But You invite
her and entreat her so earnestly so as to inflame her even more
and thus make her worthy, not in the way that she supposes,
but as it pleases You, of precisely that which she so much
desires."

This *veni de Libano* can also be taken in the sense that
Ven. Teresa of J. M. (p. 38) understood it: "Come from the
Lebanon of the body and the world, from the caves of lions and
the mountains of leopards, which are the passions of the
sensitive soul. Come and you will be crowned with three crowns
that the three Divine Persons will give you. It seemed to me that
when the Person of the Father crowned me, He communicated
a new being to me . . . transforming the essence of my soul into

His divinity; giving me the inheritance of the adopted sons of God and co-inheritors with Christ, the natural Son, Who is all His attributes and divine perfections . . . The Person of the Son crowned my understanding uniting it with Himself, communicating to it a ray of His infinite knowledge . . . of that divine essence of His Father, which He alone comprehends . . . The Holy Spirit crowned my will with charity and flames of love uniting it and making it one with Him, bringing it into the enjoyment of its Lord, thus partaking in that mutual love and friendship of the Divine Persons: everything being love and enjoyment, the will receiving and cooperating in so far as its capacity allows."

The Hebrew is even more expressive. It reads: "With me, from Lebanon, O Bride, with me from Lebanon, come . . ." This is the first time that He addresses her with this sweet name of *Bride*, which expresses better than any other the new relationship uniting her to Him and the conditions of this new life to which He calls her. For this reason it is repeated more than once.

All this was most necessary so as to oblige her to abandon her beloved solitude and the delights of her hidden retreat, and to force her, in spite of the lowly idea she has of herself and the sentiments that her modesty and humility inspire in her, to go out into the public and expose herself to many dangers.

The Blessed Raymond of Capua (*Life*, Part 2, 1), writes of St. Catherine of Siena that "whenever the Lord ordered her to leave her retreat and converse with men she felt deeply pained, and her heart seemed as though it were going to break into pieces. Only God was capable of making her obey." In order to subdue and console her Our Lord would say to her: "Be calm, My dearly beloved daughter. Justice must be fulfilled and My grace must be made to bear fruit in you and in others . . . Far from leaving you, I want to be united even more through the love of your neighbor . . . In these times when men's pride is so great . . . I will send women who are ignorant and naturally wretched but who through My grace are wise and powerful, to confound this pride."

This same repugnance that the soul has for exposing herself will bring her to walk in safety, without stumbling, where so many uncautious and presumptuous souls trip and fall. For as Thomas à Kempis says (*Imitation of Christ*, 1, 20): *No man can safely appear in public but he who loves seclusion*. So that the true saints and servants of God need this repeated call to go out and occupy honorable positions and bear responsibilities which are especially dangerous. The Church needs it now, and needed it at the beginning when, as Scio says, "through baptism and the coming of the Holy Spirit she was wholly beautiful . . . The Spouse, showing the ardent love that He has for the well being of all, invites her not once but three times . . . to come out from Jerusalem and to go over those mountains; that is to say, through all the regions and provinces of the world, fearing neither lions nor leopards; namely, her enemies and persecutors, being assured of victory and the crown."

In this going to where she is called consists her true progress. And in this way, says St. Thomas, she will come to be perfect in everything, in contemplation and action, in thoughts, words and works.

Overcoming herself and sacrificing herself wholly and in all things for the love of her Spouse, she will come to win the whole of His divine heart, filling Him with pleasure in all that she does, says and thinks, however small it may be.

v. 9)   *You have wounded my heart, my sister, my Bride,*
        you have wounded my heart with one of your eyes,
        with one lock from your neck.

"The eye of the right intention which inspires her in all her works, directing them to the great glory of God, together with her thoughts that are always directed to God, represented by the lock of hair; please the heavenly Spouse so much that He says He has been wounded in His heart" (Maria Dolorosa).

"The soul has two eyes," says Fr. Gracian, "one, the eye of natural reason, the other the eye of living faith. With one she attains wisdom, prudence and human discretion; and with the other, divine wisdom and love of God . . . Let us imagine, then, that . . . the Spouse looks at her from one side, seeing only one of her eyes — the eye of living faith. This pleases the Lord so much that He says: *You have wounded my heart with one of your eyes* . . .

You wound My heart with your thoughts placed in the mouth of your desire, when their only wish is to please and serve Me . . . From this living faith and unity of thought come the two intentions of loving God and one's neighbor, together with the practice of exemplary virtues. For this reason they are far superior to those aspirations that spring from the soul of human wisdom and discretion.

"*Vulnerasti cor meum* . . . , as though the Divine Spouse were telling me," writes Sr. Teresa of J.M. (*Commentaries*, I p. 27): " 'My Sister and Bride, you have wounded My soul with the eye of your self-knowledge and humility, with your hair of affections and desire for suffering, with compassion for My passion; thus this wounded and stricken Soul surrenders Himself to you as an inseparable companion." And I was given to understand that He, united to my body, would in a certain way govern my life . . . ."

With respect to the Church, if her hair represents the faithful, souls advanced in virtue must be signified by this long lock which falls down to the collar, the symbol of her faith which is so pleasing to the Spouse.

A thousand times happy is the soul who thus succeeded in wounding or ravishing the Sacred Heart . . . ! In this way she will become mistress of His infinite treasures and to a certain extent, queen and lady of all creation; being the true and faithful *Bride*, as well as *sister*, of the eternal King . . . God lets Himself be enamored by the least adornment or *necklace* of this holy soul, by a single lock around her neck; that is to say, by any of her works, however small it might be, and He takes greater pleasure in it than in others which are greater but done with less love. She wounds and ravishes Him with a glance, or with one of her eyes, the right eye of her single and upright intention which looks on God alone and rests only in Him.

It is not at all strange that she should be called so insistently by Him Who declared He has been wounded by her. O how wonderful is the love of the Word! What marvels are worked in souls by God's love, marvels that are unknown except to those who experience them!

"The power and the tenacity of love is great," exclaims St. John of the Cross (*Spirit. Cant.*, Introdu. to Stanza 32), "for love captures and binds God Himself. Happy is the loving soul, since she possesses God for her prisoner, and He is surrendered to all her desires. God is such that those who act with love and friendship toward Him will make Him do all they desire, but if they act otherwise there is no speaking to Him nor power with Him, even though they go to extremes. Yet by love they bind Him with one hair."

"This hair," he adds (*ibid.*, stanza 30), "is her will and the love she has for the Beloved . . . She says only one hair, and not many, in order to point out that now her will is alone, detached from all other strands of hair, that is, from all extraneous loves."

Neither the Latin language nor the Greek, writes Calmet, has words which adequately convey the force of the original. St. Jerome translates it: *You have wounded my heart*. The Septuagint: *You have stolen my heart*. Which means: I am a prisoner enchained by your love, because with a single glance you stole my heart; and you have captured Me with the smallest lock of hair around your neck and I can no longer leave your side . . .

Thus captured by her beauty, He will perhaps say to her as He said to St. Rose of Lima: "Rose of My heart, be My Bride . . ." To another saint He saw fit to declare the great love

He had for her saying: "I carry My Rose in the most intimate part of My heart, for she is all Mine and I have peaceful possession of her."

In a very similar way, He would speak two centuries later to another wonderful Dominican, Sr. María Josefa Kumi (1763 — 1817), telling her (*Life*, Ch. 9): "I have a bride to My heart's liking. She is like Me and her garments are the same color as Mine . . . The darts of her love wound My heart. Hers is always open so that I can come whenever I want and take solace in her tenderness and soothe the injuries that I receive from men. Her good will has so pleased Me, that I appoint her as the mistress of My treasures. She is enriched with the gold of My pure love . . . she is on earth but does not touch it . . . Every day she grows more and more in the perfection of love, as she feels more and more her own nothingness. I have her impressed in My Heart, and I am impressed in hers."

"I do not know what to call you now," He said to Sr. Benigna Consolata in December, 1915. "I have already called you My lily, My dove, My queen. Now I call you the pupil of My eye, and the heart of My Heart."

But if the faithful soul thus wounds the Sacred Heart with darts of love, the unfaithful wound It so often with their sins, imperfections, coldness and ingratitude . . . This wound is clear for all to see, for it was made on the cross before the whole world and is preserved in Heaven. There on the cross . . . it is the source of health and life, where all who want can come and be refreshed, (*Is.* 12, 2-3), heal and beautify their souls (*Zech.* 13, 1). In Heaven it is a triumphant sign and glorious testimony of the tender love with which He loved us, adopting for our sakes a heart capable of suffering and of being wounded by us in this way . . . Thus in one way or another He can say to all of us: *You have wounded my heart, my sister, my bride.* Let us try to ensure, then, that this wound is of pure love and not of pain . . .

"Who would dare to say this," asks Fr. La Puente (*Guía,*

tr. 3, Ch. 9), "if the Lord Himself were not to say to His Bride: *You have wounded my heart with one of your eyes?* The eyes of the contemplative soul are knowledge and love, and her hair is the thoughts that spring from her memory. When the memory and the understanding recollect all their thoughts in God so that the will can love Him; when the will centers all its affections in God so that the understanding can know and penetrate Him; then these faculties are united and with this union they wound the Sacred Heart. For just as darts when thrown forcefully, pierce the insides and become joined and caught on to them, so, in the same way, knowledge and love penetrate the depths of God . . . Then God Himself, being wounded, receives and holds them within Himself; deeply loving the soul that looks at Him with these two eyes, so well matched and united, undistracted by anything that can disturb or trouble the purity of her love."

This simple gaze comes from a pure and single intention that truly wounds and captures Him with darts of love and compassion. That, as St. Lawrence Justinian says, will bring Him to wound the soul again with the fire of His divine charity, bringing her to burn with living flames, and to shine with new lights and gifts, finally binding her more closely to Him.

v. 10)   *How beautiful are your loves, my sister, my Bride!*
         Your loves are more delicious than wine,
         and your perfumes more fragrant than all other scents.

The mystical *breasts,* as the Vulgate translates it, these beautiful, divine loves, the love of God and of one's neighbor, are now so well developed and perfected in the Bride's heart that they are not content with mere affections, desires and good words; they produce marvelous works and sustain Christ Himself and foster Him in other souls. Thus, when speaking of those who do the will of God, He said that such souls are His brothers and also His *mother* (*Matt.* 12, 49-50). This soul is the "mother of Christ", giving birth to Him again in other souls (*Gal.* 4, 19). The Spouse calls her *sister,* because she is very similar to Him — being a true daughter of His Eternal Father, for in all things she is possessed and moved by His divine Spirit; and *Bride,* because she has become one spirit with Him. This is how she is continually exhaling the incomparably sweet fragrance of Christ with which she wins so many hearts for Him, pleasing and delighting His own.

"More beautiful than wine . . . That is to say," writes Fr. Gracian, "they are more beautiful and perfect than all discretion, prudence and human wisdom, which is what is represented by the wine. Souls who live in this way, loving God and their neighbor, with truth and sincerity of mind, do much good in the Church of God with the holy example of their lives. Their conversation and companionship is so good, so spiritual and edifying, that it is clear it springs from prayer. This is what is meant by *The scent of your garments is like the scent of incense.* It is called the scent of garments because the soul is dressed in exterior communication . . . and it is very clear from exterior behavior whether one has true prayer or not."

Quae pulchrae sunt mammae tuae . . . "This Bride's two breasts," says St. Teresa (*XIV,*) "the love and fear with which she proceeds, please and delight Him so much that it seems He will never stop praising and extolling them, as if there is nothing with which He can compare them. After praising her so lavishly and admiringly, telling her how beautiful her breasts are, He then goes on to add: *they are more beautiful than wine.* If the Spouse were speaking here of material wine, He would be doing little to extol her beauty, for wine has things more worthy of praise than its beauty. But since the wine here means love, He seems to mean: although the love they have for Me is very beautiful in My estimation and moves My heart, its beauty is far greater when it is accompanied by fear than when it is not. Thus, when they are together like two breasts, they seem more beautiful to me than if they were just one, and this like wine. From these two breasts comes a balsam-like liquid that smells more fragrant than all the sweet-smelling things that exist in the world: *et odor unguentorum tuorum super omnia aromata.* And thus, with this ointment I shall anoint My head much better than Aaron anointed his, as David said: *sicut unguentum in capite* . . . When I place this ointment on My head, since I am the High Priest according to the order of Melchisedek, this divine and fragrant ointment will spread over My face and over My whole body until it reaches the edge of My garments, like dew descending to Me, Mount Zion, from the small mountain of Hermon, My Bride . . . All this is extremely pleasing to Me and I pour a thousand blessings on My Bride, and I order and promise her an eternal life with Me: *Quoniam illic mandavit Dominus benedictionem* . . . This was the result of the two brothers, love and fear, dwelling within her in unity (*Ps.* 133)."

v. 11)   *Your lips, my bride, are the filtering of the honey-comb,*
           Honey and milk are under your tongue,
           and the scent of your garments
           is like the scent of incense.

He again calls her His *Bride,* because she really is His Bride, through the deep love with which she raises her many spiritual children, feeding them with the sweetness of milk and honey proper to young children. In the primitive Church the newly baptized were given milk and honey, being infants in Christ.

With the words of eternal life that come from her lips, the Bride feeds the many souls that she has attracted and won and for God by the fragrance of the virtues adorning her; exhaling the sweet scent of the incense of continual prayer.

In this way we can see what these beautiful *loves* or mystical *breasts* are that He has just mentioned. They are the breasts of perfect charity with which to nourish children, not with material milk but with the spiritual milk of holy self-denial and the edifying conversation of a kind and loving companionship which captivates hearts. They are the milk of her continual examples of heroic virtue, her sweet words of truth and grace, and her fervent prayers that are so effective in winning hearts and heaping them with riches.

"The words of souls who love God," says Maria Dolorosa,

"have the unction of grace that is as sweet as honey, producing a kind of delight in those who hear them. There is also milk in them, because the word of God is pure and nourishes the spirit. Finally, the garments smelling like incense represent the outer conduct of loving souls . . . a conduct that is so modest and edifying."

This *milk and honey* could also be interpreted as the doctrine proper to infants and to adults. According to St. Gregory, Our Lord would seem to be saying to the Church: your words, My Bride, are appropriate to everyone's condition, being honey to the perfect, but milk to those who are imperfect; for this is what the Apostle meant when he said that he fed milk to those who were still children in Christ, but he taught the perfect the highest mysteries: "perfectis vero sublimiora et divina mysteria instar mellis communicabat."

He sometimes mixes honey with the infants' milk so they can begin to taste and crave for such desirable sweetnesses.

"Mihi, tamen interim non desplicet," says Soto Mayor, "ut per labia sponsae melle et lacte manantia intelligamus etiam orationes, preces et supplicationes, hymnos, seu laudes et gratiarum actiones, quibus Ecclesia Christi Catholica ubique gentium et ubique locorum in re divina utitur, sive publice sive etiam privatim, sive ore sive etiam corde tenus. Cujusmodi sermones . . . divino Sponso . . . melle dulciora sunt."

The Spouse tells her, then: "How beautiful are your loves! Your ointments and oils and the other scents that you bring with you, conquer the whole world . . . All your words are honey, and your tongue seems completely bathed in milk and honey, and nothing but sweetness, softness and grace comes from your lips. Even your garments, apart from fitting and adorning you most becomingly, have such a sweet scent that you seem like Mount Lebanon." All this contributes to increasing the estate I entrusted to you, the scent of your virtues drawing so many lost sheep after you and leading them to my fold . . .

These faithful souls not only exhale, but now truly are, *the sweet scent of Christ* (II *Cor.* 2, 15), and *their very leaves,* that is their outer conduct, *are for the healing of nations (Rev.* 22, 2).

That is how Christ delights in His faithful Bride who watches over His honor, guards His estate, increases His family and preaches His praise! This is how He celebrates and extols the breasts with which she rears so many spiritual children, the milk with which she nourishes them, the care with which she suckles them . . . He praises her lips of grace that speak words of celestial teaching. He rejoices in the sweet fragrance of the virtues with which He Himself had prepared her for active life. In this scent that she exhales as she passes through the world, He perceives above all the scent of incense; for it was in the retreat of prayer and contemplation that she truly prepared herself for the apostolate, that is, for profitable action. It was there that she learned not to be distracted in the midst of worldly occupations and thereby to fulfill perfectly the commandment *to pray at all times* and places *without ever weakening.* It was there also that she so sweetly wounded and won the Sacred Heart, and where her lips began to distill milk and honey. Who would not be inspired by this to persevere in prayer, to enter into intimate contact with that wonderful Lover of souls Who lets Himself be won by them, and to try to merit those ineffable sweetnesses and inestimable communications that He has reserved for those who please Him in this way, surrendering themselves totally and unconditionally to Him . . . ?

In the Church these lips distilling honey are the good preachers who nourish souls with true and hidden sweetness, giving them, according to whether they are beginners or advanced, the milk and honey that they have hidden under their tongues, while false preachers boast of a sweetness and wisdom that they do not possess.

v. 12) *You are an enclosed garden, my sister, my bride,*
        an enclosed garden, a sealed fountain.

The Bride's heart is completely sealed off from every other affection but that of her Beloved, His Will and service. There He has His recreations and delights, and no one will be permitted to enter there unless by His command.

It is impossible for anyone who does not maintain interior and exterior recollection and does not hide the gifts, graces, and mercies he receives from God to persevere very long in the love of God . . . For this reason the Spouse calls His beloved an *enclosed garden.* " The soul encloses and guards herself with prudence, recollection, enclosure, confinement, silence, solitude and fear; and God visits those souls who live like this in solitude and speaks to their hearts . . . Whoever, then, wants to preserve the graces and mercies that he is given and to receive even greater ones, must keep them in his heart and place the seal of secrecy upon them . . ." (Fr. Gracian)

A sealed fountain, as though reserved only for the Master . . . Only God can take out water, or allow water to be taken out from this mystical fountain.

"The words *enclosed garden* and *sealed fountain,*" says St. Lawrence Justinian, "are rightly applied to the soul who, carefully examining her interior, corrects her faults, washes away her stains, orders her affections and movements, and guards and subjects her senses; so that Wisdom can come and dwell in her as in His Own mansion, completely enlightening her and taking delight in the sweet scent of her virtues. For from here spring sweet waters of divine words which will satisfy and gladden hearts.

The Church is also an enclosed garden for the faithful, filled with flowers and fruits, which are the various and good works of her children. The fountain which waters this garden is the doctrine of salvation enclosed in the Sacred Scriptures which, because of the hiddenness and profundity of the meanings they enclose, are like a sealed fountain. The guardians of this garden must open it and distribute its waters . . . (*Petit-Calmet*).

v. 13)   *Your shoots are a paradise of pomegranate trees*
         with all kinds of fruits, camphor and spikenard,
         saffron, calamus and cinnamon
         with all the trees of Lebanon,
         myrrh and aloes, with all the most precious perfumes.

These are beautiful symbols of the virtues with which the divine Spouse now sees the soul adorned, a soul that is always growing, sprouting new shoots to become a flowery garden where, among the most precious and fragrant plants and flowers of virtues, He takes His delight.

"Your shoots or flowerings: *emissiones tuae*" or as Scio interprets it: "all that you emit and . . . send out, all the trees you grow . . . meaning, the innumerable great and beautiful things in your garden are like an orchard of pomegranates with its fruit of sweetness, which are the apples; where there is also camphor and spikenard etc., so that what He plants is truly a delightful garden. He compares this loveliness to His Bride for such is her beauty and grace."

"Souls in love with Christ," writes María de la Dolorosa, "are an enclosed garden because they do not allow other loves to enter their hearts. In this way they become sealed fountains, not allowing other loves to drink the waters of their affections." such souls as these, she adds, "do not allow any crowd of worldly cares to enter in and ruin the flowers of virtues and the fruits of good habits, or to trouble the water of their pure intention in accomplishing their work. It is for this reason that their words and fervent example, when transplanted into the souls that hear them, produce the fruit of amendment and of virtuous actions . . ."

The *camphor and the spikenard* denote the harmony between the active and contemplative life, by which the soul tries to compensate and console the Spouse for sinners who are hindering Him, making herself more and more perfect in His eyes.

"Jesus is here praising all the virtues of the loving soul

represented by the *spikenard* . . . and all the trees of Lebanon; it is because of these that she exhales a sweet fragrance and makes herself most acceptable to her Spouse. Chief among these virtues and the *myrrh and aloes,* symbols of suffering, and the *finest perfumes,* symbols of the theological virtues; because a virtue cannot be called such if it has not been refined by suffering and if it in the slightest way resists faith, hope and charity."

"All just men," says St. Gregory the Great, "whether in time of peace, or in the frenzy of persecutions, are growing plants and shoots of various kinds of virtues, thereby creating a delightful garden of pleasant fruits and exquisite scents. In order to make known its fecundity and the abundance of this spiritual garden, the Holy Spirit gives a very life-like picture of the number and variety of all these virtues, using plants as symbols . . . The mixture and collection of all these virtues and good works produce the sweet fragrance of Jesus Christ in holy souls at all times and places, and are a most efficient remedy for restoring the sick to health."

"All these precious things," noted St. Ambrose (*De Isaac,* Ch. 5), "are the gifts of the Divine Spouse Himself, and they not only spread the scent of His good name and reputation everywhere, but they service the soul as a shield and defence against dangers. Some of these plants like the *calamus* and *cinnamon* symbolize the fragrance of the virtues with which she becomes pleasing in the eyes of her Spouse, and also in the eyes of the whole world; others, like the *myrrh* and the *aloes,* with their bitterness, represent the mortification that is needed for the soul to be kept from corruption.

"These precious ointments," says Fr. Gracian (*In Cant.,* 4) "represent the seven ways of the spirit . . . that the glorious Virgin taught us in the divine song of the *Magnificat.* The first is the esteem of God and His works and the gratefulness to Him, which is found in the loving soul, as in these words: *Magnificat anima mea Dominum.* The second, joy and spiritual rejoicing in

God: *Exultavit spiritus meus in Deo salutari meo.* The third: profound humility and recognition of one's own wretchedness: *Quia respexit humilitatem ancillae suae.* The fourth, gratitude for all the benefits received, the soul valuing them very highly since they are given by the hand of God: *Quia fecit mihi magna qui potens est.* The fifth, reverential fear, which is the respect of the soul as she sees herself before such a great and powerful God: *Timentibus eum. Fecit potentiam,* etc. The sixth, the fervent hungering and thirsting after justice, uprightness in the service of God, by which the soul is filled with riches: *Esurientes replevit bonis . . .* The seventh, and last, union with Christ, receiving and bringing Him within: *Suscepit Israel puerum suum,* etc. These seven spirits, or fruits of loving prayer are said to be in the Bride when the Spouse says *The Camphor and spikenard,* etc."

Thus the devout soul, being betrothed to Christ, is a well guarded and defended garden, being completely closed off from strangers and open only to her true Lord, the Divine Spouse. She is a fountain sealed by her Spouse Himself so that no one can make its crystal waters muddy. The countless gifts and graces that adorn this soul form a kind of precious garden, where there is nothing useless and where everything, besides being delightful, offers special blessings to all.

"In the just man and in virtue," writes Fr. Luis de León, "delight, profit, happiness and all other riches are to be found together, there being nothing that is not useful and valuable. Moreover, the just man not only has and produces delicious fruit that delights the taste, but also green leaves, the scent of a good reputation with which to delight and benefit the soul of his neighbor . . . All these trees . . . are a wonderful sight and have an excellent fragrance, thus confounding the nonsense of those who say that ceremonies and exterior works are not necessary."

"Come," said Our Lord to Sr. Nativity of Fougères (*Revelations,* II, Ch. 5), "come and enter the interior of my most beloved Bride, and you will see the purest pleasure and the ineffable delight that I have in her heart, in this *enclosed garden* where no one except I ever enters . . .

"O what a wonderful dwelling-place is this delightful garden! The beneficient rays of a temperate sun fill it with a continual verdure. The trees are laden with flowers and fruits, which are the sum of the virtues that adorn the Bride, and of the good works produced by constant practice . . . all of which are infinitely valuable in the eyes of the Heavenly Spouse. There the entire atmosphere is perfumed with the fragrance of these virtues, and all that is breathed is divine love . . .

"My beloved's heart," He told me, "is like a garden adorned with all kinds of sweet-smelling flowers and with a dazzling brilliance. I am delighted by its appearance and I never tire of looking upon it. Here humility is like the violet that grows under the feet of the passer-by. Her kindly modesty is like the lily of the field; the ardor of her love is like the splendor of the rose, as a beautiful spring day begins to dawn. Her separation from the world, the purity of intention with which she directs everything to Me, the care she takes not to do or think anything that might displease Me, her affection, her confidence, her complete surrender . . . all this, and a thousand other virtues which stem from this, is to Me a garden with the most pleasing fragrance and the most delightful appearance. That is why her conduct is so beautiful in My eyes and everything about her attracts Me so much. With a single glance she has wounded My heart. She is My beloved, chosen from among thousands, for she has preferred Me to everything. I take her under My protection in a very special way. The singular favors that I so genersouly give her are due to her for having chosen Me for her Spouse, for the faithfulness she continually shows Me and for the ardent love with which she ceaselessly sighs for Me. I am the absolute Master of her heart, of her free will and of all her faculties. She has nothing that is not Mine, and it is right that she should experience My goodness and not

be deprived of any of My favors . . . As a reward for your
victory, I surrender to you this Heart that you have
wounded . . ."

"Hence these loving conversations, these exchanges of
tenderness, these expressions of love, made between the Spouse
and the beloved Bride . . . What a reward for a creature!
Nothing less than the Heart of a God, who loves her to this
extreme, assuring her that she is in His love and His grace! . . . O
what mysteries are contained in the spiritual effusion that takes
place between the soul and her God!

"And what was my surprise to hear from the very lips of
Jesus Christ Himself that *no one is excluded from this degree of
perfection,* that even the worst sinners can hope to attain it
through grace and will only remember their sins in order to
celebrate the glorious efforts by which they triumphed over
everything! Who would not strive to reach such a desirable
state?"

Thus, the mystical Bride, or the loving soul, and above all,
holy Church are like a flowery garden filled with the fragrances
of all the virtues blended together, each giving a special delight
to the Lord, Who, as He takes His recreation there, could say
the same words spoken by Isaac as he blessed Jacob, only
more fittingly (*Gen.* 27): *Ecce odor filii mei sicut odor agri
pleni . . .*

St. Gregory comments very well on these words saying (*In
Ezech., Hom.* 6): "One of these scents is that of the vine, which
symbolizes the preachers who are full of the heavenly doctrine
that produces deep delights; another, that of the olive,
represents the mercies that are of such comfort to the weak;
another, that of the rose, the love of martyrs, whose
wonderfully sweet-scented examples embalm the world;
another, the scent of violets, the shyness of the humble, who,
hidden from the worldly, lead a supernatural life; and finally,
the scent of the spikenard, the symbol of perfect souls and
saints who have reached maturity in all kinds of good works."

It should also be noted that here (v. 13) Christ compares the soul to the appletree or its fruits, that is, to the same thing to which she had earlier compared Him (Ch. 2, v. 3). And this seems to indicate the *transformation* this happy soul has undergone on being raised to the mystical betrothal; consequently she must now be modeled on Him, and become one with Him. Thus, through her likeness to Him and her participation in His life she will become changed into a living store and source of graces.

v. 15)   *(You are) a fountain for gardens, a well of living waters that flow down impulsively from Lebanon.*

Shortly before He called her a *sealed fountain,* because this soul was now completely His. Now He calls her a *fountain for gardens* because of the great profit derived by many souls from the abundant graces that she received and which, surrendering herself and all her possessions, she lets flow freely, following the impulses of the Holy Spirit. For she irrigates these souls, like so many gardens, with the fullness that overflows from the waters of life and salutary wisdom. This is how *the impulse of the* divine *River,* that is to say, of the Holy Spirit, the mysterious *River of the water of life that proceeds out of the throne of God and of the Lamb (Rev.* 22, 1) not only gladdens this city of God *(Ps.* 46, 5), but converts it into a living store and a mystical *spring welling up to eternal life (John* 4, 14) and from which *rivers of living water (ibid,* 7, 38) will pour; and next to these waters many just souls can prosper and bear fruit, being always in leaf, and always producing the proper fruit in due season *(Ps.* 1, 3).

All these waters *flow down impulsively from Lebanon,* that is to say, from the fullness received in Baptism and increased in Confirmation, a fullness that impelled us all towards holiness, and finally, with our faithful cooperation, poured forth and flowed out in abundance to our own good and to that of others.

"An interior soul," writes Jesus' 'secretary', Benigna

Consolata, at His command, "through her union with God exercises a much greater apostolate than could ever be exercised by any exterior soul . . . An interior soul emerges from prayer as though completely embalmed in the fragrances of heaven. She is like a person who has spent some time in an atmosphere saturated with perfumes: without intending to she becomes impregnated with them and spreads them all around her . . .

"If the soul wants to become ever more interior and discover new horizons, for God communicates Himself to the soul that is ready to receive Him," the Blessed Virgin told her, "she must surrender herself to the power of Love, speaking very little to creatures and very much to God."

"Loving souls," says María Dolorosa, "are fountains that water the gardens of faithful hearts with prayer and good example; they are wells of living waters that flow from the spring of grace. Since these waters flow in this way from Lebanon they do not allow the soul to remain in the same state but speed her on her way towards perfection."

Progressing in this way she draws many others along with her through her prayer and example. Because of this, while in the eyes of the world these souls are considered selfish, egoistic and useless, everything that they possess, and they possess priceless riches and infinitely valuable graces, apart from greatly pleasing the Divine Spouse, is not only useful and delightful to them, but also to many others who do not even know them by name and who never discover the source of the abundant riches they receive . . . They are truly a *Fountain for gardens,* as well as *a Paradise of delights* . . . where all the Persons of the Blessed Trinity take recreation, seeing in them Their own Image. For there they shine with the virtue of the Father, the wisdom of the Son, and the goodness and charity of the Holy Spirit.

This is how they become worthy of hearing with ineffable pleasure this series of wonderful praises that are offered to them by their Divine Spouse Who is the very essence of Truth.

"The soul, who had never observed herself except to see

her own faults and defects," writes M. Angeles Sorazu (*Spiritual Life*, Ch. 19), "and who had never been able to listen to the praises that creatures might have lavished upon her, without a feeling of repugnance, fear and painful distress, now not only consents to the praises of her God and Divine Spouse . . . but is also immensely glad and most humbly grateful for the gifts and graces she possesses and the exceptional state that the divine light reveals to her. She feels that she is more loved by God than the immense majority of pious souls and that she is the special object of His predilections; she understands the high degree of divine union enjoyed by her almost boundless capacity to know and love her God; she understands the value this lends to her works and prayers in view of her exceptional state and the divine perfections in which she participates. She understands the gifts and privileges that she enjoys and that the Lord has given her so that she might work for the salvation of the souls that He wishes to sanctify through her; and she especially appreciates the wonderful mystical fecundity of her spirit united with that of God in producing the virtues practised in the external life and, above all, in the inner life, that is to say, in her relations with God during the course of her spiritual life, especially after being raised up to union with Him. This communication fills her with an ardent desire to save souls and a profound longing to share with them the graces that she treasures up and the happiness she enjoys in her union with God. She understands that *her lips are like the distilling of the honeycomb* and that *honey and milk are under her tongue.* Through her union with God, she possesses inexhaustible treasures of divine charity and knowledge, supernatural, ineffable and divine longings and aspirations, and the spirit of grace and truth which inspires her to utter words imbued with divine life, which, springing from her lips, penetrate, the souls of those who hear them. She desires to use this gift to the glory of God and for the good of souls, as she was instructed by her spiritual director . . . She feels that she is *a fountain for gardens, a well of living waters that flow down impulsively from Lebanon.* Her soul is a deep and living well that collects the torrential waters that perpetually flow from God, not in order to hold them, but so as to transmit them to souls who ask for them and who, through her, seek justice and holiness, or the development of their supernatural life. She does not want to set dikes around these living waters that God sends through her to souls who cannot receive them directly, but rather wants to let them follow their own course so that they can reach their destination."

v. 16)   *Rise up, north wind, and come, south wind,*
                and blow upon my garden,
                to spread its sweet smell around.

This could be the voice of the Spouse expelling the cold north wind that shrivels the flowers so they cannot grow, and telling the moderate south wind to come and open the flowers, and embalm the whole of His Bride's beautiful garden, His favorite property, where He so loves to come and take His delight. And it is perhaps the voice of the Bride herself, asking the warm humid wind of the Holy Spirit to blow over her and with His sweet breath to fill her with new fragrance; to stir her flowers and make them exhale those delightful scents that please the divine Lover so much and that succor so many souls, encouraging piety and inspiring fervor and the love of purity in the hearts of all.

"The Holy Spirit," says St. Mary Magdalen de Pazzi (*Part 3, Ch.* 4), "by ardent desires and enkindled words attracts to Himself His chosen ones who desire to be like God and to enkindle all hearts in His love — words and desires which the Spirit Himself has inspired. He brings them before the throne of the Eternal Father, and then spreads them over the earth yielding wonderful fruits for the Church."

Rise up, north wind . . . The Spouse says these words, according to Fr. Gracian, because what obstructs the love of God and the increase of grace and virtue is sin, the devil, coldness of spirit and all that is contrary to fervor. This is called here the north wind from which all evil is born in consciences, as is stated in these words (*Jer.* 1): *Ab Aquilone pandetur omne malum.* The south wind represents divine inspirations that give rise to grace, charity and the spirit of devotion.

That is why this divine breath is so desirable. To blow in this way through the mystical garden, that is to say, "to breathe through the soul," says St. John of the Cross (*Cant.* Stanza 17), "is to touch and put into motion the virtues and perfections already given, renewing and moving them in such a way that they of themselves afford the soul a wonderful fragrance and sweetness . . . Since the soul is not always experiencing and enjoying the acquired or infused virtues actually . . . they remain within her in this life like flowers enclosed in the bud or like aromatic spices whose scent is not perceived until shaken or uncovered. God sometimes grants these favors to the soul, His bride; He breathes through her flowering garden, opens all these buds of virtues, and uncovers these aromatic spices of gifts, perfections, and riches, and, disclosing this interior treasure and wealth, He reveals all her beauty. Then it is a wonderful sight to behold and pleasant to experience: the richness of her gifts unveiled the soul and the beauty of these flowers of virtues now in full bloom. The fragrant scent which each one of these with its own characteristic sweetness gives to her, is inestimable. She calls this the flowering of the garden's fragrance . . .

"Sometimes the fragrance is so abundant in the soul that it seems she is clothed with delight and bathed in inestimable glory, to such an extent that the experience is not only within her, but overflows and becomes manifest outwardly, those capable of recognizing it are aware of her experience. It seems to them that she is in a pleasant garden filled with the delights and riches of God. This is observable in holy souls, not only when the flowers open, but almost always; for they have a certain air of grandeur and dignity which inspires the beholders with awe and reverence. And so the Bride has an immense longing . . .

that the south wind come . . . for then the soul gains an accumulation of graces . . . This divine breeze of the Holy Spirit should be greatly desired. *Let each soul petition that He breathe through her garden* so that this divine fragrance might be diffused. Since this is so necessary . . . the Bride desires and ask for it . . . saying: *Arise north wind, come south wind . . .* The soul desires this not for her own pleasure and glory, but because she knows her Bridegroom is charmed with it, and it is a preparation and foretaste of the coming of the Son of God to take His delight in her."

When applied to the Church this passage gives a very good illustration of those days when the first disciples were in seclusion and, together with the Blessed Virgin Mary, cried out for the coming of the consoling Spirit . . .

"Some," remarks Scio, "explain the words *Rise up,* in this way: *Rise up, North wind and come and blow with the South wind;* for the Lord wanted the tribulations . . . to be the way in which His Bride would become grounded in humility, would recognize her own weakness and inability since she cannot sustain herself without the breath and assistance of the Spirit of God, and that she would thus cease to trust in herself and turn solely to God in all her needs . . . These same trials and tribulations give her occasion to spread the sweet scent and fragrance of all virtue everywhere."

Indeed, God sometimes — and this could also be the meaning here — allows souls to be shaken by the storms of tribulations and adversity, so that they exhale the scents of their virtues that were hidden and unknown to all . . . "Quomodo stellae in nocte lucent, in die latent; sic vera virtus, quae saepe in prosperis non apparet, eminet in adversis." (St. Bernard, *Serm.* 27)

"After she has learned her vocation and destiny," comments M. Sorazu (*Spiritual Life,* Ch. 19), "she listens to the voice of her God summoning two entirely contrary winds, the Divine Spirit and the diabolical wickedness of man; commanding the first to blow through the enclosed garden, the soul herself, and to spread the fragrance of the flowers and fruits that adorn and enrich it; and the second, to visit her with temptation so that she has occasion to exercise the virtues she possesses, and He, of showing her the affection and esteem He has for her, by the paternal Providence and wonderful protection that He affords her."

Synopsis

After completely surrendering herself and all she possesses to her Divine Spouse, after hearing Him lavish such praises upon her, and seeing herself now favored with the breath of His Spirit, she beseeches Him to come quickly and take recreation in His garden which for so many reasons belongs to Him, and to enjoy its most precious fruits. He accepts such a sincere offer and comes as absolute Master, bringing many guests with Him to this mystical harvest and mysterious feast given at the expense of the Bride.

V. 1   The Bride's sleep, watched over by her heart which hears the voice of her Beloved; the moving call of God

V. 2   and the Bride's humble excuses

V. 3   The Lord's sweet violence and the efficacy of His loving touch

V. 4-5   God's game with the soul; the painful absence and wretched abandonment

V. 6   The terrible trials and adversities that the soul searching for her Beloved suffers at the hands of those who ought to help her.

V. 7   The relief and comfort she seeks from the daughters of Jerusalem

V. 8   Their inability to understand these mysteries of love; their pity, but belief that she is mentally afflicted, this gives rise to the necessity of her making known the perfections of the

Spouse.
V. 9-16 In this way they, too, are enkindled in divine love.

THE BRIDE

(ch. 4,16) *Let my Beloved come into his garden*
and let him eat the fruit of its apple trees.[a]

(ch. 5, v. 1)

I came into my garden, my sister, my Bride
I gathered my myrrh with my scents[b]
I ate my honeycomb with my honey[c]
I drank my wine with my milk,
Eat, friends, and drink,
and inebriate yourselves, my dearly loved ones.

THE BRIDE

v. 2)   *I sleep, but my heart keeps vigil:*
           (it is) the voice of my Beloved calling.

THE SPOUSE

Open to me, my sister, my love,
my dove, my immaculate one;[d]
for my head is filled with dew
and my locks with the drops of the night.

THE BRIDE

v. 3)   *I have taken off my tunic; how shall I put it on?*
           I have washed my feet; how shall I soil them?

v. 4)   *My Beloved put his hand through the hole in the door*[e]
           and the depths of my being trembled at his touch.

v. 5)   *I rose to open to my Beloved;*
           myrrh ran off my hands
           the purest myrrh off my fingers. [f]

a.   The Hebrew text joins this with v. 16 of the preceding chapter.
b.   Hebrew: I come-or will come-to my garden ... I will gather my myrrh ...
c.   Hebrew: I will eat my honeycomb ...
d.   Hebrew: my perfect one.
e.   Through the small hole in the door that was used to run back the bolt and
       open it.
f.   Hebrew and the Septuagint: "Pure myrrh adhered from my fingers on to the
       bolt." They thus join the word *bolt* with v. 5, and begin v. 6 with "I opened to
       my Beloved ..." Fr. Luis de Leon: "and my hands dripping myrrh — and
       from fingers, myrrh that runs over the hingers of the door-latch."

v. 6)   *I opened the bolt of my door to my Beloved,*
         But he had gone from there and had left.
         My soul melted on hearing him speak[g]
         I sought him but did not find him,
         I called to him and he gave me no answer.

v. 7)   *The watchmen that go about the city found me.*[h]
         They beat me and wounded me;
         the keepers of the walls took my mantle from me.

v. 8)   *I charge you, daughters of Jerusalem,*
         if you should find my Beloved
         that you tell him that I am sick with love[i]

THE DAUGHTERS OF JERUSALEM

v. 9)   *What makes your Beloved better than other beloveds,*
         O loveliest of women?
         What makes your Beloved better than other beloveds,
         that you give us a charge like this?

THE BRIDE

v. 10)   *My Beloved is white and ruddy,*
         outstanding among thousands[j]

v. 11)   *His head is of the purest gold;*
         his hair like palm shoots,
         and black as a raven.

v. 12)   *His eyes are like doves by the brooks of waters*
         that are washed with milk
         and dwell near the abundant streams[k]

v. 13)   *His cheeks are like a bed of spices,*
         a bank of sweet-smelling plants.
         His lips are lilies distilling the purest myrrh.

g.   Hebrew: "My soul left me when he spoke" or "after him."
h.   Hebrew: "My veil." The mantle worn by Orientals covers them completely.
i.   Hebrew and the Septuagint: "What must you tell him . . . ? That I am sick
     with love."
j.   Hebrew: "Outstanding among ten thousand." "The Hebrew can also be
     translated:"and bears the banner among ten thousand. As though to say: there
     is no need for me to tell you who he is, for among ten thousand he stands out
     like the standard bearer." (Scio)
k.   Hebrew: "resting in abundance."

v. 14)   *His hands are rounded, golden*
          full of hyacinths.
          His breast is of ivory
v. 15)   *His legs are pillars of marble*
          set in sockets of gold.
          His appearance is like that of Lebanon
          tall like the cedars.
v. 16)   *His throat is most sweet*[m]
          and he is altogether desirable.
          Such is my Beloved, and he is my friend,
          O daughters of Jerusalem.

THE DAUGHTERS OF JERUSALEM

v. 17)   *Where did you Beloved go?*
(ch. 6, 1) *O loveliest of women?*
          Which way did your Beloved turn,
          that we may seek Him with you?

Exposition

ch. 4, v. 16   *Let my beloved come into his garden*
                and let him eat the fruit of his trees.

This verse, intimately linked with the last verses of the
previous chapter, is an eloquent expression of the Bride's
complete surrender of herself and her possessions to the Spouse,
of the exchange of shares earned, and of the strong impulses of
love that are now born in her. Carried along by these impulses
and faithful to her promises, she wants everything for her
Beloved; and being well founded in humility and self-knowledge
she knows that all the gifts and graces that she possesses and
that have been heaped upon her are not hers; thus she zealously
places everything in the hands of Him Who is Master of all. As
soon as she perceives the perfumes of this mystical garden
passing in great abundance, she invites the Beloved to come to
it. She calls it her Beloved's garden and not her own because

---

l.   Hebrew: "His hands are rings of gold, full of jewels of Tarshish. His belly is a
      work of ivory covered with sapphires."
m.   Hebrew: "This palate, sweetness . . ."

there is nothing there now that is not God's. She no longer invites Him with sweet-smelling flowers of virtues but with seasoned, precious fruits of holiness and all kinds of good works, which are what Our Lord chiefly comes to look for and encourage, and which most delights and refreshes Him in His visits.

Let us see what is meant by this divine visit. "It is said that God comes to the soul," writes Fr. Gracian (*in Cant.* 5, 1), "although He never leaves her 'In Ipso vivimus . . .', because the soul herself moves and goes towards God. This going of the soul to God and coming of God to the soul happens in many ways. The first, through faith; the second, through grace; the third, through love; the fourth, through actual contemplation; the fifth, through the affection of the will and the inner act of charity; the sixth, through a way of experiencing the presence of God within her that makes her attentive, reverential, loving, and fearful of offending Him, These and others are ways in which God comes to the soul and the soul goes to God. Following this, the soul's invitation to the Spouse to come (as though He were absent) is as much as saying: 'Lord, give me faith, give me grace, give me love; may I contemplate Your greatness, feel Your presence within me, and then I shall do inner acts that are pleasing to Your divine Majesty.' "

Recognizing the noble and sincere sentiments of this soul now so totally His, and seeing how faithful she is to the generous surrender of self that she has so often made to Him, Jesus gladly accepts this loving invitation. He promises to come or comes there straightway to take recreation and to regale His friend, but at the cost of great privations and sacrifices that He asks of her, and at the cost of the apparently extreme poverty to which He sometimes reduces her.

The soul learns that severe tests await her and accepts them with filial submission and even with enthusiasm. She longs for the moment when she will be submitted to the temptation and tribulation she awaits. Since she cannot forestall the house

of Providence, and since it would not be right to precipatate
these adversities which she sees coming towards her at a pace
extremely slow to her impatient longing, she seeks to renounce
the happiness that she enjoys in her relations with God and to
suffer the privation of His divine consolations. She invokes God
asking Him to come to His garden and eat the fruit of His
apple trees; that is to say, to strip her of the treasures of virtue
deposited in her, or rather, to deprive her of the realization of
these treasures in the inferior part of her soul so as to leave her
in absolute poverty . . . stripped of all riches save God Himself
Whom she possesses." M. Sorazu (*loc. cit.*)

v. 1)   *I came into my garden, my sister, my Bride,*
         I gathered my myrrh with my scents;
         I ate my honeycomb with my honey
         I drank my wine with my milk.
         Eat, friends, and drink,
         and inebriate yourselves, my dearly loved ones.

"He calls her sister and bride," says St. John of the Cross
(*Canticle*, stanza 22), "because she was a sister and bride in the
love and surrender she had made of herself to Him before He
called her to this state . . . where, as He says, He has now
gathered His fragrant myrrh and aromatic spices, which are the
fruits of the flowers now ripe and ready for the soul. These are
the delights and grandeurs which of Himself and in Himself He
communicates to her in this state."

"But what is most wonderful and delightful," observes the
Ven. Fr. La Puente (*Guía*, tr. 1, Ch. 20), "is to see the joy with
which our sovereign God makes these visits and distributes these
gifts, saying not so much that He gives them as that He receives
them, as though He were profiting by them . . . What is Christ's
going to His garden, says St. Gregory, but His visiting the souls
in whom He takes delight? What is this gathering of His myrrh
with the other aromatic species but His delight in the scent of
mortification, and in the fragrance of the other virtues that they
exercise? And what else is His eating His honeycomb with His

honey but, His joy at seeing truths put into practice to the delight of the souls themselves? What is His drinking His wine with His milk but His rejoicing at seeing how love unites with purity, how zeal combines with discretion and knowledge. He calls all this His, because His is the myrrh of mortification, and His are the honeycomb, the wine and milk of the meditations, affections and holy exercises that seethe in the soul with the sweetness that accompanies them. He causes all this by His visit: we receive it all from Him, and His banquet is to see His gifts in us and to see us profit from them. He eats and drinks these works when He approves them and delights in them, considering them His . . . O Spouse of chaste souls, since You find such pleasure in our works, come to my garden, and eat the fruit of my apple trees! Visit me, Lord, with Your sweet presence, not because of the pleasure I receive but because of that which You receive. Give me the gifts of Your grace not only that I may consume them, but also that You may receive great glory and praise because of them."

The Beloved replies, accepting the property of the garden and showing Himself as the true Master of all: They invite Him alone and He brings friends. They offer Him apples and other sweet fruits and He replies: *I gathered — or will gather — my myrrh,* etc. adding: *Eat, friends, and drink* . . . specifying in this way the virtues and good works that He most desires to gather from this soul and the use He is going to make of them, if not harvesting the soul herself who is now fully ripe and bearing her off to the garden of glory.

He began by gathering the myrrh of self-denial and sweet-smelling mortification, which is what He most needed to distribute to many hearts that He might heal them or preserve them from the corruption to which they were exposed. Then He ate and drank and offered to others the *honey* and *honeycomb* of sweetness and gentleness distilled from the Bride's lips, and the wine of mystical wisdom that intoxicates with love and fills with Heavenly gladness, and with which He inspires and consoles advanced souls. He drinks it with the milk of spiritual infancy with which He feeds and regales beginners so that they "grow in health" as they "taste how sweet the Lord is" (I *Peter* 2, 2-3). The Spouse gathers the best flowers of the garden and collects many aromatic plants and the precious fruits that He like most, thus leaving the sweet Bride apparently impoverished. But she is never richer than at that moment, never are her gifts better won than when she loses them in this way, when He takes them for Himself and distributes them to so many souls who are hungering after truth and justice.

   I gathered my myrrh . . . I drank my wine . . . "In these words," adds Fr. Gracian, "Christ makes known the effects of His divine loving presence in the soul that He visits. The first mortifies her, enlightening her as to her imperfections and curbing her faults. The second raises her spirit inspiring her to perform acts of exemplary virtue (represented by the scents). The third gives her a sweetness and richness that is like honey. The fourth gives her spiritual wine with its strong desires. And the fifth communicates to her the milk of doctrine that is necessary for her salvation. He also says that He eats the honey and drinks the milk and wine within the soul; for all this the Spouse finds delightful, there being nothing sweeter to Christ than to be alone with His Bride enjoying His love (*Prov.* 8). So, let no one think that when a servant of God spends a long time in mental prayer or contemplation, he is wasting his time or losing favor, as long as God is not calling him to other things. For, although he might appear to be idle and to be doing nothing, there is no occupation more pleasing and gratifying to God than that of the soul that contemplates and loves Him.

   "Your heart," said Our Lord to Sr. Susana María de Rianst (*Life,* Part 1, Ch. 12), is this garden where I have gathered the myrrh that the bitterness of suffering had poured into it. It is also a honeycomb that contains the honey of My grace. The wine represents this powerful grace which, mixed with the milk of My gentleness, makes it victorious. The doorways to this heart have been opened to receive the effects of My justice. Now I promise you that it will be closed to the vanities of the world and sensible only to My love and to Eternal Truths. You must stand before My Father like an empty vessel, ready to receive all kinds of liquids; but His justice will pursue you until you are completely purified . . . It is in Me that you must gather strength and light . . . Souls lifted up above all creation and above themselves like sacred eagles contemplate the Divinity in Its Essence and discover Its infinite perfections. But those who only see these perfections in the dark night of creatures receive a very poor impression of them."

"It seemed to me," writes Sr. Teresa of J. M. (*Comment.* I), "that the Divine Spouse was telling me: I will come to My garden, which is you, and entering into it, I will gather my myrrh, which is your soul, and is to Me like the most precious and sweetest scented myrrh, because of its perfect and continual mortification, which produces the fragrance of many other virtues. *I will eat my honeycomb with my honey,* that is to say, I will eat the will with its sweet, loving affections . . . *I will drink my wine with milk,* which is as much as to say: I will absorb your understanding and its knowledge. And He says that all this is His, because this soul's faculties are now His through union, and all that they contain has been placed there by Him. In this way He again united my soul and faculties with Himself."

"There is certainly some mystery," says Soto Mayor, "in the marked repitition of the pronoun *mine,* with which He seems to glory in the fact that everything belongs to Him . . . Videtur . . . quodammodo gloriari omnia bona, . . . nempe *hortum* ipsum, et *myrrham* cum caeteris aromatibus, et *mel* et *vinum,* et *lac* propria sua esse, id est, proprio suo jure se cuncta haec abunde possidere, non tanquam mercenarium aut custodem, sed tanquam verum et legitimum Dominum . . .

"Per vinum commode sublimiorem et arcaniorem doctrinam, per lac vero doctrinam illam rudiorem, qua recens baptizati *tanquam modo geniti infantes* in Ecclesia imbuuntur, seu initiantur, accipimus. Infantes enim et parvuli propter teneram aetatem nondum capaces sunt solidioris cibi, id est, perfectioris doctrinae, quae per vinum significatur."

Without this celestial wine the devout soul cannot be satisfied. "Desideramus," says St. Augustine (*De agone Christiano*, Ch. 9), "ipsum vitae fontem, ubi sobria ebrietate inundemur. Dicit enim Spiritus S.: *'Filii autem hominum in tegmine alarum tuarum sperabunt. Inebrianbuntur ab ubertate domus tuae, et torrente voluptatis tuae potabus eo'*. Talis enim ebrietas non everit mentem, sed tamen rapit sensum, et oblivionem praestat omnium terrenorum."

Eat friends . . . Since the Bride's invitation was so sincere, the Spouse brings his friends with Him and they eat all that she has there. And she resigns herself to this spiritual barrenness and hardship through love of her Beloved. She is even grateful, delighting and rejoicing at the sight of His pleasure in her and how He deigns to relish the sweetness of the things she has produced.

"One day when the love of God made itself felt in a very intense and intimate way," wrote one soul in May, 1915, "He asked me to give the joyful part of this love to souls who do not love Him, together with all that is most sensitive, leaving myself with the substantial part of suffering. I shuddered because it seemed as if God were placing before my eyes a picture of the suffering that awaited me. It seemed to me as if the three Divine Persons of the Blessed Trinity were each kissing my soul. What I felt and heard in my heart is too intimate to be described. For eight days I rested completely in God: it seemed that He was nourishing me, that He was more my soul than my soul itself. Afterwards . . . what happened? I don't know, but it seemed that I had lost everything, being left with just a feeling of nothingness and of chilling death . . . It seemed as though I had fallen into a very deep, dark well where I could not see, hear or know anything . . . ; I felt as though I had lost God, faith hope, love, as though I had never known them. I felt like an imbecile, unable to suffer or to desire . . .

"Some days," she added in November, "I have had some respite. One night when I felt such a great longing and hunger for God that, had I let myself go, I would have said and done a thousand foolish things, I seemed to hear His voice telling me so sweetly and silently: 'If I am the air you breath, if you are in Me and I am in you, why are you looking for Me?' And at once I felt so close to God that I could never describe it . . ."

Then the soul's desires are satisfied as she sees herself made one with Him for Whom she was longing, receiving His Spirit of love, which is the mystical kiss that she prayed for from the beginning and through which she will participate in His sentiments and above all, in His spirit of sacrifice.

"For this I exist," she adds, "to be at the mercy of God and like the host, to be sacrificed for my brethren; for He wants me to look on them as my children and that they be truly so, for His praise and glory . . . I have come to see that Jesus has many souls who sacrifice themselves for the good of their neighbors, who work for their salvation, etc., but that He has very few *mothers* of souls: there are very few to give these souls substance to nourish and form them, etc. . . . And He wants me to be a mother in this way, completely at their disposal, undergoing hunger so that they can eat: they are more truly my children than I could ever say. It is true that I have many cares of my own . . . but if this occurs to me as I suffer, I seem to feel Him saying to me: 'Remember, take care of Me and I will take care of you.' The two ideas of host and mother of souls are so similar that only the Eucharist makes them understandable. Looking at the sacred Host everything is fully explained to me . . . !" (September)

Here, then, is a sample of the delights that God has in souls where He reigns at His pleasure . . . ! This is how He takes recreation, how He gives pasture and feeds among the lilies and how He gathers His precious myrrh . . . !

These mystical fruits with which the Bride invites and regales the Spouse are shared in by nearly all the true friends of Jesus, that is by all the faithful who live in His grace; for all share in and enjoy the merits of the others by virtue of the *Communion of saints.*

"With these words Our Lord also makes known," says Fr. La Puente (*Perf. Gener.* tr. 4, Ch. 6), "the order the chosen ones must have in imitating Him so as to receive Him. First, gathering the myrrh of mortification, and also the virtues which, like aromatic spices, yield the fragrance of good works. Once this has been done in great abundance (as is indicated by the word *gather*), He invites them to eat *His honeycomb with His honey* — or as the Septuagint interprets it, *His bread with His honey* — and His wine with His milk; this bread and wine representing, as St. Ambrose states, His most Sacred Body and Blood as in the Blessed Sacrament, together with the ineffable sweetness that is communicated with it. With this food and drink He invites His friends and dear ones who love Him, hoping they will eat and drink and fill themselves with such an excess of love that they become intoxicated, like one who has drunk more than his weak nature can withstand, 'For,' as St. Gregory says (*Hom. 10 in Ezech.*), 'to become intoxicated is to change one's opinion about what one previously felt, to gain renewed strength to do what one was previously unable to do, exchange the sentiments and judgements of the world for those of Christ, and the strength of the flesh for the strength of the spirit.' "

"He first gathers the myrrh," observes María Dolorosa, "so as to indicate that He is more pleased by the sufferings than by the sweetness of the honey and milk of spiritual consolations, so that, if we want to be lovers of Christ, we must also be lovers of the Cross. The tender Spouse wants all the faithful to approach not only the feast of the Eucharist but also that of prayer. In prayer, some eat and drink the divine word contained in devout books by means of meditation, others are enraptured in the sweetness of contemplation."

Thus, although all participate in this feast, not all do so in the same way. For, as St. Bonaventure (*De 7 Donis* SS., Part 2, s.7, c.6) and Richard of St. Victor point out, while the friends "eat and drink", the *dearly beloved become intoxicated* or *enraptured*, transported beyond themselves in lofty contemplation, enjoying the fullness in which they receive the sweet wine of mystical wisdom that brings them the sum total of all virtues and riches. Those who have never merited such a happy rapture of love, however "perfect" they consider themselves to be, "love less and are loved less: *Quandiu hujusmodi ebrietatem et excessum mentis non sentimus, quid aliud de nobis sentire debemus nisi quia minus deiligimur, et nisi quia minus diligimus?"*

St. Gregory remarked, we must not here be content with simply eating, but must aspire to this mystical intoxication which is more sanctifying: to this rapture where the soul becomes transformed and made one with the heart of the Spouse.

"There are two kinds of divine love," writes Fr. Gracian with respect to this, "one, of His ordinary friends, and the other, of His dearly beloved and much cherished friends. By His ordinary friends I mean those servants of God who are content with keeping His commandments and pursuing an ordinary kind of meditation . . . His dearly beloved and cherished friends are the very fervent, spiritual and contemplative souls, who, by persevering at great length in prayer and through sweet love, attain to joys, ecstasies, raptures, visions, revelations and other supernatural mercies and singular graces of God. Making known then, this diversity of love, the Spouse says: *Eat and drink, friends, but drink and inebriate yourselves, my dearly loved ones.* Which is as much as to say: you who are my friends through the usual, average degree of grace and charity, eat the bread . . . of doctrine and ordinary meditation; but you, my dearly loved and cherished ones, come and drink such strong spirit that you are transported out of yourselves and your faculties are left behind, so that you become, as it were, intoxicated, unaware of anything on earth."

There are, however, in these mystical wine-cellars bitter wines which intoxicate without the soul feeling any of the Lord's sweetness; but instead, an apparent harshness, repulsion and withdrawal from Him, abandonment, solitude and a very pungent bitterness . . . Nevertheless, she sleeps in peace and lives only for God, oblivious of herself and thus living in holy intoxication . . .

"Whoever is intoxicated," adds María Dolorosa, "feels inspired and does not hesitate to risk herself in any kind of danger. Thus, the soul inebriated by divine love heeds nothing and, in spite of all the obstacles, directs herself to wherever zeal for the Spouse's honor indicates."

Indeed, this wine of contemplation always intoxicates souls in such a way that it makes them truly sober and chaste, oblivious of the world and transported up to heavenly things: *"Sic mentes inebriat,"* says St. Cyprian (*Ep.* 63), *"ut sobrios faciat, ut mentes ad spiritualem sapientiam redigat, ut a sapore isto saeculari ad intellectum Dei unusquisque resipiscat."*

"Sobria illa ebrietas," adds St. Bernard (*Tr. de Dilig. Deo*), vero *non mero ingurgitans: non madens vino, sed ardens Deo."*

"But this intoxication," adds Gracian, "occurs in many ways . . . The spirit is sometimes so great and so powerful that the inebriation reaches that profound sleep more properly called ecstasy . . . Here . . . the exterior and interior faculties cease; for the senses of sight and hearing, etc., do not see or hear; the imagination ceases, as do the interior appetites; only the understanding and the will . . . in a certain way keep vigil . . . And because the understanding and the will (which is the free will and called the soul's heart) are penetrating and loving and all the other faculties are asleep, alienated and ceasing to function, the Bride says: *I sleep and my heart keep vigil.* For, were the free will to cease operating, loving and understanding, there would be no merit in a soul when she is thus enraptured . . ."

v. 2)   *I sleep and my heart keeps vigil . . .*

This is what the Bride exclaims, says St. Ambrose, as she falls into a sweet sleep of love, enraptured while contemplating the great mysteries the Lord communicates to Her: *Hausit anima fidelis mysteriorum ebrietatem coelestium, et velut soporata vino, et quasi in excesu vel stupore posita, dicit:* Ergo dormio . . .

"The favor of enabling the heart to keep watch while the soul sleeps," says Fr. La Puente (*Guia*, tr. 1, Ch. 19), following the opinion of St. John Climacus (*Escl. Esp.* gr. 19), "Our Lord usually concedes to those who give themselves to this sovereign exercise (of prayer) with great fervor and perseverance. And it is good to ask Him for it, saying: O Eternal God, Who are the heart and love of the just who converse with You, watch over me while I sleep, and give me such a sleep that it becomes the source of fervent prayer when I am awake."

In this *Song* the Bride three times says that she sleeps, but in different tones, as the sleep of contemplation becomes more and more intimate and profound. Before she dreamt while she slept; now she sleeps, but her heart keeps watch, and thus she at once hears the voice of her sweet Lord Who is knocking at the door. O how delicate this knock or touch is! What wonders this divine Voice works in the soul!

> *The voice of my beloved calling!*
> *Open to me, my sister, my love,*
> *my dove, my immaculate one;*
> *for my head is filled with dew*
> *and my locks with the drops of the night.*

This occurs when souls have reached the mystical union and, above all, the state of betrothal, and to whom the Lord so often comes, now to rest, now to ask for sacrifices, now to find consolation for the neglect, disdain and irreverence with which the worldly treat Him. For such souls are always and everywhere thinking of Him and seeking the best way of pleasing Him. Thus, even when asleep, they are constantly praying and in this way are always ready to hear His most delicate voice. The sleep in question here is the sleep of lofty contemplation. Enraptured with the wine of love of the mystical banquet, these souls sometimes fall asleep, or so it would seem to the profane and, to a certain extent, to the spiritual as well, for these souls more or less lose the use of their senses. However, it is then that their hearts are most awake, and so they hear more clearly and distinctly than ever the voice of the Lord as He comes to them as their most loving Spouse, and tells them of His solitude and of the great longing He has for their love. For it was in order to be loved by all that He came into the world and suffered such rigors and torments from the stable of Bethlehem to the Garden of Olives and Calvary. He invites them not only to console Him and receive Him with the deepest affection, but sometimes even to leave the very rest of contemplation and go out with Him to win souls that will love Him and cease to offend Him.

"O Christ's Bride," says Fr. Gracian, "let us now see in what way this sleep benefits you. What is this *I hear the voice of my Beloved: Open to me my sister . . .* ?

"O Divine Spouse, what lofty doctrine You teach us, and how necessary if we are to understand what perfect love is . . . ! I can see two kinds of love, which we can call *pleasurable love* and *zealous love*. Pleasurable love they call fruitive love . . . and it is very good when placed in God, for, since He is my ultimate End, I am well occupied in enjoying His presence with pleasure and delight . . . Zealous love is a strong, efficacious and practical love whose purpose is the glory and honor of God and the salvation of souls, and doing and suffering everything it can to ensure that Christ receives more honor and glory . . . When the soul is in ecstasy — which is normally the result of pleasurable love — Christ is not content with that love alone, but calls her to engage in zealous love, to do good to souls, to practice works of mercy and to suffer trials and abuse for His love. And so He tells her to open her heart and to expand her desires in imitation of Him . . . It usually happens that those souls dearly loved by Christ, who experience ecstasies and raptures, visions and revelations, come to be very profitable to the Church, suffering great trials for the Lord, as was true in the case of St. Francis, St. Dominic, St. Clare, St. Teresa of Jesus and other founders and reformers of Orders.

On other occasions He invites them to renounce themselves more and more and to surrender into His hands, leaving themselves so as to be lost completely in the abyss of His infinite greatness and beauty . . . In all events, He comes full of grace like a divine dew, with which to refresh, bathe, beautify and enrich all who receive Him with love; but He usually comes in a hurry and, as it were, just passes through. So we must always be ready to receive Him promptly, so as not to lose such a happy opportunity which, if well used, would bring us unspeakable joy, producing a wonderful renewal within us that would give us a foretaste of eternal happiness and a precious "taste of eternal life", being the pledge of further and yet more ineffable favors.

"The coming of the Spouse," says Ruysbroeck (*Adorno de las bodas* 1.3. Ch. 3), "is sudden and swift, for His coming is timeless and accompanied by immense riches; He always comes anew, personally manifesting Himself more clearly as if He had never come before; for His timeless coming consists in a certain *nunc* or everlasting present, and He is always received with a new hunger and a new enjoyment. What gifts then, and what joys the Spouse brings with His coming! . . . They are infinite and immense because they are the Spouse Himself. The spiritual eyes with which the soul carefully contemplates and looks upon her Spouse are so opened that they never close, because the attentive contemplation of the spirit with which she gazes upon the hidden manifestation of God, lasts forever."

Here He calls her not only in order to favor her, but also to be favored by her: to be consoled and sheltered, to have His sick or needy members cared for, and to help those liable to perish forever.

Thus we see that "with the most affectionate words He asks to be admitted," writes María Dolorosa, "so that she might understand that with every effort of her good will she must not only receive the dew of His grace, but also comfort and console Him for the rejection He has received in His pursuit of sinners (represented by the dampness of the night).

It is wonderful to see how tenderly and with what moving words of affection He now calls to her, being so weary of knocking in vain at so many doors! What love and labor He puts into His efforts to enter souls who want to be faithful to Him, but who are not generous and who resist Him in many ways. And how much guilty resistance He encounters as He tries to take possession of hearts . . . !

Lope de Vega expresses it well when he writes:

How often my angel would tell me:
"Soul, run to the window and see
With what love He insistently calls to you . . . !"
And how often, O Sovereign Beauty,
My reply would be: "let's open tomorrow . . ."
And tomorrow again make the same reply!

And yet, He continues calling over and over again with tenderest expressions, telling the soul: "Open to me, *My sister,* for that is what you are through the grace of baptism, when, through My merits, you were raised to the dignity of a true *daughter* of My Eternal Father; *My love,* because of My excessive charity for you and because of so many demonstrations of My affection for you; *My dove,* because of the abundant gifts and fruits of the Holy Spirit with which I enriched and beautified you; *My immaculate one,* because of the wonderful purifications with which I washed and cleansed you. So, open now the door of your heart to Me Who love you so much, and Who, tired and weary, knock at so many doors, waiting to see if they will finally give entrance just as I waited for you outside, during the *night* of neglect and forgetfulness when you pretended not to hear Me . . . Open to Me and come out and dry My hair and console Me by word and example for all the insults I receive."

"The Savior's dew-filled hair," says St. Augustine (*Tr. 57 in Joan.*) and St. Gregory, "are those Christians whose charity is so cold, that although they remain on His head, far from protecting Him, are bringing Him trouble and cold . . ."

And yet He goes on calling the heart of man, using the sweetest and tenderest ways to attract it. Although He encounters resistance, He does not go away, but continues calling and hoping.

Such neglect and resistance is more often found in beginners, for whom the Divine Lover waits so patiently, suffering in this way the agony of so many nights of icy indifference. Here the Bride's delay comes from other reasons which often cause even very fervent souls to resist Him without their realizing it.

"If the soul is so just and perfect," writes Fr. La Puente, (*Perf. Est. Ecles.* tr. 4, Ch. 6), "how is it possible for God to be outside her house, knocking at the door, asking to be admitted, for God is always within the just . . . ? But both arguments are true and correct. For Our Lord is present within souls through the effects that He works in them. After entering through justification, He repeatedly calls to them asking them to open to Him and to allow Him to come in and do all the work necessary for their profit and perfection. When this has been done, He again calls to them to let Him in to produce within their hearts a great love of their neighbor and the zeal to go out and work for the salvation and perfection of all. As long as He does not produce these effects and as long as the soul fails to prepare herself to receive them, He is detained outside her, knocking with the touches of His inspirations in the hope that she will let Him in by clearing away the obstacles that prevent her from receiving such a great favor. Who could explain the names He calls her as He asks her to open to Him . . . ? Remember, He says, that I made you *My sister* through grace, *My love* through charity, *My dove* through union with the Holy Spirit, and *My beautiful one,* through purity of heart. Will you not open to Me Who bestowed on you such great mercies, Who desires to come in so as to communicate further mercies to you just as great? Do not be content to possess this good as your own: open to Me, so that we can go out and win other brothers, other friends, other doves and other beautiful souls, so as to spread My glory and the glory of My Father . . .

He addresses her in the name of charity because of the needs of her neighbors, saying to her: "see how My head is filled with dew . . ." *The head of Christ* as a man, said St. Paul (I *Cor.* 11, 3) is God; and His head, says St. Gregory (in *Cant. 5),* is full of dew or frost when His holy name is blasphemed by the ungodly, despised by sinners and treated with little respect by the lukewarm. The hair on His head is the Christians united to it through faith; for they are full of the drops of the night when they are lacking in charity . . . If you love Christ and have the means to help Him in this need, how can you fail to hear His call and devote yourself as far as you can to withhold the blasphemies, insults and sins that fall upon His head, working for His honor, ridding the faithful of the drops of so many sins and consoling the afflicted in their suffering? Note the third term of expression He uses, when He speaks of the profit and reward He offers for this service, for this, as St. Paulino says (*Epist.* 4), is what is also meant by saying that His head is full of dew . . . the dew representing the abundance of graces and Heavenly gifts with which the Divinity of Christ is filled . . . "So if you wish to be enriched with Heavenly blessings, open to Me," says the Savior, "and consent to what I ask of you."

Let us now take an example and see what He usually asks of the soul and to what He calls her.

One day on the eve of Corpus Christi the Lord appeared to María Brotel (*Life,* Append. I), saying to her: "My daughter, not everything will be enjoyment. There has to be suffering. Are you ready to come with Me?" Finding her ready He led her, as she says:

"First, to the tabernacle where He dwells, telling me: 'come and see where I live through love of men.' I went with Him, but I had to suffer greatly. Such forgetfulness and such coldness! From there I saw so many millions of souls entering churches in a distracted, preoccupied state of mind, scarcely thinking of Jesus Who, through His love for them dwells there. How can You stay here, I said to Him . . . ? 'My daughter,' He replied, 'I have lived here through love of men ever since the beginning of the Church, and here I shall remain night and day until the end of the world.'

"Second, He led me to those souls who receive Him in Communion in a state of mortal sin. When I saw that soul open her mouth to receive Him (I say 'soul' but there were thousands of them) I stood shocked and cried out: 'let us go; I cannot stay here,' 'Patience, my daughter,' replied Jesus, 'let us remain.' And then I saw the interior of that soul. In every corner and at every turn there were demons of passions . . . Jesus made me see the terrible state of those who had eaten and drunk to their own damnation; I saw that in His just wrath He was about to hurl them into the abyss . . . As many as four times He said to me 'Let us leave here.' I asked Him to send these unfortunate souls His light, contrition and zealous confessors. And in His ineffable love He promised me to send them many graces . . .

"Third, He led me to the lukewarm souls. O, what lack of feeling! I almost suffered more there than with the previous ones. Since they are hardened by their luke-warmness, graces slip off them without penetrating. Jesus enters them, but He makes no impression. Then I cried out to Him saying: 'Frighten them, terrify them with the fear of hell, make them shudder.' 'I have already done all this, My daughter,' He replied. 'I send them all kinds of graces, illnesses, fears, loneliness, but it is all in vain. I am about to get rid of them.' I begged Him to have mercy on them.

"Fourth, He then led me to souls who are good, but who, nonetheless, receive Him without sufficient preparation and fervor and with very little gratitude. 'You see, My daughter,' said Jesus, 'what graces I should like to give them, and yet I am unable. I cannot work freely within them.' What riches they deprive themselves of through their lack of generosity! I saw Jesus' immense desire to dwell within these souls and to heap His favors upon them; but He is continually prevented by their half-hearted response.

"Fifth, He led me finally to souls who receive Him with fervent love. He had a golden key and as He opened the door of these souls He said to me: 'Let us go in.' What rest I found there! Jesus also rested and said: 'Here I am at home and do with these souls what I will.' I saw what graces He was pouring upon them, extending and expanding them until they became as large as the world, transforming them into Himself so that they would gradually become completely divine, being one with Him."

He will charge these happy souls who are His true Brides to carry on His own reparatory and expiatory mission, instituting them fully in His work of salvation. Thus, in 1805 Our Lord caused His faithful servant Sr. María Josepha Kumi, O.P., to see the transgressions of sinners and the lamentable state of avaricious nations, saying to her: "Are you ready to take upon yourself the punishments they deserve?" And since she showed herself to be prepared for everything, He appeared to her again a short while after, carrying a very heavy cross and a crown of thorns with which He crowned her, adding: "I take away from you every perceptible consolation so as to let you feel your own nothingness. The time has come when you will have no inner refreshment nor the least satisfaction from men, not even from your confessor. You will be truly abandoned on the cross. Dead to yourself, penetrated with the realization of your own nothingness, turn then your desire and love toward Me. Give yourself for sinners, like a holocaust completely devoured by the fire of love. And with this suffering many souls will be saved."

But not all His Brides reply with the same generosity, offering, under one pretext or another, some kind of resistance.

v. 3) *I have taken off my tunic, am I to put it on again?*
       I have washed my feet, am I to soil them again?

Many blame the Bride far too much here, for not wanting to open the door, considering this behavior to be very rude and discourteous. But her Beloved does not seem to reprimand her so severely or to be displeased, for this hesitation does not spring from a lack of love, but from an excessive fear of displeasing Him Whom she loves so much and, at the same time, from the humble and lowly opinion she has for herself. *I have taken off my tunic,* that is to say, I have denied myself all contact with the world and with creatures. How could I put on my tunic again without exposing myself to the contagion of worldly conversation? How can I obey Your order to return again to Egypt . . . ? *I have washed my feet* of the imperfections that accumulated during such dealings. Why do You ask me to expose myself once again to the danger of soiling them? Do not force me to do something through which I fear I will again stain myself and displease You. Leave me in the sweet darkness of solitude and in the secure humility of oblivion. This is the resistance the soul offers when asked to accept high, conspicuous and honorable positions, or great missions and difficult works of devotion that do not seem to suit her state and condition and all those other occupations which cause distractions or may sully the soul. Among others, remember the resistance offered by the wonderful St. Catherine of Siena when asked to leave her humble retreat, until she saw clearly the definite will of the Lord Who wanted such great things from her and Who lovingly triumphed over every adverse power through her.

"When there are serious obstacles," says the Ven. María de San José, C.D. (*Recreaciones,* 3), "the Divine Spouse knocks patiently at the door, and while waiting suffers His hair to be filled with the dew of the night. Moreover He is even pleased . . . when people say to Him 'How can this be' if the thing asked is beyond human comprehension, as happened with the Virgin Mary when the angel told her she was going to be the Mother of God."

The faithful soul can well join M. Sorazu in saying: "I do not refuse to reply to the divine calling, but I stop to think, fearing to expose myself to the danger of staining the purity of my soul or of losing the infinite Good which I possess in the mystical bed of divine contemplation."

Notwithstanding the tender call to help her needy neighbors, observes St. Lawrence Justinian (*Lignum vitae*, tr. 13, *de. Orat.*, Ch. 1), the soul wisely considers the advantages of her solitude and the dangers of action: *"Sagaciter se provanti pandit suae quietis profectum, nec non et actionis defectum: ut haec audiens Sponsum volentibus infestare devotionem contemplationis imperet, dicens: Adjuro vos . . ."*

"Being humble," he adds elsewhere, "she does not trust in herself and fears staining herself; since she is rich in merits, she sees how many dangers to which she is exposing herself. Only those who are very holy, and she thinks herself far from being such, can undertake to look after others without doing harm to themselves."

"Although the soul understands this truth that it is more pleasing to God to love God and to join to this love the love of one's neighbor and zeal for the salvation of souls," writes Fr. Gracian . . ."yet in spite of this, she so much desires purity and so much wants to keep from distraction and sin and avoid any occasion for these that, seeing all the dangers there are in dealing with creatures, she excuses herself saying: 'I have taken off my tunic . . .' As though saying: 'I have had experience of the harm that comes from dealing with souls and I have put aside this dangerous work and have sought recollection and solitude . . . I have washed my feet of inordinate affections and . . . other soiled things that evolve from dealing with the world . . . Why Lord, do You want me to enter into contact with these again?'

"The Spouse is not satisfied with this reply, and since He finds that the soul is *pure* and that *she loves Him* — the two things necessary for her to produce fruit in other souls — He forces her with a zeal that *moves her to the core*, and places His hand on her heart with such tender violence that He seems to take this heart out of her flesh and place in it the hearts of her nieghbors so as to bring her to truly love them. With this violence He makes her leave her secure solitude . . . For surely, those who see souls redeemed by the blood of Christ and falling into hell, will they not go and help them if possible, even if it means denying themselves the quiet of prayer?" (*Lk.* 14)

v. 4) *My beloved put His hand through the hole in the door,*
        and the depths of my being trembled at his touch.

Since the Bride's opposition was not caused by indifference or lack of love, but by humility, the Spouse does not pay much attention to it. In spite of everything He tries to enter in, as though it were His own house. Thus, in order to open the door Himself, He does her sweet violence, putting His loving hand through the hole in the door of that good will which He knows is sincerely surrendered to Him . . . But the powerful touch of this divine hand makes the Bride's inmost being tremble, because, as St. John of the Cross says, "this ineffable touch of God *tastes of eternal life*, and thus produces *violent impulses of love* which penetrate, soften and transform hearts, destroying their own wishes and making them will what God wills and accomplish that will in the way He wishes, so that it is no longer she who lives but He dwelling within her."

"When God lets Himself be felt in such a special way, as the very life of the soul," wrote a soul not long ago (February 11, 1919) who was beginning to receive this grace, "all the other communications she may have been receiving do not cease, as these things are what is meant by *feeling God*. What we have here is *God living in the soul* in a way . . . that I cannot explain."

She explains the effects that this produces when she adds: "One lives as though one were no longer on earth. I now have great peace and tranquillity and desire to fulfill the will of God in all things. But my soul longs for that great good which it once felt and so I ask Jesus not to give me anything but love and the cross."

"His putting His hand through the hole in the door so as to try to open it Himself," writes Scio, "represents the strength and efficacy of divine grace in removing the hardness of hearts."

"Jesus touches her," says María Dolorosa, "by reminding her of the immense suffering He underwent in redeeming her. She is moved by this, and repents of having resisted the inspirations of God."

"Sweet Jesus," exclaims St. Francis de Sales, "in spite of this resistance You continue to press her to let You in; then with the hand of a greater inspiration You slide back the bolt . . . The soul is so moved by this . . . and feels such sorrow for her hesitation in opening the door that she spills the jar of myrrh; that is to say, she becomes completely filled with penitence . . ."

Instead of the words *at his touch,* the Septuagint and the Hebrew text have *over Him,* as though the Bride's depths were moved to see Him make such great efforts to induce her to open to Him in spite of all the trouble she was causing Him.

v. 5)   *I rose to open to my beloved;*
          Myrrh ran off my hands,
          and my fingers were full of the purest myrrh.

In her haste, according to many commentators, the Bride stumbles over a jar of myrrh she had prepared there as a gift for her Spouse; and spilling it over her hands, her fingers become full of it. But is seems more likely that they distill the sweetest fragrance by merely touching the bolt where the Lord had placed His hand; for this divine hand perfumes all that it touches in this way.

In struggling with the latch He left it so drenched with myrrh that when the Bride later went to open the door, her fingers became covered with it, and became perfumed and embalmed with its divine fragrance. "This indicates," writes Scio, "the new spirit that she received. Perceiving the sweetness and holy scent of this new grace, she found herself pervaded with renewed energy and strength, and saw that her own fingers now exhaled the fragrance of her Spouse." Because of this she began to lament her delay in opening to Him. "The myrrh," he adds, "here represents the repentance and loving affections of her soul."

"It is a very sure sign of a good spirit," writes Fr. La Puente (*Guía*, tr. 1, Ch. 24), "if His visits give rise to the complete and perfect mortification of the passions ... For when God knocks at the door of our hearts and speaks to our spirit, our hands distill myrrh and our fingers are filled with the choicest myrrh; that is, we then experience the fragrant scent and taste the sweetness of mortification, we resolve to subdue the passions, restrain the senses, curb the tongue and punish the flesh."

Thus, when the soul hurries out of the mystical bed of prayer to go as quickly as she can to where her Spouse calls her she finds, without knowing how, that her hands are distilling precious myrrh and that her fingers are so full of it that they cannot fail to communicate a most redolent scent to all her works, which come to be, as it were embalmed in myrrh ...

The *myrrh* of mortification and spirit of sacrifice is such, that it will prevent her from being tainted while having these new dealings with the world and will make sure that there is no corruption in her works nor in all those who have the good fortune to be in contact with her.

"It is no small mortification," writes Fr. Gracian, "to abandon spiritual joys, the solitary, loving communication with God, the inner rest and the sweet sleep, reclining in the arms of the Beloved; to go out to help souls . . . or preach, or hear confessions or give advice, or write books for the good of one's neighbor. So when the Bride arises from her solitude, she says: *My hands distilled myrrh* . . . She says this because great suffering is involved in turning to assist her neighbors — the greatest and worthiest of all possible sacrifices. And this can be seen from experience for I saw this to be so in the case of St. Teresa of Jesus and others of her daughters, who were very happy and glad to do whatever penance was asked of them; but when they were told to be Superiors they wept many tears and their souls were deeply moved for they knew how little strength they had to govern those under them . . ."

But eventually, knowing that it is the will of God, the soul gives in and lifts the door-latch by her consent; and she gives herself to love without measure or reserve, taking the light out from under the measure so as to light up all who are in the house, for the Lord wants it that way, there being no other consolation save that of knowing that it is the will of God.

Since, by divine enlightenment, adds Fr. La Puente (*Perf. Es. Ecles.,* tr. 4, Ch. 6), the soul sees "the extreme need of the faithful, the aid that God offers her in order to help them and the loving way in which He asks her, her whole heart and being are moved and softened with affections of love and compassion. She at once rises up to open to her Beloved, rousing herself from her idleness and showing the true love she has for Him. But how does she rise up? *My hands,* she says, *distilled myrrh* . . . Because of the help that the powerful hand of God gave her, her hands, which are faculties, began to distil the myrrh of excellent mortification, filling the fingers of her affections and special works with a great abundance of myrrh, very discreetly removing all the obstacles she encountered. And so she says: *With my hands I opened the bolt of my door to my Beloved.* With the hand of His omnipotence Our Lord could very well have opened it Himself and done all the work, but He wanted the soul to rise up too, and to join her hands with the hands of God . . .

She caused her hands to be filled with myrrh, and not just any myrrh, but the purest and choicest kind, *myrrha probatissima,* for this is what the penance of Prelates and Apostolic men must be like: mortifying idleness and pleasure and honor, their own will and opinions, and also their excessive love of recollection and quiet and spiritual delights; for self-love usually feeds on these things when souls hesitate to go where God orders them. And she does not say that her mouth distilled myrrh but that her hands did; for she must first practise mortification before preaching it . . .

"And this," says Rupert, "also means that she removed the bolt from the door, which is the silence in which she had dwelt. Previously through love of contemplation, she had resolved to adopt the virtue of silence and not to speak by entering into conversations with her neighbors. But knowing that the Will of God was calling her to this office, she removed the bolt, broke the silence and began to preach and deal with everyone so as to win and edify them."

In spite of all this, as soon as she rises up, her Beloved flees away and hides from her. What games God plays with souls . . . !

Although these excuses sprang from humility and holy desires, and so instead of offending her Divine Lover seemed to some extent to have pleased Him, He carried on without paying any attention to them; nevertheless, since they were motivated at the same time by an excessive love for that very sacred repose to which she was now attached, she had to pay dearly for her hesitation in answering His divine call. For it was enough to cause His complete abandonment of her, His utter desertion in which state she would have to suffer some of the most painful trials of the terrible *night of the spirit,* to which, for a long period of time she was so mercifully subjected. Thus was she able to realize the full renewal and transformation that was wrought in her in order to reach the unbroken and perfect union of the *Spiritual Marriage.*

"Jesus has withdrawn and gone on ahead," writes María de la Dolorosa, "for divine inspiration is like the wind touching leaves and passing on. Whoever is prepared to receive it, pleases God and merits His immediate entrance with the abundance of His graces. Whoever is indolent and sleepy, unconsciously rejects Him and even loses much of what he had before." Thus, "oh devout souls," exclaims one commentator (Petit), "always be ready to hear the voice of your Divine Spouse and open the door of your hearts to Him without delay or excuses. Do not let it happen that because you make Him wait, He withdraws and leaves you to suffer in His, absence, like the Bride, or rejects you like He did the foolish virgins (*Matt.* 25). Always have your loins girded and your lamps burning so that you can go out and receive Him whenever He comes; for in this way you will surely be happy" (*Luke* 12, 25).

Whoever, under specious pretexts reject the favors of God, find themselves obliged to go in search of them for a long period of time and through great trials, to ask with unutterable groans, for what was before offered to them without their asking. "I can seek for You," says St. Ambrose (in *Ps.* 118, 22 n. 32). "but I cannot find You unless You so will me to find You. And You do not let Yourself be found, until You have been sought for a long time and with great diligence: *Et Tu quidem vis inveniri; sed vis, Diu quaeri, vis diligentius indigari.*"

v. 6)   *I opened the bolt of my door to my beloved,*
          but he had gone from there and had left.
          My soul melted on hearing him speak;
          I sought him but did not find him,
          I called to him and he gave me no answer.

"But, O beloved Bride," continues Fr. Gracian, "did you not expect as a result of this good resolve to receive some reward, or inner consolation, and on opening the door to embrace Him and receive from Him the sweet kisses of inner delights that He usually gives you? O Lord, there is no one who can understand Your ways! For this time the soul usually finds herself drier, colder and more disconsolate than ever; it seems to her that God has left her heart, ever since the cares of her neighbor (born of zeal for souls) entered it. And complaining of this she says: *He had gone from there and had left me.* And because of His absence my heart became as if hardened; for I lost that loving presence that melted it just as the sun softens and melts wax. It is true that I heard several inner words consoling me, giving me light, telling me how much it pleases the Spouse when the soul foregoes the pleasurable love of God in order to possess zealous love. *My soul melted on hearing my Beloved speak.* But it desires to be joined with Him once again as it used to be when it was in the state of quiet, and wants Him to reply to her with the same sweet words He formerly used when she spoke to Him in prayer . . . *I sought Him but did not find Him, I called to Him and He gave me no answer."*

These divine games, these withdrawals, touches and intimate communications of God bring about the liquefaction of the soul, wounding and consuming her, burning and melting her and, as it were, putting her to death, so as to truly re-create or reform her and completely restore and revivify her. Thus, St. John of the Cross marvels at and blesses this work, exclaiming: (*Living Flame of Love*)

> O sweet burn,
> O delightful wound!
> O gentle hand! O delicate touch
> That tastes of eternal life
> And pays every debt!
> In slaying You changed death to life.

"When the Bride sees that her Beloved has left her, she remembers with both pain and joy her reaction when she heard His voice . . . It is when the Lord withdraws that souls feel most intensely, and realize fully, the good that His sweet presence did them. When He withdraws the dart with which He wounded them, they feel as though He is also tearing out their hearts with it, now wholly enkindled and melted by love. In this way they constantly desire this wonderful pain, for the sharper and more agonizing it is, the greater the spiritual delight and sweetness it produces." (St. Teresa, *Life*, Ch. 29)

When the soul feels herself to be so lovingly wounded and sweetly dissolved, she goes out of herself exclaiming and sighing for Him Who ravished her heart, knowing that her wound of love can only be healed by that sweet hand that caused it. Thus she joins St. John of the Cross in crying: (*Spiritual Canticle*)

Where have You hidden,
Beloved, and left me moaning?
You fled like the stag
After wounding me;
I went out calling You, and You were gone . . .

"These spiritual wounds of love," he then notes (Stanza 1), "are very delightful and desirable. The soul would desire to be ever dying a thousand deaths from these thrusts of the lance, for they make her go out of herself and enter into God . . . Thus the wounded soul, strengthened by the fire caused by the wound, went out after her Beloved Who wounded her, calling for Him, that He might heal her. This spiritual departure, it should be pointed out, refers to the two ways of seeking God: one consists in a departure from all worldly things, effected through a contempt for them; the other, in going out from herself through self-forgetfulness, which is achieved by her love for God. When the love of God really touches the soul in this way, it so raises her up that it not only impels her to leave self in this forgetfulness, but even draws her away from her natural supports, attractions, and inclinations, inducing her to call after God."

". . . *And You were gone* is like saying: At the time I desired to hold You fast I did not find You, and the detachment from myself without attachment to You left me suspended in air and suffering, without support from You or from myself . . . By the rising of the soul, the Bride . . . is meant her ascent from her lowly condition and natural love to the sublime love of God."

"This liquefaction of the soul, then, is another way of going out of herself solicited by the Lord" as Ruysbroeck remarks (*loc. cit.*, Ch. 4), adding: "Then, after this divine visit, during which the Spirit of God has secretly liquefied our spirit, He whispers to us saying: *'Go out'* that is to say, to perpetual contemplation that is divine and produces its fruit in a divine manner. Through love, we possess all the riches that the Beloved has by nature; and God bestows them on us through that immense love which is the Holy Spirit in Whom the soul is permitted to enjoy all and more than can be desired. Through this same love we become dead to ourselves, and dissolved in His love which overflows and passes into the Essence Which is devoid of all form; into a light so sublime that it causes darkness, and the spirit remains motionless in the Arms of the Most Blessed Trinity, deified and enjoying the very Unity of the Godhead . . . Thus, interior and contemplative souls will in an extraordinary way go out into the divine contemplation through this infinite Light . . . transcending reason, discernment and their own created essence. They will almost be transformed by this infinite light given by the Spirit of the Lord and will become one with this Light which so dazzled them until . . . with a simple gaze of divine clarity they will contemplate God in Himself and in all things without difference . . . In this contemplation souls become masters of themselves and can freely advance step by step in the sublimity of their inner life."

But because she has *gone out of herself* and finds herself in this mystical darkness, she says that she looks for her sweet Beloved but does not find Him; she calls to Him and He does not answer . . .

She undoubtedly looks for Him in pious readings and in works of devotion and ordinary practices of the Christian life; and she no longer finds Him there. She calls to Him in prayer, meditating on the marvels of nature and invoking Him through

them, but no one replies; everything appears dark and silent
without her hearing even an echo in her soul. Eventually,
instead of her Beloved, the guards of the city come out and
meet her, wound and upset her, rather than give her
directions . . . Even though it seems to her that she cannot find
Him Whom she desires so much, and although she fears that He
has abandoned her or refuses to answer her because she is
unworthy, she nonetheless has Him hidden within her; and He is
much pleased to see how diligently she searches for Him, while
He, during this apparent absence is inflaming her ever more in
His love and preparing her for new favors and more intimate
communications.

     For this reason she anxiously asks for Him or sends Him
her amorous complaints, joining St. John of the Cross in crying
out:
     Shepherds, you that go
     Up through the sheepfolds to the hill,
     If by chance you see
     Him I love most,
     Tell Him that I sicken, suffer and die . . .
     . . . Why, since You wounded
     This heart, don't You heal it?
     And why, since You stole it from me,
     Do you leave it so,
     And fail to carry off what You have stolen? (*Spiritual Cant.*)
     She now begins to look for Him with redoubled
earnestness that is given her by a love that is so much greater
than at first (III, 2). But since fortitude also grew with love, her
sweet Lord sends her greater trials, allowing even His own
ministers and representatives, who before helped her by giving
her some degree of light, to now insult, wound and even, at
times discredit her in their confusion and by their erroneous
conclusions; aggravating her suffering instead of encouraging her
and watching over her . . . Here, indeed, the soul suffers the
pangs of love and undergoes an indescribable torment, like a

cruel sword being run through her. For having felt God so intimately and affectionately, it is impossible for her to live without this sweet assurance that He infused into her, and at the loss of which all other consolations become an unbearable martyrdom for her. This is the pain that St. John of the Cross says the soul cannot endure without relief or dying; and yet it is prolonged and made worse by other kinds of sufferings and adversities often caused by her greatest friends and even by those from whom she could reasonably expect some relief or support.

This poor little soul, then, is fully introduced into that most painful phase that the mystics call the *night of the spirit*, and which, because of its extreme importance, deserves further explanation. As we said in the *Mystical Evolution*, although the union of betrothal is so wonderful, so real and so continued, it is not completely stable, much less indissoluble: absences, darknesses and desolations are possible, and they are more painful in proportion to the ardor of her love, and the intensity of her desires to achieve a complete transformation in which she will truly become one with her Beloved. What is worse, she realizes the possibility of even now, succumbing under certain trials. The terrible fear of falling into such dangers is what troubles her most.

"The absences of the Beloved, which the soul suffers in this state of spiritual espousals," says St. John of the Cross (*Spiritual Canticle*, Introd. to Stanza 17), "are very painful; some are of such a kind that there is no suffering comparable to them. The reason for such affliction is that since the soul has such a singular and intense love for God in this state, His absence causes a singular and intense torment. Added to this torment is the disturbance caused at this time by any kind of converse or communication with creatures. Since she is constrained by her insatiable desire for union with God, any delay whatever is very burdensome and disturbing."

But in order for this intimate union to be hers in a stable

way and be established in such a fashion that she thereby
becomes absolutely certain of never being moved again, the soul
needs to be submitted to other new and more terrible
purifications that penetrate to the very core of her being, and,
like a burning fire and a very powerful lye (*Malachi* 3, 2)
consume all the dross and remains of stains within her, leaving
her completely purified, renewed and transformed into a new
creature all resplendent with holiness and justice.

Until this happens, however much she strives, she still has,
without hardly realizing it and without being able to do
anything about it on her own (Cf. St. John of the Cross, *Dark
Night* II, Ch. 2), quite a number of hidden imperfections and a
certain attachment to divine consolations; this is so, because of
a very subtle and disguised self-love through which she seeks her
own ends, at times preferring her own ideas and convenience, to
the greater service of God and the good of her neighbors. This is
most likely what happened to the mystical Bride when she
hesitated to answer the call to leave her retreat, hastening when
it was too late to where she was called. Because of this
resistance we now see her punished by being deprived of what
she so much desires: the sweet presence of her Beloved, Whose
speech melted her with love and Whose delicate touch infused
in her such intense desires to possess Him that they became her
martyrdom.

Added to this martyrdom is that produced by an excess of
divine light that is mysteriously poured into her, a penetrating
and painful light which discloses the most hidden corners and
recesses of her heart, making evident her multiple imperfections, her nothingness and wretchedness, and leaving her
unmoved and insensible to all that might have consoled her.
This wonderful light, while consoling her, plunges her into a
horrible *darkness,* where she thinks she is lost, not knowing
what to do. In order to increase her fear and torment He makes
her see in the distance the infinite beauties and fascinating
attractions of the Supreme Good, producing within her the

most intense longings and ardent desires to possess them, but which are all inaccessible to her . . . This reaction together with the sight of herself as imprisoned in her own impotence and laden with meanness and imperfections that set her against Him, cause such pain that it can only be compared to that of an injury, making her suffer a real purgatory and almost a hell . . . Love itself now becomes her cruel executioner making her feel very deeply the ugliness of her sins, her poor response to His divine favors, her inadequate use of His graces, and all the sorrow she caused the Holy Spirit by being so weak and remiss in following His inspirations. All this, apart from many other trials which then beset her, torment her, as John says, in a *wonderful* way, to the extent that St. John of the Cross (*Dark Night,* II Ch. 6-8), considers the sufferings here endured by the soul to be no longer merely *terrible,* but rather, *intolerable.* And this is basically what other great mystics like the Ven. John Tauler (*Div. Inst.,* Ch. 11) and St. Teresa (*Sixth Mansion,* Ch. 1) have to say about them. It is necessary to pass through this purgatory in order to be able to enjoy Heaven on earth. But once the soul has passed through it and seen the fruit she has derived from it, she never ceases to bless the Lord for having made her endure it here with such great gain and merit and with such relative mildness, rather than deferring it to the hereafter, where, being obligatory, it would not increase her merit and would be much more rigorous.

It is there that they are truly purified of all dross and all the virtues are tested, especially the three theological virtues which are to unite them with God. They now believe themselves to be completely lost, abandoned by God and wholly deprived of those virtues with which they could please Him or win back His favor. Yet, although they do not realize it, they love Him with a pure and unalloyed love, solely because He is Who He is. They hope against all hope for the fulfillment of His promises, telling themselves, like Job: *Even though He kill me I shall place my hope in Him;* and they firmly believe in Him as the absolute and infallible Truth. This dark faith guides them in the midst of thick darkness; this unshakable hope, like an anchor of salvation, holds them firm during these trials; this ardent charity causes their triumph over everything even over the Sacred Heart Itself . . .

This indicates some of the anguish and pain suffered by the soul that has been dissolved and consumed in love and who is utterly unable to find the One and only One in Whom she lives and for Whom she longs with all her heart, sighing with inexplicable moans . . . She searches for Him with all the means at her disposal and in no way is able to find Him. Neither spiritual readings nor the examples of the Saints who suffered similar straits are now sufficient to give her any knowledge of Him. She calls to Him with the most urgent desires and with continual prayers. And He prefers not to utter even a single word in reply . . .

"This is not the only catastrophe that has happened as a result of her hesitation to abandon the sweet love she enjoyed in her solitude, that she might take up a zealous love and have dealings with souls. For even with the most important people, especially those who are wisest and who govern, I have encountered opposition and have in this way lost their favor. For when I ask learned people, preachers, confessors and prelates how I could return to my quiet and rest, they murmur about me and reprove me for involving myself in the business of souls, and they deny me the favor which they could have given me so that I could do good in the Church" Fr. Gracian.

Not finding Him then, inside, she goes out to look for Him, hoping no doubt to find, as on other occasions, some advice or assistance that would help her to find Him; she exposes herself to thousands of obstacles to which she no longer gives heed.

v. 7) *The watchmen that go about the city found me.*
They beat me and wounded me;
the keepers of the walls took my mantle from me.

The watchmen, that is to say, the very ministers of the Church are the ones who are maltreating her here . . . Before, they showed her where she could find her Beloved. But now that she is more advanced, for her greater purification and chastisement, God often permits it to happen that they not only fail to help, but they decidedly turn against her, strike and wound her, take from her the mantle of their protection and even that of her good name, causing her to lose her peace of soul and to experience great anguish and confusion. Often they consider her to be mad or deluded or even to be a fraud and a hypocrite. This can be seen in the case of many saints who were treated in this way by the very persons who pass or pretend to pass, as the most zealous defenders of Holy Church, but who, through lack of knowledge and discretion, sometimes fear when there is no need to fear and do not fear when there is real danger. So they regard as disguised heretics or evident *Illuminati* and *Quietists* these true friends of God whose spirit they fail to understand and perhaps do not even wish to do so. Meanwhile they are in accord with her persecutors and all those who employ their energies and talents in destroying the ways of Zion and bringing them into disrepute (*Lm.* 1, 4). This causes the angels of peace to weep bitterly (*Is.* 33, 7-8) as they behold the paths of the sanctuary blocked and the gates barred, while the watchmen, holding in their hands the keys to the Kingdom and the knowledge that leads to it, neither go in themselves, nor do they allow fervent souls to enter (*Lk.* 11, 52). It often happens that it is not the poor soul who asks the question, for she already knows through experience not to place herself in the hands of the blind leading the blind (*Matt.* 15, 14), but they themselves, who, with an indiscreet zeal that is far from being *secuudum scientiam,* interfere without being asked, questioning, judging and passing sentence on things they do not understand and reviling things they do not comprehend.

Thus, the very ones who should have been most compassionate, helpful and encouraging in such a difficult

THE SONG OF SONGS

situation, and from whom she should have received some relief, are, at times, by the permission of God, those who afflict and torment her most. Failing to understand these madnesses of love, they never stop calling the poor soul deluded, fanatical, unbalanced and other similar "epithets" however well she behaves in everything. St Teresa records this as having happened to her (*Life,* Ch. 32-33; *Interior Castle* VI, Ch. 1), just as it happened to many other privileged souls as Fr. Weiss observes (*Apology,* 10).

"O God, how common this is! For there are so many ambitious and avaricious persons in the world who seek to govern others that they may be admired or possess a worthwhile income; when therefore, they see a servant of God who has lived in seclusion . . . become a superior or become involved in the concerns of his neighbor, especially if he hampers them in their worldly pursuits, they say: 'Who told so and so to meddle in such matters? Let him stay in his own domain for he has not the talent to govern, write books, direct souls, found monasteries, or convert heretics; this apostolate is not for women or uneducted people.' I know a servant of God, a great contemplative (Dona Luisa de Caravajal), who, urged by this zealous love, left the quiet of Spain, and went to England to convert the souls of heretics and to sustain the faith of many who secretly were Catholic. She carried on her apostolate with so much virtue, ardor and profit to souls, that it fills all those who know of it with admiration. Yet her zeal has been criticized, even by many learned leaders, as if she had done something extremely evil." (Fr. Gracian)

"It is very true," writes Scio, "that all who anxiously seek Christ encounter great obstacles and opposition. It is a cause for much wonder that those whose duty it is to guard, protect and take charge of the public good and in whom virtue should find all its rightful protection, are on many occasions the very ones who persecute and maltreat her." What is worse, at times they even go so far as to indiscreetly publicize the intimate secrets of her soul, thereby taking from the *mantle* of her good reputation and exposing her to all kinds of insults, slander, gossip and jibes of the profane, bringing her to be like her Spouse, the Divine Word.

"The Word," said St. Mary Magdalen of Pazzi (*Works*, Part 1, Ch. 4), "was stripped of His garments, and this is true of the soul when she is prevented from advancing along the path mapped out for her by God . . . and is obliged to take a different course. She is deprived, like the Word, of all assistance and protection and stands alone in her humiliation."

In this way the afflicted soul will think herself not only abandoned by God, but also rejected and reproved by the very persons she sought as mediators and conciliators. For when they do not have the necessary spiritual light, her most faithful friends and companions and even her worthiest confessors and directors who should have known her better, easily become her enemies, their human judgments and appreciation being confused by these wonders of grace and divine love (Cf. St. Teresa, loc. cit.).

This beating and stripping can also be interpreted as having a good meaning. Both St. Gregory and St. Thomas maintain that good directors and prelates stab the soul with the knife of the word of God, thereby wounding her with the wounds of love or with pain caused by the sight of sin; these wounds enable her to search for the Lord with renewed longings. That she might follow Him with greater freedom, they remove many obstacles and impediments from her, stripping her of the mantle of worldly concerns.

Then the soul cannot help but confess: "These faithful guardians of the interests of Jesus have not stripped me of the mantle that adorns me, but of that one which covered my imperfections, my hidden self-love. Had they not been so charitable as to strip me of this mantle covering my wretchedness, I would never be able to find the Beloved of my soul, Whom I am as determined to look for as they are to help me, for they know that this is also what the Spouse desires."

"But worldly Prelates," says Fr. La Puente (*Perf. Est. Ecles.*, tr. 7, Ch. 17), "fail to watch for the good of the souls in their care and instead seek their own convenience and evil inclinations. They even wound the conscience of these souls who are dependent upon them, and do not protect them. In this sense many doctors join the Bride in saying that those whose duty it was to be guards . . . , by their bad example scandalized and wounded her soul and took from her the mantle of good works with which she covered herself and the hood of temporal goods under which she was sheltered."

"By guards," explains Fr. Gracian, "she means the learned and Prelates. She says that they wounded and injured her with their malicious tongues. What is worse is that some that were to have given favor, encouragement and advice to servants of God who desired to do great things for the Church, rather oppose, discourage and abandon them when they see them persecuted, and thus they cause many zealous, spiritual men, who could do good, to return to their seclusion. The favor and consolation which men who are responsible for guarding the walls of the Republic are to give to those who desire to work for the good and salvation of souls, is the hood which protects the Bride, and this is taken from her shoulders by the very persons who should have placed it upon her with their blessings."

The faithful soul does not weaken at anything and derives good from everything. Her heart enkindled with love, she scorns and forgets all that she suffers from the hands of men, and does not stop until, in one way or another she finds the sweet Beloved for Whom she ceaselessly sighs. She looks for the light wherever God sees fit to offer it to her, even from any passer-by, being unable to conceal any longer her sufferings and desires.

"It should be carefully noted," says Scio, "that the Bride weeps only at the absence of her Spouse and she cries over this without remembering the injuries done to her, without complaining of her Beloved and without reducing in the slightest the intensity of her desires to look for and find Him. This shows how ardent her love is, how invincible her patience and how fully she submits herself to the will of her Spouse."

v. 8)   *I charge you, daughters of Jerusalem,*
             if you should find my beloved
             that you tell him that I am sick with love.

"Wounded and stripped of her mantle, she does not feel the harm they have done her, she is so transported in love . . . ! She will be easily consoled, provided her Spouse knows that she loves Him. This is what she wants to tell Him through all those that she encounters on her path." (Bossuet)

"I charge you, daughters of Jerusalem," exclaims Palafox (*Varón de deseos,* Part 3, 1), "if you should find my Beloved that you tell Him I am dying of love. Do not tell Him for whom, for He knows very well for Whom I am dying. Tell Him that of the pains I suffer, the greatest is that of not knowing whether I am dying of love for Him, for although my heart feels His love alone, I do not dare to assure myself of this, let Him come and see if the wound is His and heal this wounded heart . . ."

I am sick with love; that is to say: *I am wounded with charity.* "Whoever is wounded or sick," writes Fr. La Puente (*Guía,* tr. 3 Ch. 9), "does not go without suffering, although love makes it so sweet that he would never want to be without it as long as he lives. The wounds of charity are the ardent desires to love and please God greatly . . . The wounds of charity are also the desires that God be glorified and served by everyone, desires which bring great sorrow to the heart because they are unable to see fulfilled what they desire so much, and burn with zeal because of the injuries done to the Beloved. The wounds of charity are also the vehement longings to see God and be united with Him in His glory without fear of ever falling from His grace again . . . Just as a man with a painful wound or a very strong thirst is always thinking of what can bring him

relief, so the soul wounded by charity, and thirsting for God
always has her thoughts on Him, longing for His sweet
company, sending messengers up to Heaven with many sighs
and prayers to tell Him how sick she is with love. The creatures
she sees remind her of her God Who has made them, and this
thought of Him, like a bow, sends darts of love at her heart,
which, quickened by these very gifts of His, burns to be united
with the Giver of such gifts."

"The devout soul," says St. Ambrose (in *Ps.* 118) "has
only one true desire — her sweet Spouse Jesus. She longs for
Him with all the yearnings of her heart and she goes toward
Him with all her strength . . . , so that the more ardently she
longs to be united with Him, the greater are her sighs and faints.
Although this fainting reduces the strength of her body, it
increases and fortifies all the virtues of her spirit . . . The soul
who denies herself in all things, so as to be perfectly united with
Christ, does in fact suffer a kind of fainting."

These souls can well unite in singing the "songs of
the night" (*Job* 35, 10), and repeat with Sr. María de la Antigua
(*Desengano de Religiosos,* 1,5 c. 28):

> Lost, I go out in search of Him,
> But I consider that I am won,
> For when I lose myself, I win,
> And when I find myself, I'm lost.

Since the Bride now sees that the ministers of God whom
she meets do not give her the slightest help in finding her
Beloved, and since she feels that without Him she will faint
away, "knowing," says Fr. Gracian, "that all good counsel,
favor and comfort is to be found in her Beloved, Jesus Christ,
and that when she finds Him she will have the light she desires,"
she turns to faithful friends or to the first one whom she meets,
for God often uses the last people one would imagine to make
up for the deficiences of His representatives. As María de la
Dolorosa writes, "in this state she turns to other pious souls
that they might help her with their prayers to find Jesus." So

we see her, on this occasion, approach even the daughters of Jerusalem who are so ignorant of these mysteries. Nevertheless, God wants them to reply to her more kindly than they had in the past.

v. 9) *What makes your beloved better than other beloveds,*
O loveliest of women?
What makes your beloved better than other beloveds,
that you give us a charge like this?

Being unable to understand such extremes of divine love, the superficial repeatedly ask similar questions when they meet a truly holy soul who is consumed by this celestial fire, being amazed and astonished to see her, as they put it, "so upset over such a small thing". They fail to understand how such a discreet person and one adorned with great virtues and excellent gifts which at times they cannot help but acknowledge, can do such *odd and peculiar things* that in their opinion, border on madness. So, full of astonishment they ask her: *What makes your beloved better than other beloveds,* to make you lose your mind in this way?

This question can also be taken in a more favorable way as it shows that they want to know the features of her Beloved, to see whether they can recognize Him by them and give her some news of Him; although up until verse 17 we do not see them make any definite move to join her in her search and give her this consolation.

In all events they are forced to admit that she is very virtuous and worthy of respect, for they call her the *loveliest of women.* Though at the same time they wonder whether she is quite in her right mind. So they ask her: What does your Beloved have that makes you lose yourself and go madly in search of Him?

Since they give her this opportunity to speak and since she is unable to embrace her Beloved, the faithful Bride vents her feelings in listing His perfections and celebrating that incomparable beauty, with which He steals and captivates the hearts of all those who have converse with Him. Her description is the most beautiful commentary on the words of the Psalmist (*Ps.* 45, 3): *Speciousus forma prae filiis hominum.*

v. 10)   *My beloved is white and ruddy*
                 outstanding among thousands.

In just the words *white* and *ruddy* the Bride believes she is giving sufficient details for Him to be recognized and distinguished from out of thousands and millions of men; for He stands out among them all and, as the Hebrew says, *He carries the banner.* These words indicate His absolute purity and innocence, together with His infinite charity and the magnificent splendors of His Divinity, since He is the effulgence of the glory of the Father (*Heb.* 1,3), all of which causes Him to exceed by far in beauty the children of men (*Ps.* 44,3) and even the choirs of angels.

"My Beloved," says Sr. Teresa of J.M., "is white and so pure that He is the very whiteness and purity of eternal and inaccessible light. He is ruddy and inflamed because He is the very fire and sphere of love" (*Meditations*).

It can also be understood to mean that His natural color was really *white and ruddy,* as many earlier writers suppose.

This, according to the tradition of the Fathers, says Fillion, is the picture of the Word Incarnate after His glorious Humanity has been restored: *Candidus et rubicundus.*

But not content with this, full of enthusiasm and enkindled with love, she celebrates His wonderful perfections one by one, describing the parts of the Spouse in order. This we see Holy Mother Church doing every year; for, since in all of them she sees Him mocked because of His love for us, in all of them she desires to make a special tribute to His honor, while receiving from each of His mysteries that special grace He won for us in each.

Thus the devout soul also tries to be like the Shulamite who, according to St. Francis de Sales (*Love of God,* 1,6, Ch. 1), "goes flying like a mystical bee, now to the eyes, now to the lips, now to the cheeks, now to the hair of her Beloved, to take the sweetness of a thousand affections from all these parts, listing in detail all that she finds to be wonderful in Him."

In order to describe Him in this astonishing way, the soul needs a certain very clear knowledge of the marvelous perfections of the Divine Spouse, and these are revealed to her in the consoling visits and happy *meetings* which, according to St. John of the Cross and St. Teresa, tend to occur very often in the state of mystical *Betrothal,* and especially, in a very heightened form, in the darkness of the terrible *Night.* For, submerged in that divine darkness which serves as a throne for the Eternal One Whose dazzle and splendor increases as the apparent darkness grows deeper, the soul is gradually introduced to the incomprehensible grandeurs of the "hidden God", and in this way continually receives most pleasing and unspeakable surprises . . . There God Himself shows her one after another His ineffable attributes, bringing her to see new and wonderful delights in each of them. It is there in the abyss of the Divinity that the true greatness of the Word Incarnate is revealed.

So, looking from these heights, she begins to describe Him in a way that might shock and disturb whoever gazes with merely "human eyes", but which captivates and enraptures hearts enkindled by a higher light and burning with His love.

"The most essential doctrine of love taught in these songs," writes Fr. Gracian, "is that which now follows, wherein two things are made known: 1st, Who Christ is, and His beauty, for this greatly moves the soul to love Him; 2nd, in what way the Bride is to imitate Him, for this true imitation of Christ constitutes perfect love, which inspires union and zeal . . . *White and ruddy.* To resemble the Crucified Christ the Bride must unite purity and love, becoming white through purity and ruddy through love: white, because she does not allow in herself anything against the will of God, and ruddy, because she has resolved to suffer even to the extent of shedding her blood of

Him, never to offend Him and always to do His will . . . There are many souls who, staying in their corner and not conversing with their neighbors . . . are white and pure. There are many others who are ruddy through their zeal and works . . . But few there are who, without losing their spirit of recollection can go to assist other souls; few can be occupied in business and remain in the presence of God. That is why the Bride says: *Chosen among thousands,* because there are few whose service of mankind is the fruit of their ever-abiding union with Christ."

"The Bride," adds St. Francis de Sales, "depicted Jesus Christ so precisely that it is impossible to describe Him more. As God, He is the whiteness of light itself; but He became man to redeem us with the purple of His Blood . . . and as a man He is so wonderful that He can be recognized among a thousand. His charity, which is the head of the other virtues, can be said to be golden, that is, very precious; and the graces and favors which proceed from it like countless hairs, are the first fruits of the palm . . .

Having given a general indication of His beauty she now passes on to individual features, saying:

v. 11)   *His head is of the purest gold;*
                his hair like palm shoots,
                and black as a raven.

The Head of Christ, says the Apostle (I *Cor.* 11,3) is God Who is all love (I *John* 4,8), and is represented by gold. Christ Himself is our Head (*Eph.* 4,16), full of grace and truth, of Whose fullness we all receive (*John* 1,14); for all the supernatural riches that we receive come from this most rich and precious fountain of His *capital grace.*

"Just as the head is joined and united to the body . . . ," says Fr. Gracian "so the Divinity of the Word is united with the Humanity, and from this stems the infinite merit of the works of Christ. In reproducing the beauty of her Redeemer, let the soul who desires to love Him perfectly have Christ as her Head, let her be united with Him, let her live in Him, and let all her works proceed from Christ so that she can say: *Omni opera nostra operatus es in nobis, Domine.*"

His beautiful *hair* represents the inestimable gifts and graces that adorn His most sacred Humanity. At the same time it can also represent the saints who are so intimately united with Him, as though to a true Head in Whom they live and upon Whom they are completely dependent.

Christ's hair also represents the faithful who are, in varying degrees, united to Him through love, and who live in Him like *palm shoots* that are *black,* undoubtedly because of the sufferings that they constantly endure; for *anyone who tries to live devoted to Christ will suffer persecution* (II *Tim.* 3,12). They are the Savior's hair, says St. Gregory the Great, because living in grace they are joined to Him as though to His head, and serve to adorn Him. By comparing them to palm shoots the Bride indicates their continual rising up to Heaven and their complete and perfect victory assisted by grace. She adds that they are as black as a raven for, however just they may be they always consider themselves as sinners.

Moreover, since "the head f Christ is God," His black hair must be His divine, lofty thoughts, which are therefore inaccessible and *obscure* to us.

"His hair," says María de la Dolorosa, "is like the flowers of the palm-tree, because when He ran towards the mountain of salvation, He took the palm of victory only for Himself and for His chosen ones."

In Christ, says St. Paul, *are hidden all the treasures of knowledge and wisdom.* "Christ's wisdom being the supreme and most exalted wisdom," says Fr. Gracian, "is compared to the highest part of the palm-tree, but because it is obscure to us and we cannot understand or comprehend it, it is said to be as black as a raven. In imitation of this, the thoughts of the perfect soul (which are her hair) must be lofty and strong, so that she is able to say: *I can do all things in Him Who strengthens me . . .* This love-stricken soul only has thoughts of giving and suffering to the utmost."

His head is also *of the finest gold* because, according to Fr. La Puente, (*Perf. est. segl.* tr. 4 Ch. 1), "in those who are to govern His Mystical Body the perfection of charity must shine forth abundantly in its two wonderful modes of expression, the love of God and the love of one's neighbor. It is not sufficient for the head to be of any sort of gold, but it must be of the choicest kind. They must not be content with a perfunctory charity, but with its supreme degree, even going so far as to give their lives if necessary in the service of their Lord, and in fulfilling the obligations of their office. If the head must be of the finest gold, what disorder would there be if it were of breakable clay, concerned only with gaining human acclaim . . . ?"

"*Caput ejus aurum optimum,* His head, symbolizes His infinite charity, the attribute most communicated to men. It is of the purest and choicest gold, and always shining forth with a thousand glorious marvels which accomplish His designs of love. *His hair* signifies His thoughts determining the destinies of men, and is two-fold. One part, lofty and white like the crown of the palm-tree, represents His most holy and inscrutable judgments by which He predestines His chosen ones, and prepares and ordains the means whereby they cooperate with Him to achieve its blessed fulfillment.

"The other part is black like the raven and signifies the thoughts of His divine justice to punish and condemn the wicked. These thoughts are shown to be black because if it were possible for God to be sad, He would be so about this alone: that those on whom He will have to execute His justice will be submerged in the shadows and darkness of death eternally. The blackness of the raven represents more than anything else the thoughts by which God determines the condemnation and punishment of sinners. He waits for them from one day to another, yet they always seem to be saying *cras* instead of *hodie*. He defers the blow, hoping that the sinner will

avoid it by repentance. These are my Beloved's thoughts and
hair." Sr. Teresa of J.M.
v. 12)   *His eyes are like doves by the brooks of waters*
         that are washed with milk,
         and dwell near the abundant streams.

This denotes the beauty of His most holy soul, adorned
with the fullness of the graces and gifts of the Holy Spirit.
Through His sweet gaze shine His holiness and dove-like
simplicity and an ineffable purity that is infused into those
souls who are given to drink from these abundant streams of
living waters.

Jesus' eyes, which are the essence of purity, says María
Dolorosa, take delight in pure souls who are purified with the
milk of grace and regularly receive the sacraments, represented
here by the abundant streams.

Through His most beautiful eyes, that are compared, not
to the eyes of a dove, but to the dove itself, which is the symbol
of the Holy Spirit, and which is bathed in milk because of its
singular whiteness, shine forth the charms of the Divinity.

His eyes are like doves . . . That is to say, His wisdom,
represented by His eyes, is very, very simple like doves. He sees
and knows all of the past, present, and future with a simple
gaze, just like doves looking at themselves in the water. He has
no need of many concepts, nor does He need to make any
reflection whatever, but with a straight forward gaze He
embraces and comprehends everything from end to end. (Sr.
Teresa)

Since we must model ourselves on Our Lord in everything,
our eyes, says St. Gregory of Nyssa, must always be simple and
innocent, clear and free from all impurity and every extraneous
image, constantly fixed on the great currents of the waters of
the Scriptures.

As far as the marvelous effects of His gaze are concerned,
here is how they were described in 1882 by someone who knew
them from experience: "However little it is perceived," he said,

"this wonderful gaze brings light, unction and peace to the soul, strengthening, consoling, calming and uplifting it. If before she was forsaken, in a moment it fills her with joy . . . The way in which this sweet Lord looks at a soul is sufficient to bring about a change in her . . ."

"The eyes of the Spouse," says Fr. Gracian, "represent His Divine Providence with which He looks at us and the concern that He shows for souls. She says they are like doves bathed in milk, because of the charity, sweetness and goodness with which He cares for human actions . . . These doves are said to be on the water and to live near the rivers. When the dove sees in the water the reflection of the goshawk or sparrow-hawk flying in the air, she quickly gathers her young and leads them to a safe place. This must be understood to refer to the great care and providence that Christ shows in preventing harm and danger from coming to His beloved ones. The eyes of the soul are her intention, and these . . . must be sincere and free from malice, full of tenderness, sweetness, gentleness and desires for goodness, for this is what is meant by being bathed in milk. Above all, in the ministry for the salvation of souls she must be guided by what is written in the Scriptures and what is set out by the holy doctors, which are represented by the brooks and streams."

v. 13)   *His cheeks are like a bed of spices,*
                 a bank of sweet-smelling plants.

This indicates the sweetness and delight of His loving presence and the exquisite fragrance that is breathed when standing before Him. These little gardens — beds, patches, *parterres* or plots — of perfumes, or of red and white aromatic flowers, says Fr. Luis de León, were planted in a very pleasing order; thus, in the Spouse everything is ordered and full of the rich perfume of His graces.

"*His cheeks* represent His beauty, for it is the cheeks that fill and embellish the face and that are the most beautiful part of it. The beauty of my Beloved, although in itself infinite, only reveals itself to me as though in very little plots or gardens, and these I perceive not by looking at them, but by smelling them. That is why I say they are planted with aromatic spices, for these spices are what faith communicates to me through the Sacred Scriptures, and also through prophets, apostles and evangelists, that is, men chosen by God to plant the faith in these divine and fragrant spice-beds. Through this faith I can come to know and perceive some of His divine beauty which, in spite of the fact that I can attain to so little, wounds and steals my heart." Sr. Teresa of J.M.

His lips are lilies distilling the purest myrrh.

The Psalmist (*Ps.* 45, 2) says of these divine lips that "all grace is poured out from them;" from them spring words of eternal life which renew and delight souls and keep them from sin. Even His enemies admitted that "No man ever spoke like this Man" (*John* 6, 69; 7, 46). His doctrine is pure and beautiful and full of delights, but distills the myrrh of bitter penitence, of self-denial and of the spirit of sacrifice.

Lilies distilling myrrh, "for just as the lily is white with strands of gold," says Fr. La Puente (*Guía*, tr. 4. Ch. 14), so "His words shone in wisdom and holiness, discretion and purity, distilling the choicest myrrh, not only because they called for an utter extirpation of defects, but because they in themselves contained the most perfect mortification, one which is necessary for speaking and having control over the tongue. O sovereign Master, open Your most blessed lips and teach me the way of speaking that You had!"

"The lips of Christ," says Scio, "also distilled myrrh when they censured sinners and urged them to do penance and deny themselves. Here a very important piece of advice is given to preachers of the Gospel, telling them not to separate, in the vain desire to please men, the sweetness of the Gospel's message from the holy severity of the law."

"His lips and mouth," says Sr. Teresa of J.M., "represent the attribute of His justice: St. John saw Him in the Apocalypse with a sharp sword coming out of His mouth. He does not appear to me with His avenging sword, but with purple lips like lilies, which represent the great zeal He has for my love, my justice and holiness. That this holiness may increase every day and win the crown of justice, as St. Paul said, these divine lips are distilling the myrrh of suffering the bitterness which, nevertheless, I hold to be very precious, and I value it so highly that I would it were distilled in greater abundance."

v. 14)   *His hands are rounded, golden,*
                  full of hyacinths.

"His hands," continues the same contemplative soul, "represent the attribute of His goodness that is all love, and ever ready to be communicated and poured into souls. This attribute in particular is extremely communicative and displays God's riches, represented by the hyacinths. It is in bountiful and, as it were, rounded hands so that they will thus necessarily give and communicate what they have and will always be doing so."

"They are of gold," observes Scio, "because the works symbolized by them are divine or *teandricas;* and full of charity, because these works have no other motive but love of His Father and of us. The Fathers often give the word *tornatiles* an active sense, interpretating it as *dexterous* in so far as, without the slightest difficulty and in an instant He is able to do whatever He likes in Heaven and on earth."

They are *rounded,* then, through the extreme ease and perfection with which they practice all kinds of good works and are disposed to bless us. They are of gold because of the charity with which they favor us and pour out their mercies over us. These hyacinths with which they are filled, like red stones, represent the precious wounds through which His graces and blessings pour out so abundantly.

For the Bride's hands to be similar, she must proceed and work in all things through the pure love of God; in all her works she must be molded by the faithful exercise of the most perfect virtues.

His breast is of ivory
overlaid with sapphires.

The ivory symbolizes the purity, candor and innocence of His sacred *breast* . . . and the sapphires, with their blue color, recall the graces, virtues and celestial gifts with which, for our benefit, His loving heart is filled and adorned.

v. 15)   *His legs are pillars of marble*
set in sockets of gold.

"His bright, golden footwear," says Petit, "is like the sockets of His legs which are as beautiful and firm as pillars of marble . . . Aquila and Teodocion translate it as: *His legs are like pillars of marble from Paros, set in sockets of gold.*"

These legs can mean the apostles and prophets who support the Mystical Body, of which Christ Himself is the Head and *Cornerstone.* The Church is cemented and founded as though in a socket of the purest gold of His divine charity (*Eph.* 2,30; 3,17; 4, 15-16).

Against the firmness of this *Cornerstone,* all the anger of God's enemies will come and be crushed.

His legs, says Sr. Teresa, "represent the attributes of His omnipotence and fortitude which are set in golden sockets because He uses these attributes, not in order to devastate and destroy, but for works of love and for our good."

"Duo sunt Sponsi crura," says Juan de J.M., "genus humanum velut corpus impositum sustinentia et columnas marmoreas rectitudine ac elagantia imitantia, *meritum et satisfactio.* Horum columnarum bases duae aurae, *justia* sunt et *misericordia,* ex quibus tamquam ex basi columnae, opera meriti ac satisfactiones assurgunt . . . His corpus suum mysticum, quod prae culparum pondere ferebatur in tartarum, tamquam duabus fermisimis columnis . . . sustinebat et gestabat."

This shows how far Christ's empire differs from worldly ones, represented by that pompous statue with feet of clay that the prophet Daniel saw (2, 33).

His feet of gold, being always moved by His love for His
Eternal Father and by the love He bears for souls, are more
precious and beautiful than the feet of all those who have
spread the Gospel of peace in His name (*Is.* 52, 7).

> *His appearance is like that of Lebanon,*
> *tall like the cedars.*

He is wholly beautiful, full of majesty and, even as a man,
more exalted than all purely human beings or angels, just as Mt.
Lebanon stands out above all the other mountains. Moreover,
Christ is equal to and consubstantial with the Father through
His divine nature, so in this way He is outstanding among
thousands and thousands, being the only One worthy of
captivating us by His beauty. The whole of Him from head to
foot, is full of divine delights.

His appearance is like that of Lebanon where as Soto
Mayor says, at every step more and more mighty trees are to be
found: "Ita sunt opera Dei Sponsi, et divina mysteria."

"His grace and beauty are lofty like Mt. Lebanon, and He
is select like the cedar because He alone is incorruptible by
nature and the corruption of sin cannot touch Him." Sr. Teresa.

"Lebanon," observes Fr. Gracian, "means whiteness which
is purity. The cedar is tall and sweet-smelling, which indicates
that Christ is extremely holy and great. The Bride that is to
imitate Him must be pure and brave."

"Whoever gazes at the face of Jesus and contemplates His
majesty," says María Dolorosa, "cannot fail to be delighted by
His kindliness. His lips are like lilies because they communicate
purity filled with love; but lilies which distill myrrh, because
they make sure that the angelic virtue is observed through
perfect interior and exterior mortification. His golden, rounded
hands denote the action of His grace in souls when enflaming
them with His love. His breast denotes the fecundity of His
grace which brings great numbers of souls to the perfection of
purity and the firmness of charity, gifts which are represented
by the whiteness and strength of ivory. The sapphires are the

prayers and merits of Jesus, imprinted on the soul through the imitation of His virtues." His hands can also be said to be full of hyacinths, she adds, "in so far as they denote the rigors of His Providence which, in order to attract us to Himself, He sends to us with frequent trials. These seem repulsive but in fact they are precious stones which come from His hands to make us good. His breast of ivory, inlaid with sapphires, represents the immaculate purity of the body of Jesus Christ, adorned with the sapphires of His blood, which He continually offers on the altar to His Father in expiation for our sins."

v. 16)   *His throat is most sweet,*
            and he is altogether desirable.
            Such is my beloved, and he is my friend,
            O daughters of Jerusalem.

His throat is most sweet, repeats Sr. Teresa, and thus His words are so sweet that the prophet David says (*Ps.* 119): *Quam dulcia faucibus meis eloquia tua, super mel ori meo.* The whole of Him is to be desired, longed for, and loved. His words are very sweet and full of consolations; He is wholly lovable and desirable, since He is goodness and kindness itself, enrapturing and captivating the upright in heart. Such is my Lord and my only Beloved Whom all souls ought to love and desire because He is the One Who truly loves them and Who can satisfy them, establishing everlasting, intimate relations with them. He is in fact *my friend,* which means that despite His greatness and excellence and in spite of His infinite perfections He does not think it beneath Him to become a true and affectionate friend of all. So, daughters of Jerusalem, how can I help but look for Him Whom my soul loves if He is wholly desirable and if, being so beautiful and majestic, He yet deigns to establish a loving friendship with me . . . ? And how could you help but love Him ardently, you yourselves, seeing what He is like? How can you fail to be inspired also, to seek Him with extreme diligence?

"Your eyes, Jesus," exclaims Bl. Suso (*Letter V*), "are brighter than the sun's rays, Your mouth is sweet and distills honey, Your face is like lilies and roses, and the whole of Your virginal beauty infinitely exceeds all that is beautiful, delightful and desirable in the universe. The more I contemplate You Who are beyond time and matter, the more I delight in You in raptures of ecstasy; the more I hear You, the more I know how good, kind and gentle of heart You are. *Such is my beloved and he is my friend.* O how happy you will be if you have Jesus as your friend."

"Such is my beloved . . . The devout soul likes to tell others about the excellent features of Christ which God gives her to understand." (Gracian)

"Could there by any greater sweetness," says María de la Dolorosa, "than that which is to be found in the words of the Divine Spouse? These not only enrapture souls with heavenly consolations, but they also delight the body with the sweetness of His grace. Yes, indeed! Our loving Jesus is wholly lovable. Now He consoles us, now He brings us pain, but it is all for our own good. How desirable it is to know Him! We love Him so little because we do not know Him well. Oh, if only we knew Him at least as much as the Cherubs know Him, so as to be able to love Him more, even though this very love would be nothing in comparison to what He deserves."

"O my Divine Spouse!" exclaimed St. Mary Magdalen of Pazzi (*Part.* 5, excl. 7), "how sweet and loving and merciful You are! Let all look at the Word, my Spouse, and admire His goodness, His greatness, His majesty! His face shines like the sun! What am I saying? — the sun is darkened in His presence. O Spouse! O Word! Your affections and desires are the Bride's adornments. She cannot understand Your greatness, Your beauty, Your magnificence and Your glory, because these are qualities of Your Divine Being; but they are reflected in her, nonetheless, glorifying and consoling her. O my Spouse! You are so great that Your greatness cannot be comprehended; in this resides my greatest glory, and in this I can rightfully delight. But of what use to the Bride are all the Spouse's prerogatives and all these precious adornments if she does not come to be united with Him?"

Thus, the loving soul praises Him and seeks to tell everyone about Him, and tries to win for Him as many souls as she can, working with zeal, and almost without realizing it, in the very enterprise that a short while before, lacking faith in herself, she had been so unwilling to undertake. In this way the Lord triumphs over this innocent resistance, and brings everything to redound to the greater good of His chosen ones!

"With these words," adds María Dolorosa, "the soul in love with Jesus, enkindles those that hear with keen desires to forsake all worldly vanity and to accompany her in her search for the Spouse."

"It is very good," writes Fr. Gracian, "to associate with devout and spiritual persons because their conversation encourages one to seek God and to pursue prayer and the life of the spirit."

v. 17)   *Where did your beloved go,*
(ch. 6, 1)   *O loveliest of women?*
                Which way did your beloved turn,
                that we may seek Him with you?

How efficacious are the words of souls touched by God! For the very ones who at the beginning almost considered the Bride's desires to be madness now begin to experience them. Enchanted with what they heard about her Divine Lover, they not only show sincere compassion for this soul who, after knowing Him, lost Him, but also offer to join her in her search, undoubtedly hoping to find Him for themselves as well.

Eventually the constancy of love triumphs over everything and on many occasions succeeds in converting its chief opponents into allies. Thus, we see here how the very *daughters of Jerusalem*, these continual rivals or declared enemies of the mystical Bride, who until now have given her so much trouble because, not experiencing the attractions and delights of the interior life that she leads are ignorant of its mysteries and wonders, eventually become moved to compassion and pity upon seeing her great sufferings. Constrained by her zeal and holy converse they not only begin to look upon her with great sympathy, but admire her and desire to imitate her. They seek to emulate and listen to her as an experienced teacher, being now enkindled with divine love.

They have seen the moral beauty of this soul, the delights of her mystical life which the world considers dull and strange and for this reason they are irresistably drawn to the Heavenly Spouse. Thus we realize how even those who through their lack of faith fail to understand the pains and bitterness suffered by contemplative souls in their abandonment, by conversing with them and listening to them with simplicity, eventually become *infected* with the same pains of love and feel something of what they feel . . . Souls close to God truly do inspire and inflame with their sweet words of life and fire, showing that it is lovable and desirable to follow Christ faithfully.

Hence, as St. Thomas points out, the importance of supernatural conversation and of association with fervent persons capable of enkindling us with their words and of teaching and edifying us with their exemplary lives; thus also the need to live in intimate union with the Church, the true Bride of the Divine Lamb, so as to learn to find Him and to enjoy His communications of love.

Synopsis

The Bride indicates the place where her Beloved is usually to be found, which is the garden of Holy Church and in pure hearts. She openly declares how she wholly belongs to the One Who pastures in these places and Who loves with such perfect goodness (v. 2). Thereupon her sweet Lord suddenly shows Himself to her, taking pleasure in her as never before, and makes known to her the new perfections of virtues and graces which she has gained during His absence by faithfully following Him and making Him known. Above all He celebrates this divine fortitude that makes her fearful to her enemies and by which she also captivates Him (v. 3-7). He has many other souls serving and loving Him, but none that has given the same proof of love and faithfulness as she; so that, being His favorite and most perfect Bride, she now merits being united to Him forever in spiritual marriage (v. 8-9). Other pious souls, far from envying her, praise and admire her, seeing her now as though transformed into the very Sun of Justice (v. 9-10). She says that she is busy watching over the property of her Spouse which she now considers her own, and tells of what she suffered as a result (v. 11-12). But her friends beg her to return to them so that they may see her when they please (v. 13).

THE BRIDE

v. 2)   *My Beloved went down to his garden,*
          to the bed of spices,

> to pasture[a] in the gardens
> and gather lilies

v. 3)   *I am my beloved's and my beloved is mine.*
       He pastures among the lilies.

THE SPOUSE

v. 4)   *You are beautiful as Tirzah, my love,*
       and fair as Jerusalem,
       and terrible as an army in battle array.

v. 5)   *Turn your eyes away from me*
       for they make me flee away.[b]
       Your hair is like a flock of goats
       that appear from Gilead.

v. 6)   *Your teeth are like a flock of sheep*
       as they come up from washing.
       Each one has its twin
       and not one among them is barren.

v. 7)   *Your cheeks are like a piece of pomegranate*
       without what is hidden within you.[c]

v. 8)   *There are sixty queens and eighty concubines*
       and the maidens are countless.

v. 9)   *My dove, my perfect one, is but one,*
       the only done of her mother,[d]
       the favorite of the one that bore her.
       The daughters saw her, and proclaimed her most blessed,
       and even the queens and concubines praised her.

CHOIR OF FRIENDS

v. 10) *Who is this advancing like the rising dawn,*
       beautiful as the moon,

a.   The Hebrew can be interpreted in both the active and the passive sense (i.e.
       pastures his flock" and "pastures"). The Septuagint takes it in the active
       sense: *pastures his flock.*
b.   Hebrew: "For they disturb me." The Septuagint: "for they have transported
       me."
c.   Hebrew: "Your cheeks are like half a pomegranate, behind a veil." Fr. Luis de
       León: ". . . within your hair."
d.   Hebrew and Septuagint: "For her mother."

select[e] *like the sun,*
terrible like an army in battle array?

THE BRIDE

v. 11) *I went down to the nut garden,*
to see the fruits of the valleys.[f]
to see if the vine was in blossom
and if the pomegranate trees had sprouted.[g]

v. 12) *I did not know; my soul disturbed me*
because of the chariots of Aminadib.[h]

THE FRIENDS OF THE BRIDE

v. 13) *Return, return, O Shulamite,*
Return, return, that we may gaze on you.[i]

Exposition

v. 2)   *My beloved went down to his garden,*
to the bed of spices,
to pasture in the gardens
and gather lilies.

Being truly faithful in guarding the honor of her Spouse
and in caring for His interests, the mystical Bride not only
praises Him and makes Him known to others, but she wins and
inflames them in His love and in the desire to seek Him with the
firm assurance of being able to find Him. So, unlike what
usually happens in selfish love which gives rise to jealousy, what
holy, Heavenly love produces is an ardent zeal for the greater
glory of God, with burning desires to see Him served, loved and
possessed by everyone . . . The mystical Bride is not afraid that

e.   Hebrew: "Pure."
f.   Hebrew: "the greenery of the valley."
g.   Hebrew and Septuagint: "If the pomegranate trees are in flower." The
      Septuagint adds: "There I will give you my love." Cf. VII, 13.
h.   The Hebrew could be translated: "I do not know, my desire, or my soul, made
      me like the chariots of Aminadib (or of my noble people)," or else "my desire
      put me in the chariot of Aminadib."
i.   In the Hebrew and the Septuagint this verse (v. 13) is placed at the beginning
      of Chapter 7.

the Supreme Good she is in love with will be any less loved, or
will not love her as tenderly, because this Good is being
communicated to other souls at the same time; for, since It is
infinite, this Love is in no way diminished when It is lavishly
poured out. Each soul is loved as though it were the only one,
and each and everyone of them can be filled with ineffable
delights.

Forgetting herself and the anguish into which His absence
has plunged her, she takes advantage of the first opportunity to
make known to those who ask her the precise place where He
usually goes to find recreation, *to take pasture* and to pasture
His faithful sheep, and where He must be sought by all who sigh
for Him.

This mystical garden to which the Divine Lover went down
is, as we said before, first of all the Blessed Virgin Mary, the
true enclosed garden where He has His greatest delights; in her
and through her and with her everyone can find Him, just as the
Shepherds and Wise Men found Him (*Lk.* 2, 16): *Invenerunt
Mariam et ... Infantem ...* So that all who find her find life
(*Prov.* 8, 35), together with the very Author of life, for in her is
to be found "the grace of every way and truth, and all hope of
life and of virtue" (*Eccles.* 24, 25), since she has in her breast
Him Who is at one and the same time *the Way, the Truth and
the Life.*

The garden of the Spouse also refers in a very special way
to the Holy, Catholic Church, being full, as it is of all the gifts
and blessings of the Holy Spirit, enriched with all the graces of
the sacraments, and made beautiful and embalmed with the
prodigious virtues of so many pure and holy souls and of as
many religious institutions as have flourished and will always
flourish within it; these institutions being represented by the
little plots or beds of spices within the grandiose garden of the
Church, beds to which the Divine Spouse so loves to come, take
His recreation and to pasture, picking as He pleases the most
fragrant lilies ... All those who still do not know Him and who

desire to know Him fully must come to the Holy Catholic Church to look for Him and not to the dissident churches, which through schism or heresy have become uncultivated land where Jesus cannot find pleasure. For He no longer finds there these fragrant beds of spices, which are the institutions that are most observant and most filled with the spirit of prayer and sacrifice, nor the precious little gardens of pure and devout souls where He takes pleasure and delight. It is there with the preaching of pure truth, the efficacy of holy example and the marvelous works of devotion, charity and mercy that flower within it that He pastures His sheep; and it is there that the Sanctifying Spirit pours forth His favors and blessings.

Let us try not only to live within the Holy Catholic Church, but to live very close to these delightful little gardens which the Lord so frequently visits, to share in the blessings that He pours in and around them. Let us also try to see that our hearts, like those of the saints, are a true enclosed garden, and the Lover of souls will undoubtedly come there very often as to a delightful haven.

The mystical Bride now comes to experience Him when she thought she was most abandoned by Him. Speaking from her own experience, she seems to be saying: the sure way to find our sweet Lord Jesus is to cultivate all the virtues within ourselves, and especially those that are most precious and most pleasing to Him, so that our hearts diffuse His sweetest fragrance like beds of aromatic flowers. He will then come at once and pasture and feed His flock in these mystical gardens, gathering for His delight, or for the good and consolation of His friends, some of the most beautiful and sweetest-smelling lilies or "His myrrh and perfumes", which are the purest, most fervent and most self-denying hearts.

This, says St. Thomas, is how the Divine Spouse goes down to the garden of His Church and to the plots or beds of spices.

From the reply that the Bride has just given to the daughters of Jerusalem it is inferred, or it could well be inferred, that at times these very souls who get lost in search of the Lord, feel in the most intimate part of their being that He is really hidden deep within them; dwelling gladly there, taking pasture in the garden of their spirit, picking the lilies that spring from this simplicity and inner nakedness, this self-denial and continual self-sacrifice, from which they receive no delight, since the Spouse picks and reaps all the delightful flowers for Himself and for His most needy friends. These souls who are as poor as they are fortunate, being completely enamored, cannot help but lament the lack of ardent and unitive affection with which God lets Himself be felt by them in the delight of interior communication. It is for this reason that they so anxiously ask for Him Whom they already possess, and so ardently search for Him Whom they have already found. Thus, in spite of all their abandonment and solitude they, full of love and trust, surrender themselves to Him, repeating over and over again:

v. 3)   *I am my beloved's and my beloved is mine.*
             He pastures among the lilies.

Let all souls try to be such that the Divine Spouse can come and feed and pasture His flock within them. Let them continually search for Him, not in dissipation or amid the turmoil of people and the clamor of unnecessary business, but deep in these intimate gardens of the heart where He is so pleased to dwell and come for His recreation and to pasture in secret. For there they will find Him if, as St. John of the Cross says, they perservere in looking for Him and faithfully serve Him. Do you desire to have Him Who pastures among the lilies keep you company? says St. Bernard. Well, make your heart a garden of them and you will see how He will come to it . . . *Cura habere lilia penes te, si vis habere hunc habitatorem liliorum habitantem in te. Opus tuum studium tuum desiderium tuum lilia esse protestentur (Serm. 71 in Cant.).*

As the Bride reflects on these things, says an experienced soul (M. Sorazu), Jesus reveals Himself to her in His mystical garden (the breast of the Church), and in the bed of spices (the

Eucharist); and through His ministries she sees Him pasturing in the gardens, gathering the virginal lilies to transplant them to the rich land of the religious cloisters. There the soul comes to understand the designs of God for her, contemplates Him in the New Testament and the Liturgy, and looks for Him in the commands and instructions of her spiritual director. In this way she will become "Christofied" through the devotion she will experience for the son of God. And "He associates her in His filial relations with God the Father, and to a certain extent shares with her the glory of hypostatic union." She is thus obliged to say: *Ego dilecto meo* . . .

She can well repeat these words over and over again: *I am my beloved's* . . . etc., because with the same zeal with which she tries to praise Him and make Him known to others, He deigned to reveal Himself to her, to let His presence be felt and even to speak to her heart. In this way, through her own experience she now understands that she is really wholly His and that He Himself is wholly hers; for He takes pleasure in her as in a garden of delights, and He cherishes and praises her with much love, causing her to rejoice in Him.

"In this state of life so perfect," says St. John of the Cross (*Living Flame,* II, n. 36), "the soul always walks in festivity, inwardly and outwardly, and it frequently hears on its spiritual tongue a new song of great jubilation in God, a song always new, enfolded in a gladness and love arising from the knowledge the soul has of its happy state . . . There is no need to be amazed that the soul so frequently walks amid this joy, jubilance, fruition and praise of God. Besides the knowledge it has of the favors received, it feels in this state that God is so sollicitous in regaling it with precious, delicate and enhancing words, and in extolling it by various favors, that He has no one else in the world to favor nor anything else to do, that everything is for the soul alone. With this feeling it proclaims like the Bride in the Song: *Dilectus meus mihi et ego illi* . . ."

"This is her greatest joy," says St. Lawrence Justinian, "to see that she is no longer her own but wholly His. From this springs her magnanimity and strength, her peace and trust, her profound humility, together with the most enkindled charity which causes her to sacrifice herself wholly to Him Who is everything to her, and Who has won all her heart."

Ego dilecto meo . . . Before, in her first love, she gloried in possessing her Good, saying: *My beloved is mine* . . . Now that she is united to Him in a much more intimate way, a way she can no longer doubt, she begins to exclaim gladly that *she is wholly His;* she now knows for certain what before she could not know for sure . . . In the same way, later on (7, 10) she will repeat the same phrase again and with even better reason: *I am my beloved's* . . . "This," writes St. Bernard (*Serm.* 69), "is what *perfect* souls say: Who these are is known to God; but you must listen so that you can reach such happiness . . . Give me a soul who loves only God and those things related to Him that should be loved, who can not only say that her life is in Christ, but who for some time has had Christ dwelling within her, who in her works and holy repose longs only to have the Lord always before her eyes to conform to His most holy will in all things; give me such a soul as this, and I assure you that she will be worthy of the Spouse's care and of His Divine Majesty's favors and attentions: *Da, inquam, talem animam et ego non nego dignam Sponsi cura majestatis respectu, dominantis favore, solictudine gubernantis."*

"Happy the soul that has merited the intimate friendship of the Heavenly Spouse not for a short time but forever! . . . (For His words:) *Desponsabo te mihi* (*Hosea* 2,19) . . . indicate the infinite desire He has for this betrothal to be brought about, and assures us that it is His will, and that if the soul does not reject Him, He is now hers. This state is well known by the soul who says: *Dilectus meus mihi.* He is wholly mine and I am wholly His. He is my Spouse and I am His Bride. The words of Hosea speak of the future, those of the Song speak of the present: He is mine and I am His. He has given Himself to me, and I give myself to Him . . ." (Fray Juan de los Angeles, *in Cant.* 2, 16).

"Whoever is united to God in this transformation," says Ruysbroeck (*Kingdom of those who love God,* Ch. 29), "experiences incomprehensible delights and ineffable joy although not all enjoy the same blessings; for each soul is sublime, illustrious and noble according to her hunger and holy impatience for love and the loftiness of her virtues; and although each one is given a like good, each one is inundated more or less, depending on how hungry and impatient she is for love. But there is always more than enough for everyone, for the inexhaustible gifts that they receive are altogether immense and without measure . . . and constitute the very Essence of God."

I am my beloved's . . . "O what contentment the Lord derives from this kind of exchange," exclaims Fr. Gracian, ". . . and how beautiful the soul seems to Him who resolves in this way to serve Him. Fair as Jerusalem, because there is nothing in this life more similar to a soul enjoying beatitude than the soul who truly loves the Lord. Beatitude has twelve delights which are: the vision of the Divine Essence, fruition of love, eternal security, etc.; twelve other similar blessings are enjoyed in this life by the soul who resolves to do the will of God in all things. She enjoys a sublime contemplation which is born of faith, an inner security which comes from hope and a joyful and delightful love. Although not all souls experience supernatural and miraculous gifts in the body, there are some who, through the love of God and their life of virtue, receive good health and a kind of lightness, clarity and levity that lifts them miraculously into the air . . . But even when God does not work these miracles in the body, perfect souls nonetheless possess a keeness of mind, a quickness of thought, a clarity of judgment and an impassiveness that are in some way or other very much like the four qualities of the bodies of the blessed. Instead of the three crowns, God gives them three fervent desires: chastity, martyrdom and zeal for souls. Finally, as St. Paul says (*Phil.* 3): *they have their conversation in Heaven* with the saints that they bring with them into the presence of God and wherever they go they enjoy a quiet which in some way is like that of Heaven. Some people decide to call God's servants blessed because of this, indicating that they have already reached beatitude in this world."

v. 4)   *You are beautiful as Tirzah, my love,*
                 fair as Jerusalem,
                 and terrible as an army in battle-array.

The Bride was looking for her Spouse, believing Him to be absent, writes St. Thomas, and He reveals Himself to her within, praising and delighting her with such sweet words.

This is praise from God Himself and as St. Augustine says (*Soliloquies,* Ch. X), the only praise to be desired and the only praise that is always true ... The soul received this radiant beauty after being purified and refined like gold in the crucible, in the terrible trials that He Himself made her endure for this purpose. Gentleness and grace are communicated to her by the love with which she is enkindled, which also gives her fortitude and makes her frightening to the world and to the devil. The devil trembles before her and flees in terror, as is narrated in the lives of many saints, especially noted by St. John of the Cross and St. Teresa.

Thus we see how, even in this world, God rewards those who love Him truly and who, for His love, bravely and trustingly endure all the trials He sends them, and how eventually He always yields and surrenders to the sighs and longings of all who search for Him with all their hearts.

Now that the soul who is to become forever and indissolubly united with Him has been perfectly purified and molded into the form which He desires, it is time to show her the ardent charity with which He loves her and which moved Him to put her to the test ... The storm that enveloped the soul has now abated, and an unalterable peace has begun for her. The frightening and terrible *dark night* has eventually passed and the divine Sun of Justice has dawned in her heart. In this marvelous light that foretells the light of glory, she very clearly sees, admires and blesses the wonderful work that, in the midst of the darkness in which she believed herself to be lost, the fire of the Divine Spirit had been bringing about within her; renewing and transforming her until she had become completely transformed, converted into a new creature with divine instincts, tendencies and actions, just as a sluggish, groveling worm, enclosing itself in the cocoon it builds for itself, becomes a beautiful butterfly which lives in the air and feeds on flowers.

There is nothing strange, then, that the Divine Spouse should so joyfully celebrate this marvel worked by His Own Spirit. In order to demonstrate even more clearly the new beauty of this soul He compares her to most beautiful and highly populated city, or rather, following the Hebrew text, which we kept when translating this verse, He compares her to the two strongest, most beautiful and highly populated cities of Palestine, Tirzah and Jerusalem, which present the Church, formed as it is by the union of the two great nations, the Gentiles and the Jews. This soul, indeed, enjoys within her all the delights which, as Fr. Luis de León says, "in the strength of their location, the magnificence of their buildings, the greatness and beatuy of their riches, the variety of their arts and offices," were possessed by these cities.

This is not all, for He compares her to a powerful army in battle-array or with banner unfurled, before which all must surrender. "Thus, to extol her all the more," adds the same commentator, "He tells the Bride that she fills Him with astonishment and that He is so beside Himself because of her extreme degree of loveliness that He is enraptrue . . . . . . there being no power or resistance against the Bride's strength and extreme beauty.

The soul has become so perfect through the trials she has suffered that the divine Lover shows Himself to be captivated and overcome by her. Thus she is frightening, like a well-ordered army, not only because of her great victories over herself, the world and the devil; but also because she is strong with God, Whom she persuades not to punish men as they deserve, she captivating and overcoming Him through love. For this reason the Spouse then adds:

v. 5)   *Turn your eyes away from me,*
              for they make me flee away.

Or as others translate it: *Turn away your eyes for they have overcome me.*

He tells her to turn away her eyes, to avert them a little from the contemplation of His divine beauty, so as to go where He calls her and do what He wants her to do, which is to win souls for Him and to work for His greater glory; or else not to imagine that she can comprehend Him.

Turn away your eyes ... "As though to say," writes Fr. Gracian, "your desire to comprehend and completely penetrate My mysteries with the eyes of your natural reason makes Me fly and depart from your presence, leaving your soul which is involved in a kind of investigation, without the fruit of love and contemplation."

This can also be interpreted to mean that this soul is not only overpowering to men, but also to God Himself. Thus He tells her to turn away her eyes, that is to say, not to do Him violence with them, not to impose her intercession, but to let Him carry out His justice. For, very often these lofty souls are like divine lightning conductors which channel off the currents of God's wrath and hold back His avenging arm He says to them as He said to Moses (*Ex.* 32, 10): *Leave Me* ... ! as though He could not continue as long as they intercede with their humble requests. But these holy souls persist because they know very well that God desires to see Himself forced by their loving complusion not to punish as our sins deserve, and allow mercy to prevail over the strictness of justice. For this reason He delights over and over again in contemplating and celebrating the fine gifts and the singular beauty of the mystical Bride, repeating:

> *Your hair is like flocks of goats,*
> *that come up from Gilead.*

v. 6)
> *Your teeth are like a flock of sheep*
> *that came out from washing.*
> *Each one has its twin*
> *and not one among them is barren.*

v. 7)
> *Your cheeks are like a piece of pomegranate*
> *without what is hidden within you.*

The Spouse here repeats the same expressions with which He earlier praised the Bride's beauty (4, 2-3), for perfection is always one and the same, even though it increase in degree, as in this soul. Also perhaps, as Fr. Luis de León says, "because these similes are so outstanding that they cannot be surpassed." Thus He shows her how pleased He is by the diligence with which the soul places all her thoughts in Him and the singular care with which she absorbs holy doctrine so as to assimilate it fully and be able to communicate it to others with ardent love.

"The Spouse again praises the Bride for the hair of her thoughts, the teeth of her meditations, the cheeks of her appearance, as we have explained above. He says how few are the souls who manage to reach this sovereign union and perfect love of God" (Fr. Gracian).

v. 8)
> *There are sixty queens and eighty concubines*
> *and the maidens are countless.*

Here we see that the perfect or very advanced souls, although relatively few, are more numerous than is normally believed, By "queens", the Divine Spouse, in our humble opinion, is referring to perfect and innocent souls; by "concubines" or legitimate but second class wives, He refers to those who are also perfect and who even at times surpass the first in ardor of charity, but who are not of royal descent; that is who, through an excess of divine kindness and mercy, or through penance and faithfulness to new grace, have deserved to

THE SONG OF SONGS

be elevated to the mystical betrothal in spite of not having kept intact, as the others have, the treasure of their baptismal innocence, or their virginity and innocence.

According to St. Gregory, the *queens* are holy souls who, serving the Lord in all faithfulness and purity of love, raise many spiritual children whose pure and innocent hearts they will prove to be truly *royal* . . . *Concubines* are those who serve Him with hypocrisy and vile self-interest, seeking their own satisfaction and convenience.

According to the V. Teresa of J.M.. (*Comment.* XV), "sixty are the queens who have reached the state of spiritual marriage . . . and eighty the concubines who have only reached the state of betrothal. The beautiful and pure souls who did not reach either of these two states are beyond counting."

The countless maidens, then, are the many souls who have been admitted by the Lord into His palace and introduced into His first *rooms,* and who begin to taste there some of the delights of supernatural contemplation. Together with these, there are others, more or less fervent, who also aspire to these favors and to the celebration one day of the mystical marriage; although unfortunately many of them, through lack of preparation, faithfulness, generosity, and perserverance are eventually rejected as the foolish virgins were, fulfilling in this way the words of the Savior when He said (*Matt* 22,14), that although so many were *called,* few were *chosen.* Fr. Godinez maintains that no less than 99 out of 100 fail at the first trial, above all because they lack a good director to encourage, correct and guide them. St. Teresa states that there are many who reach the prayer of *quiet* and very few who pass beyond (*Life,* Ch. 15). In the *Interior Castle* (5, Ch. 4) she adds that she saw some very loftly souls in the state of *union* fall.

But to fall back or to fail is our fault alone, for God, as St. Teresa repeats on many occasions, invites everyone and would like to have His delights in every soul, and does not favor certain persons. She adds, (*ibid.* and *Way,* Ch. 31-32), the soul that is given the graces of the prayer of quiet is given it to lift it to greater heights provided that it does not offer any resistance. So that, in spite of everything, the souls who reach the *Betrothal* are as many as eighty in number. Although there could be incomparably more of them were there not so many obstacles, in this spiritual marriage uniqueness is always preserved.

v. 9) *My dove, my perfect one, is but one*
       the only one of her mother
       the favorite of the one that bore her.
       The daughters saw her and proclaimed her most blessed,
       and even the queens and concubines praised her.

The Holy Catholic Church is indeed the perfect one, as is the Immaculate Virgin Mary, the favorite soul, and the lovely Bride. For God has His delights in each devout soul as though He loved her alone, and Christ died for her as though He died for her alone; and there is enough love in this divine breast that He would die for each soul separately if this were necessary, just as He died once to save every soul. So that although the Brides are many, the marriage is unique, for all the Brides together are one "with one heart and one soul in the Lord," and each perfect soul is treated as though it were *the only one,* always possessing something special that makes it a *favorite.*

"This statement that she is the most beautiful," writes the Ven. Mariana de San José (in *Cant.* 1), "could distress us if it was not known from long experience that the Lord deals with many souls and treats each as if she were the only one and the much loved Benjamin.

"Just as merits must vary, for the glory given in Heaven to those that dwell there varies, so here in this world their singular beauty is due to that attribute in which they excel, for each soul is the most beautiful in that particular thing in which she excels; whatever her happiness and good fortune, she is very precious for she achieved this grace in the loving eyes of the Spouse, Who makes this known and praises her as the most beautiful of all."

There is no rivalry or envy in these loves, for it is clear here that they all praise the Bride, sincerely recognizing her prerogatives and singular beauty. For in her they always admire and praise the living image of the Spouse Whose love, unlike what happens in worldly love, the saintly soul wants all her sisters to enjoy (*Song* 1, 2-3; 2, 9; 3,11). In this way the blessed delight in God not only by reason of their own gifts, but also by seeing Him in the gifts of others.

"*The only one of her mother* (or, *for her mother*), — *the favorite of the one that bore her;* that is, of the Church, and also of the Virgin Mary who is the Mother who gave birth to us and raised us in grace, giving to each soul the love she bore for her Only-Begotten, as He Himself charged her to do on the cross. After modeling her upon her Son, the sweet Mother of beautiful love looks upon the holy soul as unique, as her favorite, as the one chosen to be the worthy Bride of her Son, to Whom she will be presented *with much rejoicing* (*Ps.* 45,15).

v. 10)   *Who is this advancing like the rising dawn*
              beautiful as the moon,
              select like the sun,
              terrible like an army in battle-array?

These words are said by the daughters of Jerusalem who are now converted into faithful friends, admirers and disciples of the Bride, or else by the friends of the Spouse who marvel at seeing this happy soul rise up and advance majestically like the dawn which shines more and more until the perfect day is reached (*Prov.* 4,18), without ever declining or halting in its course. In the way of the spirit the one who tires least is he who runs most and stops least; for in relaxing or taking short steps, even under the pretext of taking a brief rest, we in fact see that their spiritual strength is always lessened instead of renewed.

The holy soul not only advances like the dawn, but is also *beautiful as the moon,* that is, is similar to the Blessed Virgin, the true *Moon* of the mystical Heaven lighting up our darkness and watching over our *nights* . . . The moon does not have its own light, but receives it from the sun; so this soul tries to be like Mary and always to receive the divine rays of her Sun Jesus, so as to become, under His continual influence, another new sun; in this way she seems pure and select like Him. For she shines so much with the clarity that she receives, and reflects His divine light so much when enlightening other souls, that she seems to mirror Him and to look like a real sun.

No longer ordinary people in general, but even the friends of the Spouse and the angels themselves praise this singular and privileged soul, marveling at her delightful beauty, her generosity, valor and magnanimity. They watch her at the very dawn of her spiritual life when she first began to rise up and scatter sweet sparks of light; they watch her as she advances, laden with gifts and riches, and beautiful as the mystical moon; that is very similar to the sublime Mother of divine grace, and receiving from the Divine Sun a most abundant clarity that she communicates to many others; and finally they see her very similar in splendor to the Sun Himself, upon Whom she becomes modeled.

She does good to everyone: she enlightens all with Heavenly wisdom, she seeks to enkindle all in divine love and to some extent, impresses all with her sublime virtues, driving away all who resist such salutary influences. Her greatness and power is such that she seems like a well-ordered army that overcomes and terrifies its enemies, triumphing over everything. For the souls in this state of such intimate union with the Word, are not only frightening to demons who flee from her in terror and confusion, but also to men, however furious and inimical they are. This can be seen in the case of so many saints and especially in that of St. Catherine of Siena who, by their very presence alone change hearts and make their enemies put down their arms . . . Here they are truly seen to be working with a divine power, for it is God Himself Who manifests Himself and works through them, while at the same time taking His delight in them.

"Blessed be He." exclaims the Ven. Mariana de San José (in *Cant.* 2,4), "Who, being the God of infinite majesty, nonetheless desires to communicate Himself to us in an infinite manner. If this were not so, He would never deign to look at us nor raise a common and unworthy slave to the happy state of being His Bride and friend, nor would He make her one with Himself, the two becoming one single will; so that, through participation in this union, the creature becomes a god, and a mirror in which the true God sees Himself and which, reflecting the rays of His light, seems to be the light itself, so that the soul becomes the light of Light and the Lord can call her the light of His eyes . . . O Lord, what hidden and yet what patent truths! Hidden, to souls who do not prepare themselves, but to those who are prepared and who surrender themselves into Your hands, how evident and how full of glory."

But although hidden, they make themselves felt just as the mystical Bride succeeds in making herself felt.

The soul who before was attached to the earth now sees herself lifted out of herself and above all that is worldly, and not only has the *true Light of life* for herself, but with her edifying conversation, begins to serve as a luminary for many others. So that, as St. Gregory says, as her light shines more and more, she is compared first to the moon, because with her good conduct she begins to point out the straight path to those that lie in the darkness or in the shadows of death; and then to the Sun Itself, for she is now able to enlighten with beautiful and brilliant examples no only sinners, but also the just and the very advanced.

"When the soul leaves the night of sin," observes Fr. Gracian, "she always tries to progress; at first she is like the morning, where there is not so much light and much coldness until the sun warms the earth; and she is like this because the souls of beginners are ignorant of many things and often cold in spirit. They enter the active life, which is compared to the moon, because . . . the soul receives the light of her instructor's teaching and has increases and decreases of virtue . . . After having exercised herself in these works of ascetical life, she ascends to the contemplative life that overflows with light like the sun. Finally, from the contemplative life she ascends to the unitive stage where, united to God and to all creatures in Heaven and on earth, like an army lined up in squadrons, she fulfills the desires and mercies of God."

Who is this, they will all ask, who is beautiful as the sun, through the purity of her chastity, who patiently shines at night in the midst of the adversities of this life without losing her splendor because of them? Who is this, select like the sun, firm and stable in her virtuous exercises . . . which she regulates like a resplendent army . . . becomes terrifying to devils . . . ? Who is this soul who always ascends and never halts, abandoning all worldly things so as to have her conversation in Heaven . . . ? O how lofty Christian life is . . . and with what wonder it fills the angels themselves ! " (La Puente, *Guia,* tr. 4, Ch. 12).

Terrible like an army . . . The powers of this world therefore surrender themselves to the holy soul; and even kings do not think it beneath them to consult her and to follow her advice, as someone of the stature of Philip II did with the Blessed Fr. Francisco of the Child Jesus who was, moreover, a very simple and uneducated little man; as Philip V did later on with the Ven. Agreda, and as Attila had done with St. Leo, and even Herod with St. John the Baptist.

v. 11)   *I went down to the nut garden*
             to see the fruits of the valleys,
             to see if the vine was in blossom
             and if the pomegranate trees had sprouted.

v. 12)   *I did not know; my soul disturbed me*
             because of the chariots of Aminadib.

These two verses which we attribute to the Bride present considerable difficulties. Some, and Fr. Luis de León among them, attribute verse 10 to the Spouse arguing that this is how

"He replies to the secret complaint that the Bride (it is supposed) quite likely has against Him, for having knocked at the door and then passed on, thus causing her to go out losing herself in search of Him; and . . . He replies that since she took so long in opening to Him, He decided to see the state of His garden in the meantime." In verse 11 the Bride's reply would be that she did not know this, or did not realize this and that she was frightened when she heard the sound of the chariots of Aminadib that seemed to be pursuing her. Or else: "I do not know what it was, nor what You did in leaving me like that, nor what it was that moved You to do it. I do not know anything, except my desire and the profound love that I have for You brought me to go and look for You as soon as I heard You, flying along as though travelling by post . . . It seems as though I have come in one of those very swift carriages used by the princes and the powerful men of my country." (Cf. *Ibid.* in *h.* 1).

But this hardly makes any sense and does not fit in with the preceding verses. It seems very unlikely that the Spouse would say in the darkest part of the night He had gone *to see the state of His garden* . . . Moreover this supposed explanation by the Spouse would come too late, and would serve no purpose in view of all the praise that He has just directed to the Bride, who, receiving such singular favors cannot help but forget all her troubles and thinks only of thanking Him and of responding to such kindness. Thus, it seems to us that both verses are spoken by the Bride, who in this way shies away from the praise, telling her Spouse how concerned she had been when she learned of the state of Christendom, watching and praying so as to assist the many needs of the Church and of souls, especially to care for those who can and should produce certain fruits with which to feed the faithful nations, and these are represented by the *nut garden.* Thus, she *went down to see the fruits of the valleys,* to visit the possessions and property of the Spouse, which she now considers her own, taking care to see to the needs that she notices there; interceding with her prayers and sacrifices so as to provoke and encourage piety in some, to enkindle zeal and fervor in others, to win souls for God, to make them grow in virtue and holiness and thereby to increase the wealth and glory of her Beloved, which is the true Bride's only consideration. Although she is interested in the good and prosperity of all the faithful, she shows special pleasure in seeing the fruits of the valleys; that is, the good works of the humble, and a very singular interest in watching over the *chosen vine,* the symbol of religious families, and also over the *pomegranate trees* which represent privileged souls and all those who can procure the good of others.

It is no doubt because she had just exercised herself in such works of devotion that, without realizing it, she was now advancing so beautifully and impressively (v. 10).

Of verse 12: *Nescivi,* "I did not know, my soul was upset etc.," many varied and obscure interpretations exist. We have already seen that from Fr. Luis de León; and there are others fairly similar which also fail to satisfy. Some suppose that verse 9 does not refer to the Bride but to the ceremony with which the Divine Spouse arrives; and that in verse 10 He replies by telling how He came down from the height of Heaven to visit the precious mystical garden of His Church, and that the richer the merits and fruits of virtues that He saw there, the greater were the rejoicing and the demonstrations of joy. This divine ceremony leaves the Bride terrified (v. 12), and this does not seem to them to be applicable to one who was *terrible as an army.* So they think that verse 9 should be translated not as *Who is this . . . ?* but rather *What is this . . . ?* referring to this ceremony (Gietmann).

The whole of this verse could refer to that growing divine splendor and marvelous power with which the Lord advances (*Hab.* 3,4), Who first appears as the light of dawn, then as that of the moon and of the sun, and eventually appears as an army . . . But it all fits the Bride much better, who is really

formidable with divine virtue. When this virtue is partly taken
from her, she feels the weight of her own weakness and her
nothingness, and thus is brought to rely always on Him Who is
her strength and Who comforts her in such a way that she is
able to do all things in Him (*Phil.* 4,3). In this way she can glory
in the Lord, joining the apostle in saying (II *Cor.* 12,10): *Cum
infirmor, tunc potens sum* . . .

So that it should read: *Who is this* . . . ? just as it should
later (8,5) when it says quite clearly that *she came up leaning
upon her beloved.*

According to St. John of the Cross, by this *Nescivi: I did
not know* the Bride could be meaning that the communication
which she then received from God was so lofty and spiritual and
so far transcended all human means that she found herself
obliged to say:

I entered into *unknowing,*
And there I remained *unknowing,*
Transcending all knowledge.

"The good of the man who reaches this suspension is so
incomparable," says the Ven. Fr. Miguel de la Fuente (*The
Three Lives of Man*, 1,3), "that while on earth he lives in a
peaceful paradise full of spiritual lilies and very beautiful
flowers, of virtues and other Heavenly gifts; here he breathes
the sweet air of divine consolations, and enjoys the true peace
of the Spirit which surpasses all understanding. Here he tastes
the sweet liquids of charity, and all this, says St. Bernard, is the
true *return of the hundred-fold which God promised to His own
in this life,* apart from the glory which He is to give them in
eternity."

Thus the soul enraptured in this heavenly love *does not
know* what is happening . . . and is transported out of herself.

This divine wisdom also causes her to find everything that
is not God strange and foreign. After tasting this wisdom to an
exalted degree she cannot help but exclaim instinctively
Nescivi: I did not know; She feels a lethargy in everything here

below and this prepares her to be a faithful instrument of the Lord, who will become her virtue and wisdom working everything in her and through her.

When explaining the words of Psalm 73, 22: *I was brought to nothing, and I knew not,* the great mystical Doctor writes (*Spirit. Canticle,* Stanza 1), that "the soul, through love, is brought to nothing, and knows nothing save love." Therefore, although in this way she learns to fulfill all her duties with marvelous perfection, she nevertheless fails to understand many of the things that she sees . . ."The reason," he adds later (Stanza 26), "is that the draught of highest wisdom makes her forget all worldly things. It seems that her previous knowledge, and even all the knowledge in the world, in comparison with this enlightment is pure ignorance . . . When the soul is brought into this lofty knowing, she understands by means of it that all other knowledge which has not the taste of this clear perception of truth is not knowledge but ignorance . . . Hence the wise men of God and the wise men of the world are foolish in the eyes of the other, for the one group finds the wisdom and knowledge of God imperceptible, and the other finds the same of the knowledge of the world. Wherefore the knowledge of the world is ignorance to the knowledge of God, and the knowledge of God is ignorance to the knowledge of the world . . . On the other hand, that elevation and immersion of the mind in God, in which the soul is as though carried away and absorbed in love, entirely transformed in God, does not allow attention to any worldly thing. She is not only annihilated before God and estranged from all things, but even from herself . . . Thus, the Bride . . . refers to this unknowing in which she was left by the word, *nescivi* (I did not know) . . . In a way, the soul in this state resembles Adam in the state of innocence, who did not know evil. For she is so innocent that she does not understand evil, nor does she judge anything in a bad light. She will hear very evil things and see them with her own eyes and be unable to understand that they are so, since she does not have within herself the habit of evil by which to judge them; for God, by means of the perfect habit of true wisdom, has destroyed her habitual imperfections and ignorances which include the evil of sin; and so too, in regard to this *she no longer knew anything.*

This expression can also refer to the astonishment the devout soul feels when presented with certain things and actions of some of the Lord's ministers as St. Teresa *(Life,* Ch. 21) and her faithful daughter, St. Thérèsè of the Child Jesus (*Life,* Ch. 6) point out, are often far from being what they ought to be, and from what one would imagine them to be, that is completely holy, and living images of Him Whom they represent. Thus, when she goes down to her Spouse's property to see to His interests and be solictous for His honor and glory, she often encounters nothing but opposition and scorn from those from whom she hoped to receive support, direction and encouragement; she notes how few in actual fact are the faithful workers who seek this divine glory in everything, and have this as their sole consideration in all they do, and she is greatly surprised and astonished and disconcerted. *She does not understand,* nor is she able to understand how preachers, for example, can abandon the simplicity of the Gospel and cease to preach as the apostles preached only Christ and Christ Crucified. She fails to understand, and is surprised and greatly distressed to see, that in the office of preaching and in the pastoral ministry, etc., human prudence is introduced, together with worldly conversations and a certain outward ceremony or pompous display which, while it seeks to add dignity, in fact reduces it. These, then, are the *chariots of Aminadib,* or the *princes of her people who trouble her soul.* Aminadib was, indeed, a descendant of Juda and a predecessor of Our Lord; and the name means either willful people or prince of my people. So, these chariots represent not, as some suppose, the enemy, but the ministers or representatives of God who, instead of encouraging devout souls, frighten and disconcert them as we have just seen, or at least fill them with astonishment and repugnance.

This is what causes the great mystical Doctor to exclaim (*Life*, Ch. XXI): "Oh, what it is for a soul which finds itself in this state (*ecstatic union* with God) to have to return to intercourse with all, to look at this farce of a life and see how ill-organized it is . . . It is wearied by everything; *it cannot run away;* it sees itself chained and held captive . . . It wanders about like one who has been sold into a strange land; its chief trouble is finding so few to join in its complaints and prayers . . . Its mind is now so used to thinking upon *eternal Truths* that anything else seems to it mere child's play. It sometimes enjoys a quiet laugh when it sees serious people . . . making a great fuss about niceties concerning their honor . . . They say that discretion demands this and that the more they have of the authority due to their positions the more good they can do. But the soul knows very well that if they subordinated the authority due to their positions to the love of God they would do more good in a day than they are likely to do as it is in ten years. So the life of this soul continues, a troubled life, never without crosses, but a life of great growth."

When applied to the Church, this verse indicates the agitation and confusion of its good and faithful ministers before the obstinate and pompous opposition that they frequently encounter in unworthy companions who are possessed by the spirit of the world or by other evil influences. Thus, the devout commentator, Fr. Placido Vicente does well to point out: "In spite of the Bride's holy zeal in watching over the harvest of the valleys, the flowers in the vineyard and the fruits of the pomegranate trees, until the end of time she will always find Aminadib's chariots; that is false brothers and unfaithful companions . . . who will intimidate and upset her in the fervent exercise of her duties, in such a way that at times she does not know what is happening to her. What clearer proof of her confusion than the sad state in which she found herself in the stormy days of the Athanasius' and Basils when the noisy din of

the *chariots of Aminadib* (that is of the Arian Bishops) filled
the simplicity and good faith of her children with confusion,
sowing discord among her princes and priests?"

"While the victorious Church," says María de la Dolorosa,
"was examining the virtue of the faithful, new persecutions
arose in the form of heretical writings which oppose its belief,
and which, as though in chariots, carry souls to hell. She is
astonished and disquieted, and would seem to be saying: Is it
possible, after so many solemn testimonies to the truth I
profess, that they can persist in persecuting me?"

But through this opposition, the mystical Bride shows even
more clearly the singular beauty of her heart, now so closely
patterned on the divine Model, and in this way once again
arouses the admiration of all.

These words: *I did not know, my soul was disturbed* can
nevertheless . . . also be attributed to the daughters of
Jerusalem, marveling at the wealth and riches that they see in
the Bride. In this way St. Thomas attributes these words to the
Synagogue: "quae videns," he says, "tantam in Ecclesia gratiam,
inspecta veritate Evangelii, dolet quod non antea cognoverit
fidem Christi. Conturbata est, inquit, anima mea, *propter
quadrigas Aminadab.* Aminadab . . . interpretatur *populus meus
spontaneus.* Ideoque significat Christum, qui populi sui
spontaneus fuit . . . Et est sensus: Conturbata inquit, sum
propter Evangelii subitam praedicationem quae veluti velocis-
simae quadrigae totum subito mundum pervolavit. Et bene hanc
praedicationem non currum, sed quadrigam appellat; quia
Evangelii praedicatio quatuor Evangelistarum auctoritate
consistit, et quatuor Evangelia quasi quadrigae sunt Novi
Testamenti, cui praesidet auriga ipse Christus temperans et
disponens ipse cursum Evangeliorum."

Others understand the *nescivi* to be a kind of holy fear in
the soul, or a distrust and contempt of herself before the heroic
examples of virtue that she has seen in her excursion through
her Spouse's property, and especially in the drivers of these

triumphant chariots of Aminadib. So, confused and reduced to nothing, she seeks to withdraw to where no one will see her. But her friends and disciples cannot suffer her absence and cry out: Return . . .

Fr. Gracian writes: "One of the greatest anxieties and troubles that the soul enamored of Christ has, it that of not knowing whether she is on the right road, especially when she considers the difference between her own life and the lives of the saints and martyrs. She is always troubled by this fear suspicion and worry, and this mars the enjoyment of the divine gifts she receives. *I did not know* . . . As though saying: However many gifts I receive from God . . . I still do not know whether my way of prayer is true or false; I do not know whether I will persevere, for I seem so weak that the slightest temptation will make me fall. I do not know whether my resolutions are true, for every day I make them and then break them. I do not know whether future trials will draw me away from the love of God and from the pleasure I have in communicating with Him . . . From this lack of light springs anguish, displeasure, distrust, fear and suspicion that trouble my soul, especially when I see what Aminadib's charioteers did (to the saints and martyrs). For when Moses divided the waters of the Red Sea to allow the children of Israel to pass through, the first tribe to pass in their chariot was that of Aminadib; and the drivers were not afraid or worried, even though they saw mountains of water before them, that seemed to engulf them. Thus, the saints and martyrs of the Church are very rightly called the chariot drivers of Aminadib. Seeing how different her life and troubles are from those of the saints and martyrs, the soul becomes upset and distressed, not knowing whether she is on the right road or the wrong.

"When suffering like this, she would like to withdraw from the world and go to a desert where no one can see her, not showing anyone her interior or writing down any of her ideas for others to read. For she thinks everything to be false and counterfeit and she does not want to scandalize her neighbors with the example of her wicked life and spirit. But God does not want this, nor are her neighbors pleased, rather they ask her to return and converse with them. She must not retire, but enlighten them as to what is passing in her soul, other saints have done. They plead: *return, return* . . . as though saying: O devout soul who has a life of prayer, do not hide, but return and converse with us that we may know what is happening within you, and imitate you."

v. 13)   *Return, return, O Shulamite,*
             return, return, that we might gaze on you.

        This is spoken by the chorus of friends, symbolizing most devout souls, both beginners and advanced, who would always like to have at their side the true saints and the great servants of God that they have had the good fortune to know and converse with, so as better to contemplate and admire their excellent virtues and divine heroism; and to derive greater benefit from the examples of their lives and from their holy conversation. This choir could also be the choir of angels who, wondering at the beauty of this worthy Bride of the Lamb, wish to contemplate her graces and perfections at their pleasure. They call her *Shulamite,* the name derived from *Solomon,* meaning *peaceful,* for she is the Bride of this divine Solomon Whose qualities she shares; thus she can and does pacify, frequently establishing peace between men, and peace also between men and God.

        The most devout Fr. Hoyos tells (*Life,* p. 86) how in one of the communications of the Word to his soul, he was crowned with the very crown of the Divine Spouse. And when the saints who were present saw this, they exclaimed: *Return, O happy soul; return and let us see you with this richest crown!* . . .

Synopsis

The Spouse asks the daughters of Jerusalem what they have seen in the Shulamite, and turning to her He pays her the most wonderful praise, extolling her from her feet to her head (v. 1-6). Admiring her perfection and beauty He compares her to a dove, seeing how she triumphs over everything, and her breasts to clusters of grapes, since she can now fill many with holy intoxication by her teaching (v. 7-8). He adds that He is going to gather the fruits of her victories; but the friends of the Bride, it seems, interrupt to praise her wonderful milk and the fragrance of her life that they received from her. They meditate on the sweetness of her addresses that are worthy of delighting the Beloved (v. 9-10). She repeats that she belongs wholly to Him Who so generously responds to her (v. 11); thus, considering the Spouse's riches to be her own, she invites Him to go out with her and lodge in the houses of the country, and see the state of His property and enjoy the fruit of her self-sacrificing love (v. 12-13). The profit derived from these visits (v. 14).

THE SPOUSE

v. 1)   *What will you see in the Shulamite*
        but choirs of squadrons?
v. 2)   *How beautiful your steps are*
        with shoes, O prince's daughter!
        The joints of your thighs are like bracelets

v. 3) *worked by a master hand.*[a]
Your breast is like a rounded cup
which never lacks drink.
Your stomach is like a heap of wheat
surrounded with lilies.[b]

v. 4) *Your two breasts are like two young roes that are twins.*

v. 5) *Your neck is like an ivory tower.*
Your eyes, like the pools of Heshbon[c]
that are by the gate of Bathrabbim.
Your nose is like the tower of Lebanon
which looks toward Damascus.

v. 6) *Your head is like Carmel*
and the hair of your head like the purple
of a king, bound in channels.[d]

v. 7) *How beautiful you are and how pleasant,*
O dearest one in delights.[e]

v. 8) *Your stature is like a palm tree,*[f]
and your breasts like clusters of grapes.

v. 9) *I said: I will go up to the palm tree*

a.   Hebrew: "Why do you look at the Shulamite as if you were looking at the dance of choirs (or the dance of Mahamaim)? How beautiful your feet are in your sandals, O Prince's daughter! The shape — or pillar — of your thighs is like that of a necklace, the handiwork of an artist." The title of *Prince's daughter* can be given her because she really is a princess, or because she is quite rightly to be considered *noble, distinguished* or *generous-hearted* and *magnanimous* — which is what the word *Nadib* means, translated here as *Prince*. In Hebrew it is customary to use the expression *son (or daughter) of something* when this quality belongs to the subject in a special way.

b.   Fr. Arintero writes: We translate it in this way out of consideration for certain ears which are at times overly delicate.

c.   Heshbon, the famous city in Trans Jordan (cf. *Num.* 21, 25-30). Its large pools are mentioned in II *Machabees* 12, 16

d.   Hebrew: "Your head is like Carmel — and the hair of your head is like purple; a king is held captive in the tresses." It seems to allude to the custom of tying the tresses with strings of purple. Amat translates: "and her hair like fringes of royal purple."

e.   Hebrew: O my love in the midst of my delights! or, O my dearest daughter of delights!

f.   Hebrew: Your form or disposition.

and will pick its fruits;[g]
and your breasts will be like clusters of the vine,
and the scent of your mouth like that of apples.

THE FRIENDS OF THE BRIDE

v. 10)   *Your throat like choice wine,*[h]
worthy for my beloved to drink,
and to be savored between his lips and teeth[i]

THE BRIDE

v. 11)   *I am my beloved's,*
and his affection is for me.

v. 12)   *Come, my beloved, let us go into the country*
and dwell in country-houses.

v. 13)   *In the early morning let us go to the vineyards,*
let us see if the vine has blossomed,
if the flowers produce fruit,
if the pomegranate trees are yet in flower.
There I will give you my love.

v. 14)   *The mandrakes already yield their scent.*
At our doors (there are) all kinds of fruits,
the new and the old, my beloved,
I shall keep them for you.

Exposition

v. 1)   *What will you see in the Shulamite*
but choirs of squadrons?

Some attribute this to the Bride herself, and others to the
friends who follow behind in wonder, looking at her as though
she alone formed an harmonious choir, a choir of war-

---

g.   Hebrew: "I will grasp the clusters." The Septuagint: "the tops"
h.   Hebrew: "Your palate." Since the pronoun is in the feminine, the words are
definitely spoken to the Bride by the friends, or perhaps by the Spouse
Himself.
i.   Hebrew: "Which runs sweet or straight for my beloved — (or through my
palate) — and which passes through the lips of those who sleep (or between
my teeth and lips)."

experienced squadrons that sing hymns of praise to God,
vanquish enemies and put them to flight.

If these words were spoken by the Bride it would mean
that she was shying away from applause, as though saying that
they could not see in her anything worthy of admiration except
what was purely the result of her Beloved's generosity, as for
example the guarding and protection of the angelic choirs with
which He favored her. We believe that they are spoken by the
Spouse Himself, as He begins in this way the new sequence of
praise that follows, in which He extols the singular beauty of
the mystical Bride; that is to say, of the Blessed Virgin, the
Catholic Church and the holy soul, describing her from her feet
to her head in such a detailed, shocking and apparently, such a
realistic way that it was undoubtedly done so deliberately by
the Holy Spirit, so that, without pausing over anything material,
it being unworthy of the loftiness of this Song, we might
straightway transcend the humble symbol and enter the exalted
regions of the great mysteries that are symbolized by it.

This is the most sublime praise that has been paid to the
Immaculate Virgin, and therefore the most perfect and
wonderful model that could be offered to us, serving as a very
clear mirror in which all souls who truly wish to follow her
closely can see themselves.

Those who, by renouncing themselves and constantly
fighting against the three great concupiscences that plague the
world (I *John* 2, 16), finally triumph over all their enemies and
eventually become established in true peace. Like Mary and our
holy Mother the Church they deserve to bear the most honored
name of Brides of the King of Peace, of *Shulamite*, that is
Peaceful whose mission it is to pacify, pouring everywhere a
thousand graces and blessings from Heaven. Such a soul as this
is capable of saving a whole city, a whole province, a whole
nation; and God uses them for the edification of His Church,
for the destruction of Satan's empire, for the confusion of all
His enemies and for His own recreation. For in them He has

ineffable delights, thus compensating all the insults and ingratitude that He receives from sinners and from the luke-warm.

In order to imitate Mary better or to imitate the soul who is closely modeled on her, these maidens (or pious souls who long to be consecrated to Him and to deserve to be called His brides), wish to gaze at her, and turn towards her again and again. This pleases the Divine Lover, for He Himself begins to praise her, saying to them: *What will you see in the Shulamite but choirs of squadrons?*

Words worthy of such a Lover! Words that are as sublime and delightful to those who succeed in understanding them, as they are shocking perhaps to ears that are unrefined. They summarize all that can be said of the mystical Bride, and all that He will go on to detail as He describes her part by part, directing His attention to her so as to applaud and entertain her with the greatest affection and enthusiasm.

She is very rightly compared to "a choir of squadrons", for she certainly appears to be one, to judge by the way in which she is continually singing the most pleasing hymns of praise to God, at all times and in all places lifting up her pure hands towards Him in ceaseless prayer, while with her words and her exemplary life she wins countless hearts for Him and confounds and overcomes the cunning and power of her enemies; so that she alone comes to form a squadron, through the sum of her virtues which truly constitute an "angelic militia".

"In the Church," says Maria de la Dolorosa, "these military choirs are its martyrs, who, assisted and comforted by the grace of Jesus Christ, leapt for joy amid the most terrible torments and sang hymns of praise to the holy name of God."

The Hebrew has it in the plural: What are you looking at so carefully, as if it were the dance of *Manhanaim*? This seems to allude to the two camps of angels pointed out to Jacob in the place which he called by this name (*Gen.* 32,2). Thus, the Bride comes to be compared to these choirs of Heavenly squadrons.

This comparison praises in a very special way the true squadrons of the Holy Church formed by its most zealous ministers, and by all souls, who, rising above what is worldly, live only for the glory of God and for the good of their neighbors. This is especially true in the Religious Orders which are completely dedicated to working for the good of Christianity, that is to say, to spreading the Kingdom of God and to bringing about the triumph of His justice; for these souls truly form *sicut choros castrorum*.

"Just as the sweetness of the choir," remarks Fr. La Puente (*Perf. Est. Ecl.*, tr. 1, Ch. 8), "and the strength of the army consist in the harmony of the singers and soldiers, so the sweetness and strength of the ecclesiastical ministers and the whole success of their apostolate, rests on the harmony of the hearts united with one another and with Christ, Who is called the peaceful King. Since she is His Bride, the Church is also called peaceful, and it is right that those who form such an important part of her should fulfill what her name indicates. But because peace in this life is never without a war whereby peace is preserved, they must fight like courageous soldiers against the enemies who would seek to break this peace and destroy the harmony. They generously mortify all disordered passions and affections which are the cause of discord, especially ambition for prestige and honor, desire for worldly interests and wealth, coveting of other person's progress and prosperity and anger and revenge for one's own injuries and humiliations.

This sweet Guest continually dwells in the soul who is united with God and who is possessed by the Holy Spirit; and "as sovereign Artist playing as though on an incomparable harp," as St. Gregory Nazianzen says, "with His delicate touch He creates harmonies that are more than angelic and which only He can produce." Thus, in the heart of the Shulamite, of the soul who is truly *Preaceful* like Mary, each thought, each affection, each feeling, each movement or work however small, each breath, each sign, each desire, each prayer, each look, each longing and aspiration, by her perfect faithfulness to grace goes to form a divine harmony, or a series of divine harmonies or concertos whose delightful, sacred melodies give great pleasure to the Lord and cause Him to forget the transgressions of sinners. This is the *silent music* which, according to St. John of the Cross, is continually to be heard in the *sounding solitude* of the enamored heart which has triumphed over all its enemies and been established in true peace. Oh, if only there were an abundance of these wonderful Shulamites Who thus bring comfort to all, even to the divine Heart of Jesus Itself, outraged by our sins . . . ! We would then certainly not be menanced by such terrible punishments, nor would we see ourselves plunged into such bloody strife, but would enjoy that peace of Jesus which the world cannot give . . .

"Feeling my extreme weakness and lack of virtue," writes Sr. Teresa of J.M. (*Comment.* 1, p. 45), "I heard interiorly . . . *Quid videbitis in Sulumite* . . . and my soul wondered more and more that this should be said about her . . . and again humbled herself . . . I was given to understand that nothing of mine had remained except my body and that there, in some way, Christ Our Lord had placed His soul, together with all the squadrons and armies of His virtues; and that within it was His Divinity with all the squadrons of His attributes and divine perfections, so that who could see anything else in me *nisi choros castrorum*? Then my soul rested in great peace and silence, feeling intimate friendship with God and a love communicated by the Holy Spirit with which to love Him . . . *Terribilis ut castrorum acies ordinata.* Not only can choirs of armies be seen in you, but you yourself are terrible like the armies and squadrons, possessing as you do all My divine perfections and attributes . . ."

To this general eulogy the Divine Lover adds a very detailed expression of praise in which He extols one by one the principle beauties and perfections of His mystical Bride. Before He praised her by beginning with her head and working down to her feet; now He studies her from her feet to her head, beginning with the beauty of her wonderful footwear and of her superhuman step.

"He begins," says Fr. Luis de León, "with her feet whose lightness and swiftness He has just witnessed, and He works up to her head, going from the least to the greatest, which is a splendid way to give praise." Thus He says:

v. 2)   *How beautiful your feet are in your shoes!*

Or else: *How graceful your walk is, O prince's daughter* (or generous and noble-hearted one). Her feet are, indeed, beautiful and her steps are graceful, since they are perfectly ordered by faithful obedience to the will of God, made beautiful by charity and directed, like those of Mary, in the Visitation, to seek the good of souls and to make known the glories of her Heavenly Spouse, bringing many to share in some way in the lights she has received in contemplation. This beauty is highlighted by that of her footwear, formed no doubt, following the examples of the saints, by *charity* and *humility* and *evangelical* poverty. For it is on the foundation of a very strong love of God, of true self-knowledge and of a complete disregard for all that is earthly that a holy apostlelate must be founded, so that the soul can then be concerned only with what effects the greater glory of God and the good of her neighbor. All who see the minister of the divine word, the bearer of the message of peace, raised up above all human misery and conversing more in Heaven than on earth, cannot help but exclaim: *How beautiful on the mountains are the feet of one who brings good news, who heralds peace, brings happiness and proclaims salvation!* (*Is.* 52, 7).

"What are these feet," asks Fr. La Puente (*Perf. Est. Ecl.,* tr. 4, Ch. 2), "but the two affections of the love of God and of one's neighbor, and the steps taken by them in contemplation and in preaching, climbing the mountain so as to contemplate and descending to the plains so as to preach? He quite rightly praises the beauty of her feet and not of her face, mouth or hands, because her beauty in other works proceeds from these affections and steps. So when Our Lord praises the Bride who is now perfect, He begins with her feet, saying: *O how beautiful are your steps . . . because of the footwear* with which you cover your feet! This refers, as St. Gregory says, to the witness of the saints who died for the love of God and their neighbor, with which she encourages herself to continue her steps.

Thus, wherever the mystical Bride, the Shulamite or *Peaceful One* goes, she always carries on the mission of the Holy Spirit Who vivifies, moves and possesses her, producing in her His twelve most precious fruits in great abundance, to crown her one day with twelve stars. In this way her mission is wholly one of peace, charity, kindness, faith, joy, modesty . . . chastity. She is called a Prince's daughter to denote her divine filiation which is visible in her upright, beautiful and majestic walk . . .

The blessed steps of these superhuman souls whom the Lord heaps with such blessings of sweetness, virtue and fortitude to make them worthy keepers of His honor and propagators of His Kingdom, are eventually admired and praised by all, for all come to share in some degree in her favors.

"How tremendous will be the might," declares St. John of the Cross (*Spirit. Cant.,* Stanza 30), "of this soul that is all clothed with strong virtues and has them so fastened and interwoven that no ugliness or imperfection can get between them. By its strength every virtue adds strength to the soul; by its beauty it adds beauty, by its value it enriches her, and by its majesty it imparts power and grandeur to her. How marvelous, then, to the spiritual eye will this Bride-soul appear, at the right hand of the King, her Bridegroom, in the charm of these gifts. *How beautiful are your steps in sandals, O prince's daughter . . .* He calls her 'prince's daughter' to denote her royal inheritance. If He calls her beautiful because of her sandals, what will be the beauty afforded by her garment! Not only does her beauty in this robe of flowers stir one's admiration, but the strength she possesses from the orderly arrangement of these flowers and the interspersion of both emeralds and innumerable divine gifts fills one with terror. On this account the Groom declares of her ... *You are terrible* ... As these virtues and gifts of God give refreshment by their spiritual fragrance, so too, when they are joined together in the soul, they impart strength by their substance."

These mysterious sandals in Mary represent her most ardent, fragrant and loving affections, together with most perfect detachment from the world and from herself, whereby she was always able to walk completely pure and unsullied, without the slightest stain, always progressing in the paths of perfect justice and holiness of life, doing in all things what was most pleasing to God, without ever deviating a single step to one side or to the other, and without ever picking up even an atom of worldly dust on the soles of her blessed feet. Thus was her walk always extremely noble and *distinguished,* as befitted this happy daughter of the King of kings and Prince of peace Who, being pleased with her, heaped upon her glory and riches. He tells us: *I walk in the ways of justice and enrich those who love Me ... (Prov.* 8, 20-21).

The Wise Man says (*Wisdom* 10, 10), "the Lord leads the just along straight paths, He shows him the Kingdom of God, and teaches him the knowledge of holy things." Those who are in all things led and moved by the Holy Spirit, the very Essence of Love, are in all truth the children of God (*Rom.* 8, 14), for it is the beatitude of the peacemaker (*Matt.* 5, 9). The detached soul is promised the joy of true peace that belongs to the sons of the Most High; thus she will always be a peacemaker, bringing gladness to all those who approach her, always carrying the message of peace and love everywhere.

Since Sacred Scripture normally uses the feet to represent the affections of the soul making her move in one direction or another, when the Blessed Virgin appeared at Lourdes wearing only two golden roses on her feet, she undoubtedly wanted to reveal a great mystery of her love and purity to us, showing us how her steps were always directed and ordered by her most perfect love for God and her neighbor, symbolized by the gold; how in her walk she left everything perfumed and embalmed with her divine fragrance, represented by the roses . . . In this way she teaches her faithful children how they must always proceed in imitating her, spreading everywhere the heavenly fragrance of the sweet scent of Jesus and exercising this two-fold love, since this is what is most lacking in a world that is so corrupt, so divorced from God and so devoured by satanic hatred.

He then praises the most perfect obedience of the true Shulamite, and her wounderful submission to the motions and touches of the Holy Spirit. The Bride dwells always in the peace of Jesus, which is achieved through the constant victories of her complete obedience. This lovely model can always be offered to all who make a vow or promise of obedience by which to learn truly to renounce themselves, their own judgment and will; to relinquish even their own ideas, endeavors, initiatives and human ways of proceeding in prayer and everywhere, to become gradually possessed and governed by the Spirit of the Lord.

v. 2)   *The joints of your thighs are like bracelets,*
            worked by a master hand.

This verse tells us that the soul is now perfect in all things. By her victorious obedience she is ready for everything, since she has been elevated to *spiritual marriage* with the Divine Word. Her knees are as ready to bend in adoration before the divine Majesty as they are to run after the lost sheep and to work with zeal for the glory of her Beloved. Who was the consumate Artist and brilliant Craftsman Who succeeded in achieving this masterpiece, but the Sovereign Spirit of wisdom and knowledge, counsel and intelligence, Who polished and chiseled her until she became a docile instrument in His hands to do all that He might ask of her?

She is now ever attentive to the inspirations of this divine

Consoler and Teacher of all truth, so as never to distress Him, nor resist in the slightest His sweet motions and delicate touches. Wherever the impulse of this Holy Spirit leads her, she follows, without ever turning back (*Ezechial* 1, 12), without deviating or hesitating for a single moment. When Mary was made Mother of the Word, see how promptly she followed the divine impulse of charity, rose up and went out to help her cousin Elizabeth . . . !

In the Church this well-ordered form of the legs and thighs represents, according to St. Gregory, the harmony of the preachers who unite and lead the Christian people.

After this brief praise of the soul's complete detachment from all worldly things and from herself, which allows her to walk in a direct path towards God, and in all things to obey the voice and follow the motions of the Holy Spirit; this wonderful *Song* begins to extol in an incomparable way the most perfect chastity and inviolable integrity of the mystical Bride, a perfection that must be sought by all souls who aspire to be His Bride. These virgins contract by the vow of chastity a very special union with the divine Word, Whom they must always follow, *wherever He goes,* thus coming to possess Him in such a way that they can even communicate Him to others.

To prove this, the Song uses two mysterious symbols that are apt to disconcert all human modesty, but which are as noble and meaningful as they would appear to be humble and vulgar. These symbols are that of the cup and of the heap of wheat.

v. 3)　　　*Your breast is like a rounded cup,*
　　　　　which never lacks drinks.

This cup is said to be "rounded" to denote her faultless perfection; and "never lacking" because she never allows the inestimable treasures she possesses to empty away.

Since both the original and the Vulgate expressly mention the humble organ whereby the child is fed from the maternal breast, "this comparison," says Scio, "shows the great care the Church takes in giving her children the necessary food."

With respect to each soul, this verse undoubtedly indicates the abundant baptismal graces which heap riches and blessings upon her, creating within her a kind of *fountain welling to eternal life* (*John* 4,14), giving her the being and life proper to an adopted daughter of God, and enabling her, with the infused virtues and gifts of the Holy Spirit, to one day reach the state of the perfect man, that is to say, "the measure of the fullness of Chirst," and thus celebrate mystical marriage with Him. The Heavenly Spouse, here praises that beginning of divine life which has reached such an exalted degree in His worthy Bride; for being a true *sealed fountain,* she has succeeded in becoming a mystical *fountain for gardens* (*Song* 4,15), her heart sending forth those mysterious *rivers* that He Himself describes through St. John (7,38).

When applied to the Holy Virgin, this comparison seems to refer to the Immaculate Conception when she became so full of grace that she deserved to be called *blessed among all other women,* for her fullness, like an immense overflowing cup can be shared not just by many but all.

In the eyes of God, her blessed soul was a most precious cup, full of the most exquisite drinks with which she could always satisfy her own thirst, that of others, and also refresh her Divine Spouse. It was always full and rounded because of the perfect faithfulness with which she responded to the graces and used the gifts received, and because of the inexpressible integrity of this most pure Virgin, whose capacity God Himself continually increased to go on filling her more and more making her a living store of graces, that all might ceaselessly receive from her as from an incomparable *fountain for gardens and from a well of living waters that flow down impetuously from Lebanon.*

Finally, applied to the Church, it possibly refers to her *embryonic* or nascent state in the Cenacle where, on the day of Pentecost the Spirit of Love poured Himself with exceeding abundance over her, bestowing lights, graces and gifts upon her, enrapturing her with divine delights and favoring her with the tenderest Mother (*Is.* 66, 11-13).

What are we to see here, but the ineffable consolations with which the Divine Paraclet nourishes, comforts and refreshes the heavenly offspring recently born from the "imaculate womb of the divine font" (*John* 1, 13; 3, 5), urging them to proceed as new born babes, *sicut modo genitit* (I *Peter* 2, 2), until the light appears fully and Christ is formed within them? (*Gal.* 4, 19).

v. 3)   *Your stomach is like a heap of wheat,*
                       surrounded with lilies.

This wheat symbolizes the Holy Eucharist, which is the mystical *Bread of Life* and the precious *wheat of the chosen* which the Holy Virgin grew and prepared for us in her pure breast, together with that sweet wine that produces virgins (*Zech.* 9, 14). Thus, It is surrounded with lilies not only in the Virgin because of her immaculate purity, but in all those who worthily receive It as true nourishment for their souls, whereby to grow in grace and virtue. There is a superabundance for all, symbolized by the *heap of wheat* or granary. Provided that souls offer no resistance It will communicate Its divine purity, according to the disposition of each soul. The Eucharist, indeed, intimately unites the Christian with Christ, and setting the copy against the model, It produces a wonderful impression in the soul, stamping her with new features of divine filiation and bringing her to be more and more closely patterned on the Savior. It is like a divine ferment which transforms us into Its own substance and communicates to us Its Own properties, so that we can then communicate them to those around us. There, wholly and without reserve, Jesus Christ Himself surrenders Himself to our souls, that they too might surrender themselves to Him in the same way, and, finding all their nourishment in Him, might live only in Him and by Him in a life that is truly divine. In this way, possessing the very Word of God, the true "Living Bread that came down from Heaven", they have a kind of spiritual granary in their hearts; and with this spiritual *Living Bread,* that is, with words of life, they are to feed all the hungry and needy who approach them, bringing them to breathe an air that is as though scented with lilies. As we shall see, that is how, with their continual aspirations, they can be always communicating to other souls not only the Word of God, but also the Holy Spirit with His most precious gifts. For, since this Divine Word, as St. Thomas says, is "a Word Who breathes Love," all who receive Him are enkindled in Him.

The same is even more true of Holy Church which, with such love and respect, keeps this *Bread of Life* in the ciborium, as though in the very center of her heart, where fervent and pure souls, today represented by the *Marys* and *Johns* and the *worshippers* in general, try to approach Him like so many lilies, standing guard near this *Bread of Life.*

By these two symbols, the *rounded cup,* that is, her perfection and fullness resulting from her inviolable faithfulness and integrity, and that of the *heap of wheat surrounded by lilies,* Christ makes known to His faithful Bride the abundant and pure food with which she was nourished in her spiritual infancy and adolescence, and with which she herself in her maturity, as a true mother, must try to nourish the many souls that she must raise for Him. First of all, she gives them only drinks which overflow from this *full cup* and which are the only proper food for this early age; then she gives them "the food of adults", that is, the *Bread of the strong* with which they can come to be such, modeling themselves on the suffering Christ. She will try to feed each one according to his state and condition, as the apostle said (I *Cor.* 3, 1-2): *Being infants in Christ, what I fed you with was milk not solid food, for you were not ready for it.* Solid food is for perfect souls (*Heb.* 5,14) who, with the strength they receive from the mysterious Bread of Life, can, like Elias, reach the holy mountain of God, where they will receive the virtue and zeal they need to win and raise many spiritual children for Him.

St. Gregory says this mystical *breast* of the Church represents holy preachers who, with celestial drink, nourish the little ones from their own overflowing abundance.

The belly or stomach of the Church, according to Origin, refers to Sacred Scripture, a kind of spiritual granary, from which the holy Doctors have been able to extract bread, and surround it with a beautiful, lily-like doctrine to feed our souls."

Ezekiel criticized the Synagogue for its despicable origin, saying that its father had been an Amorite and its mother a Hittite; when it was born its umbilical cord had not been cut, nor had it been washed with water . . . (*Ezek.* 16, 3-4). But the Church, the contary, is here presented, says Petit, as a very beautiful queen, a prince's daughter, and distinguished among many. "Her breast is full of a wonderful liquid, denoting the sacrament of baptism whereby we are elevated to the condition of children of God and are cleansed of the stains of the children of Adam . . . The Church is a chaste and fertile Bride who carries within her the *wheat of the chosen,* the sacraments, the doctrine of Jesus Christ, and all the faithful who are like a heap of pure, choice wheat with which to fill the granaries of Heaven."

Acervus . . . "The symbol of fertility and chastity. The Church is a virgin and the mother of so many children." (*Filion*).

Thus, these two symbols, which at first sight seem so surprising, give us a very concise account of the inestimable treasures and spiritual riches that fill the heart of the divine Shulamite, of the mystical Bride who, in her inexhaustible supplies, always finds some way of satisfying with *the water of salutary wisdom and the bread of life and understanding* (*Si.* 15,3), the many hungering and thirsting after justice who frequently come to her, especially when there are so many children asking for bread and there is no one to give it to them. For man does not live by material bread alone, but by every word which comes from the mouth of God (*Deut.* 8,3).

Today, when this spiritual livelihood has become extremely scarce, much more so than any other; when our Lord seems to have sent to the world, as the prophet Amos declared (8,11), a great hunger and thirst, not for bread and water but for the true word of God which, as in the time of Samuel (I *Kings* 3, 1), has become highly *valued* and extremely "precious" to us. Today more than ever, the world needs these wonderful followers of the Divine Lamb called Shulamites, these fountains of blessings, these generous souls who have completely surrendered themselves to the Lord and in Him have found true peace and every treasure. These treasures, contained in this mysterious *cup* and the spiritual *granary,* can satisfy or quench this great hunger and thirst that we suffer, purify with their fragrant lilies the pestilential air that stifles us, and resist the wave of filth which, in the form of indecent fashions and customs, the dragon seeks to hurl at us (*Rev.* 12, 12-17).

In this way, as worthy Brides of Jesus Christ, they succeed in raising a great many children for Him in complete health and in a wonderful atmosphere of purity, thus deserving, like Mary and Holy Church, the honorable name of *spiritual mothers* or *mothers of souls* and as such, also "ever-virgin mothers".

Note that this description of the Bride (v. 12) offers a certain analogy with the description she herself made earlier of the Spouse (5, 14-15). In the earlier example it was the fullness of His grace, His majesty and His firmness that were being praised; while here, it is the Bride's beauty, purity and fertility.

v. 4)   *Your breasts are like two young roes that are twins.*

We have already explained (Ch. 4, v. 5) what these breasts signify: the love of God and zeal for the good of souls, inseparable in the mystical Bride. These two loves are twins because they are born simultaneously from the same principle, divine charity poured into our hearts by the Holy Spirit, Who makes them both graceful and swift as roes. The soul enraptured with divine love feels a consuming zeal and a

mother's desire to rush to the needs of her neighbors, ready to
sacrifice herself for them and for many other children in the
Lord. In this way she becomes such a source of goodness and
such a providential help that, at times she alone is able to save
whole cities and kingdoms.

v. 5)   *Your neck is like an ivory tower.*

This indicates the strength here attained by the soul who is
not rough and coarse but pleasing and beautiful and, through the
sum of virtues that this presupposes, refined and well-polished
like ivory. All this is the result of her purity, her submission to
the divine will, her simplicity, humility, and fortitude. Moreover,
her constancy in prayer gives her, together with her magnanimity, this delightful purity and splendor, this mysterious
firmness and tranquillity by which she meets all the attacks of
her enemies without suffering any harm, but rather vanquishes
them.

To compare the neck to an ivory tower, says Fr. Luis de
León, "is to call it tall, smooth and well-made, the qualities
needed to be beautiful... The neck, into which food is
received and speech emitted, represents in the Church her
preachers who receive the breath of the Holy Spirit and
communicate it to others through preaching. Therefore they
must be like an ivory tower, that is, their doctrine must be firm,
pure as white ivory, without stain or falsehood. They must be
fearless, failing neither by avoiding to preach openly what they
should, nor by obscuring the simplicity and purity of sacred
doctrine with affected coloring."

For this reason, as St. Gregory says, "they must be tall
through contemplation, strong through the exercise of good
works, and beautiful through the gift of wisdom."

"The Church is compared to a tower of the purest, most
delicate and precious ivory," writes Sr. Teresa (*Com.* XII),
"because it is very tall, in which contemplative souls gaze upon
and reflect the glory of the Divinity, as St. Paul says (II *Cor.* 3,
18) ... Brought to maturity in this tower, they are so intimate

with God that it seems they can almost see Him face to face; that is, *with faces unveiled*. Contemplating the glory of the Lord Who is Master of this tower, they become transformed into His image from light to light; that is, from the resplendent beauty of the Sacred Humanity to that of the Divinity abiding within them."

The Blessed Virgin can also, and even more fittingly, be likened to the *neck of the Church* who united us with our Head, Jesus Christ, for she is the true "ivory tower" and stronghold where the whole Christian nation can find safety, protection and true refuge. It is not without reason we call her *Refugium Christianorum*. She is so lofty a tower as to be the true *Gate of Heaven*.

> *Your eyes, like the pools of Heshbon*
> *that are by the gate of Bathrabbim.*

In her eyes, many souls can see themselves as though in a very clear mirror; for, just as the sky is reflected in lakes and pools, so the eyes of the saints see within their own souls the glorious image of Him Who they ceaselessly contemplate, while others, in this same light see their own imperfections and those things they need to correct or achieve. We can say that God Himself takes pleasure and delight in gazing at this crystal-clear mirror of the pure and fervent soul, wherein He sees His Own glory reflected. He is especially delighted when looking at the eyes of Mary. How Jesus must see Himself in them . . . ! How He must also see Himself in the eyes of those who faithfully reproduce His divine image . . . ! How He watches to see that this image is not stained or disfigured . . . !

"It seemed to me," says Ven. Mariana de San José (*Life* 1,2, Ch. 15), "that my soul became a mirror wherein God was gazing at Himself, where the Three Divine Persons saw Themselves, and I saw Them, within my soul, made to His image. I myself seemed to disappear. This vision of the Lord afforded me great advantage, for He was in my soul with His resplendent light. It seemed to me that He was happy there, giving orders as Lord, and working mercies with wonderful unheard of and unspeakable glory and joy...If only it were known ... what it is for any of these "apples of His eye" to be touched by any stain, thus marring His beloved image . . . !"

Your eyes like the pools of Heshbon ... "It is as though saying," writes Fr. Gracian, "let your intentions be pure and clear, full of many noble desires, even if, taking into consideration your strength, condition and health, you do not put them into practice ..." He compares them to these fountains (pools), because it is from a pure and lucid motive that the faculties must extract the waters of merit. Calling that gate 'the daughter of the multitude', understanding by this the many people who would gather in that square on market-day, signifies that, even if the soul can do very little, she should not limit herself by repressing her desires to ask God for great things, but rather propose to do them if it were in her power. Without leaving her convent, a religious can, in her cell . . . have the intention of converting all the souls in the world."

> *Your nose is like the tower of Lebanon,*
> *which looks toward Damascus.*

This tower served as a watch-tower to keep he people of God safe from the invasion of their enemies, the kings of Syria, whose capital was Damascus. Thus souls who reach the mystical betrothal become like sentinels of the Church. The Lord usually communicates to them a most delicate *spiritual sense of smell* with which, in their innocence, they not only distinguish between spirits, but discover even the most distant dangers, and, even scarcely recognizing them, they already stand guard lest they be taken by surprise. In this way they keep themselves safe and teach others to be vigilant and defend themselves. We read in *Ecclesiasticus* (37, 18) that *the spiritual man's soul often forewarns him better than seven watchmen perched on a watchtower.*

"In Hebrew," observes Fr. Gracian, "Lebanon means whiteness, and Damascus, blood. The devout soul of true discretion chooses pure works to do and pure words to speak, manifesting that dangers come not from the spirit but from flesh and blood, so as to combat them, being always on the frontier against whatever can do harm."

v. 6)   *Your head is like Carmel*
             and the hair of your head like the purple
             of a king, bound in channels.

This means through contemplation your head is beautiful, elegant and lifted high, like Carmel, a lofty, luxuriant mountain, rich in fruits and pasture. All your works and enterprises and the noble ideas or thoughts and intentions which adorn you like a beautiful head of hair are *like the purple of the king,* for they are dyed and made precious by the blood which runs in streams through the very hair and beard of Christ. For this reason each one of your hairs can capture a heart and, as the Hebrew text says, does capture the heavenly King Himself. Just as this famous mountain rises majestically above all the neighboring mountains and can be seen from far out at sea, so this soul rises above her companions and at times can be discerned from afar by those sailing in the stormy sea of the world, serving as a protection and guide for them. Also as the orchards and vineyards extend in profusion across the sides and slopes of the mountain like seductive locks of beautiful hair falling in wonderful waves down the neck and face, in like manner rich and abundant fruits of holiness bedeck this fertile head, fruits whose delicate scent and sweet taste attract and win countless souls and fill the Spouse with much delight.

When applied to the Church, writes María Dolorosa, "her invisible Head is Jesus Christ, Who, because of the splendor of His Divinity and the eminence of His Humanity, is compared to Carmel. The visible head is the Pontiff at Rome to whom Jesus Christ, when making him His Vicar, gave spiritual dominion over all the earth. The head of hair represents the faithful who, united to Christ through love, look like a royal purple cloth tied and placed in the dyers' vats, that is, dyed with the merits of

His Precious Blood. As the hair adorns the head, so the fervent, faithful souls adorn the Head of the Church."

v. 7)   *How beautiful you are and how pleasant,*
             O dearest one in delights!

After having praised in such a varied and richly colored way each part of His sweet Bride, and admitting defeat before such beauty, the Spouse ends with this wonderful phrase which summarizes everything, as though saying: "why go on enumerating your graces, for it overpowers one to see how irresistable you are in everything; in all your words and deeds, how sweet and beautiful and delightful, for are you not the very pinnacle of sweetness and beauty? (Fr. Luis de León).

What are these delights in which she appears so beautiful to the eyes of all and so pleasing to those of her sweet Beloved . . . ? This is something the world cannot grasp or understand; it is understood only by those who have experienced it, for it is the true *hidden manna*. The soul enamored of the Divine Lamb enjoys the greatest delights precisely where she encounters the purest suffering. The cross of Christ, considered scandalous by the Jews and follish by the gentiles, this is the fountain of delights for the soul who has been enraptured in the mystical wine-cellars of the Spouse . . . !

It is there that she becomes modeled on the Crucified Christ and gathers the fruit of His victories. It is there that she prepares herself to enter into intimacy with Him, and merits sharing in His ineffable secrets, receiving with unspeakable pleasure the knowledge of His mysteries, thus enjoying the incomparable delights of His loving company and tasting the sweetness which He has reserved for those that fear Him. These sweetnesses enable her to follow Him to the very summit of His holy mountain which, as St. Gregory says, it would be impossible to reach without enjoying to some degree these divine delights.

The worldly see only the bitterness of the cross, and do not even suspect the ineffable sweetness contained within the

bitter shell of its precious fruits ... But devout souls who
sincerely contemplate and admire the singular beauty that these
privileged Brides of the Divine Lamb receive in the intimate
communications with God, suspect and discern something of the
sweetness of the cross and therefore truly begin to embrace and
bless it. Thus their greatest delights consist in loving Jesus, trying
to win all possible glory and pleasure for Him, never refusing
Him any sacrifice. For they know that He has His pleasures, as
St. Margaret Mary says (*Works*, Vol. 2), "in finding *love,
suffering and silence* in a heart".

v. 8)   *Your stature is like a palm tree
             and your breasts like clusters of grapes.*

        That is to say, the clusters of grapes are supported by the
palm tree, so that the grapes are as if hanging from it.

        These words seem to be spoken by the Spouse, for,
together with those in the previous verse, they give a very fine
conclusion to the tableau of praise and complete the list of
perfections that He is pleased to see in His Bride who faithfully
imitates Him. They could also be spoken by friends, or pious
souls, when they see how wonderfully she is praised, and how
closely united and assimilated she is to Christ, the true Palm
Tree of our victories, seeing a divine disposition and deportment
within her that make her in all ways very similar to her sweet
Spouse, upon Whom she has become molded to such an extent
that her breasts, like Him Who is *better than wine,* are
comparable to clusters of grapes ... They now receive from
them not only the sweet food of infancy, but also a certain
spiritual intoxication which the very advanced receive from the
breasts of the Church formed by her holy Fathers and Doctors
and by all those who, like the Castilian Mystical Doctor, have
received the gift of being able to nourish others with their
heavenly doctrine.

        The "breasts of the Church", according to María de la
Dolorosa, can also refer to the holy sacraments which, she says,
"are like clusters of abundant graces which, with their juice,

enrapture us in the holy love of God and comfort us with their fragrance of sweetness."

The holy soul, observes St. Gregory, is like the palm tree because it grows broader and broader as it grows higher and becomes increasingly capable of greater things.

"We can rightly compare," says Fr. La Puente (*Guía*, 3), "spiritual life to the palm tree which in its lower part, the part nearest the earth, is narrow, rough and has spikes . . . for the beginnings of spiritual life are often rough and difficult. As it develops it grows broader and fuller like the palm tree, having at its summit very sweet and abundant fruits. Whoever has begun to climb it through exercises of mortification and prayer must not halt until he has these fruits in his hands.

"He must take not only the dates, which are the fruit of the palm tree, but also the clusters of grapes of the vines that climb up attached to it. This is why the Holy Spirit added: *Your breasts will be like clusters of the vine and the scent of your mouth like that of apples.* The purpose of climbing to the peak of spiritual life must be not only to pick the fruits of contemplation, which are the heroic acts of the unitive way, but also the wonderful fruits produced by the other virtues attached to it, clusters of very holy works and sweet-scented words to the glory of God, the edification of the Church and the good of one's neighbor."

In this happy soul everything is perfect, as in the beautiful and regular form of the palm tree. Everything is productive, as in this tree from which many poor families derive all they need: shade, protection, clothing and food. In this way the holy soul is everything for everyone (*I Cor.* 9, 22), all who turn to her find a true and effective cure for all their needs (*II Cor.* 6, 10). The fruits of life which she produces, like clusters of grapes, not only feed and refresh her neighbor but also delight God Himself.

The palm tree, the symbol of victory, recalls the triumph won by Christ on the cross. From this blessed tree reddened with the Divine Blood, hanging like the dates from the palm tree and the clusters of grapes from the vine wrapped around it, are suspended the fruits of the sacred passion, especially that most precious fruit of the Eucharist whereby the soul becomes united with, and conformed to the suffering Christ, Who is the "true vine" (*John* 15, 1)United and assimilated to Him in this way, the perfect soul can not only feed others with the milk of spiritual infancy, that is to say, with doctrine for beginners, but can even enrapture them with the effusions of love and the strength of spirit that she is continually receiving from the very breasts of Christ.

What are the Savior's breasts but that wonderful love with which He loved His Father and was obedient to Him even unto death, and with which He loved His own to the extent of giving them His Body and Blood and dying for them? How sweet it is for the Bride to be able to approach these most loving breasts and intoxicate herself in the wound of His side with that precious nectar of His infinite charity!

Let us poor children, who through our own weakness have not yet been able to enjoy this supernatural intoxication, and experience this exquisite fragrance of a godly life, at least respectfully approach the delicate fragrance emanating from souls so enraptured, bursting forth in transports of love. Let us listen to the loving words they speak; these will comfort us like precious wine and will inflame us with desires to ascend to the divine heights with the Bride, as St. Bernard says (*In Cant. Serm.* 67). It could very well be she, who, shying away from all this praise, exclaims:

v. 9)   *I said: I will go up to the palm tree*
         and will pick its fruits
         and your breasts will be like clusters of the vine,
         and the scent of your mouth like that of apples.

Through contemplation the mystical Bride does, indeed, go up to the true Palm Tree, Whose flowering must be imitated by all who aspire to be just (*Ps.* 91,13), to the real symbol of our victories: Christ on the cross. She partakes of the precious fruits of the Tree of Life, and from the open breast of her crucified Lover she imbibes the wine with which she must nourish and fortify her love for Him. When thus fortified she herself will be able to comfort and uplift many souls. In order to do this she will have to climb up to receive from His Own divine mouth the loving kiss and message of peace that she must carry to men. There she perceives a very sweet, divine perfume *like that of apples,* which frees souls from the evil caused by that other apple. The effect of the seven words spoken by Christ on the cross, therefore, is to inspire, comfort, and restore . . .

When they hear the Bride speak it seems as if her friends hurry to interrupt her and, without letting her finish, add the last phrases of this verse themselves, saying: *and your breasts will be like clusters of the vine, and the scent of your mouth like that of apples.* For they can now really perceive this fragrant life in her, as she feeds them with great sweetness at her breast and leaves them enraptured in love . . .

Nevertheless, it is generally believed that all these words are spoken by the Divine Spouse Who continues telling how He mounted the cross, the palm tree of His victories, to gather for us — or within us, as from so many palm trees of His triumph — the fruits of Redemption. With these fruits her breasts, which were sterile before, can now be compared to clusters of grapes, and her mouth can exhale a sweet vivifying scent "like that of apples."

For now all the Bride's words are really not so much flowers of virtue as true "fruits of honor and purity"; that is to say, of healthy life, whose fragrance of holiness comforts, perfumes and embalms hearts, counteracting the scent of death produced by the fatal apple. This was true of our Father St. Dominic, of whom it is written that "he spoke only with God or of God", and whose conversation attracted, fascinated and won for the Lord all who had the good fortune to hear him. It can also be seen to a greater or lesser extent in all the just whose mouths *meditate wisdom* (*Ps.* 37,30), so as to utter with their tongues the *judgment* of redeeming truth . . .

In this happy state the Lord can come and gather from the soul the fruits of His victories. Once she has reached this lofty degree of perfection and holiness in which she resembles Him greatly in everything, she can, as His worthy Bride, offer Him not only sweet milk (that is, the food proper to spiritual infancy, represented by the dates or fruits of the palm with which she is to rear many children for Him), but also the true and precious wine of heavenly doctrine and the words of mystical wisdom, with which the "adults in Christ" or the very advanced –– whose spiritual senses are now well developed and awakened and who are able to understand the divine language of the perfect –– can be strengthened and enraptured in divine love. For being so assimilated and united to Him, and possessing as she does the very Word of God with all His graces and gifts, she feels moved to communicate to the rest the incomparable treasures with which she is enriched. This is how she will come to communicate to everyone, adults and children alike, this Divine Word of life; and with Him, also His Spirit, as occurred in the Visitation of the Virgin to St. Elizabeth, and will always occur in souls full of God, in a Catherine of Siena, a Teresa of Jesus, a Rose of Lima, or a Margaret Mary, etc. . . .

The Lord also, and in a very special way, comes to gather these fruits from the palm tree in times of great triumphs, that is to say, in times of persecutions and trials endured with love and patience and joy in the Holy Spirit. "From all eternity," says Maria Dolorosa, "the Divine Spouse had decreed to allow His Church to be persecuted, so as to bring her to triumph over her enemies; for He wanted to mount the palm tree and gather from the martrys the precious fruits of His blood. The sweetness of the dates symbolizes that which Christians, strengthened with the grace of Jesus Christ, experience when sacrificing their lives in bearing witness to the truth of the Catholic religion."

He seeks to gather the same fruits from all the hearts that He comes to visit, longing to see them triumphing over everything, but only in Mary's heart did He always find everything He wanted, so that she alone is completely deserving of all this.

v. 10)   *Your throat like choice wine,*
          worthy to be drunk by my beloved,
          and to be savored between his lips and teeth.

This seems quite clearly to be spoken by the chorus of friends who, captivated by the Bride's fragrant life and holy conversation, cannot help but tell her openly that her throat, that is to say, the words that spring from her, have such sweetness that they not only captivate and enrapture all who are able to hear them, but even delight the Spouse in such a way that, like a very precious wine, they bring Him to forget the offences and insults of the sinners and to taste the ineffable consolation that an enamored soul can provide His adorable Heart.

And what will be the consolation given Him by the holy preaching of the Church which enraptures so many hearts with divine delights and brings them to forget all worldly things . . . ? For it is when the Church brings this exquisite wine to be savored in this way by her mystical members that the Spouse is really regaled and refreshed. He savors it with His teeth and lips, says St. Gregory, when the perfect reconsider what they have heard, break it down and slowly meditate over it, so as better to appreciate its value, feel its virtue, fully assimilate it and faithfully put it into practice.

"The thought of the Church," writes Maria Dolorosa, "is the divine word which gladdens and comforts the spirit like precious wine, a wine worthy to be drunk by the Beloved Who is so pleased to hear His faithful speak of Him. The lips and teeth are the priests who must offer this word to the faithful after it has been well ruminated and prepared, so that they can then ponder and reflect upon it and derive from it all the benefit that they should."

If the words of a virtous soul, or of anyone who exercises this sacred ministry in a holy way, are so pleasing, comforting and at times even fascinating, what must Mary's be like, the Lord having poured into her blessed lips all His grace and all His blessings . . . ? All Christ's devout and faithful souls and all His Brides and even the entire Holy Church so enjoy savoring them that they will never cease repeating them over and over again in the *Magnificat,* asking her for her own soul so as to *magnify the Lord* and her *spirit* so as to *rejoice in God their Savior,* trying at the same time to be inspired with her feelings of gratitude and humility so as to become worthy like her of the gaze of the Most High.

Thus, the holy Bride seeks at all costs to reject the praise she receives for her works and words, and tries to bring everything to redound to the greater glory of her sweet Master, by Whom she now finds herself so lovingly possessed and to Whom she wants always to belong, wholly and without the slightest reservation.

Some, attributing to the Spouse all that has been said up to the first words of verse nine, believe that when she hears Him tell her that her throat is choice wine, she is unable to contain her love and gratitude and, in order to make it known at once that she owes everything to Him and wants everything for Him, she interrupts Him adding: worthy to be drunk by my Beloved . . . And not content with this she goes on to announce that in all things she wants to belong to Him Who shows her such profound affection.

FOURTH SECTION
God with the Soul, and the soul made one with Him:
Spiritual Marriage.

v. 11)   *I am my Beloved's*
                          and his affection is for me.

The Hebrew can be translated as: *I am for my beloved and his authority (as spouse) is over me.* That is to say, I depend upon Him as a true Spouse (cf. *Gen.* 3,16). "Such," says Petit, "is the submission of the Church to Jesus Christ ... It is completely inspired by His Spirit, led by His orders and decides according to His instructions, teaching nothing but His doctrine nor speaking any language but His; from Him she receives all her authority, all her glory and all her prerogatives."

Such also, as Fr. Luis de León observes, is "the holy soul's humble recognition that all the good and wealth she possesses is from God and for God. And so she says: if I am anything it is through the goodness of my Beloved that I am thus, and it is His desire and love for me that beautifies and enriches me."

The mystical Bride no longer makes mention of lilies as she did before when saying something similar, for all this is now taken for granted; and in this state of spiritual marriage she loses herself and all that is hers "leaving her cares —— forgotten among the lilies", as St. John of the Cross so divinely expressed it. Here the soul enjoys the continual presence of the Holy Trinity and scarcely does she recollect herself than she experiences this ineffable union and divine operation, that is, the very life of God infused into her own, and sees Him working and living in her as the soul of her life and the life of her soul. Before such wonders of divine love she enjoys ineffable delights, although she no longer loses the use of her senses and is comforted in such a way that she can receive these communications without neglecting the interests of her Spouse, but to all the rest she is as though alienated and oblivious. For this reason it does not occur to her to speak of lilies when they surround the "heap of wheat" with which she herself can feed many.

He never forgets or abandons this happy soul but rather delights her and converses with her in such intimacy that it seems as though He has reserved all His affection and tenderness for her alone, as though He had no others to converse with, always looking at her, turning towards her with extreme pleasure to entertain and delight her and even, in some way or other, to serve her as His Queen and the Mistress of His Heart.

Ad me conversio ejus . . . "This," wrote the V. Mariana de San José (*Life* 1:3, c. 17), "is a state in which the soul derives so much from the Lord that it appears as though He forgets Himself in cherishing and regaling her to whom He wishes to unite Himself. And He does so in such sweet, friendly and merciful ways that they are far beyond our powers of description and can be understood only to a limited degree . . . His love and mercies are very strong chains and very swift wheels which rush the soul along into the arms of Him Who so sweetly calls her and so strongly binds her to Himself that even death itself cannot snatch her from Him. This is what the Bride means when she says that *she is her beloved's and he has become wholly converted to her* . . . which is the way in which the Lord inclines Himself and all riches to the soul, for it seems to Him that there is nothing richer than this soul, nor ever could there be. She is the mistress of the wealth of her Lord and God, Whose power pacified all the people in her house who had caused in her such a state of disturbance . . . From now on she is so devoid of anything that is her own, that she no longer considers the love she feels in her soul to be her own, but to belong to her Master Who completely possesses her; thus the gifts which until now she seemed to be receiving are no longer 'things received', but are sure possessions."

"In this interior union," writes St. John of the Cross (*Spirit. Cant.*, Introd. Stanza 27), "God communicates Himself to the soul with such genuine love that no mother's affection, in which she tenderly caresses her child, nor brother's love, nor friendship is comparable to it. The tenderness and genuiness of the love by which the infinite Father favors and exalts this humble and loving soul reaches such a degree —— O wonderful thing worthy of all our awe and admiration! —— that the Father Himself becomes subject to her in His exaltation . . . And He is as solicitous in favoring her as He would be if He were her slave and she His god . . . For in this communication of love, He exercises in some way that very service that He says in the gospel He will render to His elect . . . that is: girding Himself . . . He will minister to them (*Luke*, 12,37). He is occupied here in favoring and caressing the soul like a mother who ministers to her child and nurses it at her own breasts. The soul thereby comes to know the truth of Isaias' words: *You shall be carried at the breast of God and upon His knees you will be caressed* (*Is.* 66,12). What then will be the soul's experience among such sovereign graces! How dissolved she will be in love! . . . Aware that she has been set among so many delights, she makes a complete surrender of herself and gives Him the breast of her will and love . . . saying to her Bridegroom: *I turn to my beloved and his turning is toward me. Come my beloved, let us go into the field . . . there will I give you my breasts* (that is, I shall employ the delights and strength of my will in Your love.)"

"Giving one's breast to another," he adds later, "signifies the giving of love and friendship to another and the revealing of secrets to him as a friend."

At these heights of spiritual marriage not only does the soul belong wholly to the Spouse and the Spouse wholly to the soul but, apart from belonging to one another, they come to be inseparable and 'cohabit', as it were, always looking after and attending to one another: *Ego dilecto meo —— et ad me conversio ejus.*

"So that," writes Fr. Juan de los Angeles (in *Cant.* 2:16), "all that I am, all that I am worth and can do; all this comes from the Beloved; all my virtue, all my power, and all my strength . . . *He watches for me and attends to me.* This certainly is something to be greatly wondered at by anyone who carefully considers the two: a soul and the Divine Word . . . The soul who sees God is seen by Him as if she were the only one upon whom He could fix His gaze; then she becomes modeled on Him and is transformed in His image. Full of trust she says that He is attending to her and she to Him . . . O Lord, how good You are to the soul who looks for You and who affectionately, discreetly and vigorously loves You! You betroth Yourself to her and go out to meet her with arms and heart open wide. O happy the soul who merits the blessing of such sweetness and who is given to experience the close and intimate embrace of such goodness! Do you not see how great a thing love is, returning always to its beginning, to its origin or source, from which it always receives, from which it always flows? Renouncing all other affections or attachments, the soul quite rightly occupies herself entirely in love, since love must be repaid with nothing but love."

Ad me conversio ejus: 'His gaze is turned towards me': or, as the Hebrew has it: *His ardent desire is for me,* as though saying: All the affection of the Spouse is reserved for me, His heart is mine, in me He has His delights, and I am the sole object of all His thoughts and desires . . . It seems to every saintly soul —— and this is how she is treated —— as if the Divine Lover had no other soul to entertain; for infinite Love is communicated to each soul as if she were the *only one.*

"Now it seems to me," wrote the V. Mariana de San José about herself in Nov. 1915 (cf. *Life* 1:3, C.30), "that never will He leave me nor I leave Him, because the bonds of His love are very tight, and communication is of a much greater perfection than that known until now. It is such a brotherly and friendly relationship that it is impossible to make any meaningful comparison with any enjoyed in this life. Recently He seems to thank me in a very pleasing way for what I do through my own efforts, showing Himself to be indebted to me when I look to my own salvation and sanctification; and He brings me to feel this in such a way that I forget I am a part of it, that it has to do with me, as if I were nothing more than a neighbor whose health and well-being I am concerned about, seeing how much this Lord loves her. In this way He has given me such great dominion that in all truth and security I tend to my own needs through this Lord Who so lovingly cares for me . . . He has taught me how I must give assistance through Him and not from my own resources, and has done so in words so tender that they cannot be repeated, nor have I the strength to do so."

Here, then, all the soul's desires are satisfied, in as far as this is possible in this miserable life; for she has now succeeded in receiving the mystical kiss for which she so longed, and has become so intimately united with her God —— her only source of happiness —— that she has become one single spirit with Him (I *Cor.* 6,17). She now not only *works* in all things with the power of Christ, and is moved by His Spirit, but is so possessed of this Divine Spirit as *Lord and Giver-of-Life,* that she seems to live the life of Christ; He living in her rather than she in herself. This demands such an intimate kind of renewal and transformation that it affects not only the faculties but also the very essence of the soul, for it is a true process of *deification.*

All the great mystics agree that no words are able to communicate the perfection of this state and the intimacy of this most happy union. They compare the soul to a sponge soaked in the water of the sea, to an iron placed in the fire, to two candles standing so close together that they give off a single flame . . . but they believe they are still far from explaining it. St. Teresa (*Int. Cast.* 7th Mansion Ch. 2) can find only some remote resemblance in a drop of water which falls and joins the water of a river from which it can never be separated, or in the light which, entering through two windows, lights up a room: "It is impossible to say more than that; as far as one can understand, the soul (I mean the spirit of this soul) is *made one with God.*"

"Here the holy soul" says Blosius (*Inst. Spir.* C.12), "dissolves and swoons; dead to herself, she now lives only for God . . . So that she who previously was cold now burns; she who was dark now shines; she who was hard-hearted is now soft."

"The *spiritual marriage* between the soul and the Son of God," writes St. John of the Cross (*Spirit. Cant.* Stanza 22), "is incomparably greater than the spiritual *espousal,* for it is a total *transformation* in the Beloved in which each surrenders the entire possession of self to the other with a certain consummation of the union of love. The soul thereby becomes *divine,* becomes *God through participation,* insofar as is possible in this life."

In spite of such intimate union, there is still a difference between the two which obliges the soul to recognize her own insignificance and the infinite holiness of Him Who sought to elevate her in this way. "The union wrought between the two natures and the communication of the divine to the human in this state is such that even though *neither change their being,* both appear to be God."

"The man who is in God in this exalted and ineffable way," writes Bl. Henry Suso (*Eternal Wisdom,* 32), "becomes one with Him, retaining nevertheless, his individual, natural being. He does not lose his human nature but is given the power to possess and enjoy God *in a divine way.*"

This transformation is so extensive that it effects the outward appearance and shows in the face, as it did in our Father St. Dominic, in St. Catherine of Siena, in St. Francis de Sales, whose features were like those of Christ, so firmly was He impressed in their souls!

Because of the intimacy and stability of this union many distinguished mystical writers believe that this implies confirmation in grace and also, according to St. John of the Cross (loc. cit.) exemption from the sufferings of purgatory, since these must already have been endured during the *night of the spirit* (cf. *Mystical Evolution,* Part 2, Ch. 5).

The soul now lives in the *perfection of pure love.* The first effect of spiritual marriage, adds St. Teresa (Seventh Mansion, Ch. 3), "is a self-forgetfulness which is so complete that it really seems as though the soul no longer existed, because it is such that she has neither knowledge nor remembrance that there is either Heaven or life or honor for her, so entirely is she employed in seeking the honor of God."

"Thus all her sighs and longings," as the V. Maria de la Encarnación said, "are for her most beloved Master."

With these she attracts Him to her and also His Divine Spirit so that she can mysteriously communicate Them to others.

"Each of the perfect soul's aspirations,' writes St. Mary Magdalen de Pazzi (Part 1, Ch. 3), "in some way draws the Divine Word from the bosom of the Father into her own. Possessing the Word in this way, she becomes like another Word through her intimate and loving union with Him. Just as the Word greatly longs to communicate Himself to all His creatures, so she feels an ardent desire to communicate herself to others, that is, to communicate to them the Word which she possesss within her together with all His gifts and graces."

"The Word," she adds (ibid. Ch. 4), "sends the Holy Spirit; and in a certain way the soul in union with the Word also sends the Holy Spirit for, having attracted Him to herself with her ardent sighs, she then pours forth His spiritual communications and exhortations into other souls who are ready to receive them."

v. 12)   *Come, my Beloved, let us go into the country,*
          and dwell in the country-houses.

v. 13)   *In the early morning let us go to the vineyards,*
          let us see if the vine has blossomed,
          if the flowers produce fruit,
          if the pomegranate trees are yet in flower.
          There I will give you my love.

A natural effect of this intimate union and communication in which there is pefect reciprocal giving is that the soul should consider all the possessions of her beloved Spouse as her own. The more she forgets herself and her own personal interests the more deeply she becomes occupied with those of her Spouse. While previously she found it so very difficult to leave the quiet of contemplation, now she does so with the greatest ease, as though moved by a higher force which urges her to help the needs of her neighbors. She now has no other ambitions or desires but those of her sweet Master.

For this reason she herself now invites the Spouse to go and visit His property and see the state of His possessions and to meet whatever needs are encountered. She now wants to go, not to her garden, but into the country, everywhere, so that all will be made to feel the beneficial influence of His presence and the fountain of blessings that she now carries within her always. Although she seems to travel the world alone, and seems to have abandoned the sweet retreat of contemplation, she in fact has excellent company, being accompanied in inner recollection by her Beloved Whom she never ceases to contemplate and Who bestows virtue and efficacy upon all her works. Thus, she enjoys more or less the continual presence and sweet company of Jesus and communicates it to others without ever separating herself from Him for a single moment.

"Those who have reached a very high degree of perfection," said Our Lord to St. Catherine of Siena (*Dialogues,* Ch. 78), "and who are completely dead to their own will, are the ones who *continually feel Me resting in their hearts and souls;* so that, as often as they want to unite themselves with Me through a look of love, they are able to do so, for their desire unites them in such a way that nothing can separate us. They find every moment and every place suitable for prayer, for their conversation is raised up above the world and is fixed on Heaven . . . The perfect soul is made one with Me and no one can separate her from Me. Nor do I ever withdraw My presence from her as I did with the others so as to bring them to perfection. For once they have reached this state I stop playing the game of love by alternating visits and absences."

Now seeing herself always so lovingly accompanied by Him, she says to Him: *Let us go out . . . Let us see . . .* Previously God worked *in her* but now He is pleased to work *with* her, bringing her to join Him in His work.

Let us go into the country . . . "The country," said one
soul, "is a quiet place where love can be enjoyed more at one's
pleasure. It is not distracted by company nor by caring for
personal needs. Lovers can enjoy one another without any
worry, in all simplicity and sincerity. When the soul, who is
surrounded by a thousand concerns (among them the urgings of
her own natural spirit which seeks to make self attractive and to
adorn herself), feels the attractions of the Spouse, she,
understanding nothing but love, asks Him to remove her from
the influence of these surroundings so that, finding Him in all
simplicity and without the insignias of His Majesty and Royalty,
she might enjoy Him at her pleasure."

Commoremur —— let us dwell. "This," says Fillion, "is a
very important word. What the Bride now seeks is not a fleeting
visit but a stable union . . . From now on they will belong to, or
be possessed by, one another in the solitude of the fields. What
they will do in this happy sojourn is indicated when she adds:
Mane surgamus . . . videamus si floruit vinea . . . ," which means
to say, as Maria de la Dolorosa notes, "in the morning (the
symbol of vigilance) let us rise up and go out to the 'cultivation'
of hearts which form the vine planted by You. Let us see if this
vine of grace has blossomed with good desires, if these flowers
which sprang from the Word of God are producing the fruits of
solid virtues, and if the pomegranate trees are in flower, that is,
love for God and one's neighbor. There I will give You my love;
for I will praise Your Holy Name and will try to make known to
other souls how sweet and beneficial Your love is."

"This," she adds, "is what fervent priests and all loving
souls say . . . Ah! The love of God is a very powerful fire which,
when finding itself within a soul, refuses to be kept shut up
within her and searches out and opens up a thousand ways to
spread its blaze; in this way she will speak all she can of her
Beloved to enkindle all hearts in His love . . . She wants
everyone to know and to love Him, and unable to keep silent,
she repeats: *Let us go into the country* and speak everywhere of

God without fear and without concern for human considerations. Let us speak the whole truth revealed by Him and confirmed by so many wonders. Love is indeed brave and fears no dangers."

But she nonetheless invites her Beloved to go out with her for she cannot live without Him, and she knows that without His assistance she can do nothing. Enkindled by love, she invites and calls Him so as to better fulfill His holy will and to always enjoy His presence; for although she ardently wishes to visit the Spouse's vineyards, she does not want to go alone but rather in His sweet company because she fears she would become weak. Being sure of taking Him with her in some way, it is not at all difficult for her to leave the delights and repose of contemplation in order to take up active work. During this work she is, in fact, never completely deprived of the intimate embraces of her God Whose presence she is always conscious of when she recollects herself, even very slightly, in the midst of her activity; and actually she is able to see Him working not only through her, but *in her* and *with her.*

These vineyards that they go to visit are those inherited by the Spouse: the flowers and fruits that she considers are the advances made by souls in their various states and conditions; souls for which she should make reparation and for whose progress she should be concerned and sacrifice herself.

There, she says, she will give Him her breasts; that is, all her heart, and thus will show Him her love, for love is demonstrated not simply in words, but in works, sacrifices and sufferings. These are precisely the only things which the creature can give to God and which He needs to receive from her in order to perpetuate the sacrifice of the cross in a body capable of suffering and to apply it efficaciously to so many who are in need. There she gives Him her breasts, nursing Him in many souls, winning and uplifting them for Him. And she rejoices in doing this.

When applied to the Church we can join St. Thomas in

saying that "descendit at hortum nucum Ecclesia, quando per Doctores suos vitas singulorum considerat. Unde sequitur: *Ut viderem poma convallium.* Poma convallium sunt virtutes quae humilitate condiuntur. Descendi, inquit, ut viderem poma convallium, id est, considerarem sanctos, excellentia quidem virtutum praeditos sed humilitate depressos; ut inspicerem *si floruisset vinea,* hoc est, considerarem qui in studio sanctarum virtutum proficeret. *Et, germinassent mala punica.* Hoc est, ut eos quoque perquirerem qui jam apti sunt ad imitandum passionem Christi. Nam mala punica mysterium Dominicae Passionis significant. Considerat ergo Ecclesia per praelatos suos qui in virtutibus crescunt; vel qui jam ita perfecti sunt, ut imitantes passionem Christi, pro illo quoque idonei sunt sanguinem fundere."

"From the beginning," writes Scio, "the Church's entire concern has been, and will continue to be throughout the centuries, that of ceaselessly watching the various stages and degrees of virtue in the faithful . . . *The vine in flower* or *in blossom* represents the state of those who are beginning to walk in the ways of the Lord, in whom it is possible to see the kind of fruit that can be hoped for from the good desires that they display and from the relatively easy acts of virtue in which they exercise themselves. The flowers, from which they are now forming fruits, symbolize those who are making progress in virtue and, although at the cost of great effort and exhaustion, are putting their good desires into practice. Finally, the pomegranate trees . . . represent the state of the perfect."

She shows Him the greatness of her love, says Gietmann, by no longer visiting just the urban garden of Palestine but going out into the fields and villages of the gentiles.

v. 14)   *The mandrakes already yield their scent.*
              At our doors there are all kinds of fruits
              the new and the old, my beloved,
              I shall keep them for you.

The mandrakes seem to symbolize the active life that is

rich in good works, as though saying that these works now yield
a very sweet scent. Thus, these are all symbols of the fertility
that accompanies this holy soul, and of the perfect faithfulness
and purity of intention with which she proceeds. In her
presence everything flourishes, everything exhales a fragrance
and yields abundant fruit, giving great glory to God. Nothing
clings to her for she flees in horror from worldly praise and is
not even mindful of herself; in this way she is able to take care
of the fruits for her Beloved, both the new fruits and the old.
This means, says Maria Dolorosa, "in order to honor You, my
Supreme God, I have employed the gifts of grace and nature
that I have received from You, all the spiritual gifts and natural
talents."

"The new fruits," says Fr. La Puente (*Guia,* tr. 4 Ch. 11),
"are the supernatural works that spring from charity, in
accordance with the new law, the law of grace . . . The old fruits
are works of nature (which is older than grace) such as eating,
sleeping, seeing, speaking, etc., which conform to our own
natural inclination. You must offer both to your Beloved . . .
doing these works because He enjoys them and in order to
please Him. They are not for you St. Paul deliberately makes
mention of them when he says (I *Cor.* 10,31): *whether you eat,
whether you drink, whatever you do, do it all for the glory of
God.* Everything, I repeat, without exception, for every single
fruit must be for the Beloved. How much this represents for
Him and His glory, since she is wholly His! His is the garden, His
the trees, His the virtue with which they produce and His the
fruit that they bear; so, in the soul's natural and supernatural
works let His be the glory; and may I dwell with them not for
myself but for Him."

"Happy is the life and state," exclaims St. John of the
Cross (Stanza 28), "and happy the person who attains it, where
everything is now the substance of love and the exaltation and
delight of espousal. The Bride in this state can indeed say to the
divine Bridegroom those words . . . of pure love . . . *All the new*

522

THE SONGS OF SONGS

and old apples I have kept for You, which is equivalent to saying: My Beloved, all that is rough and toilsome I desire for Your sake, and all that is sweet and pleasant I desire for Your sake."

"The virtues and graces of the Bride," he adds (Introd. to Stanza 30), "as well as the grandeurs and graces of the Bridegroom, the Son of God, are brought to light. They both display these riches in order to celebrate the feast of their espousal, and they mutually communicate their goods and delights with a wine of savory love in the Holy Spirit . . ."

The visit to the Lord's possessions, then, could not have been more profitable. The mandrakes, the symbol of fertility, give off a sweet fragrance. And at the very doors of the house they already find very abundant fruits which the diligent Bride hastens to gather and give to her Beloved.

Fruits new and old: "Because the works of the saints of old and those of our day have such an efficacious effect on the soul that by imitating them she will produce the fruits of . . . an increase in virtues and . . . a strength to resist the temptations and persecutions of men and the devils." (Fr. Gracian).

These brilliant images give an excellent picture of the immense good accomplished in the world by the apostolate and works of devotion of souls truly united with Jesus, communicating to others what they have contemplated and bearing everywhere the message of peace . . . As they pass, everything seems to regain life; just one of these divine Shulamites is often enough to produce a profound and extensive reform . . . The fire that they carry in their breasts sets many other hearts ablaze and tends to bring about a divine conflagration.

Synopsis

The soul's longing, even in the midst of external activity, to enjoy the perfect and complete possession of the Lord (v. 1). The invitation which she offers Him and the knowledge she desires to possess (v. 2). The Bride's mystical sleep and the Spouse's final commission (v. 3-4). The friends' admiration (v. 5). The manner in which the soul is reminded of the grace of redemption and His request for a worthy response from her: the laws of love (v. 6-7). The concern of the Bride with the formation of one of her little sisters, and her request for advice from the Spouse (v. 8). He shows her how natural deficiencies will be overcome by supernatural gifts (v. 9); admission to the fact that she is adorned with these gifts and greatly ennobled by the condescension of Him Who has brought her to find peace (v. 10). The beautiful parable of the vineyards (v. 11-12). The song of the mystical gardener and her sweet farewell to the Spouse (v. 13-14).

THE BRIDE

v. 1)   *Who will give me you for my brother*
sucking the breasts of my mother,
so I can find you outside and kiss you
without anyone despising me?[a]

---

a.   Hebrew: "If you could be my brother —— nursed at the breasts of my mother! I would find You outside, I would embrance You and they would not despise me." This is a subjunctive sentence which amounts to saying: 'would that you were' ... ! Since he has often called her by the sweet name of sister, she wishes that she were really so." (Fillion, h. 1.)

v. 2)   *I will take you and lead you to my mother's house*[b]
         there you will instruct me,
         and I will give you spiced wine to drink,
         and the juice of my pomegranates.

v. 3)   *His left hand under my head*
         and his right hand will embrace me.

THE SPOUSE

v. 4)   *I charge you, daughters of Jerusalem,*
         not to stir my love or rouse her
         until she please

THE CHORUS OF FRIENDS

v. 5)   *Who is this coming up from the desert*
         full of delights[c], *leaning on her Beloved?*

THE SPOUSE

         I awakened you under the apple tree,
         there where your mother was corrupted[d]
         there where she who gave birth to you was violated[e]

v. 6)   *Set me like a seal upon your heart*
         like a seal upon your arm;
         for love is strong as death,
         jealousy cruel as hell.
         Its ardors are lamps
         of fire and divine flames[f].

v. 7)   *Love no flood can quench*

b.   The Septuagint adds: "To the bedroom of her who conceived me."
c.   *Full of delights:* this is missing in the Hebrew; in the Septuagint: "with
     dazzling whiteness."
d.   The Septuagint: "There your mother gave birth to you." Hebrew, literally:
     "there your mother had pains of you."
e.   Hebrew: "there she who gave birth to you had pains." In Hebrew all this and
     the following verse seems to be spoken by the Bride since the pronouns *you,*
     your, are in the masculine; the Jewish scholars attribute these lines to her. But
     the majority of the Fathers and latin interpreters attribute them to the
     Spouse.
f.   Hebrew: "Its ardors are ardors of fire —— the flame of Jehovah;" or, "Its darts
     are darts of fire —— darts of Johovah."

no rivers drown.
Were a man to offer all the riches of his house[g] *for love,*
love would utterly despise them.

THE BRIDE

v. 8)   *Our sister is small*[h]
And she has no breasts.
What shall we do for our sister
on the day when she is spoken for?[i]

THE SPOUSE

v. 9)   *If she is a wall,*
let us build upon it battelements of peace;
if she is a door,
let us adorn it with planks of cedar.

THE BRIDE

v. 10) *I am a wall*
and my breasts are like a tower
since I was made in His eyes like one who finds peace[j].

v. 11) *The Peacemaker had a vineyard at Baalhammon*[k].
He entrusted it to the guards,
each one bringing a thousand pieces of silver for its fruit.

v. 12) *My vineyard stands before me*[l]
The thousand pieces for you, O Peacemaker[m],
and two hundred for those who guard its fruit.

THE SPOUSE

v. 13) *O you who dwell in the gardens*
the friends are listening,

g.   The Septuagint: "His whole life."
h.   Hebrew: "We have a little sister."
i.   Hebrew and Septuagint: "on the day when she is spoken for."
j.   Hebrew: "Then I was in His eyes like one who finds peace."
k.   This name means Master, possessor of abundance, just as Solomon means
     peacemaker. (In the Vulgate the meanings are given instead of the name.)
l.   I do not lend it, I myself guard and cultivate it.
m.   Hebrew and Septuagint: "Solomon".

let me hear your voice[n].

THE BRIDE

v. 14)   *Haste away, my Beloved,*
         and be like the roe, the young stag,
         on the mountains of spices.

Exposition

v. 1)   *Who will give me you for my brother*
         sucking the breasts of my mother,
         so that I can find you outside and kiss you,
         without anyone despising me?

Feeling the very close and intimate embrace of the Divine
Word, the Bride yearns to be continually responding to Him
with the tenderest effusions and the greatest transports of love,
even in the midst of the greatest activity and in the sight of
everyone, so that all might love Him Who loves us so much and
Who so much deserves to be loved by all; that, seeing the
caresses with which He favors her, they might help her in giving
Him fitting thanks, in blessing Him and in praising Him for His
infinite goodness and mercy.

Divine love has this special quality, that the more it is
enjoyed, the more keenly it is appreciated and the more
intensely it is desired. When the soul finds herself alone with her
sweet Jesus she responds to His wonderful familiarity —
stupenda nimis —— with the intimacy that is not subject to the
laws and opinions of men but conforms to the divine operations
of the Spirit of piety and love Who inspires and directs her,
filling her with this glorious *freedom proper to the children of
God.* However when she has intercourse with the world, she
notices that her Beloved tends to withdraw a little from her, or
loosens the sweet bond of union which so enraptured her, to let
her devote herself to the ministries that He entrusts to her; and
she would like, if it were possible, to be always feeling and

n.   Hebrew and Septuagint: "The friends listen to your voice, let me hear it."

enjoying Him in the same way as formerly. Even if she sometimes finds Him outside the same as before, she fully understands the need to restrain herself slightly so as not to shock or attract attention too much, for the world is far from understanding these ineffable effusions of infinite love, these wonderful *extravagances of divine love*. In view of the blindness of the world, she addresses the Lord in a language similar to that here used by the Bride, at times in order to give some relief to her heart, than again in order to see if she is making these mysteries of heavenly love more accessible to other souls.

"This verse," says Maria Dolorosa, "sets forth the great desire that souls free from worldly affections have for perfect union with the Divine Spouse. Ah! these souls having exhausted themselves seeking the spiritual good of their neighbors, frequently feel such vehement impulses of tender love for Jesus that they are constrained to say: 'My God, make Yourself visible to me as though You were my little brother so that, finding You without the veil of faith, I could kiss You without being despised when others see me delirious with love of You.!'"

Since the fire in which these happy souls burn contrasts so strongly with the coldness of the world, many times during the day they will feel half forced to repeat the words of that wonderful *Madman,* the "Poor One of Assisi" when he cried: *No one loves Love!* . . . or else to break forth in expressions of affection that might scandalize the irreligious. But the same circumspection that restrains these impulses makes the soul desire that this Divine Lover would become a tender suckling child, a little brother whom she could find whenever she wishes and treat in the way she desires; so that out in the street, before everyone, as well as at home alone, she could, without anyone noticing or maligning her, lavish all the affection she might wish upon Him and at the same time receive all His affection for her.

Thus, the patriarchs and prophets and all the ancient saints ardently longed to see the promised Messiah; and the shepherds and Wise Men and the elderly saints Simeon and Anna, had the good fortune to see Him newly born and caress Him at their pleasure ... This is how He sometimes reveals Himself even today to His faithful brides in whose hearts and on whose lips the Holy Spirit places identical or very similar words.

"The desires of the Synagogue, the prayers of the patriarchs, the laments of human nature have now been heard; Jesus *is our Brother*. We can embrace Him, caress Him, follow Him, give to Him and ask of Him every demonstration of affection without fear of being scorned, except by worldly men, whose scorn and insults should be our glory and joy" (Petit).

Just as God made Himself accessible to all of us by becoming man, so the holy soul tries to make His love and generosity more accessible to others by making Him known in this tender way. She attempts to speak to the world of the ineffable kiss that she receives from the very mouth of God, not by describing the most profound depths of His love but by its manifestations in Christ and in the Child Jesus Who in this state moves souls more easily to tenderness. For, if His greatness makes Him extremely worthy of praise, as the Psalmist says: *Magnus Dominus, et laudabilis nimis (Ps.* 47;2). His littleness as a Child, born for us, as St. Bernard observes, makes Him extremely lovable to us: *Parvulus, et amabilis* ... This is how the Bride can relieve her heart without scandalizing the world.

At the same time she very keenly feels the need she has to possess the Son and the Mother together, and for this reason she searches for Him sucking the virginal breast, and later seeks to bring Him into the house of the sweet *Mother of beautiful wine.*

Ardently desiring to reproduce within herself the mysteries of Jesus and Mary, from the Expectancy to the Cenacle, Calvary, the Resurrection and Ascension, she endeavors to read the heart of Our Lady and live within her, so as to imitate her in all things and to become so inspired by what she learns that she may thereby give more pleasure to Jesus, and refresh Him with these most pleasing manifestations of her love. In this way she will come to do everything in union with the Virgin Mother.

"In a mysterious way," an experienced soul said recently, "through Mary and with Mary, the Bride participates in the life of the Son of God, until eventually she sees Jesus enthroned; His whole physical and moral being is contained in the form of a Child or Divine Infant and feeling possessed by Him she is filled with happiness."

Then she sees Him in the plenitude of His life as He mysteriously brings her to join in all His works for the good of souls, for He now seems to want to identify her with Himself in everything.In this way she is able to satisfy this ardent desire to treat Him as her little brother and lavish her purest kisses and caresses upon Him.

"In calling Him brother," writes St. John of the Cross (stanza 22), "she indicates the equality of love between the two in the espousal before this state is reached . . . And there kiss you alone, that my nature now alone and stripped of all temporal, natural and spiritual impurity may be united with You alone, with Your nature alone, through no intermediary. This union is found only in the spiritual marriage, in which the soul kisses God without contempt or disturbance from anyone. For in this state neither the flesh, the world, the devil, nor the appetites molest her.

Surely they are not able to molest her now that she dwells within her Mother Mary as in a place of refuge, a mansion of peace and of divine delights.

v. 2) *I will take you and lead you to my mother's house,*
      there you will instruct me,
      and I will give you spiced wine to drink,
      and the juice of my pomegranates.

Seeing Him so small and enchanting, whenever she found Him she would be ready to embrace Him in the tenderest way. To enjoy Him more at her pleasure she would bring Him into her house, that is, into her mother's house; she would bring Him into her very breast, would "enthrone" Him in the most intimate part of her heart and there would entertain Him with the most delightful and exquisite things that love can contrive. While He, in His turn, in His sweet infant voice, would speak to her and make known to her His incomprehensible ways and adorable designs, instructing her in a wonderful way concerning the ineffable mysteries of the Incarnation and the Redemption, so as to bring her to join Him in His divine work . . . For it seems, says St. John of the Cross, that He does not want to conceal anything from these souls who are His faithful consorts and so He reveals wonderful things to them.

Let us all be like the Bride and try to make a worthy resting-place for Him in our hearts. Then He will not delay in coming to teach us also.

"The loving soul," adds Maria Dolorosa, "wants to take the Divine Spouse and lead Him into the house of her own heart. There, He would be her Teacher and she, being united with Him, could offer Him the spiced wine of her affection and the sweet juice of pomegranates, that is, of the merits of His Precious Blood from which she has derived power for such an intimate union."

"I will take You," she says, "I will take You with the affection of my enamored will which God, even though Omnipotent, cannot resist, and I will lead You into my mother's house, which is none other than Your Own. Mary is the true Mother of all the children of God. My whole interior is dedicated to her, so that as its queen and Mother of divine grace and beautiful love, she might dispose everything within me in the way that is most pleasing to You, and teach me to delight and caress You. Thus, I shall be able *to give you spiced wine to drink and the juice of my pomegranates,* while You teach me to know You, to love You and to please You in all things."

These expressions are symbols of the mysterious feast which the souls celebrates with the Divine Spouse in this state of spiritual marriage in which she gives God all that she is and all that she possesses; and He, in a certain way, reciprocates, giving her all that He is and all that He has thus enabling her to

once again offer Him the infinite treasures which she is receiving
from Him and love Him with His Own divine love . . . This is the
ebb and flow of the life of God in the soul and of the soul in
God, a movement so ineffable that every one who has had the
good fortune to experience it cannot describe it. If she does try
to explain it, she later has remorse for, as the Bl. Angela de
Foligno observes, it seems to her that she is blaspheming
because our language is so inappropriate to the expression of
such divine concepts. Therefore, lacking suitable terms, she uses
these images of the *instruction,* of the *spiced wine* and of the
juice of pomegranates, so as to indicate as far as she is able the
delights of a knowledge that is completely divine, of a love
which enraptures pure hearts and delights God Himself,
refreshing Him with its exquisite fragrance and its truly
heavenly sweetness.

There You will teach me, writes St. John of the Cross
(Stanza 26), "wisdom and knowledge and love; and *I shall give
You a drink of spiced wine,* my love spiced with Yours,
transformed into Yours.

"Thus I will be able to say," adds Sr. Teresa de J.M., "that
I am giving You the Holy Spirit to drink, which is the kind of
wine that You drink, my Spouse."

This precious wine of divine love is also spiced with the
spices of all the virtues of this state of perfection. She also
wants to give Him the juice of pomegranates, which represents
the good works now done in a spirit of great sacrifice, that even
reaches the degree of heroism, as she tries to imitate and
perform the works of the Savior, reproducing within herself all
His mysteries.

"O God!" exclaims Fr. Gracian, "who could describe this
spiced wine, this juice of herbs and the love with which the
enamored soul says to Christ: 'I know, Lord, and confess that
You are my Father and I must revere You as my father . . . You
are my Spouse . . . my King and my God; I am Your daughter,
Your mother, (Mark 3), Your sister, Your Bride, Your love,

Your disciple, Your subject, Your soldier, Your companion, Your slave, Your vassal and Your creature. Lord, let me love You with reverence, tenderness, trust, oneness, fervor, understanding, obedience, fortitude, sweetness, humility, fear, adoration, etc. Moreover, not only is this wine of pomegranates made all at once and by the union of all these loves, but the soul also prolongs this prayer for many days, varying the loving names of Christ that she meditates upon, and lavishing her affections upon them . . . This spiced wine and pomegranate juice normally give rise to ecstasy and rapture."

The *pomegranates* from which this juice is taken, writes St. John of the Cross (stanza 37), "stand for the mysteries of Christ, the judgments of the wisdom of God and the virtues and attributes revealed in the knowledge of these innumerable mysteries and judgments . . . The juice . . . is the fruition and delight caused by the love of God overflowing from the knowledge of His attributes . . . It is the drink of the Holy Spirit which with glowing tenderness of love she at once offers to her God, the Word, her Spouse. She had promised Him this divine drink . . . if He would make her capable of imbibing such lofty knowledge, saying: *There you will instruct me, and there I will give you . . . the juice of my pomegranates!* She calls the pomegranates (the divine knowledge) her own because, even though they are His, God has given them to her. She offers her Divine Spouse this drink of the wine of love as an expression of her gratitude for the attainment of the knowledge she had solicited . . . Tasting it Himself, He gives it to her to taste; and she in tasting it turns and offers it to Him, and they both taste it together."

In these two lines, says Scio, the Holy Fathers all recognize the voice of the just who lived before the Incarnation, longing to see the Word made man and, as such, their Brother. With these longings they made Him come down from the bosom of His Father into the Synagogue, His mother, so that He could give to the one He had chosen for His Bride the Church those divine instructions that only He could give, teaching her the new law of grace and love . . . In gratitude for His teaching the Church promises a greater number of chosen men who will show Him their extraordinary love by the faithful practice of every virtue and by the generosity with which they will shed their blood for Him. This is the generous wine and pomegranate juice that the mystical Bride offers Him and with which she herself will become intoxicated.

v. 3)   *His left hand under my head*
            and his right hand will embrace me.

This is spoken by the holy soul as she is caught up into a much higher rapture than what she experienced in the other stages of contemplation. She no longer loses the use of her senses as formerly, nor does she suffer abandonment, aridity or other similar trials in which previously the Lord supported her as though with His left hand to prevent her from losing consciousness. His left hand here represents the sufferings of Chirst, in which the soul is now made to participate so that, united to Him in His passion and death, she may cooperate with Him in His apostolic work for souls, and in making reparation to the Divine Majesty. His right hand represents the exalted delights she now receives from this embrace which, as St. John of the Cross says, "tastes of eternal life and pays every debt."

"In the taste of eternal life which it enjoys here," notes the same saint (*Living Flame of Love*, II), "the soul is rewarded for the trials she passed through in order to reach this state. She feels not only that she has been compensated and amply satisfied but that she has been rewarded far beyond her expectations . . . There is no tribulation, or penance, or trial which she has endured to which there does not correspond a hundred fold of consolation and delight even in this life" (*Matt.* 19:23).

"When the soul sees the Spouse's Justice in His left hand and His Mercy in His right," writes Maria Dolorosa, "she wants Him to place His left hand under her head, that is, to forget the time when through her own sins she had forced Him to use His justice with her, and now to embrace her with His mercy." As far as it applies to the Church she adds that "through its visible head, the Church begs Jesus not only to support it but to bring it to rest next to His Heart, communicating to it the abundance of His graces and the holiness of His divine affections."

v. 4)   *I charge you, daughters of Jerusalem,*
          not to stir my love or rouse her
          until she please.

This is the third and last time that the Spouse orders that His Love be not awakened. So great is the value that He attaches to this divine sleep of prayer that, even in such an exalted state as this, when the soul's works are so beneficial and essential to the Church, He refuses to allow it to be cut short. He orders them to leave her in peace and not to stir or rouse her until she please; and since her will is now one with His, this will be when He moves her to do so. Meanwhile, as St. John of the Cross remarks, she does more, both for the glory of Him to Whose Love she is completely surrendered, and for the good of souls, than she would by working; just as Moses did more for the victory of His people by simply lifting his hands up to God in prayer than could have been achieved by the bravest warriors who were fighting; and just as the Blessed Virgin accomplished more by praying, then the very apostles by preaching.

In order to be productive, this sacred ministry must always be accompanied by the exercise of prayer where lights and blessings are received from on high in great abundance. Just as the body, so also this life of great spiritual activity needs to be refreshed with food and rest. It is this spiritual repose that the soul is now enjoying as she rests lovingly in the arms of her Beloved, filling Him with delights while at the same time being fed by Him with the knowledge, lights, gifts and strength that she needs. The great saints, however busy they are or however demanding their apostolate, never abandon this absolute essential of prayer, this better part which consists in the contemplation of the Supreme Good. Rather, the greater their tasks, the more they try to seek support and quiet in the presence of the Lord. This is what the apostles themselves did when they left temporal cares to others so as to devote themselves more diligently to prayer and to the service of the word of God (Acts 6,4); and this is what our Father St. Dominic did when, having spent the whole day in preaching, in teaching, and in the confessional, would spend the night in prayer and, like the Spouse, request his sons to go and recollect themselves and not to disturb him during this his mystical sleep.

The Lord earnestly entreats that no one stir His Love, the holy soul, from this intimate communion with Him for since she is now wholly His, He seeks His delight in her, thus finding compensation in her pure heart for the unkindness with which He is treated by so many others. He no longer charges others by the roes and the deer of the fields, but simply because this is His wish, His absolute and sovereign Will and His divine pleasure.

Nevertheless, later He will return the soul to those who desire to have her always at their side or occupied in working for their profit, and the fruit, of which she had seemed to deprive them during her long hours of rest will then be a hundred times greater. As a result, they will begin to marvel at the elevations of the soul which she now experiences and the prodigies she will perform by this intimate union and communication with the Word.

FINAL SECTION
Consummate Perfection

v. 5)　　　*Who is this coming up from the desert,*
full of delights, leaning on her Beloved?

While in the eyes of the world the mystical Bride seems to be submerged in a profound sleep or to be needlessly wasting time, the holy angels, faithful friends and those who know the intimate secrets of the Spouse see her rising up, supported by Him through the contemplation of His mysteries, to such heights that they are filled with wonder to see a soul rise to such lofty summits from this abject and miserable exile.

"O happy spirits," exclaims the V. Fr. La Puente (*Guia*, tr. 3, Ch. 9), "you have good reason to wonder that such a weak creature could have the courage and strength to do so much for God . . . That she should ascend full of heavenly gifts and delights is not so surprising considering the rest . . . for since she has abandoned the delights of the flesh it is to be expected that the Beloved will give her the favors of the Spirit. How could she ascend in this way if she did not share in the joys of her Beloved? And how could she be content to be so closely united with Him in love and yet not have any part in His infinite satisfaction? She sees Him Whom she loves, she feels Him, enjoys Him, is joined and united with Him. Is it, then, at all surprising that when He ascends she also ascends, He uniting her to Him as He goes? Is it surprising that when she ascends He does also, since He dwells within her and the two are of one spirit united by the bond of love . . . ?

"Let us not overlook another marvelous feature of this blessed soul who, as she ascends full of delights, relies neither on these gifts nor on herself but on her Beloved; for . . . the more that the soul who contemplates God experiences and knows Him in these joys, the more she knows herself and realizes that these favors are not from her. Nonetheless, she continues to value them, not because of the pleasure they give but because they are bestowed on her by her Beloved as a means whereby she can exercise her love for Him."

For this reason she now advances with such grace, majesty and glory that often she cannot fail to arouse the admiration of all and even to overcome her greatest enemies. She no longer advances in this way in appearance only, as she did before (3, 6) but now ascends leaning sweetly and firmly on her Beloved from Whom she can never more be separated; and so she moves radiant with His divine beauty and enjoying His happiness with delights that are a foretaste of Glory.

Full of delights: Who could count the joys, gifts and

sweetnesses which she receives from Christ as she rises in spirit and ascends from virtue to virtue. This fact fills other devout souls with wonder and they ask: *Who is this . . .* ? The spiritual delights and pleasures of loving souls are many. Let us here mention seven. The first is *joy* which is a kind of smile which visits the soul and then passes away, something she cannot describe except to say that she receives it (*Rev.* 3). Happy is he who knows it from experience, as it is written in the Psalm (*Ps.* 88): *Beatus populus qui scit jubilationem*. The second is *spiritual happiness,* from the love of God, as a result of which the soul, interiorly and exteriorly, constantly walks joyfully in the Lord, with a serene and peaceful countenance, with a happiness of which St. Paul says (*Phil.* 4) *Guadete in Domino semper.* The third is *spiritual rapture* which is an impulse of great joy which transports the soul out of herself and inebriates her so that she can understand nothing but God, and depriving her of all human discretion. The fourth is *sensible devotion* effected by the love of God which reaches even the soul's appetite through which she offers herself to Christ . . . The fifth is *sweet tears* which come from meditating on the passion of Christ which enkindles love. The sixth is a *tenderness* and inner liquefaction which seemingly causes to dissolve at the breath of the Spirit and words of love that come to her from God, as it is written (*Ps.* 147) *Emittet verbus suum et liquefaciet ea, flabit spiritus ejus, et fluent aquae.* The seventh is the pleasing *company* of the Spouse, for it seems to the soul that she has Him in her heart and is enjoying His presence with great delight . . . These, together with many others that are ineffable, are the delights and pleasures of love. But greater than all of them is the union of all the faculties with Christ, when the soul no longer seems to walk on her own feet or to work with her own strength but all that she thinks, speaks and does is as though Christ *were living within her and doing all her works* (*Phil.* 1). This is what is meant when it says she ascends *on the arm of her Beloved"* (Fr. Gracian).

"In this state," says Maria de la Dolorosa, "the soul clearly shows that she belongs to the Lord in a special way, for things that are undoubtedly supernatural are revealed within her. This is recognized even by men. The people who converse with her are surprised to see her always full of joy through the Holy Spirit Who dwells within her, and leaning on her Beloved, without Whose arm she would undoubtedly be unable to do what she does."

Leaning on the Lord in this way, there is no fear that His bride the Holy Church will weaken. "Thrones will be cast down," adds the same servant of God, "nations will be scattered and cities destroyed, but the Church will always stand firm, for it knows how faithful the Spouse is Who supports it. Jesus, moreover, supports the Church in relation to the future life, heaping all kinds of supernatural delights and graces so that it will lift itself up from the desert of this world to the bridal-chamber of the eternal wedding that He has prepared in Heaven."

With respect to the soul, who can say what she feels, sees and enjoys with such delight in this stage of her life . . . ? Very frequently she has continuous fruition and truly rests in the arms of her Spouse and God, savoring the first-fruits of eternal joy. At other times she will be permitted to contemplate divine beauty through a very luminous obscurity, which mysteriously brings her to experience the strongest and, apparently, the most opposed affections: an intolerable suffering (reproducing that endured by the *Man of Sorrows*), combined with ineffable delights. For this reason the angels, as though astonished, ask: *Who is this . . . ?*

The Lord interrupts them, either to prevent her from becoming even slightly puffed up because of this admiration and praise and from such exalted mercies; or to move her to even greater love and gratitude, by reminding her of her origin and of that original sin because of which we are born children of wrath and as such sentenced to eternal death, from which He so lovingly freed us, raising us up to the condition of children of God who share in His very nature and inherit His glory.

> *I awakened you under the apple tree,*
> *there where your mother was corrupted,*
> *there where she who gave birth to you was violated.*

"Here," says Maria Dolorosa, "the Spouse makes known to the soul that He, through an act of pure charity, roused her from the sleep of her past life, beneath the tree of the cross; that is, by virtue of His passion, and brought her to the state of perfection in which she now finds herself. Remember, He adds, that human nature, your mother, was also corrupted under a tree and that Eve your ancestor was contaminated there, passing on to you her evil inclinations."

In this way He reminds her of her own wretchedness and of how, when He roused her from that sleep of death, He did so beneath the sacred tree on which He gave His Own blood as so to produce the fruit of life with which to overcome the evil that the apple had brought about within her through Eve. He thus puts before her the mystery of Redemption, the source of all the graces with which she is enriched and the cause of this wonderful condition to which she has been raised. Beneath that mystical apple-tree, He tells her, I roused you and lifted you up: there, in the very place where your mother Eve was seduced, through My holiness and mercy you were raised up from that miserable state of death, to life, from the servitude of Satan to the glorious freedom of the children of God. Thus, I forbid you to attribute anything to yourself, for it is not yours; but rather to give Me eternal thanks for everything and to respond to Me with humility, love and generosity, clothing yourself in My Own affections and dispositions.

This reminder, far from being a painful reprimand for the soul, is, according to St. John of the Cross, one of the most pleasing communications that she receives. "In this high state of spiritual marriage," he writes (*Introd.* to Stanza 23), "the Bridegroom reveals His wonderful secrets to the soul, as to His faithful consort, with remarkable ease and frequency, for true and perfect love knows not how to keep anything hidden from the beloved. He communicates to her mainly, sweet mysteries of His Incarnation and of the ways of the Redemption of mankind, which is one of the loftiest of His works and thus most delightful to the soul. And so . . . in speaking to the soul He says:

> *Beneath the apple tree;*
> *there I took you for my own,*
> *there I offered you my hand*
> *and restored you,*
> *where your mother was corrupted.*

"The bridegroom explains to the soul . . . His admirable plan of redeeming and espousing souls to Himself through the very means by which human nature was corrupted and ruined, telling her that as human nature through Adam was ruined and corrupted by means of the forbidden tree in the Garden of Paradise so on the tree of the cross it was redeemed and restored when He gave it, through His passion and death, the hand of His pardon and mercy . . . *Beneath the apple-tree,* that is, under the protection of the tree of the cross (referred to as the apple tree), the Son of God redeemed human nature and consequently espoused it to Himself and then espoused each soul by giving it through the cross, grace and the pledge of this espousal . . . If, therefore, your mother brought you death under the tree, I, under the tree of the cross, brought you life. In such a way God manifests the decrees of His wisdom; He knows how to draw good from evil so wisely and beautifully, and to ordain to a greater good what was a cause of evil."

It is to be noted that, as Fillion writes, "in the present Hebrew text all the pronous are in the masculine, which would seem to indicate that these words are spoken by the Bride, but we follow the Syrian version and agree with the fathers and the majority of ancient commentators in attributing them to the Spouse since this makes much better sense. *Sub arbore malo . . .*

In the Hebrew there is a very significant article here: beneath *the apple tree* or *this apple tree,* as the mystical Brides were passing by they encountered this very tree which brought them such moving memories. It was there that the first words of love were spoken to her *(suscitavi te:* I roused your affection . . .). Another detail more clearly expressed in the Hebrew is that 'there your mother gave birth to you, there she who bore you brought you forth . . .' This mysterious or symbolical tree which had witnessed the birth of the Shulamite (baptism) and her first pangs of love, according to the Fathers, represents the redeeming cross under whose shadow the Church was born and later became enamored with the love of her Divine Deliverer."

Even when attributed to the Bride, as the Hebrew text suggests, these words, according to Scio, can be interpreted almost in the same way, namely: As I ate the forbidden fruit beneath the tree of the knowledge of good and evil, I awakened You and moved You to come into the world and wash away my sins; there your mother (that is, Eve) conceived and gave birth to You (that is, to human nature.)"

But the words of the Hebrew text can also be attributed to the Blessed Virgin as she suffers at the foot of the cross, saying: *Beneath the apple tree I awakened you; there your mother had pains because of you; there she who gave birth to you, suffered.* There she did, indeed, suffer intensely because of Him and because of us, her adopted children. And there the very love of His Bride made Him awake from the sleep of death "raised to life for our justification." (*Rom.* 4,25). So this awakening beneath the apple tree can refer to that which takes place in Paradise where the same sin awakened and moved Him to compassion, enkindling Him with new love that "where sin abounded there grace did more abound." The Bride, kneeling at the foot of the cross, contemplating Him hanging there and moved to pity for His Holy Mother, also awakens a new love within Him with which He will come and enrapture her in these intimate communications.

v. 6)   *Set me like a seal upon your heart*
                 like a seal upon your arm;
                 for love is strong as death,
                 jealousy cruel as hell.
                 Its ardors are lamps
                 of fire and divine flames.

This is equivalent to His saying to her: "Be grateful for My
love, then; set Me like a seal upon your heart, loving no one but
Me, and only in Me loving everything lovable that presents itself
to your eyes. Set Me also like a seal on your arm, so that all
your works are done only through Me. In this way you will
always be Mine and I will always be yours. In this way you will
prefer to suffer death rather than do anything which offends
Me. The flames of love are very much alive and ardent. The
Divine Spouse shows a truly special love for each one of these
souls that He, through His adorable designs has particularly
chosen for Himself. But whoever loves greatly, desires greatly to
have this love reciprocated; so that He makes them feel that if
they are especially loved by Him they must respond to His love
in a special way" (María Dolorosa).

Here, then, the Divine Spouse imposes on the soul the laws
of faithful reciprocation and true love, as though saying to her:
"Take note, My cherished bride, of the greatness of My love and
the vastness of My sufferings for your love. I charge you never
to let Me out of your heart and never to fail to love Me; so that
My image, and My image alone, might be carved in your heart.
Make Me as secure within it as the image on the seal . . . and let
them break it into pieces rather than allow them to change My
image which is carved on it. I not only want you to carry Me in
your heart and mind, but I also forbid you to look at or listen
to anything but your Spouse; so that you see Me in everything
and are aware of My presence there. This you must do by
always having Me present before your eyes, like those who are
in the habit of sealing their secret papers and writings, always
carry it with them in a kind of ring on their hand so that no one

will steal or falsify it. And know, My spouse, that I have good reason to ask this of you because of what I have done for you, moved by your love which is in My breast, a love which is so strong and has compelled Me so forcefully without My being able to resist; that death itself, against which there is no human defense, is not as strong as the love I have for you . . . My bride, I also want you to love Me alone, loving no one else, not only because My love deserves this; but also because of the torment of jealously that is suffered by those who love as I do . . . He says that the fire of love which burns in His breast burns with red-hot coals and a strong flame. This fire is greater and more ardent than material fire because if you throw a little water on material fire, it is extinguished. But the fire of His love is stronger than all torrents. If you throw water on it, it burns even more passionately and fiercely, although entire rivers were to be poured upon it. Divine love is so strong that all the power in the world is not sufficient to overcome it, nor is it willing to allow itself to be allured and captivated by gifts . . . If someone were to be offered all the wealth and belongings that even the wealthiest man possessed in exchange for his love, he would not only be unmoved by esteem for these but he would even despise the man who offered them to him . . . Since My love for you is like this, it is only fitting that you should respond by loving Me with the same strength and to the same degree" (Fr. Luis de León).

The God Who so often calls Himself a *jealous God* — *Dominus zelotes nomen ejus,* (*Exodus* 34, 14) — is jealous of these souls in a very special way; not allowing the slightest foreign affection to enter the hearts of His brides, nor the slightest conscious imperfection to enter their works. Thus He strictly orders them to have Him always fixed in their hearts and on their arms, dedicating all their affection to Him and seeking nothing but the greater glory of God and the good of their neighbors in their works. He has abundant reason to do this, for it cost Him dearly to win them for Himself, redeeming

them, purifying them, beautifying them and lifting them up to
such heights that they might be worthy to be called His sisters
and brides. The excessive trials and torments of His life and
sacred passion were all directed towards this superabundance of
grace; and if all this seems slight to Him in view of the extreme
love He had for them, it is only fitting that He should demand
such a faithful and perfect response. Since His love proved to be
stronger than death with all its horrors, His jealously has to be
equally strong, terrible and relentless as hell itself. Hence the
unspeakable rigor with which He tries and purifies His chosen
souls in the frightful *night of the spirit;* especially when He
perfects those three very precious theological virtues which will
unite them to Himself impressing upon them His ineffable
attributes, among them that of His infinite holiness and
justice . . .

But it is there that, through the power of the Holy Spirit,
they will eventually become truly modeled on their Spouse, and
carry Him everywhere as a seal upon their heart. The soul
already had this seal impressed or fixed within her to some
extent in baptism, and even more so in Confirmation, when the
image of Christ was engraved upon her so as to endow her with a
holy life. But it must become increasingly more deeply impressed
as she is transformed in Him through the continual action of His
Spirit (*II Cor.* 3,18). As long as the soul is not prepared and
pliable enough to receive this action, this soul cannot fail to
find it most distressing and painful. By surrendering herself into
the hands of this divine Craftsman allowing Him to engrave her
as He wishes she will eventually become completely renewed
and entirely transformed, stripped of the old man and clothed
with the new. This is the wonderful work that is accomplished
through intense suffering in the *night of the spirit* already
referred to.

Now it is *day* and she is free from the works of darkness
which she has cast off and is clothed in the armor of light
(*Rom.* 13,12). She is extremely delighted to find herself so well

sealed, and so perfectly modeled on her Beloved, as she sees how, by being united with Him, she has truly become one spirit with Him (*I Cor.* 6,17), radiant with His very clarity and glory, as the perfect daughter of the Eternal Father from Whom she is always receiving new life.

"When the intimate contemplator," says Ruysbroeck (*Adornment of the Wedding,* 1.3, Ch. 5), "obtains His eternal image and, in this purity and sincerity, reaches and possesses the bosom of God the Father through the Son, he becomes enlightened with divine truth, and at all hours enjoys a divine rebirth; and in this light enters into divine contemplation, that loving encounter with God in which our supreme good and happiness principally consist . . .

"But this delightful divine encounter is actively and ceaselessly renewed within us; for the Father is given in the Son, and the Son in the Father, in a mutual and eternal union in a most loving embrace that is continually renewed through the bond of love. For just as the Father ceaselessly contemplates Himself anew in the generation of His Son, so all things are loved anew by the Father and the Son in the pouring forth of the Holy Spirit; the Holy Spirit is the active agent Who brings about this encounter of the Father and the Son Who lovingly embrace us in eternal charity."

Here the words of the Savior are fulfilled (*John* 17,26), *Father, I have made Your name known to them, so that the love with which You loved Me may be in them.* "What is this love by which the Father loves the Son," asks Massoulie (*Love of God,* Part 3 Ch. 4), "but an eternal immense and infinite Love, namely, the Holy Spirit, the love of the Father and the Son? It is this same Love that enters the hearts of the blessed . . . (and which can in some way be enjoyed even in this life) . . . Oh how sacred and exceedingly wonderful are the mysteries of the Christian religion! The Father and the Son love one another through the Holy Spirit, Who is Their reciprocal love; and through this same love the Three Divine Persons love us: 'Pater et Filius dicuntur diligentes Spiritu Sancto et se et nos' (St. Thom., P. 1, Q. 37, a. 2). God gives Himself to us and so we can say without fear: *Deus meus,* my God is wholly mine. This word *mine* indicates a possession *denotat possessionem;* but it is the Holy Spirit Who is especially called *Gift of the Most High . . .* Together with the charity that He pours forth into our hearts, the very Person of the Holy Spirit is communicated to us as a Gift that belongs to us and Whom we can freely enjoy . . . This is the joy of a soul who can say that, through the grace that Jesus Christ has won for her, she has the same Love with which the Father loves the Son and with which the Son loves the Father; has the same Love that constitutes all the joy and happiness of the Holy Trinity. This is the other promise that Jesus Christ made to His disciples (*John* 15, 11): *I have told you this so that My own joy may be in you and your joy be complete.* What is the joy of the Father and the Son but that of loving and of being loved, loved as God loves and can be loved . . . ? This is the essential joy of the Holy Trinity . . . This same joy takes possession of the hearts of the blessed. They love God, they are loved by Him; and the Love which unites Himself to them to make them love, is God. Thus the soul finds rest and her happiness is complete when she enters into this joy and this joy enters into her, when she feels that she loves and is loved in this way, and is loved as God *loves Himself."*

This divine, glorified love is enjoyed here in advance . . . ! For this reason the Divine Spouse here charges the soul to attend carefully to this divine seal that is imprinted within her, to keep her heart closed to affections alien to divine love, living like a chest sealed by His loving hand in which she keeps His treasures, and not using her arms for anything save the works of His divine service.

"With considerable mystery," writes Fr. La Puente (*Guia,* tr. 2, Ch. 11), "He compares Himself to the image and impression on a seal which, unlike other portraits which serve only to please the eye or to recall to mind the person depicted there, is principally used to impress its own form or figure on the thing that is sealed so that it will be known whose it is, or so that it will be well protected . . . For what is Christ doing when He tells you to place Him like a seal on your heart and arm, but informing you that you must impress His divine image on your understanding and will through the affections of love and of the interior virtues, and on your senses and faculties through exterior works, completely transforming yourself into His living image, just as the wax is transformed into the figure of the seal . . . ? O beloved of my soul, I beg You to imprint Yourself as a seal upon my whole spirit, for without You I am unable to do so. Set Yourself as a seal upon my faculties, impressing them with the image of who You are, so that I may know You, love You and imitate You and be totally transformed in You, and that You may live in me."

"I offer You my heart like soft wax ready to receive Your seal," he adds (Ch. 14). "Apply it and press it hard so that the seal will be fixed securely even if it means great trials and sufferings for me, for if it cost You so much to become the seal for Your elect, it is very little that they should suffer something in being sealed. From now on I shall join the apostle in saying: *So that I can now live only for God I have been crucified with Christ on the cross. (Gal. 2,20).* The Crucified Christ will be my seal, the imprint of the wounds which He bears in His body I will also carry in mine, the thorns which crowned His head will crown mine . . . *O God forbid that I should glory in anything save in the cross of Our Lord Jesus Christ" (Gal. 6, 14).*

"From now on," the Savior Himself told Mary of the Divine Heart in 1890 (*Life,* Ch. 3), "you must have no will of your own. Put Me in the place of your will so that I may freely work in you. Whenever you work it is I Who am working in you, and whenever you rest it is I Who am resting in you. Since My greatest desire has always been to suffer, I shall also suffer in you and through you. Prepare yourself, then, and be ready to suffer. In this way I continue My passion and apply it to souls, suffering in My chosen ones."

He reminds her that love is as strong as death, that it fears nothing, that the suffering and torment to which jealousy submits it does not frighten it, even though this suffering may at times be comparable to that of hell itself; instead it overcomes everything and sweeps away the obstacles that impede the divine union that it ardently longs for. The fire of this love produces living flames which are like the lamps of the mystical wedding, flames of a divine conflagration that nothing can extinguish and which flare up with a multitude of good works (*Matt.* 5, 16); "living flames of love that tenderly wound," that continually light up and burn and consume the self-love and impurities of our own nature, leaving it resplendent and pure; flames that not even death can extinguish, for it is then that this divine fire burns most brilliantly and most resplendently, causing no suffering whatsoever but rather unspeakable happiness.

"Perfect charity is as strong as death because," as Fr. La Puente says (*Guia,* tr. 2, Ch. 14) "it overcomes all other affections and keeps the heart withdrawn from them. But love's victory goes beyond this, for its jealousy is as cruel as the grave and as hard as hell — which demonstrates another of its excellent qualities. The grave and hell are two of the hardest and cruelest enemies met with after death. The grave is very hard on the body, consuming it; but hell is very torturous to the soul that enters there. Both are so hard and relentless in holding on to their prisoner, that they do not leave off until they have had complete vengeance. The love of God is similarly hard on the soul that it loves with a tender and unviolable cruelty. For, not content with having killed all the disordered affections within her, it goes even further in its persecution and strips her of all the exterior things she possessed. It makes her leave her parents, friends and acquaintances and forsake the world . . . so as to imitate her Beloved Jesus Whose jealous love was as cruel as the grave on Him since it destroyed and consumed

Him . . . and even abandoned Him on a cross, humiliated, naked and dead. O would that my soul could die this happy death of love and could enter this loving grave, closed and sealed with the seal of the Beloved!"

Its ardors or lamps, he adds, *are fire and flames* "because love always shines forth in wonderful heroic works and with burning affections; and these affections do not rest at the bottom like hot coals, but climb up high like flames, carrying the spirit with them up to their Beloved in Heaven, longing to be united with Him in eternal love. The excellence of love is made known through the wonderfully appropriate comparison of fire and lamps which burn and radiate at their own expense; for love does not mind using up and consuming all that it is in itself in order, to illuminate and burn, in its excellent work in the service of the Beloved. When He was on the cross, He burned like a lamp, sending out flames of great splendor and heat, capable of enkindling and inflaming our cold hearts. O sweet Savior Who cried from the furnance of the cross: *I have come to bring fire to the earth and how I wish it were already blazing* (*Luke* 12,49). Throw one of these hot coals into the earth of my heart that it may become enkindled with the fire of Your love, and may lift its flame up high, passing from my spirit into Yours, with love making the two one."

"This flame of love," says St. John of the Cross (*Living Flame,* Stanza 1), "is the Spirit of its Bridegroom, which is the Holy Spirit. *The soul feels Him within itself* not only as a fire which has consumed and transformed it, but as a fire that burns and flares within it . . . And that flame, every time it flares up, bathes the soul in glory and refreshes it with the quality of divine life. Such is the activity of the Holy Spirit in the soul transformed by love; the interior acts He produces shoot up like flames for they are acts of inflamed love, in which the will of the soul ignited by that flame, made one with it, loves most sublimely. These acts of love are most precious; *one of them is more meritorious and valuable than all the deeds a person may have performed in his whole life* without this transformation, however great they may have been ... In this state the soul cannot make acts because the Holy Spirit makes them all and moves it to perform them. As a result all the acts of the soul are divine ... Hence it seems to a person that every time this flame shoots up, making him love so profoundly and divinely, it is giving him eternal life."

These are the inextinguishable fires of love and the lamps of divine flames with which from now on this happy soul will burn and flare up before the Lord, as He communicates Himself to her more and more and always in a renewed way, bringing her to share in His infinite perfections. With this foretaste of glory, then, what must her ineffable joys, delights and happiness be like?

"The truest idea of beatitude that can be given us," writes Fr. Massoulie (*Love of God,* Part 2, Ch. 4), "is to be told that a man shares the same ineffable rapture that the three Persons of the Holy Trinity cause in one another. The Father has ineffable joy in the happiness of the Son; in return the Son receives infinite satisfaction from the happiness of the Father; and the Father and the Son enjoy equal delectation in the happiness of the Holy Spirit. This indivisible communication of greatness, glory, power and essence is, in our opinion, the basis of the mutual love between the adorable Persons. Each One says to the Other: *All I have is Yours and all You have is Mine (John 17, 9).* Now, it was the participation in this communication; that is, in this fullness of delight and joy that Jesus charged His disciples to pray for: *Petite ... ut gaudium vestum sit plenum (John 16, 24).* The fullness of this joy is the fruition of the reciprocal rapture of the Holy Trinity. Such is the torrent of joy with which God gratifies the desires of the blessed."

Such also is the joy with which the mystical Bride's desires are here satiated!

"O my Lord!" exclaims the Ven. Mariana de San José (*In Cant.,* 2, 4), "what obscure and profound depths of loving light You reveal here to the soul, as You cauterize her so sweetly that almost without realizing it she becomes the cautery itself. Turned into fire she feels the movement of Your flame which fills her more and more with You, my Lord; for when she gives You everything, You return everything to her again with renewed manifestations of Yourself that are so sweet and loving and You completely fill her with communications so wonderful that just one would be sufficient to enrich a soul."

"Since all these lamps of the knowledge of God," adds St. John of the Cross (ibid. stanza 3), "illumine you in a friendly and loving way, O enriched soul, how much more light and happiness of love will they . . . beget in you! How remarkable, how advantageous, and how multificated will be your delight; for in all and from all you receive fruition and love, since God communicates Himself to your faculties according to His attributes and powers! . . . Being omnipotent, He loves omnipotently and does good to you; being all-wise, He loves and does good to you with wisdom . . . ; being merciful, mild and clement, you experience His mercy, mildness, clemency. Since He is pure and undefiled, you know that He loves you in a pure and undefiled way. Being truth, you realize that He loves you in truthfulness; being liberal, you experience His liberality and favor, given without any personal profit, only in order to do good to you . . . ; gladly revealing Himself to you in these ways of knowledge, with His countenance filled with graces, and with His lips telling you of this union, with great rejoicing: *I am yours and for you and delighted to be what I am so as to be yours and give Myself to you.*

"Who, then, will be able to express your experience, O happy soul, since you know that you are so loved and exalted? Your bosom, which is your will is . . . similar to a sheaf of wheat, covered with and surrounded by lilies. For while you are enjoying the grains of the bread of life, the lilies, or virtues, surrounding you also provide you with delight. These are the King's daughters mentioned by David, who will delight you with myrrh, stacte, and other aromatic spices; for you know that the graces and virtues, which the Beloved communicates to you are His daughters. You so overflow with these and are so engulfed in them that you likewise become a well of living waters which flow impetuously from Mount Libanus, that is, from God. Your whole soul made harmonious by these (graces and virtues), became wonderfully joyful and even your body participates in it. O marvelous thing, that the soul at this time is flooded with divine waters, abounding in them like a plentiful fount overflowing on all sides! Although it is true that this communication under discussion is the light and fire from the lamps of God, yet this fire here is so gentle that being a divine conflagration, it is like the waters of life, which safisfy the thirst of the spirit with that impetus which the spirit desires to give. Hence these lamps of fire are living waters of the Spirit, like those that descended upon the apostles (*Acts.* 2, 3); although they are lamps of fire, they are clear and pure waters as well. The prophet Ezechiel referred to them in this fashion when he prophesied the coming of the Holy Spirit: *I will pour out upon you,* God is speaking, *clean waters and will put my spirit in the midst of you* (*Ez.* 36, 25) . . . Thus the Spirit of God, insofar as it is hidden in the veins of the soul, is like soft refreshing water, which satisfies the thirst of the spirit; and insofar as this love is exercised by sacrifice, it is like living flames of fire . . .

"All that can be said of this stanza is much less than the reality, for the transformation of the soul in God is indescribable. Everything can be expressed in this statement: The soul becomes God from God through participation in His life and in His attributes, which are termed *lamps of fire.*"

Although these wonders of divine love cannot be described since they surpass all human understanding "sometimes the souls that receive these riches," adds the Ven. Mariana (loc. cit.), "do not receive them in an obscure way, but rather with such clarity that these riches are much clearer to them without any comparison than what they see with their bodily eyes. In this state they know and distinguish between the

divine and the human; they know the workings of the three
Divine Persons and Their communications, they comprehend
the knowledge He gives to the soul, and the love with which He
loves her, and the impossibility of the Lord's love and kindness
ever ceasing to love her or to communicate Themselves to her in
this state. Thus this communication cannot be compared to any
stream or river, however rapid and overflowing; nor is this
communicable goodness to be compared to torrents which
cannot be retained. All the love of creatures put together is no
more than a very small drop of water in comparison with this
sea of love which is infinite. If this is so, if this love pours itself
wholly into the Bride's will (which is that of a limited creature),
what will be the outcome of these divine onslaughts of love if
not to transform her into love itself, submerged in each light or
flash that is revealed to her and illumines her. Thus the delights
are beyond measure, and the pleasures of this life in comparison
are disgusting and worthless. The effects it produces are
inestimable . . . for each joy and delight that the Spouse here
communicates is a burning flame of ardor and divine love, and
each one communicates knowledge and love. In this way the
soul grows in grace and wisdom, in purity and virtue. The
virtues which are here exercised in an exalted and divine way,
are governed by love, and there is a harmony of the sweetest
music that is heard and enjoyed only by these two faithful
lovers . . . as they embrace one another . . ."

"O my sweet, good Jesus!" exclaims St. Augustine (*Medit.,*
Ch. 35), "I beg You to fill my heart continually with this
inextinguishable fire . . . so that, like a blazing furnace, my
whole being may burn in the sweetness of Your love which
innumerable streams of opposition could never extinguish . . .
Enkindle me, my Jesus and God, in this Your love, in Your
sweetness and delectation, in Your joy and happiness, in this
delight and profound desire for You, which is so holy and so
good, so chaste and pure, so quiet and secure; so that,
completely filled with the sweetness of Your love and wholly

enkindled in the flame of Your charity, I may love You, my
Lord and God, with all my heart and with the very depths of
my being; carrying You within me, on my lips and before my
eyes at all times and in all places, so that no false and adulterous
love can ever find a place in my heart."

v. 7)   *Love no flood can quench,*
          no rivers drown.
          Were a man to offer all the riches of his house for love,
          love would utterly despise them.

Once this mutual fidelity has been confirmed by the
solemn celebration of the spiritual marriage between God and
the soul, there is no force capable of extinguishing or
diminishing the divine fires of that love that is capable
of anything; nor are there riches which do not seem worthless
compared to it.

The Septuagint, the Hebrew text and some of the ancient
Vulgate manuscripts read: *If a man gives all his property for
love, they will despise Him.* That is, he will be considered
unwise, strange, eccentric or foolish. This, indeed, is what
happens every day to those who renounce worldly riches for the
love of the Divine Spouse; they are despised, ridiculed and
treated as odd, foolish or eccentric by the worldly who are
blind to the infinite treasures that are contained in divine love.

It is this most precious and ardent love that inspires
resistance to the onslaughts and inundations of suffering and
tribulation that the Lord allows to beset His friends. After these
friends have worked and suffered greatly for Him, this love
makes them say: *We are useless servants . . .* always attributing
little importance to their trials and adversities since by them
they have been able to prove their loyalty and faithfulness, and
have succeeded in tasting His ineffable sweetness. Now that
they have found God it seems to them that they have found
Him without cost, for they see by experience that all the trials
they can suffer are not worthy to be compared to the glory and
happiness that await them. They join the apostle in saying:

Nothing can come between us and the love of Christ, neither tribulation, distress . . . persecution nor the sword . . . I am certain that neither death nor life, . . . nor any creature will be able to separate us from the love of God, which is in Christ Jesus our Lord. (*Rom.* 8, 35-39).

O Christian souls who are made for such happiness! Here you have the inestimable hidden treasure; here is the precious pearl that the Lord speaks of in His Holy Gospel. Do not hesitate to give all you are and all you possess in order to acquire it, because in it you will find whatever you sacrificed to acquire it, deified and multiplied a hundred times. This perfect and consummate union of mystical marriage is a kind of foretaste of glory and the greatest blessing that can be had in this life. According to St. John of the Cross (*Spirit. Cant.*, Stanza 22), it implies *confirmation in grace* and *exemption from the suffering of Purgatory,* inasmuch as those who die in this happy state have nothing which needs purifying, having completed all their purification in this life in accordance with God's plan. Thus their death is a precious victory, being a manifestation of the hidden glory of the children of God, and their presence in the world is like a fountain of blessings.

v. 8)   *Our sister is small,*
             and she has no breasts.
             What shall we do for our sister
             on the day when she is to be spoken for?

Very great is the concern shown by these worthy Brides of Christ for other souls who are like so many sisters to them, and above all for those who must soon devote themselves to the public ministry and to labor for the glory of the Lord, but who are not yet ready or fully prepared. They offer continual prayers and sacrifices for them, each one telling Jesus in their own special way: Lord, see how our poor little sister still does not have breasts, that is, sufficient maturity, virtue, zeal, discretion and knowledge for the difficult office to which she will soon be appointed. What shall we do for her so that she can properly fulfill her duty and come forth triumphant when she has to present herself in public, is consulted and required to speak and communicate to others the milk of salutary and holy doctrine which she still does not possess?

Before being brought into the *secret rooms* where the ineffable sweetness of God is first tasted, the soul is like a *little child* in Christ, whose *spiritual senses* still have to be exercised; (*Hebr.* 5, 13-14); and thus neither is she able to speak the language of wisdom and justice nor is she scarcely able to understand it, and therefore she herself needs to be fed with the milk of infancy (*ibid.* and *I Cor.* 3, 1-2). Until she succeeds in entering the *mystical wine-cellar* where souls are inebriated with divine love, and ascends to that lofty contemplation where souls learn the secrets of the Spouse and penetrate the mysteries of the interior life; that is, until she reaches the stage of *prayer of union* in which she acquires true zeal and learns divine truth, it can not be said of her that she has reached full adult age, attained sufficient perfection and holiness to be able to communicate to others the spiritual milk of contemplative truth (cf. *Mystical Questions,* Part 4). Since true Christian perfection, in the ordinary opinion of the saints, implies a full mystical state — consisting in fact, as St. Thomas says, in having the spiritual senses well exercised — how can a soul who has not reached this state of development raise other souls to God if she herself perhaps still needs to be fed on milk and does not have breasts with which to feed them? What will she do if she finds herself obliged to exercise these functions of a spiritual mother, and what can we do for her to remedy her deficiencies . . . ?

When this ministry is imposed through obedience and the soul recognizes her own incapacity, constantly asking God for assistance, He will know how to bring ministerial grace to bear fruit within her; with this, and with the wisdom that He never refuses to those who sincerely ask Him for it (*James* 1, 5) and does give to them in abundance, she will be able to remedy and supply for her ignorance and deficiency; until, through the exercise of an active life, she will become progressively more practiced in all things, grow in virtue and in the knowledge of God and thus prepare herself to enter into contemplative life. and attain to spiritual adulthood.

v. 9)   *If she is a wall,*
             let us build upon it battlements of peace;
             if she is a door
             let us adorn it with planks of cedar.

With these words, then, the Divine Spouse satisfies the holy desires and concerns of the Bride, as though saying to her: With divine art I will meet all these natural or supernatural deficiencies. Because of your love I will give this poor soul who is still so young, the knowledge and strength she needs, and with My right hand I will protect her so as to fortify her little virtue. If they send her to a place where she has to serve as a wall to protect other souls and to give them somewhere to rest, that is, if they give her the responsibility of directing and governing others, let Us build battlements of peace upon this wall; let Us shed abundant heavenly light of infused doctrine upon her, and instruct her fully in Holy Scripture; and let Us starve her senses, illuminating and strengthening them with special gifts and graces so that she may better watch over her subordinates, protecting and defending them against the assaults of their enemies. If they make her serve as a door to a spiritual building where she will have to live in contact with the world in order to defend others, let Us adorn her with a true spirit of mortification and a continual remembrance of the examples of the saints. With these virtues she will be able to block all worldly influence, being better defended than if she were protected with incorruptible planks of cedar . . .

Notice that He does not use the singular "I will build," but the plural: *let us build, let us adorn*. . . for He now really wants to associate the Bride with Himself in all He does. Having given her the needed virtues and strength, He wills that she take part in these wonderful works.

In this way we are given a divine description of what the formation of a religious should be. *Let us build upon it battlements of silver.* "Because of its purity and resonance, silver is a symbol of holy doctrine, or doctrine inspired by God. This line amounts to saying: let us teach her scriptural doctrine and give her a profound knowledge of divine truth, communicating to her the enlightnment she needs so as to be able to understand and then propound it. There are some," observes Fr. Gracian, "who teach their novices . . . doctrine which they themselves invent or which they read in books compiled by human genius. Many seek to lead their disciples along the same path that they themselves have discovered. This is the cause of considerable error and ignorance, because true knowledge of salvation and of the love of God is that communicated by the Holy Spirit. When saints write in order to guide souls, their doctrine is always based on Sacred Scripture . . . Just as towers and battlements are built on top of walls . . . so, when a disciple . . . seeks knowledge we must teach him the rules of Holy Scripture by which he can resist the temptations of the devil and defend himself against the evil doctrine of mistaken people. The verb *let us build* is also in the plural because the preacher, confessor or teacher, etc., must never preach or teach without having Christ at his side; neither must he ever attribute his knowledge to his own talents, for the principal teacher is God."

The planks of cedar can be interpreted as the solid virtues in which the soul must exercise herself if she is to become stable and well adorned. Thus, the two rules that the Lord gives her to ensure that a novice may quickly reach the desired maturity are, as Fr. Gracian adds, to teach her "the solid doctrine of Holy Scripture . . . and to exercise her in true virtue."

v. 10)   *I am a wall*
           and my breasts are like a tower
           since I have been made in his eyes like one
           who has found peace.

This is spoken by the holy Bride as she clearly sees in herself the fullness of perfection and the pricelessness of the gifts she has received, attributing nothing to herself but making known the source of so many riches. This is what the merciful eyes of her Spouse beholds together with the ineffable peace produced in her soul when, with perfect surrender and enkindled love, she lets herself be enveloped by this divine gaze that renews and transforms her, vivifying and deifying her, as St. John of the Cross sings:

> When You looked at me
> Your eyes imprinted Your grace in me;
> For this You love me ardently;
> And thus my eyes deserved
> To adore what they beheld in You.

Thus, humble and grateful like the Apostle (*I Cor.* 15, 10), she recognizes how, through the goodness and mercy of God and in spite of her former weakness, she has been made into a very solid wall and a very powerful tower. She feels that she possesses impregnable strength and that she is so enriched with higher knowledge and so furnished with salutary doctrine that she can, in fact, serve as a support and provide sustenance to many souls.

"The wall," writes Fr. Gracian, "refers to the strength possessed by the soul who is perfected in love and established in solid principles. Of her it may be said that she is *placed as a wall by the house of Israel* to ward off evil . . . Her two breasts of the love of God and her neighbor are like a tower."

All of this, however, she owes to the peace which came with the mystical *kiss* she received from her sweet Spouse, and to having been made in His eyes as far as possible, like unto her who *found grace before the Lord* and deserved to be called *blessed among all women* for having brought to us the peace of Heaven and for having crushed the head of the enemy.

" 'I am a wall,' replies the perfected Bride," according to Maria Dolorosa, " 'because the things of the world now make no impression on me, and my breast, like a tower, is impregnable.' She confesses that she owes everything to her Spouse since before she was not, as she is now, transformed by His grace. She has received so many favors from Him that she has become a kind of wall, built by His grace; and her breast has become like a tower for, jealously carrying His heart within her, she is no longer capable of any desire which is opposed to her consecrated state. Such is the perfection of these souls who have reached union with the heavenly Spouse, for it is He Who works within them and through them."

It seems as if she were saying: "Since, in spite of what I was, You made me so powerful and so *peaceful,* I do not doubt that You will do the same for my little sister, that is, for many other souls, provided they do not place any obstacles in Your way. You have the power and love to work in them, if they so wish, the same wonders that You have worked in me. As you desire, now all my concern is to watch and pray for Your Holy Church, the garden of Your delights and Your chosen vine, and for all the beds of spices that You have there."

The Church, writes St. Thomas, can very well say: *"Ego murus,* quia super firmam petram fundata sum et glutino divinae charitatis solidata. Sive murus sum; quia de vivis lapidibus et electis, hoc est sanctis, sum aedificate. *Et ubera mea quasi turris;* quia tales intra me contineo, qui vice uberum alios nutrire possunt spirituali doctrina; et vice muri et turris defendere et munire; quosque sicut turres muniunt et defendunt, ita merito doctrinae et conversationis inter reliqua membra praecellunt. Hoc autem non meis meritis . . . , sed dono et gratia Sponsi mei. *Ex quo facta sum coram eo quasi pacem* reperiens. Id est, ex quo ille suum sanguinem pro me fudit . . . mihique coelestia pacificavit. Ex quo ergo hanc pacem reperi, murus esse et habere ubera vice turrium merui."

This is an affectionate warning to walk in fear which is given to those of us who, through our vocation, must be walls and doors of the house of God, and who lack those mystical breasts full of the milk of salutary and holy doctrine acquired in lofty contemplation, and the strength, discretion and edifying virtue that our ministry demands . . .

v. 11)   *The peacemaker had a vineyard at Baalhamon,*
         He entrusted it to the guards,
         each one bringing a thousand pieces for you,
         O peacemaker,
         and two hundred for those who guard its fruits.

This brief parable makes it very clear why the Lord is so concerned to preserve the quiet and tranquillity of souls enjoying the holy rest of contemplation, even to the extent of three times charging overly active souls not to disturb them (II, 7; III, 5; VIII, 4). As we noted above, it is there that they receive the knowledge and grace that they need in order to be able to guard His vineyard and correct the negligence of many of His servants and guards. This vineyard is Holy Church, the property of the true Peacemaker (or Solomon) Who is Jesus Christ Our Lord. They have this vineyard in a place called Baalhamon, which means, *in the possession or dominion of many: quae habet populos.* It is put in the care of all His servants, but especially in that of His priests, so that by cultivating it and taking care of it without self-interest, they may make it produce abundant fruits for the common good. It happens, though, that many of them come to work as wage-earners or as colonists concerned only about their own profit; paying God only the rent demanded, they keep all the other produce and income for their own profit and enjoyment. It very frequently happens that among these colonists, laborers or guards, there are some who seriously fail to carry out their duties, allowing the vineyard to become overgrown with brambles so that they are scarcely able to reap enough to pay the lease. Having failed to contribute to the common good they themselves are reduced to a state of want.

When these anxious Brides see this damage from the heights of contemplation to which they are elevated, they try to remedy it as best they can, by following the example of Ann Catherine Emmerich. By means of mystical prayer they now uproot many thistles from the Lord's vineyard; now watch over it and obtain abundant rain or blessings for it from Heaven, now help with their own hands to cultivate it. In this way they zealously look after it, never letting it out of their sight; furthermore, after paying their Master all the rent, there is still enough income left to help even the tenants and laborers.

This is very evident today when so many faithful Brides from the retreat of the cloister, not only serve as lightning conductors of His anger and as walls and towers of His vineyard, but also become its guards and cultivators; now serving as teachers among Christians, now as assistants to the dying, now as missionaries among the heathens, thereby demonstrating daily as many works of devotion as true piety can conceive. Together with all this prodigious activity that the weaker sex displays to us, inspired and guided by that charity that moves them, they often confound and put to shame the "stronger" sex, while also remedying or compensating, as far as possible, for so many neglected ministries and duties caused by indolence and indifference. In this way, the Lord's vineyard continues and will continue to prosper.

As she always has it before her eyes, the mystical Bride is now far from having to say, as she did at the beginning: *They made me look after the vineyards — Had I only looked after my own!*

Like her, we must all try to keep before us the vineyard of our soul — and of the others that are perhaps entrusted to us — so that, cultivating them properly, they may yield all the abundant and precious fruit that Our Lord seeks to gather from them. In this way, we will appear before His Divine Majesty as diligent and faithful servants . . . He entrusts His property to souls, but many of these, since they tend and cultivate it, keep the profit for themselves. However, the faithful Bride which, as St. Bernard says, is every soul who loves with a pure and delicate love, diligently and selflessly looking after the vineyard for the glory of the Beloved and forgetful of her own profit and need, endeavors to keep all the fruit for Him, both *the old and the new* ... By doing this, far from losing her own income, she multiplies it beyond words, as also her merits. For the glory of the Lord is so essential in the spiritual life that it becomes the source of all true happiness.

For this reason it is especially necessary that the soul forget herself and her own satisfactions, opinions and interests, and serve such a good Lord simply because *He is Who is,* and because His Majesty and holiness deserve that we should live our whole life for Him, completely surrendering our whole heart and soul to Him ... In this way the soul shall find its all in Him, and be infinitely enriched.

When applied to the mystical Gardener, the Blessed Virgin, this verse (V. 12) has a wonderful meaning. Interior souls are daily becoming more and more aware of this as they experience her presence within themselves where she cooperates in an ineffable way in the purifying, illuminating and sanctifying action of the Holy Spirit, as the Bl. Louis Grignon de Montfort, T.O.P. explains in *The True Devotion to the Blessed Virgin.*

v. 13) *O you who dwell in the gardens*
the friends are listening,
let me hear your voice.

Let me hear your voice in the gardens of My Church, singing My praises, preaching My glories, celebrating My perfections, instructing souls by your words and example ... This was Jesus Christ's farewell to each one of His Apostles when, as He was about to ascend to His Heavenly Father, He charged them to preach His Gospel throughout the world. The same farewell which He made then to His Bride the Church, He seems to repeat to each devout soul when she seeks to dedicate herself fully to the apostolate.

He says this in a very special way to the Blessed Virgin, the Heavenly Gardener of souls, who in some way dwells within these souls, so as to cultivate them and help towards their sanctification, as the true Bride of the Holy Spirit, the Mother of divine grace and dispenser of all the blessings of Heaven.

Every soul who, like Mary, is so full of grace and enkindled in love that she can fittingly speak of His abundance and communicate His treasures to the rest, is invited by the Spouse to sing a song that is forever new, delighting His ears with sounds of praise, and at the same time to pour over so many hearts thirsting for knowledge and truth the life-giving word that they need. He urges her, through her love for Him, to dedicate herself fully to the apostolate, communicating to others what she has learned in contemplation. *Let me hear your voice . . .* ! He tells her continually.

When the Lord sees the soul thus forgetful of her own interests and ready to leave her quiet so as to look after the vineyard of the Church, and "seeing that there are people who will be eager to hear her doctrine," says Fr. Gracian, "He invites her to go out and preach and teach. He tells her to carry out this office perfectly, bearing in mind that when she preaches and teaches, she has Christ Himself as a listener and disciple and that she is carrying out this office in the presence of God . . ."

"The friends are listening; let me hear your voice," as though to say to her: "although you are recollected, see how *the harvest is rich, but the laborers are few* (*Luke* 10). It is my friends who are waiting for you to give them the word of truth; do not preach . . . in order to please men and win the reputation of being wise . . . but speak as though there is no one in the congregation but Me."

"The Heavenly Spouse," writes María Dolorosa, "shows how pleased He is when souls who are united to Him speak to their neighbor of His love. Their communications greatly benefit those who are travelling the way of the spirit. *'O you,'* He says to her, *'who dwell in the gardens of My Church,* if you are a priest, preach to Me; if you are not, speak to others about Me. *The friends are listening, let me hear your voice.'* How true it is that when two or three people speak of God, He is present in the midst of them."

So then, speak Bride, and sing and go to work in the Spouse's vineyard, for the harvest is rich and the laborers are few. Cry out and pray to the Lord to send many faithful cultivators to His vineyard. Make Him continually hear your voice in this way, for not only is its sound so sweet, but it is such that it captivates the Sacred Heart and moves Him to pour His blessings over souls who are then enraptured, subdued and led to the feet of the Good Shepherd.

The life of the perfect Bride of Christ, then, must be a life that is in some way *apostolic*. In one form or another they must dedicate themselve to cultivating and making productive the vineyard of the Spouse and to watching over His interests. Just as He came into the world in order to save souls, so they, wishing to imitate and please Him in all things and seeking to perpetuate His work, live as though this was their sole or principal occupation. That they may be able to give themselves fully to this work, God sees fit to moderate slightly the torrent of His consolation, and at times, even the souls themselves ask Him to do this . . . but only for a few hours.

v. 14)   *Haste away, my beloved*
                and be like the roe and the young stag
                on the mountains of spices.

When the soul sees that the Spouse is beginning to withdraw so as to leave her working alone in His vineyard, she fulfills the desire that He has recently made known to her, *that she work while delighting Him with her voice* or, as the Apostle says (*Col.* 3, 16), *singing in her heart.* She does this by singing a very sweet melody which serves as a farewell and gives a very happy ending to this incomparable *Song.*

Many believe that she who began by so ardently sighing for the Lord and longing for His loving kiss and intimate communication, could not possibly end by telling Him to go away. They say that this *flee* must mean the same as *runs,*

hasten back to me . . . This would amount to her saying to Him:
Since now You are determined to withdraw from me, fleeing
from me and leaving me alone and completely occupied in
working for Your glory; and since I must forego the sweet
communing with You in contemplation so as to perform the
apostolic work You have entrusted to me, let Your will be
done; haste away, if that is what You think is right, even though
I will suffer so much during Your absence. But notice that my
love cannot bear the loneliness of Your absence. Since You are
determined to flee, at least do so like the stag that frequently
turns round to look back and often lets itself be seen on the
mountain heights. Give me this consolation from time to
time . . ."

This could very well be interpreted here as a simple act of
perfect resignation or submission to the will of God manifested
in this flight. But it seems rather to be a true and generous
request made by the soul that He withdraw a little and restrain
the external effect of His joy-filled inundations, in as much as
they prevent her from attending to the work entrusted to her.
We read what St. Ephrem, St. Francis Xavier and so many other
saints did, asking Him to moderate slightly the abundance of
consolation, which would prevent them from living, and still
more, from working as pilgrims should who are yet on the way.
The sacrifice which at the beginning they could not make, they
now offer gladly to Him.

The soul is asked for a song which will please the ears of
her sweet Master and console His friends who are eager to hear
it. Complying with the desires of the Spouse, she begins to sing a
song similar to that which she sang for Him at the very
beginning (II, 17), but altering it is a very significant way so as
to indicate the very pure and spiritual love that she now has for
Him, a love far superior to the sensible love she then had in
which she still selfishly sought to enjoy Him, while now she
thinks only of pleasing Him, however much it costs. Previously
she began by saying *Return* . . . ! Now she tells Him *Haste*

away . . . ! if that is what you want.

"It is a very frequent temptation in many," observes Fr. Gracian, "when they are enjoying their spiritual gifts, such as peace in their souls, and the attention and presence of God, to be disinclined to study, preach or hear confessions so as not to be distracted ... The Bride, however, realizing that leaving prayer for study is more pleasing to God ... asks her Spouse to withdraw and leave her in dryness with only her understanding alert so that she can study well; but to do this in such a way that He will later return with greater gifts and spiritual riches ... As though saying: "Lord, if You want me to study, allow me to leave Your presence for a short while; but return from time to time to console me ... with the swiftness of a mountain-goat, and allow me to have loftiness of spirit and the sweet scent of good example, even if for a short time I become distracted through study."

The saints apply this to the Church by maintaining that she invites Him to ascend into Heaven to enjoy His victories while she continues working for His glory and the spread of His Kingdom.

Its application to souls can be clearly seen in the many who ask Him to condescend to reduce or to moderate slightly the torrents of ineffable joy produced in them by His divine presence; to withdraw Himself a little from them so that they can work with greater ardor and care in the cultivation of His vineyard, that is, in the apostolic work He has entrusted to them, works which so much concern His honor and glory, and greatly console His faithful friends.

It seems as if she were saying to Him: "If You want me to go and work for Your glory, flee a little from me, my sweet Good, let me free myself from Your loving arms so as to hasten to where You Yourself call me. Do not keep my faculties so absorbed and captivated that I cannot use them as You wish, in Your holy service. I want to sacrifice my pleasure for Yours and to fulfill Your will, not mine in all things. I no longer take into account the enjoyment of Your love, but simply Your love itself, which You have placed in souls. Flee, yes, but like the young stags who often turn round to look back. Thus, my sweet Love, turn and look back often so as not to deprive me of Your divine gaze, for in it I have placed not only all my strength, but even my life."

She asks Him not to withdraw so much that she completely ceases to feel His loving presence, and that He at least let her see Him whenever in the midst of her duties, she is able to retire a little into the fragrant mountains of prayer.

"Haste away, she tells Him," writes María de la Dolorosa, "otherwise, being so enraptured by Your words, how am I able to speak to my neighbor? Flee from my contemplation with the speed of the roe and the young stag; and set Yourself on the mountain of spices, that is, in my heart. Then if You order me to speak of Your love, You Yourself will be inspiring my words, embalming them with the fragrance of Your grace; and in this way they will serve for Your glory, my merit and the spiritual benefit of my neighbors."

She can also say this at times when a deep feeling of her own wretched and abject condition takes possession of her and moves her to lovingly beseech the Lord to go away and take recreation in hearts that are pure and fervent, to flee from her because she is so unworthy.

Flee . . . "As though saying," writes the Fr. La Puente, (*Guia,* tr. 1. Ch. 20), "although I greatly desire Your visit, when I consider my lowliness and unworthiness I beseech You to go to the fragrant mountains of the great saints . . . where You will find the welcome and rest You desire. Even though the soul may say this in humility, God will not flee from her nor will the soul flee from the Beloved or move away from Him in the slightest, but rather will regale Him by conversing with Him . . . Only on two occasions is He told to flee: the first, when the grace of devotion is so abundant that it exhausts her physically through its very excess, for then God Himself wants us to cease and to tell Him to flee . . . just like St. Ephrem when he said: *Sufficit mihi, Domine:* 'Enough, Lord! or else the jar will break with the ferment of the juice . . .' The second is when obedience or charity obliges us to leave Him in order to turn to other external works or to attend to the good of souls; we can then tell Him to flee, in a way extremely pleasing to the Lord Himself, begging Him to visit other just souls who are occupied in offering Him the sweet fragrance of prayers and good works, while we do without His visit and sweet contemplation so as to attend to the conversion of His brothers."

He rewards this generosity, bestowing on the soul, even in the midst of all the activity of her apostolate and ministry, new communications which are much more sublime, delightful and exalted.

It is reported of the Ven. Hoyos (*Life,* p. 206) that one Christmas night (1731), feeling as though wounded and possessed by great impulses of love which drove him into ecstasy, he "immediately asked the Child Who was wounding him in this way, to withdraw a little from him, so that he could render the services needed during Mass and Communion for that holy night. The blessed Child complied at once to his request, but communicated to the intimate part of his soul all the favors which He had given him in previous years."

Later on, when preparing himself to celebrate his first Mass (January 6, 1735), this young saint himself tells how "I asked Jesus to withdraw from everything external and not to allow His interior communications to appear exteriorly, I was certain that I could not hold that Divine Lover in my hands, Who was the object of all my longings, unless He withdrew or reduced the clarity of His enlightenment and the activity of His love" (*ibid.,* p. 304). "The Lord, indeed, "he adds (p. 306), "prevented everything external, communicating all His favors to me in a most exalted and insensible way, producing the loftiest feelings that were very gratifying, but at the same time very solid. From that point on, the Lord seems to have changed His conduct within my soul; for while the sensible favors, revelations and enlightenments are not so frequent, these other favors and higher lights are continuous. Just as my priestly office has placed me in a higher sphere, so the Lord's graces belong to a sphere that is equally lofty and firm."

Thus, we see how when souls reach the *spiritual marriage* they completely cease to have exstasies and raptures; and even in the midst of their communications with their neighbors they receive the loftiest spiritual graces without any external evidence.

It is at this point then that the soul gladly leaves God, for God's sake. But the more generously she is able to forego all sensible consolations and deprive herself of this enjoyment and profit, the more surely He dwells within her and at intervals makes known His presence ever more intimately. Here, the mystical Bride, having received from the very mouth of God the kiss of peace so longed for at the beginning — and for which she properly prepared herself with the kiss of His feet, hands and side — and having found her happiness on earth, she flies off like a white dove to carry to her neighbor this peace of Heaven she has received.

So with her sweet voice she goes forth billing and cooing to her Divine Spouse, and singing, for the joy and comfort of His friends as well, ceaseless spiritual hymns and loving canticles of praise (Col. 3,16), if not with her lips, at least in the sanctuary of her heart, which she keeps completely reserved for Him. However, when she has a free moment she will quickly recollect herself, and will fly up to the fragrant heights of contemplation, that is, to the "mountains of spices" where she is now absolutely sure of being able to find her Beloved at any hour . . .

May He give us His efficacious grace so that, attending to Him with extreme care and heeding His sweet calls, we may be able to follow Him generously, and reach the sublime degree of perfection and union to which He invites us all, saying: *Be perfect like Your Heavenly Father,* and repeating to us over and over with ineffable love: *Come to Me all of you . . . and you will find rest for your souls.*

Let us all join St. Augustine in ceaselessly repeating (*Medit.*, Ch. 35): "Sweet Lord, give me the grace to truly love You and, moved by the desire for Your glory, to rid myself of the heavy burden of all my carnal desires and worldly appetites that so obstruct and drag down my poor soul; running swiftly and freely so that I may attain the sweet fragrance of Your spices, and guided by Your divine grace, my soul may soon find its fulfillment and be completely satiated by the sight of Your beauty."

AMEN.